Mastering Modern Psychological Testing

Cecil R. Reynolds • Robert A. Altmann
Daniel N. Allen

Mastering Modern Psychological Testing

Theory and Methods

Second Edition

 Springer

Cecil R. Reynolds
Austin, TX, USA

Robert A. Altmann
Minneapolis, MN, USA

Daniel N. Allen
Department of Psychology
University of Nevada, Las Vegas
Las Vegas, NV, USA

First edition published by Pearson Education. Authors have written release from Pearson to publish a new edition elsewhere.

ISBN 978-3-030-59457-2   ISBN 978-3-030-59455-8   (eBook)
https://doi.org/10.1007/978-3-030-59455-8

This Springer imprint is published by the registered company Springer Nature Switzerland AG
The registered company address is: Gewerbestrasse 11, 6330 Cham, Switzerland

Contents

List of Figures

List of Tables

List of Special Interest Topics

Introduction to Psychological Assessment

1

Why do I need to learn about testing and assessment?

Abstract

Psychological testing and assessment are important in virtually every aspect of professional psychology. Assessment has widespread application in health, educational, occupational, forensic, research, and other settings. This chapter provides a historical and theoretical introduction to psychological testing, discussing basic terminology, major types of psychological tests, and types of scores that are used for interpreting results. Assumptions that underlie psychological assessment are considered as well as the rationale for using tests to make important decisions about people. Common applications and common criticisms of testing and assessment are reviewed, and characteristics of those involved in the testing process are presented. The chapter ends with a discussion of expected changes to current testing to meet new demands for test applications in the twenty-first century.

Supplementary Information The online version of this chapter (https://doi.org/10.1007/978-3-030-59455-8_1) contains supplementary material, which is available to authorized users.

Learning Objectives

After reading and studying this chapter, students should be able to:
1. Describe major milestones in the history of testing.
2. Define test, measurement, and assessment.
3. Describe and give examples of different types of tests.
4. Describe and give examples of different types of score interpretations.
5. Describe and explain the assumptions underlying psychological assessment.
6. Describe and explain the major applications of psychological assessments.
7. Explain why psychologists use tests.
8. Describe the major participants in the assessment process.
9. Describe some major trends in assessment.

Most psychology students are drawn to the study of psychology because they want to work with and help people, or alternatively to achieve an improved understanding of their own thoughts, feelings, and behaviors. Many of these students aspire to be psychologists or counselors and work in clinical settings. Other psychology students are primarily interested in research and aspire to work at a university or other research institution. However, it is only a minority of psychology students that have a burning desire to specialize in psychological tests and measurement. As a result, we often hear our students ask, "Why do I have to take a course in tests and measurement?" This is a reasonable question, and when we teach test and measurement courses, we spend some time explaining to our students why they need to learn about testing and assessment. This is one of the major goals of this chapter. We want to explain to you why you need to learn about testing and assessment, and hopefully convince you that this is a worthwhile endeavor.

> Psychological testing and assessment are important in virtually every aspect of professional psychology.

Psychological testing and assessment are important in virtually every aspect of professional psychology. For those of you interested in clinical, counseling, or school psychology, research has shown assessment is surpassed only by psychotherapy in terms of professional importance (e.g., Norcross, Karg, & Prochaska, 1997; Phelps, Eisman, & Kohout, 1998). However, even this finding does not give full credit to the important role assessment plays in professional practice. As Meyer et al. (2001) observed, unlike psychotherapy, formal assessment is a unique feature of the practice of psychology. That is, while a number of other mental-health professionals provide psychotherapy (e.g., psychiatrists, counselors, and social workers), psychologists are the only mental-health professionals that routinely conduct formal assessments. Special Interest Topic 1.1 provides information about graduate psychology programs that train clinical, counseling, and school psychologists.

The use of psychological tests and other assessments is not limited to clinical or health settings. For example:

Special Interest Topic 1.1: How Do Clinical, Counseling, and School Psychologists Differ?

In the introductory section of this chapter, we discussed the important role that testing and assessment plays in professional psychology. The American Psychological Association (APA) accredits professional training programs in the areas of clinical, counseling, and school psychology. While there are many other types of psychology programs (e.g., social psychology, quantitative psychology, and biological psychology), most psychologists working with patients or clients are trained in a clinical, counseling, or school psychology program. Some refer to these programs as "practice-oriented" because their graduates are trained to provide psychological health-care services. There are currently 248 doctoral-level clinical programs, 75 counseling programs, 69 school programs, and 14 combined programs that are all accredited by the APA (2019). Graduates of these doctoral programs typically qualify for equivalent professional benefits, such as professional licensing, independent practice, and eligibility for insurance reimbursement (e.g., Norcross, 2000). However, there are some substantive differences between clinical, counseling, school, and combined programs. Another important distinction is the program degree. Some programs offer a Ph.D. (Doctor or Philosophy) while others offer a Psy.D. (Doctor of Psychology).

If you are considering a career in psychology, and you would like to work in applied settings with individuals with emotional or behavioral problems, then these distinctions are important for you. PhD programs provide broad training in both clinical and research applications (i.e., scientist-practitioner model) whereas PsyD programs typically focus on clinical training and place less emphasis on research. The American Psychological Association (APA) accredits both PhD and PsyD programs in clinical, counseling, and school psychology. Approximately two-thirds are PhD programs (APA, 2019). The relative merits of the PhD versus the PsyD are often fiercely debated and we will not delve into that debate at this time. We do encourage you to seek out advice from trusted professors and advisors as to which degree is most likely to help you reach your career goals.

For counseling, clinical, and school programs, the historic distinction is that clinical psychology programs trained psychologists to work with clients with the more severe forms of psychopathology (e.g., schizophrenia, bipolar disorder, dementia), counseling psychology programs trained psychologists to work with clients with less severe problems (e.g., adjustment disorders, career and educational counseling, couple/marriage counseling), and school psychology programs prepare psychologists to work in school settings. You still see distinctions between clinical and counseling programs to some degree, but the differences have diminished over the years. In fact, the APA stopped distinguishing between clinical and counseling psychology internships many years ago. Clinical and counseling programs have similar program descriptions, faculty, and student characteristics, as well as similar

(continued)

admissions requirements and training objectives (Morgan & Cohen, 2008). Some notable differences do continue to exist (Karazsia & Smith, 2016; Morgan & Cohen, 2008; Norcross, 2000). These include:

- In terms of psychological assessment, clinical programs typically require more coursework in assessment compared to counseling programs. Clinical psychologists tend to use more personality assessments while counseling psychologists use more career and vocational assessments.
- In terms of theoretical orientation, clinical training programs are more likely to endorse a cognitive behavioral orientation, while counseling programs tend to favor client-centered or humanistic approaches. Clinical programs are almost exclusively housed in psychology departments, while counseling programs are more often found in departments of education.
- Clinical psychologists are more likely to work in private practice, hospitals, or medical schools, while counseling psychologists are more likely to work in university counseling centers and community mental-health settings.
- Students entering clinical and counseling programs are similar in terms of GRE scores and undergraduate GPA. However, it is noted that more students with masters degrees enter counseling programs than clinical programs (67% for PhD counseling programs versus 21% for PhD clinical programs).
- Clinical psychology programs have more professional training opportunities in medical and inpatient settings and place greater emphasis on research investigating mental illnesses compared to counseling programs.
- If you're considering applying to a psychology doctoral program, advanced training in psychopathology, diversity, and scientific methods is preferred by all programs. However, faculty in clinical psychology PhD programs prefer students who have more training in assessment, psychopathology, and life sciences, while counseling psychology PhD programs prefer more training in diversity.

In summary, even though clinical and counseling psychology programs have grown in similarity in recent years, some important differences still exist. We will now turn to the field of school psychology. School psychology programs prepare professionals to work with children and adolescents in school settings. Clinical and counseling programs can prepare their graduates to work with children and adolescents; however, this is the focus of school psychology programs. School psychology programs also provide extensive training in psychological assessment (cognitive, emotional, and behavioral) and learn to consult with parents and other professionals to promote the school success of their clients.

This discussion has only focused on doctorate-level training programs that are accredited by the APA but these programs share substantial overlap with doctoral-level professional counseling programs that are accredited by the Council for Accreditation of Counseling and Related Educational Programs

(continued)

(CACREP) and clinical psychological science programs accredited by the Psychological Clinical Science Accreditation System (PCSAS). There are many more masters-level psychology programs that also prepare students for careers as mental-health professionals. Because professional licensing is controlled by the individual states, each state determines the educational and training criteria for licensing, and this is something else one should take into consideration when choosing a graduate school.

You can learn more details about these areas of psychological specialization at the website of the American Psychological Association (http://www. apa.org). The official definitions of each specialty area are housed here as well as other archival documents that describe each specialty in detail that have been accepted by the APA's Commission for the Recognition of Specialties and Proficiencies in Professional Psychology (CRSPPP).

- Industrial and organizational psychologists devote a considerable amount of their professional time developing, administering, and interpreting tests. A major aspect of their work is to develop assessments that will help identify prospective employees that possess the skills and characteristics necessary to be successful on the job.
- Research psychologists also need to be proficient in measurement and assessment. Most psychological research regardless of its focus (e.g., social interactions, child development, psychopathology, or animal behavior) involves measurement and/or assessment. Whether a researcher is concerned with behavioral response time, visual acuity, intelligence, or depressed mood (just to name a few), he or she will need to engage in measurement as part of their research. In fact, *all* areas of science are very concerned and dependent on measurement. Before one can study any variable in any science, it is necessary to be able to ascertain its existence and accurately measure important characteristics of the variable, construct, or entity.
- Educational psychologists, who focus on the application of psychology in educational settings, are often intricately involved in testing, measurement, and assessment issues. Their involvement ranges from developing and analyzing tests that are used in educational settings to educating teachers about how to develop better classroom assessments.

In summary, if you are interested in pursuing a career in psychology, it is likely that you will engage in assessment to some degree, or at least need to understand the outcome of testing and assessment activities. Before delving into contemporary issues in testing and assessment, we will briefly examine the history of psychological testing.

1.1   Brief History of Testing

As Anastasi and Urbina note (1997), the actual "roots of testing are lost in antiquity (p. 32)." Some writers suggest the first test was actually the famous "Apple Test" given to Eve in the Garden of Eden. However, if one excludes Biblical references, testing is usually traced back to the early Chinese. The following section highlights some of the milestones in the history of testing.

The earliest documented use of tests is usually attributed to the Chinese who tested public officials to ensure competence.

1.1.1   Earliest Testing: Circa 2200 BC

The earliest documented use of tests is usually attributed to the Chinese who tested public officials to ensure competence (analogous to contemporary civil service examinations). The Chinese testing program evolved over the centuries and assumed various forms. For example, during the Han dynasty, written examinations were included for the first time and covered five major areas: agriculture, civil law, geography, military affairs, and revenue. During the fourth century, the program involved three arduous stages requiring the examinees to spend days isolated in small booths composing essays and poems (Gregory, 2004).

1.1.2   Eighteenth- and Nineteenth-Century Testing

1.1.2.1   Carl Frederich Gauss

Carl Frederich Gauss (1777–1855) was a noted German mathematician who also made important contributions in astronomy and the study of magnetism. In the course of tracking star movements, he found that his colleagues often came up with slightly different locations. He plotted the frequency of the observed locations systematically and found the observations to take the shape of a curve—the curve we have come to know as the normal curve or normal distribution (also known as the Gaussian Curve). He determined that the best estimate of the precise location of the star was the mean of the observations and that each independent observation contained some degree of error. While Gauss is not typically recognized as a pioneer in testing, we believe his formal recognition of measurement error and its distributional characteristics earn him this recognition.

1.1.2.2   Civil Service Examinations

Civil service tests similar to those used in China to select government employees were introduced in European countries in the late eighteenth and early nineteenth centuries, including the introduction of civil service examinations by the East Indian Trading Company in 1829 (Huddleston & Boyer, 1996). In 1883, the U.S. Civil Service Commission started using similar achievement tests to aid selection of government employees (Anastasi & Urbina, 1997).

1.1.2.3 Physicians and Psychiatrists

In the nineteenth century, physicians and psychiatrists in England and the United States developed classification systems to help classify individuals with intellectual disabilities (previously known as mental retardation) and other mental problems. For example, in the 1830s, the French physician *Jean Esquirol* was one of the first to distinguish between insanity (i.e., emotional disorders) from mental deficiency (i.e., intellectual deficits present from birth). He also believed that intellectual disabilities existed on a continuum from mild to profound and observed that verbal skills were the most reliable way of identifying its degree. In the 1890s, *Emil Kraepelin* and others promoted the use of free-association tests in assessing psychiatric patients. Free-association tests involve the presentation of stimulus words to which the respondent responds "… with the first word that comes to mind." Later, *Sigmund Freud* expanded on the technique of encouraging patients to freely express any and all thoughts that came to mind in order to identify underlying thoughts and emotions.

1.1.3 Brass Instruments Era

Early experimental psychologists such as Wilhelm Wundt, Sir Francis Galton, James McKeen Cattell, and Clark Wissler made significant contributions to the development of cognitive ability testing. One of the most important developments of this period was the move toward measuring human abilities using objective procedures that could be easily replicated. These early pioneers used a variety of instruments, often made of brass, to measure simple sensory and motor processes based on the assumption that they were measures of general intelligence (e.g., Gregory, 2004). Some of these early psychologists' contributions were so substantive that they deserve special mention.

1.1.3.1 Sir Francis Galton

Sir Francis Galton is often considered the father of mental tests and measurement. One of his major accomplishments was the establishment of an anthropometric laboratory at the International Health Exhibition in London in 1884. This labo-

> Galton is considered the father of mental tests and measurement and was responsible for first large-scale systematic collection of data on individual differences.

ratory was subsequently moved to a museum where it operated for several years. During this time, data were collected including physical (e.g., height, weight, head circumference), sensory (e.g., reaction time, sensory discrimination), and motor measurements (e.g., motor speed, grip strength) on over 17,000 individuals. This represented the first large-scale systematic collection of data on individual differences (Anastasi & Urbina, 1997; Gregory, 2004). Another of his noteworthy accomplishment was proposing the idea of "psychometry" which he defined as "….the art of imposing measurement and number upon operations of the mind" (Galton, 1879, p. 149). Now referred to as "psychometrics," this area of study is foundational for development and interpretation of psychological tests.

1.1.3.2 James McKeen Cattell

James McKeen Cattell shared Galton's belief that relatively simple sensory and motor tests could be used to measure intellectual abilities. Although later research demonstrated this belief was too simplistic, Cattell was instrumental in opening psychological laboratories and spreading the growing testing movement in the U.S.A. He is thought to be the first to use the term "mental test" in an article he published in 1890. In addition to his personal professional contributions, he had several students that went on to productive careers in psychology, including E.L. Thorndike, R.S. Woodworth, and E.K. Strong (Anastasi & Urbina, 1997; Gregory, 2004). Galton and Cattell also contributed to the development of testing procedures such as standardized questionnaires and rating scales that later became popular techniques in personality assessment (Anastasi & Urbina, 1997).

1.1.3.3 Clark Wissler

Clark Wissler was one of Cattell's students whose research largely discredited the work of his famous teacher. Wissler found that the common sensory-motor measures being used to assess intelligence had essentially no correlation with academic achievement. He also found that the sensory-motor tests had only weak correlations with each other. These discouraging findings essentially ended the use of the simple sensory-motor measures of intelligence and set the stage for a new approach to intellectual assessment that emphasized more sophisticated higher-order mental processes. Ironically, there were significant methodological flaws in Wissler's research that prevented him from detecting moderate correlations that actually exist between some sensory-motor tests and intelligence (to learn more about this interesting turn of events, see Fancher, 1985 and Sternberg, 1990). Nevertheless, it would take decades for researchers to discover that we might have dismissed the importance of psychophysical measurements in investigating intelligence, and the stage was set for Alfred Binet's approach to intelligence testing emphasizing higher-order mental abilities (Gregory, 2004).

1.1.4   Twentieth-Century Testing

1.1.4.1 Alfred Binet: Bring on Intelligence Testing!

Alfred Binet initially experimented with sensory-motor measurements such as reaction time and sensory acuity, but became disenchanted with them and was a pioneer of using measures of higher-order cognitive processes to assess intelligence (Gregory, 2004). In the early 1900s, the French government commissioned Binet and his colleague Theodore Simon to develop a test to predict academic performance. The result of their efforts was the first *Binet-Simon Scale*, released in 1905. The scale contained some sensory-perceptual tests, but the emphasis was on verbal items assessing comprehension, reasoning, judgment, and short-term memory. Binet and Simon achieved their goal and developed a test that was a good predictor of academic success. Subsequent revisions of the Binet-Simon Scale were released in 1908 and 1911. These scales gained wide acceptance in France and were soon translated and standardized in the United States, most successfully by Louis Terman at Stanford University. This resulted in the Stanford-Binet Intelligence Scale, which has been revised numerous times (the fifth revision, SB5, remains in use today). Ironically, Terman's version of the Binet-Simon Scale became even more popular in France and other parts of Europe than the Binet-Simon Scale!

> The Binet-Simon Scale was released in 1905 and was the first intelligence test that was a good predictor of academic success.

1.1.4.2 Army Alpha and Beta Tests

Intelligence testing received another boost in the United States during World War I. The U.S. Army needed a way to assess and classify recruits as suitable for the military and to classify them for jobs in the military. The American Psychological Association (APA) and one of its past presidents, Robert M. Yerkes, developed a task force that devised a series of aptitude tests that came to be known as the *Army Alpha and Army Beta*—one was verbal (Alpha) and one nonverbal (Beta). Through their efforts and those of the Army in screening recruits literally millions of Americans became familiar with the concept of intelligence testing. Because most intelligence tests up to that time were administered individually, like the Binet scales, the Army Alpha and Beta tests also introduced and popularized group intelligence testing.

1.1.4.3 Robert Woodworth: Bring on Personality Testing!

In 1918, Robert Woodworth developed the *Woodworth Personal Data Sheet* which is widely considered to be the first formal personality test. The Personal Data Sheet was designed to help collect personal information about military recruits. Much as the development of the Binet scales ushered in the era of intelligence testing, the introduction of the Woodworth Personal Data Sheet ushered in the era of personality assessment.

1.1.4.4 Rorschach Inkblot Test

Hermann Rorschach developed the Rorschach inkblots in the 1920s. While there has been considerable debate about the psychometric properties of the Rorschach (and other projective techniques), it continues to be one of the more popular personality assessment techniques in use at the beginning of the twenty-first century.

1.1.4.5 College Admission Tests

The College Entrance Examination Board (CEEB) was originally formed to provide colleges and universities with an objective and valid measure of students' academic abilities and to move away from nepotism and legacy in admissions to academic merit. Its efforts resulted in the development of the first Scholastic Aptitude Test (SAT) in 1926. The American College Testing Program (ACT) was initiated in 1959 and is the major competitor of the SAT. Prior to the advent of these tests, college admission decisions were highly subjective and strongly influenced by family background and status, so another purpose for the development of these instruments was to make the selection process increasingly objective.

1.1.4.6 Wechsler Intelligence Scales

Intelligence testing received another boost in the 1930s, when David Wechsler developed an intelligence test for adults that included measures of verbal ability and nonverbal on the same test. Prior to Wechsler, and the Wechsler-Bellevue I, intelligence tests typically assessed verbal or nonverbal intelligence, not both. The latest versions of the Wechsler scales continue to be widely used today!

1.1.4.7 Minnesota Multiphasic Personality Inventory

The *Minnesota Multiphasic Personality Inventory (MMPI)* was published in the early 1940s to aid in the diagnosis of psychiatric disorders. It is an objective personality test (i.e., can be scored in an objective manner) and has been the subject of a large amount of research. Its second edition, the MMPI-2 continues to be one of the most popular (if not the most popular) personality assessments in use today!

1.1.5   Twenty-First-Century Testing

The last 60 years have seen an explosion in terms of test development and use of psychological and educational tests. For example, a recent search of the *Mental Measurements Yearbook,* which contains information for English-language tests, resulted in the identification of over 600 tests listed in the category on personality tests and over 400 in the categories of intelligence and aptitude tests. Many of the chapters in this textbook will be devoted to the development and use of different types of tests. Later in this chapter, we will examine some current trends in assessment and some factors that we expect will influence the trajectory of assessment practices in the twenty-first Century. We have summarized this time line for you in Table 1.1.

Table 1.1   Milestones in testing history

Circa 2200 BC	• Chinese test public officials
Eighteenth and nineteenth century	• Carl Frederich Gauss discovers the normal distribution when evaluating measurement error • Civil service examinations used in Europe and the United States • Physicians and psychiatrists assess mental patients with new techniques • Brass Instruments Era—Emphasis on measuring sensory and motor abilities • Early attention to questionnaires and rating scales by Galton and Cattell
1905	• Binet-Simon Intelligence Scale released—Ushers in the era of intelligence testing
1917	• Army alpha and Beta released—First group intelligence tests
1918	• Woodworth Personal Data Sheet released—ushers in the era of personality assessment
1920s	• Scholastic Aptitude Test (SAT) and Rorshach inkblot test developed—Testing expands its influence
1930s	• David Wechsler releases the Wechsler-Bellevue I—Initiates a series of influential intelligence tests
1940s	• The Minnesota Multiphasic Personality Inventory released— Destined to become the leading objective personality inventory

1.2   The Language of Assessment

We have already used a number of relatively common but somewhat technical terms. Before proceeding it would be helpful to define the common ones for you: tests, measurement, and assessment.

1.2.1   Tests

A *test* is a device or procedure in which a sample of an individual's behavior is obtained, evaluated, and scored using standardized procedures (AERA, APA, & NCME, 2014). This is a rather broad or general definition, but at this point in our discussion, we are best served with this broad definition. Rest assured that we will provide more specific information on different types of tests in due time. Before

> A test is a procedure in which a sample of an individual's behavior is obtained, evaluated, and scored using standardized procedures (AERA et al., 2014).

proceeding, we should elaborate on one aspect of our definition of a test: that a test is a sample of behavior. Because a test is only a sample of behavior, it is important that tests reflect a representative sample of the behavior you are interested in. For example, a math test designed to measure knowledge of simple addition will only include a small number or "sample" of all possible addition problems. The importance of the concept of a representative sample will become more apparent as we proceed with our study of testing and assessment, and we will touch on it in more detail in later chapters when we address the technical properties of tests.

1.2.2   Standardized Tests

A *standardized test* is a test that is administered, scored, and interpreted in a standard manner. Most standardized tests are developed by testing professionals or test publishing companies. The goal of standardization is to ensure that testing conditions are as nearly the same as is possible for all individuals taking the test. If this is accomplished, no examinee will have an advantage over another due to variability in administration procedures, and so assessment results will be comparable across individuals.

> Measurement is defined as a set of rules for assigning numbers to represent objects, traits, attributes, or behaviors.

1.2.3   Measurement

Measurement can be defined as a set of rules for assigning numbers to represent objects, traits, attributes, or behaviors. A psychological test is a measuring device and therefore involves rules (e.g., administration guidelines and scoring criteria) for assigning numbers that represent an individual's performance. In turn, these numbers are interpreted as reflecting characteristics of the test taker. For example, the number of items endorsed in a positive manner (e.g., "True" or "Like Me") on a depression scale might be interpreted as reflecting a client's experience of depressed mood. Few items endorsed would indicate "no" or "mild" depression, while many items endorsed would indicate "severe" depression.

1.2.4   Assessment

Assessment is defined as a systematic procedure for collecting information that can be used to make inferences about the characteristics of people or objects (AERA et al., 2014). Assessment should lead to an increased understanding of these characteristics. Tests are obviously one systematic method of collecting information and are therefore one set of tools for assessment. Reviews of historical records, interviews, and observations are

> Assessment is defined as any systematic procedure for collecting information that can be used to make inferences about the characteristics of people or objects (AERA et al., 2014).

also legitimate assessment techniques, and all are maximally useful when they are integrated. In fact, assessment typically refers to a process that involves the integration of information obtained from multiple sources using multiple methods. Consider the assessment of an adult who complains of memory problems. This assessment typically involves review of occupational and medical records, interviews with the client and significant others, and formal standardized testing often focused on behavior at home and at work, memory, attention, and other cognitive abilities. Therefore, assessment is a broader, more comprehensive process than testing.

Meyer et al. (2001) further contrast psychological testing and psychological assessment, observing that testing is a relatively straightforward process where a specific test is administered to obtain a specific score. In contrast, psychological assessment integrates multiple scores, typically obtained using multiple tests, with information collected by reviewing records, conducting interviews, and conducting observations. The goal is to develop a better understanding of the client, answer referral questions (e.g., Why is this student doing poorly at school?), and communicate these findings to the appropriate individuals.

McFall and Treat (1999) go a bit further and remind us the "... aim of clinical assessment is to gather data that allow us to reduce uncertainty regarding the probabilities of events" (p. 215). Such an "event" in a clinical setting might be the probability a patient has depression versus bipolar disorder versus dementia, all of which require treatments. In personnel psychology, an event might be the probability that an applicant to the police force will be successful in completing the police academy, a very expensive training. For these events, useful tests are those that allow us to be more accurate in diagnosing depression or predicting who will successfully complete police academy training. The more general principle is that tests are only useful if they improve decision making. Because professionals in all areas make errors the goal is to minimize the number and magnitude of these mistakes. In psychology, testing and assessment done properly greatly reduce these errors.

1.2.5   Are Tests, Measurement, and Assessment Interchangeable Terms?

Now that we have defined these common terms, with some reluctance, we acknowledge that in actual practice many professionals use testing, measurement, and assessment interchangeably. Recognizing this, Popham (2000) noted that among many professionals assessment has become the preferred term. "Measurement" sounds rather rigid and sterile when applied to people and tends to be avoided. "Testing" has its own negative connotations. For example, hardly a week goes by when newspapers don't contain articles about "teaching to the test" or "high-stakes testing," typically with negative connotations. Additionally, when people hear the word "test," they usually think of paper-and-pencil tests. In recent years, as a result of growing dissatisfaction with traditional paper-and-pencil tests, alternative testing procedures have been developed (e.g., performance assessments and portfolios). As a result, "testing" is not seen as particularly descriptive of modern practices. That leaves us with "assessment" as the contemporary popular term.

1.2.6   Other Important Terms

There are some additional terms that you should be familiar with. *Evaluation* is a term often used when discussing assessment, testing, and measurement-related issues. Evaluation is an activity that involves judging or appraising the value or worth of something. For example, assigning formal grades to students to reflect their academic performance is referred to as summative evaluation. *Psychometrics* is the science of psychological measurement, and a *psychometrician* is a psychological or educational professional who has specialized in the area of testing, measurement, and assessment. You will likely hear people refer to the psychometric properties of a test, and by this, they mean the measurement or statistical characteristics of test scores. These measurement characteristics include reliability and validity. *Reliability* refers to the stability, consistency, and relative accuracy of the test scores. On a more theoretical level, reliability refers to the degree to which test scores are free from measurement

> Reliability refers to the stability or consistency of test scores.

errors. Scores that are relatively free from measurement errors will be stable or consistent (i.e., reliable) and are thus more accurate in estimating some value. *Validity*, in simplest terms, refers to the appropriateness or accuracy of the interpretations of test scores. If test scores are interpreted as reflecting intelligence, do they actually reflect intellectual ability? If test scores are used to predict success on a job, can they accurately predict who will be successful on the job? In order for tests to be useful, they must be both reliable and

> Validity refers to the accuracy of the interpretation of test scores.

valid. To illustrate, one can very accurately (i.e., reliably) measure your height, but that does not mean that your height is not a good indicator of your intelligence. Here, while the measurement or test has high reliability, it has low validity and so not useful for assessing intelligence.

1.3   Types of Tests

We defined a test as a device or procedure in which a sample of an individual's behavior is obtained, evaluated, and scored using standardized procedures (AERA et al., 2014). You have probably taken a large number of tests in your life, and it is likely that you have noticed all tests are not alike. For example, people take tests in schools that help determine their course grades, driving tests to obtain a driver's license, interest inventories to help make educational and vocational decisions, admissions tests when applying for college, examinations to obtain professional certificates and licenses, and personality tests to gain personal understanding. This brief list is clearly not exhaustive!

Our brief list does highlight substantial differences in test format, structure, content, and use, and it is reasonable to ask whether there are more general test characteristics that explain these differences. One major difference between tests is whether they are maximum performance or typical response measures (Cronbach, 1990). *Maximum performance tests* are designed to measure the upper limits of an examinee's knowledge and abilities, while *typical response tests* attempt to measure routine or day to day characteristics. Maximum performance tests are also referred to as ability tests and achievement tests. For example, maximum performance tests can be designed to assess how well a student can perform selected tasks (e.g., 3-digit multiplication) or has mastered a specified content domain (e.g., American history). Intelligence tests and classroom achievement tests are common examples of maximum performance tests. On these and other maximum performance tests, items are usually scored as either "correct" or "incorrect" and examinees are encouraged to demonstrate their very best performance. In contrast, typical response tests often are referred to as personality tests, and in this context, "personality" is used broadly to reflect a host of noncognitive characteristics such as attitudes, behaviors, emotions, and interests (Anastasi & Urbina, 1997). These tests often employ a true–false or yes–no item format and examinees are typically instructed to select the response option that describes them. Some individuals reserve the term "test" for maximum performance measures, while using terms such as "scale" or "inventory" when referring to typical performance measures. In this textbook, we will use "test" in its broader sense, applying it to both maximum performance and typical response procedures.

1.3.1   Maximum Performance Tests

Maximum performance tests are designed to assess the upper limits of the examinee's knowledge and abilities. Within the broad category of maximum performance tests, there are a number of subcategories.

First, maximum performance tests are often classified as either achievement tests or aptitude tests. Second, maximum performance tests can be classified as either objective or subjective. Finally, are often described as either speed or power tests.

> Maximum performance tests are designed to assess the upper limits of an examinee's knowledge and abilities.

These distinctions, while not absolute in nature, have a long historical basis and provide some useful descriptive information.

1.3.1.1   Achievement and Aptitude Tests

The first categorical distinction between maximum performance tests is achievement versus aptitude. ***Achievement tests*** are designed to assess the knowledge or skills of an individual in a content domain in which he or she has received instruction. In contrast, ***aptitude tests*** are broader in scope and are designed to measure the cognitive skills, abilities, and knowledge that an individual has accumulated as the result of overall life experiences (AERA et al., 2014). In other words, achievement tests are linked or tied to a specific program of instructional objectives, whereas aptitude tests

> Achievement tests measure knowledge and skills in an area in which instruction has been provided (AERA et al., 2014).

> Aptitude tests measure cognitive abilities and skills that are accumulated as the result of overall life experiences (AERA et al., 2014).

reflect the cumulative impact of life experiences as a whole. This distinction, however, is not absolute and is actually a matter of degree or emphasis. Most testing experts today conceptualize both achievement and aptitude tests as measures of developed cognitive abilities that can be ordered along a continuum in terms of how closely linked the assessed abilities are to specific learning experiences.

Another distinction between achievement and aptitude tests involves the way their results are used or interpreted. Achievement tests are typically used to measure what has been learned or "achieved" at a specific point in time. In contrast, aptitude tests usually are used to predict future performance or reflect an individual's potential in terms of academic or job performance. However, this distinction is not absolute either. As an example, a test given at the end of high school to assess achievement might also be used to predict success in college. Although we feel it is important to recognize that the distinction between achievement and aptitude tests is not absolute, we also feel the achievement/aptitude distinction is useful when discussing different types of abilities.

1.3.1.2 Objective and Subjective Tests

Objectivity typically implies impartiality or the absence of personal bias. Cronbach (1990) notes that the less test scores are influenced by the subjective judgment of the person grading or scoring the test, the more objective the test is. In other words, objectivity refers to the extent that trained examiners who score a test will agree with each other and score responses in the same way. Tests with selected-response items (e.g., multiple-choice, true–false, and matching) that can be scored using a fixed key and that minimize subjectivity in scoring are often referred to as *objective tests*. In contrast, *subjective tests* are those that rely on the personal judgment of the individual grading the test. For example, essay tests are considered subjective because the person grading the test relies to some extent on their own subjective judgment when scoring the essays. Most students are well aware that different teachers might assign different grades to the same essay item. Essays and other test formats that require the person grading the test to employ their own personal judgment are often referred to as "subjective" tests. It is common, and desirable, for those developing subjective tests to provide explicit scoring rubrics in an effort to reduce the impact of the subjective judgment of the person scoring the test.

1.3.1.3 Speed and Power Tests

The last categorical distinction between maximum performance tests is speed versus power. On a pure *speed test*, performance only reflects differences in the speed of performance. A speed test generally contains items that are relatively easy and has a strict time limit that prevents any examinee from successfully completing all the items. Speed tests are also commonly referred to as "speeded tests." On a

> On speed tests, performance reflects differences in the speed of performance.

> On power tests, performance reflects the difficulty of the items the examinee is able to answer correctly.

pure *power test*, the speed of performance is not an issue. Everyone is given plenty of time to attempt all the items, but the items are ordered according to difficulty, and the test contains some items that are so difficult that no examinee is expected to answer them. As a result, performance on a power test primarily reflects the difficulty of the items an examinee is able to answer correctly.

Well-developed speed and power tests are designed so no one will obtain a perfect score. They are designed this way because perfect scores are "indeterminate." That is, if someone obtains a perfect score on a test, the test failed to assess the very upper limits of that person's ability. To access adequately the upper limits of ability, tests need to have what test experts refer to as an "adequate ceiling." That is, the difficulty level of the tests is set so none of the examinees will be able to obtain a perfect score.

As you might expect, the distinction between speed and power tests is often one of degree. Most often a test is not a *pure* speed test or a *pure* power test, but incorporates some combination of the two approaches. For example, the Scholastic Assessment Test (SAT) and Graduate Record Examination (GRE) are considered power tests, but both have time limits. When time limits are set such that 95% or more of examinees will have the opportunity to respond to all items, the test is still considered to be a power test and not a speed test.

1.3.2 Typical Response Tests

As noted, *typical response tests* are designed to measure the typical behavior and characteristics of examinees. Typical response tests measure constructs such as personality, behavior, attitudes, or inter- ests. In traditional assessment terminol-

> Typical performance tests are designed to measure the typical behavior and characteristics of examinees.

ogy, "personality" is a general term that broadly encompasses a wide range of emotional, interpersonal, motivational, attitudinal, and other personal characteristics (Anastasi & Urbina, 1997). Tests that measure conscientiousness, agreeableness, psychopathy, depression, anxiety, dominance, sensitivity, perfectionism, or sensation seeking would all be considered personality tests. When describing personality tests, most assessment experts distinguish between objective and projective techniques. Although there are some differences, this distinction largely parallels the separation of maximum performance tests into "objective" or "subjective" tests. These two approaches are described next.

1.3.2.1 Objective Personality Tests

As with maximum performance tests, in the context of typical response assessment objectivity also implies impartiality or the absence of personal bias. *Objective per- sonality tests* are those that use selected-response items (e.g., true–false) and are

> Objective personality tests use items that are not influenced by the subjective judgment of the person scoring the test.

scored in an objective manner. For example, a personality test that includes true– false items such as "*I enjoy parties*" is considered objective. The test taker simply responds "true" if the statement describes them and "false" if it does not. By consci- entiously using a scoring key, there should be no disagreement among scorers regarding how to score the items.

1.3.2.2 Projective Personality Tests

Projective personality tests typically involve the presentation of unstructured or ambiguous materials that can elicit an almost infinite range of responses from the examinee. For example, the clinician may show the examinee an inkblot and ask: "What might this be?" Instructions to the examinee are minimal, there are essentially no restrictions on the examinee's response, and there is considerable subjec- tivity when scoring the response. Elaborating on the distinction between objective and projective tests, Reynolds (1998) noted:

> It is primarily the agreement on scoring that differentiates objective from subjective tests. If trained examiners agree on how a particular answer is scored, tests are considered objec-

tive; if not, they are considered subjective. Projective is not synonymous with subjective in this context but most projective tests are closer to the subjective than objective end of the continuum of agreement on scoring (p. 49).

What is unique to projective tests is what is referred to as the *"projective hypothesis."* In brief, the projective hypothesis holds that when an examinee responds to an ambiguous stimulus, they respond in a manner that reflects their genuine unconscious desires, motives, and drives without interference from the ego or conscious

> Projective personality tests involve the presentation of ambiguous material that elicits an almost infinite range of responses. Most projective tests involve subjectivity in scoring.

mind (Reynolds, 1998). Projective techniques are extremely popular, but they are the focus of considerable controversy. This controversy focuses on the subjective nature of this approach and the lack of empirical evidence supporting the technical qualities of the instruments. In other words, although the tests are popular, there is little evidence that they provide reliable and valid information.

Table 1.2 depicts the major categories of tests we have discussed. Although we have introduced you to the major types of tests, this brief introduction clearly is not exhaustive. While essentially all tests can be classified according to this scheme, there are other distinctions possible. For example, a common distinction is made between **standardized tests** and **nonstandardized tests**. Standardized tests are professionally developed tests that are administered, scored, and interpreted in a standard manner. The goal of standardization is to make sure that testing conditions are as nearly the same for all the individuals taking the test as is possible. Part of the

Table 1.2   Major categories of tests

---
1. Maximum performance tests
    (a)   *Achievement tests*: Assess knowledge and skills in an area in which the examinee has received instruction
        1.   *Speed tests* (e.g., a timed typing test)
        2.   *Power tests* (e.g., a spelling test containing words of increasing difficulty)
    (b)   *Aptitude tests*: Assess knowledge and skills accumulated as the result of overall life experiences
        1.   *Speed tests* (e.g., a timed test where the test taker quickly scans groups of symbols and marks symbols that meet predetermined criteria)
        2.   *Power tests* (e.g., a test of nonverbal reasoning and problem-solving that requires the test taker to solve problems of increasing difficulty)
    (c)   *Objective or Subjective tests*: When the scoring of a test does not rely on the subjective judgment of the individual scoring it, it is said to be objective. If the scoring of a test does rely on subjective judgment, it is said to be subjective
2. Typical Response Tests
    (a)   *Objective personality tests* (e.g., a test where the test taker answers true–false items referring to the personal beliefs and preferences)
    (b)   *Projective personality tests* (e.g., a test where the test taker looks at an inkblot and describes what he or she sees)
---

process of standardizing most tests also involves administering it to a large, representative sample that represents the types of individuals to whom examinees are to be compared. This group, typically referred to as the standardization sample, is used to establish "norms" that facilitate the interpretation of test results by comparing the score of the individual to that of the group. Examples of standardized tests include the Stanford-Binet Intelligence Scales, Fifth Edition (SB5: Roid, 2003), a popular intelligence test, and the Minnesota Multiphasic Personality Inventory, Second Edition (MMPI-2: Butcher, Dahlstrom, Graham, Tellegen, & Kaemmer, 1989) a widely used objective personality test. Nonstandardized tests are those developed in a less formal manner. Administration guidelines may not be explicitly stated, and there is often not a standardization sample. The most common type of nonstandardized test is the classroom achievement tests that are administered in large numbers in schools and universities on an almost daily basis.

Finally, it is common to distinguish between individual tests (i.e., tests designed to be administered to one examinee at a time) and group tests (i.e., tests administered to more than one examinee at a time). This is an important distinction that applies to the administration of the test rather than the type of the test. For example, individual aptitude tests and group aptitude tests are both aptitude tests, they simply differ in how they are administered. Individual and group neuropsychological tests are also available to assess the effects of concussion in athletes. This is true in the personality domain as well wherein some tests require one-on-one administration but others can be given to groups. Group tests can be advantageous when large numbers of examinees take the same test, and when it is not important to understand how a person goes about solving a problem or choosing an answer. Individual tests can be advantageous when a response to one item might trigger the next items that are asked, or when an examinee might need more individualized instruction or prompting when solving test items.

1.4   Types of Scores

Almost all tests produce scores that reflect or represent the performance of the individuals taking the tests. There are two fundamental approaches to understanding scores: the norm-referenced approach and the criterion-referenced approach. With *norm-referenced score interpretations,* an examinee's performance is compared to the performance of other people, often

> Norm-referenced score interpretations compare an examinee's performance to the performance of other people.

those in a standardization sample. For example, if you say that a student scored better than 95% of his or her peers, this is a norm-referenced score interpretation. The standardization sample serves as the reference group against which performance is judged.

With ***criterion-referenced score interpretations***, the examinee's performance is not compared to that of other people. Instead, it is compared to a specified level of performance. The emphasis is on what the examinees know or what they can actually do, not their standing relative to other people. One of the most common examples of criterion-referenced scoring is the percentage of correct responses on a classroom exami-

> Criterion-referenced score interpretations compare an examinee's performance to a specified level of performance.

nation. For example, if you report that a student correctly answered 95% of the items on a classroom test, this is a criterion-referenced score interpretation. In addition to percent correct, another type of criterion-referenced interpretation is a ***cut score***. Cut scores can be used to define a level of mastery in the area being assessed; performance is usually reported with an all-or-none score such as a pass/fail designation. For example, on a licensing examination for psychologists, the cut score might be 70%, and all examinees earning a score of 70% or greater will receive a designation of "pass," representing a desired level of mastery or expertise in psychology. Conversely, if an examinee earned a score of 69%, they would receive a designation of "fail."

Norm-referenced interpretations are relative (i.e., relative to the performance of other examinees) whereas criterion-referenced interpretations are absolute (i.e., compared to an absolute standard). People often refer to norm-referenced and criterion-referenced tests, but this is not technically correct. The terms norm-referenced and criterion-referenced actually refer to the interpretation of test scores, not a type of test. Although it is most common for tests to produce either norm-referenced or criterion-referenced scores, it is possible for a test to produce both norm- and criterion-referenced scores. Table 1.3 depicts salient information about norm- and criterion-referenced scores.

Table 1.3 Norm- and criterion-referenced scores

Type of score	Description	Example
Norm–referenced scores	• An examinee's performance is compared to that of other people • Interpretation is relative to that of other people	• An examinee earns a percentile rank score of 50, meaning they scored better than 50% of the individuals in the standardization sample
Criterion–referenced scores	• An examinee's performance is compared to a specified level of performance • Interpretation is absolute (not relative)	• A student correctly answers 50% of the items on a test • On a licensing examination, an examinee obtains a score greater than the cut score and receives a passing score

1.5   Assumptions of Psychological Assessment

Now that we have introduced you to many of the basic concepts of psychological assessment, this is an opportune time to discuss some basic assumptions that underlie psychological assessment. These assumptions were adapted in part from Cohen and Swerdlik (2002) who note, appropriately, that these assumptions actually represent a simplification of some very complex issues. As you progress through this text, you will develop a better understanding of these complex and interrelated issues.

1.5.1   Assumption #1: Psychological Constructs Exist

In assessment terminology, a **construct** is simply the trait or characteristic (i.e., variable) that a test is designed to measure. In psychology, we are often interested in measuring a number of constructs, such as

> Constructs are the traits or characteristics a test is designed to measure (AERA et al., 2014).

a client's intelligence, level of depression, or attitudes. This assumption simply acknowledges that constructs like "intelligence," "depression," or "attitudes" exist.

1.5.2   Assumption #2: Psychological Constructs Can Be Measured

Cronbach (1990) notes that there is an old, often quoted adage among measurement professionals that go "If a thing exists, it exists in some amount. If it exists in some amount, it can be measured (p. 34)." If we accept the assumption that psychological constructs exist, the next natural question is "Can these constructs be measured?" As you might predict, assessment experts believe psychological and educational constructs can be measured.

1.5.3   Assumption #3: Although We Can Measure Constructs, Our Measurement Is Not Perfect

While assessment experts believe they can measure psychological constructs, they also acknowledge that the measurement process is not perfect. This is usually

> Some degree of error is inherent in all measurements.

framed in terms of **measurement error** and its effects on the reliability of scores. Some degree of error is inherent in all sciences, not just psychology and social sciences, and measurement error reduces the usefulness of measurement. As you will learn, assessment experts make considerable efforts to estimate and minimize the effects of measurement error.

1.5.4   Assumption #4: There Are Different Ways to Measure Any Given Construct

As you will learn in this text, there are multiple approaches to measuring any psychological construct. Consider the example of social anxiety. A client's level of social anxiety can be assessed using a number of different approaches. For example, a psychologist might interview the client and ask about their level of anxiety in different social settings. The psychologist might observe the client in a number of different social settings. The psychologist might have individuals familiar with the client complete behavioral rating scales that address symptoms of social anxiety. The psychologist might also administer a number of typical response tests, both objective and projective, to assess the client's level of social anxiety. All of these different assessment procedures can help the psychologist understand the client's experience of social anxiety.

1.5.5   Assumption #5: All Assessment Procedures Have Strengths and Limitations

While acknowledging that there are a number of different approaches to measuring any construct, assessment experts also acknowledge that all assessment procedures have their own specific set of strengths and limitations. One assessment approach might produce highly reliable scores, but not measure some aspects of a construct as well as another approach that produces less reliable scores. As a result, it is important that psychologists understand the specific strengths and weaknesses of the procedures they use. The relatively simple idea that professionals should be aware of the limitations of their assessment procedures and the information obtained from them is a key issue in ethical assessment practice.

> There are multiple approaches to measuring any given construct, and these different approaches have their own unique strengths and weaknesses.

1.5.6   Assumption #6: Multiple Sources of Information Should Be Part of the Assessment Process

Given that there are different approaches to measuring any given construct and that each approach has its own strengths and weaknesses, it only follows that psychological assessment should incorporate information from different approaches. Important decisions *should not be based on the results of a single test or other assessment procedure*. For example, when deciding which applicants should be admitted to a college or university, information such as performance on an admissions test (e.g., SAT or ACT), high school

> Important decisions should not be based on the result of a single test or other assessment procedure.

grade-point-average (GPA), letters of recommendation, evidence of extracurricular activities, and a written statement of purpose should be considered. It would be inappropriate to base this decision on any one source of information.

1.5.7 Assumption #7: Performance on Tests Can Be Generalized to Non-Test Behaviors

Typically, when we give a test we are not interested simply in the individual's performance on the test but the ability to generalize from test performance to non-test behaviors. For example, it is not an individual's score on the SAT that is in itself important to a college admission officer, but the fact that the score can be used to help predict performance in college. The same applies to a test designed to detect depression. It is not really the client's response to the items on a depression inventory that is of importance, but that their responses to the items on this inventory reflect their personal subjective level of depression. This assumption holds that test performance is important, not in-and-of-itself (with some very specialized exceptions), but because of what it tells us about the test taker's standing on the measured construct and the relationship of this standing to other constructs.

> Information obtained from assessment procedures can help educators make better decisions.

1.5.8 Assumption #8: Assessment Can Provide Information that Helps Psychologists Make Better Professional Decisions

The widespread use of psychological assessments is based on the premise that the information obtained can help psychologists make better decisions. For psychologists working in clinical settings,

> Psychological assessments are not perfect, but they can provide useful information.

these decisions might include accurately diagnosing a client's disorder and developing and monitoring effective treatment plans. Research psychologists use a variety of tests to collect data and test their scientific hypotheses. Psychologists working in industrial and organizational settings often use tests to help select the most qualified employees. Educational psychologists use tests and other assessments to determine which educational programs are effective and which are not. In these, and a multitude of other situations, tests provide valuable information that helps psychologists make better professional decisions. We will elaborate on the many ways assessments help psychologists make better decisions later in this chapter.

1.5.9 Assumption #9: Assessments Can Be Conducted in a Fair Manner

Although many critics of testing might argue against this assumption, contemporary assessment experts spend considerable time and energy developing instruments that, *when used with a population the test was designed for, administered according to proper procedures, and interpreted according to guidelines*, are fair and minimize bias. Nevertheless, tests can be used inappropriately and when they are it discredits or stigmatizes assessment procedures in general. However, in such circumstances, the culprit is the person using the test, not the test itself. At times, people criticize assessments because they do not like the results obtained. In many instances, this is akin to "killing the messenger," since tests are not the cause of observed differences among groups, for example, they just document them.

1.5.10 Assumption #10: Testing and Assessment Can Benefit Individuals and Society as a Whole

Although many people might initially argue that the elimination of all tests would be a positive event, on closer examination most will agree that tests and other assessment procedures make significant contributions to education and society as a whole. Consider a world without tests. People would be able to present themselves as surgeons without ever having their ability to perform surgery competently assessed. People would be given drivers' licenses without having their ability to drive assessed. Airline pilots would be flying commercial jets without having to demonstrate their competence as pilots. All of these examples should give you reasons to consider the value of tests. Although typically not a matter of life-and-death, the use of psychological tests also has important implications that can benefit society. When a psychologist is able to diagnose accurately a client's problem, they are more likely to develop an effective treatment plan. Similarly, when a psychologist helps a client better understand their personal preferences and career interests, the client is more likely to pursue educational and training activities that lead to a happier life and successful career.

These assumptions are listed in Table 1.4. As we noted, these seemingly simple assumptions represent some complex and controversial issues, and there is considerable debate regarding the pros and cons of testing and assessment. Many of the controversies surrounding the use of tests result from misunderstandings and the

Table 1.4 Assumptions of psychological assessment

1.	Psychological constructs exist
2.	Psychological constructs can be measured
3.	Although we can measure constructs, our measurement is not perfect
4.	There are different ways to measure any given construct
5.	All assessment procedures have strengths and limitations
6.	Multiple sources of information should be part of the assessment process
7.	Performance on tests can be generalized to non-test behaviors
8.	Assessment can provide information that helps psychologists make better professional decisions
9.	Assessments can be conducted in a fair manner
10.	Testing and assessment can benefit individuals and society as a whole

improper use of tests and their results. As we noted in Assumption #3, tests and all other assessment procedures contain some degree of measurement error. Tests are not perfect and they should not be interpreted as if they were perfect. However, this limitation is not solely limited to psychological measurement; all measurement is subject to error. Chemistry, physics, and engineering all struggle with imperfect, error-laden measurement that always, to some extent, limits the advancement of the discipline. An example most of us can relate to involves the medical profession. There is error in medical assessment procedures such as blood pressure tests or tests of blood cholesterol level, but they still provide useful information. The same is true of psychological assessment procedures. They are not perfect, but they still provide useful information. While you probably will not hear anyone proclaim that there should be a ban on the use of medical tests, you will hear critics of educational and psychological testing call for a ban on, or at least a significant reduction in, the use of psychological tests. On balance, testing experts spend considerable time and effort studying the measurement characteristics of tests. This process allows us to determine how accurate and reliable tests are, provides a basis for guidelines that govern their appropriate interpretation and use, and results in the development of more accurate assessment procedures (e.g., Friedenberg, 1995).

Assumption #9 suggests that tests can be used in a fair manner. Many people criticize tests, claiming that they are biased, unfair, and discriminatory against certain groups of people. Although it is probably accurate to say that no test is perfectly fair to all examinees, neither is

> Well-made tests that are appropriately administered and interpreted are among the most equitable methods of evaluating people.

any other approach to selecting, classifying, or evaluating people. The majority of professionally developed tests are carefully constructed and scrutinized to minimize bias, and when used properly actually promote fairness and equality. In fact, it is probably safe to say that well-made tests that are appropriately administered and interpreted are among the most equitable methods of evaluating people particularly when compared to subjective judgments. Consider the example of the tests used to help select students for admission to universities. Without tests, admission officers might make arbitrary decisions based solely on their personal likes and dislikes. In fact, the SAT was developed to increase the objectivity of college admissions, which in the first quarter of the twentieth century depended primarily on family status. Research has demonstrated that as the level of subjectivity of any selection process increases, the probability of bias in the process increases. Nevertheless, the improper use of tests can result in considerable harm to individual test takers, institutions, and society.

1.6   Why Use Tests?

Since psychological assessment can incorporate a number of procedures in addition to tests (e.g., interviews, observations), it is reasonable to ask "Why do psychologists use tests so often in their professional practice?" The answer is simple: *People (including psychologists) are not very good at judging other people objectively, and most "non-test" assessment procedures involve subjective judgment.* If you are like most people, on more than one occasion your first impression of someone later proved to be totally

> People are not very good at judging other people objectively, and most "non-test" assessment procedures involve subjective judgment.

wrong. Someone that initially seemed aloof and uncaring turns out to be kind and considerate. Someone that initially appeared conscientious and trustworthy ends up letting you down. The undeniable truth is that people are not very good at judging other people in the absence of months and perhaps even years of consistent exposure to them. The reason is that all of us are susceptible to a host of biases and prejudices that undermine our judgment. For example, if someone is initially judged to be outstanding on one trait (or extremely negative on a trait), that single evaluation tends to color our overall impression of the person. As a result, a person that is viewed as physically attractive might also be considered smart, trustworthy, and personable. In contrast, someone that is viewed as physically unattractive might be considered uneducated, lazy, and boring. This is a well-documented cognitive bias that is referred to as the "halo effect." It is by no means the only bias that impairs our ability to accurately judge other people.

To illustrate the fallibility of our subjective judgments with a clinical example, Dahlstrom (1993) shared a story about one of his clients whose initial diagnosis was significantly impacted by a negative halo effect. When working as an intern, Dr. Dahlstrom had a 15-year-old female client who was described as "Not very attractive, poorly dressed and disheveled, she was silent, withdrawn, and unresponsive to questioning by the psychiatric resident who admitted her. As his preliminary diagnosis, he entered into her chart: mental retardation and possible schizophrenia. (p. 2)." Dr. Dahlstrom was not convinced that this diagnosis was accurate and coaxed his young client into completing some intelligence tests that did not require verbal responses. Her nonverbal IQ was approximately 115, which is better than about 84% of the population! Clearly the diagnosis of retardation (now referred to as intellectual disability) was inaccurate. He then had her complete a subjective personality inventory that suggested depression and social introversion, but not schizophrenia. In summary, objective testing quickly revealed that the initial diagnostic impression of intellectual disability and schizophrenia, which was based on an interview and observation, was inaccurate. With proper treatment, the patient was able to overcome the depressed state and went on to excel as an artist and become an administrator of an art institute. This is a good example of McFall and Treat's (1999) notation discussed earlier that tests are valuable because they allow us to act with less error than we would act without the information provided by the tests.

Over the years, a number of authors (e.g., Meyer et al., 2001) have delineated how formal tests can help psychologists make better clinical and diagnostic decisions. These include:

- Patients are notoriously poor historians and may present biased information. Some clients will attempt to minimize their difficulties in order to appear more competent and/or socially acceptable. This is referred to as "faking good." Other clients, particularly those involved in legal proceedings, may exaggerate their symptoms in hope of gaining a financial reward. This is referred to as "faking bad." These tendencies to misrepresent one's true characteristics are typically referred to as response biases. To address these, many contemporary tests incorporate specific validity scales that are designed to help the clinician detect a response bias and when present, consider its impact on test scores.
- Many psychological tests are designed to assess a large number of characteristics or traits, and as a result, they may help ensure that important clinical issues are not overlooked. For example, a pediatric behavior rating scale may cover such rare behaviors as "fire-setting" and "cruelty to animals," topics that might be overlooked in a clinical interview.
- Psychological tests typically provide quantitative information that allows more precise measurement of important characteristics. Additionally, many psychological tests are interpreted in such a way that each client is compared to a group of their peers. This allows the psychologist to determine how common or unusual a client's responses or performance actually are. For example, based on a clinical interview, a skilled clinician might conclude that a client has a deficit in short-term memory. The use of a memory test might indicate that the client's performance is two standard deviations below the mean (i.e., below that of 98% of their peers). In this case, the use of the test confirms the clinician's impression and also helps document how severe the deficit is. Many seasoned clinicians claim they have developed "internal norms" that allow them to judge how extreme a client's complaints or behaviors are. This might be the case if you work with a limited range of patients (e.g., adolescent males), but it would be very difficult for a psychologist to develop internal norms for the wide range of clients one typically sees in modern clinical settings.
- The process and content of clinical interviews and observations often vary considerably from client to client. For example, a clinician might ask one set of questions to one client and an entirely different set of questions to another. In contrast, psychological tests have standardized stimuli (i.e., questions or items), administration (e.g., instruction and time limits), and scoring procedures. Since all clients are presented the same stimuli under the same conditions with the same scoring criteria, we can have increased confidence that observed differences are the result of true differences in our clients, not simply differences in the questions they were asked.
- Finally, the use of tests, in addition to interviews and observations, helps ensure that multiple sources of data are included.

Dahlstrom (1993) notes that the fallibility of human judgment is one of the main reasons that psychological tests have become increasingly popular over the past century.

> The fallibility of human judgment is one of the main reasons that psychological tests have become increasingly popular over the past century.

This does not mean that psychologists should eschew the use of clinical interviews and observations, just that they should use multiple sources of information whenever making professional decisions. When there is consistency in the information we obtain using multiple sources of information (e.g., interviews, observations, tests), then we can have increased confidence in our findings. When the results of different assessment procedures are inconsistent, we must systematically generate and test different hypotheses until we determine what is the most accurate explanation. This process is often complex, requires extensive professional skill, and is the hallmark of psychological assessment when done in a competent, professional manner.

We are advocates of a philosophy or model of assessment that incorporates psychometric sophistication, clinical insight, knowledge of psychological theory, and thoughtful reasoning. The goal is to design and conduct an assessment that enhances the client's life (Reynolds & Fletcher-Janzen, 2002). With this model, assessment involves a dynamic evaluation and synthesis of information that is obtained in a reliable and valid manner from multiple sources using multiple procedures. Kaufman (1994) suggests that a psychologist conducting an assessment should assume the role of a "detective" that collects, evaluates, and synthesizes information and integrates that information with a thorough understanding of psychological theories of development, psychopathology, and individual differences. When performed appropriately, psychological assessment is a very demanding and sophisticated process.

1.7   Common Applications of Psychological Assessments

Now that we have introduced you to some of the basic terminology, concepts, and assumptions involved in testing and assessment, we will describe some of the major applications of psychological assessment. Tests and other assessments have many uses, but underlying practically all of these uses is the belief that they provide information about important psychological constructs, and that this information can help psychologists and other professionals make better decisions. Below are brief descriptions of prominent applications of assessment procedures (Table 1.5).

> We use tests because they provide information about important psychological constructs that can help psychologists make better decisions.

1.7.1   Diagnosis

Diagnosis is implied when a health-care professional specifies the nature and/or cause of a disorder, disease, or injury. In psychology and psychiatry, the diagnostic process typically incorporates information obtained using a variety of assessment procedures (e.g., tests, interviews, observations, record reviews) and utilizes the Diagnostic and Statistical Manual of Mental Disorders, Fifth Edition (DSM-5)

Table 1.5 Major applications of psychological assessments

Application	Examples
Diagnosis	Psychologists often use a variety of assessment procedures to help understand the client's history, identify their current level of functioning, and document the presence of clinical symptoms. These procedures may include a review of historical records, clinical interviews and observations, and formal tests. The information obtained will help the psychologist rule-out competing diagnoses and establish treatment needs
Treatment planning and effectiveness	Ideally, diagnosis should provide information that allows the clinician to customize the treatment for the individual client. Not all clients with a depressive disorder will present with the same pattern of clinical symptoms, and treatment is optimal when interventions are selected that target specific symptoms. Ongoing assessment can monitor the effectiveness of treatment and indicate if modifications are needed
Selection	Colleges and universities typically establish admission criteria that help determine which students will be admitted. These criteria often include scores from tests such as the American College Test (ACT) and the Scholastic Achievement Test (SAT)
Placement	Based on performance on tests and other assessments, students in a school may be assigned to different instructional programs (e.g., remedial, regular, and honors)
Classification	Students in special education may be classified as learning disabled, emotionally disturbed, speech disabled, or some other category of handicapping conditions based on the results of an assessment
Self–understanding	Psychological assessment can help clients enhance their self-understanding in order to make better decisions about educational and career goals. Assessments used in premarriage counseling can help couples identify and address possible areas of conflict before they create problems
Evaluation	Summative evaluation involves the formal evaluation of performance, often taking the form of a numerical or letter grade (e.g., A, B, C, D, or F). Formative evaluation involves evaluative activities that are aimed at providing feedback to facilitate and guide learning
Licensing	Many professions require that applicants pass licensing examinations in order to be licensed (e.g., physicians, lawyers, psychologists, and teachers). Additionally, some fairly common activities such as driving a car require an examination
Program evaluation	Program evaluation involves the formal evaluation of a service delivery program in order to evaluate its effectiveness. This can range from the effectiveness of a specific curriculum being used in a classroom to the efficiency of a large federal program
Scientific method	The scientific method involves measurement and the collection of empirical data. Scientists use a wide variety of tests and other assessments in order to test their hypotheses

(American Psychiatric Association, 2013) as the guiding taxonomy. Ideally, diagnosis involves more than simply specifying a diagnostic category (e.g., Generalized Anxiety Disorder), but informs about potential underlying causes of the disorder, explains the nature of the problem the client is experiencing, and guides the development of a treatment plan. As a result, diagnosis is an integral part of effective treatment.

1.7.2   Treatment Planning and Treatment Effectiveness

As noted in the previous section, psychological assessments can provide important information that helps psychologists and other professionals tailor their interventions to meet the specific needs of the individual client. For example, not all clients with dyslexia will exhibit the same pattern of cognitive strengths and weaknesses. Similarly, not all clients with a depressive disorder will present with the same set of symptoms. When developing treatment plans, it is important to consider the client's specific needs and develop a program that is most likely to produce the maximum benefit. Repeated testing or measurement of a variable targeted for change can reveal the relative effectiveness (or ineffectiveness) of treatment.

1.7.3   Selection, Placement, and Classification

The terms selection, placement, and classification are often used interchangeably, but technically they have different meanings. Nitko (2001) notes that *selection* refers to decisions by an individual or institution to either accept or reject an applicant for some position (e.g., hiring employees). With selection decisions, the key factor is that some individuals are "selected" while others are "rejected." In contrast, *placement* decisions involve situations where individuals are assigned to different programs or tracks that are ordered in some way. With placement, there are no actual rejections because all individuals are placed. For example, if all the students in a school are assigned to one of three instructional programs (e.g., remedial, regular, and honors), this is a placement decision. Finally, **classification** refers to situations in which individuals are assigned to different categories that are not ordered in any way. For example, special education students may be classified as Learning Disabled, Emotionally Disturbed, Speech Handicapped, or some other category of handicapping conditions, but these categories are not ordered in any particular manner, they are simply descriptive. You might have noticed that classification and diagnosis are related procedures. There are, however, some significant differences. Diagnosis is a more elaborate process that goes beyond simple classification. Additionally, when properly executed, diagnosis involves a thorough description and/or explanation of the condition under study.

1.7.4 Self-Understanding

Psychological and educational assessments can provide information that promotes self-understanding and helps individuals plan for their future. For example, there are a number of career assessments that are designed to help an individual select a college major and/or career that matches their personal interests, preferences, and strengths. There are also tests that help couples considering marriage evaluate their commonalities and differences.

1.7.5 Evaluation

Educators often use a variety of assessment procedures to monitor the academic progress of their students. In schools, probably the most common use of assessments involves assigning grades to students to reflect their academic progress or achievement. This type of evaluation is typically referred to as ***summative evaluation***. In the classroom, summative evaluation typically involves the formal evaluation of student performance, commonly taking the form of a numerical or letter grade (e.g., A, B, C, D, or F). Summative evaluation is often designed to communicate information about student progress, strengths, and weaknesses to parents and other involved adults. Another prominent application of student evaluation is to provide feedback to students in order to facilitate or guide their learning. This type of evaluation is referred to as ***formative evaluation***. Optimally, students need to know both what they have mastered and what they have not mastered. This type of feedback serves to facilitate and guide learning activities and can help motivate students. It is often very frustrating for students to receive a score on an assignment without also receiving feedback about what they can do to improve their performance in the future. Formative evaluation involves evaluative activities that are aimed at providing feedback to students. Evaluation decisions are not limited to educational settings. For example, industrial-organizational psychologists help develop assessments used to evaluate the performance of employees in work settings.

1.7.6 Licensing

Tests and other assessments are used in licensing decisions ranging from who qualifies for a driver's license to who qualifies for a medical license.

1.7.7 Program Evaluation

In addition to providing information about individuals, assessment can also provide information about the quality and usefulness of programs. Cronbach (1990) notes that in this context, "programs" typically refers to a plan or model for delivering some type of services. For example, job-training programs help prepare people for employment. Therefore, it is important to determine if job-training programs are actually helping people obtain jobs and succeed in the workforce. Programs can be as narrow as the curriculum program implemented by an individual teacher in his/her classroom or as large as a federal program for delivering services to millions of people (e.g., Social Security, Medicaid).

1.7.8   Scientific Method

Tests and other assessments play promi-nent roles in the scientific process. Regardless of what hypothesis is being tested, measurement is typically involved. While scientists may use commercial tests in their research (e.g., a standardized intelligence test), it is also common for researchers to develop tests that specifi-cally address the hypotheses they are interested in testing.

> Tests and other assessments impact many aspects of modern life, and while tests clearly have their oppo-nents, they are likely to continue to impact our lives for many years to come.

This brief list of common applications of tests and assessments is clearly not exhaustive. Tests and other assessments impact many aspects of modern life, and while tests clearly have their opponents, they are likely to continue to impact our lives for many years to come.

1.8   Common Criticisms of Testing and Assessment

It is no secret that we are staunch advocates for the use of tests and formalized assessment. This book serves as a testament to our commitment for encouraging knowledgeable assessment practice, covering important topics that necessitate a basic level of understanding by those partaking in the field of testing and assess-ment. As passionate as we are about the merits of formalized testing and assess-ment, it is not hard to find those who are just as passionate in their opposition to it. Unfair, biased, discriminatory, unjust, inaccurate, irrelevant, crooked, right-winged, political, evil—These are all words that are commonly used by testing and assess-ment opponents. A simple web search will assuredly reveal numerous stories and blogs proclaiming the detrimental effects testing and assessment has on our society, particularly in the world of education.

Throughout this book, we intend to provide you with the background informa-tion needed to understand many of the arguments commonly presented when evalu-ating the utility of testing and assessment. For arguments where there is a lot of supporting evidence for an argument, we present our interpretation of that evidence, and make conclusions accordingly. For areas where the evidence is mixed, we stop short of drawing conclusions. In either case, you ultimately will draw your own conclusions on these issues, which is entirely appropriate and acceptable, as the evidence doesn't always point in a single direction.

Criticisms against testing and assessment can be very general or very specific. Here are some of the common ones that are addressed in the book. We encourage you to keep them in the back of your minds as you advance through the book. We will help you access them from the recesses of your mind by bringing them up at appropriate times as we go through the chapters.

- Tests are not fair to everyone. Perhaps one of the most pervasive and frequent arguments against testing is that tests do not give everyone who takes them an equal opportunity to perform well on the test, due to some characteristic about a person or a person's background and experiences. We will present evidence that this often is not the case, and in fact standardized testing results in a fairer process and more accurate results than do other less objective methods of evaluating a performance area.
- The items included in tests are bad. This criticism is very broad and may refer to a number of different things. Oftentimes, it refers to the perception that an item is irrelevant to a given test, or that a test item doesn't seem fair to all those taking the test. While there are likely to be many tests that have some bad items on them, we will show that good test development practices require several steps to ensure that test items are important representations of the underlying constructs being measured, that they are fair to those taking the test, and that they are at least indirectly related to the overall skill or performance area the test is designed to measure.
- Everyone should have the same chance to score well on a test. We agree— Everyone should have an equal opportunity to perform well on a test. However, that doesn't mean all will receive a high or passing score, which is often what is really meant by this criticism. It is important to remember that one of the primary purposes of a power test is to differentiate individuals based on their knowledge or abilities in a particular area. Those who are very knowledgeable in an area or who have high skill levels should attain higher scores than those with lower levels of knowledge or skills. For this reason, tests that result in similar scores for individuals with very different skills or abilities are not good tests.
- Tests don't capture all of the important information about a person or what he or she knows. One of the biggest challenges in developing a test is determining how long it should be. Many factors go into that decision: Are there a minimum number of skills that need to be covered (e.g., as in a licensure or certification test)? How much testing time can the examinee reasonably handle? What will the test results be used for? How sophisticated or complex is the underlying construct(s) being measured? These are just a few of the things that might be considered when developing a test, but all else being equal, shorter tests are preferable to longer tests for a number of reasons. We will discuss in this book a variety of techniques that test developers use to shorten tests while still adequately measuring those constructs that tests are designed to assess.
- Tests are used so large companies can make a lot of money and politicians can get political donations from them. This criticism has been repeatedly levied against companies developing tests in educational settings (e.g., state-wide assessments of learning). Ultimately, such tests are very expensive to develop

and generate scores and reports. We will explore some of the reasons for this and will attempt to correct some of the fallacies associated with them.

- Tests can be easily faked. Personality tests and attitudinal surveys often ask personal questions whose answers are only known by the individual providing responses. Such questions can be of a sensitive nature and may cause a person to think twice about what information to share. For example, preemployment tests that ask about previous illicit activities (e.g., employee theft, recreational drug use, etc.) or about one's social prowess might result in responses based on what the job applicant thinks the potential employer wants to hear, rather than the applicant's actual beliefs or activities. While no test can guarantee candid responses, we will review several methods used on tests to minimize and detect biased or deceptive responses.
- You can learn as much or more from talking to a person than you can by testing them. While in some cases this statement is plausible, we will review some advantages of the methodical and standardized way information is gathered and interpreted via test administration. We will also review how formats that use an interview-based approach can result in undesirable response sets that might not exist in approaches that allow the examinee to respond more "privately" (e.g., on a piece of paper).

1.9   Participants in the Assessment Process

When you consider who is involved in the assessment process, the person who administers the test (examiner) and the person takes the test (examinee) immediately come to mind. But there are other individuals involved in the assessment process and we spend some time discussing them in the next sections (e.g., AERA et al., 2014).

1.9.1   People Who Develop Tests

Can you guess how many new tests are developed in a given year? Although the exact number is unknown, the American Psychological Association (1993) estimated that up to 20,000 new psychological, behavioral, and cognitive tests are developed every year. Most people are surprised by the magnitude of this number, but it includes only those tests published by commercial test publishers, tests developed by professionals hoping to have their instruments published, and tests developed by researchers to address specific research questions. When you consider the vast number of tests that are developed by teachers and professors in our schools and universities to assess the achievement or progress of their students, the actual number is substantially larger. For tests to be of high

> The "Standards for Educational and Psychological Testing" is the most influential and comprehensive set of guidelines for developing and using psychological and educational tests.

quality, there are minimal standards they should meet, whether developed by an assessment professional, a graduate student completing a thesis, or a professor assessing the achievement of students in a test and measurement course. Numerous professional organizations have developed guidelines to provide standards for the

---

Special Interest Topic 1.2: Making the Test

Police officer, lawyer, doctor, engineer—Most of you have probably heard these career choices from a family member or friend. Test developer? Probably not, but that doesn't mean it is a bad idea! As discussed throughout this book, tests are used across a variety of interesting fields: employment/workplace, education, clinical practice, medicine, military, and a host of others. Although job titles can change depending on the setting, the testing industry offers several typical job types, including positions like those listed below.

1. *Research Director*. Research directors are typically responsible for overall test development projects. Often having specialized training in assessment and testing (e.g., like that obtained by individuals holding a graduate degree in psychology) and/or the content area of the test (e.g., speech/language pathology, neuroscience, nursing, etc.), the research directors work to define the parameters of the test, conduct background research, develop the test items, plan each stage of test development, conduct/review data analysis results and make final item decisions, write supporting technical documentation, training test users, etc. This role is best for individuals who like a high degree of task variety, and who like to problem-solve on a daily basis. Communication skills are a must since this person is often a formal leader of a development team that is comprised of many individuals from various parts of a company (such as the roles described below). Excellent writing skills are a must, as is the ability to make challenging material accessible to an audience with a wide range of experience in the content area.

2. *Psychometrician*. In the last decade, psychometricians have been one of the most sought-after positions in the education and testing industry, resulting in a number of perks (e.g., competing job offers, higher salaries that can be in the six-figure range, entry-level positions that are high in the organizational hierarchy, etc.). The position often requires a Ph.D. in psychometrics or statistics, and extensive knowledge of a variety of statistical software packages (that is often acquired along the way of obtaining the degree). Psychometricians are responsible for ensuring that the questions being addressed in a research study can be answered by the statistical analysis being used, as well as carrying out the analyses and summarizing their results. One of the biggest challenges a psychometrician can face starts prior to running any statistical routines, when "cleaning" the data file occurs. In large projects, data files contain tens of thousands of test records, each of which has responses on hundreds of variables. As is quickly

(continued)

learned, no data file is ever complete and most contain unexpected responses. All of the problematic responses have to be resolved prior to analyzing item and test scores. Individuals who are successful at this position possess a high level of attention to detail, enjoy technical and methodological problem-solving, enjoy writing analysis code, and are comfortable working under project deadlines. While they play a more "behind-the-scenes" role in a development project, the impact of their work is central to the overall success of test.

3. *Development Specialist*. Like a research director, the development specialist can play a number of different roles in a development project. These individuals might hold a specialized or advanced degree, but can be from a host of different areas. For employment tests, these positions can be held by someone who previously was a member of the field in which the test is being used (e.g., teacher, technical support helpdesk). For a math test, it can be held by someone who used to be a math teacher. These positions are for those who like to role their sleeves up, get into the details, and deal with whatever comes their way.

4. *Software Engineer*. Software engineers (aka programmers) play an increasingly large role in the development of new tests. The level of sophistication of the software can vary widely, from simple digital adaptions that provide the test taker with an experience that resembles a paper-and-pencil test administration, to implementing complex digital test items with features and scoring that are not possible using a traditional paper-and-pencil format (e.g., how long the examinee spent looking at an item, how long it took to respond to the item, whether a response was changed, where on the screen a person was looking). In addition, software engineers are responsible for developing the scoring and reporting platform that can be easily used by those responsible for interpreting the test results. Persons with dual expertise in testing/assessment and computer programming are poised to make significant advances in digital testing, an area that will assuredly continue to grow for the foreseeable future.

5. *Design Specialist*. The main role of a design specialist is to optimize the testing materials and ultimately the testing experience for both the examiner and the examinee. On paper-and-pencil materials, this covers a variety of areas, such as the readability and usability of the forms, as well as the overall look of the materials. However, there is increasing development of digital-native tests (tests developed specifically for a digital implementation) as well as transformation of test that started in a paper-pencil format to computer platforms. As a result, designers will need to further combine their creative expertise with technical software expertise in coming years. Design specialists often have a design-related degree, as well as expertise in using a variety of software programs that enable the development of complex visual materials.

(continued)

6. *Editor.* Most tests do not simply consist of a booklet that contains the test items and responses. Other test materials include answer keys, test manuals, technical reports, reports for parents, software reports—just to name a few. It is crucial for testing materials to be accurate and clearly written. The editor plays a key role in ensuring that all materials are error-free, and written in a way that they can be easily understood by user of the material (e.g., a student, a parent, a teacher). Editors can also play a role in the development of test items particularly when the content of the test overlaps with an editor's area of expertise (e.g., a reading test). Editors typically have a degree in English or related field. There is a high demand for editors who are multi-lingual, particularly in Spanish or other languages commonly spoken in various regions of the United States.

7. *Data Collection Specialist.* The data collection specialist is responsible for overseeing the large-scale testing projects. For tests that offer nationally based norms, there are often thousands of completed test forms that have to be collected throughout the United States, in proportions that approximate the demographics of the U.S. population. There can be hundreds of data collection sites and even more testing coordinators/examiners. The role of the data collection specialist is to recruit the coordinators and test examiners, assign test cases that match the desired demographic targets for the overall sample, ensure testing materials are delivered in a timely fashion, and ensure they are securely returned. (Security is crucial because there is often a bootleg market for test items that appear on "high-stakes" tests, such as college entrance examinations, intelligence tests, etc.) While an advanced degree is typically not required for such positions, "people skills," organization ability, and attention to detail are must-haves for those who want to be successful in this role.

development and use of psychological tests, educational tests, and other assessment procedures. The most influential and comprehensive set of guidelines is the ***Standards for Educational and Psychological Testing*** that is published by the American Educational Research Association, the American Psychological Association, and the National Council on Measurement in Education (hereinafter referred to as the Standards, 2014). We have referenced this document numerous times earlier in this chapter and will do so many more times throughout this text. Special Interest Topic 1.2 illustrates the growing need for test development experts in modern society!

1.9.2 People Who Use Tests

The list of people who use tests includes those who select, administer, score, interpret, and use the results of tests and other assessment procedures. Tests are used in a wide range of settings by a wide range of individuals. For example, psychologists and counselors use tests to understand their clients better and to help refine their diagnostic impressions and develop treatment plans. Employers use tests to help select and hire skilled employees. States use tests to determine who will be given drivers' licenses. Professional licensing boards use tests to determine who has the knowledge and skills necessary to enter professions ranging from medicine to real estate. Teachers use tests in schools to assess their students' academic progress. This is only a small sampling of the many settings in which tests are used. As with the development of tests, some of the people using these tests are assessment experts whose primary responsibility is administering, scoring, and interpreting tests. However, many of the people using tests are trained in other professional areas, and assessment is not their primary area of training. As with test development, the administration, scoring, and interpretation of tests involve professional and ethical standards and responsibilities.

1.9.3 People Who Take Tests

We have all been in this category many times in our lives. In public school, we take an untold number of tests to help our teachers evaluate our academic progress, knowledge, and skills. You probably took the SAT or ACT to gain admission to college. When you graduate from college and are ready to obtain a professional license or certificate, you will probably be given another test to evaluate how well prepared you are to enter your selected profession. While the other participants in the assessment process have professional and ethical responsibilities, test takers have a number of rights. The Joint Committee on Testing Practices (JCTP, 1998) notes that the most fundamental right test takers have is to be tested with tests that meet high professional standards and that are valid for the intended purposes. Other rights of test takers include the following:

> The most fundamental right of test takers is to be tested with tests that meet high professional standards and are valid for the intended purpose.

- Test takers should be given information about the purposes of the testing, how the results will be used, who will receive the results, accommodations available for individuals with disabilities or language differences, and any costs associated with the testing.
- Test takers have the right to be treated with courtesy, respect, and impartiality.
- Test takers have the right to have tests administered and interpreted by adequately trained individuals who follow professional ethics codes.
- Test takers have the right to receive information about their test results.
- Test takers have the right to have their test results kept confidential.

1.9.4   Other People Involved in Assessment Process

Although the preceding three categories probably encompass most participants in the assessment process, they are not exhaustive. For example, there are individuals who market and sell assessment products and services, those who teach others about assessment practices, and those who conduct research on assessment procedures and evaluate assessment programs (NCME, 1995).

1.10   Psychological Assessment in the Twenty-First Century

The field of psychological assessment is dynamic and continuously evolving. There are some aspects of the profession that have been stable for many years. For example, classical test theory has been around for almost a century and is still very influential today. However, many aspects of psychological assessment are constantly evolving as the result of a number of external and internal factors. Some of these changes are the result of theoretical or technical advances, some reflect philosophical changes within the profession, and some are the result of external societal, economic, and political influences. It is important for assessment professionals to stay informed regarding new developments in the field and to consider them with an open mind. To illustrate some of the developments the profession is dealing with today, we will briefly highlight a few contemporary trends that are likely to continue to impact assessment practices as you enter the teaching profession.

1.10.1 Computerized Adaptive Testing (CAT)

The widespread availability of fairly sophisticated and powerful personal computers has had a significant impact on many aspects of our society, and the field of assessment is no exception. One of the most dramatic and innovative uses of computer technology has been the emergence of *computerized adaptive testing (CAT)*. In CAT, the test taker is initially given an item that is of medium difficulty. If the test taker correctly responds to that item, the computer selects and administers a slightly more difficult item. If the examinee misses the initial item, the computer selects a somewhat easier item. As the testing proceeds the computer continues to selects items on the basis of the test taker's performance on previous items. CAT continues until a specified level of precision is reached. Research suggests that CAT can produce the same levels of reliability and validity as conventional paper-and-pencil tests, but because it requires the administration of fewer test items, assessment efficiency can be enhanced (e.g., Weiss, 1982, 1985, 1995).

1.10.2 Other Technological Applications Used in Assessment

CAT is not the only innovative application of computer technology in the field of assessment. Some of the most promising applications of technology in assessment involve the use of technology to present problem simulations that cannot be realisti-cally addressed with paper-and-pencil tests. For example, flight-training programs routinely use sophisticated flight simulators to assess the skills of pilots. This tech-nology allows programs to assess how pilots will handle emergency and other low--incidence situations, skills that were previously difficult if not impossible to assess accurately. Another innovative use of technology is the commercially available instrumental music assessment systems that allow students to perform musical pieces and have their performances analyzed and graded in terms of pitch and rhythm. Online versions of these pro-grams allow students to practice at home and have their performance results for-warded to their instructors at school. Although it is difficult to anticipate the many ways technology will change assessment practices in the twenty-first century, it is safe to say that they will be dramatic and sweeping.

> Although it is difficult to anticipate the many ways technology will change assessment practices in the twenty-first century, it is safe to say that changes will be dramatic and sweeping.

1.10.3 "Authentic" Assessments

Although advances in technology are driving some of the current trends in assess-ment, others are the result of philosophical changes among members of the assess-ment profession. This is exemplified in the current emphasis on performance assessments and portfolios in educational settings. Performance assessments and portfolios are not new creations, but have been around for many years (e.g., perfor-mance assessments have been used in Industrial and Organizational Psychology for decades). However, the use of performance assessments and portfolios in educa-tional settings has increased appreciably in recent years. Traditional testing formats, particularly multiple-choice and other selected-response formats (e.g., true–false, matching) have always had their critics, but their opposition has become more vocal in recent years. Opponents of traditional test formats complain that they emphasize rote memorization and other low-level cognitive skills and largely neglect higher--order conceptual and problem-solving skills.

To address these and related shortcomings, many assessment experts have pro-moted the use of more "authentic" or complex-performance assessments, typically in the form of performance assessments and portfolios. Performance assessments require test takers to complete a process or produce a product in a context that closely resembles real-life situations. For example, a graduate student in a clinical psychology program might be required to interview a mock client, select tests and other assessment procedures, provide a diagnosis, and develop a treatment plan. Portfolios, a form of performance assessment, involve the systematic collection of student work products over a specified period of time according to a specific set of guidelines (AERA et al., 2014). Artists, architects, writers, and others have long used portfolios to represent their work, and in the last decade, portfolios have become increasingly popular in the assessment of students. While performance assessments have their own set of strengths and weaknesses, they do represent a significant addition to the assessment options available to teachers.

1.10.4 Health-Care Delivery Systems

So far, we have described how technological and philosophical developments within the profession have influenced current assessment practices. Other changes are the result of political, societal, and economic influences, and this can be seen in the way managed care is influencing the practice of psychology. Managed care is a generic name for health-care systems (e.g., Health Maintenance Organization [HMO] or a Preferred Provider Organization [PPO]) that control expenses by managing programs in which health-care professionals accept lowered compensation for their services and patients accept limitations in their choice of health-care providers. Managed care systems also limit the services that health-care professionals provide, including the number of psychotherapy or counseling sessions a client receives and the types of assessments that can be employed. In the past, it was common for psychologists to use a comprehensive battery of time-consuming tests with their patients. However, due to managed care's emphasis on time-limited and problem-focused interventions, current assessment practices are starting to emphasize the use of briefer and less expensive behavioral and problem-oriented assessments (Maruish, 2004).

1.10.5 High-Stakes Assessment

Societal and political forces are also influencing assessment practices in our public schools. Although parents and politicians have always closely scrutinized the public schools, over the last three decades the public demands for increased accountability in the schools have reached an all-time high. To help ensure that teachers are teaching what they are supposed to be teaching and students are learning what they are supposed to be learning, all 50 states and the District of Columbia have implemented statewide testing programs (Doherty, 2002). These testing programs are often referred to as "high-stakes testing" because they produce results that have direct and substantial consequences for both the students and schools (AERA et al., 2014). Students who do not pass the tests may not be promoted to the next grade or allowed to graduate.

However, the "high stakes" are not limited to students. Many states publish "report cards" that reflect the performance of school districts and individual schools. In some states low-performing schools can be closed, reconstituted, or taken over by the state, and administrators and teachers can be terminated or replaced (Amrein & Berliner, 2002). Proponents of these testing programs maintain that they ensure that public school students are acquiring the knowledge and skills necessary to succeed in society. To support their position, they refer to data showing that national achievement scores have improved since these testing programs were implemented. Opponents of high-stakes testing programs argue that the tests emphasize rote learning and generally neglect critical thinking, problem-solving, and communication skills. Additionally, these critics feel that too much instructional time is spent "teaching to the test" instead of teaching the vitally important skills teachers would prefer to focus on (Doherty, 2002). This debate is likely to continue for the foreseeable future, but in the meantime accountability and the associated testing programs are likely to play a major role in our public schools. In fact, the trend is toward more,

---

Special Interest Topic 1.3: What Does the Twenty-First Century Hold for the Assessment Profession?

Dr. Susan Embretson presented a lecture titled "The Second Century of Ability Testing: Some Predictions and Speculations" at the Educational Testing Service (ETS) in Princeton, New Jersey in January 2001. In this presentation, she started by reviewing the history of ability testing which dates back approximately 100 years. She noted that by 1930, most of the key psychometric principles were firmly established and that the remainder of the twentieth century was largely spent applying and refining those principles. As the profession enters its second century, she predicts changes in the way tests are developed, the way abilities are measured, and the aspects of ability that are measured. Below is a brief summary of some of her key points.

The Way Tests Are Developed. Dr. Embretson believes that technological advances will significantly impact the way tests are developed. For example, currently test revision is an expensive and labor-intensive process where tests are revised and renormed every few years. In the future, she anticipates tests will undergo continuous test revisions. As more assessments are administered via computers and data collection is centralized, test developers will be able to try out new items and update normative data on an ongoing basis. Computer-administered tests and centralized data collection will also facilitate automated validity studies and even allow items to be developed through the use of artificial intelligence.

The Way Abilities Are Measured. Based on technological and theoretical advances, Dr. Embretson predicts ability tests will become both shorter and more reliable. She also predicts that there will be a broader conceptualization of test items. For example, ability testing will incorporate more essays and other work-products that had previously been difficult to evaluate in a reliable and economical manner. In recent years, computer programs have been developed that can score written essays and graphical problems and these initial efforts show considerable potential.

The Aspects of Ability That Are Measured. During the twentieth century, normative interpretations of ability predominated, but Dr. Embretson expects new interpretive models to become increasingly popular. For example, she

(continued)

believes domain-referenced interpretations will emerge where abilities will be interpreted in reference to the cognitive processes and structures that are required to solve the assessment problems or tasks. Instead of focusing almost exclusively on quantitative aspects of performance, future assessments will focus more on the qualitative aspects of test performance. Finally, she believes dynamic testing will become an increasingly important force in ability testing. Dynamic testing measures how responsive the examinee's performance is to changes in conditions as the assessment proceeds.

Although Dr. Embretson expects changes to occur rapidly over the next few decades, she also believes that the basic psychometric principles that have been with for almost a century will still be important. Therefore, even though some exciting changes are in store for the assessment profession, the basic principles and concepts that are presented in this textbook will continue to be fundamental aspects of the profession.

If you are interested in reading this intriguing paper, it can be accessed at http://www.ets.org/Media/Research/pdf/PICANG7.pdf or you can purchase a copy for $3.00 by contacting the ETS Policy Information Center, MS-04R, Rosedale Road, Princeton, NJ651-0001.

rather than less, standardized testing in public schools. For example, the Elementary and Secondary Education Act of 2001 (No Child Left Behind Act) requires that states test students annually in Grades 3 through 8. Because many states typically administer standardized achievement tests in only a few of these grades, this new law will require even more high-stakes testing than is currently in use (Kober, 2002).

This has been a brief and clearly incomplete discussion of some current trends in the field of assessment. To complicate the situation, some of these trends have opposing results. For example, while managed care is placing limits on the use of assessments by psychologists working in many health-care settings, the trend toward more high-stakes assessments programs in the public schools results in the increased use of standardized tests in these settings. Special Interest Topic 1.3 provides a commentary by a respected assessment expert about what she expects to evolve during the next century.

1.11   Summary

This chapter provides a broad introduction to the field of psychological assessment. Milestones in the history of testing began with the use of "civil service" type tests in China as early as 2200 BC and concluded with the development of seminal tests in the twentieth Century. Common terms used in the psychological assessment literature include test, measurement, and assessment. A test is a procedure in which a sample of an individual's behavior is obtained, evaluated, and scored using standardized procedures. Measurement is a set of rules for assigning numbers to represent objects, traits, attributes, or behaviors. Assessment is any systematic procedure for collecting information that can be used to make inferences about the characteristics of people or objects. Evaluation, reliability, and validity are other important terms. Evaluation is an activity that involves judging or appraising the value or worth of something. Reliability refers to the stability or consistency of test scores. Validity refers to the accuracy of the interpretations of test scores.

There are different types of tests. Most tests are classified as either maximum performance or typical response. Maximum performance tests assess the upper limits of the examinee's knowledge and abilities whereas typical response tests measure the typical behavior and characteristics of examinees. Maximum performance tests are often classified as achievement tests or aptitude tests. Achievement tests measure knowledge and skills in an area in which the examinee has received instruction. In contrast, aptitude tests measure cognitive abilities and skills that are accumulated as the result of overall life experiences).

Maximum performance tests can also be classified as either speed tests or power tests. On pure speed tests performance reflects only differences in the speed of performance while on pure power tests performance reflects only the difficulty of the items the examinee is able to answer correctly. In most situations, a test is not a measure of pure speed or pure power, but reflects some combination of both approaches.

Finally, maximum performance tests are often classified as objective or subjective. When the scoring of a test does not rely on the subjective judgment of person scoring the test, it is said to be objective. For example, multiple-choice tests can be scored using a fixed scoring key and are considered objective (multiple-choice tests are often scored by a computer). If the scoring of a test does rely on the subjective judgment of person scoring the test, it is said to be subjective. Essay examinations are examples of subjective tests.

Typical response tests measure constructs such as personality, behavior, attitudes, or interests and are often classified as being either objective or projective. Objective tests use selected-response items (e.g., true–false, multiple choice) that are not influenced by the subjective judgment of the person scoring the test. Projective tests involve the presentation of ambiguous material that can elicit an almost infinite range of responses. Most projective tests involve some subjectivity in scoring, but what is exclusive to projective techniques is the belief that these techniques elicit unconscious material that has not been censored by the conscious mind.

Most tests produce scores that reflect the test takers' performance. Norm-referenced score interpretations compare an examinee's performance to the performance of other people. Criterion-referenced score interpretations compare an examinee's performance to a specified level of performance. Typically, tests are designed to produce either norm-referenced or criterion-referenced scores, but it is possible for a test to produce both norm- and criterion-referenced scores.

There are also basic assumptions that underlie psychological assessment including:

- Psychological constructs exist.
- Psychological constructs can be measured.
- Although we can measure constructs, our measurement is not perfect.
- There are different ways to measure any given construct.
- All assessment procedures have strengths and limitations.
- Multiple sources of information should be part of the assessment process.
- Performance on tests can be generalized to nontest behaviors.
- Assessment can provide information that helps psychologists make better decisions.
- Assessments can be conducted in a fair manner.
- Testing and assessment can benefit individuals and society as a whole.

The use of psychological assessments is predicated on the belief that they can provide valuable information that helps psychologists make better decisions. Prominent uses include:

- Diagnosis
- Treatment Planning
- Selection, Placement, and Classification
- Self-understanding
- Evaluation
- Licensing
- Program Evaluation
- Scientific Research

Major participants in the assessment process include those who develop tests, use tests, and take tests.

Trends in psychological assessment at the beginning of the twenty-first century include the influence of computerized adaptive testing (CAT) and other technological advances, a growing emphasis on authentic assessments, the influence of managed care on assessment practices, and the growing emphasis on high-stakes assessment.

References

American Educational Research Association, American Psychological Association, & National Council on Measurement in Education. (2014). *Standards for educational and psychological testing*. Washington, DC: American Educational Research Association.

American Psychiatric Association. (2013). *Diagnostic and statistical manual of mental disorders* (5th ed.). Arlington, VA: Author.

American Psychological Association. (1993). Call for book proposals for test instruments. *APA Monitor, 24*, 12.

American Psychological Association. (2019). Retrieved from https://www.accreditation.apa.org/accredited-programs.

Amrein, A. L., & Berliner, D. C. (2002). High stakes testing, uncertainty, and student learning. *Education Policy Analysis Archives, 10*(18). Retrieved from https://epaa.asu.edu/ojs/article/viewFile/297/423.

Anastasi, A., & Urbina, S. (1997). *Psychological testing* (7th ed.). Upper Saddle River, NJ: Prentice Hall.

Butcher, J. N., Dahlstrom, W. G., Graham, J. R., Tellegen, A., & Kaemmer, B. (1989). *MMPI-2: Manual for administration and scoring*. Minneapolis, MN: University of Minnesota Press.

Cohen, R. C., & Swerdlik, M. E. (2002). *Psychological testing and assessment: An introduction to tests and measurement*. New York, NY: McGraw-Hill.

Cronbach, L. J. (1990). *Essentials of psychological testing* (5th ed.). New York, NY: HarperCollins.

Dahlstrom, W. G. (1993). Tests: Small samples, large consequences. *American Psychologist, 48,* 393–399.

Doherty, K. M. (2002). Education issues: Assessment. *Education Week*. Retrieved from http://www.edweek.org/context/topics/issuespage.cfm?id=41.

Fancher, R. E. (1985). *The intelligence men: Makers of the IQ controversy*. New York, NY: Norton.

Friedenberg, L. (1995). *Psychological testing: Design, analysis, and use*. Boston, FL: Allyn & Bacon.

Galton, F. (1879). Psychometric experiments. *Brain: A Journal of Neurology, 11,* 149–162.

Gregory, R. (2004). *Psychological testing: History, principles, and applications*. Needham Heights, MA: Allyn & Bacon.

Huddleston, M. W., & Boyer, W. W. (1996). *The Higher Civil Service in the United States: Quest for reform*. Pittsburgh, PA: University of Pittsburgh Press.

Joint Committee on Testing Practices. (1998). *Rights and responsibilities of test takers: Guidelines and expectations*. Washington, DC: American Psychological Association.

Karazsia, B. T., & Smith, L. (2016). Preparing for graduate-level training in professional psychology: Comparisons Across Clinical PhD, Counseling PhD, and Clinical PsyD Programs. *Teaching of Psychology, 43*(4), 305–313.

Kaufman, A. S. (1994). *Intelligent testing with the WISC-III*. New York, NY: Wiley.

Kober, N. (2002). Teaching to the test: The good, the bad, and who's responsible. *Test Talk for Leaders* (Issue 1). Washington, DC: Center on Education Policy. Retrieved from http://www.cep-dc.org/testing/testtalkjune2002.htm.

Maruish, M. E. (2004). Introduction. In M. Maruish (Ed.), *The use of psychological testing for treatment planning and out comes assessment* (General considerations) (Vol. 1, 3rd ed., pp. 1–64). Mahwah, NJ: Erlbaum.

McFall, R. M., & Treat, T. T. (1999). Quantifying the information value of clinical assessment with signal detection theory. *Annual Review of Psychology, 50,* 215–241.

Meyer, G. J., Finn, S. E., Eyde, L. D., Kay, G. G., Moreland, K. L., Dies, R. R., … Reed, G. M. (2001). Psychological testing and psychological assessment: A review of evidence and issues. *American Psychologist, 56,* 128–165.

Morgan, R. D., & Cohen, L. M. (2008). Clinical and counseling psychology: Can differences be gleaned from printed recruiting materials? *Training and Education in Professional Psychology, 2*(3), 156–164.

National Council on Measurement in Education. (1995). *Code of professional responsibilities in educational measurement*. Washington, DC: Author.

Nitko, A. J. (2001). *Educational assessment of students*. Upper Saddle River, NJ: Merrill Prentice Hall.

Norcross, J. C. (2000). Clinical versus counseling psychology: What's the diff? *Eye on Psi Chi, 5*(1), 20–22.

Norcross, J. C., Karg, R. S., & Prochaska, J. O. (1997). Clinical psychologists in the 1990s: Part II. *Clinical Psychologist, 50,* 4–11.

Phelps, R., Eisman, E. J., & Kohout, J. (1998). Psychological practice and managed care: Results of the CAPP practitioner survey. *Professional Psychology: Research and Practice, 29,* 31–36.

Popham, W. J. (2000). *Modern educational measurement: Practical guidelines for educational leaders*. Boston, MA: Allyn & Bacon.

Reynolds, C. R. (1998). Fundamentals of measurement and assessment in psychology. In A. Bellack & M. Hersen (Eds.), *Comprehensive clinical psychology* (pp. 33–55). New York, NY: Elsevier.

Reynolds, C. R., & Fletcher-Janzen, E. (2002). Intelligent testing. In C. R. Reynolds & E. Fletcher-Janzen (Eds.), *Concise encyclopedia of special education* (2nd ed., pp. 522–523). New York, NY: Wiley.

Roid, G. H. (2003). *Stanford-Binet Intelligence Scale* (5th ed.). Itasca, IL: Riverside.

Sternberg, R. J. (1990). *Metaphors of mind: Conceptions of the nature of intelligence*. Cambridge, England: Cambridge University Press.

Weiss, D. J. (1982). Improving measurement quality and efficiency with adaptive theory. *Applied Psychological Measurement, 6*, 473–492.

Weiss, D. J. (1985). Adaptive testing by computer. *Journal of Consulting and Clinical Psychology, 53*, 774–789.

Weiss, D. J. (1995). Improving individual difference measurement with item response theory and computerized adaptive testing. In D. Lubinski & R. Dawis (Eds.), *Assessing individual differences in human behavior: New concepts, methods, and findings* (pp. 49–79). Palo Alto, CA: Davies-Black.

Recommended Reading and Internet Sites

American Educational Research Association, American Psychological Association,, and National Council on Measurement in Education. (2014). *Standards for educational and psychological testing*. Washington, DC: American Educational Research Association. In practically every content area this resource is indispensable!

American Psychological Association. www.apa.org. In addition to general information about the Association, this site has much information on psychology as a field of study, current reviews, and archival documents such as specialty definitions and practice guidelines. Links to the divisions' websites are provided here as well as applications for student membership.

The Basic Statistics of Measurement

2

One does not need to be a statistical wizard to grasp the basic mathematical concepts needed to understand major measurement issues.

Abstract

Measurement is at the heart of all psychological testing and assessment. A number of statistical tests and procedures can be used to help evaluate how well a test measures what it is supposed to measure. The information presented in this chapter provides a solid foundation of basic statistical methods and concepts used in measurement. Rules for assigning numbers to represent objects and concepts are presented, involving four types of scales: nominal, ordinal, interval, and ratio. This chapter also describes how numbers are used to represent scores from individuals or groups of people, forming a distribution of scores. Various descriptive statistics are presented, such as measures of central tendency and measures of variability. Correlation coefficients are discussed in depth, along with an introduction to linear regression.

Supplementary Information The online version of this chapter (https://doi.org/10.1007/978-3-030-59455-8_2) contains supplementary material, which is available to authorized users.

© Springer Nature Switzerland AG 2021
C. R. Reynolds et al., *Mastering Modern Psychological Testing*,
https://doi.org/10.1007/978-3-030-59455-8_2

Learning Objectives

After reading and studying this chapter, students should be able to:
1. Define measurement.
2. Describe different scales of measurement and give examples.
3. Describe measures of central tendency and their appropriate use.
4. Describe measures of variability and their appropriate use.
5. Correctly interpret descriptive statistics.
6. Explain the meaning of correlation coefficients and how they are used.
7. Explain how scatterplots are used to describe the relationships between two variables.
8. Describe major types of correlation coefficients.
9. Distinguish between correlation and causation.
10. Describe how linear regression is used to predict performance.
11. Explain what the Standard Error of Estimate represents and how it is used to create confidence intervals around predicted scores.

Every semester, when one of us teaches a course in tests and measurement, we inevitably hear a common moan. Students are quick to say they fear this course because they hear it involves "a lot of statistics" and they are not good at math, much less statistics. The truth is you do not have to be a statistical wizard to comprehend the mathematical concepts needed to understand major measurement issues. In fact, Kubiszyn and Borich (2003) estimate that less than 1% of the students in their testing and assessment courses performed poorly entirely because of insufficient math skills. Nevertheless, all measurements in psychology have mathematical properties, and those who use tests and other assessments need to understand the basic mathematical and statistical concepts on which these assessments are predicated. In this chapter, we will introduce these mathematical concepts. Generally, we will emphasize the development of a conceptual understanding of these issues rather than focusing on mathematical computations. In a few instances, we will present mathematical formulas and demonstrate their application, but we will keep the computational aspect to a minimum.

In developing this textbook, our guiding principle has been to address only those concepts that psychology students really need to know to select, administer, and interpret assessments in clinical settings. We recognize that most of our students do not desire to become test development experts, but because psychologists use and interpret assessments, they need to be competent in their use. In this chapter, we will first discuss scales of measurement and show you how different scales have different properties or characteristics. Next, we will introduce the concept of a collection or distribution of scores and review the different statistics available to describe distributions. We will then introduce the concept of correlation, how it is measured, and what it means. Finally, we will briefly introduce and illustrate the use of linear regression (due to its importance to prediction), the standard error of estimate, and confidence intervals.

2.1 Scales of Measurement

2.1.1 What Is Measurement?

We defined *measurement* as a set of rules for assigning numbers to represent objects, traits, attributes, or behaviors. Psychological tests are measuring devices, and as such, they involve rules (e.g., specific items, administration, and scoring

> Measurement is defined as a set of rules for assigning numbers to represent objects, traits, attributes, or behaviors.

instructions) for assigning numbers to an individual's performance that are interpreted as reflecting characteristics of the individual. For example, the number of items on a depression inventory that a client endorses in a specific manner may be interpreted as reflecting the client's subjective level of depression. Similarly, the number of digits a client can remember and repeat might be interpreted as reflecting his/her short-term auditory memory. As you will learn in this course, there are a vast number of psychological tests available that are designed to measure a vast number of psychological constructs.

When we measure something, the units of measurement have a mathematical property called the scale of measurement. A scale is a system or scheme for assigning values or scores to the characteristic being measured (e.g., Sattler, 1992). Stevens (1946) originally proposed a taxonomy that specified four scales of measurement. These different scales have distinct properties and convey unique types of information. The four scales of measurement are nominal, ordinal, interval, and ratio. The scales form a hierarchy, and as we progress from nominal to ratio scales, we are able to perform increasingly sophisticated measurements that capture more detailed information.

2.1.2 Nominal Scales

Nominal scales are the simplest of the four scales. Nominal scales provide a qualitative system for categorizing people or objects into categories, classes, or sets. In most situations, these categories are

> Nominal scales classify people or objects into categories, classes, or sets.

mutually exclusive. For example, sex is an example of a nominal scale that assigns individuals to mutually exclusive categories. Another example is assigning people to categories based on their college academic major (e.g., psychology, biology, chemistry). You may have noticed that in these examples, we did not assign numbers to the categories. In some situations, we do assign numbers in nominal scales simply to identify or label the categories; however, the categories are not ordered in a meaningful manner. For example, we might use the number one to represent a category of students who list their academic major as psychology, the number two for the academic major of biology, the number three for the academic major of chemistry, and so forth. Notice that no attempt is made to order the categories. Three is not greater than two, and two is not greater than one. The assignment of numbers is completely arbitrary. Another individual might assign a new set of numbers that would be just as useful as ours. In fact, in nominal scales, the numbers just serve as names for the categories. We could just as easily call them red, blue, green, or eagles, sparrows, and robins. Because of the arbitrary use of numbers in nominal scales, nominal scales do not actually quantify the variables under examination. Numbers assigned to nominal scales should not be added, subtracted, ranked, or otherwise manipulated. As a result, most common statistical procedures cannot be used with nominal scales so their usefulness is limited.

2.1.3   Ordinal Scales

Ordinal scale measurement allows you to rank people or objects according to the amount or quantity of a characteristic they display or possess. As a result, ordinal scales enable us to quantify the variables under examination and provide substan-

> Ordinal scales rank people or objects according to the amount of a characteristic they display or possess.

tially more information than nominal scales. For example, ranking people according to height from the tallest to the shortest is an example of ordinal measurement. Traditionally, the ranking is ordered from the "most" to the "least." In our example, the tallest person in the class would receive the rank of 1, the next tallest a rank of 2, and so on. Although ordinal scale measurement provides quantitative information, it does not ensure that the intervals between the ranks are consistent. That is, the difference in height between the person ranked 1 and 2 might be 3 in. while the difference between those ranked 3 and 4 might be 1 in. Ordinal scales indicate the rank-order position among individuals or objects, but they do not indicate the extent by which they differ. All the ordinal scale tells us is that 1 is taller than 2; it tells us nothing about how much taller. As a result, these scales are somewhat limited in both the measurement information they provide and the statistical procedures that can be applied. Although you will see it done, it rarely makes sense to add, subtract, multiply, or divide such scores. Nevertheless, the use of these scales is fairly common in many settings.

2.1.4   Interval Scales

Interval scales provide more information than either nominal or ordinal scales. Interval scale measurement allows you to rank people or objects like an ordinal scale, but on a scale with equal units. By

> Interval scales rank people or objects like an ordinal scale, but on a scale with equal units.

equal scale units, we mean the difference between adjacent units on the scale is equivalent. For example, the difference between 70 and 71 °F is the same as the difference between 50 and 51° (or 92 and 93, 37 and 38, etc.). Many psychological tests are designed to produce interval-level scores. Let's look at an example of scores for three people on an intelligence test. Assume individual A receives a score of 100, individual B a score of 110, and individual C a score of 120. First, we know that person C scored the highest followed by B then A. Second, given that the scores are on an interval scale, we also know that the difference between individuals A and B (i.e., 10 points) is equivalent to the difference between B and C (i.e., 10 points). Finally, we know the difference between individuals A and C (i.e., 20 points) is twice as large as the difference between individuals A and B (i.e., 10 points). Interval-level data can be manipulated using common mathematical operations (e.g., addition, subtraction, multiplication, and division) whereas lesser scales (i.e., nominal and ordinal) cannot. A final advantage is that most statistical procedures can be used with interval scale data.

As you can see, interval scales represent a substantial improvement over ordinal scales and provide considerably more information. Their one limitation is that interval scales do not have a true zero point. That is, on interval scales a score of zero does not reflect the total absence of the attribute. For example, if an individual were unable to answer any questions correctly on an intelligence test and scored a zero, it would not indicate the complete lack of intelligence, but only that he or she was unable to respond correctly to any questions on this test. (Actually, intelligence tests are designed so no one actually receives a score of zero. We just use this example to illustrate the concept of an arbitrary zero point.) Additionally, ratios are not meaningful with interval scales. For example, even though an IQ of 100 is twice as large as an IQ of 50, it does not mean that the person with a score of 100 is twice as intelligent as the person with a score of 50. For such a statement to be accurate, we would need to have a true zero point.

Despite this limitation, some school districts and agencies continue to use some form of a "percentage discrepancy" between actual and predicted achievement or an IQ. In such a circumstance, the difference between two values, such as an obtained achievement score of say 75, is subtracted from the student's predicted achievement score of 100. The difference score is then used to calculate a percentage of deficiency in the area of academics covered—various formulas are in use to do this, but simplistically, one might take this difference of 25 points, divide it by 100 (the predicted score), and decide the student has a 25% deficiency in the area in question. Such a percentage is nonsensical, regardless of the formulas used to make the determination because a percentage is a ratio of two numbers—and ratios are uninterpretable in interval scaling because we have no true zero point for reference in interval scaling. To calculate these percentages, ratio scales are required as described in the next section.

With behavioral variables like intelligence or even personality characteristics like friendliness, we do not know where the true zero point lies. With physical characteristics like height and weight, a zero point is well defined, and we measure beginning at zero and go up. When the zero point is unknown, the only place we can begin measuring accurately is the middle of the distribution. Interval scales are derived by first locating the midpoint of a variable, usually taken to be the mean score of a population or sample, and then measuring outward in each direction, above and below, as far as we can establish scores with reasonable accuracy. We never reach the true bottom or true top of what we are measuring (although a particular test may bottom-out or top-out, the construct being measured continues). Remember that the interval scale, the most common scale used in psychology and education, begins measuring in the middle, the only point we can initially define, and then measures toward the two ends of the distribution, never reaching either end. In psychology, interval scale scores are most commonly seen in the form of a special type of score called a standard score. There are several types of standard scores used in psychology, which will be discussed in the next chapter.

2.1.5 Ratio Scales

Ratio scales have the properties of interval scales plus a true zero point that reflects the complete absence of the characteristic being measured. Miles per hour,

> Ratio scales have the properties of interval scales plus a true zero point.

length, and weight are all examples of ratio scales. As the name suggests, with these scales, we can interpret ratios between scores. For example, 100 miles per hour is twice as fast as 50 miles per hour, 6 ft is twice as long as 3 ft, and 300 pounds is three times as much as 100 pounds. Ratios are not meaningful or interpretable with the other scales we discussed. As we noted, a person with an intelligence quotient (IQ) of 100 is not twice as intelligent as one with an IQ of 50. Given the enormity of human intelligence, an IQ of 100 may only represent a 1%, 5%, or 10% increase over an IQ of 50. This holds in achievement as well; a person with a standardized math achievement test score of 120 does not know "twice as much" as one with a score of 60. The key point being that absent a ratio scale for intelligence, achievement, or any other psychological construct, we cannot know the magnitude of differences in absolute terms. With the exception of the percent of items correct and the measurement of behavioral responses (e.g., reaction time), there are relatively few ratio scales in psychological measurement. Fortunately, we are able to address most of the measurement issues in psychology adequately using interval scales.

Table 2.1 gives examples of common nominal, ordinal, interval, and ratio scales used in psychological measurement. As we noted, there is a hierarchy among the scales with nominal scales being the least sophisticated and providing the least information and ratio scales being the most sophisticated and providing the most information. Nominal scales allow you to assign a number to a person that associates that person with a set or category, but other useful quantitative properties are missing. Ordinal scales have all the positive properties of nominal scales with the addition of the ability to rank people according to the amount of a characteristic they possess. Interval scales have all the positive properties of

Table 2.1 Common nominal, ordinal, interval, and ratio scales

Scale	Example	Sample scores
Nominal	Sex of participant	Female = 1
		Male = 2
	Ethnicity	African American = 1
		White = 2
		Hispanic American = 3
		Native American = 4
		Asian American = 5
	Location	Northeast = 1
		Southeast = 2
		Midwest = 3
		Southwest = 4
		Northwest = 5
		Pacific = 6
Ordinal	Preference for activity	1 = Most preferred
		2 = intermediate preferred
		3 = least preferred
	Graduation class rank	1 = valedictorian
		2 = salutatorian
		3 = third rank
		etc.
	Percentile rank	99th percentile
		98th percentile
		97th percentile
		etc.
Interval	Intelligence scores	IQ of 100
	Personality test scores	Depression score of 75
	Graduate record exam	Verbal score of 550
Ratio	Height in inches	60 in. tall
	Weight in pounds	100 pounds
	Percentage correct on classroom test	100%

ordinal scales and also incorporate equal scale units. The inclusion of equal scale units allows one to make relative statements regarding scores (e.g., the difference between a score of 82 and a score of 84 is the same as the difference between a score of 92 and 94). Finally, ratio scales have all of the positive properties of an interval scale with the addition of an absolute zero point. The inclusion of an absolute zero point allows us to form meaningful ratios between scores (e.g., a score of 50 reflects twice the amount of the characteristic as a score of 25). Although these scales do form a hierarchy, this does not mean the lower scales are of little or no use. If you want to categorize students according to their academic major, a nominal scale is clearly appropriate. Accordingly, if you simply want to rank people according to height, an ordinal scale would be adequate and appropriate. However, in most measurement situations, you want to use the scale that provides the most information.

2.2   The Description of Test Scores

An individual's ***raw score*** on a test, taken in isolation, typically provides very little information. For example, if you know that an individual endorsed 50% of the items on a depression inventory in a manner indicating depressive symptoms, you still know very little about that person's level of depression. To interpret or describe test scores meaningfully you need to have a frame of reference. Often the frame of reference is how other people performed on the test, which is referred to as norm-referenced interpretation. For example, if you knew that in a large representative sample, less than 2% of the sample endorsed 50% or more of the items in a manner indicating depressive symptoms you would likely interpret it as reflecting a high or at least unusual level of depression symptoms. In contrast, if more than 50% of the sample endorsed at least 50% of the items in a manner indicating depressive symptoms you would likely interpret it as reflecting a normal level of depressive symptoms (unless of course, your sample was composed mostly of people with a diagnosis of Major Depressive Disorder). The following sections provide information about score distributions and the statistics used to describe them. In the next chapter, we will use many of these concepts and procedures to help you learn how to describe and interpret test scores.

2.2.1   Distributions

A *distribution* is simply a set of scores. These can be scores on an intelligence test, scores on a measure of abstract reasoning, or scores

> A distribution is a set of scores.

on a career interest inventory. We can also have distributions reflecting physical characteristics such as weight, height, or strength. Distributions can be represented in a number of ways, including tables and graphs. Table 2.2 presents scores for 20 students on an exam similar to what might be recorded in a teacher's grade book. Table 2.3 presents an ungrouped frequency distribution of the same 20 scores. Notice that in this example, there are only seven possible measurement categories or scores (i.e., 4, 5, 6, 7, 8, 9, and 10). In some situations, there are so many possible scores that it is not practical to list each potential score individually. In these situations, it is common to use a ***grouped frequency distribution***. In grouped frequency distributions, the possible scores are "combined" or "grouped" into class intervals that encompass a range of possible scores. Table 2.4 presents a grouped frequency distribution of 250 hypothetical scores that are grouped into 5-point class intervals.

Frequency graphs, also known as ***histograms***, are also popular and provide a visual representation of a distribution of scores. When reading a frequency graph, scores are traditionally listed on the horizontal axis (commonly called the *x*-axis) and the frequency of scores is listed on the vertical axis (commonly called the *y*-axis). Figure 2.1 presents a graph of the set of scores listed in Tables 2.2 and 2.3. In examining this figure, you see that there was only one score of 10 (reflecting perfect performance) and there was only one score of 4 (reflecting correctly responding to

Table 2.2 Distribution of scores for 20 students

Student	Test score
Cindy	7
Raul	8
Paula	9
Steven	6
Angela	5
Robert	6
Kim	10
Mario	9
Julie	9
Kareem	9
Karen	8
Paul	4
Teresa	5
Freddie	6
Tammy	7
Shelly	8
Aisha	8
Johnny	7
Jose	8
Randy	5
Mean = 7.2	
Median = 7.5	
Mode = 8.0	

Table 2.3 Ungrouped frequency distribution

Score	Frequency
10	1
9	4
8	5
7	3
6	3
5	3
4	1

Note. This reflects the same distribution of scores depicted in Table 2.2

only four questions). Most of the students received scores between 7 and 9. Figure 2.2 presents a graph of a distribution that might reflect a large standardization sample. Examining this figure reveals that the scores tend to accumulate around the middle with their frequency diminishing as we move further away from the middle.

Another characteristic of the distribution depicted in Fig. 2.2 is that it is symmetrical. By **symmetrical** we mean if you divide the distribution into two halves, they will mirror each other. Not all distributions are symmetrical. When a

Table 2.4 Grouped
frequency distribution

Class interval	Frequency
125–129	6
120–124	14
115–119	17
110–114	23
105–109	27
100–104	42
95–99	39
90–94	25
85–89	22
80–84	17
75–79	13
70–74	5

Note. This presents a grouped frequency distribution of 250 hypothetical scores that are grouped into 5-point class intervals

Homework Score

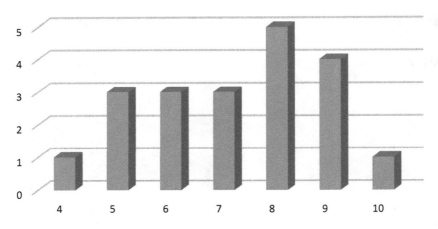

Fig. 2.1 Histogram graph of the homework scores

distribution is not symmetrical, it is referred to as *skewed*. Skewed distributions can be either negatively or positively skewed. A negatively skewed distribution is one with few scores at the low end as illustrated in Fig. 2.3; it points toward the y or vertical axis. When a maximal performance test produces scores that are negatively skewed, it is probable that the test is too easy because there are many high scores and relatively few low scores. A positively skewed distribution is one with few scores at the high end as illustrated in Fig. 2.4; it points away from the y or vertical

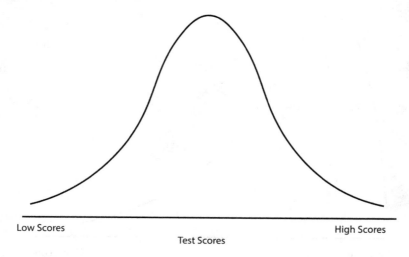

Fig. 2.2 Hypothetical distribution of large standardization sample

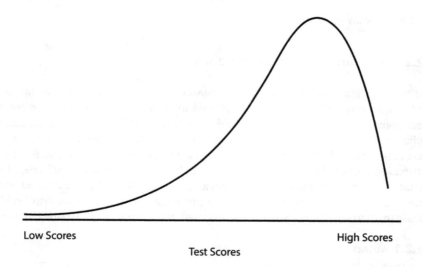

Fig. 2.3 Negatively skewed distribution

axis. If a maximal performance test produces scores that are positively skewed, it is likely that the test is too difficult because there are many low scores and few high scores. Later in this chapter, we will talk more about a special type of distribution referred to as the normal or bell-shaped distribution and describe how it is used to help interpret test scores. First, however, we will describe two important character-istics of distributions and the methods we have for describing them. The first char-acteristic is central tendency and the second is variability.

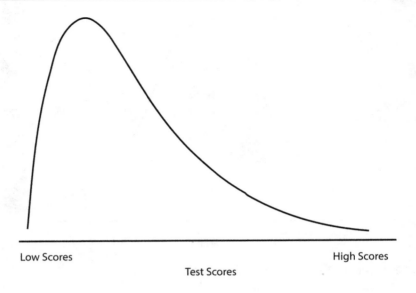

Low Scores   High Scores

Test Scores

Fig. 2.4 Positively skewed distribution

2.2.2   Measures of Central Tendency

The scores in many distributions tend to concentrate around a center, and statistics used to summarize this tendency are referred to as *measures of central tendency*. Three common descriptive statistics used to summarize this tendency are the mean, median, and mode. We refer to these and other statistics as *descriptive statistics* because they describe basic features of the data, in this case where the middle of the distribution tends to be. The mean, median, and mode are frequently referenced in mental and in physical measurements, and all psychologists should be familiar with them. It is likely that you have heard of all of these statistics, but we will briefly discuss them to ensure that you are familiar with the special characteristics of each.

2.2.2.1 Mean

Most people are familiar with the *mean* as the simple arithmetic average. Practically, every day you will hear multiple discussions involving the concept of the average

> The mean is the arithmetic average of a distribution.

amount of some entity. Meteorologists give you information about the average temperature and amount of rain, politicians and economists discuss the average hourly wage, educators talk about the grade point average, health professionals talk about the average weight and average life expectancy, and the list goes on. Formally, the mean of a set of scores is defined by the equation:

$$\text{Mean} = \frac{\text{Sum of Scores}}{\text{Number of Scores}}$$

The mean of the test scores listed in Table 2.2 is calculated by summing the 20 scores in the distribution and dividing by 20. This results in a mean of 7.20. Note that the mean is near the middle of the distribution (see Fig. 2.1). Although no student obtained a score of 7.20, the mean is useful in providing a sense of the central tendency of the group of scores. The mean of a distribution is typically designated with $\overline{X}$ or M for sample data and the Greek symbol *mu* (μ) for a population.

Several important mathematical characteristics of the mean make it useful as a measure of central tendency. First, the mean is meaningful for distributions containing interval and ratio level scores (though it is not applicable for nominal or ordinal scores). Second, the mean of a sample is a good estimate of the mean for the population from which the sample was drawn (assuming you did a good job of drawing a random sample). This is useful when developing tests in which standardization samples are tested and the resulting distribution is believed to reflect characteristics of the entire population of people with whom the examinee or test taker is to be compared (see Special Interest Topic 2.1 for more information on this topic). Another positive characteristic of the mean is that it is essential to the definition and calculation of other descriptive statistics that are useful in the context of measurement.

Special Interest Topic 2.1: Population Parameters and Sample Statistics

While we try to minimize the use of statistical jargon whenever possible, at this point, we feel it is useful to highlight the distinction between population parameters and sample statistics. Statisticians differentiate between populations and samples. A population is the complete group of people, objects, or other things of interest. An example of a population is "all of the secondary students in the United States." This is a very large number of students and it would be extremely difficult to study a group this large. Due to these types of constraints researchers often are unable to study entire populations. Instead, they study samples. A sample is just a subset of the larger population that is thought to be representative of the population. By studying samples, researchers are able to make generalizations about populations. For example, while it might not be practical to administer a questionnaire to all secondary students in the United States, it is possible to select a random sample of secondary students and administer the questionnaire to them. If we are careful selecting this sample and it is of sufficient size, the information we garner from the sample may allow us to draw some conclusions about the population.

Now we will address the distinction between parameters and statistics. Population values are referred to as parameters and are typically represented with Greek symbols. For example, statisticians use *mu* (μ) to indicate a population mean and *sigma* (σ) to indicate a population standard deviation. Since it is often not possible to study entire populations, we often don't know population parameters and have to estimate them using statistics. A statistic is a value that is calculated based on a sample. Statistics are typically represented with Roman letters. For example, statisticians use $\overline{X}$ to indicate the sample mean (some statisticians use M to indicate the mean) and SD (or S) to indicate the sample standard deviation. Sample statistics can provide information about the corresponding population parameters. For example, the sample mean ($\overline{X}$) may serve as an estimate of the population mean (μ). Of course, the information provided by a sample statistic is only as good as the sample the statistic is based on. Large representative samples can provide good information while small or biased samples will provide poor information. While we don't want to go into detail about sampling and inferential statistics at this point, we do want to make you aware of the distinction between parameters and statistics. In this and other texts, you will see references to both parameters and statistics and understanding this distinction will help you avoid a misunderstanding. Remember, as a general rule, if the value is designated with a Greek symbol, it refers to a population parameter, but if it is designated with a Roman letter, it is a sample statistic.

An undesirable characteristic of the mean is that it is sensitive to unbalanced extreme scores. By this, we mean a score that is either extremely high or extremely low relative to the rest of the scores in the distribution. An extreme score, either very large or very small, tends to "pull" the mean in its direction. This might not be readily apparent so let's look at an example. In the set of scores 1, 2, 3, 4, 5, and 38, the mean is 8.8. Notice that 8.8 is not near any score that actually occurs in the distribution. If 38 is excluded, the mean is 3. As the example illustrates, the extreme score of 38 pulls the mean in its direction. The tendency for the mean to be affected by extreme scores is particularly problematic when there is a small number of scores. The influence of an extreme score decreases as the total number of scores in the distribution increases. For example, the mean of 1, 1, 1, 1, 2, 2, 2, 2, 3, 3, 3, 3, 4, 4, 4, 4, 5, 5, 5, 5, and 38 is 4.7. In this example, the influence of the extreme score is reduced by the presence of a larger number of scores.

2.2.2.2 Median

The *median* is the score or potential score (formally referred to as the "point") that divides the distribution in half. When the number of scores in a distribution is an odd number, the median is simply the

> The median is the score or potential score that divides a distribution in half.

score that is in the middle of the distribution when the distribution is listed in ascending or descending order. For example, for the set of scores 1, 4, 7, 8, and 9, the median is 7 because it the middle of the ordered distribution. When the number of scores in a distribution is an even number, to find the median, simply take the two middle numbers in an ordered (ascending or descending) distribution and average them. For example, in a distribution of scores 4, 5, 7, and 10, take 5 + 7 = 12, divide by 2, and the median is 6. In the distribution of scores depicted in Table 2.3, there are 20 scores in the distribution. The point that divides the distribution in half (i.e., where the top 10 scores and the bottom 10 scores meet) is 7.5 (8 + 7 = 15, divide by 2, is 7.5). When the data have been arranged as a grouped frequency distribution, a process referred to as interpolation is used to compute the median. Interpolation is illustrated in practically every basic statistics textbook, but we will not go into detail about the process.

The median can be calculated for distributions containing ratio, interval, or ordinal level scores, but it is not appropriate for nominal level scores. A desirable characteristic of the median is that it is insensitive to extreme scores. For example, in the set of scores 1, 2, 3, 4, 5, and 38, the median is 3.5 (as opposed to a mean of 8.8). The median is a useful and versatile measure of central tendency that is particularly useful for many common descriptive purposes.

2.2.2.3 Mode

The *mode* of a distribution is the most frequently occurring score. Refer back to Table 2.3 that presents the ungrouped frequency distribution of 20 students on a

> The mode is the most frequently occurring score in a distribution.

test. By examining these scores, you will see that the most frequently occurring score is 8. These scores are graphed in Fig. 2.1, and by locating the highest point in the graph, you are also able to identify the mode (i.e., 8). An advantage of the mode is that it can be used with nominal data (e.g., the most frequent college major selected by students) as well as ordinal, interval, and ratio data (Hays, 1994). However, the mode does have significant limitations as a measure of central tendency. First, some distributions have two scores that are equal in frequency and higher than other scores (see Fig. 2.5). This is referred to as a *"bimodal"*

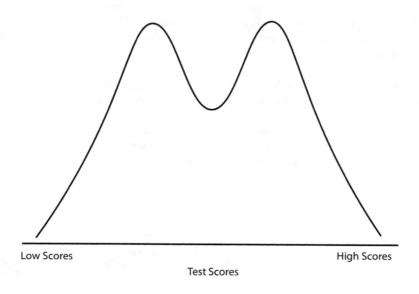

Fig. 2.5 Bimodal distribution

distribution, and here, the mode is ineffective as a measure of central tendency. Second, the mode is not a stable measure of central tendency, particularly with small samples. For example, in the distribution depicted in Table 2.3, if one student who earned a score 8 had earned a score of 9, the mode would have shifted from 8 to 9. As a result of these limitations, the mode is often of little utility as a measure of central tendency.

2.2.2.4 Choosing Between the Mean, Median, and Mode

A natural question is which measure of central tendency is most useful or appropriate? As you might expect, the answer depends on a number of factors. First, as we noted when discussing the mean, it is essential when calculating other useful statistics. For this and other rather technical reasons (see Hays, 1994), the mean has considerable utility as a measure of central tendency. However, for purely descriptive purposes, the median is often the most versatile and useful measure of central tendency. When a distribution is skewed, the influence of unbalanced extreme scores on the mean tends to undermine its usefulness. Figure 2.6 illustrates the expected relationship between the mean and the median in skewed distributions. Note that the mean is "pulled" in the direction of the skew. That is, the mean is lower than the median in negatively skewed distributions and higher than the median in positively skewed distributions. To illustrate how the mean can be misleading in skewed distributions, Hopkins (1998) notes that due to the influence of extremely wealthy individuals, about 60% of the families in the United States have incomes below the national mean. For example, in 2008 the median family income was $50,303 while the mean income was $68,424 (http://www.census.gov/). In this situation, the mean is pulled higher by the extremely high income of some individuals (e.g., select actors, athletes, and CEOs) and is somewhat misleading as a measure of central tendency. Finally, if you are dealing with nominal level data, the mode is the only measure of central tendency that provides useful information.

At this point, you should have a good understanding of the various measures of central tendency and be able to interpret them in many common applications. However, you might be surprised how often individuals in the popular media demonstrate a fundamental misunderstanding of these measures. See Special Interest Topic 2.2 for a rather humorous example of how a journalist misinterpreted information based on measures of central tendency.

Fig. 2.6 Relationship between mean, median, and mode in normal and skewed distributions

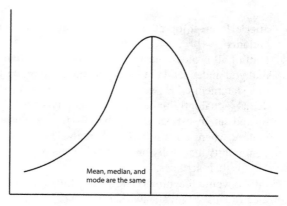

Mean, median, and mode are the same

Normal Distribution

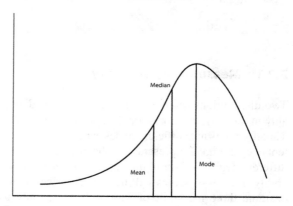

Median

Mean

Mode

Negatively Skewed Distribution

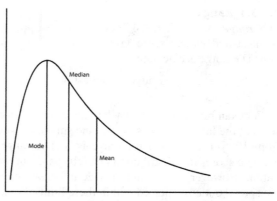

Median

Mode

Mean

Positively Skewed Distribution

Special Interest Topic 2.2: A Public Outrage: Physicians Overcharge Their Patients

Half of all professionals charge above the median fee for their services. Now that you understand the mean, median, and mode you recognize how obvious this statement is. However, a few years back a local newspaper columnist in Texas, apparently unhappy with his physician's bill for some services, conducted an investigation of charges for various medical procedures in the county where he resided. In a somewhat angry column, he revealed to the community that "fully half of all physicians surveyed charge above the median fee for their services."

We would like him to know that "fully half" of all professionals, plumbers, electricians, painters, lawn services, hospitals, and everyone else we can think of also charge above the median for their services. We wouldn't have it any other way!

2.2.3 Measures of Variability

Two distributions can have the same mean, median, and mode yet differ considerably in the way the scores are distributed around the measures of central tendency. Therefore, it is not sufficient to describe a set of scores solely by measures of central tendency. Figure 2.7 presents graphs of three distributions with identical means but different degrees of variability. *Measures of variability*, dispersion, or spread variability of a set of scores will help us describe the distribution more fully. We will examine three measures of variability commonly used to describe distributions: range, standard deviation, and variance.

2.2.3.1 Range

The *range* is the distance between the smallest and largest score in a distribution. The range is calculated:

> The range is the distance between the smallest and largest score in a distribution.

$$\text{Range} = \text{Highest Score} - \text{Lowest Score}$$

For example, in referring back to the distribution of scores listed in Table 2.3 you see that the largest score is 10 and the smallest score is 4. By simply subtracting 4 from 10, you determine the range is 6. The range considers only the two most extreme scores in a distribution and tells us about the limits or extremes of a distribution. However, it does not provide information about how the remaining scores are spread out or dispersed within these limits. We need other descriptive statistics, namely the standard deviation and variance, to provide information about the dispersion or spread of scores within the limits described by the range.

2.2.3.2 Standard Deviation

The mean and standard deviation are the most widely used descriptive statistics in psychological testing as well as research in the social and behavioral sciences. The *standard deviation* is a measure of the average distance that scores vary or deviate from the mean of the distribution. The

> The standard deviation is a measure of the average distance that scores vary from the mean of the distribution.

larger the standard deviation, the more scores differ from the mean and the more variability there is in the distribution. If scores are widely dispersed or spread around the mean, as in Fig. 2.7b, the standard deviation will be large. If there is relatively

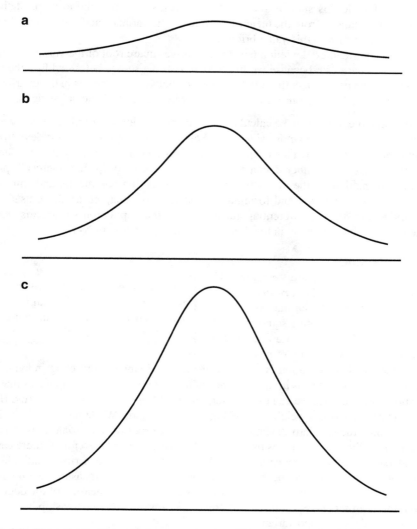

Fig. 2.7 Three distributions with the same mean but different degrees of variability

little dispersion or spread of scores around the mean, as in Fig. 2.7c, the standard deviation will be small. The standard deviation is computed with the following steps which are illustrated in Table 2.5 using the scores listed in Table 2.2:

- *Step 1*: Compute the mean of the distribution.
- *Step 2*: Subtract the mean from each score in the distribution in order to determine how far the scores vary or deviate from the mean. (This will yield some negative numbers and if you add all of these differences, the sum will be zero. To overcome this, we simply square each difference score because the square of any number is always positive; see Step 3).
- *Step 3*: Square each difference score.
- *Step 4*: Sum all the squared difference scores.
- *Step 5*: Divide this sum by the number of scores to derive the average of the squared deviations from the mean. This value is the variance and is designated by σ^2 (we will return to this value briefly).
- *Step 6*: The standard deviation (σ) is the positive square root of the variance (σ^2). It is the square root because we first squared all the scores before adding them. To now get a true look at the standard distance between key points in the distribution, we have to undo our little trick that eliminated all those negative signs.

This example illustrates the calculation of the population standard deviation designated with the Greek symbol *sigma* (σ). You will also see the standard deviation designated with SD or *S*. This is appropriate when you are describing the standard deviation of a sample rather than a population (refer back to Special Interest Topic 2.1 for information on the distinction between population parameters and sample statistics). The discussion and formulas provided in this chapter are those used in descriptive statistics. In inferential statistics when the population variance is estimated from a sample, the N in the denominator is replaced with N-1.

2.2.3.3 Variance

In calculating the standard deviation, we actually first calculate the *variance* (σ^2). As illustrated in Table 2.5, the standard deviation is actually the positive square root of the variance. Therefore, the variance is also a measure of the variability of scores. The

> The variance is a measure of variability that has special meaning as a theoretical concept in measurement theory and statistics.

reason the standard deviation is more frequently used when interpreting individual scores is that the variance is in squared units of measurement which complicates interpretation. For example, we can easily interpret weight in pounds, but it is more difficult to interpret and use weight reported in squared pounds. While the variance is in squared units, the standard deviation (i.e., the square root of the variance) is in the same units as the original scores from which it was derived and therefore is more easily understood. Although the variance is difficult to apply when describing individual scores, it does have special meaning as a theoretical concept in measurement theory and statistics. For now, simply remember that the variance is a measure of the degree of variability in scores. Special Interest Topic 2.3 examines the relationship between the standard deviation and variance.

Table 2.5 Calculating the standard deviation and variance

Student scores	Difference (score − mean)	Difference squared
7	$(7 - 7.20) = -0.20$	0.04
8	$(8 - 7.20) = 0.80$	0.64
9	$(9 - 7.20) = 1.80$	3.24
6	$(6 - 7.20) = -1.20$	1.44
5	$(5 - 7.20) = -2.20$	4.84
6	$(6 - 7.20) = -1.20$	1.44
10	$(10 - 7.20) = 2.80$	7.84
9	$(9 - 7.20) = 1.80$	3.24
9	$(9 - 7.20) = 1.80$	3.24
9	$(9 - 7.20) = 1.80$	3.24
8	$(8 - 7.20) = 0.80$	0.64
4	$(4 - 7.20) = -3.20$	10.24
5	$(5 - 7.20) = -2.20$	4.84
6	$(6 - 7.20) = -1.20$	1.44
7	$(7 - 7.20) = -0.20$	0.04
8	$(8 - 7.20) = 0.80$	0.64
8	$(8 - 7.20) = 0.80$	0.64
7	$(7 - 7.20) = -0.20$	0.04
8	$(8 - 7.20) = 0.80$	0.64
5	$(5 - 7.20) = -2.20$	4.84
Sum = 144		*Sum* = 53.20
Mean = 7.20		Variance $= 53.20 / (n)$
		$= 53.20 / 20$
		$= 2.66$
		Standard deviation $= \sqrt{\text{Variance}}$
		$= \sqrt{2.66}$
		$= 1.63$

Special Interest Topic 2.3: Is the Variance Always Larger Than the Standard Deviation?

In this chapter, we show that the standard deviation is the positive square root of the variance. For example, if a distribution has a variance of 100, the standard deviation is 10. If the variance is 25, the standard deviation is 5. Can you think of any situations where the variance is not larger than the standard deviation?

It might surprise you but there are situations where the variance is not larger than the standard deviation. If the variance is 1.0, the standard deviation is also 1.0. In the next chapter, you will learn about z-scores that have a mean of 0 and a standard deviation of 1.0. It is also possible for the standard deviation to actually be larger than the variance. For example, if the variance is 0.25, the standard deviation is 0.50. While it is not common to find situations where the variance and standard deviation are decimals in educational assessment, it is good to be aware of the possibility.

2.2.3.4 Choosing Between the Range, Standard Deviation, and Variance

As we noted, the range conveys information about the limits of a distribution, but does not tell us how the scores are dispersed within these limits. The standard deviation indicates the average distance that scores vary from the mean of the distribution. The larger the standard deviation, the more variability there is in the distribution. The standard deviation is very useful in describing distributions and will be of particular importance when we turn our attention to the interpretation of scores in the next chapter. The variance is another important and useful measure of variability. Because the variance is expressed in terms of squared measurement units, it is not as useful in interpreting individual scores as is the standard deviation. However, the variance is important as a theoretical concept, and we will return to it when discussing reliability and validity in later chapters.

2.2.4   The Normal Distribution

The *normal distribution* is a special type of distribution that is very useful when developing and interpreting tests. The normal distribution, which is also referred to as the Gaussian or bell-shaped distribution, is a distribution that characterizes many variables that occur in nature (see Special Interest Topic 2.4 for information on Carl Frederich Gauss, who is credited with discovering the bell-shaped distribution). Gray (1999) indicates that the height of individuals of a given age and gender is an example of a variable that is distributed normally. He noted that numerous genetic and nutritional factors influence an individual's height, and in most cases, these various factors average out so that people of a given age and gender tend to be of approximately the same height. This accounts for the peak frequency in the normal distribution. In referring to Fig. 2.8, you will see that a large number of scores tend to accumulate or "pileup" around the middle of the distribution. However, for a relatively small number of individuals, a unique combination of factors results in them being either much shorter or much taller than the average. This accounts for the distribution trailing off at both the low and high ends, but never touching the axis at the ends. Theoretically, the normal curve ends at a value of infinity so it is known as asymptotic to its axis.

Special Interest Topic 2.4: Whence the Normal Curve?
Carl Frederich Gauss (1777–1855) was a noted German mathematician who is generally credited with being one of the founders of modern mathematics. Born in 1777 in Brunswick, he turned his scholarly pursuits toward the field of astronomy around the turn of the Century. In the course of tracking star movements and taking other forms of physical survey measurements (at times with instruments of his own invention), he found to his annoyance that students and colleagues plotting the location of an object at the same time, noted it to be in somewhat different places! He began to plot the frequency of the observed locations systematically and found the observations to take the shape of a

(continued)

curve. He determined that the best estimate of the true location of the object was the mean of the observations and that each independent observation contained some degree of error. These errors formed a curve that was in the shape of a bell. This curve or distribution of error terms has since been demonstrated to occur with a variety of natural phenomena, and indeed has become so commonplace that it is most often known as the "normal curve" or the normal distribution. Of course, you may know it as the Bell Curve as well due to its shape, and mathematicians and others in the sciences sometimes refer to it as the Gaussian Curve after its discoverer and the man who described many of its characteristics. Interestingly, Gauss was a very prolific scholar and the Gaussian Curve is not the only discovery to bear his name. He did groundbreaking research on magnetism and the unit of magnetic intensity is called a gauss.

To be fair, some writers (e.g., Osterlind, 2006) credit the discovery of the normal distribution to Abraham de Moivre. They suggest that Abraham de Moivre's studies of probability theory laid the foundation for Gauss' subsequent "discovery" of the normal distribution. Additionally, de Moivre is credited with developing the concept of the standard deviation.

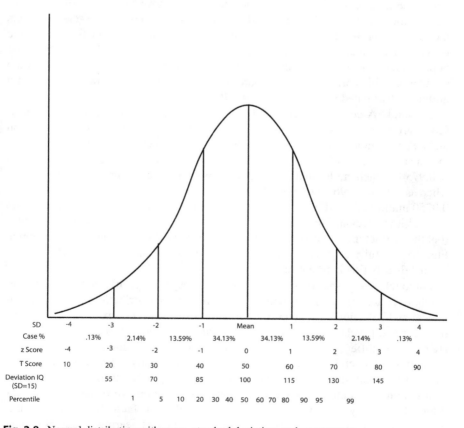

Fig. 2.8 Normal distribution with mean, standard deviation, and percentages

Although the previous discussion addressed only observable characteristics of the normal distribution, certain mathematical properties make it particularly useful when interpreting scores. First, the normal distribution is a unimodal distribution in which the mean, median, and mode are all equal. It is also symmetrical, meaning that if you divide the distribution into two halves, they will mirror each other.

> The normal distribution is a symmetrical unimodal distribution in which the mean, median, and mode are all equal.

Probably the most useful characteristic of the normal distribution is that predictable proportions of scores occur at specific points in the distribution. Referring to Fig. 2.8 you find a normal distribution with the mean and standard deviations (σ) marked (Fig. 2.8 also indicates percentile ranks [PR] which will be discussed later). Because we know that the mean equals the median in a normal distribution, we know that an individual who scores at the mean scored better than 50% of the sample of examinees (remember, earlier we defined the median as the score that divides the distribution in half). Because approximately 34% of the scores fall between the mean and 1 standard deviation above the mean, an individual whose score falls 1 standard deviation above the mean performs at a level exceeding approximately 84% of population (i.e., 34 + 50% below the mean). A score two standard deviations above the mean will be above 98% of the population. Because the distribution is symmetrical, the relationship is the same in the inverse below the mean. A score 1 standard deviation *below* the mean indicates that the individual exceeds only about 16% (i.e., 50 − 34%) of the population on the attribute in question. Approximately two-thirds (i.e., 68%) of the population will score within 1 standard deviation above and below the mean on a normally distributed variable (i.e., 34 + 34%).

Appendix A contains a table that allows you to determine what proportion of scores are below any given point in a distribution by specifying standard deviation units. For example, you can use these tables to determine that a score 1.96 SD *above* the mean exceeds 97.5% of the scores in the distribution (i.e., 1.00 − 0.0250 = 0.9750, which multiplied by 100 to convert to a percentage, equals 97.5%) whereas a score 1.96 SD *below* the mean exceeds only 2.5% of the scores (i.e., 0.0250 multiplied by 100 to covert it to a percentage equals 2.5%). Although we do not feel it is necessary for you to become an expert in using these statistical tables (but the instructor of your statistics course might), we do encourage you to examine Fig. 2.8 carefully to ensure you have a good grasp of the basic properties of the normal distribution before proceeding.

Although many variables of importance in psychology like achievement and intelligence are very close to conforming to the normal distribution, not all psychological and behavioral variables are normally distributed. For example, aggressive behavior and psychotic behavior are two variables of interest to psychologists that are distinctly different from the normal curve in their distributions. Consider physical aggression in children. Most children are not physically aggressive, so on measures of physical aggression, most children tend to pile up at the left side of the distribution (i.e., obtain low scores indicating few aggressive behaviors) whereas those who are only slightly aggressive may score relatively far to the right. Likewise, few people ever experience psychotic symptoms such as hearing voices of people who are not there or seeing things no one else can see. Such variables will each have their own unique distribution, and even though one can, via statistical manipulation, force these score distributions into the shape of a normal curve, it is not always desirable to do so. We will return to this issue later, but at this point, it is important to refute the common myth that all human behaviors or attributes conform to the normal curve; clearly, they do not!

2.3   Correlation Coefficients

Most psychology students are somewhat familiar with the concept of correlation. When people speak of a correlation, they are referring to the relationship between two variables. The variables can be physical such as weight and height or psychological variables such as intelligence and academic achievement. For example, it is reasonable to expect height to demonstrate a relationship with weight. Taller individuals tend to weigh more than shorter individuals. This relationship is not perfect because there are some short individuals who weigh more than taller individuals, but the tendency is for taller people to outweigh shorter people. You might also expect more intelligent people to score higher on tests of academic achievement than less intelligent people, and this is what research indicates. Again, the relationship is not perfect, but as a general rule, more intelligent individuals perform better on tests of academic achievement than their less intelligent peers.

Technically, a *correlation coefficient* is a quantitative measure of the linear relationship between two variables. The common correlation coefficient was developed

> A correlation coefficient is a quantitative measure of the relationship between two variables.

by **Karl Pearson** (1857–1936) and is designated by the letter r. Correlation coefficients can range from -1.0 to $+1.0$. When interpreting correlation coefficients, there are two parameters to consider. The first parameter is the sign of the coefficient. A **positive correlation** coefficient indicates that an increase in one variable is associated with an increase in the other variable. For example, height and weight demonstrate a positive correlation with each other. As individuals get taller, their weight tends to increase. A **negative correlation** coefficient indicates that an increase in one variable is associated with a decrease in the other variable. For example, because lower scores denote superior performance in the game of golf, there is a negative correlation between the amount of tournament prize money won and a professional's average golf score. Professional golfers with the lowest average scores tend to win the most tournament prize money.

The second parameter to consider when interpreting correlation coefficients is the magnitude or absolute size of the coefficient. The magnitude of a coefficient indicates the strength of the relationship between two variables. A value of 0 indicates the absence of a relationship between the variables. As coefficients approach an absolute value of 1.0, the strength of the relationship increases. A coefficient of 1.0 (either positive or negative) indicates a perfect correlation, one in which change in one variable is accompanied by a corresponding and proportionate change in the other variable, without exception. Perfect correlation coefficients are rare in psychological measurement, but they might occur in very small samples simply by chance.

There are numerous qualitative and quantitative ways of describing correlation coefficients. A qualitative approach is to describe correlation coefficients as weak, moderate, or strong. Although there are no universally accepted standards for describing the strength of correlations, we offer the following guidelines: <0.30 Weak; 0.30–0.70 Moderate; and >0.70 Strong (these are just guidelines and they should not be applied in a rigid manner). This approach is satisfactory in many situations, but in other contexts, it may be more important to determine whether a correlation is "statistically significant," meaning that it is likely not to have a value of zero in the population. Statistical significance is determined by both the size of the correlation coefficient and the size of the sample. A discussion of statistical significance would lead us into the realm of inferential statistics and is beyond the scope of this text. However, most introductory statistics texts address this concept in considerable detail and contain tables that allow you to determine whether a correlation coefficient is significant given the size of the sample. In measurement, one typically

---

Special Interest Topic 2.5: Are Weak Correlations Useless or of No Practical Value?

Suppose you could do the following:

- Reduce the number of heart attacks among those at high risk by 8–10%;
- Reduce the number of citizen complaints against police officers by 8–10%;
- Reduce the turnover rate in hiring at a large corporation by 8–10%?

Do you think any of these would be useful or beneficial to the parties involved? The first one is the easiest—of course, we would like to reduce heart attacks by any amount and a reduction of 8–10% is certainly meaningful, especially if you or a member of your family were among this 8–10%! The others are important as well. Certainly, hiring police officers who perform their jobs well and abide by the rubric of "serve and protect" is also an important goal. However, it also reduces costs to the public significantly in terms of human outcomes but also in terms of dollars and cents—it costs a great deal of money to recruit, train, and employ police officers and even more to investigate complaints against them. Dismissing officers who act inappropriately is an expensive and time-consuming process as well and often means a series of citizens has been mistreated in some way by the offending officer. Job turnover is also a significant expense in the private employment sector. Employers want to place the right people into their employ, people who are competent at the job and who will be happy in their work and remain on the job for as long as possible.

(continued)

If we look at these effects expressed as a correlation, the value ranges from 0.28 to 0.31. Most people would consider such correlations to be low and complain that they only account for 8 to 10% of the association between two variables. Yet in each of the instances above, the observed correlations are in fact very important and tell us what level of effects we can expect to obtain. For heart attacks, this is about the percentage reduction one can expect from taking low dose aspirin on a daily basis. In the other two cases, these are about the effects we see from using sound psychological tests as a component of the hiring process.

Still, we might question whether such small effects are worth the costs. In making a judgment, we should consider a variety of factors including the costs of doing nothing as well as the cost of the procedure—e.g., whether taking aspirin or taking a psychological test! We also need to ask, "Is there a better way to accomplish this goal or a way to improve upon it?"

In the case of hiring decisions, we are always looking to create better employment tests that predict long-term job performance and factors such as turnover—and, for some jobs, we do have tests that perform better. We also have to consider how difficult it may be to measure some constructs and the limits of our current knowledge about how variables are in fact related. Some psychological constructs are just far more difficult to measure reliably than are others, just as some outcomes are far more difficult to predict than are others. In some instances, such as those cited above, these so-called weak correlations are quite good and are very practical in terms of saving costs as well as human suffering. On the other hand, if we want to predict academic achievement levels and the test used for predictions only correlated 0.30, we would likely discard the test as not being very useful, since it is relatively easy to find aptitude measures that correlate twice as high (0.60) or more with academic outcomes. If we were to develop a test that added to this prediction by another 8–10% and was cost-effective in terms of its time and cost of administration, we still might use it due to the incremental validity it would add to the prediction of achievement.

The value of a correlation may also be very important to test validation as well as theory building when it is low in value or considered weak. For example, if we build a test to measure intelligence, and it correlates too highly with extraneous variables such as motor speed and fine motor coordination, then we know that the test is too confounded with other constructs to be a good measure of intelligence. We would prefer that the test of intelligence have weak correlations with motor speed and coordination.

Do not dismiss weak correlations—always view them in the context in which they were derived and the research questions trying to be answered. Even a correlational value of zero has something to tell us!

wants to consider magnitude as well as statistical significance—even weak correlations can be quite useful (see Special Interest Topic 2.5).

Another way of describing correlation coefficients is by squaring it to derive the coefficient of determination (i.e., r^2). The *coefficient of determination* is interpreted as the amount of variance shared by the two variables. In other words, the coefficient of determination reflects the amount

> The coefficient of determination is interpreted as the amount of variance shared by two variables.

of variance in one variable that is predictable from the other variable, and vice versa. This might not be clear so let's look at an example. Assume the correlation between an intelligence test and an achievement test is 0.60 (i.e., $r = 0.60$). By squaring this value, we determine the coefficient of determination is 0.36 (i.e., $r^2 = 0.36$). This indicates that 36% of the variance in one variable is predictable from the other variable. Additionally, if you subtract the coefficient of determination from 1.0 (i.e., $1 - r^2$), the result is the amount of variance in one variable that is *not* predictable from the other variable. This is the coefficient of nondetermination. Using our example examining the relationship between intelligence and achievement, we find that 64% of variance in one variable is not predictable from the other variable. In the discussion of scatterplots that follows, we provide some additional examples to help understand the usefulness of the coefficient of determination.

2.3.1 Scatterplots

As noted, a correlation coefficient is a quantitative measure of the linear relationship between two variables. Examining scatterplots may enhance our understanding of the linear relationship between variables. A *scatterplot* is simply a graph that visually displays the relationship between two variables. To create a scatterplot, you need to have two scores for each individual. For example, you could graph each individu-

> A scatterplot is a graph that visually displays the relationship between two variables.

al's weight and height. In the context of psychological testing, you could have scores for research participants on two different measures of cognitive ability. In a scatterplot, the X-axis represents one variable and the Y-axis the other variable. Each mark in the scatterplot actually represents two scores, an individual's scores on the X variable and the Y variable.

Figure 2.9 shows scatterplots for various correlation values. First, look at Fig. 2.9a that shows a hypothetical perfect positive correlation (+1.0). Notice that with a perfect correlation all of the marks will fall on a straight line. Because this is a positive correlation, an increase in one variable is associated with a corresponding increase in the other variable. Because it is a perfect correlation, if you know an individual's score on one variable you can predict the score on the other variable with perfect precision. In this example, the coefficient of determination would also be +1.0, indicating the line passes through 100% of the marks in the scatterplot.

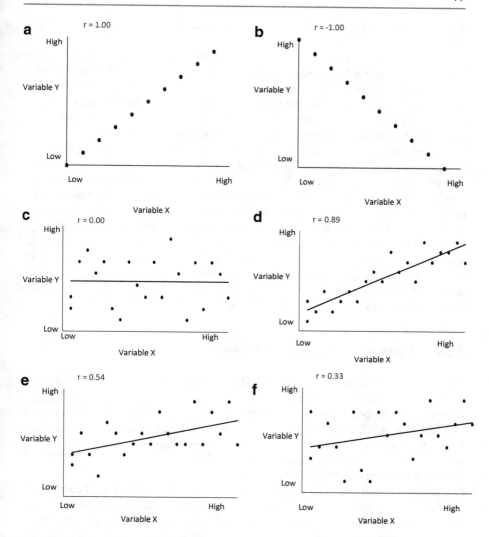

Fig. 2.9 Scatterplot of different correlation coefficients

Next examine Fig. 2.9b which illustrates a perfect negative correlation (−1.0). Being a perfect correlation, all the marks fall on a straight line, but because it is a negative correlation, an increase in one variable is associated with a corresponding decrease in the other variable. Given a score on one variable, you can still predict the individual's performance on the other variable with perfect precision. Now examine Fig. 2.9c which illustrates a correlation of 0.0. Here, there is not a relationship between the variables. In this situation, knowledge about performance on one variable does not provide any information about the individual's performance on the other variable or enhance prediction. The coefficient of determination would also be

0.0, and if one were to plot a line on the scatter plot, it would not pass through any of the marks.

So far we have examined only the scatterplots of perfect and zero correlation coefficients. Examine Fig. 2.9d which depicts a correlation of +0.89. Notice that the marks clearly cluster along a straight line. However, they no longer all fall on the line, but rather around the line. As you might expect, in this situation knowledge of performance on one variable helps us predict performance on the other variable, but our ability to predict performance is not perfect as it was with a perfect correlation. Finally examine Fig. 2.9e and Fig. 2.9f which illustrate coefficients of 0.54 and 0.33, respectively. As you can see a correlation of 0.54 is characterized by marks that still cluster along a straight line, but there is more variability around this line than there was with a correlation of 0.89. Accordingly, with a correlation of 0.33, there is still more variability of marks around a straight line. In these situations, knowledge of performance on one variable will help us predict performance on the other variable, but as the correlation coefficients decrease so does our ability to predict performance. It is also worth mentioning that because the coefficient of determination is based on the correlation, higher correlations result in higher coefficients of determination. In these scatterplot examples, as the coefficient of determination increases, the greater percentage of marks the line will pass through.

2.3.2   Types of Correlation Coefficients

There are specific correlation coefficients that are appropriate for specific situations. The most common coefficient is the *Pearson product-moment correlation*. The Pearson coefficient is appropriate when the variables being correlated are measured on an interval or ratio scale. Table 2.6 illustrates the calculation of the

> There are specific correlation coefficients that are appropriate for specific situations.

Pearson correlation coefficient. Although the formula for calculating a Pearson correlation may appear rather intimidating, it is not actually difficult and we encourage you to review this section if you are interested in how these coefficients are calculated (or if your professor wants you to be familiar with the process). *Spearman's rank correlation coefficient*, another popular coefficient, is used when the variables are measured on an ordinal scale. The *point-biserial correlation coefficient* is also widely used in test development when one variable is dichotomous (meaning only two scores are possible, e.g., pass or fail, true or false, 0 or 1, etc.) and the other variable is measured on an interval or ratio scale. A common application of the point-biserial correlation is in calculating an item-total test score correlation. Here the dichotomous variable is the score on a single item (e.g., right or wrong) and the variable measured on an interval scale is the total test score. A large item-total correlation is taken as evidence that an item is measuring the same construct as the overall test measures (more on this in later chapters).

Table 2.6 Calculating a Pearson correlation coefficient

There are different formulas for calculating a Pearson Correlation coefficient, and we will illustrate one of the simpler ones. For this illustration, we will use two sets of test scores, represented by X and Y. The formula is:

$$r_{xy} = \frac{N\Sigma XY - (\Sigma X)(\Sigma Y)}{\sqrt{N\Sigma X^2 - (\Sigma X)^2}\sqrt{N\Sigma Y^2 - (\Sigma Y)^2}}$$

ΣXY = sum of the XY products

ΣX = sum of X scores

ΣY = sum of Y scores

ΣX^2 = sum of squared X scores

ΣY^2 = sum of squared Y scores

Test 1 (X)	X^2	Test 2 (Y)	Y^2	(X)(Y)
6	36	7	49	42
7	49	8	64	56
7	49	9	81	63
3	9	4	16	12
8	64	6	36	48
8	64	7	49	56
7	49	9	81	63
8	64	8	64	64
9	81	9	81	81
8	64	7	49	56
10	100	9	81	90
5	25	6	36	30
4	16	6	36	24
8	64	7	49	56
6	36	6	36	36
6	36	5	25	30
7	49	7	49	49
5	25	6	36	30
7	49	8	64	56
8	64	7	49	56
$X = 137$	$X^2 = 993$	$Y = 141$	$Y^2 = 1031$	$XY = 998$

$$r_{xy} = \frac{20(998) - (137)(141)}{\sqrt{20(993) - (137)^2}\sqrt{20(1031) - (141)^2}}$$

$$r_{xy} = \frac{19{,}960 - 19{,}317}{\sqrt{19{,}860 - 18{,}769}\sqrt{20{,}620 - 19{,}881}}$$

$$r_{xy} = \frac{643}{\sqrt{1091}\sqrt{739}}$$

$$r_{xy} = \frac{643}{(33.030)(27.185)}$$

$$r_{xy} = 0.72$$

2.3.3 Factors that Affect Correlation Coefficients

There are a number of factors that can impact the size of correlation coefficients and need to be considered when interpreting correlation coefficients. Below we will briefly discuss two of these factors that are of special concern in the context of psychological measurement.

2.3.3.1 Linear Relationship

We noted that a correlation coefficient is a quantitative measure of the *linear relationship* between two variables. It is important to highlight the fact that there is the assumption of a linear relationship between the variables. By linear relationship, we mean the relationship is best represented by a straight line. For example, when discussing scatterplots, we noted that with a correlation coefficient of 1.0 all of the marks fall on a straight line. Many variables of interest to psychologists do demonstrate linear relationships. For example, the relationship between intelligence and academic achievement is linear. So is the relationship between height and weight. However, not all variables of interest to psychologists demonstrate linear relationships. For example, it is generally accepted that there is a relationship between anxiety and performance. For many people, some anxiety about performance helps them focus on the task at hand, and ultimately, they do better on the task. However, too much anxiety can be debilitating, and thereby decreases task performance. This is an example of a curvilinear relationship, and it is shown in Fig. 2.10. The use of correlation coefficients such as the Pearson or Spearman coefficients would produce spuriously low estimates of the relationship. However, there are special procedures that are appropriate for examining nonlinear relationships. It is usually possible to detect nonlinear relationships by carefully examining scatterplots. This highlights the importance of routinely examining scatterplots prior to analyzing and

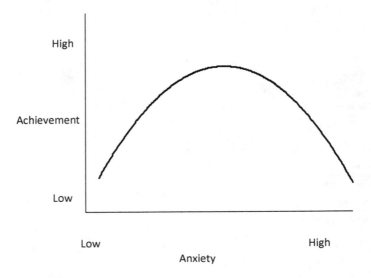

Fig. 2.10 Curve to fit a scatterplot of curvilinear data

interpreting the data. It should be noted that nonlinear relationships are not limited to clinical psychology variables. For example, Latané (1981) describes a number of social psychology studies that found nonlinear relationships between variables.

2.3.3.2 Range Restriction

The values we obtain when calculating coefficients are dependent on characteristics of the sample or group of individuals upon which the analyses are based. One characteristic of the sample that can significantly impact the coefficients is the degree of variability in performance (i.e., variance). More precisely, coefficients based on samples with large variances (referred to as heterogeneous samples) will generally produce higher correlation coefficients than those based on samples with small variances (referred to as homogeneous samples). When correlation coefficients are based on a sample with a restricted range of variability, the coefficients may actually underestimate the relationship between the variables. For example, if you calculate a correlation coefficient between two cognitive variables (e.g., short-term memory and vocabulary) among students at a prestigious university, you will receive lower coefficients than if the analyses were based on a more heterogeneous sample (e.g., one that included people with all levels of education, including those that did not complete the 12th grade). As a result, it is important to consider that the possibility of range restriction when interpreting or comparing correlation coefficients.

2.3.4 Correlation Versus Causation

Our discussion of correlation has indicated that when variables are correlated, information about an individual's performance on one variable enhances our ability to predict performance on the other variable. We have also seen that by squaring a correlation coefficient to get the coefficient of determination we can make statements about the amount of variance shared by two variables. In later chapters, we will show how correlation coefficients are used in developing and evaluating tests. *It is, however, a common misconception to believe that if two variables are correlated one is causing the other.* It is possible that the variables are causally related, but it is also possible that a third variable explains the relationship. Let's look at an

> Correlation analysis does *not* allow one to establish causality.

example. Assume we found a correlation between the amount of ice cream consumed in New York and the number of deaths by drowning in Texas. If you were to interpret this correlation as inferring causation, you would either believe that people eating ice cream in New York caused people to drown in Texas or that people drowning in Texas caused people to eat ice cream in New York. Obviously, neither would be correct! How would you explain this relationship? The answer is that the seasonal change in temperature accounts for the relationship. In late spring and summer when it is hot, people in New York consume more ice cream and people in Texas engage in more water-related activities (i.e., swimming, skiing, boating) and consequently drown more frequently. This is a fairly obvious case of a third variable explaining the relationship between ice cream consumption and drowning;

however, identifying the third variable is not always this easy. It is fairly common for individuals or groups in the popular media to attribute causation on the basis of a correlation. So the next time you hear on television or read in the newspaper researchers found that consuming vitamin X is correlated with improved cardiovascular health, and that this correlation means that vitamin X consumption improves heart health, you will not immediately go to your nearest health food store and spend your hard-earned money to purchase the vitamin, because you understand that correlation does not equal causation, i.e., vitamin X consumption does not cause improved heart health. In fact, whenever you hear a report that a correlation between variable A and variable B means that variable A causes variable B, you will not be fooled. Special Interest Topic 2.6 presents a historical example of when interpreting a relationship between variables as indicating causality resulted in an erroneous conclusion. Although correlation analysis does not allow us to establish causality, certain statistical procedures are specifically designed to allow us to infer causality. These procedures are referred to as inferential statistics and are covered in statistical courses, and we provide a brief overview of one such procedure (linear regression) given its importance to psychological assessment.

Special Interest Topic 2.6: Caution: Drawing Conclusions of Causality

Reynolds (1999) related this historical example of how interpreting a relationship between variables as indicating causality can lead to an erroneous conclusion. He noted that in the 1800s a physician noted that a large number of women were dying of "childbed fever" (i.e., puerperal fever) in the prestigious Vienna General Hospital, one of the premier medical facilities of its day. Curiously, more women died when they gave birth in the hospital than when the birth was at home. Childbed fever was even less common among women who gave birth in unsanitary conditions on the streets of Vienna. A commission studied this situation and after careful observation concluded that priests who came to the hospital to administer last rites were the cause of the increase in childbed fever in the hospital. The priests were present in the hospital, but were not present if the birth was outside of the hospital. According to the reasoning of the commission, when priests appeared in this ritualistic fashion, the women in the hospital were frightened and this stress made them more susceptible to childbed fever.

Eventually, experimental research debunked this explanation and identified what was actually causing the high mortality rate. At that time, the doctors who delivered the babies were the same doctors who dissected corpses. The doctors would move from dissecting diseased corpses to delivering babies without washing their hands or taking other sanitary precautions. When handwashing and other antiseptic procedures were implemented, the incidence of childbed fever dropped dramatically.

In summary, it was the transmission of disease from corpses to new mothers that caused childbed fever, not the presence of priests. While the conclusion of the commission might sound foolish to us now, if you listen carefully to the popular media you are likely to hear contemporary "experts" establishing causality based on observed relationships between variables. However, now you know to be cautious when evaluating this information.

2.4   Linear Regression

In discussing correlation coefficients, we mentioned that when variables are correlated, knowledge about performance on one variable can help us predict performance on the other variable. A special mathematical procedure referred to as *linear regression* is designed precisely for this purpose. Linear regression allows you to predict values on one variable given information on another variable. For

> Linear regression is a mathematical procedure that allows you to predict values on one variable given information on another variable.

example, if our research shows that indeed X and Y are related, linear regression will allow us to predict the value of Y if we know the value of X. Retaining X and Y as we have used them so far, the general form of our equation would be:

$$Y = a + bX$$

This equation goes by several names. Statisticians are most likely to refer to it as a regression equation. Practitioners of psychology who use the equation to make predictions may refer to it as a prediction equation. However, somewhere around the eighth or ninth grade, in your first algebra class, you were introduced to this expression and told it was the equation of a straight line. You maybe even learned to graph this equation and use it to determine a value of Y for any given value of X. What algebra teachers typically do not explain at this level is that they were actually teaching you the statistical concept of regression!

Let's look at an example of how this equation works. For this example, we will let X represent some individual's score on a predictor test (e.g., job screening test) and Y the person's score on a criterion to be measured in the future (e.g., supervisor's performance rating). To determine our actual equation, we would have to test a large number of people with the predictor test (X) and then measure their actual job performance (Y). We then calculate the correlation between the two sets of scores. One reasonable outcome would yield an equation such as this one:

$$Y = 10 + 0.5X$$

In determining the relationship between X and Y, we calculated the value of a to be 10 and the value of b to be 0.5. In your early algebra class, a was referred to as the Y-intercept (the starting point of your line on the y-axis when $X = 0$) and b as the slope of your line. We have graphed this equation for you in Fig. 2.11. When $X = 0$, Y is equal to 10 ($Y = 10 + 0.5(0)$), so our line starts on the y-axis at a value of 10. Since our slope is 0.5, for each increase in X, the increase in Y will be half or 0.5 times as much. We can use the equation or the prediction line to estimate or predict the value of Y for any value of X, just as you did in that early algebra class. Nothing has really changed except the names. Instead of the Y-intercept, we typically refer to a from our equation as a constant, since it is always being added to bX in the same amount on every occasion. Instead of "slope," we typically refer to b as a regression coefficient or a beta weight. If you look at Fig. 2.11, you can see that for a score of

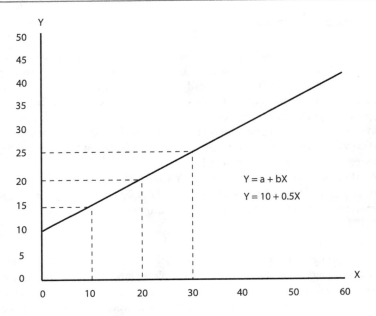

Fig. 2.11 Example of a graph of the equation of a straight line, also known as a regression line or prediction line. Note: $Y = a + bX$ when $a = 10$ and $b = 0.5$. For example, if X is 30, then $Y = 10 + (0.5)\ 30 = 25$

10 on our predictor test, a score of 15 is predicted for job performance rating. A score of 30 on our predictor test, a 20-point increase, predicts a job performance rating of 25, an increase on Y equal to half the increase in X. These values are the same whether we use our prediction line or use our equation—they are simply differing ways of showing the relationship between X and Y. Table 2.7 presents an example of the calculation of linear regression using the data originally presented in Table 2.6 where we illustrated the calculation of the Pearson correlation coefficient.

2.4.1   Standard Error of Estimate

If we had variables that had perfect correlations with each other (i.e., 1.0), our prediction would be perfect. However, in the real world when we are predicting Y from X, our prediction is never perfect since perfect correlations among psychological test scores don't exist. As a result, for any one person, there will always be some amount of inaccuracy in predicting future criterion performance. Our linear regression model actually is telling us the mean or average score on Y of all the individuals in the research study at each score on X. For example, using the data displayed in Fig. 2.11, 25 was the average performance rating for employees with a predictor test score of 30. We know that not all of the employees who earned a 30 on the predictor test will receive a job performance rating of 25. Nevertheless, the mean

Table 2.7 Calculating linear regression

The general form for a regression equation is:

$Y' = a + bX$

where:

Y' = predicted score on Y—i.e., Criterion
X = score on X variable—i.e., Predictor

a = Y-intercept or Constant. Calculated as $a = \bar{Y} - (b)\bar{X}$
b = slope or Regression Coefficient. Calculated as $b = r_{xy}(\sigma_y/\sigma_x)$
Using the X and Y scores presented in Table 2.6, we have:

$\bar{X}$ = 6.85 (i.e., mean of Test 1 [X]; 137 ÷ 20)
$\bar{Y}$ = 7.05 (i.e., mean of Test 2 [Y]; 141 ÷ 20)
r_{xy} = 0.72
σ_x = 1.69
σ_y = 1.39
b = 0.72 (1.39/1.69) = 0.875
a = 7.05 − (0.875)6.85 = 1.05

For example, if an individual received a score of 6 on the test $\bar{X}$ (i.e., predictor), the regression equation is:

$Y' = 1.05 + 0.875(6)$

$Y' = 6.3$

A simple way to check the accuracy of your regression equation is to use $\bar{X}$ as your predictor score and verify that the result is the mean of the Y scores. This is illustrated below

$Y' = 1.05 + 0.875(6.85)$

$Y' = 7.04$ (which is within rounding error of our $\bar{Y}$ mean of 7.05)

Below is a scatterplot with regression line for these data

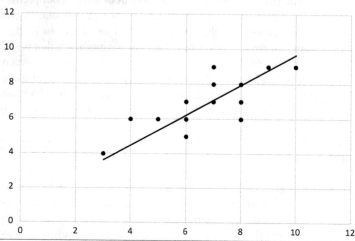

Table 2.8 Calculating the standard error of the estimate

The standard error of the estimate is designated by S_E and is computed as:

$$S_E = \sigma_y \sqrt{1 - r^2}$$

Work with the data presented in Table 2.7, we have the following results.

$$S_E = 1.39\sqrt{1 - (0.72)^2}$$

$$S_E = 1.39\sqrt{0.482}$$

$$S_E = 1.39 \times 0.694$$

$$S_E = 0.96$$

Based on this, if an individual's predicted score on Y is 7, we are 68% confident their actual score 2 weeks later will be between 6.04 (7 − 0.96) and 7.96 (7 + 0.96). This 68% confidence level is the result of you creating a 1 SD interval around your predicted score. It is rare for people to be satisfied with a 68% confidence interval, and test publishers typically report 90% or 95% confidence intervals (or both). To do this, they multiply the S_E by 1.64 for 90% confidence intervals and 1.96 for 95% confidence intervals. These calculations are illustrated below:

90% Confidence Interval = $Y' \pm (1.64)(0.96) = Y' \pm 1.57$

95% Confidence Interval = $Y' \pm (1.96)(0.96) = Y' \pm 1.88$

For our example involving a predicted score on Y of 7, the results are:

90% Confidence Interval = 5.43–8.57

95% Confidence Interval = 5.12–8.88

performance rating (i.e., Y) is used because it results in the smallest amount of error in all our predictions when making predictions using the predictor test (i.e., X).

In practice, we would also be highly interested in just how much error exists in our predictions and this degree of error would be calculated and reported. The **standard error of estimate** is the statistic that reflects the average amount of error in our predictions and is designated as S_E. Once we know the standard error of estimate in our regression model, we can make statements about how confident we are in our predictions. For example, if the standard error of estimate is 2 points, we might say that based on John's score of 30 on X, we are 68% confident that his score on Y will be between 23 and 27 and 95% confident that it will fall between 21 and 29. We refer to these intervals as *confidence intervals* since they reflect a range of scored within which we expect the client's actual score to fall with a specified degree of confidence (Table 2.8).

2.5   Summary

In this chapter, we survey basic statistical concepts and procedures essential to understanding psychological measurement. Measurement is a set of rules for assigning numbers to represent objects, traits, or other characteristics. Measurement can involve four different scales: nominal, ordinal, interval, and ratio. Each scale has distinct properties which are summarized here:

- *Nominal Scale*: a qualitative system for categorizing people or objects into categories. In nominal scales, the categories are not ordered in a meaningful manner and do not convey quantitative information.

- *Ordinal Scale*: a quantitative system that allows you to rank people or objects according to the amount of a characteristic possessed. Ordinal scales provide quantitative information, but they do not ensure that the intervals between the ranks are consistent.
- *Interval Scale*: a system that allows you to rank people or objects like an ordinal scale but with the added advantage of equal scale units. Equal scale units indicate that the intervals between the units or ranks are the same size.
- *Ratio Scale*: a system with all the properties of an interval scale with the added advantage of a true zero point.

These scales form a hierarchy and allow more sophisticated measurements as we move from nominal to the ratio scales.

We next turn our attention to distributions. A distribution is simply a set of scores and distributions can be represented in number of ways, including tables and graphs. Descriptive statistics have been developed that help us summarize and describe major characteristics of distributions. For example, measures of central tendency are frequently used to summarize distributions. The major measures of central tendency are:

- *Mean*: the simple arithmetic average of a distribution. Formally, the mean is defined by the equation: Mean = Sum of Score/Number of Scores
- *Median*: the score or potential score that divides the distribution in half.
- *Mode*: the most frequently occurring score in the distribution.
- *Measures of variability* (or dispersion) comprise another set of descriptive statistics used to characterize distributions. These measures provide information about the way scores are spread out or dispersed. They include:
- *Range*: the distance between the smallest and largest score in a distribution.
- *Standard Deviation*: a popular index of the average distance that scores vary from the mean.
- *Variance*: another measure of the variability of scores, expressed in squared score units. Less useful when interpreting individual scores, but important as a theoretical concept.

We then discuss correlation coefficients. A correlation coefficient is a quantitative measure of the linear relationship between two variables. Correlation coefficients provide information about both the direction and strength of a relationship. The sign of the coefficient (i.e., + or −) indicates the direction of the relationship while the magnitude of the coefficient indicates the strength of the relationship. Scatterplots are used to illustrate correlations, and there are several types of correlation coefficients commonly used in psychological statistics and psychometrics. While correlations are extremely useful in the development and evaluation of tests, they do not imply a causal relationship.

The study of correlation also has important implications in the context of predicting performance on tests and other criteria. The stronger the correlation between two variables the better we can predict performance on one variable given information about performance on the other variable. Linear regression is a statistical procedure that allows us to predict performance on one variable (i.e., the criterion) given performance on another variable (i.e., the predictor) when a linear relationship exists between the variables. When there is a perfect correlation between two variables (either positive or negative), you can predict performance with perfect precision. Since there are no perfect correlations among psychological variables, our prediction is always less than perfect. We have a statistic called the standard error of estimate that reflects the average amount of error in prediction and allows us to specify a range of scores within which we expect the client's actual score to fall with a specified degree of confidence.

Practice Items

1. Calculate the mean, variance, and standard deviation for the following score distributions. For these exercises, use the formulas listed in Table 2.5 for calculating variance and standard deviation.

Distribution 1	Distribution 2	Distribution 3
10	10	9
10	9	8
9	8	7
9	7	7
8	6	6
8	6	6
8	6	6
7	5	5
7	5	5
7	5	5
7	4	4
6	4	4
5	3	3
4	2	2
4	2	1

2. Calculate the Pearson correlation coefficient for the following pairs of scores

Sample 1		Sample 2		Sample 3	
Variable X	Variable Y	Variable X	Variable Y	Variable X	Variable Y
9	10	9	10	9	7
10	9	9	9	9	7
9	8	8	8	8	8
8	7	8	7	8	5
9	6	7	5	7	4
5	6	7	5	7	5
3	6	6	4	6	5
7	5	6	3	6	5
5	5	5	4	5	4
4	5	5	5	5	4
7	4	4	4	4	7
3	4	4	3	4	8

Sample 1		Sample 2		Sample 3	
Variable X	Variable Y	Variable X	Variable Y	Variable X	Variable Y
5	3	3	2	3	5
6	2	2	3	2	5
5	2	2	2	2	5

References

Gray, P. (1999). *Psychology*. New York, NY: Worth.

Hays, W. (1994). *Statistics* (5th ed.). New York, NY: Harcourt Brace.

Hopkins, K. D. (1998). *Educational and psychological measurement and evaluation* (8th ed.). Boston, MA: Allyn & Bacon.

Kubiszyn, T., & Borich, G. (2003). *Educational testing and measurement: Classroom application and practice* (7th ed.). New York, NY: Wiley.

Latané, B. (1981). The psychology of social impact. *American Psychologist, 36*(4), 343–356.

Osterlind, S. J. (2006). *Modern measurement: Theory, principles, and applications of mental appraisal*. Upper Saddle River, NJ: Pearson.

Reynolds, C. R. (1999). Inferring causality from relational data and design: Historical and contemporary lessons for research and clinical practice. *The Clinical Neuropsychologist, 13*, 386–395.

Sattler, J. M. (1992). Assessment of children. In *rev* (3rd ed.). San Diego, CA: Author.

Stevens, S. S. (1946). On the theory of scales of measurement. *Science, 103*, 677–680.

Recommended Reading

Hays, W. (1994). *Statistics* (5th ed.). New York, NY: Harcourt Brace. This is an excellent advanced statistics text. It covers the information covered in this chapter in greater detail and provides comprehensive coverage of statistics in general.

Nunnally, J. C., & Bernstein, I. H. (1994). *Psychometric theory* (3rd ed.). New York, NY: McGraw-Hill. An excellent advanced psychometric text. Chapters 2 and 4 are particularly relevant to students wanting a more detailed discussion of issues introduced in this chapter.

Reynolds, C. R. (1999). Inferring causality from relational data and designs: Historical and contemporary lessons for research and clinical practice. *The Clinical Neuropsychologist, 13*, 386–395. An entertaining and enlightening discussion of the need for caution when inferring causality from relational data. Contains both historical and contemporary examples, including a lawsuit where hundreds of billions of dollars changed hands.

Internet Sites of Interest

http://data.gov. This site provides easy access to all open data from the United States federal government.

http://nces.ed.gov/. This is the site for the National Center for Education Statistics, the primary federal agency responsible for collecting and analyzing data related to education.

http://unstats.un.org/. This is the United Nations Statistics Division Homepage. It contains information on the population and demographics of regions, countries, and cities.

http://www.ncaa.org. This site is great for the sports enthusiasts! It provides access to sports statistics compiled by the National Collegiate Athletic Association for sports ranging from baseball to lacrosse.

The Meaning of Test Scores

3

> *Scores are the keys to understanding an examinee's performance on tests and other assessments. As a result, thoroughly understanding the meaning of test scores and how they are interpreted is of utmost importance.*

Abstract

Test scores produced by psychological tests are extremely important because they are the basis on which to interpret an examinee's performance. There are many different types of scores, and each has its own unique properties. Raw scores are not very useful for interpreting test performance but transformed scores are quite useful and so are covered in some detail. The two main approaches to score interpretation involve comparing an examinee's test score to the scores of other people (norm-referenced interpretation) or to a preestablished criterion or cut-off (criterion-referenced interpretation). The type of interpretive approach and the kind of scores used to reflect test performance are selected based on the purpose of the test and the questions the examiner wants to answer.

Supplementary Information The online version of this chapter (https://doi.org/10.1007/978-3-030-59455-8_3) contains supplementary material, which is available to authorized users.

Learning Objectives

After reading and studying this chapter, students should be able to:

1. Describe raw scores and explain their limitations.
2. Define norm-referenced and criterion-referenced score interpretations and explain their major characteristics.
3. List and explain important criteria for evaluating standardization data.
4. Describe the normal curve and explain its importance in interpreting test scores.
5. Describe major types of standard scores.
6. Transform raw scores to standard scores.
7. Define normalized standard scores and describe major types of normalized standard scores.
8. Define percentile rank and explain its interpretation.
9. Define grade equivalents and explain their limitations.
10. Describe some common applications of criterion-referenced score interpretations.
11. Describe Item Response Theory and properties of IRT or Rasch-type scores.
12. Read and interpret information on standardization and scores presented in a test manual.

Test scores are a mathematical representation of the performance or ratings of the individuals completing a test. Because test scores are the keys to interpreting and understanding the examinees' performance, their meaning and interpretation are extremely important topics and deserve careful attention. As you will see, there is a wide assortment of scores available for our use and each format has its own unique characteristics. Possibly the simplest type of score is a raw score. A *raw score* is simply the number of items scored or coded in a specific manner such as correct/incorrect, true–false, and so on. For example, the raw score on a classroom math test might be the number of items the student answered correctly. The calculation of raw scores is usually fairly straightforward, but raw scores are often of limited use to those interpreting the test results; they tend to offer very little useful information for the following reasons. Let's say a student's score on a classroom math test is 50. Does a raw score of 50 represent poor, average, or superior performance? The answer to this question depends on a number of factors such as how many items are on the test, how difficult the items are, how other students did on the same test, and the like. If the test contained only 50 items and the student's raw score was 50, the student demonstrated perfect performance. If the test contained 100 items and the student's raw score was 50, he or she answered only half of the items

> A raw score is simply the number of items scored or coded in a specific manner such as correct/incorrect, true–false, and so on.

correctly. However, we still do not know what that really means. If the test contained 100 extremely difficult items and a raw score of 50 was the highest score in the class, this would likely reflect very good performance. Because raw scores, in most situations, have little interpretative meaning, we need to transform or convert them into another format to facilitate their interpretation and give them greater meaning.

These *transformed scores*, typically referred to as derived scores, standard scores, or scaled scores, are pivotal in helping us interpret test results. There are a number of different derived scores, but they can usually be classified as either norm-referenced or criterion-referenced. We will begin our discussion of scores and their interpretation by introducing you to these two different approaches to deriving and interpreting test scores, norm-referenced and criterion-referenced score interpretations. Another score format is available based on Item Response Theory, but we will wait until the end of the chapter to discuss it.

3.1   Norm-Referenced and Criterion-Referenced Score Interpretations

To help us understand and interpret test results, we need a frame of reference. That is, we need to compare the examinee's performance to "something." Score interpretations can be classified as either norm-referenced or criterion-referenced, and this distinction refers to the "something" to which we compare the examinee's performance. With *norm-referenced score interpretations,* the examinee's performance is compared to the performance of other people (i.e., the typical performance or "norm" by which to compare a score against). For example, scores on tests of intelligence are norm-referenced. If you report that an examinee has an IQ of 100, this indicates he or she scored higher than 50% of the people in the *standardization* (or norm) *sample*. This is a norm-referenced interpretation. The examinee's performance is being compared with that of other test takers. Personality tests also typically are reported as norm-referenced scores. For example, it might be reported that an examinee scored higher than

> With norm-referenced score interpretations the examinee's performance is compared to the performance of other people.

98% of the standardization sample on some traits such as extroversion or sensation seeking. With all norm-referenced interpretations, the examinee's performance is compared to that of others.

With *criterion-referenced score interpretations*, the examinee's performance is not compared to that of other people; instead, it is compared to a specified level of performance (i.e., a criterion). With criterion-referenced interpretations, the emphasis is on what the examinees know or what they can do, not their standing relative to other test takers. Possibly the most common example of a criterion-referenced score is the percentage of correct responses on a classroom examination.

> With criterion-referenced score interpretations the examinee is compared to a specified level of performance.

If you report that a student correctly answered 85% of the items on a classroom test, this is a criterion-referenced interpretation. Notice that you are not comparing the student's performance to that of other examinees; you are comparing it to a standard, in this case perfect performance on the test.

Norm-referenced interpretations are relative because they are relative to the performance of other examinees, whereas criterion-referenced interpretations are absolute because they are compared to an absolute standard. Norm-referenced score interpretations have many applications and the majority of published standardized tests produce norm-referenced scores. Nevertheless, criterion-referenced tests also have important applications, particularly in educational settings. Although people frequently refer to norm-referenced and criterion-referenced tests, this is not technically accurate. The terms norm-referenced and criterion-referenced actually refer to the interpretation of test scores; they are not an attribute of the test. Although it is most common for tests to produce either norm-referenced or criterion-referenced scores, it is actually possible for a test to produce both norm- and criterion-referenced scores. We will come back to this topic later. First, we will discuss norm-referenced and criterion-referenced score interpretations and the types of derived scores associated with each approach.

> Norm-referenced interpretations are relative whereas criterion-referenced interpretations are absolute.

3.1.1   Norm-Referenced Interpretations

3.1.1.1 Norms and Reference Groups

To understand an examinee's performance on a psychological test, it is often useful to compare their performance to the performance of some preselected group of individuals. Raw scores on a test, such as the number correct, take on special meaning when they are evaluated relative to the performance of a ***normative or reference group***. To accomplish this, when using a norm-referenced approach to interpreting test scores, raw scores on the test are typically converted to derived scores based on information about the performance of a specific normative or reference group. Probably the most important consideration when making norm-referenced interpretations involves the relevance of the group of individuals to whom the examinee's performance is compared. The reference group from which the norms are derived should be representative of the type of individuals expected to take the test or the group to which the examinee is to be compared or referenced. Most often these groups are the same, but they can be different. When you interpret an examinee's performance on a test or other assessment, you should ask yourself, "Are these norms appropriate for this examinee and for this use with this examinee?" For example, it would be reasonable to compare a student's performance on a test of academic achievement to other students of the same age, grade, and educational background. However, it would probably not be particularly useful to compare a student's performance to younger students who had not been exposed to the same curriculum, or to older students who have received additional instruction, training, or experience. For norm-referenced interpretations to be meaningful you need to compare the examinee's performance to that of a relevant reference group or sample.

When creating a test, one of the first steps a test publisher or developer must take is to define clearly the population for whom the test is designed. Once defined, a random sample from the reference population can be selected and tested. The normative reference group most often used to derive scores is called a national standardization sample. Most test publishers and developers select a national standardization

> Standardization samples should be representative of the type of individuals expected to take the test.

sample using a procedure known as *population proportionate stratified random sampling*. This means that samples of people are selected in such a way as to ensure that the national population as a whole is proportionately represented on important variables. In the United States, for example, tests are typically standardized using a sampling plan that stratifies the sample by gender, age, education, ethnicity, socio-economic background, region of residence, and community size based on population statistics provided by the U.S. Census Bureau. If data from the Census Bureau indicate that 1% of the U.S. population consists of African American males in the middle range of socioeconomic status residing in urban centers of the southern region, then 1% of the standardization sample of the test is drawn to meet this same set of characteristics. Once the standardization sample has been selected and tested, tables of derived scores are developed. These tables are based on the performance of the standardization sample and are typically referred to as normative tables or "norms." Because the relevance of the standardization sample is so important when using norm-referenced tests, it is the responsibility of test publishers to provide adequate information about the standardization sample. Additionally, it is the responsibility of every test user to evaluate the adequacy of the sample and the appropriateness of comparing the examinee's score to this particular group. In making this determination, you should consider the following factors:

- Is the standardization sample representative of the examinees with whom you will be using the test? Are demographic characteristics of the sample (e.g., age, race, sex, education, geographical location, etc.) similar to those who will take the test? In lay terms, are you comparing apples to apples and oranges to oranges?
- Is this the correct reference group for this application of this test? For example, if I want to know how Maria's current level of reading skills in English compare to that of the general population of children of the same age and grade in the USA, then a population proportionate stratified random sample of children of the same age and grade would be the appropriate reference group. This would be true even if Maria were a recent immigrant to the USA with limited English proficiency. Some would argue this is an unfair comparison because so few if any such children would be present in the "national standardization sample" and that Maria's reading skills should be evaluated by comparing her to other recently immigrated children with limited English proficiency. The latter comparison is very likely a useful one, but so is the former. These two comparisons to different reference groups answer different questions about Maria's reading skills—and

that is our point. Comparing Maria's reading skills to children-at-large describes her progress in learning English relative to all children in the schools. Comparing Maria to other recently immigrated children who are just learning English tells us about her relative progress compared to similar children. Both pieces of information are useful, and for these purposes, both samples are appropriate for answering their respective questions.

- Is the sample current? Participants in samples from 20 years ago may have responded quite differently from a contemporary sample. Attitudes, beliefs, behaviors, and even cognitive abilities change over time, and to be relevant, the normative data need to be current (see Special Interest Topic 3.1 for information on the "Flynn Effect" and how intelligence changes over time).

- Is the sample size large enough to provide stable statistical information? Although there is no magic number, if a test covers a broad age range, it is common for standardization samples to exceed 1000 participants. Otherwise, the number of participants at each age or grade level may be too small to produce stable estimation of means, standard deviations, and the more general distribution of scores. For example, the Woodcock Reading Mastery Test—Third Edition (WRMT; Woodcock, 2011) has 2600 participants in the standardization sample, with a minimum of 200 at each grade level (i.e., kindergarten through Grade 12).

> Normative data need to be current and the samples should be large enough to produce stable statistical information.

Special Interest Topic 3.1: The "Flynn Effect"

Research has shown that there were significant increases in IQ during the twentieth century. This phenomenon has come to be referred to as the "Flynn Effect" after the primary researcher credited with its discovery, James Flynn. In discussing his research, Flynn (1998) notes:

> Massive IQ gains began in the nineteenth century, possibly as early as the industrial revolution, and have affected 20 nations, all for whom data exist. No doubt, different nations enjoyed different rates of gains, but the best data do not provide an estimate of the differences. Different kinds of IQ tests show different rates of gains: Culture-reduced tests of fluid intelligence show gains of as much as 20 points per generation (30 years); performance tests show 10–20 points; and verbal tests sometimes show 10 points or below. Tests closest to the content of school-taught subjects, such as arithmetic reasoning, general information, and vocabulary show modest or nil gains. More often than not, gains are similar at all IQ levels. Gains may be age specific, but this has not yet been established and they certainly persist into adulthood. The fact that gains are fully present in young children means that causal factors are present in early childhood but not necessarily that they are more potent in young children than older children or adults (p. 61)

So what do you think is causing these gains in IQ? When we ask our students, some initially suggest that these increases in IQ reflect the effects of evolution or changes in the gene pool. However, this is not really a plausible

(continued)

explanation because it is happening much too fast. Currently, the most widely accepted explanation—and the one Flynn supports—is that changes in our environment that is largely the result of global modernization have increased our ability to deal with abstract concepts, an ability that is reflected to a large degree in contemporary IQ tests. Nevertheless, the underlying reason for the Flynn Effect remains controversial, and while virtually all researchers accept its existence, there is no universal agreement as to its causes.

Consider the importance of this effect in relation to our discussion of the development of test norms. When we told you that it is important to consider the date of the normative data when evaluating its adequacy we were concerned with factors such as the "Flynn Effect." Due to the gradual but consistent increase in IQ, new normative data makes tests more demanding. In other words, an examinee must obtain a higher raw score (i.e., correctly answer more items) each time a test is renormed in order for their score to remain the same. Kamphaus (2001) suggests that as a rule of thumb, IQ norms increase in difficulty by about 3 points every 10 years (based on a mean of 100 and standard deviation of 15). Consequently, the same performance on IQ tests normed 10 years apart would result in IQ scores about 3 points apart, with the newer test producing the lower scores. As a result, he recommends that if the normative data for a test is more than 10 years old one should be concerned about the accuracy of the norms. This is a reasonable suggestion, and test publishers are becoming better at providing timely revisions. For example, with the Wechsler Intelligence Scale for Children, the number of years between the second edition of the test (the WISC-R) and the third edition (WISC-III) was 17 years; the number of years between the latest edition (WISC-V) and its predecessor (WISC-IV) was 11 years. What do you think the social implications of the Flynn Effect might be? The time period in which normative data were collected might well affect whether or not a test taker receives a diagnosis of intellectual disability, for example. This has many ramifications for a person's life including receiving disability payments and other forms of public assistance, access to specialized educational and vocational training programs, and in the criminal arena, even whether one can be eligible to receive the death penalty, since persons with intellectual disability are fully exempted from such a punishment. What other social implications occur to you?

While a nationally representative sample is the most common type of reference group used by developers of major standardized tests, other reference groups are sometimes selected. For example, the standardized achievement tests used in many school districts provide local normative data that are based on students in individual school districts. This allows school officials and parents to be sure that their students are being compared with students that are comparable to many important variables.

Other types of normative data are provided with some standardized tests. For example, the Behavior Assessment System for Children Third Edition (Reynolds & Kamphaus, 2015a) includes normative data based on clinical samples as well as general population norms. These clinical norms are often helpful in refining or narrowing in on a diagnostic impression (see Special Interest Topic 3.2 for an example of how clinical norms are used). Whenever special normative group data are provided, the publisher should describe the normative group thoroughly in the test manual so psychologists can make informed decisions about how appropriate they are for a given examinee and for a given purpose. Different normative or reference samples answer different questions.

Special Interest Topic 3.2: Using Clinical Norms?
Reynolds and Kamphaus (2015a) note that clinical norms are most useful when an examinee's performance is extreme when compared to the general population. They give the example of a child referred for significant emotional and behavioral problems. Since the referred child's scores are extreme relative to the general population, a profile of his or her scores will indicate the overall degree of the problem, but the profile might appear flat and not help the clinician identify the specific nature of the problem. The figure below illustrates this concept using an example from the Behavior Assessment System for Children, third Edition. In this figure, the child's profile based on the general norms is represented by the dotted line. This profile indicates that the child's behavior is extreme, about four or more standard deviations above the mean, but it is relatively flat and does not reveal the specific nature of the child's problem. With this information, the clinician knows the child's behavior is deviant, but not what the most salient problems are. The profile based on the clinical norms (the solid line) demonstrates more variability. That is, it is not flat but has peaks and valleys. By examining the profile based on clinical norms, you see that the child's most extreme Externalizing Problems score is on Conduct Problems, and the most extreme Internalizing Problems score is on Somatization. In both of these examples, the clinical norms helped differentiate pervasive problems identified by the general norms, providing insight that clinicians can use to develop more effective intervention and treatment protocols.

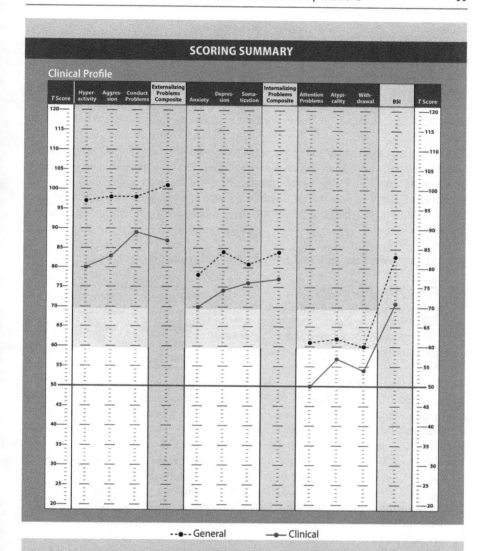

Source. Reynolds, C.R., & Kamphaus, R.W. (2015). *Behavior Assessment System for Children* (3rd ed.), Fig. 2.1, p. 18, © NCS Pearson. Reproduced by permission of NCS Pearson

A final consideration regarding norm-referenced interpretations is the importance of ***standardized administration***. The normative sample should be administered the test under the same conditions and with the same administrative procedures that will be used in actual practice. Accordingly, when the test is administered in clinical or educational settings, it is important that the test user follows the administrative procedures precisely. For example, if you are administering standardized tests, you need to make sure that you are reading the directions verbatim and closely adhering to time limits. It obviously would not be reasonable to compare your examinee's performance on a timed test to the performance of a standardization sample that was given either more or less time to complete the items. (The need to follow standard administration and scoring procedures actually applies to all standardized tests, both those with norm-referenced and criterion-referenced interpretations.)

Many types of derived scores or units of measurement may be reported in "norms tables," and the selection of which derived score to employ can influence the interpretation of scores. In Chap. 2, we introduced you to the normal distribution. If you are not confident that you thoroughly understand the material presented on the normal distribution, we encourage you to review it before proceeding to the next section of this chapter.

3.1.1.2 Derived Scores Used with Norm-Referenced Interpretations

3.1.1.2.1 Standard Scores

As we have noted, raw scores such as the number of items correct are difficult to work with and interpret. Raw scores therefore typically are transformed to another unit of measurement or derived score. With norm-referenced score interpretations, *standard scores* (sometimes

> Standard scores are transformations of raw scores to a desired scale with a predetermined mean and standard deviation.

called scaled scores) are often the preferred type of derived score. Transforming raw scores into standard scores involves creating a set of scores with a predetermined mean and standard deviation that remains constant across some preselected variables such as age (termed *scaling* because we change the underlying metric or rescale the scores). Although we are going to describe a number of different standard score formats, they all share numerous common characteristics. All standard scores use standard deviation units to indicate where an examinee's score is located relative to the mean of the distribution. Often, standard scores are simply linear transformations of raw scores to a desired scale with a predetermined mean and standard deviation. In a linear transformation, the following generic equation is applied to each score:

$$\text{Standard Score} = \overline{X}_{ss} + \text{SD}_{ss} * \frac{\left(X_i - \overline{X}\right)}{\text{SD}_x}$$

where

X_i = raw score of any individual taking the test i
$\overline{X}$ = mean of the raw scores for the entire sample
SD_x = standard deviation of raw scores for the entire sample
SD_{ss} = desired standard deviation of the derived standard scores
$\overline{X}_{ss}$ = desired mean of the derived or standard scores

This transformation is known as a *linear transformation*, and standard scores computed using it retain a direct relationship with the raw scores and the distribution retains its original shape (the importance of this statement will become more evident when we discuss normalized standard scores). Table 3.1 provides an example of how this formula is applied to raw scores to transform them into standard scores.

> Standard scores calculated using linear transformations retain a direct relationship with raw scores and the distribution retains its original shape.

As we noted, there are different standard score formats that have common characteristics. They differ in means and standard deviations. Here are brief descriptions of some of the more common standard score formats. This is not an exhaustive list, and it is possible to create a new format with virtually any mean and standard

Table 3.1 Transforming raw scores to standard scores

In this chapter, we provided the following formula for transforming raw scores to z-scores

$$z\text{-score} = \frac{X_i - \overline{X}}{SD}$$

where X_i = raw score of any individual i

$\overline{X}$ = mean of the raw scores

SD = standard deviation of the raw scores

Consider the situation where the mean of the raw scores ($\overline{X}$) is 75, the standard deviation of raw scores (SD) is 10, and the individual's raw score is 90

$$z\text{-score} = \frac{90 - 75}{10}$$

$$= \frac{15}{10}$$

$$= 1.5$$

If you wanted to convert the individual's score to a *T*-score, you would use the generic formula:

$$\text{Standard Score} = \overline{X}_{ss} + SD_{ss} * \frac{X_i - \overline{X}}{SD_x}$$

where X_i = raw score of any individual taking the test i

$\overline{X}$ = mean of the raw scores

SD_x = standard deviation of raw scores

SD_{ss} = desired standard deviation of the derived standard scores

$\overline{X}_{ss}$ = desired mean of the derived or standard scores

In this case, the calculations are:

$$T\text{-score} = 50 + 10 * \frac{90 - 75}{10}$$

$$= 50 + 10 * 1.5$$

$$= 50 + 15$$

$$= 65$$

deviation you desire. However, test authors and publishers typically use these common standard score formats because psychologists are most familiar with them.

- **z-scores**: z-scores are the simplest of the standard score formats and indicate how far above or below the mean of the distribution the raw score is in standard deviation units. z-scores are simple to calculate and a simplified equation can be used:

$$z \text{ - score} = \frac{X_i - \bar{X}}{SD}$$

where

X_i = raw score of any individual i,

$\bar{X}$ = mean of the raw scores,

SD = standard deviation of the raw scores.

z-scores have a mean of 0 and a standard deviation of 1. As a result, all scores above the mean will be positive and all scores below the mean will be negative. For example, a z-score of 1.6 is 1.6 standard deviations above the mean (i.e., exceeding 95% of the scores in the distribution) and a score of −1.6 is 1.6 standard deviations *below* the

> z-scores are the simplest of the standard scores and indicate how far above or below the mean on the distribution the raw score is in standard deviation units.

mean (i.e., exceeding only 5% of the scores in the distribution). As you see, in addition to negative scores, z-scores involve decimals. This results in scores that many find difficult to use and interpret. As a result, few test publishers routinely report z-scores for their tests. However, researchers commonly use z-scores because scores with a mean of 0 and a standard deviation of 1 make statistical formulas easier to calculate.

- **T-scores**: T-scores have a mean of 50 a standard deviation of 10. Relative to z--scores, they have the advantage of all scores being positive and without decimals. For example, a score of 66 is 1.6 standard deviation above the mean (i.e., exceeding 95% of the scores in the distribution) and a score of 34 is 1.6 standard deviation *below* the mean (i.e., exceeding only 5% of the scores in the distribution).

- **IQ scores**: Most intelligence scales in use today employ a standard score format with a mean of 100 and a standard deviation of 15 (e.g., Kaufman Assessment Battery for Children, 2nd Edition, Reynolds Intellectual Assessment Scales, 2nd Edition, Stanford-Binet Intelligence Scale, Fifth Edition, and all current Wechsler Scales). Like T-scores, this IQ format avoids decimals and negative values. For example, a score of 124 is 1.6 standard deviation above the mean (i.e., exceeding 95% of the scores in the distribution) and a score of 76 is 1.6 standard deviation *below* the mean (i.e., exceeding only 5% of the scores in the distribution). This format has become very popular and most aptitude and individually administered achievement tests report standard scores with mean of 100 and standard deviation of 15. Special Interest Topic 3.3 provides a historical discussion of how we came to interpret IQs using a mean of 100 and standard deviation of 15.

As we noted, standard scores can be set to any desired mean and standard deviation, with the fancy of the test author frequently being the sole determining factor.

Special Interest Topic 3.3: Why Do IQ Tests Use a Mean of 100 and Standard Deviation of 15?

When Alfred Binet and Theodore Simon developed the first popular IQ test in the late 1800s, items were scored according to the age which half the children got the answer correct. This resulted in the concept of a "mental age" for each examinee. This concept of a mental age (MA) gradually progressed to the development of the IQ which at first was calculated as the ratio of the child's MA to their actual or chronological age multiplied by 100 to remove all decimals. The original form for this score, known as the Ratio IQ was:

$$MA / CA \times 100$$

where

MA = mental age
CA = chronological age

This score distribution has a mean fixed at 100 at every age. However, due to the different restrictions on the range of Mental Age possible at each Chronological Age (e.g., a 2-year-old can range in MA only 2 years below CA but a 10-year-old can range 10 years below the CA), the standard deviation of the distribution of the ratio IQ changes at every CA! At younger ages, it tends to be small and it is typically larger at upper ages. The differences are quite large, often with the standard deviation from large samples varying from 10 to 30! Thus, at one age, a Ratio IQ of 110 is one standard deviation above the mean, while at another age, the same Ratio IQ of 110 is only 0.33 standard deviations above the mean. Across age, the average standard deviation of the now archaic Ratio IQ is about 16. This value was then adopted as "the" standard deviation for the Stanford-Binet IQ tests and was the standard until David Wechsler scaled his first IQ measure in the 1930s to have a standard deviation of 15 which he felt would be easier to work with. Additionally, he selected a standard deviation of 15 to help distinguish his test from the Stanford-Binet test, which was the dominant test of that time. The Stanford-Binet tests have long abandoned the Ratio IQ in favor of a true standard score, but remained tethered to the standard deviation of 16 until the Stanford-Binet Fifth Edition was published in 2003. With the Fifth Edition its new primary author, Gale Roid, converted to the far more popular scale with a mean of 100 and standard deviation of 15.

Table 3.2 Relationship of different standard score formats

z-scores $\overline{X} = 0$ SD = 1	T-scores $\overline{X} = 50$ SD = 10	IQs $\overline{X} = 100$ SD = 15	Percentile rank
2.6	76	139	>99
2.4	74	136	99
2.2	72	133	99
2.0	70	130	98
1.8	68	127	96
1.6	66	124	95
1.4	64	121	92
1.2	62	118	88
1.0	60	115	84
0.8	58	112	79
0.6	56	109	73
0.4	54	106	66
0.2	52	103	58
0.0	50	100	50
−0.2	48	97	42
−0.4	46	94	34
−0.6	44	91	27
−0.8	42	88	21
−1.0	40	85	16
−1.2	38	82	12
−1.4	36	79	8
−1.6	34	76	5
−1.8	32	73	4
−2.0	30	70	2
−2.2	28	67	1
−2.4	26	64	1
−2.6	24	61	1

$\overline{X}$ = mean, SD standard deviation

Fortunately, the few standard score formats we just summarized will account for the majority of standardized tests in education and psychology. Table 3.2 illustrates the relationship between various standard score formats. If reference groups are comparable, Table 3.2 can also be used to help you equate scores across tests to aid in the comparison of a student's performance on tests of different attributes using different standard scores. Table 3.3 illustrates a simple formula that allows you to convert standard scores from one format to another (e.g., z-scores to T-scores).

It is important to recognize that not all authors, educators, or clinicians are specific when it comes to reporting or describing scores. That is, they may report "standard scores," but not specify exactly what standard score format they are using. Obviously, the format is extremely important. Consider a standard score of 70. If this is a T-score, it represents a score 2 standard deviations *above* the mean (exceeding approximately 98% of the scores in the distribution). If it is a Wechsler IQ (or

Table 3.3 Converting standard scores from one format to another

You can easily convert standard scores from one format to another using the following formula:

$$\text{New Standard Score} = \bar{X}_{ss2} + SD_{ss2} * \frac{\left(X - \bar{X}_{ss1}\right)}{SD_{ss1}}$$

where X = original standard score

$\bar{X}_{ss1}$ = mean of original standard score format

SD_{ss1} = standard deviation of original standard score format

$\bar{X}_{ss2}$ = mean new standard score format

SD_{ss2} = standard deviation of new standard score format

For example, consider the situation where you want to convert a z-score of 1.0 to a T-score. The calculations are:

$$T\text{-score} = 50 + 10 * \frac{(1-0)}{1}$$
$$= 50 + 10 * \frac{1}{1}$$
$$= 50 + 10 * 1$$
$$= 50 + 10$$
$$= 60$$

comparable score), it is 2 standard deviation *below* the mean (only exceeding approximately 2% of the scores in the distribution). Be sure you know what standard score format is being used so you will be able to interpret the scores accurately!

3.1.1.2.2   Normalized Standard Scores

Our discussion about standard scores and their relationship to population percentages thus far applies primarily to scores from distributions that are normal (or that at least approximate normality) and were computed using a linear transformation. As noted earlier, although it is commonly held that psychological and educational variables are normally distributed, this is not always the case. Many variables such as intelligence, memory skills, and academic achievement will closely approximate the normal distribution when well measured. However, many variables of interest in psychology and education, especially behavioral ones (e.g., aggression, attention, and hyperactivity), may deviate substantially from the normal distribution. As a result, it is not unusual for test developers to end up with distributions that deviate from normality. In these situations, test developers may elect to develop normalized standard scores.

Normalized standard scores are standard scores based on underlying distributions that were not originally normal, but were transformed into normal distributions. The transformations applied in these situations are often nonlinear transformations, meaning there is no longer a direct relationship with the original raw scores and the shape of the now normalized score distribution. Although the relationship between the normalized standard scores and the original score distribution is different, this does not mean that normalized standard scores are undesirable. In situations in which the obtained distribution is not normal because of small

sample size, sampling error, or choice of subjects, normalization can enhance the usefulness and interpretability of the scores because it can be used to counteract the inadequacies of the original sample. In situations in which the obtained distribution is not normal because the variable is not normally distributed, normalization is not gener-
ally useful and indeed may be misleading,
resulting in over- or underestimates of the prevalence of a score with respect to the population.
Thus, it is desirable to know what type of scores
you are working with and how they were
calculated.

> Normalized standard scores are standard scores based on underlying distributions that were not originally normal, but were transformed into normal distributions.

In most situations, "normalized" standard scores are interpreted in a manner similar to other standard scores. In fact, they often look strikingly similar to linear standard scores. For example, they may be reported as normalized z-scores or normalized T-scores and often reported without the prefix "normalized" at all. In this context, they will have the same mean and standard deviation as their counterparts derived with linear transformations. However, there are several types of scores that traditionally have been based on nonlinear transformations and are normalized standard scores. These include:

- **Stanine scores**. Stanine (i.e., *standard nine*) scores divide the distribution into nine bands (1 through 9). Stanine scores have a mean of 5 and standard deviation of 2. Because stanine scores use only nine values to represent the full range of scores, they are not a particularly precise score format. As a result, some professionals avoid their use. However, certain professionals prefer them *because* of their imprecision. These professionals are concerned with the imprecision inherent in all psychological measurement and choose stanine scores because they do not misrepresent the precision of measurement (e.g., Popham, 2000). Special Interest Topic 3.4 briefly describes the history of stanine scores.

Special Interest Topic 3.4: The History of Stanine Scores
Stanines have a mean of 5 and a standard deviation of 2. Stanines have a range of 1–9 and are a form of standard score. Because they are standardized and have nine possible values, the contrived, contracted name of stanines was given to these scores (*stan*dard *nine*). A stanine is a conversion of the percentile rank that represents a wide range of percentile ranks at each score point. This system was developed by the U.S. Air Force during World War II when a simple score system was needed that could represent scores as a single digit. On older computers, which used cards with holes punched in them for entering data, the use of stanine scores not only saved time by having only one digit to punch, but also increased the speed of the computations made by computers and conserved computer memory. Stanines are now only used occasionally and usually only in statistical reporting of aggregated scores (from Reynolds, 2002).

- *Wechsler scaled scores*. The subtests of the Wechsler Intelligence Scale for Children—Fifth Edition (WISC-V: Wechsler, 2014) and predecessors are reported as normalized standard scores referred to as scaled scores. Wechsler scaled scores have a mean of 10 and a standard deviation of 3. This transformation was performed so the subtest scores would be comparable, even though their underlying distributions may have deviated from the normal curve and each other.
- *Normal Curve Equivalent (NCE)*. The Normal Curve Equivalent is a normalized standard score with a mean of 50 and standard deviation of 21.06. NCE scores range from 1 to 99 and were designed to approximate percentile ranks. However, being normalized standard scores, they are equal-interval scores, which is an advantage over percentile ranks which are ordinal-level scores. Because school districts must report NCE scores to meet criteria as part of certain federal education programs, many test publishers report these scores for tests used in educational settings.

3.1.1.2.3   Percentile Rank

One of the most popular ways to interpret and report a test score is the *percentile rank*. Like all norm-referenced scores, the percentile rank simply reflects an examinee's performance relative to a specific group. Percentile ranks range from 1 to 99, and a rank of 50 indicates the median performance (in a perfectly normal distribution it is also the mean score). A key benefit of the percentile rank is it directly tells us how common (or uncommon) a score is compared to those in the normative sample. However, a problem with interpreting percentile ranks is the variability (or lack of specification) in how they are computed.

The Standards for Educational and Psychological Testing (AERA et al., 2014) defines percentile rank as the rank of a given score based on the percentage of scores in a specified score distribution that is below the score being ranked (p. 221). For example, a percentile rank of 80 indicates that 80% of the individuals in the standardization sample scored below this score. A percentile rank of 20 indicates that only 20% of the individuals in the standardization sample scored below this score. As the definition in the *Standards* implies, percentile rank is computed by determining the percentage of scores in the normative distribution that falls below an obtained score.

> One of the most popular and easily understood ways to interpret and report a test score is the percentile rank. Percentile ranks reflect the percentage of individuals scoring below a given point in a distribution.

Other methods exist for calculating (and thus defining) percentile ranks (Crawford, Garthwaite, & Slick, 2009). For example, percentile ranks can be defined as the percentage of scores that fall at or below the score of interest. In this case, all of the scores found in the normative sample at the score of interest are included in the calculation of the percentile rank. Alternatively, percentile ranks can be defined as the percentage of scores that fall below the score of interest, where only half of those obtaining the score of interest are included in the percentage. In this case, only half of the scores found in the normative sample are included in the percentile rank calculation. For both of these variants, the percentile rank is interpreted in a similar manner to the definition provided in the *Standards*; what differs is the referent group mentioned in the description (e.g., a percentile rank of 80 indicates that 80% of the standardization sample scored at or below this score). It is beyond the scope of this chapter to provide the computational formulas and arguments for which method is superior (interested readers can refer to Crawford et al., 2009). While the differences between methodologies appear to be subtle, psychometrics is a precise science, and you should be aware of the distinctions. It is important to know how test authors and publishers approach the calculation of percentile ranks so users can interpret them accordingly.

Regardless of the methodology used to calculate them, the fact that percentile ranks simply describe how a score ranks compared to the normative population makes them fairly easy to explain and allows them to be understood by individuals without formal training in psychometrics. Whereas standard scores might seem somewhat confusing, a percentile rank is often more understandable. For example, a parent might believe an IQ of 75 is in the average range, generalizing from their experiences with classroom tests whereby 70–80 is often interpreted as representing average or perhaps "C-level" performance. However, explaining that the child's score exceeded only approximately 5% of the standardization sample or scores of other children at the same age level might clarify the issue. There is one common misunderstanding that may arise when using percentile ranks. When discussing results in terms of percentile rank, it is important to ensure that they are not misinterpreted as "percent correct" (Kamphaus, 1993). That is, a percentile rank of 60 means that the examinee scored better than 60% of the standardization sample, not that the examinee correctly answered 60% of the items.

Although percentile ranks can be interpreted easily, they do not represent interval-level measurement. That is, percentile ranks are not equal across all parts of a distribution. Percentile ranks are compressed near the middle of the distribution, where there are large numbers of scores, and spread out near the tails where there are relatively few scores (you can see this in Fig. 3.1 by examining the line that depicts percentiles). This implies that small differences in percentile ranks near the middle of the distribution might be of little importance, whereas the same difference at the extreme might be substantial. Therefore, it is often noted that the use of percentile ranks will exaggerate small differences near the mean and obscure large differences near the tails of the distribution. However, because the pattern of inequality is predictable, this can be taken into consideration when interpreting scores and it is not particularly problematic, so long as the user is aware of this particularity of percentile ranks.

There are two formats based on percentile ranks that you might come across, most often in educational settings. Some publishers report **quartile scores** that divide the distribution of percentile ranks into four equal units. The lower 25% receives a quartile score of 1, 26–50% a quartile score of 2, 51–75% a quartile score of 3, and the upper 25% a quartile score of 4. Similarly, some publishers report **decile-based scores**, which divide the distribution of percentile ranks into ten equal parts. The lowest decile-based score is 1 and corresponds to scores with percentile

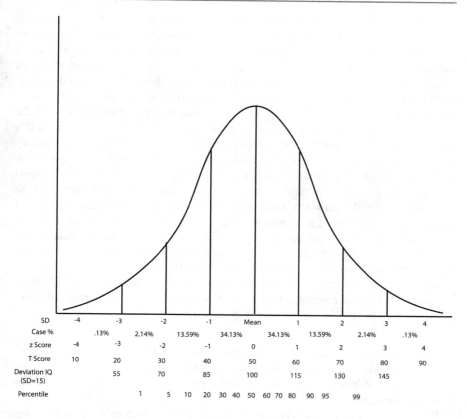

SD	-4	-3	-2	-1	Mean	1	2	3	4
Case %		.13%	2.14%	13.59%	34.13%	34.13%	13.59%	2.14%	.13%
z Score	-4	-3	-2	-1	0	1	2	3	4
T Score	10	20	30	40	50	60	70	80	90
Deviation IQ (SD=15)		55	70	85	100	115	130	145	
Percentile		1	5	10 20 30 40	50 60 70 80	90 95	99		

Fig. 3.1 Normal distribution illustrating the relationship among standard scores

ranks between 0 and 10%. The highest decile-based score is 10 and corresponds to scores with percentile ranks between 90 and 100% (e.g., The Psychological Corporation, 2002).

3.1.1.2.4   Grade Equivalents

Grade equivalents are norm-referenced derived scores that identify the academic "grade level" achieved by the examinee. Although grade equivalents are very popular in some settings and *appear* to be easy to interpret, they actually need to be interpreted with considerable caution. To understand grade equivalents, it is helpful to be familiar with how they are calculated. When a test is administered to a group of children, the mean raw score is calculated at each

> Grade equivalents are norm-referenced scores that identify the academic grade level achieved by the examinee. Although grade equivalents are very popular and appear to be easy to interpret, they actually need to be interpreted with considerable caution.

grade level and this mean raw score is called the "grade equivalent" for raw scores of that magnitude. For example, if the mean raw score for beginning third graders on a reading test is 50, then any examinee earning a score of 50 on the test is assigned a grade equivalent of 3.0 regardless of their age. If the mean score for fourth graders is 60, then any examinee earning a score of 60 is assigned a grade equivalent of 4.0. It becomes a little more complicated when raw scores fall between two median grade scores. In these situations, intermediate grade equivalents are typically calculated using a procedure referred to as *interpolation*. To illustrate this procedure with a straightforward example, consider a score of 55 on our imaginary reading test. Here, the difference between a grade equivalent of 3.0 (i.e., raw score of 50) and a grade equivalent of 4.0 (i.e., raw score of 60) is divided into 10 equal units to correspond to 10 months of academic instruction. In this example, since the difference is 10 ($60 - 50 = 10$), each raw score unit corresponds to one-tenth (i.e., 1 month) and a raw score of 55 would be assigned a grade equivalent of 3.5. In actual practice, interpolation is not always this straightforward. For example, if the difference between a grade equivalent of 3.0 and 4.0 had been 6 points (instead of 10), the calculations would have been somewhat more complicated.

Much has been written about the limitations of grade equivalents, and the following list highlights some major concerns summarized from several sources (Anastasi & Urbina, 1997; The Psychological Corporation, 2002; Popham, 2000; Reynolds, 1998).

- The use of interpolation to calculate intermediate grade equivalents assumes that academic skills are achieved at a constant rate and that there is no gain or loss during the summer vacation. This tenuous assumption is probably not accurate in many situations.
- Grade equivalents are not comparable across tests or even subtests of the same battery of tests. For example, grade equivalents of 6.0 on a test of reading comprehension and a test of math calculation do not indicate that the examinee has the same level of proficiency in the two academic areas. Additionally, there can be substantial differences between the examinee's percentile ranks on the two tests.
- Grade equivalents reflect an ordinal-level scale of measurement, not an interval scale. As discussed in the previous chapter, ordinal-level scales do not have equal scale units across the scale. For example, the difference between grade equivalents of 3.0 and 4.0 is not necessarily the same as the difference between grade equivalents of 5.0 and 6.0. Statistically, one should not add, subtract, multiply, or divide such scores because their underlying metrics are different. It is like multiplying feet by meters—you can multiply 3 ft by 3 m and get 9, but what does it mean?
- There is not a predictable relationship between grade equivalents and percentile ranks. For example, examinees may have a higher grade equivalent on a test of reading comprehension than of math calculations, but their percentile rank and thus their skill relative to age peers on the math test may actually be higher. For

example, a student in Grade 10.0 may have a grade equivalent of 8.0 on a reading test and 8.0 on a math test, but the percentile rank for the reading score could easily be 30 and for the math score 5, indicating very different levels of potential academic problems in these content areas.

- A common misperception is that children should receive instruction at the level suggested by their grade equivalents. Parents may ask "Johnny is only in the fourth grade but has a grade equivalent of 6.5 in math. Doesn't that mean he is ready for sixth-grade math instruction?" The answer is clearly "No!" Although Johnny correctly answered the same number of items as an average sixth grader, this does not indicate that he has mastered the necessary prerequisites to succeed in math at the sixth-grade level.

- Unfortunately, grade equivalents tend to become standards of performance. For example, lawmakers might decide that all students entering the sixth grade should achieve grade equivalents of 6.0 or better on a standardized reading test. If you will recall how grade equivalents are calculated, you will see how ridiculous this is. Because the mean raw score at each grade level is designated the grade equivalent, 50% of the standardization sample scored below the grade equivalent. As a result, it would be expected that a large number of students with average reading skills would enter the sixth grade with grade equivalents below 6.0. It is a law of mathematics that not everyone can score above the average!

As the result of these and other limitations, we recommend that you avoid using grade equivalents. **_Age equivalents_** are another derived score format that indicates the age, typically in years and months, at which a raw score is the mean or median. Age equivalents have the same limitations as grade equivalents, and we again recommend that you avoid using them. Many test publishers report grade and age equivalents, and occasionally you will find a testing expert that favors them (at least at the lower grade levels). Nevertheless, they are subject to misinterpretation and should be avoided when possible. If you are required to use them, we recommend that you also report standard scores and percentile ranks and emphasize these more precise derived scores when explaining test results.

> We recommend that you avoid using age and grade equivalents.

3.1.2 Criterion-Referenced Interpretations

As noted previously, with criterion-referenced interpretations, the examinee's performance is not compared to that of other people, but to a specified level of performance (i.e., a criterion). Criterion-referenced interpretations emphasize what the examinees know or what they can do, not their standing relative to other test takers, but their standing relative to an absolute standard or criterion. Although some authors appear to view criterion-referenced score interpretations as a relatively new approach dating back to only the 1960s or 1970s, criterion-referenced interpretations actually predate norm-referenced interpretations. For example, educators were scoring their students' papers and tests using "percentage correct," a criterion-referenced interpretation, long before test developers started developing norm-referenced scores. Nevertheless, since the 1960s, there has been renewed interest in and refinement of criterion-referenced score interpretations. A number of different labels have been applied to this type of score interpretation in the last 40 years, including content-referenced, domain-referenced, and objective-referenced. In this text, we will be using the term criterion-referenced because it is probably the broadest and most common label.

> Criterion-referenced interpretations emphasize what the examinee knows or what he or she can do, not the person's standing relative to other test takers.

Perhaps the most common example of a criterion-referenced score is "percent correct." For example, when a teacher reports that a student correctly answered 85% of the problems on a classroom test assessing the student's ability to multiply double digits, this is a criterion-referenced interpretation. Although there are a variety of criterion-referenced scoring systems, they all involve an absolute evaluation of examinees' performances as opposed to a relative evaluation. That is, instead of comparing their performances to the performances of others (a relative interpretation), a criterion-referenced interpretation attempts to describe what they know or are capable of doing—the absolute level of performance.

In addition to percent correct, another type of criterion-referenced interpretation is referred to as **_mastery testing_**. Mastery testing involves determining whether the examinee has achieved a specific level of mastery of the knowledge or skills domain and is usually reported in an all-or-none score such as a pass/fail designation (AERA et al. 2014). Most of us have had experience with mastery testing in obtaining a driver's license. The written examination required to obtain a driver's license is designed to determine whether the applicant has acquired the basic knowledge necessary to operate a motor vehicle success-

> Mastery testing involves determining whether the examinee has achieved a specific level of mastery of the knowledge and skills domain and is usually reported in an all-or-none score such as a pass/fail designation.

fully and safely (e.g., state motoring laws and standards). A **_cut score_** had been previously established, and all scores equal to or above this score are reported as "pass" whereas scores below it are reported as "fail." If the cut score requires correctly answering 85% of the items, all examinees with scores of 84% or below fail and all with 85% and above pass. There is no practical distinction in such a decision between an examinee answering 85% of the items correctly and one who answered 100% correctly. They both pass! For many educators, mastery testing is viewed as the preferred way of assessing mastery or proficiency of basic educational skills. For example, a teacher can develop a test to assess students' mastery of multiplication of fractions or addition with decimals. Likewise, a teacher can develop a test to assess students' mastery of spelling words on a third-grade reading list. In both of these situations, the teacher may set the cut score for designating mastery at 85%

and all students achieving a score of 85% or higher will be considered to have mastered the relevant knowledge or skills domain.

Another common criterion-referenced interpretative approach is referred to as **standards-based interpretations**. Whereas mastery testing typically results in an all-or-none interpretation (i.e., the student either passes or fails), standards-based interpretations usually involve three to five performance categories. For example, the results of an achievement test might be reported as basic, proficient, or advanced. An old variant of this approach is the assignment of letter grades to reflect performance on classroom achievement tests. Many teachers assign letter grades based on the percentage of items correct on a test, which is another type of criterion-referenced interpretation. A grades might be assigned for percentage correct scores between 90 and 100%, Bs for scores between 80 and 89%, Cs for scores between 70 and 79%, Ds for scores between 60 and 69%, and Fs for scores below 60%. Note that with this system a student with a score of 95% receives an A regardless of how other students scored. If all of the students in the class answered 90% or more of the items correctly, they would all receive A grades on the test.

> The most important consideration with criterion-referenced interpretations is how clearly the knowledge or skill domain is specified or defined.

As noted previously, with norm-referenced interpretations the most important consideration is the relevance of the group that the examinee's performance is compared to. However, with criterion-referenced interpretations, there is no comparison group and the most important consideration is how clearly the knowledge or skill domain being assessed is specified or defined (e.g., Popham, 2000). For criterion-referenced interpretations to provide useful information about what a student knows or what skills they possess, it is important that the knowledge or skill domain assessed by the test be clearly defined. To facilitate this, it is common for tests specifically designed to produce criterion-referenced interpretations to assess more limited or narrowly focused content domains than those designed to produce norm-referenced interpretations. For example, a test designed to produce norm-referenced interpretations might be developed to assess broad achievement in mathematics (e.g., ranging from simple number recognition to advanced algebraic computations). In contrast, a math test designed to produce criterion-referenced interpretations might be developed to assess the students' ability to add fractions. In this situation, the criterion-referenced domain is much more focused, which allows for more meaningful criterion-based interpretations. To illustrate, if a student successfully completed 95% of the fractional addition problems, you would have a good idea of their math skills in this limited, but clearly defined area. In contrast, if a student scored at the 50th percentile on the norm-referenced broad mathematics achievement test, you would know that their performance was average for their age. However, you would not be able to make definitive statements about the specific types of math problems the student is able to perform. Although criterion-referenced interpretations are most applicable to narrowly defined domains, they are often applied to broader, less clearly defined domains. For example, most tests used for licensing professionals such as physicians, lawyers, teachers, or psychologists require broad knowledge but involve criterion-referenced interpretations.

3.1.3   Norm-Referenced, Criterion-Referenced, or Both?

Early in this chapter, we noted that it is not technically accurate to refer to norm-referenced tests or criterion-referenced tests. It is the interpretation of performance on a test that is either norm-referenced or criterion-referenced. As a result, it is possible for a test to produce both norm-referenced and criterion-referenced interpretations. That being said, for several reasons, it is usually optimal for tests to be designed to produce either norm-referenced or criterion-referenced scores. Norm-referenced interpretations can be applied to a larger variety of tests than criterion-referenced interpretations. We have made the distinction between maximum performance tests (e.g., aptitude and achievement) and typical response tests (e.g., interest, attitudes, and behavior). Norm-referenced interpretations can be applied to both categories, but criterion-referenced interpretations are typically applied only to maximum performance tests. That is, because criterion-referenced score interpretations reflect an examinee's knowledge or skills in a specific domain, it is not logical to apply them to a typical response test like a personality measure. Even in the broad category of maximum performance tests, norm-referenced interpretations tend to have broader applications. Consistent with their focus on well-defined knowledge and skills domains, criterion-referenced interpretations are most often applied to educational achievement tests or other tests designed to assess mastery of a clearly defined set of skills and abilities. Constructs such as aptitude and intelligence are typically broader and lend themselves best to norm-referenced interpretations. Even in the context of achievement testing, we have alluded to the fact that tests designed for norm-referenced interpretations often cover broader knowledge and skill domains than those designed for criterion-referenced interpretations.

> It is not technically accurate to refer to norm-referenced or criterion-referenced tests. It is the interpretation of performance on a test that is either criterion-referenced or norm-referenced.

In addition to the breadth or focus of the knowledge or skills domain being assessed, test developers consider other factors when developing tests intended primarily for either norm-referenced or criterion-referenced interpretations. For example, because tests designed for criterion-referenced interpretations typically have a narrow focus, they are able to devote a relatively large number of items to measure each objective or skill being measured. In contrast, because tests designed for norm-referenced interpretations typically have a broader focus, they may devote only a few items to measuring each objective or skill. When developing tests intended for norm-referenced interpretations, test developers will typically select items of average difficulty and eliminate extremely difficult or easy items (this will be explained in detail in Chap. 6: Item Development). When developing tests intended for criterion-referenced interpretations, test developers match the difficulty of the items to the difficulty of the knowledge or skills domain being assessed.

> Tests can be developed that provide both norm-referenced and criterion-referenced interpretations.

Table 3.4 Characteristics of norm-referenced and criterion-referenced scores

Norm-referenced tests	Criterion-referenced tests
Compare performance to a specific reference group—a relative interpretation	Compare performance to a specific level of performance—an absolute interpretation
Useful interpretations require a relevant reference group	Useful interpretations require a carefully defined knowledge or skills domain
Usually assess a fairly broad range of knowledge or skills	Usually assess a limited or narrow domain of knowledge or skills
Typically have only a limited number of items to measure each objective or skill	Typically will have several items to measure each test objective or skill
Items are typically selected that are of medium difficulty and maximize variance, very difficult and very easy items typically are deleted	Items are selected that provide good coverage of content domain; the difficulty of the items matches the difficulty of content domain
Example: Percentile rank—a percentile rank of 80 indicates that the examinee scored better than 80% of the subjects in the reference group	Example: Percentage correct—a percentage correct score of 80 indicates that the examinee successfully answered 80% of the test items

Although our discussion to this point has emphasized differences between norm-referenced and criterion-referenced interpretations, they are not mutually exclusive. Tests can be developed that provide both norm-referenced and criterion-referenced interpretations. Both interpretive approaches have positive characteristics and provide useful information (see Table 3.4). Whereas norm-referenced interpretations provide important information about how an examinee performed relative to a specified reference group, criterion-referenced interpretations provide important information about how well an examinee has mastered a specified knowledge or skills domain. It is possible, and sometimes desirable, for a test to produce both norm-referenced and criterion-referenced scores. For example, it would be possible to interpret a student's test performance as "… by correctly answering 75% of the multiplication problems, the student scored better than 60% of the students in the class." Although the development of a test to provide both norm-referenced and criterion-referenced scores may require some compromises, the increased interpretive versatility may justify these compromises (e.g., Linn & Gronlund, 2000). As a result, some test publishers are beginning to produce more tests that provide both interpretive formats. Nevertheless, most tests are designed for *either* norm-referenced or criterion-referenced interpretations. Although the majority of published standardized tests are designed to produce norm-referenced interpretations, tests producing criterion-referenced interpretations play an extremely important role in educational and other settings.

3.2   Scores Based on Item Response Theory

To this point, we have focused our discussion of norm-referenced and criterion-referenced score interpretations. In recent years, theoretical and technical advances have ushered in new types of scores that are based on ***Item Response Theory*** (IRT).

IRT is a modern test theory that has greatly impacted test development, and we will discuss it in more detail in Chap. 7. For now, we can define IRT as a theory or model of mental measurement that holds that the responses to items on a test are accounted for by latent traits. A latent trait is some ability or characteristic that cannot be assessed directly; it is inferred to exist based on theories of behavior as well as observable evidence of its existence. Intelligence is an example of a latent trait. It is assumed that each examinee possesses a certain amount of any given latent trait and that its estimation is not dependent on any specific set of items or any assessment procedure. Central to IRT is a mathematical model that describes how examinees at different levels of ability (or whatever latent trait is being assessed) will respond to individual test items. IRT is fundamental to the development and application of *computer adaptive testing* (CAT). What is most important to us at this point (i.e., a chapter on the interpretation of test scores) is that IRT allows the calculation of scores that do not fit the common norm-referenced/criterion-referenced classification scheme.

> In recent years, theoretical and technical advances have ushered in new types of scores that are based on item response theory (IRT).

To illustrate the basics of the *IRT model*, consider this simple example. Envision a scale reflecting vocabulary skills (i.e., ability to specify the meaning of words correctly). On the left side of the scale are words that most people can define. As we progress up the scale, the words get increasingly more difficult. The words on the far right side of the scale are difficult and few people, only those with strong vocabulary skills, can define them. This is illustrated in the following figure:

cat	**table**	**greater**	**venture**	**posit**	**esoteric**

In this example, most examinees can define "cat" while very few can define "esoteric." In this illustration, we only use six words reflecting six items; however, in the development of an actual test, many word items would be included (e.g., a 100 or more).

In the IRT model, this scale can also be considered a scale reflecting the ability level of examinees. The specific ability level of an examinee is defined as the level on this scale where the examinee can get half of the items correct. In IRT terminology, an examinee's ability level is designated by the Greek letter theta (θ). Consider Johnny who is 7 years old and in the second grade. He easily defines "cat" and "table," and while he correctly defines "greater," he misses half of the other items at the same difficulty level as "greater." Now consider Sally who is a junior in college. Her vocabulary skills are understandably better developed than Johnny, and her ability level is at approximately the level of the word "posit." These ability levels of these two examinees are identified in the following figure.

> Scores based on the IRT model are similar to the raw scores on tests developed using classical test theory, but they have a distinct advantage in that they are equal-interval-level scores and have stable standard deviations across age groups.

	Johnny			**Sally**	
cat	table	greater	venture	posit	esoteric

The scores assigned to reflect an individual's ability level in an IRT model are similar to the raw scores on tests developed using traditional models (i.e., Classical Test Theory, described in Chap. 4). For example, they can be transformed into either norm or criterion-referenced scores. However, they have a distinct advantage in that, unlike traditional raw scores, they are equal-interval-level scores (i.e., having equal intervals between values) and have stable standard deviations across age groups. These *IRT scores* go by different names, including *W*-scores, growth scores, and Change Sensitive Scores (CSS). *W*-scores are used on the Woodcock-Johnson IV (Schrank, Woodcock, McGrew, & Mather, 2014) and are set so a score of 500 reflects cognitive performance at the beginning fifth-grade ability level. *W*-scores have proven to be particularly useful in measuring changes in cognitive abilities. For example, they can help measure gains in achievement due to learning or declines in cognitive abilities due to dementia. In terms of measuring gains, if over time an examinee's *W*-score increases by 10 units (e.g., from 500 to 510), they can now complete tasks with 75% probability of success that they originally could only complete with a 50% probability of success. Conversely, if an examinee's *W*-score decreases by 10 W units (e.g., 500 to 490), they can now complete tasks with only 25% probability of success that originally could complete with 50% probability of success. These IRT-based scores are not available for many published tests, but they will likely become more widely available in the future. They are often referred to generically as Rasch or *Rasch-type scores* after the originator of the mathematical models on which they are based.

3.3   So What Scores Should We Use: Norm-Referenced, Criterion-Referenced, or Rasch-Based Scores?

So, what scores should we use? Just as different reference groups or standardization samples provide us with different kinds of information, allowing us to answer different questions, dif-

> Different types of test scores answer different questions.

ferent types of test scores also answer different questions. Prior to being able to answer the question of which scores should we use, we need to know what it is we want the test score to tell us.

- Raw scores tell us the number of points accumulated by a person on a measure and can tell us their relative rank among test takers (assuming we know everyone's raw score). Raw scores typically provide us only with ordinal scale measurement.
- Traditional norm-referenced standard scores address the general question of how does this person's performance compare to the performance of some specified reference group and typically reflect interval scale measurement.

- Criterion-referenced scores tell us whether or not or to what extent a person's performance has approached a desired level of proficiency.
- Rasch or IRT-based scores are on an equal-interval scale that reflects position on some underlying or latent trait. These scores are particularly useful in evaluating the degree of change in scores over time and in comparing scores across tests of a common latent trait.

To illustrate how the use different types of test scores might address different questions, consider the issue of whether or not a student's performance in reading has changed following the introduction of specialized teaching methods after it was discovered the student was having great difficulty acquiring reading skills. In such a circumstance, a student, John, would be administered a reading test prior to initiating an intervention or specialized reading methods in order to obtain a baseline level of performance. After some period of specialized instruction, John would be tested a second time to determine whether or not his skills in reading had changed. If the test used provided one of the four types of scores noted above, what would each of these scores tell us about John's change in reading skill?

- Common standard scores that are norm-referenced by age group would answer the following question: How has John's reading performance changed relative to the average rate of change of other children the same age?
- Rasch-type scores would answer the question: How has John's reading performance changed relative to the starting point of his specialized instruction?
- Raw scores would answer this question as well, but are not on an equal-interval scale. This makes it difficult to estimate by how much John's reading performance has really changed. The advantage of a Rasch-type score in this circumstance is that the distance between each score point is the same throughout the entire range of scores so it is possible to estimate how much John's reading performance changed.
- Criterion-referenced scores answer a different question. Criterion-referenced scores address the question: Has John's performance in reading reached a predetermined level of proficiency or a set goal for his instructional progress?

All of these questions may be important but they are in fact quite different and different types of scores are required to answer each of these questions. To understand the difference in the types of information provided, consider if John were running a race instead of learning to read.

- Norm-referenced standard scores would reflect John's position in the race relative to all other runners at any given time.
- Rasch scores would indicate accurately his distance from the starting point but would not allow us to assess his progress relative to other runners without also knowing their Rasch score. Raw scores would indicate distance from the starting point as well, but unlike measurement in feet or meters in a race, when used with psychological or educational variables, would not indicate the distance accurately at each point of progress.
- A criterion-referenced score would let us know when John had passed specific points on the racetrack or had reached the finish line.

So here we see that each type of score provides us with a different type of information. Which score we should use is dependent upon the type of information we desire.

For purposes of evaluating change, in some circumstances, standard scores that are age corrected are the most appropriate but in other circumstances, criterion-referenced scores or even Rasch scores may be more appropriate. In an educational environment where we are looking to assess improvement in academic achievement levels of an individual student, the question of acquisition of academic skills relative to an age appropriate peer group would be the most appropriate question to address in nearly all instances. That is, it is important to know if a student is making progress or keeping pace relative to other students the same age and not just relative to the starting point. If we only considered progress relative to a starting point and only looked at changes in raw scores or some other form of growth score such as reflected in a Rasch scale, we could certainly determine if a student was making progress; however, the student may be progressing at a rate that is less than that of classmates, and as a result is falling further and further behind. By using age-corrected standard scores, we see easily whether the student is progressing at a lesser rate, the same pace, or more quickly than other students of the same age.

In a therapeutic environment, we have very different concerns. A person who is in psychotherapy being treated for depressive symptoms may be making progress; however, we would not want to discontinue therapy until a specific criterion point had been reached. In such cases, we would be more interested in the absolute level of symptomatology present or absolute level of distress experienced by the patient as opposed to their relative level of change compared to some peer group.

3.4 Qualitative Description of Test Scores

Test developers commonly provide qualitative descriptions of the scores produced by their tests. These qualitative descriptors help professionals communicate results in written reports and other formats. For example, the Stanford-Binet Intelligence Scale, Fifth Edition (SB5: Roid, 2003), provides the following qualitative descriptions:

> Qualitative descriptions of test scores help professionals communicate results in written reports and other formats.

IQ score range	Classification
145 and above	Very gifted or highly advanced
130–144	Gifted or very advanced
120–129	Superior
110–119	High average
90–109	Average
80–89	Low average
70–79	Borderline impaired or delayed
55–69	Mildly impaired or delayed
40–54	Moderately impaired or delayed

You will note that descriptors are typically presented for a range of scores rather than individual scores, so that for the SB5 and many other intelligence tests, scores between 90 and 109 are considered Average. These qualitative descriptors help professionals communicate information about an examinee's performance in an accurate and consistent manner. That is, professionals using the SB5 should consistently use these descriptors when describing test performance.

A similar approach is often used with typical response assessments. For example, the Behavior Assessment System for Children (BASC; Reynolds & Kamphaus, 2015a) is a comprehensive set of rating scales that measure adaptive and problem behaviors in children and adolescents. It provides the following descriptions of the clinical scales such as the depression or anxiety scales:

T-score range	Classification
70 and above	Clinically significant
60–69	At-risk
41–59	Average
31–40	Low
30 and below	Very low

3.5   Reporting Information on Normative Samples and Test Scores

The *Standards for Educational and Psychological Testing* (AREA et al., 2014) devotes an entire chapter to the discussion of test norms and scores. In terms of normative data, the *Standards* (2014) specify that "It is then important that norms be based on technically sound, representative sample of test takers of sufficient size (p. 97)." The Standards stipulate that test developers should report specific information about the normative sample and how the data were collected. They also require that test developers provide information on the meaning and interpretations of test scores and their limitations. (In this and subsequent chapters we often will devise illustrations based on tests developed by one of the authors of this text [CRR]. This is done because of our expertise with these instruments and our ability to access technical information about the tests as well as other information that otherwise may be difficult to obtain.)

To illustrate how information on normative data and test scores is reported in test manuals, we will use examples from the **Reynolds Intellectual Assessment Scales, Second Edition** (RIAS–2; Reynolds & Kamphaus, 2015b). The RIAS–2 is an individually administered intelligence test for clients 3–94 years. The RIAS–2 contains a two-subtest Verbal Intelligence Index (VIX) and a two-subtest Nonverbal Intelligence Index (NIX). The two verbal subtests are *Guess What (GWH)* and *Verbal Reasoning (VRZ)*. The two nonverbal subtests are *Odd-Item Out* (OIO) and *What's Missing (WHM)*. All four subtests are combined to form the *Composite Intelligence Index (CIX)*. It takes approximately 20–25 minutes to administer the four intelligence scale subtests. The RIAS–2 also includes a conormed, supplemental measure of memory that is composed of two memory subtests that yield a

Table 3.5 Comparison of U.S. population and RIAS–2 standardization sample: age and gender

Age (years)	Male			Female			Total n
	n	Weighted %	U.S. census %	n	Weighted %	U.S. census %	
3	49	50.5	50.2	48	49.5	49.8	97
4	51	51.5	51.8	48	48.5	48.2	99
5	51	51.0	51.4	49	49.0	48.6	100
6	47	50.5	50.9	46	49.5	49.1	93
7	49	51.6	51.1	46	48.4	48.9	95
8	45	50.6	51.3	44	49.4	48.7	89
9	45	50.6	50.7	44	49.4	49.3	89
10	45	51.7	51.4	42	48.3	48.6	87
11	45	50.6	50.8	44	49.4	49.2	89
12	46	51.7	51.6	43	48.3	48.4	89
13	47	50.5	50.6	46	49.5	49.4	93
14	46	51.1	51.1	44	48.9	48.9	90
15	46	51.1	51.1	44	48.9	48.9	90
16	46	51.7	51.9	43	48.3	48.1	89
17	42	51.2	51.1	40	48.8	48.9	82
18	39	50.0	50.7	39	50.0	49.3	78
19	43	51.2	50.3	41	48.8	49.7	84
20–29	48	50.0	50.1	48	50.0	49.9	96
30–39	45	48.9	49.3	47	51.1	50.7	92
40–49	44	48.9	49.2	46	51.1	50.8	90
50–59	43	48.3	48.5	46	51.7	51.5	89
60–69	42	47.2	47.4	47	52.8	52.6	89
70–79	39	44.8	44.6	48	55.2	55.4	87
80–94	31	39.7	39.2	47	60.3	60.8	78
Total	1074	49.8	49.8	1080	50.2	50.2	2154

Composite Memory Index (CMX). The two memory subtests are *Verbal Memory (VRM)* and *Nonverbal Memory (NVM).* The administration of the memory subtests requires approximately 10–15 min. Finally, the RIAS–2 includes a conormed, supplemental measure of processing speed that is composed of two subtests that yield a *Speeded Processing Index (SPI).* The two processing speed subtests are the *Speeded Naming Task (SNT)* and the *Speeded Picture Search (SPS),* which can be completed in approximately 10 minutes.

The RIAS–2 was standardized on a national sample of 2,154 individuals that is representative of the U.S. population. Tables 3.5 and 3.6 compare the demographic characteristics of the standardization sample to that of the U.S. population. These data illustrate that the RIAS–2 standardization sample is representative of the general population.

The RIAS–2 Professional Manual (Reynolds & Kamphaus, 2015b) provides a description of how the age-adjusted subtest T-scores were derived. This includes a fairly technical description of sample weighting and continuous norming procedures that were used in developing the normalized subtest T-scores. There are also 52 tables in an appendix that allows one to convert raw scores on the subtests to T-scores. Table 3.7 reproduces the conversion table for examinees ages 8 years

Table 3.6 Comparison of U.S. population and RIAS-2 standardization sample: age and ethnicity

Age	Caucasian			African American			Hispanic			Other			Total N
	n	Weighted %	U.S. census %	n	Weighted %	U.S. census %	n	Weighted %	U.S. census %	n	Weighted %	U.S. census %	
3	49	50.5	50.3	14	14.4	14.5	25	25.8	25.5	9	9.3	9.7	97
4	50	50.5	49.8	13	13.1	13.3	26	26.3	25.5	10	10.1	11.4	99
5	51	51.0	50.3	14	14.0	13.6	25	25.0	24.8	10	10.0	11.3	100
6	49	52.7	51.6	12	12.9	13.7	24	25.8	25.4	8	8.6	9.4	93
7	51	53.7	53.0	12	12.6	12.6	24	25.3	24.9	8	8.4	9.6	95
8	48	53.9	52.7	11	12.4	13.6	22	24.7	23.7	8	9.0	10.0	89
9	49	55.1	53.5	11	12.4	13.1	21	23.6	23.6	8	9.0	9.8	89
10	49	56.3	54.9	10	11.5	12.9	21	24.1	23.2	7	8.0	9.1	87
11	48	53.9	53.1	12	13.5	14.9	21	23.6	22.8	8	9.0	9.2	89
12	50	56.2	54.5	12	13.5	14.7	20	22.5	22.1	7	7.9	8.7	89
13	52	55.9	54.9	12	12.9	13.4	22	23.7	22.8	7	7.5	8.8	93
14	51	56.7	55.9	12	13.3	13.9	20	22.2	22.0	7	7.8	8.2	90
15	51	56.7	55.2	12	13.3	13.8	20	22.2	22.0	7	7.8	8.9	90
16	50	56.2	55.5	13	14.6	15.1	19	21.3	21.4	7	7.9	8.0	89
17	46	56.1	55.9	11	13.4	14.0	18	22.0	21.8	7	8.5	8.3	82
18	44	56.4	56.3	11	14.1	14.5	17	21.8	21.0	6	7.7	8.2	78
19	47	56.0	55.9	11	13.1	13.6	18	21.4	21.7	8	9.5	8.9	84
20–29	56	58.3	57.2	12	12.5	13.3	20	20.8	20.7	8	8.3	8.8	96
30–39	54	58.7	58.3	11	12.0	12.0	19	20.7	20.5	8	8.7	9.2	92
40–49	60	66.7	64.3	10	11.1	12.0	14	15.6	16.0	6	6.7	7.7	90
50–59	65	73.0	71.3	10	11.2	11.5	10	11.2	10.9	4	4.5	6.4	89
60–69	70	78.7	76.1	8	9.0	9.9	7	7.9	8.4	4	4.5	5.6	89
70–79	72	82.8	79.2	8	9.2	8.7	4	4.6	7.3	3	3.4	4.8	87
80–94	64	82.1	82.2	6	7.7	7.3	5	6.4	6.4	3	3.8	4.2	78
Total	1276	59.5	58.4	268	12.4	12.9	442	20.3	20.2	168	7.8	8.5	2154

Table 3.7 *T*-score conversions for subtest raw scores, ages 8:0–8:3

T score	GWH	OIO	VRZ	WHM	VRM	NVM	SNT	SPS	T score
			Subtest raw score						
91	≥52		≥38				≥202		91
90		106	37	98			200–201		90
89	51						198–199		89
88		105	36				195–197		88
87	50	104		97			193–194		87
86		103					191–192		86
85	49	102	35	96			189–190		85
84		101		95	43		187–188		84
83	48	100	34	94	42		184–186		83
82		99		93	41		182–183		82
81	47		33	92			180–181		81
80		98		91	40		178–179		80
79	46	97		90	39		176–177		79
78		96	32	89			173–175		78
77	45	95		88	38		171–172		77
76		94	31	87	37	112	169–170	1	76
75	44	93		86	36	111	167–168	2	75
74		92	30	85		110	165–166	3	74
73	43	91		84	35	108–109	162–164	4–5	73
72				83	34	107	160–161	6–7	72
71	42	90	29	82	33	106	158–159	8–9	71
70		89		81		105	156–157	10–14	70
69	41	88	28	80	32	104	154–155	15–23	69
68		87		79	31	103	151–153	24–33	68
67	40	86	27	78	30	101–102	149–150	34–42	67
66		85		77		100	147–148	43–51	66
65	39	84		76	29	99	145–146	52–61	65
64			26	75	28	98	143–144	62–70	64
63	38	83		74		97	140–142	71–79	63
62		82	25	73	27	96	138–139	80–89	62
61	37	81		72	26	94–95	136–137	90–98	61
60		80	24	71	25	93	134–135	99–107	60
59	36	79		70		92	131–133	108–117	59
58		78			24	91	129–130	118–126	58
57	35	77	23	69	23	90	127–128	127–135	57
56				68	22	89	125–126	136–145	56
55		76	22	67		88	123–124	146–154	55
54	34	75		66	21	86–87	120–122	155–163	54
53		74	21	65	20	85	118–119	164–173	53
52	33	73		64	19	84	116–117	174–182	52
51		72		63		83	114–115	183–191	51
50	32	71	20	62	18	82	112–113	192–201	50

(continued)

Table 3.7 (continued)

T score	Subtest raw score								T score
	GWH	OIO	VRZ	WHM	VRM	NVM	SNT	SPS	
49		70		61	17	81	109–111	202–210	49
48	31		19	60	16	79–80	107–108	211–219	48
47		69		59		78	105–106	220–229	47
46	30	68	18	58	15	77	103–104	230–238	46
45		67		57	14	76	101–102	239–248	45
44	29	66	17	56		75	98–100	249–257	44
43		65		55	13	74	96–97	258–266	43
42	28	64		54	12	72–73	94–95	267–276	42
41		63	16	53	11	71	92–93	277–285	41
40	27	62		52		70	90–91	286–294	40
39			15	51	10	69	87–89	295–304	39
38	26	61		50	9	68	85–86	305–313	38
37		60	14	49	8	67	83–84	314–322	37
36	25	59		48		65–66	81–82	323–332	36
35		58		47	7	64	79–80	333–341	35
34	24	57	13	46	6	63	76–78	342–350	34
33		56		45	5	62	74–75	351–360	33
32	23	55	12	44		61	72–73	361–369	32
31				43	4	60	70–71	370–378	31
30	22	54	11	42	3	58–59	68–69	379–388	30
29		53		41		57	65–67	389–397	29
28	21	52		40	2	56	63–64	398–406	28
27		51	10	39	1	55	61–62	407–416	27
26	20	50		38		54	59–60	417–425	26
25		49	9	37	0	53	57–58	426–434	25
24	19	48		36		51–52	54–56	435–444	24
23			8			50	52–53	445–453	23
22	18	47		35		49	50–51	454–463	22
21		46		34		48	48–49	464–472	21
20	17	45	7	33		47	45–47	473–481	20
19		44		32		46	43–44	482–491	19
18	16	43	6	31		44–45	41–42	492–500	18
17		42		30		43	39–40	501–509	17
16	15	41	5	29		42	37–38	510–519	16
15				28		41	34–36	520–528	15
14	14	40		27		40	32–33	529–537	14
13		39	4	26		39	30–31	538–547	13
12	13	38		25		38	28–29	548–556	12
11		37	3	24		36–37	26–27	557–565	11
10	12	36		23		35	23–25	566–575	10
9	0–11	0–35	0–2	0–22		0–34	0–22	>= 576	9

Source: Reynolds, C.R., & Kamphaus, R.W. (2015). Reynolds Intellectual Assessment Scales (2nd Edition). Lutz, FL: Psychological Assessment Resources. Reprinted with permission

Table 3.8 Standard score conversions for the RIAS-2 Verbal Intelligence Index

Sum of subtest T scores	VIX	%tile Rank	Confidence interval 90%	Confidence interval 95%	T score	z score	NCE	Stanine
97–98	98	45	94–102	94–103	49	−0.13	47	5
96	97	42	93–101	93–102	48	−0.20	46	5
95	96	39	92–100	92–101	47	−0.27	44	4
94	95	37	92–99	91–99	47	−0.33	43	4
92–93	94	34	91–98	90–98	46	−0.40	42	4
91	93	32	90–97	89–97	45	−0.47	40	4
90	92	30	89–96	88–96	45	−0.53	39	4
88–89	91	27	88–95	87–96	44	−0.60	37	4

Source: Reynolds, C.R., & Kamphaus, R.W. (2015). Reynolds Intellectual Assessment Scales (2nd Edition). Lutz, FL: Psychological Assessment Resources. Reprinted with permission

0 months to 8 years 3 months. In this table, a raw score of 48 on *Guess What (GWH)* translates to a *T*-score of 83. Accordingly, a raw score of 48 on *Odd-Item Out* (OIO) translates to a *T*-score of 24. Using these tables, the examiner is able to convert raw scores to *T*-scores for all of the RIAS–2 subtests.

Once the subtest *T*-scores are calculated, the examiner is able to calculate the Index Scores. To do this, the age-adjusted *T*-scores comprising the index scores are summed. For example, the *Guess What* and *Verbal Reasoning T*-scores are summed to allow the calculation of the Verbal Intelligence Index (VIX). Once these summed scores are available, the examiner can convert them to Index scores using tables provided in the manual. These Index scores have a mean of 100 and a standard deviation of 15. Table 3.8 reproduces a portion of the table used for converting summed *T*-scores for the Verbal Intelligence Index (VIX). An examination of Table 3.8 illustrates the variety of supplemental scores available for the RIAS–2 Index Scores. These include *T*-scores, *z* scores, Normal Curve Equivalents (NCE), and Stanines.

The RIAS–2 provides computerized scoring software that generates a RIAS-2 Score Report. Figure 3.2 provides an example of a score summary and score profile that can be used to easily view an examinee's overall test results.

3.6   Summary

This chapter provides an overview of different types of test scores and their meaning. We start by noting that raw scores alone, while easy to calculate, usually provide little useful information about an examinee's performance on a test. As a result, we usually transform raw scores into derived scores. These derived scores can be classified broadly as either norm-referenced or criterion-referenced. Norm-referenced score interpretations compare an examinee's performance on a test to the performance of other people, typically those in the standardization sample. When making norm-referenced interpretations, it is important to evaluate the adequacy of

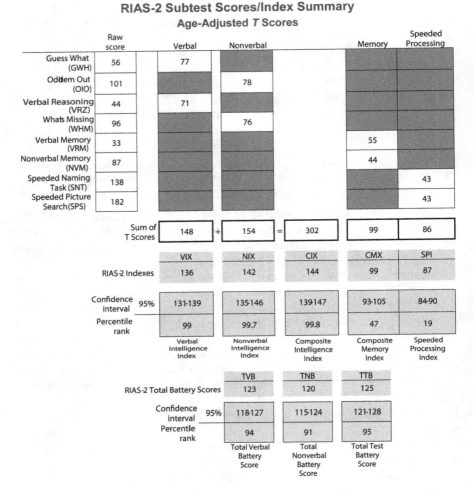

RIAS-2 Subtest Scores/Index Summary
Age-Adjusted *T* Scores

	Raw score	Verbal	Nonverbal		Memory	Speeded Processing
Guess What (GWH)	56	77				
Odd Item Out (OIO)	101		78			
Verbal Reasoning (VRZ)	44	71				
Whats Missing (WHM)	96		76			
Verbal Memory (VRM)	33				55	
Nonverbal Memory (NVM)	87				44	
Speeded Naming Task (SNT)	138					43
Speeded Picture Search (SPS)	182					43
Sum of T Scores		148 +	154 =	302	99	86

	VIX	NIX	CIX	CMX	SPI
RIAS-2 Indexes	136	142	144	99	87
Confidence interval 95%	131-139	135-146	139-147	93-105	84-90
Percentile rank	99	99.7	99.8	47	19
	Verbal Intelligence Index	Nonverbal Intelligence Index	Composite Intelligence Index	Composite Memory Index	Speeded Processing Index

	TVB	TNB	TTB
RIAS-2 Total Battery Scores	123	120	125
Confidence interval 95%	118-127	115-124	121-128
Percentile rank	94	91	95
	Total Verbal Battery Score	Total Nonverbal Battery Score	Total Test Battery Score

Fig. 3.2 Example of RIAS-2 record form. (Source. Reynolds, C. R., & Kamphaus, R. W., *Reynolds Intellectual Assessment Scales* (2nd ed.), RIAS–2 Score Report p. 2–3, p. 18, © Psychological Assessment Resources. Reproduced with permission)

RIAS-2 Profiles

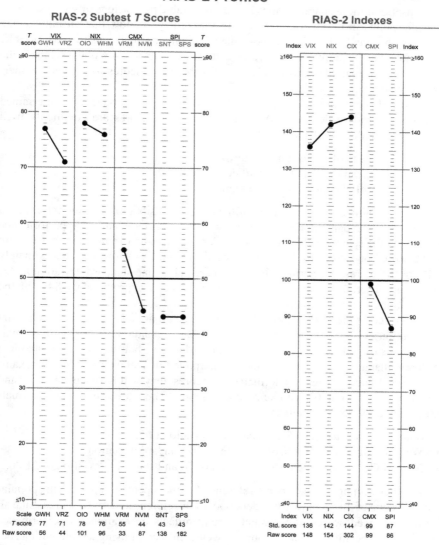

Scale	GWH	VRZ	OIO	WHM	VRM	NVM	SNT	SPS
T score	77	71	78	76	55	44	43	43
Raw score	56	44	101	96	33	87	138	182

Index	VIX	NIX	CIX	CMX	SPI
Std. score	136	142	144	99	87
Raw score	148	154	302	99	86

Fig. 3.2 (continued)

the standardization sample. This involves determining (1) if the standardization is representative of the examinees the test will be used with, (2) if the sample is current, and (3) if sample is of adequate size to produce stable statistics.

When making norm-referenced interpretations it is useful to have a basic understanding of the normal distribution (also referred to as the bell-shaped curve). The normal distribution is a distribution that characterizes many naturally occurring variables and has several characteristics that psychometricians find very useful. The most useful of these characteristics is that predictable proportions of scores occur at specific points in the distribution. For example, if you know that an individual's score is one standard deviation above the mean on a normally distributed variable, you know that the individual's score exceeds approximately 84% of the scores in the standardization sample. This predictable distribution of scores facilitates the interpretation and reporting of test scores.

Standard scores are norm-referenced derived scores that have a predetermined mean and standard deviation. A variety of standard scores are commonly used today, and we discussed some of these including:

- z-scores: mean of 0 and standard deviation of 1,
- T-scores: mean of 50 and standard deviation of 10.
- IQs: mean of 100 and standard deviation of 15.

By combining an understanding of the normal distribution with the information provided by standard scores, you can easily interpret an examinee's performance relative to the specified reference group. For example, an examinee with a T-score of 60 scored one standard deviation above the mean. You know that approximately 84% of the scores in a normal distribution are below one standard deviation above the mean. Therefore, the examinee's score exceeded approximately 84% of the scores in the reference group.

When scores are *not* normally distributed (i.e., do not take the form of a normal distribution), test publishers often use "normalized" standard scores. These normalized scores often look just like regular standard scores, but they are computed in a different manner. Nevertheless, they are interpreted in a similar manner. For example, if a test publisher reports normalized T-scores, they will have a mean of 50 and standard deviation of 10 just like regular T-scores. There are some unique normalized standard scores, including:

- Stanine scores: mean of 5 and standard deviation of 2.
- Wechsler Subtest Scaled scores: mean of 10 standard deviation of 3.
- Normal Curve Equivalent (NCE): mean of 50 and standard deviation of 21.06.

Another common type of norm-referenced score is percentile rank. This popular format is one of the most easily understood norm-referenced derived scores. Like all norm-referenced scores, the percentile rank reflects an examinee's performance relative to a specific reference group. However, instead of using a scale with a specific mean and standard deviation, the percentile rank simply specifies the percentage of individuals scoring below a given point in a distribution. For example, a percentile rank of 80 indicates that 80% of the individuals in the reference group scored below this score. Percentile ranks have the advantage of being easily explained to and understood by individuals without formal training in psychometrics.

The final norm-referenced derived scores we discussed were grade and age equivalents. For numerous reasons, we recommend that you avoid using these scores. If you are required to report them, also report standard scores and percentile ranks and emphasize these when interpreting the results.

In contrast to norm-referenced scores, criterion-referenced scores compare an examinee's performance to a specified level of performance referred to as a criterion. Probably the most common criterion-referenced score is the "percent correct" score routinely reported on classroom achievement tests. For example, if you report that a student correctly answered 80% of the items on a spelling test, this is a criterion-referenced interpretation. Another type of criterion-referenced interpretation is mastery testing. On a mastery test, you determine whether examinees have achieved a specified level of mastery on the knowledge or skill domain. Here, performance is typically reported as either "pass" or "fail." If examinees score at or above the cut score they pass; if they score below the cut score they fail. Another criterion-referenced interpretation is referred to as standards-based interpretations. Instead of reporting performance as simply pass/fail, standards-based interpretations typically involve three to five performance categories.

With criterion-referenced interpretations, a prominent consideration is how clearly the knowledge or domain is defined. For useful criterion-referenced interpretations, the knowledge or skill domain being assessed must be clearly defined. To facilitate this, criterion-referenced interpretations are typically applied to tests that measure focused or narrow domains. For example, a math test designed to produce criterion-referenced scores might be limited to the addition of fractions. This way, if a student correctly answers 95% of the fraction problems, you will have useful information regarding the student's proficiency with this specific type of math problems. You are not able to make inferences about a student's proficiency in other areas of math, but you will know this specific type of math problem was mastered. If the math test contained a wide variety of math problems (as is common with norm-referenced tests), it would be more difficult to specify exactly in which areas a student is proficient.

We note that the terms norm-referenced and criterion-referenced refer to the interpretation of test performance, not the test itself. Although it is often optimal to develop a test to produce either norm-referenced or criterion-referenced scores, it is possible and sometimes desirable for a test to produce both norm-referenced and criterion-referenced scores. This may require some compromises when developing the test, but the increased flexibility may justify these compromises. Nevertheless, most tests are designed for either norm-referenced or criterion-referenced interpretations, and most published standardized tests produce norm-referenced interpretations. That being said, tests that produce criterion-referenced interpretations have many important applications, particularly in educational settings.

We next provide a brief description of scores based on *Item Response Theory* (IRT). IRT is a modern test theory that holds that the responses to items on a test are accounted for by latent traits. The scores in this model are similar to traditional raw scores in that they can be transformed into either norm or criterion-referenced scores. However, they have an advantage in that they are interval-level scores and have stable standard deviations across age groups. This makes them particularly useful in measuring changes in cognitive and other abilities. These IRT-based scores are not currently available for many published tests, but they will likely become more widely available in the future.

We provide some guidance on determining which type of score interpretation to use. We noted that different types of test scores provide information that allows us to answer different questions. In summary:

- Raw scores tell us the number of points accumulated by a person on a measure and can tell us their relative rank among test takers (assuming we know everyone's raw score).
- Traditional norm-referenced standard scores address the general question of how does this person's performance compare to the performance of some specified reference group and typically reflect interval scale measurement.
- Criterion-referenced scores tell us whether or not or to what extent a person's performance has approached a desired level of proficiency.
- Rasch or IRT-based scores are on an equal-interval scale that reflects position on some underlying or latent trait. These scores are particularly useful in evaluating the degree of change in scores over time and in comparing scores across tests of a common latent trait.

We close the chapter by illustrating the way test developers report information on normative samples and test scores using examples from the Reynolds Intellectual Assessment Scales (RIAS–2: Reynolds & Kamphaus, 2015b).

Practice Items

1. Transform the following raw scores to the specified standard score formats. The raw score distribution has a mean of 70 and standard deviation of 10.

(a) Raw score = 85	z-score =	T-score =
(b) Raw score = 60	z-score =	T-score =
(c) Raw score = 55	z-score =	T-score =
(d) Raw score = 95	z-score =	T-score =
(e) Raw score = 75	z-score =	T-score =

2. Convert the following z-scores to T-scores.

(a) z-score = 1.5	T-score =
(b) z-score = −1.5	T-score =
(c) z-score = 2.5	T-score =
(d) z-score = −2.0	T-score =
(e) z-score = −1.70	T-score =

References

American Educational Research Association, American Psychological Association, & National Council on Measurement in Education. (2014). *Standards for educational and psychological testing*. Washington, DC: American Educational Research Association.

Anastasi, A., & Urbina, S. (1997). *Psychological testing* (7th ed.). Upper Saddle River, NJ: Prentice Hall.

Crawford, J. R., Garthwaite, P. H., & Slick, D. J. (2009). On percentile norms in neuropsychology: Proposed reporting standards and methods for quantifying the uncertainty over the percentile ranks of test scores. *The Clinical Neuropsychologist, 23*, 1173–1195.

Flynn, J. R. (1998). IQ gains over time: Toward finding the cause. In U. Neisser (Ed.), *The rising curve: Long-term gains in IQ and related measures* (pp. 25–66). Washington, DC: American Psychological Association.

Kamphaus, R. W. (1993). *Clinical assessment of children's intelligence: A handbook for professional practice.* Boston, MA: Allyn & Bacon.

Kamphaus, R. W. (2001). *Clinical assessment of child and adolescent intelligence.* Boston, MA: Allyn & Bacon.

Linn, R. L., & Gronlund, N. E. (2000). *Measurement and assessment in teaching* (8th ed.). Upper Saddle River, NJ: Prentice Hall.

Popham, W. J. (2000). *Modern educational measurement: Practical guidelines for educational leaders.* Boston, MA: Allyn & Bacon.

Psychological Corporation. (2002). *WIAT-II: Examiners manual.* San Antonio, TX: Author.

Reynolds, C. R. (1998). Fundamentals of measurement and assessment in psychology. In A. Bellack & M. Hersen (Eds.), *Comprehensive clinical psychology* (pp. 33–55). New York, NY: Elsevier.

Reynolds, C. R. (2002). *Comprehensive Trail making test: Examiner's manual.* Austin, TX: Pro-Ed.

Reynolds, C. R., & Kamphaus, R. W. (2015a). *Behavior assessment system for children* (3rd ed.). Bloomington, MN: NCS Pearson.

Reynolds, C. R., & Kamphaus, R. W. (2015b). *Reynolds intellectual assessment scales* (2nd ed.). Lutz, FL: Psychological Assessment Resources.

Roid, G. H. (2003). *Stanford-Binet intelligence scale* (5th ed.). Itasca, IL: Riverside.

Schrank, F. A., McGrew, K. S., & Mather, N. (2014). *Woodcock-Johnson IV.* Rolling Meadows, IL: Riverside.

Wechsler, D. (2014). *Wechsler intelligence scale for children* (5th ed.). Bloomington, MN: NCS Pearson.

Woodcock, R. W. (2011). *Woodcock reading mastery tests* (3rd ed.). Bloomington, MN: NCS Pearson.

Recommended Reading

Lyman, H. B. (1998). *Test scores and what they mean.* Boston, MA: Allyn & Bacon. This text provides a comprehensive and very readable discussion of test scores. An excellent resource!

American Educational Research Association, American Psychological Association, & National Council on Measurement in Education. (2014). *Standards for educational and psychological testing.* Washington, DC: AERA. For the technically minded, Chapter 5: Scores, Scales, Norms, Score Linking, and Cut Scores is must reading!

Internet Sites of Interest

Understanding Test Scores: A primer for Parents. This is a user friendly discussion of tests that is accurate and readable. A good resource for parents. http://www.teachersandfamilies.com/open/parent/scores1.cfm.

Reliability

4

> *It is the user who must take responsibility for determining whether scores are sufficiently trustworthy to justify anticipated uses and interpretations for particular uses.*
>
> AERA et al. (2014, p. 41)

Abstract

Reliability refers to the consistency in test scores. In psychological testing, scores must demonstrate acceptable levels of consistency in order for them to be meaningful. This chapter presents a variety of methods used to estimate the reliability of scores, along with an overview of how they are calculated, when they can be used, and how they can be interpreted. These methods include test-retest reliability, alternate-form reliability, inter-rater reliability, reliability of composite scores, and reliability of difference scores. Central to the measurement of reliability is measurement error, and the standard error of measurement is reviewed as one method to assess measurement error. Modern test theories, including generalizability theory and item response theory, are introduced. A practical strategy for educators to estimate reliability of classroom test scores is provided, as well as an example of how a commercially available ability test reports reliability information.

Supplementary Information The online version of this chapter (https://doi.org/10.1007/978-3-030-59455-8_4) contains supplementary material, which is available to authorized users.

Learning Objectives

After reading and studying this chapter, students should be able to:

1. Define and explain the importance of reliability in psychological assessment.
2. Define and explain the concept of measurement error.
3. Explain classical test theory and its importance to psychological assessment.
4. Describe major sources of measurement error and give examples.
5. Identify major methods for estimating reliability and describe how these analyses are performed.
6. Identify sources of measurement error reflected in different reliability estimates.
7. Explain how multiple scores can be combined in a composite to enhance reliability.
8. Describe factors that should be considered when selecting a reliability coefficient for a specific assessment application.
9. Explain factors that should be considered when evaluating the magnitude of reliability coefficients.
10. Describe steps that can be taken to improve reliability.
11. Discuss special issues in estimating reliability like estimating the reliability of speed tests and mastery testing.
12. Define the standard error of measurement (SEM) and explain its importance.
13. Explain how SEM is calculated and describe its relation to reliability.
14. Explain how confidence intervals are calculated and used in educational and psychological assessment.
15. Describe and apply shortcut procedures for estimating reliability of classroom tests.

Most dictionaries define reliability in terms of dependability, trustworthiness, or having a high degree of confidence in something. Reliability in the context of psychological measurement is concerned to some extent with these same factors, but is extended to such concepts as stability and consistency.

> In simplest terms, in the context of measurement, reliability refers to consistency or stability of assessment results.

In simplest terms, in the context of measurement, *reliability* refers to the consistency, accuracy, or stability of assessment results. Although it is common for people to refer to the "reliability of a test," in the *Standards for Educational and Psychological Testing* (AERA et al., 2014) reliability (or reliability/precision, a term introduced in the latest *Standards* revision) is considered to be a characteristic of scores or assessment results, not tests themselves. Consider the following example: A teacher administers a 25-item math test in the morning to assess the students' skill in multiplying two-digit numbers.

- If the test had been administered in the afternoon rather than the morning, would Susie's score on the test have been the same?
- Because there are literally hundreds of two-digit multiplication problems, if the teacher had asked a different group of 25 two-digit multiplication problems, would Susie have received the same score?
- What about the ambulance that went by, its siren wailing loudly, causing Johnny to look up and watch for a few seconds? Did this affect his score, and did it affect Susie's who kept working quietly?
- Joey wasn't feeling well that morning but came to school because he felt the test was so important. Would his score have been better if he had waited to take the test when he was feeling better?
- Would the students have received the same scores if another teacher had graded the test?

All of these questions involve issues of reliability of the scores obtained on the test. They all ask if the test produces stable and consistent scores.

As you can see from these examples, numerous factors can affect reliability. The time the test is administered, the specific set of questions included on the test, distractions due to external (e.g., ambulances) or internal (e.g., illness) events, and the person grading the test are just a few of these factors. In this chapter, you will learn to take many of the sources of unreliability into account when selecting or developing assessments and evaluating scores. You will also learn to estimate the degree of reliability in test scores with a method that best fits your particular situation. First, however, we will introduce the concept of measurement error as it is essential to developing a thorough understanding of reliability.

> Some degree of measurement error is inherent in all measurements.

4.1   Classical Test Theory and Measurement Error

Some degree of error is inherent in all measurements. Although measurement error has been studied largely in the context of psychological and educational tests, measurement error is clearly not unique to psychological and educational tests. In fact, as Nunnally and Bernstein (1994) point out, measurement in other scientific disciplines has as much, if not more, error than that in psychology and education. They give the example of physiological blood pressure measurement, which is considerably less reliable than many educational tests. Even in situations in which we generally believe measurement is exact, some error is present. If we asked a dozen people to time a 400-meter race using the same brand of stopwatch, it is extremely unlikely that they would all report precisely the same time. If we had a dozen people and a measuring tape graduated in millimeters, and required each person to measure independently the length of a 100-ft strip of land, it is unlikely all of them would report the same answer to the nearest millimeter. In the physical sciences, the introduction of more technologically sophisticated measurement devices has reduced, but not eliminated, measurement error.

Over the last 100 years, several theories or models have been developed to help us understand measurement issues, and the most influential is **Classical Test Theory** (CTT), which is also referred to as **True Score Theory**. Charles Spearman (1907, 1913) laid the groundwork for Classical Test Theory in the early 1900s. Other individuals such as Thurstone (1931), Guilford (1936), Thorndike (1949), Gulliksen (1950), Magnusson (1967), and Lord and Novick (1968) also made significant contributions to the development and statement of CTT. According to this theory, every score on a mental test is composed of two components: the **true score** (i.e., the score that would be obtained if there were no errors) and the **error component**. This can be represented in a very simple equation:

$$X_i = T + E$$

Here we use X_i to represent the obtained or observed score (X) of an individual (i). X_i is the score the examinee received on the test. The symbol T is used to represent an individual's true score and reflects the test taker's true skills, abilities, knowledge, attitudes, or whatever the test measures if it could be measured perfectly, with no error. Finally, E represents measurement error.

An individual only has one true score. However, they may receive different observed scores on different administrations of a test due to different amounts of measurement error. Consider these examples. On a 100-item multiple-choice test Tim actually knows the answer to 80 items (i.e., his true score) and makes lucky guesses on 5 and gets them correct (i.e., errors of measurement). His observed score is 85. Here $X_i = 85$, $T = 80$, and $E = 5$ ($85 = 80 + 5$). In this situation, measurement error resulted in an increase in his observed score. This is not always the case and measurement errors can also reduce an individual's observed score. For example, if Tim knew the answer to 80 items (i.e., true score) but incorrectly marked the answer sheet on five items, his observed scores would now be 75. Here $X_i = 75$, $T = 80$, and $E = -5$ ($75 = 80–5$). In actual practice there are a multitude of factors that can introduce error into a test score, some raising the score and some lowering the score. These errors of measurement have a cumulative or additive effect. For example, if Tim knew the answer to 80 items, correctly guessed the answer on 3, and incorrectly marked the answer sheet on two items, his observed scores would be 81. The error score component is now 1 (i.e., $3 - 2$). Here $X_i = 81$, $T = 80$, and $E = 1$ ($81 = 80 + 1$).

As noted, CTT is concerned with **measurement error** that is defined as the difference between an individual's obtained and true score. CTT focuses our attention on **random measurement error**. Random measurement error is the result of chance factors that can either increase or decrease an individual's observed score; the more random error present in the measurement of performance, the lower the reliability or precision of the resulting score. These random events vary from person to person, from test to test, and from administration to administration. There are also systematic sources of measurement error. *Systematic measurement error* involves systematic or consistent differences in test performance between groups of individuals that are the result of factors unrelated to the construct being measured. Systematic measurement error results in stable or consistent errors of measurement (i.e., the same amount of error every time); therefore, it does not impact the reliability/precision of a score. Since there is no impact on scores, CTT is concerned only with random measurement error and does not consider systematic measurement error. However, we will touch on systematic measurement error in later sections of the text, particularly when addressing test bias, since systematic error is usually associated with a detectable source and biases scores in a consistent direction.

Now that you have a grasp on the basics of CTT, we will delve a little deeper and consider some general principles or assumptions of the theory. These include:

- The mean of error scores in a population is zero. Since random measurement error is random (e.g., sometimes increasing obtained scores, sometimes decreasing the obtained scores), it balances out over a large number of test administrations. Therefore, over a very large number of test administrations random measurement error will balance out and the mean will equal zero.
- The correlation between true score and error score is zero. Since true score is without error, it does not have any systematic relationship with error. In other words, there is no relationship between an individual's level on a construct and the amount of measurement error impacting their observed score on any given administration of a test.
- The expected correlation between error scores on different measurements is zero. In other words, the amount of error in an individual's obtained score from one administration of a test is not related to the amount of error on any subsequent independent administrations of the test (or another test).

Comprehension of the basic principles of CTT is essential for understanding reliability. CTT highlights the prevalence and characteristics of random measurement error. Measurement error reduces the usefulness of measurement, our ability to generalize test results, and the confidence we have in these results (AERA et al., 2014). Practically speaking, when we administer a test we are interested in knowing the test taker's true score. However, due to the presence of measurement error, we can never know with absolute confidence the true score, so we usually refer to obtained scores or estimated true scores. CTT is also important because it presents a mathematical model that allows us to estimate the reliability of test scores. These estimates of reliability inform us about the amount of measurement error associated with test scores and how much confidence we should have in them. With information about the reliability of measurement, we can also establish intervals around an obtained

> Measurement error limits the extent to which test results can be generalized and reduces the confidence we have in test results (AERA et al., 2014).

score and calculate the probability that the true score will fall within the specified interval.

Before we proceed, we want to emphasize that our brief introduction to CTT is just that: Brief and only an introduction. A thorough discussion of CTT requires presentation of the formal mathematical proofs that underlie the model. While we will elaborate more on CTT in this chapter, we will not delve into these formal proofs. For the interested reader, more detailed descriptions are provided by Crocker and Algina (1986) and Osterlind (2006). Lord and Novick (1968) provide a detailed discussion of CTT that remains current and is well suited for readers with a more advanced background in mathematics.

4.2   Sources of Measurement Error

Because measurement error is so pervasive and significantly affects our ability to be confident that a test score is accurate, it is beneficial to be knowledgeable both about its characteristics and the methods that are available for estimating its magnitude. Generally, whenever you hear a discussion of reliability or read about the reliability of test scores, it is the score's relative freedom from measurement errors that are being discussed. Reliable assessment results are relatively free from measurement error whereas less reliable results are influenced to a larger degree by measurement error. A number of factors may introduce error into test scores and even though all cannot be assigned to distinct categories, it may be helpful to group these sources in some manner and to discuss their relative contributions. The types of errors that are our greatest concern are errors due to content sampling and time sampling.

4.2.1   Content Sampling Error

Tests rarely, if ever, include every possible question or evaluate every possible relevant behavior. Let's revisit the example we introduced at the beginning of this chapter. A teacher administers a math test designed to assess students' skill in multiplying two-digit numbers. We noted that there are literally hundreds of two-digit multiplication problems. Obviously, it would be impractical (and unnecessary) for the teacher to develop and administer a test that includes all possible items. Instead, a universe or domain of test items is defined based on the content of the material to be covered. From this domain, a sample of test questions is taken. In this example, the teacher decided to select 25 items to measure students' abilities. These 25 items are simply a sample of the item domain and, as with any sampling procedure, may or may not be representative of the domain from which they are drawn. The error that results from differences between the sample of items (i.e., the test) and the domain of items (i.e., all the possible items) is referred to as **content sampling error**. Content sampling error is typically considered the largest source of error in test scores and therefore is the source that concerns us most. Fortunately, content sampling error is also the easiest and most accurately estimated source of measurement error.

> Content sampling is typically considered the largest source of error in test scores.

The amount of measurement error due to content sampling is determined by how well we sample the total domain of items. If the items on a test are a good sample of the domain, the amount of measurement error due to content sampling will be relatively small. Using our math test example, a sampling that is considered "good" is one that would have items with a variety of difficulty levels, in proportion to the difficulty levels of items in total population (e.g., consider the item 20×10 is likely easier for most persons to solve than the item 68×74). If the items on a test are a poor sample of the domain because they are all of similar difficulty level, the amount of measurement error due to content sampling will be relatively large. The difficulty level itself is not the main concern here; tests with all easy items, all moderate items, or all difficult items will have large measurement errors due to poor content sampling. Measurement error resulting from content sampling is estimated by analyzing the degree of similarity among the items making up the test. In other words, we analyze the test items to determine how well they correlate with one another and with the examinee's standing on the construct being measured. Other considerations of similarity can also be made. How hard is it to correctly answer an item? Does the item represent a known aspect of the construct being measured, such as "being impulsive" which is often considered a core behavior of Hyperactivity? How representative are items of typical scenarios of the construct being measured, such as on a driver's test where items are included that are examples or scenarios of typical encounters (e.g., viewing stop signs, obeying speed limits) as well as infrequent encounters (e.g., engaging a parking brake if the main brakes fail)? We will explore a variety of methods for estimating measurement errors due to content sampling later in this chapter.

4.2.2 Time Sampling Error

Measurement error can also be introduced by one's choice of a particular time to administer the test. If Eddie did not have breakfast and the math test was just before lunch, he might be distracted or hurried by hunger and not perform as well as if he took the test after lunch. But Michael, who ate too much at lunch and was up late last night, was sleepy in the afternoon and might not perform as well on an afternoon test as he would have on the morning test. If during the morning testing session a neighboring class was making enough noise to be disruptive, the class might have performed better in the afternoon when the neighboring class was relatively quiet. These are all examples of situations in which random changes in the test taker (e.g., fatigue, illness, anxiety) or the testing environment (e.g., distractions, temperature) impact performance on the test. This type of measurement error is referred to as *time sampling error* and reflects random fluctuations in performance from one situation or time to another. Time sampling error limits our ability to generalize test results across different situations. As you might expect, this is a major concern for psychological testing since tests are rarely given in exactly the same environment. As you might also expect, testing experts have developed methods of estimating error due to time sampling.

Measurement error due to time sampling reflects random fluctuations in performance from one situation to another and limits our ability to generalize test scores across different situations.

4.2.3   Other Sources of Error

Although errors due to content sampling and time sampling typically account for the major proportion of random error in testing, administrative and scoring errors that do not affect all test takers equally will also contribute to the random error observed in scores. Clerical errors committed while adding up a student's score or an administrative error on an individually administered test are common examples. When the scoring of a test relies heavily on the subjective judgment of the person grading the test or involves subtle discriminations, it is important to consider differences in graders, usually referred to as *inter-rater or inter-scorer differences*. That is, would the test taker receive the same score if different individuals graded the test? For example, on an essay test would two different graders assign the same scores? These are just a few examples of sources of error that do not fit neatly into the broad categories of content or time sampling errors.

4.3   Reliability Coefficients

You will note that we refer to reliability as being *estimated*. This is because the absolute or precise reliability of assessment results cannot be known. Just as we always have some error in test scores, we also have some error in our attempts to measure reliability. However, the methods of estimating reliability we will discuss are conservative and considered to be lower bound estimates of the true reliability of test scores. In other words, the actual reliability of test scores is at least as high, and possibly higher, than the estimated reliability (Reynolds, 1999).

Earlier in this chapter, we introduced CTT which holds that test scores are composed of two components, the true score and the error score. We represented this with the equation:

$$X_i = T + E$$

As you remember, X_i represents an individual's obtained score, T represents the true score, and E represents random measurement error. This equation can be applied to the concept of variance. This application indicates that the variance of test scores is the sum of the *true score variance* plus the *error variance*, and is represented in the following equation:

$$\sigma_x^2 = \sigma_T^2 + \sigma_E^2$$

Here, σ_x^2 represents the variance of the total test, σ_T^2 represents true score variance, and σ_E^2 represents the variance due to measurement error. True score variance reflects differences in test takers due to real differences in skills, abilities, knowledge, attitudes, and so on, whereas the total score variance is made up of true score variance plus variance due to all the sources of random error we have previously described.

> Reliability can be defined as the proportion of test score variance due to true score differences.

The general symbol for the reliability of assessment results is r_{xx} and is referred to as the **reliability coefficient**. We estimate the reliability of a test score as the ratio of true score variance to total score variance. Mathematically, reliability is written:

$$r_{xx} = \frac{\sigma_T^2}{\sigma_X^2}$$

This equation defines the reliability of test scores as the proportion of test score variance due to true score differences. The reliability coefficient is considered to be the summary mathematical representation of this ratio or proportion. There is another index of reliability that is useful in the context of measurement theory. Special Interest Topic 4.1 briefly discusses this index, the Reliability Index.

Reliability coefficients can be classified into three broad categories (AERA et al., 2014). These include (1) coefficients derived from the administration of the same test on different occasions (i.e., test-retest reliability), (2) coefficients

Special Interest Topic 4.1: The Reliability Index

As noted in this chapter, reliability coefficients are designated with the symbol r_{xx} and are mathematically defined as the ratio of true score variance to observed score variance. Stated another way, reliability coefficients are interpreted as the proportion of observed score variance that is the result of variance in true scores. While we primarily focus our attention in this chapter on the interpretation of correlation coefficients, there is an equally important correlation that is integral to CTT, the *reliability index*. The reliability index is an index that reflects the correlation between true and observed scores. For example, if the reliability index is equal to 1.0, then all true scores (T) and observed scores (X) are equal and there is no measurement error.

Since true scores are not directly observable, the reliability index is a theoretical concept and cannot be calculated directly. However, we do know the mathematical relationship between the reliability coefficient and the reliability index. That is, the reliability index is the square root of the reliability coefficient. For example, if the reliability coefficient is 0.81, the reliability index is 0.90. In this example, the reliability coefficient of 0.81 indicates that 81% of the observed score variance is due to true score variance. The reliability index of 0.90 reflects the correlation between observed and true scores.

Table 4.1 Major types of reliability

Type of reliability estimate	Common symbol	Number of test forms	Number of Testing Sessions	Summary
Test-retest	r_{12}	One form	Two sessions	Administer the same test to the same group at two different sessions
Alternate forms: Simultaneous Administration	r_{ab}	Two forms	One session	Administer two forms of the test to the same group in the same session
Alternate forms: Delayed administration	r_{ab}	Two forms	Two sessions	Administer two forms of the test to the same group at two different sessions
Split-half	r_{oe}	One form	One session	Administer the test to a group one time. Split the test into two equivalent halves
Coefficient alpha or KR-20	r_{xx}	One form	One session	Administer the test to a group one time. Apply appropriate procedures
Inter-rater	r	One form	One session	Administer the test to a group one time. Two or more raters score the test independently

based on the administration of parallel forms of a test (i.e., alternate-form reliability), and (3) coefficients derived from a single administration of a test (internal-consistency coefficients). A fourth type, inter-rater reliability, is indicated when scoring involves a significant degree of subjective judgment. The major methods of estimating reliability are summarized in Table 4.1. Each of these approaches produces a reliability coefficient (r_{xx}) that can be interpreted in terms of the proportion or percentage of test score variance attributable to true variance. For example, a reliability coefficient of 0.90 indicates that 90% of the variance in test scores is attributable to true variance. The remaining 10% reflects error variance. We will now consider each of these methods of estimating reliability.

4.3.1 Test-Retest Reliability

Probably the most obvious way to estimate the reliability of a test score is to administer the same test to the same group of individuals on two different occasions. With this approach, the reliability coefficient is obtained by simply calculating the correlation between the scores on the first and second administrations. In this scenario, we could administer our 25-item math test 1 week after we initially administered it and then correlate the scores obtained on the two administrations. This estimate of reliability is referred to as *test-retest reliability*. Test-retest reliability is primarily sensitive to measurement error due to time sampling. It is an index of the stability of test scores over time, and some authors refer to coefficients obtained with this approach as stability coefficients. Because many tests are intended to measure fairly stable characteristics such as IQ, we expect tests of these constructs to produce stable scores. Test-retest reliability reflects the degree to which test scores can be generalized across different situations or over time.

> Test-retest reliability is primarily sensitive to measurement error due to time sampling and is an index of the stability of scores over time.

One important consideration when calculating and evaluating test-retest reliability is the length of the interval between the two test administrations. If the test-retest interval is very short (e.g., hours or days), the reliability estimate may be artificially inflated by memory and *practice effects* from the first administration. Practice effects refer to an improvement in test scores due to learning that results from prior exposure to the test items. If the test interval is longer, the estimate of reliability may be lowered not only by the instability of the scores but also by actual changes in the test takers during the extended period. One would expect that over the course of a year, a 5-year old's reading ability would substantially improve so it would not be surprising that her score on a reading test would also improve over the time period. In practice, there is no single "best" time interval, but the optimal interval is determined by the way the test results are to be used. For example, intelligence is a construct or characteristic that is thought to be fairly stable, so it would be reasonable to expect stability in intelligence scores over weeks or months. In contrast, an individual's mood (e.g., depressed, elated, nervous) is more subject to transient fluctuations and stability across weeks or months would not be expected. In the latter case, a test-retest study may be telling you more about the stability of the trait, state, or construct being assessed than about the stability of test scores per se. This distinction too often is overlooked in discussions of test score reliability. It is not appropriate to examine test-retest reliability over a long interval when the construct measured by the test is known to be unstable, whether due to developmental influences as is the case with reading comprehension in children, or environmental influences that contribute to changes in mood from one day to the next.

In addition to the construct being measured, the way the test is to be used is an important consideration in determining what is an appropriate test-retest interval. Because the SAT is used to predict performance in college, it is sensible to expect stability over relatively long periods of time. In other situations, long-term stability is much less of an issue. For example, the long-term stability of a classroom achievement test (such as our math test) is not a major concern because it is expected that the students will be enhancing existing skills and acquiring new ones due to class instruction and studying. In summary, when evaluating the stability of test scores, one should consider the length of the test-retest interval in the context of the characteristics being measured and how the scores are to be used.

The test-retest approach does have significant limitations, the most prominent being carryover or practice effects from the first to second testing. These practice effects result in different amounts of improvement in retest scores for different test takers. They prevent the two administrations from being independent, and as a result, the reliability coefficients may be artificially inflated. In other instances, repetition of the test may change either the nature of the test or the test taker in some subtle way

(Ghiselli, Campbell, & Zedeck, 1981). For example, a test that requires problem-solving no longer assesses problem-solving once the examinee learns how to solve the problem. Any subsequent administration of the test is more likely a test of memory (i.e.,

> The test-retest approach does have significant limitations, the most prominent being carryover effects from the first to second testing.

can the examinee remember the solution to the problem) rather than a test or problem-solving. As a result, only tests that are not appreciably influenced by these carryover effects are suitable for this method of estimating reliability.

4.3.2   Alternate-Form Reliability

Another approach to estimating reliability involves the development of two equivalent or parallel forms of the test. The development of these alternate forms requires a detailed test plan and considerable effort since the tests must be truly parallel in terms of content, difficulty, and other relevant characteristics. The two forms of the test are then administered to the same group of individuals and the correlation is calculated between the scores on the two assessments. In our example of the 25-item math test, the

> Alternate-form reliability based on simultaneous administration is primarily sensitive to measurement error due to content sampling.

teacher could develop a parallel test containing 25 different problems involving the multiplication of double digits (i.e., from the same item domain). To be parallel the items would need to be presented in the same format and be of the same level of difficulty. Two fairly common procedures are used to establish **alternate-form reliability**. One is alternate-form reliability based on simultaneous administrations and is obtained when the two forms of the test are administered on the same occasion (i.e., back-to-back). The other, alternate form with delayed administration, is obtained when the two forms of the test are administered on two different occasions. Alternate-form reliability based on simultaneous administration is primarily sensitive to measurement error related to content sampling. Alternate-form reliability with delayed administration is sensitive to measurement error due to both content sampling and time sampling.

Alternate-form reliability has the advantage of reducing the carryover effects that are a prominent concern with test-retest reliability. However, although practice and memory effects may be reduced using the

> Alternate-form reliability based on delayed administration is sensitive to measurement error due to content sampling and time sampling.

alternate-form approach, typically they are often not fully eliminated. Simply exposing examinees to the common format required for parallel tests often results in some carryover effects even if the content of the two tests is different. For example, an examinee given a test measuring nonverbal reasoning abilities may develop strategies during the administration of the first form that alters her approach to the second form, even if the specific content of the items is different. Another limitation of the alternate-form approach to estimating reliability is that relatively few tests, standardized or teacher-made, have alternate forms. As we suggested, the development of alternate forms that are actually equivalent is a time-consuming process, and many test developers do not pursue this option. Nevertheless, at times it is desirable to have more than one form of a test, as would be the case for a test designed to track memory improvement or decline in dementia, or changes in attention that result from a computerized cognitive retraining program for children with ADHD. When multiple forms exist, alternate-form reliability is an important consideration.

4.3.3   Internal-Consistency Reliability

Internal-consistency reliability estimates primarily reflect errors related to content sampling. These estimates are based on the relationship between items within a test and are derived from a single administration of the test. There are several methods for estimating internal consistency.

4.3.3.1 Split-Half Reliability

Estimating *split-half reliability* involves administering a test and then dividing the test into two equivalent halves that are scored independently. The results on one-half of the test are then correlated with results on the other half-test by calculating the Pearson product-moment correlation. Obviously, there are many ways a test can be divided in half. For example, one might correlate scores on the first half of the test with scores on the second half. This is usually not a good idea because the items on some tests get more difficult as the test progresses, resulting in halves that are not actually equivalent. Other factors, such as practice effects, fatigue, or declining attention that increases as the test progresses can also make the first and second half of the test not equivalent. A more acceptable approach would be to assign test items randomly to one half or the other. However, the most common approach is to use an odd-even split. Here all "odd" numbered items go into one half and all "even" numbered items go into the other half. A correlation is then calculated between scores on the odd-numbered and even-numbered items.

> Split-half reliability can be calculated from one administration of a test and primarily reflects error due to content sampling.

Before we can use this correlation coefficient as an estimate of reliability, there is one more task to perform. Because we are actually correlating two halves of the test, the reliability coefficient does not take into account the reliability of the test scores for the whole test but rather for only half the total number of items. In essence, this initial coefficient reflects the reliability of a shortened, half-test. As a general rule, longer tests produce scores that are more reliable than shorter tests. If we have twice as many test items, then we are able to sample the domain of test questions more accurately. The better we sample the domain the lower the error due to content sampling and the higher the reliability of our test scores. To "put the two halves of the test back together" with regard to a reliability estimate, we use a correction formula commonly referred to as the ***Spearman-Brown formula***. To estimate the reliability of scores on the full test, the Spearman-Brown formula is generally applied as:

$$\text{Reliability of scores of full test} = \frac{2*\text{Reliability of half test scores}}{1+\text{Reliability of half test scores}}$$

Here is an example. Suppose the correlation between odd and even halves of your mid-term in this course was 0.74. The calculation using the Spearman-Brown formula would go as follows:

$$\text{Reliability of scores of full test} = \frac{2*0.74}{1+0.74}$$

$$\text{Reliability of scores of full test} = \frac{1.48}{1.74} = 0.85$$

The reliability coefficient of 0.85 estimates the reliability of the full-test score when the odd-even halves correlated at 0.74. This demonstrates that the uncorrected split-half reliability coefficient presents an underestimate of the reliability of the full-test score. Table 4.2 provides examples of half-test coefficients and the corresponding full-test coefficients that were corrected with the Spearman-Brown formula. By looking at the first row in this table you will see that a half-test correlation of 0.50 corresponds to a corrected full-test coefficient of 0.67, half-test correlation of 0.70 corresponds to a corrected full-test coefficient of 0.82, and so on.

Although the odd-even approach is the most common way to divide a test and will generally produce equivalent halves, certain situations deserve special attention. For example, if you have a test with a relatively small number of items (e.g.,

Table 4.2 Half-test coefficients and corresponding full-test coefficients corrected with the Spearman-Brown formula

Half-test correlation	Spearman-Brown reliability
0.50	0.67
0.55	0.71
0.60	0.75
0.65	0.79
0.70	0.82
0.75	0.86
0.80	0.89
0.85	0.92
0.90	0.95
0.95	0.97

<8), it may be desirable to divide the test into equivalent halves based on a careful review of item characteristics such as content, format, and difficulty. Another situation that deserves special attention involves groups of items that deal with an integrated problem (this is referred to as a *testlet*). For example, if multiple questions refer to a specific diagram or reading passage that whole set of questions should be included in the same half of the test. Splitting integrated problems can artificially inflate the reliability estimate (e.g., Sireci, Thissen, & Wainer, 1991).

An advantage of the split-half approach to reliability is that it can be calculated from a single administration of a test. However, because only one testing session is involved, this approach primarily reflects only errors due to content sampling.

4.3.3.2 Coefficient Alpha and Kuder-Richardson Reliability

Other approaches to estimating reliability from a single administration of a test are based on formulas developed by Kuder and Richardson (1937) and Cronbach (1951). Instead of comparing responses on two halves of the test as in split-half reliability, this approach examines the consistency of responding to all the individual items on the test. Reliability estimates produced with these formulas can be thought of as the average of all possible split-half coefficients and are properly corrected for the length of the whole test. Like split-half reliability, these estimates are sensitive to measurement error introduced by content sampling. Additionally, they are also sensitive to the heterogeneity of the test content. When we refer to *content heterogeneity*, we are concerned with the degree to which the test items measure unrelated characteristics. For example, our 25-item math test involving multiplying two-digit numbers would probably be more homogeneous than a test designed to measure both multiplication and division. An even more heterogeneous test would be one that involves multiplication and reading comprehension, two fairly dissimilar content domains. As heterogeneity of test content increases, Coefficient Alpha and Kuder-Richardson reliabilities will generally decrease.

While Kuder and Richardson's formulas and Coefficient alpha both reflect item heterogeneity and errors due to content sampling, there is an important difference in terms of their application. In their original article, Kuder and Richardson (1937) presented numerous formulas for estimating reliability. The most commonly used formula is known as the *Kuder-Richardson Formula 20* (KR-20). KR-20 is applicable when test items are scored dichotomously, that is, simply right or wrong, scored 0 or 1. *Coefficient alpha* (Cronbach, 1951) is a more general form of KR-20 that deals with test items that produce scores with multiple values (e.g., 0, 1, or 2). Because Coefficient alpha is more broadly applicable, it has become the preferred statistic for estimating internal consistency (Keith & Reynolds, 1990). Tables 4.3 and 4.4 illustrate the calculation of KR-20 and coefficient alpha respectively.

> Coefficient alpha and Kuder-Richardson reliability are sensitive to error introduced by content sampling, but also reflect the heterogeneity of test content.

Table 4.3   Calculating KR-20

KR-20 is sensitive to measurement error due to content sampling and is also a measure of item heterogeneity. KR-20 is applicable when test items are scored dichotomously, that is, simply right or wrong, scored 0 or 1. The formula for calculating KR-20 is:

$$KR\text{--}20 = \frac{k}{k-1}\left(\frac{SD^2 - \sum p_i * q_i}{SD^2} \right)$$

where:

k = number of items

SD^2 = variance of total test scores

p_i = proportion of correct responses on item

q_i = proportion of incorrect responses on item

Consider these data for a 5-item test that was administered to 6 students. Each item could receive a score ranging from 1 or 0.

	Item #1	Item #2	Item #3	Item #4	Item #5	Total score
Student 1	1	0	1	1	1	4
Student 2	1	1	1	1	1	5
Student 3	1	0	1	0	0	2
Student 4	0	0	0	1	0	1
Student 5	1	1	1	1	1	5
Student 6	1	1	0	1	1	4
p_i	0.8333	0.5	0.6667	0.8333	0.6667	$SD^2 = 2.25$
q_i	0.1667	0.5	0.3333	0.1667	0.3333	
$p_i * q_i$	0.1389	0.25	0.2222	0.1389	0.2222	

Note: When calculating SD^2, n was used in the denominator

$\sum p_i * q_i = 0.1389 + 0.25 + 0.2222 + 0.1389 + 0.2222$

$\sum p_i * q_i = 0.972$

$$KR\text{--}20 = \frac{5}{4}\left(\frac{2.25 - 0.972}{2.25} \right)$$

$$= 1.25\left(\frac{1.278}{2.25} \right)$$

$$= 1.25(0.568)$$

$$= 0.71$$

4.3.4   Inter-Rater Reliability

If the scoring of a test relies on subjective judgment, it is important to evaluate the degree of agreement when different individuals score the test. This is referred to as inter-scorer or ***inter-rater reliability***. Estimating inter-rater reliability is a fairly straightforward process. The test is administered one time and two individuals

> If the scoring of an assessment relies on subjective judgment, it is important to evaluate the degree of agreement when different individuals score the test. This is referred to as inter-rater reliability.

Table 4.4   Calculating coefficient alpha

Coefficient alpha is sensitive to measurement error due to content sampling and is also a measure of item heterogeneity. It can be applied to tests with items that are scored dichotomously or that have multiple values. The formula for calculating coefficient alpha is:

$$\text{Coefficient alpha} = \left(\frac{k}{k-1}\right)\left(1 - \frac{\sum SD_i^2}{SD^2}\right)$$

where:

k = number of items

SD_i^2 = variance of individual items

SD^2 = variance of total test scores

Consider these data for a 5-item test that was administered to 6 students. Each item could receive a score ranging from 1 to 5

	Item #1	Item #2	Item #3	Item #4	Item #5	Total score
Student 1	4	3	4	5	5	21
Student 2	3	3	2	3	3	14
Student 3	2	3	2	2	1	10
Student 4	4	4	5	3	4	20
Student 5	2	3	4	2	3	14
Student 6	2	2	2	1	3	10
SD_i^2	0.8056	0.3333	1.4722	1.5556	1.4722	$SD^2 = 18.81$

Note: When calculating SD_i^2 and SD^2, n was used in the denominator

$$\text{Coefficient alpha} = \left(\frac{5}{4}\right)\left(1 - \frac{0.8056 + 0.3333 + 1.4722 + 1.5556 + 1.4722}{18.81}\right)$$

$$= 1.25\left(1 - \frac{5.63889}{18.81}\right)$$

$$= 1.25\left(1 - 0.29978\right)$$

$$= 1.25\left(0.70\right)$$

$$= 0.875$$

independently score each test. A correlation is then calculated between the scores obtained by the two scorers. This estimate of reliability primarily reflects differences due to the individuals scoring the test and largely ignores error due to content or time sampling. In addition to the correlational approach, inter-rater agreement can also be evaluated by calculating the percentage of times that two individuals assign the same scores to the performances of students. This approach is typically referred to as *inter-rater agreement* or percent agreement and its calculation is illustrated in Table 4.5. Many authors prefer **Cohen's kappa** over the standard percent of agreement when analyzing categorical data. Kappa is a more robust measure of agreement as it takes into consideration the degree of agreement expected by chance (Hays, 1994). A weighted kappa coefficient is also available that is appropriate for ordinal level data and takes into consideration how disparate the ratings are. For comparative purposes, kappa and weighted kappa are also reported in Table 4.5. Kappa is also used in any

Table 4.5 Calculating inter-rater agreement

The scoring of many psychological and educational assessments requires subjective judgment. For example, in academic settings students might engage in debates, compose poems, or perform pieces of music as part of their course requirements. The evaluation of these types of tasks is typically based on scoring rubrics that specify what aspects of the student's performance should be considered when providing a score or grade. Subjective scoring is not limited to educational assessments but is also common on psychological tests. For example, many intelligence and achievement tests include subtests that require subjective scoring. The Comprehension, Vocabulary, and Similarities subtests on the Wechsler Intelligence Scale for Children, Fifth Edition all involve some degree of subjective scoring. When scoring involves the subjective judgment, inter-rater reliability is an important concern. As noted in the text, one approach to estimating inter-rater reliability is to calculate the correlation between the scores that are assigned by two judges. Another approach is to calculate the percentage of agreement between the judges' scores

Consider an example where two judges rated poems composed by 25 students. The poems were scored from 1 to 5 based on criteria specified in a rubric, with 1 being the lowest performance and 5 being the highest. The results are illustrated in the following table:

Ratings of Rater #1	Ratings of Rater #2				
	1	2	3	4	5
5	0	0	*1*	*2*	4
4	0	0	*2*	3	*2*
3	0	*2*	3	*1*	0
2	*1*	1	*1*	0	0
1	1	*1*	0	0	0

You can see that there is a rating for each student in the Table. Agreements between raters are on the diagonal and are underlined, while disagreements are off the diagonal and italicized. For example, Rater 1 and 2 both gave 4 students a rating of 5, 3 students a rating of 4, *3* students a rating of 3, and so on. For examples of rater disagreements, in the third row of ratings, you'll see that *2* students were assigned a rating of 3 by Rater 1 and 2 by Rater 2, and *1* student was assigned a rating of 3 by Rater 1 and 4 by Rater 2, and so on

Once the data are recorded you can calculate Inter-Rater Agreement with the following formula:

$$\text{Inter-rater agreement} = \frac{\text{Number of cases assigned the same scores}}{\text{Total number of cases}} * 100$$

In our example the calculation would be:

$$\text{Inter-rater agreement} = \frac{12}{25} * 100$$

Inter-rater agreement = 48%

This degree of inter-rater agreement might appear low to you, but this would actually be respectable for a classroom test. In fact, the Pearson correlation between these judges' ratings is 0.80 (better than many, if not most constructed-response assessments)

Instead of requiring the judges to assign the exact same score for agreement, some authors suggest the less rigorous criterion of scores being within one point of each other (e.g., Linn & Gronlund, 2000). If this was criterion were applied to these data, the modified agreement percent would be 96% since there was only one score where the judges were not within one point of each other (Rater #1 assigned a "5" and Rater #2 a "3")

As we noted some authors prefer Cohen's kappa when calculating inter-rater reliability because it takes into consideration chance agreement and is therefore a more robust measure of inter-rater agreement. Using the data listed above, Cohen's kappa is 0.327 (interpreted as reflecting fair agreement) and the weighted kappa is 0.594. If one compares kappa to simple inter-rater agreement (i.e., 0.327 versus 0.48), it is apparent that kappa is a more rigorous approach when exact agreement is required. Similarly, if one compares the weighted kappa to the modified percent agreement (i.e., 0.594 versus 0.96), the same pattern appears instance where the agreement in classification is of interest. One such instance is when a test is administered at two different points in time to classify people into diagnostic groups (or other groups, such as those to hire and those to reject). In this case, each person would be classified or assigned to a group using the obtained test scores from each occasion and the degree of agreement across times is then compared via kappa. One could also use two different tests on the same group of people at the same point in time, and classify them separately using each set of test scores, and then compute the cross-test agreement in classification with kappa.

On some tests, inter-rater reliability is of little concern. For example, on a test with multiple-choice or true–false items, grading is fairly straightforward and any conscientious grader should produce reliable and accurate scores. In the case of our 25-item math test, a careful grader should be able to determine whether the students' answers are accurate and assign a score consistent with that of another careful grader. However, for some tests, inter-rater reliability is a major concern. Classroom essay tests are a classic example. It is common for students to feel that a different teacher might have assigned a different score to their essay. It can be argued that the teacher's personal biases, preferences, or mood influenced the score, not only the content and quality of the student's essay. Even on our 25-item math test, if the teacher required that the students "show their work" and this influenced the students' grades, subjective judgment might be involved and inter-rater reliability could be a concern.

4.3.5 Reliability Estimates Are Not Independent

We noted earlier that Coefficient Alpha is the average of all split-half-test score correlations corrected for test length. This means that it is also the average of the correlations of every test item with every other item on the test. We point this out because as a corollary, it is true that anything that reduces the average inter-item correlation also reduces the value of alpha. Thus, while we think of alpha and related reliability coefficients as estimates of the internal-consistency reliability (i.e., homogeneity of item domain sampling) of a test score, they are in reality much broader values, making alpha (as the best of its breed) the preferred reliability estimate.

In an attempt to determine the total amount of error in a test score, some researchers will sum the error due to domain sampling as estimated by alpha and the inter-rater error for example. These estimates are not independent however as inter-rater error lowers the average-inter-item correlation and is thus accounted for in Alpha due to its method of calculation. Alpha also sets limits on test-retest correlations. The theoretical maximum test-retest coefficient is the square root of alpha. While in practice it is possible to obtain a higher value due to

> Any source of error that would reduce the average inter-item correlation is reflected by coefficient alpha.

chance factors (i.e., the chance occurrence of a correlation between error terms which are actually not correlated!), the true value of a test-retest correlation cannot exceed the square root of alpha.

Not only is it unnecessary to add the estimates of error in a test across different types of error to determine the total amount of error in a test score, but it is also incorrect simply to sum them. Any potential source of error that would reduce the average inter-item correlation (e.g., administration errors, scoring errors, differing levels of effort by some examinees on hard items) is already accounted for by alpha.

4.3.6   Reliability of Composite Scores

Psychological and educational measurement often yields multiple scores that can be combined to form a composite. For example, the assignment of grades in educational settings is often based on a composite of several tests and other assessments administered over a grading period or semester. Many standardized psychological instruments contain several measures that are combined to form an overall composite score. For example, the Reynolds Intellectual Assessment Scales, Second Edition (Reynolds & Kamphaus, 2015) is composed of four subtests that are used in the calculation of the Composite Intelligence Index.

> Reliability of composite scores is generally greater than the measures that contribute to the composite.

Both of these situations involve composite scores that are obtained by combining the scores on several different tests or subtests. The advantage of composite scores is that the reliability of composite scores is generally greater than that of the individual scores that contribute to the composite. More precisely, the reliability of a composite is the result of the number of scores in the composite, the reliability of the individual scores, and the correlation between those scores. The more scores in the composite, the higher the correlation between those scores, and the higher the individual reliabilities, the higher the composite reliability. As we noted, tests are simply samples of the test domain, and combining multiple measures is analogous to increasing the number of observations or the sample size. Table 4.6 illustrates the computation of the reliability of a linear combination.

4.3.7   Reliability of Difference Scores

There are a number of situations where researchers and clinicians want to consider the difference between two scores. Here the variable of interest is a difference score that is calculated as:

$$D = X - Y$$

where X is the score on one test and Y is the score on the other test. For example, one approach to diagnosing learning disabilities involves calculating difference scores by subtracting an examinee's score on an achievement test (e.g., reading comprehension) from the IQ. The assumption is that if the discrepancy is negative and sufficiently large (e.g., two or more SDs), the examinee is not demonstrating academic achievement commensurate with aptitude. If further assessment rules out a number of explanations like inadequate educational opportunities or sensory impairment

Table 4.6 Calculating the reliability of a linear combination

Nunnally (1978) illustrated a method of calculating the reliability of a linear combination that is often used in psychometric studies. The standard score formula is:

$$r_{yy} = 1 - \frac{k - \sum r_{ii}}{\sigma_y^2}$$

where:

$\quad r_{yy}$ = Reliability of the linear combination

$\quad k$ = Number of scores in the linear combination

$\quad \sum r_{ii}$ = Sum of the reliabilities of the scores

$\quad \sigma_y^2$ = Variance of the linear combination

The only quantity in the formula that requires some extra work is σ_y^2. This may be calculated with data derived from the correlation matrix of the measures to be combined in the composite. Consider an example where we have three measures (A, B, and C) we wish to combine into a linear composite. The correlation matrix could be:

Measures	A	B	C
A	1.00	0.70	0.60
B	0.70	1.00	0.80
C	0.60	0.80	1.00

In this example, the correlation between measures A and B is 0.70, between A and C is 0.60, and between B and C is 0.80. One can calculate σ_y^2 by summing all of the values in this matrix. In this example $\sigma_y^2 = 7.2$

For this example, we will assume the reliability of the all three measures is 0.80. Therefore, $\sum r_{ii} = 2.40$ (i.e., $0.80 + 0.80 + 0.80 = 2.40$)

There are three measures, so $k = 3$

$$r_{yy} = 1 - \frac{3 - 2.40}{7.2}$$

$$= 1 - \frac{0.60}{7.2}$$

$$= 1 - 0.0833$$

$$= 0.92$$

This illustrates how three measures that produce scores with acceptable reliability (i.e., 0.80) and moderate to strong intercorrelations (i.e., between 0.60 and 0.80) can be combined to form a composite with excellent reliability

(e.g., visual or auditory problems), the discrepancy might reflect an inherent learning disability (this approach to diagnosing learning disabilities has many detractors, and that debate will be discussed in Chap. 9). Another common situation where difference scores are used is when a psychologist wants to consider gains (or losses) in test performance over time. For example, a researcher might want to determine if a specific treatment results in improved performance on a certain task. This is often accomplished by administering pre- and post-intervention tests.

> Reliability of difference scores is typically considerably lower than the reliabilities of the individual scores.

In these situations, the variable of interest is a difference score. When dealing with difference scores, it is important to remember that the reliability of difference scores is typically considerably lower than the reliabilities of the individual scores. As a general rule, the reliability of difference scores increases when the original measures have high reliabilities and low correlations with each other. For example, consider an IQ with a reliability of 0.90, an achievement test with a reliability of 0.80, and a correlation between the two of 0.50. The reliability of the difference score would equal to 0.70. While the reliabilities of the initial two measures were reasonable, the reliability of the resulting difference score is marginal at best. If the correlation between the IQ and achievement tests was 0.60 instead of 0.50, the reliability of the difference scores would fall to 0.63.

In summary, one should be cautious when interpreting difference scores. The reliability of difference scores is typically considerably lower than the reliabilities of the individual scores. To exacerbate the problem, difference scores are often calculated using scores that have fairly strong correlations with each other (e.g., IQ and achievement scores; pre- and posttest scores). Table 4.7 provides an illustration of the computation of difference scores.

Table 4.7 Calculating the reliability of difference scores

The standard score formula for calculating the reliability of a difference scores is:

$$r_{DD} = \frac{.5(r_{AA} + r_{BB}) - r_{AB}}{1 - r_{AB}}$$

where:

r_{DD} = reliability of the difference score
r_{AA} = reliability of Test A
r_{BB} = reliability of Test B
r_{AB} = correlation between the two tests

Consider the case where the reliability of Test A = 0.80, the reliability of Test B = 0.80, and the correlation between the two tests is 0.60

$$
\begin{aligned}
r_{DD} &= \frac{0.5(0.80 + 0.80) - 0.60}{1 - 0.60} \\
&= \frac{0.80 - 0.60}{0.40} \\
&= \frac{0.20}{0.40} \\
&= 0.50
\end{aligned}
$$

If the correlation between the two tests was 0.30, the reliability of the difference score would be considerably higher, as illustrated here:

$$
\begin{aligned}
r_{DD} &= \frac{0.5(0.80 + 0.80) - 0.30}{1 - 0.30} \\
&= \frac{0.80 - 0.30}{0.70} \\
&= \frac{0.50}{0.70} \\
&= 0.71
\end{aligned}
$$

This illustrates how the reliability of difference scores is influenced by the strength of the correlation between the two tests

4.3.8   Selecting a Reliability Coefficient

Table 4.8 summarizes the major sources of measurement error reflected in different reliability coefficients. As we have suggested in our discussion of each approach to estimating reliability, different conditions call for different estimates of reliability. One should consider factors such as the nature of the construct and how the scores will be used when selecting an estimate of reliability. If a test is designed to be given more than one time to the same individuals, test-retest and alternate-form reliability with delayed administration are appropriate because they are sensitive to measurement errors resulting from time sampling. Accordingly, if a test is used to predict an individual's performance on a criterion in the future, it is also important to use a reliability estimate that reflects errors due to time sampling.

> One should consider factors such as the nature of the construct being measured and how the scores will be used when selecting an estimate of reliability.

When a test is designed to be administered only one time, an estimate of internal consistency is appropriate. As we noted, split-half reliability estimates error variance resulting from content sampling whereas coefficient alpha and KR-20 estimate error variance due to content sampling and content heterogeneity. Because KR-20 and coefficient alpha are sensitive to content heterogeneity, they are applicable when the test measures a homogeneous domain of knowledge or a unitary characteristic. For example, our 25-item test measuring the ability to multiply double digits reflects a homogeneous domain and coefficient alpha would provide a good estimate of reliability. However, if we have a 50-item test, 25 measuring multiplication with double digits and 25 measuring division, the domain is more heterogeneous and coefficient alpha and KR-20 would probably underestimate reliability. In the latter situation, in which we have a test with heterogeneous content (where the heterogeneity is intended and not a mistake), the split-half method is preferred. Because the goal of the split-half approach is to compare two equivalent halves, it would be possible to ensure that each half has equal numbers of both multiplication and division problems.

We have been focusing on tests of achievement when providing examples, but the same principles apply to other types of tests. For example, a test that measures

Table 4.8   Major sources of error variance associated with types of reliability

Type of reliability	Major source of error variance
Test-retest reliability	Time sampling
Alternate-form reliability	
Simultaneous administration	Content sampling
Delayed administration	Time sampling and content sampling
Split-half reliability	Content sampling
Coefficient alpha and KR-20	Content sampling and item heterogeneity
Inter-rater reliability	Differences due to raters/scorers

depressed mood may assess a fairly homogeneous domain, making the use of coefficient alpha or KR-20 appropriate. However, if the test measures depression, anxiety, anger, and impulsiveness, the content becomes more heterogeneous and the split-half estimate would be indicated. In this situation, the split-half approach would allow the construction of two equivalent halves with equal numbers of items reflecting the different traits or characteristics under investigation.

Naturally, if different forms of a test are available, it would be important to estimate alternate-form reliability of the score. If a test involves subjective judgment by the person scoring the test, inter-rater reliability is important. Many contemporary test manuals report multiple estimates of reliability which we will illustrate in a later section of this chapter, "Reporting Reliability Information."

4.3.9 Evaluating Reliability Coefficients

Another important question that arises when considering reliability coefficients is "How large do reliability coefficients need to be?" Remember, we said reliability coefficients can be interpreted in terms of the proportion of test score variance attributable to true variance. Ideally, we would like our reliability coefficients to equal 1.0 because this would indicate that 100% of the test score variance is due to true differences among individuals on the variable assessed. However, due to measurement error, perfectly reliable measurement does not exist. There is not a single, simple answer to our question about what is an acceptable level of reliability. What constitutes an acceptable reliability coefficient depends on several factors, including the construct being measured, the amount of time available for testing, the way the scores will be used, and the method of estimating reliability. We will now briefly address each of these factors.

> What constitutes an acceptable reliability coefficient depends on several factors, including the construct being measured, the amount of time available for testing, the way the scores will be used, and the method of estimating reliability.

4.3.9.1 Construct

Some constructs are more difficult to measure than others simply because the item domain is more difficult to sample adequately. As a general rule, personality variables are more difficult to measure than cognitive abilities. As a result, what might be an acceptable level of reliability for a measure of "dependency" might be regarded as unacceptable for a measure of intelligence. In evaluating the acceptability of a reliability coefficient one should consider the nature of the variable under investigation and how difficult it is to measure. By carefully reviewing and comparing the reliability estimates of different instruments available for measuring a construct, one can determine which is the most reliable measure of the construct.

4.3.9.2 Time Available for Testing

If the amount of time available for testing is limited, only a limited number of items can be administered and the sampling of the test domain is open to greater error. This could occur in a research project in which the school principal allows you to conduct a study in his or her school but allows only 20 minutes to measure all the variables in your study. As another example, consider a district-wide screening for reading problems wherein the budget allows only 15 minutes of testing per student. In contrast, a psychologist may have two hours to administer a standardized intelligence test. It would be unreasonable to expect the same level of reliability from these significantly different measurement processes. However, comparing the reliability coefficients associated with instruments that can be administered within the parameters of the testing situation can help one select the best instrument for the situation.

4.3.9.3 Test Score Use

The way the test scores will be used is another major consideration when evaluating the adequacy of reliability coefficients. Diagnostic tests that form the basis for major decisions about individuals should be held to a higher standard than tests used with group research or for screening large numbers of individuals. For example, an individually administered test of intelligence that is used in the diagnosis of intellectual disability would be expected to produce scores with a very high level of reliability. In this context, performance on the intelligence test provides critical information used to determine whether the individual meets the diagnostic criteria. In contrast, a brief test used to screen all students in a school district for reading problems would be held to less rigorous standards. In this situation, the instrument is used simply for screening purposes and no diagnosis is to be rendered and no decisions are being made that cannot easily be reversed – only a decision about the need for a more thorough evaluation. It helps to remember that although high reliability is desirable with all assessments, standards of acceptability vary according to the way test scores will be used. High-stakes decisions demand highly reliable information!

4.3.9.4 Method of Estimating Reliability

The size of reliability coefficients is also related to the method selected to estimate reliability. Some methods tend to produce higher estimates than other methods. As a result, it is important to take into consideration the method used to produce correlation coefficients when evaluating and comparing the reliability of different tests. For example, KR-20 and coefficient alpha typically produce reliability estimates that are smaller than ones obtained using the split-half method. As indicated in Table 4.8, alternate-form reliability with delayed administration takes into account more major sources of error than other methods do and generally produces lower reliability coefficients. In summary, some methods of estimating reliability are more rigorous and tend to produce smaller coefficients, and this variability should be considered when evaluating reliability coefficients.

4.3.9.5 General Guidelines

Although it is apparent that many factors deserve consideration when evaluating reliability coefficients, we will provide some general guidelines that can provide some guidance.

- If test results are being used to make important decisions that are likely to impact individuals significantly and are not easily reversed, it is reasonable to expect reliability coefficients of 0.90 or even 0.95. This level of reliability is regularly obtained with individually administered tests of intelligence. For example, the reliability of the Full Scale IQ from the Stanford-Binet Intelligence Scales – Fifth Edition (Roid, 2003), an individually administered intelligence test, is 0.98 at some ages.

> If a test is being used to make important decisions that are likely to impact individuals significantly and are not easily reversed, it is reasonable to expect reliability coefficients of 0.90 or even 0.95.

- Reliability estimates of 0.80 or more are considered acceptable in many testing situations and are commonly reported for group and individually administered achievement and personality tests. For example, the Iowa Tests of Basic Skills (Hoover, Dunbar, & Frisbie, 2001), a set of group-administered achievement tests frequently used in public schools, has reliability coefficients for most of its subtest scores that exceed 0.80.
- For teacher-made classroom tests and tests used for screening, reliability estimates of at least 0.70 for scores are expected. Classroom tests frequently are combined to form linear composites that determine a final grade, and the reliability of these composite scores is expected to be greater than the reliabilities of the individual scores. Marginal coefficients in the 0.70s might also be acceptable when more thorough assessment procedures are available to address concerns about individual cases (e.g., when a psychologist is screening a large number of individuals in a community sample).

Some writers suggest that reliability coefficients as low as 0.60 are acceptable for group research, performance assessments, and projective measures, but we are reluctant to endorse the use of any assessment that produces scores with reliability estimates below 0.70. As you recall, a reliability coefficient of 0.60 indicates that 40% of the observed variance can be attributed to random error. How much confidence can you place in assessment results when you know that 40% of the variance is attributed to random error?

4.3.10 How to Improve Reliability

A natural question at this point is "What can we do to improve the reliability of our assessment results or test scores?" In essence, we are asking what steps can be taken to maximize true score variance and minimize error variance. Probably the most obvious approach is simply to increase the number of items on a test. In the context of an individual test, if we increase the number of items while maintaining the same quality as the original items, we will increase the reliability of the test scores obtained. This concept was introduced when we discussed split-half reliability and presented the Spearman-Brown formula. In fact, a variation of the Spearman-Brown formula can be used to predict the effects on reliability of scores achieved by adding items. This equation is:

$$r = \frac{n * r_{xx}}{1 + (n-1) r_{xx}}$$

where

r = estimated reliability of test scores with new items
n = factor by which the test length is increased
r_{xx} = reliability of the original test scores

For example, consider the example of our 25-item math test. If the reliability of the test score were 0.80 and we wanted to estimate the increase in reliability we would achieve by increasing the test to 30 items (a factor of 1.2), the formula would be:

$$r = \frac{1.2 * 0.80}{1 + ((1.2 - 1) 0.80)}$$

$$r = \frac{0.96}{1.16}$$

$$r = 0.83$$

Table 4.9 provides other examples illustrating the effects of increasing the length of our hypothetical test on reliability. By looking in the first row of this table you see that increasing the number of items on a test with a reliability of 0.50 by a factor of 1.25 results in a predicted reliability of 0.56. Increasing the number of items by a factor of 2.0 (i.e., doubling the length of the test) increases the reliability of our test score to 0.67.

> Possibly the most obvious way to improve the reliability of measurement is simply to increase the number of items on a test. If we increase the number of items while maintaining the same quality as the original items, we will increase the reliability of the test.

In some situations, various factors will limit the number of items we can include in a test. For example, teachers generally develop tests that can be administered in a specific time interval, usually the time allocated for a class period. In these situations, one can enhance reliability by using multiple measurements that are combined for an average or composite score. As noted earlier, combining multiple tests in a linear composite will increase the reliability of measurement over that of the

Table 4.9 Reliability expected when increasing the number of items

Current reliability	The reliability expected when the number of items is increased by			
	×1.25	×1.50	×2.00	×2.50
0.50	0.56	0.60	0.67	0.71
0.55	0.60	0.65	0.71	0.75
0.60	0.65	0.69	0.75	0.79
0.65	0.70	0.74	0.79	0.82
0.70	0.74	0.78	0.82	0.85
0.75	0.79	0.82	0.86	0.88
0.80	0.83	0.86	0.89	0.91
0.85	0.88	0.89	0.92	0.93
0.90	0.92	0.93	0.95	0.96

component tests. In summary, anything we do to get a more adequate sampling of the content domain will increase the reliability of our measurement.

In Chap. 7 we will discuss a set of procedures collectively referred to as "item analyses." These procedures help us select, develop, and retain test items with good measurement characteristics. While it is premature to discuss these procedures in detail, it should be noted that selecting or developing good items is an important step in developing a good test. Selecting and developing good items will enhance the measurement characteristics of the assessments you use.

Another way to reduce the effects of measurement error is what Ghiselli, Campbell, and Zedeck (1981) refer to as "good housekeeping procedures." By this, they mean test developers should provide precise and clearly stated procedures regarding the administration and scoring of tests. Such practice is also recommended in the *Standards for Educational and Psychological Testing* (AERA et al., 2014). Examples include providing explicit instructions for standardized administration, developing high-quality rubrics to facilitate reliable scoring, and requiring extensive training before individuals can administer, grade, or interpret a test.

4.3.11 Special Problems in Estimating Reliability

Reliability of Speed Tests. A speed test generally contains items that are relatively easy but has a time limit that prevents any examinees from correctly answering all questions. As a result, the examinee's score on a speed test primarily reflects the speed of his or her performance. When estimating the reliability of the results of speed tests, estimates derived from a single administration of a test are not appropriate. Therefore, with speed tests, test-retest or alternate-form reliability is appropriate, but split-half, coefficient alpha, and KR-20 should be avoided.

> When estimating the reliability of the results of speed tests, estimates derived from a single administration of a test are not appropriate.

Reliability as a Function of Score Level. Though it is desirable, tests do not always measure with the same degree of precision throughout the full range of scores. If a group of individuals is tested for whom the test is either too easy or too difficult, we are likely to have additional errors introduced into the scores. At the extremes of the distribution, where scores reflect mostly all correct or all wrong responses, little accurate measurement has occurred. It would be inaccurate to infer that a child who missed every question on an intelligence test has "no" intelligence. Rather, the test did not adequately assess the low-level skills necessary to measure the child's intelligence. This is referred to as the test having an insufficient "floor." At the other end, it would be inaccurate to report that a child who answers all of the questions on an intelligence test correctly has an "infinite level of intelligence." The test is simply too easy to provide an adequate measurement, a situation referred to as a test having an insufficient "ceiling." Both *floor effects* and *ceiling effects* indicate that a more appropriate test is needed. Generally, aptitude and achievement tests are designed for use with individuals of certain age, ability, or grade/educational levels. When a test is used with individuals who fall either at the extremes or outside this range, the scores might not be as accurate as the reliability estimates suggest. In these situations, further study of the test's reliability is indicated.

Range Restriction. The values we obtain when calculating reliability coefficients are dependent on characteristics of the sample or group of individuals on which the analyses are based. One characteristic of the sample that significantly impacts the coefficients is the degree of variability in performance (i.e., variance). More precisely, reliability coefficients based on samples with large variances (referred to as heterogeneous samples) will generally produce higher estimates of reliability than those based on samples with small variances (referred to as homogeneous samples). When reliability coefficients are based on a sample with a *restricted range* of scores, the coefficients may actually underestimate the reliability of measurement. For example, if you base a reliability analysis on students in a Gifted and Talented class in which practically all of the scores reflect exemplary performance (e.g., >90% correct), you will receive lower estimates of reliability than if the analyses are based on a class with a broader and more nearly normal distribution of scores. To be accurate, reliability estimates should be calculated using samples that are representative of the population to whom examinees are intended to be compared or referenced.

Mastery Testing. Criterion-referenced scores are used to make interpretations relative to a specific level of performance. Mastery testing is an example of a criterion-referenced score where an examinee's performance is evaluated in terms of achieving a cut score associated with a predetermined level of mastery instead of the relative degree of achievement (i.e., relative to the achievement of others). The emphasis in this testing situation is on classification. Examinees either score at-or-above the cut score and are classified as having mastered the skill or domain, or they score below the cut score and are classified as having not mastered the skill or domain. Mastery testing often results in limited variability among test takers, and

> The reliability estimates discussed in this chapter are usually not applicable to mastery tests. Because mastery tests emphasize classification, a recommended approach is to use an index that reflects the consistency of classification.

as we just described, limited variability in performance results in small reliability coefficients. As a result, the reliability estimates discussed in this chapter are typically inadequate for assessing the reliability of mastery tests. Given the emphasis on classification, a recommended approach is to use an index that reflects the consistency of classification (AERA et al., 2014). Special Interest Topic 4.2 illustrates a useful procedure for evaluating the consistency of classification when using mastery tests.

Special Interest Topic 4.2: Consistency of Classification with Mastery Tests

As noted in the text, the size of reliability coefficients is substantially impacted by the variance of the test scores. Limited test score variance results in lower reliability coefficients. Since mastery tests often do not produce test scores with much variability the methods of estimating reliability described in this chapter will often underestimate the reliability of these tests. To address this, reliability analyses of mastery tests typically focus on the consistency of classification. That is, since the objective of mastery tests is to determine if a student has mastered the skill or knowledge domain, the question of reliability can be framed as one of how consistent mastery-nonmastery classifications are. For example, if two parallel or equivalent mastery tests covering the same skill or content domain consistently produce the same classifications (i.e., mastery vs. nonmastery), we would have evidence of consistency of classification. If two parallel mastery tests produced divergent classifications we would have cause for concern. In this case, the test results are not consistent or reliable.

The procedure for examining the consistency of classification on parallel mastery tests is fairly straightforward. Simply administer both tests to a group of students and complete a table like the one listed below. For example, consider two mathematics mastery tests designed to assess students' ability to multiply fractions. The cut score is set at 80%, so all students scoring 80% or higher are classified as having mastered the skill while those scoring less than 80% are classified as not having mastered the skill. In the following example, data is provided for 50 students:

	Form B: Nonmastery (score < 80%)	Form B: Mastery (score of 80% or better)
Form A: Mastery (score of 80% or better)	4	32
Form A: Nonmastery (score < 80%)	11	3

Students classified as achieving mastery on both tests are denoted in the upper right-hand cell while students classified as not having mastered the skill are denoted in the lower left-hand cell. There were 4 students who were classified as having mastered the skills on Form A but not on Form B (denoted in the upper left-hand cell). There were 3 students who were classified as having mastered the skills on Form B but not on Form A (denoted in the lower right-hand cell). The next step is to calculate the percentage of consistency. This is accomplished with the following formula:

$$\text{Percent consistency} = \frac{\text{Mastery on both forms} + \text{Nonmastery on both forms}}{\text{Total number of students}} * 100$$

$$= \frac{32 + 11}{50} * 100$$

$$= 0.86 * 100$$

$$= 86\%$$

This approach is limited to situations in which you have parallel mastery tests. Another limitation is that there are no clear standards regarding what constitutes "acceptable" consistency of classification. Consistent with the evaluation of all reliability information, the evaluation of classification consistency should take into consideration the consequences of any decisions that are based on the test results (e.g., Gronlund, 2003). If the test results are used to make "high-stakes" decisions (e.g., awarding a diploma) a very high level of consistency is required. If the test is used only for "low-stake" decisions (e.g., failure results in further instruction and re-testing), a lower level of consistency may be acceptable.

There are more robust approaches to examine consistency of classifications. For example, one could calculate Cohen's Kappa which takes into account the degree of agreement expected by chance.

Correction for Attenuation. Statisticians and psychometricians may apply a *correction for attenuation* to correct for the unreliability of scores being correlated. For example, in a study of the relationship between visual and auditory memory, the researcher is typically only interested in the psychological constructs of visual and auditory memory and would like to eliminate measurement error. This can be achieved mathematically using a correction for attenuation. As another example, consider a test-retest reliability study. Here, both the original "test scores" and the "retest scores" contain some measurement error (e.g., due to content sampling). A test developer might decide to apply a correction for attenuation to correct for the unreliability in the original test and retest scores and focus the test-retest analysis on the stability of scores over time. These are reasonable practices as long as the researchers highlight this in their discussion of the results. It is also recommended that both corrected and uncorrected coefficients be reported. Table 4.10 illustrates the calculation of the correction for attenuation.

Table 4.10   Applying a correction for attenuation

The general formula for a correction for attenuation is:

$$C - r_{xy} = \frac{(r_{xy})}{[(\sqrt{r_{xx}})(\sqrt{r_{yy}})]}$$

where:

$C - r_{xy}$ = corrected correlation

r_{xy} = uncorrected correlation

r_{xx} = reliability of X scores

r_{yy} = reliability of Y scores

Consider this example. A researcher is examining the correlation between reading comprehension and word recognition. They decide to report both corrected and uncorrected test-retest reliability coefficients. The uncorrected correlation between the reading comprehension and word recognition scores is 0.75. The reliability of the reading comprehension scores 0.90 and word recognition scores is 0.81

$$C - r_{xy} = \frac{(0.75)}{[(\sqrt{0.90})(\sqrt{0.81})]}$$

$$C - r_{xy} = \frac{(0.75)}{[0.95 * 0.90]}$$

$$C - r_{xy} = \frac{0.75}{0.855}$$

$$C - r_{xy} = 0.88$$

Therefore, the uncorrected coefficient is 0.75 and the corrected coefficient is 0.88. This corrected coefficient can be interpreted as the correlation between true scores on the tests of reading comprehension and word recognition

4.4   The Standard Error of Measurement

Reliability coefficients are interpreted in terms of the proportion of observed variance attributable to true variance and are a useful way of comparing the reliability of scores produced by different assessment procedures. Other things being equal, you will want to select the test that produces scores with the best reliability. However, once a test has been selected and the focus is on interpreting scores, the ***standard error of measurement*** (SEM) is a more practical statistic. The SEM is the standard deviation of the distribution of scores that would be obtained by one person if he or she were tested on an infinite number of parallel forms of a test comprised of items randomly sampled from the same content domain. That definition is jam-packed with

> Reliability coefficients are useful when comparing the reliability of scores produced by different tests, but when the focus is on interpreting the test scores of individuals, the standard error of measurement is a more practical statistic.

information, so allow us to elaborate. If we created an infinite number of parallel forms of a test and had the same person take them with no carryover effects, the presence of measurement error would prevent the person from earning the same score every time. Although each test might represent the content domain equally well, the test taker would perform better on some tests and worse on others simply due to random error (e.g., chance or luck in knowing the answers to items selected for one version of a test but not another). By taking the scores obtained on all of these tests, a distribution of scores would result. The mean of this distribution is the individual's true score (T) and the SEM is the standard deviation of this distribution of error scores. Obviously, we are never actually able to follow these procedures and must estimate the SEM using information that is available to us.

4.4.1   Evaluating the Standard Error of Measurement

The SEM is a function of the reliability (r_{xx}) of test scores and standard deviation (SD) of the test scores. When calculating the SEM, the reliability coefficient takes into consideration measurement errors present in test scores, and the SD reflects the variance of the scores in the distribution. The SEM is estimated using the following formula:

$$SEM = SD\sqrt{1 - r_{xx}}$$

where:

SD = the standard deviation of the obtained scores, and
r_{xx} = the reliability of the test scores

Let's work through two quick examples. First, let's assume a test with a standard deviation of 10 and reliability of 0.90.

Example 4.1 $SEM = 10\sqrt{1 - 0.90}$

$SEM = 10\sqrt{0.10}$

$SEM = 3.2$

Now let's assume a test with a standard deviation of 10 and reliability of 0.80. The SD is the same as in the previous example, but the reliability is lower.

Example 4.2 $SEM = 10\sqrt{1 - 0.80}$

$SEM = 10\sqrt{0.20}$

$SEM = 4.5$

Notice that as the reliability of the test decreases, the SEM increases. Because the reliability coefficient reflects the proportion of observed score variance due to true score variance and the SEM is an estimate of the amount of error in test

> The greater the reliability of a test score, the smaller the SEM and the more confidence we have in the precision of test scores.

scores, this inverse relationship is what one would expect. The greater the reliability of test scores, the smaller the SEM and the more confidence we have in the precision of test scores. The lower the reliability of a test, the larger the SEM and the less confidence we have in the precision of test scores. For example, with a perfect reliability coefficient of 1.0 the SEM would equal 0, indicating no error in measurement and the obtained score is the true score. A reliability coefficient of 0 would yield an SEM equal to the SD of the obtained scores, indicating all of the test score variances are due to errors. Table 4.11 shows some additional examples of the SEM as a function of SD and reliability. Examining the first row in the table shows that on a test with a standard deviation of 30 and a reliability coefficient of 0.95 the SEM is 6.7. In comparison, if the reliability of the test is 0.90 the SEM is 9.5; if the reliability of the test is 0.85 the SEM is 11.6 and so forth. The SEM has been traditionally used in calculating intervals or bands around observed scores in which the true score is expected to fall. We will now turn to this application of the SEM.

Table 4.11 Standard errors of measurement for different levels of reliability and standard deviations

Standard deviation	Reliability coefficients					
	0.95	0.90	0.85	0.80	0.75	0.70
30	6.7	9.5	11.6	13.4	15.0	16.4
28	6.3	8.9	10.8	12.5	14.0	15.3
26	5.8	8.2	10.1	11.6	13.0	14.2
24	5.4	7.6	9.3	10.7	12.0	13.1
22	4.9	7.0	8.5	9.8	11.0	12.0
20	4.5	6.3	7.7	8.9	10.0	11.0
18	4.0	5.7	7.0	8.0	9.0	9.9
16	3.6	5.1	6.2	7.2	8.0	8.8
14	3.1	4.4	5.4	6.3	7.0	7.7
12	2.7	3.8	4.6	5.4	6.0	6.6
10	2.2	3.2	3.9	4.5	5.0	5.5
8	1.8	2.5	3.1	3.6	4.0	4.4
6	1.3	1.9	2.3	2.7	3.0	3.3
4	0.9	1.3	1.5	1.8	2.0	2.2
2	0.4	0.6	0.8	0.9	1.0	1.1

4.4.2   Calculating Confidence Intervals

A *confidence interval* reflects a range of scores that will contain the individual's true score with a prescribed probability (AERA et al., 2014). We typically use the SEM to calculate confidence intervals. When introducing the SEM, we said it provides information about the distribu-

> A confidence interval reflects a range of test scores that will contain the individual's true score with a prescribed probability (AERA et al., 2014).

tion of observed scores around true scores. More precisely, we defined the SEM as the standard deviation of the distribution of error scores. Like any standard deviation, the SEM can be interpreted in terms of frequencies represented in a normal distribution. In the previous chapter, we showed that approximately 68% of the scores in a normal distribution are located between one SD below the mean and one SD above the mean. As a result, approximately 68% of the time an individual's observed score would be expected to be within ±1 SEM of the true score. For example, if an individual had a true score of 70 on a test with a SEM of 3, then we would expect him or her to obtain scores between 67 and 73 two-thirds of the time (as long as there are no changes in performance as a function of taking the test). To obtain a 95% confidence interval we simply determine the number of standard deviations encompassing 95% of the scores in a distribution. By referring to a table representing areas under the normal curve you can determine that 95% of the scores in a normal distribution fall within ±1.96 SDs of the mean. Given a true score of 70 and SEM of 3, the 95% confidence interval would be 70 ± 3(1.96) or 70 ± 5.88. Therefore, in this situation, an individual's observed score would be expected to be between 64.12 and 75.88, 95% of the time.

You might have noticed a potential problem with this approach to calculating confidence intervals. So far we have described how the SEM allows us to form confidence intervals around the examinee's true score. The problem is that we don't know an examinee's true score, only the observed score. Although it is possible for us to estimate true scores (see Special Interest Topic 4.3), it is common practice to use the SEM to establish confidence intervals around obtained scores (see Gulliksen, 1950). These confidence intervals are calculated in the same manner as just described, but the interpretation is slightly different. In this context, the confidence interval is used to define the range of scores that will contain the individual's true score. For example, if an individual obtains a score of 70 on a test with a SEM of 3.0, we would expect his or her true score to be between 67 and 73, 68% of the time (obtained score ± 1 SEM). Accordingly, we would expect his or her true score to be between 64.12 and 75.88, 95% of the time (obtained score ± 1.96 SEM). In practice, the score delineating confidence intervals

> A major advantage of the SEM and the use of confidence intervals is that they remind us that measurement error is present in all scores and that we should interpret scores cautiously.

are rounded to the nearest whole number since most tests do not yield fractional scores. For example, "64.14–75.88" is rounded to "64–76."

Special Interest Topic 4.3: Asymmetrical Confidence Intervals

It is common practice for test developers and publishers to report confidence intervals using the procedure described in this chapter. However, to correct for true score regression to the mean, several researchers (e.g., Dudek, 1979; Glutting, McDermott, & Stanley, 1987) have suggested an approach that establishes confidence intervals based on estimated true scores and the standard error of estimation (SE_E). Using this approach, the estimated true score is obtained with the following formula:

$$\text{Estimated True Score} = \text{Mean} + r_{xx}\left(X - \text{Mean}\right)$$

where:

Mean = the mean on the standard scores
X = the observed score
r_{xx} = the reliability coefficient

The standard error of estimation is obtained using the following formula:

$$SE_E = SD\sqrt{1 - r_{xx}}\left(r_{xx}\right)$$

where the SD of the standard scores r_{xx} is the reliability coefficient.

This approach results in confidence intervals that are asymmetrical around the observed score. For example, an observed score of 120 might have a 95% confidence interval of 113–123. Note that this range extends seven points below the observed scores (i.e., 120) and only three points above it. The more common approach described in this chapter results in symmetrical confidence intervals. For example, an observed score of 120 might have a 95% confidence interval of 115–125 (i.e., observed score ±5 points).

The approach based on estimated true scores and the standard error of estimation has appealed from a technical perspective and some test developers have adopted it (e.g., Wechsler, 1997).

It may help to make note of the relationship between the reliability of a test score, the SEM, and confidence intervals. Remember that we noted that as the reliability of scores increases the SEM decreases. The same relationship exists between test score reliability and confidence intervals. As the reliability of test scores increases (denoting less measurement error) the confidence intervals become smaller (denoting more precision in measurement).

A major advantage of the SEM and the use of confidence intervals is that they serve to remind us that measurement error is present in all scores and that we should interpret scores cautiously. A single numerical score is often interpreted as if it is precise and involves no error. For example, if you report that Susie has a Full Scale

IQ of 113, her parents might interpret this as implying that Susie's IQ is exactly 113. If you are using a high-quality IQ test such as the Reynolds Intellectual Assessment Scales or the Stanford-Binet Fifth Edition, the obtained IQ is very likely a good estimate of her true IQ. However, even with the best assessment instruments, the obtained scores contain some degree of error and the SEM and confidence intervals help us illustrate this. This information can be reported in different ways in written reports. For example, Kaufman and Lichtenberger (1999) recommend the following format:

Johnny obtained a Full Scale IQ of 113 (between 108 and 118 with 95% confidence).

Kamphaus (2005) recommends a slightly different format that is illustrated below:

Susie obtained a Full Scale IQ in the High Average range, with a 95% probability that her true IQ falls between 108 and 118.

Regardless of the exact format used, the inclusion of confidence intervals highlights the fact that test scores contain some degree of measurement error and should be interpreted with caution. Most professional test publishers either report scores as bands within which the examinee's true score is likely to fall or provide information on calculating these confidence intervals.

4.5   Modern Test Theories

We have focused on Classical Test Theory in this chapter due to its prominent role in the development of tests and the estimation and reporting of reliability information. There are two newer test theories that were developed in the latter part of the twentieth century. These are Generalizability Theory and Item Response Theory. These deserve mention at this point in our discussion of reliability since they both complement and extend CTT in terms of reliability information.

4.5.1   Generalizability Theory

Lee Cronbach and colleagues (e.g., Cronbach, Rajaratnam, & Gleser, 1963) developed an extension of Classical Test Theory (CTT) known as *Generalizability Theory* in the 1960s and 1970s. CTT provides only an undifferentiated error component, but in real-life situations, more than one source of measurement error is reflected in any reliability coefficient. For example, in this chapter, we noted that internal-consistency estimates of reliability primarily reflect errors due to domain sampling. While this is true, errors due to faulty administration, errors in scoring, and errors associated with time sampling may all act to lower the average inter-item correlation which reduces the internal-consistency reliability of test scores. Likewise, test-retest coefficients are confounded by internal-consistency errors. Under CTT it is not possible to determine how much error is contributed by the different sources of error. The main advantage of Generalizability Theory is that it gives researchers the opportunity to design studies that reveal how much variance is associated with various sources of error.

The main advantage of generalizability theory is that it gives researchers the opportunity to design studies that reveal how much variance is associated with various sources of error.

Generalizability Theory typically uses analysis of variance (ANOVA) to estimate reliability coefficients and partition the error variance components. While the methods and designs for partitioning variance components in ANOVA are beyond the scope of this text, the general procedure is to use a statistical analysis program (e.g., R, SAS®, etc.) to perform such analyses. These statistical programs have analysis options that will estimate the variance components (i.e., the variances associated with each source of variation specified by the analyst). A numerical value for each source is obtained and generalizability coefficients can be calculated using rules that have been developed over the past few decades. Some psychometricians advocate simply examining the magnitude of the variances. An example of this was provided by Cronbach (1990) where he describes a researcher interested in generalizing the results of a typing test across different test passages (i.e., the selection the students are required to type) and different testing occasions (i.e., what day the test is administered). For this study, 25 students were given five different typing passages on five consecutive days (i.e., a different passage on each day). Using a two-way ANOVA design, the results indicated that the variance associated with the use of different passages on different days was small (i.e., 0.28) relative to the observed score variance (i.e., 12.4). These results indicate that the selection of a specific typing passage or a specific day to administer the test had relatively little impact on the score the students received. In other words, in this situation, it is reasonable to generalize across test passages and testing occasions. The author notes that this is a common finding when using professionally developed alternate test forms that are technically comparable. Alternate test forms developed by the typical classroom teacher might not reach as high a level of technical equivalence and the results might be different (i.e., more variance associated with the use of different test forms).

Most test manuals report information on the reliability of test scores based on Classical Test Theory. However, Generalizability Theory provides a flexible and often more informative approach to reliability analysis. Given enough information about reliability, one can partition the error variance into its components as demonstrated in Fig. 4.1. It should be noted that Generalizability Theory is an extension of CTT and the theories are not incompatible. Cronbach, who was instrumental in developing Generalizability Theory was also instrumental in developing CTT decades earlier.

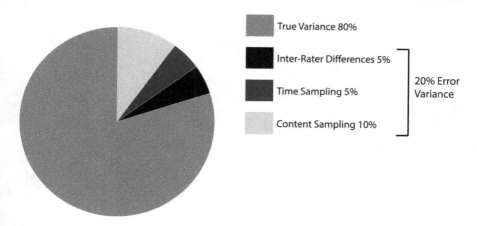

True Variance 80%

Inter-Rater Differences 5%

Time Sampling 5%   20% Error
                        Variance

Content Sampling 10%

Fig. 4.1 Partitioning the variance to reflect sources of variance

4.5.2 Item Response Theory

Another modern test theory is *Item Response Theory* (IRT). We will discuss IRT in more detail in Chap. 7: Item Analysis. For now, we can define it as a theory or model of mental measurement that posits that the responses to items on a test are accounted for by latent traits. It is assumed that each examinee possesses a certain amount of any given latent trait and that its estimation is

> In IRT, information on the reliability of scores is typically reported as a test information function (TIF) that illustrates the reliability of measurement at different points along the distribution.

not dependent on any particular set of items or any assessment procedure. Central to IRT is a mathematical model that describes how examinees at different levels of ability will respond to individual test items. IRT is fundamental to the development and application of computer adaptive testing. What is most important to us at this point (i.e., a chapter on reliability), is that in IRT information on the reliability of measurement takes a different form that either CTT or Generalizability Theory.

In IRT, information on the reliability of scores is typically reported as a ***Test Information Function (TIF)***. A TIF illustrates the reliability of measurement at different points along the distribution. This implies that the reliability of measurement in not constant across the distribution, and this is the case (as mentioned earlier in this chapter). A test (or an item) may provide more reliable measurement for examinees at one level of ability, and less reliable measurement for those at another level. TIFs can also be converted into an analog of the standard error of measurement for specific points in the distribution. Figure 4.2 shows a TIF with its analogous standard error of measurement curve. The graph shows both curves, each with a scale on different sides of the graph (i.e., TIF values on the left; standard error values on the right). This graph indicates that the most reliable information, as

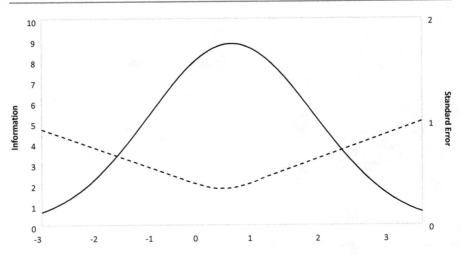

Fig. 4.2   Test information function (TIF) and standard errors (Osterlind, Figure 10.13/p. 293)

represented by higher TIF values and lower error values, is available around the middle of the distribution. At both the high and low ends of the distribution, there is more measurement error. While CTT provides only one estimate of reliability, as shown here IRT can provide information about reliability at different points along the distribution. This is an advantage of IRT. However, its mathematical complexity has been a drawback to its widespread application as well as its failure to improve on CTT models except in specialized testing models.

4.6   Reporting Reliability Information

The *Standards for Educational and Psychological Testing* (AREA et al., 2014) devote an entire chapter to the discussion of reliability and errors of measurement. This serves to emphasize the importance of information on reliability to all professionals developing and/or using tests. For test developers, the *Standards* (2014) specifies that "... developers and distributors of tests have primary responsibility for obtaining and reporting evidence of reliability/precision (p. 40)." Standard 2.3 stipulates that for all scores that are to be interpreted, estimates of relevant indices of reliability/precision should be reported. For psychologists (and all other users of tests), the *Standards* note "It is the user who must take responsibility for determining whether or not scores are sufficiently trustworthy to justify anticipated uses and interpretations (p. 41)." In other words, psychologists should carefully consider the reliability of test scores when selecting tests to administer and when interpreting test results.

Psychological researchers often use tests, questionnaires, and other assessments in conducting their research. It is important for these researchers to provide adequate information about the psychometric properties of the scores reported in their research. A task force of the American Psychological Association (Wilkinson and Task Force on Statistical Inferences, 1999) emphasized that all authors of research articles should provide information on the reliability of the measures they use in their research (e.g., reliability coefficients). They emphasize that to interpret meaningfully the size of the observed effects it is necessary to have information on the reliability of assessment scores. While information on the psychometric properties of professionally developed published tests is available typically in the professional manual or research literature, this may not be the case with instruments developed by researchers to measure constructs in their research. It is important to remember that the quality of all research is intricately tied to the quality of the measurement instruments used.

4.6.1   How Test Manuals Report Reliability Information: The Reynolds Intellectual Assessment Scales, Second Edition (RIAS-2)

To illustrate how reliability information is reported in test manuals, we will use examples from the *Reynolds Intellectual Assessment Scales, Second Edition* (RIAS–2: Reynolds & Kamphaus, 2015). The RIAS–2 is an individually administered intelligence test for clients 3 years to 94 years of age. The RIAS–2 contains a two-subtest Verbal Intelligence Index (VIX) and a two-subtest Nonverbal Intelligence Index (NIX). The two verbal subtests are *Guess What (GWH)* and *Verbal Reasoning (VRZ)*. The two nonverbal subtests are *Odd-Item Out* (OIO) and *What's Missing (WHM)*. All four subtests are combined to form the *Composite Intelligence Index (CIX)*. It takes approximately 20–25 minutes to administer the four intelligence scale subtests. The RIAS–2 also includes conormed supplemental measures of memory and processing speed. The memory measure can be completed in 0–15 min and is composed of two subtests, *Verbal Memory (VRM)* and *Nonverbal Memory (NVM)*, that yield a *Composite Memory Index (CMX)*. The processing speed measure can be completed in about 10 minutes and is composed of two subtests, the *Speeded Naming Task (SNT)* and the *Speeded Picture Search (SPS)*, that yield a *Speeded Processing Index (SPI)*. The RIAS–2 was standardized on a national sample of 2154 individuals that is representative of the U.S. population.

Chapter 5 of the RIAS-2 test manual is titled *Test Score Reliability*. To examine measurement error associated with content sampling, Reynolds and Kamphaus (2015) present coefficient alphas for all subtests and indexes. The coefficient alphas for the subtest scores are presented in Table 4.12. In this table, coefficient alphas are reported for different age groups, with median values presented in the bottom row. A review of Table 4.12 shows that the RIAS–2 subtest score alpha coefficients were 0.80 or greater for all age groups. The median coefficients for all subtests were 0.81 or greater. While the reliability estimates for the subtest scores are clearly adequate for clinical use, the authors recommend the interpretation of index scores when making clinical decisions. The reliability estimates for the RIAS–2 Indexes are presented in Table 4.13. A review of these data shows that the RIAS–2 Index alpha

Table 4.12 Coefficient alpha for RIAS–2 subtests

Age	RIAS-2 subtests							
	Guess What (GWH)	Verbal Reasoning (VRZ)	Odd-Item Out (OIO)	What's Missing (WHM)	Verbal Memory (VRM)	Nonverbal Memory (NVM)	Speeded Naming Task (SNT)	Speeded Picture Search (SPS)
3–6	0.94	0.89	0.94	0.93	0.99	0.95	0.98	0.99
7–10	0.89	0.89	0.82	0.85	0.97	0.91	0.98	0.99
11–14	0.83	0.81	0.81	0.83	0.98	0.84	0.98	0.99
15–18	0.86	0.82	0.80	0.83	0.97	0.80	0.98	0.99
19–24	0.83	0.81	0.81	0.82	0.92	0.80	0.99	0.99
25–34	0.85	0.85	0.80	0.80	0.95	0.80	0.99	0.99
35–54	0.83	0.83	0.80	0.83	0.94	0.81	0.99	0.99
55–74	0.87	0.87	0.80	0.84	0.94	0.80	0.99	0.99
75–94	0.89	0.89	0.87	0.89	0.95	0.83	0.99	0.99
Median	0.86	0.85	0.81	0.83	0.95	0.81	0.99	0.99

Table 4.13 Coefficient alpha for RIAS–2 Indexes by age group

Age	Index				
	VIX	NIX	CIX	CMX	SPI
3–6	0.95	0.95	0.97	0.96	0.99
7–10	0.93	0.89	0.94	0.93	0.99
11–14	0.88	0.93	0.91	0.93	0.99
15–18	0.90	0.92	0.93	0.90	0.99
19–24	0.90	0.90	0.93	0.86	0.99
25–34	0.92	0.90	0.93	0.90	0.99
35–54	0.90	0.88	0.93	0.86	0.99
55–74	0.93	0.88	0.94	0.87	0.99
75–94	0.94	0.92	0.96	0.91	0.99
Median	0.92	0.90	0.93	0.90	0.99

VIX Verbal Intelligence Index, *NIX* Nonverbal Intelligence Index, *CIX* Composite Intelligence Index, *CMX* Composite Memory Index, *SPI* Speeded Processing Index

coefficients for all age groups equal or exceed 0.86, with the median coefficients all 0.90 or greater. These results indicate that the RIAS–2 subtest scores and indexes provide reliable measurement, meeting or exceeding recommended standards for the recommended clinical applications.

The data just described demonstrate that the RIAS–2 subtests and indexes are reliable in the general population. The authors take an additional step by examining

Table 4.14 Standard errors of measurement of the RIAS–2 indexes by age group

Age	Index				
	VIX	NIX	CIX	CMX	SPI
3–6	3.33	3.43	2.75	2.82	1.62
7–10	3.90	4.97	3.71	3.96	1.53
11–14	5.28	3.85	4.45	3.98	1.63
15–18	4.69	4.25	4.10	4.83	1.74
19–24	4.86	4.69	4.10	5.56	1.60
25–34	4.35	4.64	3.92	4.80	1.52
35–54	4.69	5.16	3.83	5.60	1.38
55–74	4.11	5.15	3.56	5.31	1.39
75–94	3.76	4.11	3.02	4.62	1.41
Median	4.35	4.64	3.83	4.80	1.53

Reproduced by special permission of the Publisher, Psychological Assessment Resources, Inc., 16204 North Florida Avenue, Lutz, Florida 33549. Copyright 1998, 1999, 2002, 2003, 2007, 2016 by Psychological Assessment Resources, Inc. Further reproduction is prohibited without permission of PAR, Inc.

VIX Verbal Intelligence Index, NIX Nonverbal Intelligence Index, CIX Composite Intelligence Index, CMX Composite Memory Index, SPI Speeded Processing Index

the internal-consistency reliability of the RIAS–2 scores in major subgroups within the general population. Specifically, they examined the coefficient alphas of the subtests and indexes across gender and ethnic groups. While these data are not reproduced here, the results indicate consistently high coefficient alphas across ethnicity and gender.

In the next section of the chapter, the authors provide information on the standard error of measurement (SEM). The standard errors of measurement for the RIAS–2 Indexes are presented in Table 4.14. In this table, standard errors of measurement are again reported for different age groups, with median values presented in the bottom row. Examination of the data in this table indicates that the standard errors of measurement for the specific age groups range from 1.38 to 5.60. The median standard errors of measurement ranged from 1.53 to 4.80. In summary, again these data indicate highly reliable measurement.

The authors of the RIAS–2 next examine measurement error associated with temporal instability by reporting test-retest reliability coefficients (in this manual referred to as stability coefficients). Test-retest coefficients are reported for 97 examinees. The median test-retest interval was 18 days. The results are presented in Table 4.15. The coefficients for the subtests range from 0.71 (i.e., Nonverbal Memory) to 0.91 (i.e., Guess What). The coefficients for the indexes range from 0.79 (i.e., CMX) to 0.94 (i.e., VIX). The table also contains coefficients that were corrected for attenuation (i.e., C-r_{tt}). These coefficients correct for unreliability in the test and retest scores (this procedure was discussed in Special Interest Topic 4.4). As expected, the corrected coefficients are somewhat larger than the uncorrected coefficients. The authors also report test-retest coefficients for four different age groups (3–4; 5–8; 9–12; and 13–82 years). The test-retest stability coefficients across age groups are consistent with the

Table 4.15 Stability coefficients of scores for the RIAS–2 subtests and indexes

Subtest/index	First testing		Second testing		r_{tt}	C-r_{tt}
	M	SD	M	SD		
Guess What	50.07	12.32	53.35	12.41	0.91	0.99
Verbal Reasoning	50.37	12.93	53.42	12.69	0.89	0.99
Odd-Item Out	52.67	10.30	56.04	10.08	0.76	0.92
What's Missing	52.76	10.25	58.04	10.55	0.83	0.93
Verbal Memory	48.05	10.55	51.27	10.20	0.78	0.86
Nonverbal Memory	53.30	9.68	56.04	10.29	0.71	0.87
Speeded Naming Task	51.39	11.94	53.38	12.69	0.85	0.86
Speeded Picture Search	50.64	10.36	54.61	8.93	0.72	0.72
VIX	100.61	17.83	104.95	18.00	0.94	0.97
NIX	104.24	13.73	110.52	13.22	0.83	0.94
CIX	102.69	16.15	108.71	15.91	0.92	0.96
CMX	101.35	15.98	107.23	16.01	0.79	0.88
SPI	104.16	16.78	107.53	15.56	0.82	0.83

VIX Verbal Intelligence Index, *NIX* Nonverbal Intelligence Index, *CIX* Composite Intelligence Index, *CMX* Composite Memory Index, *SPI* Speeded Processing Index

Special Interest Topic 4.4: A Quick Way to Estimate Reliability for Classroom Exams

Saupe (1961) provided a quick method for teachers to calculate reliability for a classroom exam in the era prior to easy access to calculators or computers. It is appropriate for a test in which each item is given equal weight and each item is scored either right or wrong. First, the standard deviation of the exam must be estimated from a simple approximation:

$$SD = \frac{\left(\text{Sum of top 1/6 of scores} - \text{Sum of bottom 1/6 of scores}\right)}{\left(\frac{\text{Total number of scores} - 1}{2}\right)}$$

Then reliability can be estimated from:

$$\text{Reliability} = 1 - \frac{\left(0.19 * \text{Number of items}\right)}{SD^2}$$

Thus, for example, in a class with 24 student test scores, the top sixth of the scores are 98, 92, 87, and 86, while the bottom sixth of the scores are 48, 72, 74, and 75. With 25 test items, the calculations are:

$$SD = \frac{(98+92+87+86)-(48+72+74+75)}{\left(\dfrac{23}{2}\right)}$$

$$= \frac{363-269}{11.5}$$

$$= \frac{94}{11.5}$$

$$= 8.17$$

So,

$$Reliability = 1 - \frac{(0.19*25)}{8.17^2}$$

$$= 1 - 0.07$$

$$= 0.93$$

results from the total sample. Together, these results support the short-term stability of RIAS–2 scores.

In closing, the authors examine the amount of error due to examiner differences. To this end, two professionals independently scored a random sample of 35 test protocols and the subtest raw scores were correlated. The inter-rater reliability coefficients were as follows: Guess What, 1.00; Verbal Reasoning, 1.00; Odd-Item Out, 0.99; What's Missing, 1.00: Verbal memory, 0.99; Nonverbal memory, 0.99; Speeded Naming Task, 1.00; and Speeded Picture Search, 1.00. These strong coefficients support the high reliability of RIAS–2 results when scored by qualified examiners.

This example using the RIAS–2 illustrates the type of information that test manuals typically provide about the reliability of the test. You can expect some differences in the presentation of information, but the important feature is that test authors and publishers should provide adequate information for psychologists to make informed decisions about the reliability of the scores produced by a test.

4.7   Reliability: Practical Strategies for Educators

We are often asked by teachers how they can estimate reliability of their classroom test scores. First, for teachers using multiple-choice or other tests that can be scored by a computer scoring program, the score printout will typically report some reliability estimate (e.g., coefficient alpha or KR-20). If a teacher doesn't have access to computer scoring, but the items on a test are of approximately equal difficulty and

Table 4.16   KR-21 reliability estimates for tests with a mean of 80%

Number of items (n)	Standard deviation of test		
	0.10(n)	0.15(n)	0.20(n)
10	–	0.29	0.60
20	0.20	0.64	0.80
30	0.47	0.76	0.87
40	0.60	0.82	0.90
50	0.68	0.86	0.92
75	0.79	0.91	0.95
100	0.84	0.93	0.96

scored dichotomously (i.e., correct/incorrect), one can use an internal-consistency reliability estimate known as the Kuder-Richardson Formula 21 (KR-21). This formula is actually an estimate of the KR-20 discussed earlier and is usually adequate for classroom tests. To calculate KR-21 you only need to know the mean, variance, and number of items on the test. The formula is:

$$KR-21 = 1 - \frac{\bar{X}(n - \bar{X})}{ns^2}$$

where:

$\bar{X}$ = mean
s^2 = variance
n = number of items on the test

Consider the following set of 20 test scores: 50, 48, 47, 46, 42, 42, 41, 40, 40, 38, 37, 36, 36, 35, 34, 32, 32, 31, 30, 28. Here the $\bar{X} = 38.25$, $s^2 = 39.8$, and $n = 50$. Therefore,

$$KR-21 = 1 - \frac{38.25(50 - 38.25)}{50(39.8)}$$

$$= 1 - \frac{449.4375}{1990}$$

$$= 1 - 0.23 = 0.77$$

As you see, this is a fairly simple procedure. If one has access to a computer with a spreadsheet program or a calculator with mean and variance functions, you can estimate the reliability of classroom test scores easily in a matter of minutes with this formula.

Special Interest Topic 4.4 presents a shortcut approach for calculating Kuder--Richardson Formula 21 (KR-21). If one wants to avoid even these limited computations, we prepared Table 4.16 which allows you to estimate the KR-21 reliability for dichotomously scored classroom tests if you know the standard deviation and number of items (this table was modeled after tables originally presented by Deiderich,

1973). This table is appropriate for tests with a mean of approximately 80% correct (we are using a mean of 80% correct because it is fairly representative of many classroom tests). To illustrate its application, consider the following example. If your test has 50 items and a SD of 8, select the "Number of Items" row for 50 items and the "Standard Deviation" column for $0.15n$ (because $0.15(50) = 7.5$, which is close to your actual SD of 8). The number at the intersection is 0.86, which is very respectable reliability for a classroom test (or a professionally developed test for that matter).

If you examine Table 4.16 you will likely detect a few fairly obvious trends. First, the more items on the test the higher the estimated reliability coefficients. We alluded to the beneficial impact of increasing test length previously in this chapter and the increase in reliability is due to enhanced sampling of the content domain. Second, tests with larger standard deviations (i.e., variance) produce more reliable results. For example, a 30-item test with a SD of 3 (i.e., $0.10(n)$) results in an estimated reliability of 0.47, while one with a SD of 4.5 (i.e., $0.15(n)$) results in an estimated reliability of 0.76. This reflects the tendency we described earlier that restricted score variance results in smaller reliability coefficients. We should note that while we include a column for standard deviations of $0.20(n)$, standard deviations this large are rare with classroom tests (Deiderich, 1973). In fact, from our experience, it is more common for classroom tests to have standard deviations closer to $0.10(n)$. Before leaving our discussion of KR-21 and its application to classroom tests, we do want to caution you that KR-21 is only an approximation of KR-20 or coefficient alpha. KR-21 assumes the test items are of equal difficulty and it is usually slightly lower than KR-20 or coefficient alpha (Hopkins, 1998). Nevertheless, if the assumptions are not grossly violated it is probably a reasonably good estimate of reliability for many classroom applications.

Our discussion of shortcut reliability estimates to this point has been limited to tests that are dichotomously scored. Obviously, many of the assessments teachers use are not dichotomously scored and this makes the situation a little more complicated. If your items are not scored dichotomously, you can calculate coefficient alpha with relative ease using a commonly available spreadsheet tool such as Microsoft Excel. With a little effort, you should be able to use a spreadsheet to perform the computations illustrated previously in Tables 4.3 and 4.4.

4.8   Summary

Reliability refers to consistency in test scores. If a test or other assessment procedure produces consistent measurements, its scores are reliable. Why is reliability so important? As we emphasize, assessments are useful because they provide information that helps scientists and professionals make better decisions. However, the reliability (and validity) of that information is of paramount importance. For us to make good decisions, we need reliable information. By estimating the reliability of our assessment results, we get an indication of how much confidence we can place in them. If we have highly reliable and valid information, it is probable that we can use that information to make better decisions. If the results are unreliable, they are of little value to us.

Over the last century, several measurement theories have been developed that help us understand measurement error and related issues. The oldest and most widely applied theory is Classical Test Theory (CTT). We discussed CTT in some detail since it provided the foundation for most contemporary approaches to estimating reliability. We also briefly introduce Generalizability Theory and Item Response Theory, two modern test theories that have expanded our understanding of reliability and measurement error.

Errors of measurement undermine the reliability of measurement and therefore reduce the utility of the measurement. While there are multiple sources of measurement error, the major sources are content sampling and time sampling errors. Content sampling errors are the result of less than perfect sampling of the content domain. The more representative tests are of the content domain, the less content sampling errors threaten the reliability of the test. Time sampling errors are the result of random changes in the examinee or environment over time. Experts in testing and measurement have developed methods of estimating errors due to these and other sources. The major approaches to estimating reliability include:

- *Test-retest reliability* involves the administration of the same test to the same group of individuals on two different occasions. The correlation between the two sets of scores is the test-retest reliability coefficient and reflects errors due to time sampling.
- *Alternate-form reliability* involves the administration of parallel forms of a test to a group of individuals. The correlation between the scores on the two forms is the reliability coefficient. If the two forms are administered at the same time, the reliability coefficient only reflects content sampling error. If the two forms of the test are administered at different times, the reliability coefficient reflects both content and time sampling errors.
- *Internal-consistency reliability* estimates are derived from a single administration of a test. Split-half reliability involves dividing the test into two equivalent halves and calculating the correlation between the two halves. Instead of comparing performance on two halves of the test, Coefficient Alpha and the Kuder--Richardson approaches examine the consistency of responding among all of the individual items of the test. Split-half reliability reflects errors due to content sampling while Coefficient Alpha and the Kuder-Richardson approaches reflect both item heterogeneity and errors due to content sampling.
- *Inter-rater reliability* is estimated by administering the test once but having the responses scored by different examiners. By comparing the scores assigned by different examiners one can determine the influence of different raters or scorers. Inter-rater reliability is important to examine when scoring involves considerable subjective judgment.

We discuss a number of issues that are important for understanding and interpreting reliability estimates. We present some guidelines for selecting the type of reliability estimate that is most appropriate for specific assessment procedures, some guidelines for evaluating reliability coefficients, and some suggestions on improving the reliability of measurement.

While reliability coefficients are useful when comparing the reliability of different tests, the standard error of measurement (SEM) is more useful when interpreting scores.

The SEM is an index of the amount of error in test scores and is used in calculating confidence intervals within which we expect the true score to fall. An advantage of the SEM and the use of confidence intervals is that they serve to remind us that measurement error is present in all scores and that we should use caution when interpreting scores.

This chapter closes with an example of how test manuals should provide information on reliability and measurement error using the Reynolds Intellectual Assessment Scales, Second Edition (RIAS–2). We also illustrate some shortcut procedures that teachers can use to estimate the reliability of their classroom tests.

Practice Items

1. Consider these data for a 5-item test that was administered to 6 students. Each item could receive a score ranging from 1 or 0. Calculate KR-20 using the following formula:

$$\text{KR--}20 = \frac{K}{K-1}\left(\frac{\text{SD}^2 - \Sigma\, p_i * q_i}{\text{SD}^2}\right)$$

where:

k = number of items
SD^2 = variance of total test scores
p_i = proportion of correct responses on item
q_i = proportion of incorrect responses on item

	Item #1	Item #2	Item #3	Item #4	Item #5	Total score
Student 1	0	1	1	0	1	
Student 2	1	1	1	1	1	
Student 3	1	0	1	0	0	
Student 4	0	0	0	1	0	
Student 5	1	1	1	1	1	
Student 6	1	1	0	1	0	
p_i						SD^2
q_i						
$p_i * q_i$						

Note: When calculating SD^2, use n in the denominator

2. Consider these data for a 5-item test that was administered to 6 students. Each item could receive a score ranging from 1 to 5. Calculate Coefficient Alpha using the following formula:

$$\text{Coefficient alpha} = \left(\frac{k}{k-1}\right)\left(1 - \frac{\sum SD_i^2}{SD^2}\right)$$

where:

k = number of items
SD_i^2 = variance of individual items
SD^2 = variance of total test scores

	Item #1	Item #2	Item #3	Item #4	Item #5	Total score
Student 1	4	5	4	5	5	
Student 2	3	3	2	3	2	
Student 3	2	3	1	2	1	
Student 4	4	4	5	5	4	
Student 5	2	3	2	2	3	
Student 6	1	2	2	1	3	
SD_i^2						$SD^2 =$

Note: When calculating SD_i^2 and SD^2, use n in the denominator

References

American Educational Research Association, American Psychological Association, & National Council on Measurement in Education. (2014). *Standards for educational and psychological testing*. Washington, DC: American Educational Research Association.
Crocker, L., & Algina, J. (1986). *Introduction to classical and modern test theory*. Belmont, CA: Wadsworth.
Cronbach, L., Rajaratnam, N., & Gieser, G. (1963). Theory of generalizability: A liberalization of reliability theory. *British Journal of Statistical Psychology, 16*(2), 137–163.
Cronbach, L. J. (1951). Coefficient alpha and the internal structure of tests. *Psychometrika, 16*, 297–334.
Cronbach, L. J. (1990). *Essentials of psychological testing* (5th ed.). New York, NY: HarperCollins.
Deiderich, P. B. (1973). *Short-cut statistics for teacher-made tests*. Princeton, NJ: Educational Testing Service.
Dudek, F. (1979). The continuing misinterpretation of the standard error of measurement. *Psychological Bulletin, 86*(2), 335–337.
Ghiselli, E. E., Campbell, J. P., & Zedeck, S. (1981). *Measurement theory for the behavioral sciences*. San Francisco, CA: W.H. Freeman.

Glutting, J., McDermott, P., & Stanley, J. (1987). Resolving differences among methods of establishing confidence limits for test scores. *Educational and Psychological Measurement, 47*(3), 607–614.

Gronlund, N. E. (2003). *Assessment of student achievement* (7th ed.). Boston, MA: Allyn & Bacon.

Guilford, J. (1936). *Psychometric methods*. New York, NY: McGraw-Hill.

Gulliksen, H. (1950). *Theory of mental tests*. New York, NY: Wiley.

Hays, W. (1994). *Statistics* (5th ed.). New York, NY: Harcourt Brace.

Hoover, H. D., Dunbar, S. B., & Frisbie, D. A. (2001). *Iowa test of basic skills*. Itasca, IL: Riverside.

Hopkins, K. D. (1998). *Educational and psychological measurement and evaluation* (8th ed.). Boston, MA: Allyn & Bacon.

Kamphaus, R. W. (2005). *Clinical assessment of child and adolescent intelligence*. New York, NY: Springer.

Kaufman, A. S., & Lichtenberger, E. O. (1999). *Essentials of WAIS-III assessment*. New York, NY: Wiley.

Keith, T. Z., & Reynolds, C. R. (1990). Measurement and design issues in child assessment research. In C. R. Reynolds & R. W. Kamphaus (Eds.), *Handbook of psychological and educational assessment of children: Intelligence and achievement* (pp. 29–62). New York, NY: Guilford Press.

Kuder, G. F., & Richardson, M. W. (1937). The theory of the estimation of reliability. *Psychometrika, 2*, 151–160.

Linn, R. L., & Gronlund, N. E. (2000). *Measurement and assessment in teaching* (8th ed.). Upper Saddle River, NJ: Prentice Hall.

Lord, F. M., & Novick, M. R. (1968). *Statistical theories of mental test scores*. Reading, MA: Addison-Wesley.

Magnusson, D. (1967). *Test theory*. Reading, MA: Addison-Wesley.

Nunnally, J. C. (1978). *Psychometric theory* (2nd ed.). New York, NY: McGraw-Hill.

Nunnally, J. C., & Bernstein, I. H. (1994). *Psychometric theory* (3rd ed.). New York, NY: McGraw-Hill.

Osterlind, S. J. (2006). *Modern measurement: Theory, principles, and applications of mental appraisal*. Upper Saddle River, NJ: Pearson.

Reynolds, C. R. (1999). Inferring causality from relational data and design: Historical and contemporary lessons for research and clinical practice. *The Clinical Neuropsychologist, 13*, 386–395.

Reynolds, C. R., & Kamphaus, R. W. (2015). *Reynolds Intellectual Assessment Scales* (2nd ed.). Lutz, FL: Psychological Assessment Resources.

Roid, G. H. (2003). *Stanford-Binet Intelligence Scale* (5th ed.). Itasca, IL: Riverside.

Saupe, J. L. (1961). Some useful estimates of the Kuder-Richardson formula number 20 reliability coefficient. *Educational and Psychological Measurement, 2*, 63–72.

Sireci, S. G., Thissen, D., & Wainer, H. (1991). On the reliability of testlet-based tests. *Journal of Educational Measurement, 28*, 237–247.

Spearman, C. (1907). Demonstration of formulae for true measurement of correlation. *The American Journal of Psychology, 18*(2), 161–169.

Spearman, C. (1913). Correlations of sums or differences. *British Journal of Psychology, 5*, 417–426.

Thorndike, R. (1949). *Personnel selection: Test and measurement techniques*. Oxford, England: Wiley.

Thurstone, L. (1931). *The reliability and validity of tests: Derivation and interpretation of fundamental formulae concerned with reliability and validity of tests and illustrative problems*. Ann Arbor, MI: Edwards Brothers.

Wechsler, D. (1997). *Wechsler adult intelligence scale* (3rd ed.). San Antonio, TX: Psychological Corporation.

Wilkinson, L., & Task Force on Statistical Inferences. (1999). Statistical methods in psychology journals: Guidelines and explanations. *American Psychologist, 54*(8), 594–604.

Recommended Reading

American Educational Research Association, American Psychological Association, & National Council on Measurement in Education. (2014). *Standards for educational and psychological testing*. Washington, DC: AERA. Chapter 2: Reliability/Precision and Errors of Measurement is a great resource!

Feldt, L. S., & Brennan, R. L. (1989). Reliability. In R. L. Linn (Ed.), *Educational measurement* (3rd ed., pp. 105–146). Upper Saddle River, NJ: Merrill/Prentice Hall. A little technical at times, but a great resource for students wanting to learn more about reliability.

Ghiselli, E. E., Campbell, J. P., & Zedeck, S. (1981). *Measurement theory for the behavioral sciences*. San Francisco, CA: Freeman. Chapters 8 and 9 provide outstanding discussions of reliability. A classic!

Nunnally, J. C., & Bernstein, I. H. (1994). *Psychometric theory* (3rd ed.). New York, NY: McGraw-Hill. Chapter 6: The Theory of Measurement Error and Chapter 7: The Assessment of Reliability are outstanding chapters! Another classic!

Subkoviak, M. J. (1984). Estimating the reliability of mastery-nonmastery classifications. In R. A. Berk (Ed.), *A guide to criterion-referenced test construction* (pp. 267–291). Baltimore, MD: Johns Hopkins University Press. An excellent discussion of techniques for estimating the consistency of classification with mastery tests.

Validity

5

Validity refers to the degree to which evidence and theory support interpretations of test scores for the proposed uses of the test. Validity is, therefore, the most fundamental consideration in developing and evaluating tests.

Abstract

Validity is a fundamental psychometric property of psychological tests. For any given test, the term validity refers to evidence that supports interpretation of test results as reflecting the psychological construct(s) the test was designed to measure. Validity is threatened when the test does not measure important aspects of the construct of interest, or when the test measures characteristics, content, or skills that are unrelated to the test construct. A test must produce reliable test scores to produce valid interpretations, but even highly reliable tests may produce invalid interpretations. This chapter considers these matters in depth, including various types of validity and validity evidence, sources of validity evidence, and integration of validity evidence across different sources to support a validity argument for the test. The chapter ends with a practical discussion of how validity evidence is reported in test manuals, using as an example the Reynolds Intellectual Assessment Scales, second edition.

Supplementary Information The online version of this chapter (https://doi.org/10.1007/978-3-030-59455-8_5) contains supplementary material, which is available to authorized users.

Learning Objectives

After reading and studying this chapter, students should be able to:

1. Define validity and explain its importance in the context of psychological assessment.
2. Describe major threats to validity.
3. Explain the relationship between reliability and validity.
4. Trace the development of the contemporary conceptualization of validity.
5. Describe five categories of validity evidence specified in the 1999 Standards.
6. For each category of validity evidence, give an example to illustrate the type of information provided.
7. Explain how validity coefficients are interpreted.
8. Define the standard error of estimate and explain its interpretation.
9. Describe steps in factor analysis and how factor analytic results can contribute evidence of validity.
10. Explain how validity evidence is integrated to develop a sound validity argument.
11. Review validity evidence presented in a test manual and evaluate usefulness of the test scores for specific purposes.

In the previous chapter, we introduced you to the concept of the reliability/precision, (i.e., the accuracy and consistency of measurement). Now we turn our attention to validity, another fundamental psychometric property. Messick (1989) defined **validity** as "an integrated evaluative judgment of the degree to which empirical evidence and theoretical rationales support the adequacy and appropriateness of inferences and actions based on test scores or other modes of assessment" (p. 13). Similarly, the Standards for Educational and Psychological Testing (AERA et al., 2014) defined validity as "the degree to which evidence and theory support the interpretations of test scores for proposed uses of the tests" (p. 11). Reynolds (1998) defines validity similarly, arguing that validity refers to the appropriateness and accuracy of the interpretation of performance on a test, such performance usually expressed as a test score. Validity is illustrated in the following series of questions: If test scores are interpreted as reflecting intelligence, do they actually reflect intellectual ability? If test scores are interpreted as reflecting depressed mood, do they actually reflect a client's level of depression? If test scores are

> Validity refers to the appropriateness or accuracy of the interpretation of test scores.

used (i.e., interpreted) to predict success in college, can they accurately predict who will succeed in college? Naturally, the validity of the interpretations of test scores is directly tied to the usefulness of the interpretations. Valid interpretations help us to make better decisions; invalid interpretations do not!

There is a consensus in the profession of psychometrics that older concepts of validity as referring to a test are abandoned in favor of an approach that emphasizes that validity refers to the appropriateness or accuracy of the interpretations of *test scores*. In other words, it is not technically correct to refer to the validity of a test. Validity is a characteristic of the interpretations given to test scores. As a result, it is not technically correct to ask the question "Is the Wechsler Intelligence Scale for Children—Fifth Edition (WISC-V) a valid test?" It is preferable to ask the question "Is the interpretation of performance on the WISC-V as reflecting intelligence valid?" Validity must always have a context and that context is interpretation. What does performance on this test mean? The answer to this question is the interpretation given to performance and it is this interpretation that possesses the construct of validity, not the test itself.

Additionally, when test scores are interpreted in multiple ways, each interpretation needs to be validated. For example, an achievement test can be used to evaluate a student's performance in academic classes, to assign the student to an appropriate instructional program,

> When test scores are interpreted in multiple ways, each interpretation needs to be evaluated.

to diagnose a learning disability, or to predict success in college. Each of these uses involves different interpretations and the validity of each interpretation needs to be evaluated (AERA et al., 2014).

To establish or determine validity is a major responsibility of the test authors, test publisher, researchers, and even test user. A test manual presents essentially a summary of evidence for espoused interpretations of test scores, as the evidence is known at the time the manual is prepared. However, validation is a process; one that involves an ongoing, dynamic effort to accumulate evidence for a sound scientific basis for proposed test score interpretations (AERA et al., 2014; Reynolds, 1998). Validation is not then static but a constantly moving target. Validation continues in the scientific literature and test users should not be constrained by the necessary limitations imposed on information in a test manual and should follow the accumulated literature of the ongoing process of validation. This premise is also supported in the *Standards* (AERA et al., 2014) which note "validation is the joint responsibility of the test developer and test user" (p. 13).

We will alert you to the fact that this chapter is one of the longest you will read in this text—however, validity is the most important of all psychometric characteristics and misconstrued surprisingly often by practicing professional psychologists. Since we have introduced you to the central issue of validity, you might be interested in knowing how psychological tests compare to medical tests in terms of validity. You might be surprised with the answer to this question! Special Interest Topic 5.1 provides a brief overview of a research article that examines this issue.

Special Interest Topic 5.1: Are Psychological Tests as Accurate as Medical Tests?
Many if not most people assume that tests used by medical professionals are more reliable and valid than those used by psychologists. That is, medical tests such as magnetic resonance imaging (MRI), X-rays, Pap smears, and electrocardiograms provide more reliable and accurate results than common psychological tests such as intelligence, neuropsychological, and personality tests. However, Meyer et al. (2001) reviewed research that examined the validity of a large number of medical and psychological tests and concluded that psychological tests often provide results that equal or exceed the validity of medical tests. For example, the Pap smear test that is used to detect cervical abnormalities produces an effect size of 0.36 while the average ability of scores from the Minnesota Multiphasic Personality Inventory—2 to detect depressive or psychotic disorders has an effect size of 0.37 (larger effect sizes indicate superior validity). Even when you examine the validity of medical and psychological tests to detect the same disorder, psychological tests can provide superior results. For example, the effect size of MRI results in detecting dementia is 0.57 while the effect size for neuropsychological tests in detecting dementia is 0.68. This paper reports effect sizes for over 140 medical and psychological tests. So the answer to the question is *"Yes, psychological tests can provide information that is as valid as common medical tests."*

5.1 Threats to Validity

Messick (1994) and others have identified the two major threats to validity as construct underrepresentation and construct-irrelevant variance. To translate this into everyday language, validity is threatened when a test measures either less (construct underrepresentation) or more (construct-irrelevant variance) of the construct it is supposed to measure (AERA et al., 2014). ***Construct underrepresentation*** occurs when a test does not measure important aspects of the specified construct (later, in Chap. 6, we will explain in detail how to avoid this problem if you are developing a test). Consider a test

> Validity is threatened when a test measures either less or more than the construct it is intended to measure.

designed to be a comprehensive measure of the mathematics skills covered in a third-grade curriculum and to convey information regarding mastery of each skill. If the test contained only division problems, it would not be an adequate representation of the broad array of math skills typically covered in a third-grade curriculum (although a score on such a test may predict performance on a more comprehensive measure). Division is an important aspect of the math curriculum, but not the only important aspect. To address this problem, the content of the test would need to be expanded to reflect all of the skills typically taught in a third-grade math curriculum.

Construct-irrelevant variance is present when the test measures characteristics, content, or skills that are unrelated to the test construct. For example, if our third--grade math test has extensive and complex written instructions, it is possible that in addition to math skills, reading comprehension skills are being measured. If the test is intended to measure only math skills, the inclusion of reading comprehension would reflect construct-irrelevant variance. To address this problem, one might design the test to minimize written instructions and to ensure the reading level is low. As you might imagine, most tests leave out some aspects that some users might view as important and include aspects that some users view as irrelevant (AERA et al., 2014).

In addition to characteristics of the test itself, factors external to the test can impact the validity of the interpretation of results. Linn and Gronlund (2000) identified numerous factors external to the test that can influence validity. They highlight the following factors:

5.1.1   Examinee Characteristics

Any personal factors that alter or restrict the examinees' responses in the testing situation can undermine validity. For example, if examinees experience high levels of test anxiety this may impact their performance on a maximum-performance test. Low motivation might also impact the validity of interpretations based on maximum--performance tests. The same principle applies to typical response tests. For example, instead of responding in a truthful manner when completing a personality test, a client might attempt to present him or herself in either a more pathological (i.e., fake-bad) or a less pathological manner (i.e., fake-good). All of these can undermine validity.

5.1.2   Test Administration and Scoring Procedures

Deviations from standard administrative and scoring procedures can undermine validity. In terms of administration, failure to provide the appropriate instructions or follow strict time limits can lower validity. To accommodate the special needs of individuals with disabilities, there are occasions when it is appropriate to modify standard administrative procedures. However, even in these situations, it is required that examiners provide evidence that the validity of score interpretations is not compromised (Lee, Reynolds, & Willson, 2003). In terms of scoring, unreliable or biased scoring can lower validity.

5.1.3   Instruction and Coaching

In addition to the content of the test influencing validity, prior instruction and or coaching can also impact validity. For example, consider a test of critical thinking skills. If the examinees were coached and given solutions to the particular problems included on a test, validity would be compromised. Recall that a test presents a sample of the domain of potential questions related to a specific construct, so if someone takes this sample of questions and teaches the examinees how to respond, the test is no longer useful in determining where the examinee stands on the construct represented by the item sample. This is a potential problem when educators "teach the test" and when attorneys sometimes obtain copies of tests and coach their clients in particular ways to answer so as to present themselves in a way favorable to their legal case.

Additionally, the validity of norm-referenced interpretations of performance on a test is influenced by the appropriateness of the reference group, aka, standardization sample (AERA et al., 2014). As these examples illustrate, a multitude of factors can influence the validity of assessment-based interpretations. Due to the cumulative influence of these factors, validity is not an all-or-none concept. Rather, it exists on a continuum, and we usually refer to degrees of validity or to the relative validity of the interpretation(s) given to a particular measurement.

> Validity is not an all-or-none concept, but exists on a continuum.

5.2   Reliability and Validity

In the preceding chapter, we addressed the issue of the reliability of measurement. Reliability refers to the stability, consistency, and accuracy of test scores and reflects the amount of random measurement error present. Reliability is a necessary but insufficient condition for validity. A test that does not produce reliable scores cannot produce valid interpretations. However, no matter how reliable measurement is, it does not guarantee validity. From our discussion of reliability, you will remember that obtained score variance is composed of two components: true score variance and error variance. Only true score variance is reliable, and only true score variance can be related systematically to any construct the test is designed to measure. If reliability is equal to zero, then the true score variance component must also be equal to zero, leaving our obtained score to be composed only of error, that is, random variations in responses. Thus, without reliability, there can be no validity.

> Reliability is a necessary but insufficient condition for validity.

Reliability also places limits on the magnitude of validity coefficients when a test score is correlated with variables external to the test itself, e.g., if we compute the correlation between an IQ and achievement in reading. In such research, the internal consistency reliability coefficient imposes a theoretical limit on the true value of the correlation that is equal to the square root of the reliability coefficient, i.e., maximum correlation $= \sqrt{r_{xx}}$.

Although low reliability limits validity, high reliability does not ensure validity. It is entirely possible that a test can produce reliable scores but inferences based on the test scores can be completely invalid. Consider the following rather silly example involving head circumference. If we use some care we can measure the circumferences of our clients' heads in a reliable and consistent manner. In other words, the measurement is reliable. However, if we considered head circumference to be an index of intelligence, our inferences would not be valid. The measurement of head circumference is still reliable, but when interpreted as a measure of intelligence it would result in invalid inferences.

A more relevant example can be seen in the various intelligence scales that produce highly reliable verbal and nonverbal scales. There is also a rather substantial body of research demonstrating these scores are interpreted appropriately as reflecting types of intelligence. However, some psychologists have drawn the inference that score differences between the verbal and nonverbal scales indicate some fundamental information about personality and even forms of psychopathology. For example, one author argued that a person who scores higher on the verbal scale relative to the nonverbal scale by 15 points or more is highly likely to have an obsessive-compulsive personality disorder! There is no evidence or research to support such an interpretation, and, in fact, a large percentage of the population of the United States score higher on the verbal scales relative to the nonverbal scales (about 12.5% in fact on the scale in question here). Thus, while the scores are themselves highly reliable and some interpretations are highly valid (the scales measure intellectual ability), other interpretations wholly lack validity despite the presence of high reliability.

5.3   "Types of Validity" Versus "Types of Validity Evidence"

We have already introduced you to the influential *Standards for Educational and Psychological Testing* (AERA et al., 2014). This is actually the latest in a series of documents providing guidelines for the development and use of tests. At this point, we are going to trace the evolution of the concept of validity briefly by highlighting how it has been defined and described in this series of documents. In the early versions (i.e., APA, 1954, 1966; AERA et al., 1974, 1985), validity was divided into three distinct types. As described by Messick (1989), these are:

> Validity is a unitary concept.

- *Content validity* involves how adequately the test samples the content area of the identified construct. In other words, is the content of the test relevant and representative of the content domain? We speak of it being representative because every possible question that could be asked cannot as a practical matter be asked, so questions are chosen to sample or represent the full domain of questions. Content validity is typically based on professional judgments about the appropriateness of the test content.
- *Criterion-related validity* involves examining the relationships between the test and external variables that are thought to be direct measures of the construct. Studies of criterion-related validity empirically examine the relationships between test scores and criterion scores using correlation or regression analyses.
- *Construct validity* involves an integration of evidence that relates to the meaning or interpretation of test scores. This evidence can be collected using a wide variety of research strategies and designs.

This classification terminology has been widely accepted by researchers, authors, teachers, and students and is often referred to as the traditional nomenclature (AERA et al., 2014). However, in the late 1970s and 1980s, measurement professionals began moving toward a conceptualization of validity as a unitary concept. That is, whereas we previously had talked about different types of validity (i.e., content, criterion-related, and construct validity), these "types" really only represent different ways of collecting evidence to support the validity of interpretations of performance on a test, which we commonly express as a test score. To emphasize the view of validity as a unitary concept and get away from the perception of distinct types of validity, the 1985 *Standards for Educational and Psychological Testing* (APA et al., 1985) referred to "types of validity evidence" in place of "types of validity." Instead of content validity, criterion-related validity, and construct validity, the 1985 *Standards* referred to content-related evidence of validity, criterion-related evidence of validity, and construct-related evidence of validity. In the most recent editions of the *Standards* (AERA et al., 1999, 2014), validity is described as: ".....a unitary concept. It is the degree to which all of the accumulated evidence supports the intended interpretation of test scores for the proposed use" (p. 14).

While the concept remains similar (i.e., "types of validity evidence" versus "types of validity"), the terminology has expanded and evolved somewhat. The change in terminology is not simply cosmetic, but is substantive and intended to promote a new way of conceptualizing validity, a view that has gained traction over the past several decades. The 2014 *Standards* identifies the following five categories of evidence that are related to the validity of test score interpretations:

- *Evidence based on test content* includes evidence derived from an analysis of the test content, which includes the type of questions or tasks included in the test and administration and scoring guidelines.
- *Evidence based on response processes* includes evidence derived from an analysis of the processes engaged in by the examinee when answering test items, or by the examiner when recording or judging the examinee's performance on the item.
- *Evidence based on internal structure* includes evidence regarding relationships among test items and components.
- *Evidence based on relations to other variables* includes evidence based on an examination of the relationships between test performance and external variables or criteria.
- *Evidence based on consequences of testing* includes evidence based on an examination of the intended and unintended consequences of testing.

These sources of evidence differ in their importance or relevance according to factors such as the construct being measured, the intended use of the test scores, and the population being assessed. Those using tests should carefully weigh the evidence of validity and

> Sources of validity evidence differ in their importance according to factors such as the construct being measured, the intended use of the test scores, and the population being assessed.

Table 5.1 Tracing historical trends in the concept of validity

1974 Standards: validity as three types	1985 Standards: validity as three interrelated types	1999 and 2014 Standards: validity as a unitary construct
Content validity	Content-related validity	Validity evidence based on test content
Criterion validity	Criterion-related validity	Validity evidence-based relations to other variables
Construct validity	Construct-related validity	Validity evidence based on response processes
		Validity evidence based on internal structure
		Validity evidence based on consequences of testing

make judgments about how appropriate a test is for each application and setting. Table 5.1 provides a brief summary of the different classification schemes that have been promulgated over the past four decades in the *Standards*.

At this point you might be asking, "Why are the authors wasting my time with a discussion of the history of technical jargon?" There are at least two important reasons. First, it is likely that in your readings and studies you will come across references to various "types of validity." Many older test and measurement textbooks refer to content, criterion, and construct validity, and some newer texts still use that or a similar nomenclature. We hope that when you come across different terminology you will not be confused, but instead will understand its meaning and origin. Second, the *Standards* are widely accepted and serve as professional guidelines for the development and evaluation of tests. For legal and ethical reasons test developers and publishers generally want to adhere to these guidelines. Several of the major scientific journals in the field of tests and measurements (e.g., *Educational and Psychological Measurement* and *Psychological Assessment*) require all published manuscripts to conform to the language recommendations of the *Standards*. A review of recently released tests shows that many test publishers have adopted the new nomenclature as well (e.g., Reynolds & Kamphaus, 2015). However, older tests typically have supporting literature that uses the older terminology, and you need to understand its origin and meaning. When reviewing test manuals and assessing the psychometric properties of a test, you need to be aware of the older as well as the newer terminology.

5.4   Sources of Validity Evidence

5.4.1   Evidence Based on Test Content

The *Standards* (AERA et al., 2014) note that valuable validity evidence can be gained by examining the relationship between the content of the test and the construct or domain the test is designed to measure. In this context, "test content includes the themes, wording, and format of the items, tasks, or questions on a test," as well as administration and scoring rules (p. 14). Other writers provide similar descriptions. For example, Reynolds (1998) notes that validity evidence based on test content focuses on how well the test items sample the behaviors or subject matter the test is designed to measure. In a simi-

> Valuable validity evidence can be gained by examining the relationship between the content of the test and the construct it is designed to measure.

lar vein, Anastasi and Urbina (1997) note that validity evidence based on test content involves the examination of the content of the test to determine whether it provides a representative sample of the domain being measured. Popham (2000) succinctly frames it as "Does the test cover the content it's supposed to cover?" (p. 96). In the past, this type of validity evidence was primarily subsumed under the label "content validity."

Test developers routinely begin considering the appropriateness of the content of the test at the earliest stages of development. Identifying what we want to measure is the first order of business, because we cannot measure anything very well that we have not first clearly defined. Therefore, the process of developing a test should begin with a clear delineation of the con-

> Item relevance and content coverage are two important factors to be considered when evaluating the correspondence between the test content and its construct.

struct or content domain to be measured. Once the construct or content domain has been clearly defined, the next step is to develop a *table of specifications*. This table of specifications is essentially a blueprint that guides the development of the test. It delineates the topics and objectives to be covered and the relative importance of each topic and objective. Finally, working from this table of specifications the test developers write the actual test items. Professional test developers often bring in external consultants who are considered experts in the content area(s) covered by the test. For example, if the goal is to develop an achievement test covering American history, the test developers will likely recruit experienced teachers of American history for assistance developing a table of specifications and writing test items. If the goal is to develop a typical response scale to assess the presence of symptoms associated with a psychological disorder (e.g., depression, anxiety), the test developers will typically recruit expert consultants to help review the clinical and research literature and develop items designed to assess the theoretical construct being measured. If care is taken with these procedures, the foundation is established for a correspondence between the content of the test and the construct it is designed to measure. Test developers may include a detailed description of their procedures for writing items as validity evidence, including the number, qualifications, and credentials of their expert consultants.

After the test is written, it is common for test developers to continue collecting validity evidence based on content. This typically involves having expert judges systematically review the test and evaluate the correspondence between the test content and its construct or domain. These experts can be the same ones who helped

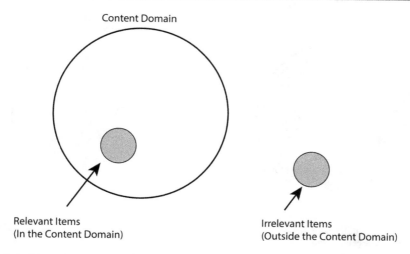

Fig. 5.1   Illustration of item relevance

during the early phase of test construction or a new, independent group of experts. During this phase, the experts typically address two major issues, item relevance and content coverage. To assess item relevance, the experts examine each individual test item and determine whether it reflects essential content in the specified domain. To assess content coverage, the experts look at the overall test and rate the degree to which the items cover the specified domain. To understand the difference between these two issues, consider these examples. For a test intended to assess obsessive--compulsive symptoms, a question about the presence and frequency of ritualistic handwashing would clearly be deemed a relevant item whereas a question about calculating algebraic equations would be judged to be irrelevant. This distinction deals with the relevance of the items to the construct or content domain. In contrast, if you examined the total test and determined that all of the questions dealt with the ritualistic behaviors and no other obsessive-compulsive symptoms were covered, you would conclude that the test had poor content coverage. That is, because obsessions and compulsions include many important symptoms in addition to ritualistic behaviors that are not covered in the test, the test does not reflect a comprehensive and representative sample of the specified construct or content domain. The concepts of item relevance and content coverage are illustrated in Figs. 5.1 and 5.2.

As you can see, the collection of content-based validity evidence is typically qualitative in nature. Test publishers might rely on traditional qualitative approaches, such as the judgment of expert judges to help develop the tests and subsequently to evaluate the completed test. However, they can take steps to report their results in a more quantitative manner. For example, they can report the number and qualifications of the experts, the number of chances the experts had to review and comment on the assessment, and their

> Content-based validity evidence is often the preferred approach for establishing the validity of achievement tests and tests used in the selection and classification of employees.

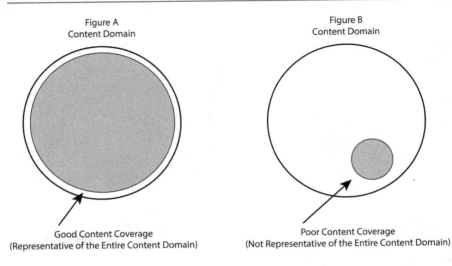

Fig. 5.2 Illustration of content coverage

degree of agreement on content-related issues. Taking these efforts a step further, Lawshe (1975) developed a quantitative index that reflects the degree of agreement among the experts making content-related judgments. Newer approaches are being developed that use a fairly sophisticated technique known as multidimensional scaling analysis (Sireci, 1998).

As we suggested previously, different types of validity evidence are most relevant, appropriate, or important for different types of tests. For example, content-based validity evidence is often seen as the preferred approach for establishing the validity of academic achievement tests. This applies to both teacher-made classroom tests and professionally developed achievement tests. Another situation in which content-based evidence is of primary importance is with tests used in the selection and classification of employees. For example, employment tests may be designed to sample the knowledge and skills necessary to succeed at a job. In this context, content-based evidence can be used to demonstrate consistency between the content of the test and the requirements of the job. The key factor that makes content-based validity evidence of paramount importance with both achievement tests and employment tests is that they are designed to provide a representative sample of the knowledge, behavior, or skill domain being measured. In contrast, content-based evidence of validity is usually less important, though certainly not unimportant, for personality and aptitude tests (Anastasi & Urbina, 1997).

5.4.1.1 Face Validity

Before leaving our discussion of content-based validity evidence, we need to highlight the distinction between it and face validity. *Face validity* is an older term that you may yet encounter. It is technically not a form of validity at all, but instead refers to a test "appearing" to measure what it is designed to measure. That is, does the test appear valid to untrained individuals who take, administer, or examine the test? Face validity really has nothing to do with what a test actually measures, just what it appears to measure. For example, does a test of personality look the way that the general public expects a personality test to look? Does a test of intelligence look like the general public expects an intelligence test to look? Naturally, the face

> Face validity is not technically a form of validity, but refers to a test "appearing" to measure what it is designed to measure.

validity of a test is closely tied to the content of a test. In terms of face validity, when untrained individuals inspect a test they are typically looking to see whether the items on the test are what they expect. Whereas content-based evidence of validity is acquired through a systematic and technical analysis of the test content, face validity involves only the superficial appearance of a test. A test can appear "face valid" to the general public, but not hold up under the systematic scrutiny involved in a technical analysis of the test content.

This is not to suggest that face validity is an undesirable or even irrelevant characteristic. A test that has good face validity is likely to be better received by the general public. If a test appears to measure what it is designed to measure, examinees are more likely to be cooperative and invested in the testing process, and the public is more likely to view the results as meaningful (Anastasi & Urbina, 1997). Research suggests that on maximum-performance tests, good face validity can increase examinee motivation, which in turn can increase test performance (Chan, Schmitt, DeShon, Clause, & Delbridge, 1997). If a test has poor face validity, those using the test may have a flippant or negative attitude toward the test, and as a result, put little effort into completing it. If this happens, the actual validity of the test can suffer. The general public is not likely to view a test with poor face validity as meaningful, even if there is technical support for the validity of the test.

There are times, however, when face validity is undesirable. These occur primarily in forensic settings in which detection of malingering may be emphasized. Malingering is a situation in which an examinee intentionally feigns symptoms of a mental or physical disorder in order to gain some external incentive (e.g., receiving a financial reward, avoiding punishment). In these situations, face validity is not desirable because it may help the examinee fake pathological responses. In fact, false forms of face validity are useful in detecting malingered responses (see Chap. 6 for an explanation).

5.4.2   Evidence Based on Response Processes

Validity evidence based on the response processes invoked by a test involves an analysis of the fit between the performance and actions the examinees actually engage in and the construct being assessed. Although this type of validity evidence has not received as much attention as some of the other approaches for establishing validity evidence, it has considerable potential, and in terms of the traditional nomenclature, it would likely be classified under construct validity. For example, consider a test designed to measure mathematical reasoning ability. In this situation, it would be important to investigate the examinees' response processes to verify that they are actually engaging in analysis and reasoning as opposed to applying rote mathematical algorithms (AERA et al., 2014). There are numerous ways of collecting this type of validity evidence, including interviewing examinees about their response processes and strategies, recording behavioral indicators such as response times and eye movements, or even analyzing the types of errors committed (AERA et al., 2014; Messick, 1989).

The *Standards* (AERA et al., 2014) note that studies of response processes are not restricted to individuals taking the test, but may also examine the assessment professionals who administer or grade the tests. When testing personnel record or evaluate the performance of examinees, it is important to make sure that their processes or actions are in line with the construct being measured. For example, many tests provide specific criteria or rubrics that are intended to guide the scoring process. The Wechsler Individual Achievement Test—Third Edition (WIAT-III; Pearson, 2009) includes a task that requires the examinee to write a short essay. To facilitate grading, the authors include an analytic scoring rubric that includes several evaluative categories, including the use of multiple paragraphs, an introduction (including a thesis statement and summary), transitions that show the relationships between ideas, reasons that support the thesis, elaborations that support each reason, and a conclusion that includes a thesis statement and a summary of the reasons presented. These rubrics help to ensure consistency of scoring by those evaluating the essays and help to avoid giving credit to irrelevant factors are not indicative of the examinee's ability to write good essays.

5.4.3   Evidence Based on Internal Structure

By examining the internal structure of a test (or battery of tests), one can determine whether the relationships between test items (or, in the case of test batteries, component tests) are consistent with the construct the test is designed to measure (AERA et al., 2014). For example, one test might be designed to measure a construct that is hypothesized to involve a single dimension, whereas another test might measure a construct thought to involve multiple dimensions. By examining the internal structure of the test, we can determine whether its actual structure is consistent with the hypothesized structure of the construct it measures. Factor analysis is a sophisticated statistical procedure used to determine the number of conceptually distinct factors or dimensions underlying a test or battery of tests. Since factor analysis is a prominent approach to collecting validity evidence based on internal structure, we will briefly discuss it.

5.4.3.1 Factor Analysis: A Gentle Introduction

As noted, factor analysis plays a prominent role in test validation. The Standards (AERA et al., 2014) defines factor analysis as:

Any of several statistical methods describing the interrelationships of a set of variables by statistically deriving new variables, called factors, that are fewer in number than the original set of variables. (p. 219)

Reynolds and Kamphaus (2003) provide a slightly more theoretical definition, noting that factor analysis is a statistical approach that allows one to evaluate the presence and structure of any latent constructs existing among a set of variables. These definitions are in agreement, because in factor analysis terminology a factor is a hypothetical variable reflecting a latent construct—the factor underlies and is at least partly responsible for the way examinees respond to questions on the variables that make up the factor. The mathematical process of factor analysis scrutinizes the intercorrelation matrix of a set of variables to see if patterns of relationships emerge that are useful in explaining any patterns of test scores that may occur. The "set of variables" mentioned in these explanations can be either the individual items of a test or the subtest scores of a test battery. For example, a hypothetical personality test with 200 individual items might be analyzed with the results indicating that five factors, or dimensions, exist among the items. In the chapter on personality assessment, we will describe the "Five-Factor Model" that posits that five major factors or dimensions underlie the construct of personality (i.e., neuroticism, extraversion, openness to experience, agreeableness, and conscientiousness). If the author of our hypothetical personality test had developed the personality test based on the Five-- Factor Model, the results of this factor analysis can be used to support the validity of the test. The test author can also develop five-factor scores that summarize examinees' responses on the test.

Factor analysis can also be applied to the subtest scores of a test battery. This is often pursued with intelligence and other maximum-performance test batteries (e.g., neuropsychological batteries). For example, the Reynolds Intellectual Assessment Scale, Second Edition (RIAS–2, Reynolds & Kamphaus, 2015) is a battery that contains eight subtests. Based on factor analytic studies, the subtests of the RIAS–2 can be used to identify five different factor-based scores:

- *Verbal Intelligence Index*: Provides a summary estimate of verbal intelligence as assessed by verbal reasoning and reflecting primarily crystallized intelligence functions.
- *Nonverbal Intelligence Index*: Provides a summary estimate of nonverbal intelligence as assessed by nonverbal reasoning and reflecting primarily fluid intellectual functions.
- *Composite Intelligence Index*: Provides a summary estimate of global intelligence, designed to estimate g, the general intelligence factor.
- *Composite Memory Index*: Provides a summary estimate of verbal and nonverbal memory functions across a broad array of memory skills.
- *Speeded Processing Index*: Provides a summary estimate of processing speed primarily involving both decision speed and reaction time while minimizing the efforts of fine motor speed.

The RIAS–2 and other intelligence tests will be discussed in more detail in the chapter on the assessment of intelligence.

Table 5.2 Correlation matrix for a hypothetical intelligence test

	Subtest			
	Story Memory	Word List Memory	Visual Analysis	Visual-Spatial Design
Story Memory	1.00	0.52	0.15	0.18
Word List Memory	0.52	1.00	0.14	0.16
Visual Analysis	0.15	0.14	1.00	0.64
Visual-Spatial Design	0.18	0.16	0.64	1.00

5.4.3.2 Factor Analysis: The Process

Factor analysis begins with a table of intercorrelations among the variables (individual items or subtests) that is referred to as a correlation matrix. Table 5.2 is a correlation matrix showing the correlations between two subtests measuring memory (i.e., Story Memory and Word List Memory) and two subtests measuring visual-spatial abilities (i.e., Visual Analysis and Visual-Spatial Design). A review of these correlations reveals that the two memory subtests showed moderate correlations with each other (i.e., $r = 0.52$), but small correlations with the visual-spatial subtests (ranging from 0.14 to 0.18). Likewise, the two visual-spatial subtests showed moderate correlations with each other (i.e., $r = 0.64$), but small correlations with the memory subtests (ranging from 0.14 to 0.18).

Several different factor analytic methods have been developed (often referred to as Factor Extraction Techniques), and each has its own supporters and detractors. For example, Principal Component Analysis (PCA) begins with the assumption that the variables have perfect reliability and places a value of 1.0 in the diagonal of the correlation matrix. With PCA all of the variances is analyzed, including shared variance (i.e., variance shared with other variables), unique variance (i.e., variance unique to individual variables), and error variance (i.e., variance due to measurement error). In contrast, Principal Factor Analysis (PFA) does not assume the variables have perfect reliability and begins by placing the squared multiple correlations of all the other variables with the variable being considered (R^2) in the diagonal of the correlation matrix. With PFA only shared variance is analyzed, with unique and error variance excluded. There are a number of other factor analytic methods available, but when the underlying factor structure is robust, it will typically emerge regardless of which extraction method is used, although the relative strength of the factors will vary across methods.

Once one has selected a factoring technique and applied it to the data, one must determine how many factors to retain. On one hand, the more factors retained, the more variance that is explained by the factor solution. On the other hand, retaining too many factors can result in a complex solution that does not facilitate interpretation. Selecting the number of factor to retain is not as straight forward a process as one might imagine, but researchers have a number of guidelines to help them. One common approach, referred to as the Kaiser-Guttman criteria, is to examine eigenvalues and retain values greater than 1.0. Eigenvalues reflect variance when each variable being analyzed contributes a variance value of 1.0. Retaining factors with

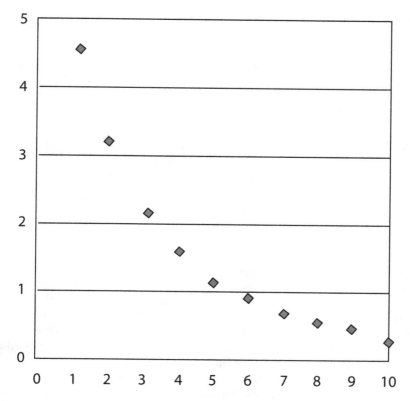

Fig. 5.3 Scree plot

eigenvalues greater than 1.0 ensure that each factor that is retained accounts for more variance than any single variable being analyzed. Another approach to determine how many factors to retain is the scree test (Cattell, 1966). Here factors are plotted on the horizontal axis and eigenvalues are plotted on the vertical axis. The research then examines the graph and looks for an "elbow," a point where previous factors explain substantially more variance than those past the point. Figure 5.3 presents a hypothetical scree plot. Examination of this plot suggests the presence of an elbow at the fifth factor. If you draw a line through the first five points you get a reasonably good fit. However, another line with a different slope would need to be drawn to fit the remaining points. Another important consideration is the interpretability of the factor solution. That is, does the factor solution make sense from a psychological perspective? Put another way, do the variables loading on a factor share a common theme or meaning? For example, on an intelligence test, all the variables loading on a single factor might be measuring verbal processing skills. On a personality test, all the variables loading on a factor might reflect a propensity to experience negative affect. A factor solution that is not interpretable has little or no practical value and will likely provide scant evidence of validity.

Table 5.3 Factor matrix for a hypothetical intelligence test

Subtest	Factor 1	Factor 2
Story Memory	0.77	−0.49
Word List Memory	0.74	−0.52
Visual Analysis	0.62	0.61
Visual-Spatial Design	0.61	0.62

Table 5.4 Rotated factor matrix for a hypothetical intelligence test

Subtest	Factor 1	Factor 2
Story Memory	0.90	0.06
Word List Memory	0.90	0.11
Visual Analysis	0.08	0.87
Visual-Spatial Design	0.09	0.87

All factor extraction methods produce a factor matrix that reflects the correlations between the variables and the factors (i.e., latent constructs). Table 5.3 presents a hypothetical factor matrix. In this example, there are two subtests that measure memory-related abilities (i.e., Story Memory and Word List Memory) and two subtests measure visual processing abilities (i.e., Visual Analysis and Visual-Spatial Design). This initial factor matrix is difficult to interpret. All the subtests have moderate-to-high loadings on Factor One. On Factor Two, first two variables having negative loadings and the second two factors have loadings that approximate their loadings on Factor One. To enhance interpretability (i.e., understanding the meaning of the factors), researchers typically geometrically rotate the axes of the factors. The goals of these rotations are typically to eliminate any large negative loadings and yield a solution where each variable has high loadings on only one factor and small loadings on all other factors (referred to as "simple structure"). If these goals are achieved, the rotated factor pattern should be easier to interpret. Table 5.4 presents a rotated factor pattern for the same subtests presented in Table 5.3. This rotated factor pattern is more interpretable, revealing that the two variables involving memory load on Factor One, and the two variables involving visual processing load on Factor Two. Researchers have a number of options when selecting a rotation method. Some rotation methods produce orthogonal factors that are not correlated. The most popular orthogonal rotation method is the Varimax technique. Other rotation techniques allow oblique factors that can be correlated. Most researchers select orthogonal rotations, but oblique rotations may be appropriate when the factors are correlated in real-world applications (e.g., ability test batteries).

5.4.3.3 Confirmatory Factor Analysis

Our discussion of factor analysis to this point has focused on exploratory factor analysis. As described, exploratory factor analysis examines or "explores" a data set in order to detect the presence and structure of latent constructs existing among a set of variables. Confirmatory factor analysis is an alternative set of procedures that had wide popularity among researchers. With confirmatory factor analysis, the researcher specifies a hypothetical factor structure and then examines the data to see if there is a reasonable fit between the actual and the hypothesized structure of the data set. There are a number of statistics available (referred to as model-fit statistics) that statistically test the fit or match between the actual and hypothesized factor structure. As Cronbach (1990) observed, a positive finding in confirmatory factor analysis does not necessarily indicate that the hypothesized structure is optimal, only that the data does not clearly contradict it. In summary, test publishers and researchers use factor analysis either to confirm or to refute the proposition that the internal structure of the tests is consistent with that of the construct being measured. Later in this chapter, we will describe the results of both exploratory and confirmatory factor analytic studies of the RIAS–2.

Factor analysis is not the only approach researchers use to examine the internal structure of a test. Any technique that allows researchers to examine the relationships between test components can be used in this context. For example, if the items on a test are assumed to reflect a continuum from very easy to very difficult, empirical evidence of a pattern of increasing difficulty can be used as validity evidence. If a test is thought to measure a one-dimensional construct, a measure of item homogeneity might be useful (AERA et al., 2014). The essential feature of this type of validity evidence is that researchers empirically examine the internal structure of the test and compare it to the structure of the construct of interest. This type of validity evidence traditionally has been incorporated under the category of construct validity and is most relevant with tests measuring theoretical constructs such as intelligence or personality.

5.4.4   Evidence Based on Relations to Other Variables

Important validity evidence also can be secured by examining the relationships between test scores and other variables (AERA et al., 2014). In describing this type of validity evidence, the *Standards* recognize several related but fairly distinct applications. These applications include the examination of test-criterion relationships, the examination of convergent and discriminant evidence, and a process known as validity generalization. For clarity, we will address these applications separately.

5.4.4.1 Test-Criterion Relationships
Many tests are designed to predict performance on some variable that is typically referred to as a criterion. The *Standards* define a **criterion** as "a measure of some attribute or outcome that is operationally distinct from the test" (p. 17). The criterion can be academic performance as reflected by the grade point average (GPA), job performance as measured by a supervisor's ratings, or anything else that is of

importance to the user of the test. Historically, this type of validity evidence has been referred to as "predictive validity," "criterion validity," or "criterion-related validity." There are two different types of validity studies typically used to collect test-criterion evidence: predictive studies and concurrent studies. In a ***predictive study,***

> There are two different types of validity studies typically used to collect test-criterion evidence: predictive studies and concurrent studies.

the test is administered, there is an intervening time interval, then the criterion is measured and the relationship between the test and the criterion is then examined. In a ***concurrent study***, the test is administered and the criterion is measured at about the same time and their relationship is examined.

To illustrate these two approaches we will consider the Scholastic Achievement Test (SAT). The SAT is designed to predict how well high school students will perform in college. To complete a predictive study, one might administer the SAT to high school students, wait until the students have completed their freshman year of college, and then examine the relationship between the predictor (i.e., SAT scores) and the criterion (i.e., freshman GPA). Researchers often use a correlation coefficient to examine the relationship between a predictor and a criterion, and in this context, the correlation coefficient is referred to as a validity coefficient. To complete a concurrent study of the relationship between the SAT and college performance, the researcher might administer the SAT to a group of students completing their freshman year and then simply correlate their SAT scores with their GPAs. Another example of these two approaches can be illustrated with the Beck Depression Inventory (BDI). In the predictive approach, one could administer the BDI, wait 9 months, and then examine the relationship between BDI score (predictor) and diagnosis of major depressive disorder 9 months later (criterion). A concurrent study would administer the BDI and correlate its score with current diagnosis

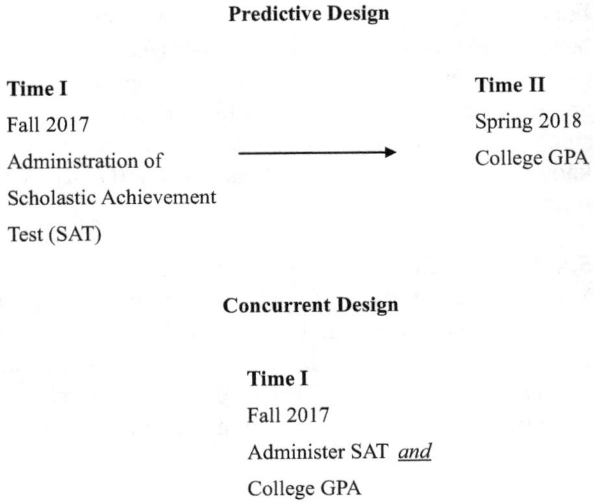

Fig. 5.4 Illustration of predictive and concurrent studies

Predictive Design

Time I

Fall 2017

Administration of

Scholastic Achievement

Test (SAT)

⟶

Time II

Spring 2018

College GPA

Concurrent Design

Time I

Fall 2017

Administer SAT *and*

College GPA

of major depressive disorder. In a predictive study, there is a time interval between the predictor test and the criterion; in a concurrent study, there is no time interval. Figure 5.4 illustrates the temporal relationship between administering the test and measuring the criterion in predictive and concurrent studies.

A natural question is "Which type of study, predictive or concurrent, is best?" As you might expect (or fear), there is no simple answer to that question. Very often in education, clinical psychology, and other settings we are interested in making predictions about future performance. Consider our example of the SAT; the question is which students will do well in college and which will not. For the BDI, you want to know who is at risk for developing major depressive disorder. Inherent in these questions is the passage of time. If you want to administer a test before students graduate from high school that will help predict the likelihood of their success in college, or before they develop depression in order to identify a group that is at increased risk, predictive studies are warranted. This is because predictive studies maintain the temporal relationship and other potentially important characteristics of the real-life situation (AERA et al., 2014).

Because a concurrent study does not retain the temporal relationship or other characteristics of the real-life situation, a predictive study is preferable when prediction is the ultimate goal of assessment. However, predictive studies take considerable time to complete and can be extremely expensive. As a result, although predictive studies might be preferable from a technical perspective, for practical reasons test developers and researchers might adopt a concurrent strategy to save time and/or money. In some situations this is less than optimal; caution is warranted when evaluating the results. However, in certain situations, concurrent studies are the preferred approach. Concurrent studies clearly are appropriate when the goal of the test is to determine current status of the examinee as opposed to predicting future outcome (Anastasi & Urbina, 1997). For example, a concurrent approach to validation would be indicated for a test designed to diagnose the presence of depression in adults. Here we are most concerned that the test gives us an accurate assessment of whether or not the individual is clinically depressed at the time of testing, not at some time in the future. The question here is not "Who will develop depression?" but "Who has depression?" In these situations, the test being validated is often a replacement for a more time-consuming or expensive procedure. For example, a relatively brief screening test like the BDI might be evaluated to determine whether it can serve as an adequate replacement for a more extensive psychological assessment or diagnostic process. However, if we were interested in selecting individuals who were at high risk of developing depression in the future, say, for participation in a prevention program, a prediction study would be in order. In this scenario, we would need to address how well or how accurately our test predicts who will develop depression or whatever disorder is in question. The other important point here is that some tests may be excellent when used in concurrent applications but poor for predictive applications. Consider a test that measures the symptoms of psychopathology. This test might do quite well in a concurrent study by demonstrating great accuracy in identifying those who currently have a psychopathology diagnosis. However, because the factors that predict the risk for developing psychopathology may be quite different than current symptoms of psychopathology, the same test may not perform well in a predictive situation.

5.4.4.1.1 Selecting a Criterion

In both predictive and concurrent studies, it is important that the criterion itself be reliable and valid. As noted earlier, reliability is a prerequisite for validity. If a measure is not reliable, whether it is a predictor test or a criterion measure, it cannot be valid. At the same time, reliability does not ensure validity. Therefore, we need to select criterion measures that are also valid. In our example of using the SAT to predict freshman GPA, we consider our criterion, GPA, to be a valid measure of success in college. In a concurrent study examining the ability of a test to diagnose depression, the criterion might be the diagnosis provided by an extensive clinical assessment involving a combination of clinical interviews, behavioral observations, and psychometric testing. Optimally the criterion should be viewed as the "gold standard," the best existing measure of the construct of interest.

5.4.4.1.2 Criterion Contamination

It is important that the predictor and criterion scores be independently obtained. That is, scores on the predictor should not in any way influence criterion scores. If predictor scores do influence criterion scores, the criterion is said to be contaminated. Consider a situation in which students are selected for a college program based on performance on an aptitude test. If the college instructors are aware of the students' performance on the aptitude test, this might influence their evaluation of the students' performance in their class. Students with high aptitude test scores might be given preferential treatment or graded in a more lenient manner. In this situation knowledge of performance on the predictor is influencing performance on the criterion. When criterion contamination has occurred any resulting validity coefficients will be artificially inflated. That is, the validity coefficients between the predictor test and the criterion will be larger than they would be had the criterion not been contaminated. The coefficients will suggest the validity is greater than it actually is. To avoid this undesirable situation, test developers must ensure that no individual who evaluates criterion performance has knowledge of the examinees' predictor scores.

5.4.4.1.3 Interpreting Validity Coefficients

Predictive and concurrent validity studies examine the relationship between a test and a criterion and the results are often reported in terms of a validity coefficient. At this point, it is reasonable to ask, "How large should validity coefficients be?" For example, should we expect validity coefficients greater than 0.80? Although there is no simple answer to this question, validity coefficients should be large enough to indicate that information from the test will help predict how individuals will perform on the

> If a test provides information that helps predict criterion performance better than any other existing predictor, the test may be useful even if the validity coefficients are relatively small.

criterion measure (e.g., Cronbach & Gleser, 1965). Returning to our example of the SAT, the question is whether the relationship between the SAT and the freshman GPA is sufficiently strong so that information about SAT performance helps predict who will succeed in college. If a test provides information that helps predict criterion performance better than any other existing predictor, the test may be useful even if its validity coefficients are relatively small. As a result, testing experts avoid specifying a minimum coefficient size that is acceptable for validity coefficients. In this context it is useful to also recall the arguments of McFall and Treat (1999):

> The aim of clinical assessment is to gather data that allow us to reduce uncertainty regarding the probabilities of events. (p. 215)

> Test scores "…have information value or are illuminating to the degree they allow us to predict or control events with greater accuracy or with less error than we could have done without them." (p. 217)

Prediction can be an outcome such as accurately receiving a clinical diagnosis, graduating from college, or completing fighter pilot training without crashing! If a test allows us to reduce the uncertainty surrounding the probability of any such event, it is useful.

We cannot overemphasize the importance of the context of assessment, measurement, and prediction (i.e., reducing the error in our estimation of the probability of some event) in deciding whether a validity coefficient is of a sufficiently large magnitude for useful application in that setting. In the prediction of classroom achievement, we tend to look for tests that have coefficients in the mid to high .50s and above before we consider them useful. However, much smaller coefficients can have enormous impacts on our ability to improve certain outcomes. For example, Hunter, Schmidt, and Rauschenberger (1984) have demonstrated the far-reaching implications on productivity of workers and subsequently the gross domestic product of the United States (reaching into the 100s of billions of dollars) if employers used employment tests to place workers in the best jobs, even if the employment tests had validity coefficients only in the .20s to .30s. Even though the validity coefficients are small for these employment tests and certainly well below what is acceptable for a reliability coefficient, the very practical relationship they have with an overall increase in gross domestic product justifies their use.

Although we cannot set a minimum size for acceptable validity coefficients, certain techniques are available that can help us evaluate the usefulness of test scores for prediction purposes. In Chap. 2 we introduced linear regression, a mathematical procedure that allows you to predict values on one variable given information on another variable. In the context of validity analysis, linear regression allows you to predict criterion performance based on predictor test scores. When using linear regression, a statistic called the standard error of estimate is used to describe the amount of prediction error due to the imperfect validity of the test. The standard error of estimate is the standard deviation of prediction errors around the predicted score and can be used to create a confidence interval within which the true

> The standard error of estimate is used to describe the amount of prediction error due to the imperfect validity of interpretation of a test score.

population correlation will fall (similar to the concept of the standard error of measurement discussed in Chap. 4).

5.4.4.2 Contrasted Groups Studies

Theory may serve as a basis for gathering validity evidence by examining how different groups (as identified by some external criterion) are expected to differ on the construct a test is designed to measure. This is referred to as a ***contrasted group study***. For example, if you are attempting to validate a new measure of intelligence, you might form two groups, individuals with intellectual disabilities and those with typical intellectual ability. In this type of study, the diagnoses or group assignment would have been made using assessment procedures that do not involve the test under consideration. Each group would then be administered the new test. The new test's validity as a measure of intelligence would be supported if as predicted, the intellectual disability group performed much worse than the typical intellectual ability group. Although the preceding example is rather simplistic, it illustrates a general approach that has numerous applications. For example, many constructs in psychology and education have a developmental component. That is, you expect younger participants to perform differently than older participants. Tests designed to measure these constructs can be examined to determine whether they demonstrate the expected developmental changes by looking at the performance of groups reflecting different ages and/or education. Or you expect a group diagnosed with a psychotic disorder like schizophrenia to endorse more psychotic symptoms than a group that has no diagnosis. In the past, this type of validity evidence has typically been classified as construct validity.

5.4.4.3 Decision-Theory Models

5.4.4.3.1 Selection Ratio and Base Rate

When tests are used for making decisions such as in student or employment selection, factors other than the correlation between the test and criterion can impact the usefulness of test scores including the selection ratio and the base rate. The ***selection ratio*** is the proportion of applicants needed to fill positions. Two computer

> Decision-theory models help the test user determine how much information a predictor test can contribute when making classification decisions.

chip makers are hiring and want to use a psychological test to help select those applicants most likely to be successful. One needs to hire ten positions but has only ten applicants, while the other needs to hire 20 positions but has 100 applicants. The first computer chip maker does not have the luxury of being selective and has to accept all the applicants (selection ratio = 1.0). In this situation, no test is useful, no matter how strong a relationship there is between it and the criterion (i.e., success as an employee) because all applicants have to be hired. However, for the computer chip maker who needs to hire 20 positions and has 100 applicants (selection ratio = 0.2), even a test with a moderate correlation with the criterion may be useful in improving hiring decisions.

The **base rate** is the proportion of applicants who have applied to the job that actually have the skills to be successful. In the case of our companies, if computer chip making is a very easy task, then almost any applicant selected will be successful at it. No test is likely to be useful for improving hiring decisions regardless of how strong a relationship there is between it and the criterion. On the other hand, if making a computer chip is very difficult, then few applicants can be successful at doing it, so even a test with a moderate correlation with the criterion may be useful.

Decision-theory models of utility take into consideration selection ratio and base rate factors (Messick, 1989). Decision-theory models help the test user determine how much information a predictor test can contribute when making classification decisions. We will not go into detail about decision theory at this point, but we will discuss the use of tests in personnel selection in some detail in Chap. 12. Other good discussions of decision-theory and selection methods for those with interests in this area can be found in Hunter, Schmidt, and Rauschenberger (1984) and Schmidt and Hunter (1998).

5.4.4.3.2   Sensitivity and Specificity

Whenever a test score (or even a clinician's opinion or conclusions) is used to classify individuals or some characteristic of an individual into groups, the sensitivity and specificity of the classification method is important. This is best illustrated in the cases of diagnosis or in making hiring decisions. The **sensitivity** of a measure to a diagnostic condition is essentially the ability of the test at a predetermined cut score to detect the presence of the disorder. The **specificity** of a measure is the ability of the test at a predetermined cut score to determine the absence of the disorder. Sensitivity and specificity may sound like mirror images of each other, but they are not. It may be very easy to tell when someone does not have a disorder—but very difficult to tell when they do! Attention-deficit/hyperactivity disorder (ADHD) is a prime example, and a controversial diagnosis. ADHD has many so-called mimic disorders—disorders that have similar symptom patterns but a different underlying cause. So it is easy to determine that a child or adolescent does not have the disorder if they are absent impulsive, overactive, and inattentive behaviors; determining they do have the disorder in the presence of these symptoms is far more difficult.

> Whenever a test score is used to classify individuals or some characteristic of an individual into groups, the sensitivity and specificity of the classification method is important.

For example, if we give a child a comprehensive measure of behavior to determine if he or she has ADHD, the manual for the measure might give a cut score of $T \geq 70$ on certain subscales as indicative of a high probability of the presence of ADHD—thus it is used to predict the presence of the disorder. Since neither test scores nor clinicians are always right, we should be interested in the relative accuracy of such predictions—which is not apparent from a correlation coefficient. Rather, a type of contingency table such as shown in Table 5.5 is used to analyze the sensitivity and specificity of classifications. Often, recommended cut scores for declaring a classification (e.g., ADHD—no ADHD, hire—do not hire) are investigated using just such tables. Cut scores are then varied and the effects of different scores on the sensitivity and specificity values are determined. Typically as cut scores are used that have increased sensitivity, specificity goes down and vice versa. The trick is to find the appropriate balance in terms of the errors we will make—false-positive errors (e.g., diagnosing ADHD when it is not present) and false-negative errors (e.g., failing to diagnose ADHD when it is present).

Given that we will always make mistakes in diagnosis or other judgments about people, which is better—a higher false-positive or higher false-negative error rate? There is no one size fits all response to this question. In making a determination of which type of error is better to make, we must ask ourselves about the consequences of each type of error for the person involved. Screening measures are designed to detect a high probability of a condition in an economical and efficient manner. If the results of the screening measure suggest the presence of the condition, more extensive and expensive testing or evaluation can be conducted. Screening measures should always emphasize sensitivity over specificity. For example, if we are screening for a deadly cancer, we would want our screener to have extremely high sensitivity so that virtually all who have the disease would be detected and receive early treatment. In this decision-making example, the cost of not detecting the cancer when it is present (false-negative errors) is deemed so high that it overshadows concerns about anxiety or worry that could result from being identified as having cancer when it is actually not present (false-positive error). On the other hand, when failing to detect a disorder is judged to have minimal consequences, we may look for better rates of specificity. We hope it is clear that in any decision-making process, there is a relative value placed on the acceptability of errors, whether they are false positive or false negative. An individual who screened positive for cancer but did not have it may have experienced significant anxiety, more extensive and expensive diagnostic procedures, with the associated life disruption. This person may very well disagree with the value judgment that false-negative errors are more important than false-positive errors.

Table 5.5 Calculating sensitivity and specificity

Test result	Actual outcome		Row totals
	Positive	Negative	
Positive	True positives (Cell A)	False positives (Cell B)	A + B = Number of predicted positive cases
Negative	False negatives (Cell C)	True negatives (Cell D)	C + D = Number of predicted negative cases
Column totals	A + C = Number of Cases with Positive Outcomes	B + D = Number of cases with negative outcome	

Sensitivity: The ability of the instrument to detect a disorder when it is present. Calculated as $A/(A+C)$

Specificity: The ability of an instrument to detect the absence of a disorder when it is absent (i.e., detect normality). Calculated as $D/(B+D)$

Positive Predictive Values (PPV): Represents the proportion of positive cases that will be detected accurately. Calculated as $A/(A+B)$

Negative Predictive Values (NPV): Represents the proportion of "normal" cases that will be detected accurately. Calculated as $D/(C+D)$

Table 5.5 demonstrates how sensitivity and specificity values are calculated. To help us interpret these values better, we also look at Positive Predictive Values (PPV) and Negative Predictive Values (NPV). PPV represents the proportion of positive cases that will be detected accurately, and NPV represents the proportion of "normal" cases that will be detected accurately. As we have noted, this type of analysis can be applied to any set of classifications where the categories to be predicted are mutually exclusive.

5.4.4.4 Convergent and Discriminant Evidence

Convergent and discriminant evidence of validity have traditionally been incorporated under the category of construct validity. ***Convergent evidence*** of validity is obtained when you correlate a test with existing tests that measure the same or similar constructs. For example, if you are developing a new intelligence test you might elect to correlate scores on your new test with scores on the Wechsler Intelligence Scale for Children—Fifth Edition (WISC-V; Wechsler, 2014). Because the WISC-V is a well-respected test of intelligence with considerable validity evidence, a strong correlation between the WISC-V and your new intelligence test would provide evidence that your test is actually measuring the construct of intelligence.

Discriminant evidence of validity is obtained when you correlate a test with existing tests that measure dissimilar constructs. For example, if you were validating a test designed to measure anxiety, you might correlate your anxiety scores with a measure of sensation seeking. Because anxious individuals do not typically engage in sensation-seeking behaviors, you would expect a negative correlation between the measures. If your analyses produce the expected negative correlations, this would support your hypothesis.

There is a related, relatively sophisticated validation technique referred to as the ***multitrait-multimethod matrix*** that combines convergent and discriminant strategies (Campbell & Fiske, 1959). This approach requires that you examine two or more traits using two or more measurement methods. The researcher then examines the resulting correlation matrix, comparing the actual relationships with a priori (i.e., preexisting) prediction about the relationships. Table 5.6 presents a hypothetical multitrait-multimethod matrix with depression, hyperactivity, and socialization as the traits, and self-report, parent report, and teacher report as the methods. The reliability coefficients are designated by r_{xx} and are along the principal diagonal (referred to as monotrait-monomethod correlations). The validity coefficients are designated by r_{xy} and are along three shorter diagonals. The validity coefficients are the correlations of scores of the same trait measured by different methods (i.e., referred to as monotrait-heteromethod correlations). In the matrix, HM indicates heterotrait-monomethod correlations that reflect relationships between different traits measured by the same method. HH indicates heterotrait-heteromethod correlations that reflect relationships between different traits measured by different methods. Campbell and Fiske note that validity coefficients should obviously be greater

> There is a relatively sophisticated validation technique referred to as the multitrait-multimethod matrix that combines convergent and discriminant strategies.

Table 5.6 A multitrait-multimethod matrix

		Self-report			Parent rating			Teacher rating		
		D	H	S	D	H	S	D	H	S
Self-Report	**Depression**	r_{xx}								
Scale	**Hyperactivity**	HM	r_{xx}							
	Socialization	HM	HM	r_{xx}						
Parent	**Depression**	r_{xy}	*HH*	*HH*	r_{xx}					
Rating	**Hyperactivity**	*HH*	r_{xy}	*HH*	HM	r_{xx}				
Form	**Socialization**	*HH*	*HH*	r_{xy}	HM	HM	r_{xx}			
Teacher	**Depression**	r_{xy}	*HH*	*HH*	r_{xy}	*HH*	*HH*	r_{xx}		
Rating	**Hyperactivity**	*HH*	r_{xy}	*HH*	*HH*	r_{xy}	*HH*	HM	r_{xx}	
Form	**Socialization**	*HH*	*HH*	r_{xy}	*HH*	*HH*	r_{xy}	HM	HM	r_{xx}

D depression, *H* hyperactivity, *S* socialization. Monotrait-monomethod values are reliability coefficients (r_{xx}), and momotrait-heteromethod values are validity coefficients (r_{xy}). **HM** indicates heterotrait-monomethod correlations, and *HH* indicates heterotrait-heteromethod correlations

than correlations between different traits measured by different measures (designated HH correlations in Table 5.6), and also greater than different traits measured by the same method (designated HM correlations in Table 5.6). In addition to revealing information about convergent and discriminant relationships, this technique provides information about the influence of common method variance. When two measures show an unexpected correlation due to similarity in their method of measurement, we refer to this as method variance. Thus, the multitrait-multimethod matrix allows one to determine what the test correlates with, what it does not correlate with, and how the method of measurement influences these relationships. This approach has considerable technical and theoretical appeal, yet difficulty with implementation and interpretation has somewhat limited its application to date.

5.4.4.5 Validity Generalization

An important consideration in educational and employment settings is *validity generalization*, or the degree to which test-criterion relationships can be generalized to new situations without further study. When a test is used for prediction in new settings, research has shown that validity coefficients can vary considerably. For example, a validation study may be conducted using a national sample, but different results may be obtained when the study is repeated using a restricted sample such as a local school district. Originally these results were interpreted as suggesting that test users were not able to rely on existing validation studies and needed to conduct their own local validation studies. However, subsequent research using a relatively new statistical procedure known as meta-analysis indicated that much of the variability previously observed in validity coefficients was actually due to statistical artifacts (e.g., sampling error). When these statistical artifacts were taken into consideration the remaining variability was often negligible, suggesting that validity coefficients can be generalized more than previously thought (AERA et al., 2014). Currently, in many situations, local validation studies are not seen as necessary. For example, if there is abundant meta-analytic research that produces consistent results, local validity studies will likely not add much useful information. However, if there is little existing research or the results are inconsistent, then local validity studies may be particularly useful.

5.4.5   Evidence Based on Consequences of Testing

Recently, researchers have started examining the consequences of test use, both intended and unintended, as an aspect of validity. In many situations, the use of tests is based largely on the assumption that their use will result in some specific benefit (AERA et al., 2014; also see McFall & Treat, 1999). For example, if a test is used to identify qualified applicants for employment, it is assumed that the use of the test will result in better hiring decisions (e.g., lower training costs, lower turnover). If a test is used to help select students for admission to a college program, it is assumed that the use of the test will result in better admissions decisions (e.g., greater student success and higher retention). This line of validity evidence simply asks the question, "Are these benefits being achieved?" This type of validity evidence often referred to as consequential validity evidence, is most applicable to tests designed for selection and promotion.

Some authors have advocated a broader conception of validity, one that incorporates social issues and values. For example, Messick (1989) in his influential chapter suggested that the conception of validity should be expanded so that it "... formally brings consideration of value implications and social consequences into the validity framework" (p. 20). Other testing experts have criticized this position. For example, Popham (2000) suggests that incorporating social consequences into the definition of validity would detract from the clarity of the concept. Popham argues that validity is clearly defined as the "...accuracy of score-based inferences" (p. 111) and that the inclusion of social and value issues unnecessarily complicates the concept. The *Standards* (AERA et al., 2014) appear to avoid this broader conceptualization of validity. The *Standards* distinguish between consequential evidence that is directly tied to the concept of validity and evidence that is related to social policy. This is an important but potentially difficult distinction to make. Consider a situation in which research suggests that the use of test results in different job selection rates for different groups. If the test measures only the skills and abilities related to job performance, evidence of differential selection rates does not detract from the validity of the test. This information might be useful in guiding social and policy decisions, but it is not technically an aspect of validity. If, however, the test measures factors unrelated to job performance, the evidence is relevant to validity. In this case, it may suggest a problem with the validity of the test such as the inclusion of construct-irrelevant factors.

Another component of this process is to consider the consequences of not using tests. Even though the consequences of testing may produce some adverse effects, these must be contrasted with the positive and negative effects of alternatives to using psychological tests. If, for example, more subjective approaches to decision making are employed, the likelihood of cultural, ethnic, and gender biases in the decision-making process will likely increase. This typically raises many controversies and many professionals in the field attempt to avoid these issues, especially at the level of training students. We disagree. We believe this issue is of great importance and address concerns related to cultural bias in testing later in this book, devoting an entire chapter to these issues.

5.5   Integrating Evidence of Validity

The *Standards* (AERA et al., 2014) state that "Validation can be viewed as a process of con-

> The development of a validity argument typically involves the integration of numerous lines of evidence into a coherent commentary.

structing and evaluating arguments for and against the intended interpretation of test scores and their relevance to the proposed use" (p. 11). The development of this validity argument typically involves the integration of numerous lines of evidence into a coherent commentary. As we have noted, different types of validity evidence are most applicable to different type of tests. Here is a brief review of some of the prominent applications of different types of validity evidence.

- *Evidence based on test content* is most often reported with academic achievement tests and tests used in the selection of employees.
- *Evidence based on relations* to other variables can be (1) test-criterion relationships, which is most applicable when tests are used to predict performance on an external criterion; (2) convergent and discriminant evidence of validity, which can be useful with a wide variety of tests, including intelligence tests, achievement tests, personality tests, and so on; or (3) validity generalization evidence, which is most useful when the same or similar tests are being used repeatedly in similar applications.
- *Evidence based on internal structure* can be useful with a wide variety of tests, but has traditionally been applied with tests measuring theoretical constructs such as personality or intelligence.
- *Evidence based on response processes* can be useful with practically any test that requires examinees to engage in any cognitive or behavioral activity.
- *Evidence based on consequences* of testing is most applicable to tests designed for selection and promotion, but can be useful with a wide range of tests.

You might have noticed that most types of validity evidence have applications to a broad variety of tests, and this is the way it should be. The integration of multiple lines of research or types of evidence results provides a more compelling validity argument. It is also important to remember that every interpretation or intended use of a test must be validated. As we noted earlier, if a test is used for different applications, each use or application must be validated. In these situations, it is imperative that different types of validity evidence be provided. Table 5.7 provides a summary of the major applications of different types of validity evidence.

Although we have emphasized a number of distinct approaches to collecting evidence to support the validity of score interpretations, validity evidence is actually

Table 5.7   Sources of validity evidence

Source	Example	Major applications
Evidence Based on Test Content	Analysis of item relevance and content coverage	Achievement tests and tests used in the selection of employees
Evidence Based on Relations to Other Variables	Test-criterion; convergent and discriminant evidence; contrasted groups studies	Wide variety of tests
Evidence Based on Internal Structure	Factor analysis, analysis of test homogeneity	Wide variety of tests, but particularly useful with tests of constructs like personality or intelligence
Evidence Based on Response Processes	Analysis of the processes engaged in by the examinee or examiner	Any test that requires examinees to engage in a cognitive or behavioral activity
Evidence Based on Consequences of Testing Structure	Analysis of the intended and unintended consequences of testing	Most applicable to tests designed for selection and promotion, but useful on a wide range of tests

broader than the strategies described in this chapter. The *Standards* (AERA et al., 2014) state:

> Ultimately, the validity of an intended interpretation of test scores relies on all the available evidence relevant to the technical quality of a testing system. Different components of validity evidence...include evidence of careful test construction; adequate score reliability; appropriate test administration and scoring; accurate score scaling; equating, and standard setting; and careful attention to fairness for test takers, as appropriate to the test interpretation in question. (p. 22)

In other words, when considering the validity of score interpretations, one should consider in totality the evidence of the technical quality of the test. Obviously, the five sources of validity evidence described in this chapter are central to building a validity argument, but other information should be carefully considered. Does the test produce reliable scores, is the standardization sample representative and of sufficient size, is there adequate standardization of both administration and scoring? In sum, is the test a well-developed and technically sound instrument? In Chap. 6 we will add to this discussion and provide practical guidance to ensuring the validity of test score interpretations. This is a process that begins when you first begin thinking about developing a test.

Finally, the development of a validity argument is an ongoing process; it takes into consideration existing research and incorporates new scientific findings. While test developers are obligated to provide initial evidence of the validity of the score interpretations they are proposing, research from independent researchers subsequent to the release of the test is also essential. A number of excellent professional journals (e.g., *Psychological Assessment, Psychometrika*) routinely publish empirical research articles covering the psychometric properties of different tests. Additionally, those using tests are expected to weigh the validity evidence and make their own judgments about the appropriateness of the test in their own situations and settings. This places the clinical practitioners using psychological tests in the final, most responsible role in the validation process.

5.6   How Test Manuals Report Validity Evidence: The Reynolds Intellectual Assessment Scales, Second Edition (RIAS–2)

To illustrate how validity evidence is reported in test manuals, we will use examples from the ***Reynolds Intellectual Assessment Scales, Second Edition*** (RIAS–2: Reynolds & Kamphaus, 2015). The RIAS–2 is an individually administered intelligence test for individuals 3–94 years of age. The RIAS–2 contains a two-subtest Verbal Intelligence Index (VIX) and a two-subtest Nonverbal Intelligence Index (NIX). The two verbal subtests are Guess What (GWH) and Verbal Reasoning (VRZ). The two nonverbal subtests are Odd-Item Out (OIO) and What's Missing (WHM). All four subtests are combined to form the Composite Intelligence Index (CIX). It takes approximately 20–25 min to administer the four intelligence scale subtests. The RIAS–2 also includes a conormed, supplemental measures of memory and of processing speed. Memory is assessed with two memory subtests, Verbal Memory (VRM) and Nonverbal Memory (NVM). They require approximately 10–15 min to administer and yield a Composite Memory Index (CMX). Processing speed is assessed with a Speeded Naming Task (SNT) and a Speeded Picture Search (SPS) task. They can be administered in 5–10 min each, and combined to form a Speeded Processing Index (SPI). The RIAS–2 was standardized on a national sample of 2154 individuals who are representative of the U.S. population.

Chapter 6 of the test manual is titled Validity of Test Score Interpretation. The authors report validity evidence using the nomenclature presented in the *Standards* (AERA et al., 2014). They start by describing Carroll's (1993) three stratum theory of intelligence, (see Chap. 9: Assessment of Aptitude and Intelligence) and note that the RIAS–2 focuses on the assessment of stratum three and stratum two abilities from Carroll's theory. The authors then describe how the different subtests and index scores of the RIAS–2 match the three stratum theory of intelligence, and hypothesize validity evidence that will support this relationship.

In terms of validity evidence based on test content, they examine the stimuli, items, and format of the individual RIAS–2 subtests. The authors note that while the individual items are new, the general formats of the subtests have a long history of use in cognitive assessment and have been thoroughly studied. They support these statements in a subtest-by-subtest manner providing citations of research supporting the validity of these tasks in intellectual assessment.

The authors also describe the item-review and item-selection process. Early in the development process a panel of minority psychologists experienced in assessment reviewed all items to determine if they were appropriate as measures of the relevant constructs and were applicable across the U.S. cultures. A second panel of psychologists with diverse training (e.g., school, clinical, neuropsychology) also reviewed the items. Items questioned by either panel were either eliminated or revised. Final items were selected based on traditional item statistics such as item difficulty, item discrimination, and item consistency (these will be discussed in detail in Chap. 8: Item Analysis). Item analyses were also conducted across age, gender, and ethnic groupings to ensure items were not biased. In summary, the

Table 5.8 RIAS–2 intelligence subtest rotated loadings for individuals 18–30 years of age

RIAS-2 subtest	Factor 1	Factor 2	Factor 3
Guess What	0.73	0.35	−0.01
Verbal Reasoning	0.79	0.30	−0.02
Odd-Item Out	0.35	0.56	−0.30
What's Missing	0.21	0.64	0.17
Verbal Memory	0.45	−0.03	0.01
Nonverbal Memory	0.08	0.62	0.12
Speeded Naming Task	−0.18	0.55	0.75
Speeded Picture Search	0.02	0.00	0.22

authors hold that a review of test content supports the validity of the RIAS–2. The test formats are longstanding, well-researched and the individual items passed multiple levels of expert and statistical review and analysis.

Validity evidence based on the internal structure is the next topic in the test manual. First, the internal consistency of the index scores is examined. It is noted that median values for Cronbach's coefficient alphas across all index scores were .90 or higher. In addition to suggesting strong reliability, these strong coefficients reflect high internal consistency among the subtests comprising the indexes. Theory-based evidence of validity is provided next, as well as evidence based on test content and response processes.

Next, the authors present a substantial amount of evidence from exploratory and confirmatory factor analyses. The results of principal factor analyses with Varimax rotations for the eight RIAS–2 subtests suggest the three-factor solution made the most psychological and psychometric sense. The three factors reflect verbal abilities, nonverbal abilities, and speeded processing. In general, the verbal subtests load on the rotated Factor 1, the nonverbal subtests load on Factor 2, and the processing subtests load on Factor 3. Table 5.8 presents the intelligence subtest loadings for individuals in the 18- to 30-year-old age group. To assess the stability of the three--factor solution across different groups, the authors examined the factor structure across age groups, gender, and ethnicity. They present tables with the factor loadings for these groups and present statistics that test the comparability of factor solutions across groups. These analyses demonstrate that the three-factor solution is stable across these groups.

A series of confirmatory factor analyses were also conducted. In these analyses, several models were examined including a one-factor solution, a two-factor solution (reflecting verbal and nonverbal abilities), a three-factor solution (reflecting verbal, nonverbal, and memory or processing speed factors), and a four-factor solution (reflecting verbal, nonverbal, memory abilities, and processing speed abilities). The results support a four-factor solution, which provides evidence of the validity of the Composite Intelligence Index (CIX), Verbal Intelligence Index (VIX) Nonverbal Intelligence Index (NIX), and Speeded Processing Index (SPI).

The authors next turned their attention to validity evidence based on relations to other variables and developmental trends. This examination found that intellectual ability grows rapidly in young children, starts to plateau in adolescence with some continued growth, and finally declines in the elderly. Correlations and plots of smoothed polynomial curves document the predicted relationship between performance on RIAS–2 raw scores and age. Correlations between RIAS–2 scores and performance and the Wechsler intelligence scales and academic achievement reveal expected relationships between RIAS–2 scores and Wechsler measures of intelligence. RIAS–2 scores were not strongly impacted by motor coordination and motor speed. Examination of RIAS-2 scores in a number of clinical groups (e.g., adults with mild Intellectual Disabilities, children with Learning Disabilities, individuals with Traumatic Brain Injury) indicated that all clinical groups performed more poorly when compared to the population mean, again supporting the validity of the RIAS–2 score interpretations.

In closing, the authors considered validity evidence based on the consequences of testing. In this context, they noted that while this category of validity evidence is most applicable to tests designed for selection purposes, evidence that the RIAS–2 can provide an accurate estimate of intelligence, memory, and processing speed across gender and ethnic groups supports the diagnostic utility of this instrument. The RIAS-2 authors also note that development of a validity argument incorporates not only the validity evidence presented in a test manual's chapter on validity, but also in the totality of information provided on the development, standardization, scaling, reliability etc. related to the test.

5.7   Summary

This chapter introduces the concept of validity. In the context of psychological tests and measurement, validity refers to the degree to which theoretical and empirical evidence supports the meaning and interpretation of test scores. In essence, the validity question is "Are the intended interpretations of test scores appropriate and accurate?" Numerous factors can limit the validity of interpretations. The two major internal threats to validity are construct underrepresentation (i.e., the test is not a comprehensive measure of the construct it is supposed to measure) and construct-irrelevant variance (i.e., the test measures content or skills unrelated to the construct). Other factors that may reduce validity include examinee characteristics, test administration/scoring procedures, and instructional and coaching procedures. There is also a close relationship between validity and reliability. For a test to be valid it must be reliable, but at the same time reliability does not ensure validity. Put another way, reliability is a necessary but insufficient condition for validity.

As a psychometric concept, validity has evolved and changed over the last half-century. Until the 1970s validity was generally divided into three distinct types: content validity, criterion-related validity, and construct validity. This terminology was widely accepted and is still often referred to as the traditional nomenclature. However, in the 1970s and 1980s measurement professionals started conceptualizing validity as a unitary construct. That is, although there are different ways of collecting validity evidence, there are not distinct types of validity. To get away from the perception of distinct types of validity, today we refer to different types of validity evidence. The most current typology includes the following five categories:

- *Evidence based on test content.* Evidence derived from a detailed analysis of the test content includes the type of questions or tasks included in the test and guidelines for administration and scoring. Collecting content-based validity evidence is often based on the evaluation of expert judges about the correspondence between the test's content and its construct. The key issues addressed by these expert judges are whether the test items assess relevant content (i.e., item relevance) and the degree to which the construct is assessed in a comprehensive manner (i.e., content coverage).

- *Evidence based on response processes.* Evidence analyzing the processes engaged in by the examinee or examiner can help determine if test goals are being achieved. For example, if the test is designed to measure mathematical reasoning, it is helpful to verify that the examinees are actually engaging in mathematical reasoning and analysis as opposed to performing rote calculations.

- *Evidence based on internal structure.* Evidence examining the relationships among test items and components, or the internal structure of the test, can help determine whether the structure of the test is consistent with the hypothesized structure of the construct it measures.

- *Evidence based on relations to other variables.* Evidence based on an examination of the relationships between test performance and external variables or criteria can actually be divided into subcategories of validity evidence, including test-criterion evidence, convergent and discriminant evidence, and validity generalization evidence. Test-criterion evidence is typically of interest when a test is designed to predict performance on a criterion such as job performance, success in college, or psychiatric diagnosis. Two types of studies are often used to collect test-criterion evidence: predictive and concurrent studies. In a predictive study, the test is administered and there is an *interval of time* before the criterion is measured. In concurrent studies, the test is administered and the criterion is measured at approximately *the same time*. The collection of convergent and discriminant evidence involves examining the relationship between a test and other tests that measure similar constructs (convergent evidence) or dissimilar constructs (discriminant evidence). If the test scores demonstrate the expected relationships with these existing measures, this can be used as evidence of validity. Validity generalization evidence is of interest when test-criterion relationships can be generalized to new situations without further study. Local validation studies might be needed if there is little existing research or the results of existing studies are inconsistent.

- *Evidence based on consequences of testing.* Evidence examining the intended and unintended consequences of testing is based on the common belief that some benefit will result from the use of tests. Therefore, it is reasonable to confirm that these benefits are achieved. In recent years this type of validity evidence has gained considerable attention with continuing debate regarding its scope. Some authors suggest that social consequences and values should be incorporated into the conceptualization of validity, whereas others feel such a broadening would detract from the clarity of the concept.

Different lines of validity evidence are integrated into a cohesive validity argument that supports the use of the test for different applications. The development of this validity argument is a dynamic process that integrates existing research and incorporates new scientific findings. Validation is the shared responsibility of the test authors, test publishers, researchers, and even test users. Test authors and publishers are expected to provide preliminary evidence supporting the validity of proposed test score interpretations whereas researchers often pursue independent validity studies. Ultimately, those using tests are expected to weigh the validity evidence and make their own judgments about the appropriateness of using a test in their own situations and settings, placing the practitioners or consumers of psychological tests in the final, most responsible role in this process. Given this responsibility, the chapters in this text are intended to equip test users to make informed decisions about test selection, administration, and interpretation.

References

American Educational Research Association, American Psychological Association, & National Council on Measurement in Education. (2014). *Standards for educational and psychological testing*. Washington, DC: American Educational Research Association.

American Educational Research Association, American Psychological Association, & National Council on Measurement in Education. (1999). Standards for educational and psychological testing. Washington, DC: American Educational Research Association.

American Psychological Association. (1954). Technical recommendations for psychological tests and diagnostic techniques. *Psychological Bulletin, 51*(2 Pt. 2), 1–28.

American Psychological Association. (1966). *Standards for educational and psychological tests and manuals*. Washington, DC: Author.

American Psychological Association, American Educational Research Association, & National Council on Measurement in Education. (1974). *Standards for educational and psychological testing*. Washington, DC: Author.

American Psychological Association, American Educational Research Association, & National Council on Measurement in Education. (1985). *Standards for educational and psychological testing*. Washington, DC: Author.

Anastasi, A., & Urbina, S. (1997). *Psychological testing* (7th ed.). Upper Saddle River, NJ: Prentice Hall.

Campbell, D. T., & Fiske, D. W. (1959). Convergent and discriminant validation by the multitrait-multimethod matrix. *Psychological Bulletin, 56*(2), 546–553.

Carroll, J. B. (1993). *Human cognitive abilities: A survey of factor-analytic studies*. New York, NY: Cambridge University Press.

Cattell, R. (1966). *Handbook of multivariate experimental psychology*. Chicago, IL: Rand McNally.

Chan, D., Schmitt, N., DeShon, R. P., Clause, C. S., & Delbridge, K. (1997). Reaction to cognitive ability tests: The relationship between race, test performance, face validity, and test-taking motivation. *Journal of Applied Psychology, 82*, 300–310.

Cronbach, L. J. (1990). *Essentials of psychological testing* (5th ed.). New York, NY: HarperCollins.

Cronbach, L. J., & Gleser, G. C. (1965). *Psychological tests and personnel decisions* (2nd ed.). Champaign, IL: University of Illinois Press.

Hunter, J. E., Schmidt, F. L., & Rauschenberger, L. (1984). Methodological, statistical, and ethical issues in the study of bias in psychological tests. In C. R. Reynolds & R. T. Brown (Eds.), *Perspectives on bias in mental testing* (pp. 41–100). New York, NY: Plenum Press.

Lawshe, C. H. (1975). A quantitative approach to content validity. *Personnel Psychology, 28,* 563–575.

Lee, D., Reynolds, C., & Willson, V. (2003). Standardized test administration: Why bother? *Journal of Forensic Neuropsychology, 3*(3), 55–81.

Linn, R. L., & Gronlund, N. E. (2000). *Measurement and assessment in teaching* (8th ed.). Upper Saddle River, NJ: Prentice Hall.

McFall, R. M., & Treat, T. T. (1999). Quantifying the information value of clinical assessment with signal detection theory. *Annual Review of Psychology, 50,* 215–241.

Messick, S. (1989). Validity. In R. L. Linn (Ed.), *Educational measurement* (3rd ed., pp. 13–103). Upper Saddle River, NJ: Merrill Prentice Hall.

Messick, S. (1994). The interplay of evidence and consequences in the validation of performance assessments. *Educational Researcher, 23,* 13–23.

Meyer, G. J., Finn, S. E., Eyde, L. D., Kay, G. G., Moreland, K. L., Dies, R. R., ... Reed, G. M. (2001). Psychological testing and psychological assessment: A review of evidence and issues. *American Psychologist, 56,* 128–165.

Pearson. (2009). *WIAT-III: Examiners manual.* San Antonio, TX: Author.

Popham, W. J. (2000). *Modern educational measurement: Practical guidelines for educational leaders.* Boston, MA: Allyn & Bacon.

Reynolds, C. R. (1998). Fundamentals of measurement and assessment in psychology. In A. Bellack & M. Hersen (Eds.), *Comprehensive clinical psychology* (pp. 33–55). New York, NY: Elsevier.

Reynolds, C. R., & Kamphaus, R. W. (2003). *Reynolds Intellectual Assessment Scales.* Lutz, FL: Psychological Assessment Resources.

Reynolds, C. R., & Kamphaus, R. W. (2015). *Reynolds Intellectual Assessment Scales* (2nd ed.). Lutz, FL: Psychological Assessment Resources.

Schmidt, F. L., & Hunter, J. (1998). The validity and utility of selection methods in personnel psychology: Practical and theoretical implications of 85 years of research findings. *Psychological Bulletin, 124*(2), 262–274.

Sireci, S. G. (1998). Gathering and analyzing content validity data. *Educational Assessment, 5,* 299–321.

Wechsler, D. (2014). *Wechsler intelligence scale for children* (5th ed.). Bloomington, MN: NCS Pearson.

Recommended Reading

American Educational Research Association, American Psychological Association, & National Council on Measurement in Education. (1999). *Standards for educational and psychological testing.* Washington, DC: American Educational Research Association. Chapter 1 is a must read for those wanting to gain a thorough understanding of validity.

Cronbach, L. J., & Gleser, G. C. (1965). *Psychological tests and personnel decisions* (2nd ed.). Champaign, IL: University of Illinois Press. A classic, particularly with regard to validity evidence based on relations to external variables!

Gorsuch, R. L. (1983). *Factor analysis* (2nd ed.). Hillsdale, NJ: Erlbaum. A classic for those really interested in understanding factor analysis.

Hunter, J. E., Schmidt, F. L., & Rauschenberger, J. (1984). Methodological, statistical, and ethical issues in the study of bias in psychological tests. In C. R. Reynolds & R. T. Brown (Eds.), *Perspectives on bias in mental testing* (pp. 41–100). New York, NY: Plenum.

Lee, D., Reynolds, C. R., & Willson, V. L. (2003). Standardized test administration: Why bother? *Journal of Forensic Neuropsychology, 3,* 55–81.

McFall, R. M., & Treat, T. T. (1999). Quantifying the information value of clinical assessments with signal detection theory. *Annual Review of Psychology, 50,* 215–241.

Messick, S. (1989). Validity. In R. L. Linn (Ed.), *Educational measurement* (3rd ed., pp. 13–103). Upper Saddle River, NJ: Merrill/Prentice Hall. A little technical at times, but very influential.

Schmidt, F. L., & Hunter, J. E. (1998). The validity and utility of selection methods in personnel psychology: Practical and theoretical implications of 85 years of research findings.
Psychological Bulletin, 124, 262–274. A must read on personnel selection!

Sireci, S. G. (1998). Gathering and analyzing content validity data. *Educational Assessment, 5*,
299–321. This article provides a good review of approaches to collecting validity evidence
based on test content, including some of the newer quantitative approaches.

Tabachnick, B. G., & Fidel, L. S. (1996). *Using multivariate statistics* (3rd ed.). New York, NY:
HarperCollins. A great chapter on factor analysis that is less technical than Gorsuch (1993).

Item Development

6

Everyone thinks it is easy to develop good test items, until they try!

Abstract

A psychological test is generally only as good as its items. While test items are often classified as objective or subjective, a more direct way of classifying items is by using a selected-response or constructed-response designation. Specific examples of these item types are reviewed throughout this chapter. This chapter also provides general item writing guidelines, along with detailed reviews of a wide range of maximum-performance test items, including multiple choice, true-false, matching, essay, and short answer. This chapter concludes by reviewing typical-response items that are often found on personality and attitude scales.

Supplementary Information The online version of this chapter (https://doi.org/10.1007/978-3-030-59455-8_6) contains supplementary material, which is available to authorized users.

Learning Objectives

After reading and studying this chapter, students should be able to:
1. Distinguish between objective and subjective items.
2. Distinguish between selected-response and constructed-response items.
3. Specify the strengths and limitations of selected-response and constructed-response items and the specific formats.
4. Understand, describe, and apply general guidelines for developing items.
5. Distinguish between maximum-performance test items and typical-response items.
6. Demonstrate entry-level skills in developing multiple-choice items.
7. Demonstrate entry-level skills in developing true-false items.
8. Demonstrate entry-level skills in developing matching items.
9. Demonstrate entry-level skills in developing essay items.
10. Demonstrate entry-level skills in developing short-answer items.
11. Demonstrate entry-level skills in developing typical-response items.

Psychological tests are made up of test items, so the goodness of the test items determines the goodness of the test. On the face of it, developing good test items may seem like a simple straightforward endeavor, but in reality, the goodness of test items is determined by careful consideration of a number of important factors combined with quantitative evaluation using specific psychometric procedures. In this chapter, we provide a practical discussion of how to develop good test items. This includes discussion of the different item formats available to test authors and some basic guidelines for developing items. We discuss development of items for maximum-performance tests and typical-response tests. You will recall that maximum-performance tests are designed to determine the upper limits of individuals' abilities or knowledge, while typical-response tests assess their routine or day-to-day characteristics. In an occupational setting, an employer could use a typical-response test to determine whether an employee is completing those daily activities that are required for the job, and a maximum-performance test to determine whether the employee has the knowledge or ability for promotion to a more complex higher-level job. Maximum-performance and typical-response tests have important roles in psychological assessment so we consider test items used in both. We start this chapter with a brief survey of the most popular item formats before proceeding to a discussion of guidelines for developing items.

6.1   Item Formats

Different authors use different classification systems or schemes to categorize test items. One historically popular approach is to classify test items as either "objective" or "subjective." This distinction usually refers to how the items are scored, either in an objective or subjective manner. If experts in the area would demonstrate a high level of agreement on whether

> One popular approach has been to classify test items as either objective or subjective.

the item is answered correctly or in the keyed direction, the item is considered objective—where much disagreement might exist, the item is classified as subjective. The relative objectivity and subjectivity of items anchor two ends of a continuum, and there is often no bright shining line for declaring an item as totally objective or subjective. However, in the context of maximum-performance tests, there should be no disagreement among individuals grading multiple-choice items. The items should be easily scored "correct" or "incorrect" according to the scoring criteria. This also applies to true–false and matching items. They can all be scored in an objective manner and are classified as objective: everyone agrees on which answers are keyed as correct and incorrect. This rationale also applies to objective items on typical-response tests. For example, true–false items are also used on typical-response tests and these can be scored in an objective manner.

In contrast, essay items are considered subjective since grading them involves subjective judgments on the part of the individuals grading the items. It is not too surprising that two graders might assign different grades to the same essay item. Another example could be an examinee's responses on an oral examination. Here there also might be considerable subjectivity in scoring and two individuals might score the response differently. Our own personal experiences in administering the oral section of state board licensing examinations for psychologists, where oral examiners are trained, provided a manual, and allowed to observe experienced examiners, and need only score the examinee's answers as pass–fail, indicates such exams to be highly subjective, with a surprising amount of disagreement among examiners. Since examinations are used for licensure in many professions (e.g., psychology, medicine, physical therapy, law, etc.) to determine who is allowed to practice and who is not, lack of correspondence between examiners about who passes and who fails is very concerning. Primarily for this reason, many licensing organizations are doing away with oral exams in favor of objective examination procedures for such critical decisions. As a result, essay, oral response, and other test item formats that involve more subjective scoring are classified as subjective.

In the context of typical-response tests, there are also item formats that require subjective judgment. For example, projective personality tests are typical-response tests that require the respondent to respond to ambiguous stimuli. The Rorschach Inkblot Test is an example of a projective personality test where the test taker is shown an inkblot and asked "What might this be?" One person might envision a boat, another sees a swan, and another sees a dragon. The scoring of this type of test typically involves considerable subjective judgment.

While the objective-subjective distinction is generally useful, there are some limitations. For example, are "short-answer" items objective or subjective? Many authors refer to them as objective items, but actually scoring short-answer items often involves considerable subjectivity. A more direct approach is to classify items as either *selected-response* or *constructed-response* items. With this approach, if an item requires an examinee to select a response from available alternatives, it is classified as a selected-response item. Multiple-choice, true–false, and matching items are all selected-response items. If an item requires examinees to create or construct a response, it is classified as a constructed-response item. Constructed-response items include *fill-in-the-blank, short-answer,* and *essay items,* and would

> A more direct approach is to classify items as either selected-response or constructed-response items, and this is the one adopted in this textbook.

also include typical *oral examination procedures* as well as *interviews.* In a broader sense, constructed-response assessments also include *performance assessments, portfolios,* and even *projective techniques.* The selected-response/constructed-response classification system is the one we will use in this textbook.

As we indicated, on selected-response items, examinees select the appropriate response from options that are provided. On a true–false item, the examinee simply selects true or false to answer the item. On multiple-choice items, they select the best response from a list of alternatives. On matching items, the examinees match premises (typically listed on the left) with the appropriate responses (typically listed on the right). The key factor is that all selected-response items provide the answer; the examinee simply selects the appropriate one. While there are considerable differences among these selected-response item formats, we can make some general statements about their strengths and limitations. Strengths include:

- Examinees generally can respond to a relatively large number of selected-response items in a limited amount of time. This means you can include more items in your test. Since tests are essentially samples of the content domain, and large samples are better than small samples, the inclusion of a large number of items tends to enhance the measurement characteristics of the test.

> Examinees generally can respond to a relatively large number of selected-response items in a limited amount of time and items can be scored in an efficient, objective, and reliable manner.

- Selected-response items can be scored in an efficient, objective, and reliable manner. A computer can often score selected-response items. As a result, scoring takes less time, there are fewer grading errors, and scorer bias has little impact on the final score. This can produce tests with desirable measurement characteristics such as more reliable test scores.
- Selected-response items are flexible and can be used to assess a wide range of constructs with greatly varying levels of complexity.
- Selected-response items decrease the influence of certain construct-irrelevant factors that can impact test scores (e.g., the influence of writing ability on a test measuring scientific knowledge).

Naturally, there are limitations associated with the use of selected-response items. These include:

- Selected-response items are challenging to write. For example, for items that provide several response options, it can be difficult to come up with alternative responses that are plausible, yet still incorrect. Alternative responses that are too easily ruled out as a correct answer can lead examinees to a correct response by a process of elimination rather than actually knowing the answer. Relative to constructed-response items, selected-response items typically take more effort and time to write. This is not to say that writing constructed-response items is an easy task—just that the development of effective selected-response items is usually more difficult and time-consuming.
- There are some constructs that cannot be measured using selected-response items. For example, if you want to measure an individual's ability to play the flute or write a poem, you need to have them actually create the response by performing. Special Interest Topic 6.1 summarizes research that examines unsubstantiated claims that selected-response items penalize creative examinees.
- Selected-response items are subject to blind guessing and random responding. Since the examinee is only required to "select" a response, they can do this randomly. When this type of responding produces a correct response, it leads to the false impression that the examinee knows something about the content domain that they do not.

Constructed-response items include short-answer items, essays, performance assessments, and portfolios. Most people are familiar with short-answer items and essays. Short-answer items require the examinee to supply a word, phrase, or number in response to a direct question. Short-answer items may also take the form of an incomplete sentence which the examinee completes (i.e., fill-in-the-blank). Essay items pose a question or problem for the examinee to respond to in a written format. Essay items can typically be classified as either restricted-response or extended-response. As the name suggests, restricted-response essays are highly structured and place restrictions on the nature and scope of the examinees' responses. In contrast, extended-response essays are less structured and provide more freedom to examinees in how they respond. While we have mentioned performance assessments previously in this text, you may not be very familiar with them. Performance assessments require

Special Interest Topic 6.1: Do Multiple-Choice Items Penalize Creative Examinees?

Critics of multiple-choice and other selected-response items have long asserted that these items only measure superficial knowledge and conventional thinking and actually penalize examinees that are creative, deep-thinkers. In a recent study, Powers and Kaufman (2002) examined the relationship between performance on the Graduate Record Examination (GRE) General Test and selected personality traits, including creativity, quickness, and depth. In summary, their analyses revealed that there was no evidence that "deeper-thinking" examinees were penalized by the multiple-choice format. The correlation between GRE scores and Depth were as follows: Analytical = 0.06, Quantitative = 0.08, and Verbal = 0.15. The results in terms of creativity were more positive. The correlation between GRE scores and Creativity were as follows: Analytical = 0.24, Quantitative = 0.26, and Verbal = 0.29 (all p's < 0.001). Similar results were obtained with regard to Quickness. The correlation between GRE scores and Quickness were as follows: Analytical = 0.21, Quantitative = 0.15, and Verbal = 0.26 (all p's < 0.001). In summary, there is no evidence that individuals that are creative, deep-thinkers, and mentally quick are penalized by multiple-choice items. In fact, the research reveals modest positive correlations between the GRE scores and these personality traits. To be fair, there was one rather surprising finding, a slightly negative correlation between GRE scores and Conscientious (e.g., careful, avoids mistakes, completes work on time). The only hypothesis the authors proposed was that "conscientious" does not benefit examinees particularly well on timed tests like the GRE that place a premium on quick performance.

examinees to complete a process or produce a product in a context that closely resembles real-life situations. An example would be having an airline pilot being required to demonstrate their aviation skills in a flight simulator that mimics the flying characteristics on a specific airplane. Portfolio assessments, a form of performance assessment, involve the systematic collection of examinee work products over a specified period of time according to a specific set of guidelines (AREA et al., 2014). Artists, architects, writers, and others have long used portfolios to represent their work. In the context of typical-response tests, projective personality tests require respondents to construct a unique response to ambiguous stimuli, not to select a response from a list of alternatives. Constructed-response assessments have their own associated strengths and weaknesses. Their strengths include:

- Compared to selected-response items, some constructed-response assessments (e.g., short-answer and essays) may be easier to write or develop. Not easy, but easier! It is important to remember that while the question might be easier to write, developing a framework for how to properly score such a response can take a considerable amount of time and effort.

- Constructed-response items are well suited for assessing higher-order cognitive abilities and complex task performance, and some tasks simply require a constructed-response format (e.g., composing a letter, demonstrating problem-solving skills). As a result, they expand the range of constructs that can be assessed.
- Constructed-response items eliminate blind guessing. Since the examinee has to actually "construct" or create a response, random guessing is nearly eliminated.

Their weaknesses include:

- Constructed-response items take more time for examinees to complete. You cannot include as many constructed-response items or tasks on a test as you can selected-response items. As a result, you are not able to sample the content domain as thoroughly.
- Constructed-response items are more difficult to score in a reliable manner. In addition to scoring being more difficult and time-consuming compared to selected-response items, scoring is more subjective and less reliable.
- While constructed-response items practically eliminate blind guessing, they are vulnerable to "feigning." For example, examinees who do not actually know the correct response might feign a response that superficially resembles a correct response (in Texas we have another name for this act that our publisher will not allow us to name here!).
- Constructed-response items are vulnerable to the influence of extraneous or construct-irrelevant factors that can impact test scores (e.g., the influence of writing ability on a test measuring scientific knowledge).

> Constructed-response items are well suited for assessing higher-order cognitive abilities and complex task performance.

As you see, selected-response and constructed-response test items have specific strengths and weaknesses, and these strengths and weaknesses deserve careful consideration when selecting an assessment format. However, typically the key factor in selecting an assessment or item format involves identifying the format that most directly measures the construct. That is, you want to select the item format or task that will be the most pure, direct measure of the construct of interest. For example, if you want to assess an examinee's writing abilities, an essay is the natural choice. If you want to assess an examinee's ability to engage in oral debate, a performance assessment would be the logical choice. However, if you wanted to predict their ability to develop such a skill with proper training, a selected-response measure of logical and deductive reasoning might work very well. While the nature of some constructs or objectives dictates the use of constructed-response items (e.g., writing skills), some can be measured equally well using either selected-response or constructed-response items. If after careful consideration you determine that both formats are appropriate, we generally recommend the use of selected-response items since they allow broader sampling of the content domain and more objective/reliable scoring procedures. Both of these factors enhance the measurement characteristics of your test. Tables 6.1 and 6.2 summarize the strengths and weaknesses of selected-response and constructed-response items.

> Selected-response and constructed-response assessments have specific strengths and weaknesses that should be considered when selecting an item format. However, typically the key factor in selecting an assessment or item format involves identifying the format that most directly measures the construct you want to measure.

6.2   General Item Writing Guidelines

In the remainder of this chapter, we will provide guidelines for developing different types of items. We recommend you apply these guidelines in a flexible manner. When creating test items, the overriding goal is to develop items that measure the specified construct and contribute to psychometrically sound tests. Many of these suggestions are tied to specific item types. For example, we will first discuss the broad topic of maximum-performance tests. In that section, we will discuss the development of both selected-response and constructed-response items. We will then turn to our attention to the development of typical-response tests. Here we will focus on the development of selected-response items. However, before providing guidelines for developing specific item types, we will provide some general guidelines that are applicable to almost all items. These general guidelines are listed below.

> The overriding goal is to develop items that measure the specified construct and contribute to psychometrically sound tests.

Table 6.1   Strengths and weaknesses of selected-response items

Strengths of selected-response items
1. You can typically include a relatively large number of selected-response items in your test. This facilitates adequate sampling of the content domain
2. They can be scored in an efficient, objective, and reliable manner
3. They are flexible and can be used to assess a wide range of abilities
4. They can reduce the influence of certain construct-irrelevant factors

Weaknesses of selected-response items
1. They are relatively difficult to write, particularly in creating reasonable response options that have a single correct answer
2. They are not able to assess all abilities (e.g., writing ability)
3. They are subject to random guessing

Table 6.2 Strengths and weaknesses of constructed-response items

Strengths of constructed-response items
1. Compared to selected-response items, they are often easier to write
2. They are well suited for assessing higher-order cognitive abilities and complex task performance
3. They help to eliminate random guessing

Weaknesses of constructed-response items
1. Since they typically require more time than selected-response items for the examinees to complete, you cannot include as many items in a test. As a result, you are not as able to sample the content domain as thoroughly
2. They are more difficult to score in a reliable manner, and require extensive time and effort in creating scoring criteria
3. They are vulnerable to feigning
4. They are vulnerable to the influence of construct-irrelevant factors

1. **Provide clear directions.** It is common for inexperienced test developers to assume that test takers understand how to respond to different item formats. This may not be the case! When developing a test always include thorough directions that clearly specify how the examinee should respond to each item format. Just to be safe, assume that the examinees have never seen a test like it before and provide directions in sufficient detail to ensure they know what is expected of them. However, overly long and detailed instructions are less desirable than short succinct ones, because too much detail may actually decrease clarity. When directions are long, examinees may not distinguish those aspects of the directions that are crucial for task performance from those that are secondary, or simply may not remember the instructions.

2. **Present the question, problem, or task in a clear and straightforward manner.** When writing items, keep it as simple as possible! Unless you are assessing reading ability, aim for a low reading level. You do not want an examinee to answer an item incorrectly due to ambiguous wording, complex syntax, or unnecessarily difficult vocabulary. This does not mean to avoid scientific or technical terms necessary to state the problem; rather, simply avoid the unnecessary use of complex incidental words.

    In addition, generally avoid using items that contain *no*, *none*, and *not*. The use of negative statements can make the statement more ambiguous, which is not desirable. Do not make vocabulary a part of the question or problem *unintentionally*. Along these same lines, you should avoid whenever possible complex, compound sentence constructions unless their understanding and comprehension are actually being assessed. Otherwise, you will almost certainly introduce construct-irrelevant variance as some people will simply be confused by the wording or have difficulty attending to such constructions when knowledge or understanding of a distinct concept is being assessed. They will then answer incorrectly for reasons irrelevant to the construct being measured.

3. **Develop items that can be scored in a decisive manner.** Ask yourself if the items have clear answers on which virtually every expert would agree. In terms of essays and performance assessments, the question may be if experts would agree about the quality of performance on the task. The scoring process can be challenging even when your items have clearly "correct" answers. When there is ambiguity regarding what represents a definitive answer or response, scoring can become much more difficult.

4. **Avoid inadvertent cues to the answers.** It is easy for unintended cues to correct responses to become embedded in a test. For example, information in one item may provide information that reveals the answer to another item. It is also possible for items to contain a clue to its own answer. Consider the following examples.

Example 1A: Poor item—stem contains a cue to the correct answer
1. Which type of validity study examines the ability of test scores to predict a criterion that is measured in the future?
   A. interval study
   B. content study
   C. factorial study
   D. predictive study   ≪

Example 1B: Better item—cues avoided
2. Which type of validity study involves a substantial time interval between when the test is administered and when the criterion is measured?
   A. interval study
   B. content study
   C. factorial study
   D. predictive study   ≪

Example 2A: Poor item—stem contains a definitive clue to the correct answer (this is an actual item taken from a classroom test administered by a physical education, not math, teacher)
1. How many quarters are there in a football game? _____

Example 2B: Better item—cues avoided
2. How many time periods of play are there in a football game? _____

In Example 1, in the first item, the use of "*predict*" in the stem and "*predictive*" in the correct alternative provides a cue to the correct answer. This is corrected in the second example. In Example 2, the vocabulary gives away the answer— *quarters* refers to 4, and indeed 4 is the correct answer.

5. **Arrange the items in a systematic manner.** You should arrange the items in your assessment in a manner that promotes the optimal performance of your examinees. If your test contains multiple item formats, the items should be arranged in sections according to the type of item. That is, place all the multiple-choice items together, all the short-answer items together, and so on. This is recommended because it allows the examinees to maintain the same mental set throughout each section. It has the added benefit of making it easier for you to score the items. After arranging the items by format, in the case of a maximum-performance measure, you should arrange the items in each section according to their level of difficulty. That is, start with the easy items and move progressively to the more difficult items. This arrangement tends to reduce anxiety,

enhance motivation, and allows examinees to progress quickly through the easier items and devote the remaining time to the more difficult items.

6. **Ensure that individual items are contained on one page.** For selected-response items, ensure that they are contained on one page. For example, for multiple-choice, true–false, and matching items, do not divide them so that part of the item is on one page, and it is completed on another. This can contribute to examinees making errors as they switch back and forth between pages, errors that are irrelevant to the construct you are measuring.

7. **Tailor the items to the target population.** Carefully consider the type of clients your test will be used with and tailor the items accordingly. For example, young children and elderly do not respond well to tasks with manipulatives and these should be avoided unless assessment of dexterity is actually the purpose of the item.

8. **Minimize the impact of construct-irrelevant factors**. Look for and minimize cognitive, motor, and other factors that are necessary to answer items correctly, but irrelevant to the construct being measured. For example, the inclusion of extensive and complex written instructions on a test intended to measure math skills will likely result in the test measuring not only math skills, but also reading comprehension. In Chap. 5 (Validity), we identified construct-irrelevant variance as one of the major threats to validity of test score interpretation.

9. **Avoid using the exact phrasing from study materials.** When preparing achievement tests, avoid using the exact wording used in the textbook or other study materials. Exact phrasing may be appropriate if rote memorization is what you desire, but it is of limited value in terms of encouraging concept formation and the ability to generalize.

10. **Avoid using biased or offensive language.** Carefully review your items for potentially biased or otherwise offensive language. We also encourage you to ask a diverse group of colleagues to review your test items. While reviewers are no better than chance at nominating or detecting culturally biased items, the language or symbols contained in a test item may be inadvertently offensive to some cultural and religious groups, and if you are not a member of the group, you may well be unaware of the issue with the item content. Commercial test publishers routinely ask members of both genders as well as ethnic and other cultural groups, including different religious denominations, to review test item content for offensiveness.

11. **Use a print format that is clear and easy to read.** Use a font size and spacing that is clear and appropriate for the examinees. For example, with tests designed for use with very young or with elderly clients a larger font size is recommended. Carefully examine the test in its final form to ensure that it is easy to follow and does not hinder performance.

12. **Determine how many items to include.** There is no simple answer to the question of how many items to include in a test. The optimal number of items to include in an assessment is determined by factors such as the time available, age of the examinees, the types of items, the breadth of the material or topics

being assessed (i.e., scope of the test), and the type of test. Let's consider several of these factors separately:

- *Time Available:* Obviously it is important to consider the amount of time available for assessment when determining how many items to include in a test. For example, if you are developing a classroom test to be administered in a standard one-hour period you must plan accordingly. If you are developing a brief screening instrument designed to screen a large number of persons for depression, it is important to limit the number of items so the test be administered in a brief time period (e.g., 15 minutes).

- *Age of examinees:* For young examinees, it is probably best to limit tests to no more than about 30 minutes in order to maximize effort, concentration, and motivation. The same might apply to elderly clients. For adolescents and most adults you can increase this period considerably, but it is probably desirable to limit most assessments to 2–4 hours in order to maximize performance. Naturally, these are just flexible guidelines. For example, when administering comprehensive achievement, aptitude, or personality assessments, more time may be necessary to assess the constructs adequately. Also, time limits may be considerably longer when tests are administered individually by a trained examiner, skilled at developing and maintaining rapport, evaluating effort, attention, and fatigue, and recognizing when breaks are appropriate.

- *Types of items:* Obviously, examinees can complete more true–false or multiple-choice items than they can essay items in a given period of time. As we have already alluded to, the inclusion of more "time-efficient" items will enhance the sampling of the content domain and produce more reliable scores.

- *Type and Purpose of the Test:* Maximum-performance tests can typically be categorized as either *speed* or *power* tests. Pure speed tests generally contain items that are relatively easy but have strict time limits that prevent examinees from successfully completing all the items. On pure power tests, the speed of performance is not an issue. Everyone is given enough time to attempt all the items, but the items are ordered according to difficulty, with some items being so difficult that almost no examinees are expected to answer them all. The distinction between speed and power tests is one of degree rather than being absolute. Most often a test is not a *pure* speed test or a *pure* power test, but incorporates some combination of the two approaches. The decision to use a speed test, a power test, or some combination of the two will influence the number and type of items you include on your test.

- *Scope of the Test*: In addition to the power versus speed test distinction, the scope of the test will influence how many items you include in an assessment. For a weekly classroom exam designed to assess progress in a relatively narrow range of skills and knowledge, a brief test will likely be sufficient. However, for a 6-week or semester assessment covering a broader range of skills and knowledge, a more comprehensive (i.e., longer) assessment is typically indicated.

When estimating the time needed to complete the test, you should also take into consideration any test-related activities such as handing out the test, giving directions, and collecting the tests. Most test professional test developers design power tests that approximately 95% of their samples will complete in the allotted time. This is probably a good rule of thumb for most maximum-performance tests. If fewer than 95% of examinees reach the final item before a time limit expires, the test is considered to be speeded, and not a true power test. The purpose of the test (i.e., what you are attempting to measure) should always be considered in determining whether you need time limits and if so, how stringent they should be. Many tests have no time limits at all. Table 6.3 provides a summary of these general guidelines for developing test items.

6.3   Maximum-Performance Tests

In the next sections, we provide guidelines for writing items for maximum-performance tests. In this section, we will focus primarily on the development of items for achievement tests that are designed to measure educational or learning objectives. However, many of these guidelines will apply to aptitude tests that use these types of items. We will first address selected-response items, then constructed-response items. In subsequent sections, we will provide suggestions for developing guidelines for typical performance tests.

Table 6.3 General item development guidelines

1. Provide clear instructions
2. Present the question, problem, or task in a clear and straightforward manner
3. Develop items that can be scored in a decisive manner
4. Avoid inadvertent cues to correct answers
5. Arrange items in a systematic manner
6. Ensure individual items are contained on one page
7. Tailor the items to the target population
8. Minimize the impact of construct-irrelevant factors
9. Avoid using the exact phrasing from study materials
10. Avoid using biased or offensive language
11. Use a print format that is clear and easy to read
12. To determine the number of items, consider factors such as the amount of time available, age of the examinees, and purpose of the test

6.3.1 Multiple-Choice Items

Multiple-choice items are by far the most popular of the selected-response items. They have gained this degree of popularity because they can be used in a variety of content areas and can assess both simple and complex objectives. Multiple-choice items take the general form of a question or incomplete statement with a set of possible answers, one of which is correct. The part of the item that is either a question or an incomplete statement is referred to as the stem. The possible answers are referred to as alternatives. The correct alternative is simply called the answer and the incorrect alternatives are referred to as distracters (i.e., they serve to "distract" examinees who don't actually know the correct response).

> Multiple-choice items are the most popular of the selected-response items largely because they can be used in a variety of content areas and can assess both simple and complex objectives.

Multiple-choice items can be written so the stem is in the form of a direct-question or an incomplete-sentence. Most writers prefer the direct-question format because they feel it presents the problem in the clearest manner. The advantage of the incomplete-statement format is that it may present the problem in a more concise manner. If the question is formatted as an incomplete statement, it is suggested that the omission occurs near the end of the stem. Our recommendation is to use the direct-question format unless the problem can be stated more concisely using the incomplete-sentence format without any loss of clarity.

Another distinction is made between multiple-choice items that have what's known as the *correct-answer format* versus the *best-answer format*. The correct-answer format is appropriate when there is only one correct answer (e.g., what is the square root of 100?). However, multiple-choice items can also be written to handle situations where there are more than one correct answer and the objective is to identify the "best-answer." Consider the following example of a best-answer item.

Example 3: Best-answer format
1. Which variable is generally thought to be the most important influence on the resale value of a house?
    A. initial cost per square foot cost
    B. the builder's reputation
    C. contemporariness of the design
    D. location   ≪

In Example 3, all the variables listed are important to consider when considering resale value of a house, but as almost any realtor will tell you, location is the most important. Most test developers prefer the best-answer format for two reasons. First, in some situations it is difficult to write an answer that everyone will agree is correct. The best-answer format allows you to frame it as an answer that most experts will agree with. Second, the best-answer format often requires the examinee to make more subtle distinctions among the alternatives, which results in more demanding items that measure more complex educational objectives. Below are more suggestions for developing multiple-choice items.

1. **Use a format that makes the item as clear as possible.** While there is not a universally accepted format for multiple-choice items, here are a few recommendations regarding the physical layout that can enhance clarity.
   - The item stem should be numbered for easy identification, while the alternatives are indented and identified with letters.
   - There is no need to capitalize the beginning of alternatives unless they begin with a proper name.
   - Keep the alternatives in a vertical list instead of placing them side by side since it is easier for examinees to scan a vertical list quickly.

2. **The item stem should contain all the information necessary to understand the problem or question.** When writing multiple-choice items, the problem or question should be fully developed in the item stem. Poorly developed multiple-choice items often contain an inadequate stem that leaves the test taker unclear about the central problem or question. One way to determine if the stem is adequate is to read the stem without examining the alternatives. If the stem is adequate, a knowledgeable individual should be able to answer the question with relative ease without needing to read the alternatives.

3. **Provide between three and five alternatives.** While there is no "correct" number of alternatives to provide, it is recommended that you use between three and five alternatives. Four is the most common number of alternatives, but some test developers suggest using five alternatives since using more alternatives reduces the chance of correctly guessing the answer when you know nothing at all about which answer is correct. For example, the chance of correctly guessing the answer with three alternatives is 1 in 3 (i.e., 33%); with four alternatives is 1 in 4 (i.e., 25%); and with five alternatives is 1 in 5 (i.e., 20%). The use of five alternatives is probably the upper limit since many computer-scoring programs only accommodate five alternatives and due to the difficulty in developing plausible distracters (the addition of distracters that are clearly wrong and not selected by any examinees does not reduce the chance of correctly guessing the answer). In some situations, three alternatives may be sufficient. It takes examinees less time to read and answer items with three alternatives instead of four (or five) and it is easier to write two good distracters than three (or four). There is even research that suggests that multiple-choice items with three alternatives can be as effective as items with four or five alternatives (e.g., Costin, 1970; Grier, 1975; Sidick, Barrett, & Doverspike, 1994).

4. **Keep the alternatives brief and arrange them in an order that promotes efficient scanning.** As we noted, the item stem should contain as much of the content as possible and should not contain irrelevant material. A correlate of this is that the alternatives should be as brief as possible. This brevity makes it easier for the examinees to scan the alternatives looking for the correct answer. When applicable, alternatives should be arranged in a logical order that promotes efficient scanning. For example, numbers should be placed in ascending order, dates ordered in temporal sequence, and nouns and names should be alphabetized. When there is no logical order for the distracters, they should be arranged randomly to avoid a pattern where one lettered distracter is more

likely to be correct over the course of the test items (e.g., many people believe that option "C" is the most frequent correct answer among 5-choice MC items).

5. **In most situations, avoid negatively stated stems.** As a general rule, we recommend to avoid using negatively stated stems. By this we mean you should limit the use of terms such as *except*, *least*, *never*, or *not*. Examinees might overlook these terms and miss the question even when they have mastered the learning objective measured by the item. Unless your intention is to measure the examinee's ability to read the items carefully and attend to details, this is not a desired outcome and the correct interpretation of the test's results is undermined. In most situations, this can be avoided simply by rephrasing the stem. Occasionally it may be necessary or desirable to state stems in the negative. For example, in some situations, it is important for examinees to know what not to do (e.g., what should you *not* do if you smell gas?) or identify an alternative that differs in some way from the other alternatives. In these situations, you should highlight the negative terms by capitalizing, underlining, or printing them in bold type.

   Double negatives should be avoided always (a word we generally detest in testing circles!). While logicians know that a double negative indicates a positive case, examinees should not have to ferret out this logic problem—nor decide if you understood it!

6. **Make sure only one alternative is correct or clearly represents the best answer.** Carefully review your alternatives to ensure there is only one correct or best answer. It is common for professors to be confronted by upset students who feel they can defend one of the distracters as a correct answer. While it is not possible to avoid this situation completely, you can minimize it by carefully evaluating the distracters. We recommend setting the test aside for a period of time and returning to it for proofing after a break. Occasionally it might be appropriate to include more than one correct alternative in a multiple-choice item and require the examinees to identify all of the correct alternatives. In these situations, it is usually best to format the question as a series of true–false items, an arrangement referred to as a cluster-type or multiple true–false item. This format is illustrated below.

Example 4: Multiple true–false item

1. Which of the following states have a coastline on the Gulf of Mexico? Underline the **T** if the state has a Gulf coastline, or **F** if the state does not have a Gulf coastline

Alabama	**T**	F
Florida	**T**	F
Tennessee	T	**F**
Texas	**T**	F

---

7. **All alternatives should be grammatically correct relative to the stem.** Another set of cues that may help the uninformed examinee select the correct answer is based on grammatical rules. These grammatical cues are usually the result of

inadequate proofreading and can usually be corrected once they are detected. Examine the following examples.

Example 5: Poor item—grammatical cue present

1. Which individuals are credited with making the first successful flights in a heavier-than-air aircraft that was both powered and controlled?
    A. Octave Chanute
    B. Otto Lilienthal
    C. Samuel Langley
    D. Wilbur and Orville Wright   ≪

Example 6: Better item—grammatical cue avoided

2. Which individuals are credited with making the first successful flights in a heavier-than-air aircraft that was both powered and controlled?
    A. Octave Chanute and Sir George Cayley
    B. Otto Lilienthal and Francis Herbert Wenham
    C. Samuel Langley and Alphonse Penaud
    D. Wilbur Wright and Orville Wright   ≪

In the first example the phrase "... individuals are..." in the stem indicates a plural answer. However, only the fourth alternative (i.e., D) meets this requirement. This is corrected in the second example by ensuring that each alternative reflects a plural answer. Another common error is inattention to the articles *a* and *an* in the stem. Review the following examples:

Example 7: Poor item—grammatical cue present

1. A coherent and unifying explanation for a class of phenomena is a _____
    A. analysis
    B. experiment
    C. observation
    D. theory   ≪

Example 8: Better item—grammatical cue avoided

2. A coherent and unifying explanation for a class of phenomena is a(n) _____
    A. experiment
    B. hypothesis
    C. observation
    D. theory   ≪

In the first example, the use of the article *a* indicates an answer beginning with a consonant instead of a vowel. An observant examinee relying on cues will detect this and select the fourth alternative (i.e., D) since it is the only one that is grammatically correct. This is corrected in the second example by using "a(n)" to accommodate alternatives beginning with either consonants or vowels.

8. **All distracters should appear plausible.** Distracters should be designed to distract unknowledgeable examinees from the correct answer. Therefore, all distracters should appear plausible and should be based on common errors. In general, distractors should also be related to the subject being tested on. For example, review the following examples:

Example 9: Poor item—unrealistic distractors

1. Which of the following is a famous female explorer known for flying throughout the world and who disappeared during a flight? _____

    A. Ariana Grande

    B. Amelia Earhart   ≪

    C. Selena Gomez

    D. Beyoncé

Example 10: Better Item—Distractors who are all female explorers

2. Which of the following is a famous female explorer known for flying throughout the world and who disappeared during a flight? _____

    A. Isabella Bird

    B. Amelia Earhart   ≪

    C. Mary Kingsley

    D. Ann Bancroft

In the first example, all distractors are popular singers/performers; in the second example, all response choices are female explorers. After you have administered the test once, analyze the distracters and determine which ones are effective and which are not. Replace or revise the ineffective distracters. There is little point in including a distracter that can be easily eliminated by uninformed examinees. Such distracters simply waste time and space. This analysis may produce some surprising results. In Example 10, the last distractor "D" Ann Bancroft is a female explorer, but Anne (with an "e") Bancroft was an American actress, screenwriter, and director. The name similarity of these two famous women may decrease the effectiveness of this distractor. Those who are familiar with the actress but not the exact spelling of her name may dismiss this a reasonable answer to the question.

9. **Use alternative positions in a random manner for the correct answer.** This guideline suggests that the correct answer should appear in each of the alternative positions approximately the same number of times. When there are four alternatives (e.g., A, B, C, and D), there is a tendency for test developers to overuse the middle alternatives (i.e., B and C). Alert examinees are likely to detect this pattern and use this information to answer questions of which they are unsure. For example, we have had examinees indicate that when faced with a question they can't answer based on the knowledge, they simply select "B" or "C." An easy way to reach this goal is to attempt random assignment when possible and once the test is complete count the number of times the correct answer appears in each position. If any positions are over or underrepresented, simply make adjustments to correct the imbalance. However, be sure that the adjustment doesn't result in a cue for the correct answer, e.g., if the response options for the other questions are listed in alphabetic or numerical order, then moving a response to a different place in the order might be a cue for the examinee; in

such a case, a distractor or distractors might need to be slightly adjusted to maintain the desired ordering of response options.

10. **Minimize the use of "none of the above" and avoid using "all of the above."** There is some disagreement among test development experts regarding the use of "none of the above" and "all of the above" as alternatives. The alternative "none of the above" is criticized because it automatically forces the item into a correct-answer format. While there are times when "none of the above" is appropriate as an alternative, it should be used sparingly. If it is used, then it is important to use it in at least a few questions; otherwise, if used only when it is a correct answer, then it might serve as a cue to the correct answer. Testing experts are more unified in their criticism of "all of the above" as an alternative. There are two primary concerns. First, an examinee may read alternative A, see that it is correct and mark it without ever reading alternatives B, C, and D. In this situation the response is incorrect because the examinee did not read all of the alternatives, not necessarily because they did not know the correct answer. Second, examinees may only know that two of the alternatives are correct and therefore conclude that "all of the above" is correct. In this situation, the response is correct but is based on incomplete knowledge. Our recommendation is to use "none of the above" sparingly and avoid using "all of the above."

11. **Limit the use of "always" and "never" in the alternatives.** The use of always and never should generally be avoided since it is only in mathematics that their use is typically justified. Savvy examinees know this and will use this information to rule-out distracters.

Multiple-choice items are the most popular selected-response format. They have numerous strengths including versatility, objective and reliable scoring and efficient sampling of the content domain. The only substantive weaknesses are that multiple-choice items are not effective for measuring all learning objectives (e.g., organization and presentation of material; writing ability; performance tasks) and they are not easy to develop. Testing experts generally support the use of multiple-choice items as they can contribute to the development of reliable and valid assessments. Table 6.4 provides a checklist for developing multiple-choice items. Special Interest Topic 6.2 summarizes research that has empirically examined the question "Is it in your best interest to change your answer on a multiple-choice test?"

6.3.2 True–False Items

The next selected-response format we will discuss is the true–false format. *True–false items* are very popular, second only to the multiple-choice format. We will use the term true–false items to actually refer to a broader class of items. Sometimes this category is referred to as *binary items, two-option items, or alternate-choice* items. The common factor is that all these items involve a statement or question that the examinee marks as true or false, agree or disagree, correct or incorrect, yes or no,

Special Interest Topic 6.2: What Research Says About "Changing your answer?"
Have you ever heard that it is usually not in your best interest to change your answer on a multiple-choice test? Many examinees *and* educators believe that you are best served by sticking with your first impression. That is, don't change your answer. Surprisingly this is not consistent with the research! Pike (1979) reviewed the literature and came up with these conclusions:

- Examinees only change their answers on approximately 4% of the questions.
- When they do change their answer, more often than not it is in their best interest. Typically there are approximately two favorable changes (i.e., *incorrect* to *correct*) for every unfavorable one (i.e., *correct* to *incorrect*).
- These positive effects tend to decrease on more difficult items.
- High-scoring examinees are more likely to profit from changing their answers than low-scoring examinees.

This does not mean that you should encourage your examinees to change their answers on a whim. However, if an examinee feels a change is indicated based on careful thought and consideration, they should feel comfortable doing so. Research suggests that they are probably doing the right thing to enhance their score.

Table 6.4   Checklist for the development of multiple-choice items

1. Are the items clear and easy to read?	_____
2. Does the item stem clearly state the problem or question?	_____
3. Are there between three and five response alternatives?	_____
4. Are the alternatives brief and arranged in an order that promotes efficient scanning?	_____
5. Have you avoided negatively stated stems?	_____
6. Is there only one alternative that is correct or represents the best answer?	_____
7. Are all alternatives grammatically correct relative to the stem?	_____
8. Do all distracters appear plausible?	_____
9. Did you use response alternative positions in a random manner for the correct answer?	_____
10. Did you minimize the use of "none of the above" and avoid using "all of the above?"	_____
11. Did you limit the use of "always" and "never" in the alternatives?	_____

fact or opinion, etc. Since the most common form is true–false, we will use this term generically to refer to all two-option or binomial items. Below are our guidelines for developing true–false items.

1. **Avoid including more than one idea in the statement.** True–false items should address only one central idea or point. Consider the following examples.

Example 11A: Poor item—statement contains more than one idea
1. T   F   The study of biology helps us understand living organisms and predict the weather.
Example 11B: Better item—statement contains only one idea
2. **T**   F   The study of biology helps us understand living organisms.

Example 11A contains two ideas, one that is correct and one that is false. Therefore it is partially true and partially false. Although the statement is false— most agree that biologists do not predict the weather—the presentation of both ideas can cause confusion as to how examinees should respond. The second example addresses only one idea and is less likely to be misleading. Even if both ideas are correct, the specificity of the item content is suspect and the test results become more difficult to interpret correctly. For example, if the examinee missed the item, was it because s/he did not know the first idea, the second idea, or neither of them?

2. **Avoid specific determiners and qualifiers that might serve as cues to the answer.** Specific determiners like *never, always, none,* and *all* occur more frequently in false statements and serve as cues to uninformed examinees that the statement is too broad to be true. Accordingly, moderately worded statements including *usually, sometimes,* and *frequently* are more likely to be true and these qualifiers also serve as cues to uninformed examinees. While it would be difficult to avoid using qualifiers in all true–false items, they can be used equally in true and false statements so their value as cues is diminished.

3. **Ensure that true and false statements are of approximately the same length.** There is a tendency among item-writers to write *true* statements (most likely to ensure their exactness) that are longer than *false* statements. To prevent statement length from serving as an unintentional cue, visually inspect your statements and ensure that there is no conspicuous difference between the length of true and false statements.

4. **Include an approximately equal number of true and false statements.** Some examinees are more likely to select *True* when they are unsure of the correct response (i.e., acquiescence set) and there are also examinees who have adopted a response set where they mark *False* when unsure of the answer. To prevent examinees from artificially inflating their scores with either of these response sets you should include an approximately equal number of *True* and *False* items. Some earlier writers recommended that in a true–false format, that 60% of the items be written so that true is the correct response. This was promulgated as a means of promoting learning since a majority of the statements the examinee would read would be accurate. This helps in only very limited circumstances,

Table 6.5   Checklist for the development of true–false items

1. Does each statement include only one idea?	_____
2. Have you avoided using specific determiners and qualifiers that can serve as cues to the answer?	_____
3. Are true and false statements of approximately the same length?	_____
4. Are there an approximately equal number of true and false statements?	_____

does not apply to typical performance tests (a common application of the binary format—some using yes–no instead of true–false), and is outweighed by the issue of response sets and guessing strategies. Balance is better.

True–false items are a popular selected-response format for maximum-performance tests. While true–false items can be scored in an objective and reliable manner and examinees can answer many items in a short period of time, they have numerous weaknesses. For example, they are often limited to the assessment of fairly simple learning objectives and are vulnerable to guessing. While true–false items have a place in maximum-performance tests, before using them we recommend that you weigh their strengths and weaknesses and ensure that they are the most appropriate item format for assessing the specific learning objectives. Table 6.5 provides a brief checklist for developing true–false items. Many of these will also apply to yes–no formats that are often used with younger individuals since these ideas are a little easier to understand.

6.3.3 Matching Items

The final selected-response format we will discuss is *matching items*. Matching items usually contain two columns of words or phrases. One column contains words or phrases for which the examinee seeks a match. This column is traditionally placed on the left and the phrases are referred to as premises. The second column contains words that are available for selection. The items in this column are referred to as responses. The premises are numbered and the responses are identified with letters.

Directions are provided that indicate the basis for matching the items in the two lists. Below is an example of a matching item.

Example 12: Matching items

Directions: Column A lists major functions of the brain. Column B lists different brain structures. Indicate which structure primarily serves which function by placing the appropriate letter in the blank space to the left of the function. Each brain structure listed in Column B can be used once, more than once, or not at all

Column A	Column B
b 1. Helps initiate and control rapid movement of the arms and legs	a. basal ganglia
g 2. Serves as a relay station connecting different parts of the brain	b. cerebellum
e 3. Involved in the regulation of basic drives and emotions	c. corpus callosum
a 4. Helps control slow, deliberate movements of the arms and legs	d. hypothalamus
c 5. Connects the two hemispheres	e. limbic system
d 6. Controls the release of certain hormones important in controlling the internal environment of the body	f. medulla
	g. thalamus

This item demonstrates an imperfect match since there are more responses than premises. Additionally, the instructions also indicate that each response may be used once, more than once, or not at all. These procedures help prevent examinees from matching items simply by elimination. Below are some additional suggestions for developing matching items.

1. **Limit matching items to homogeneous material.** Possibly the most important guideline to remember when writing matching items is to keep the lists as homogeneous as possible. By this, we mean you should base the lists on a common theme. For example, in the previous example (Example 12) all of the premises were functions served by brain structures and all of the responses were brain structures. Other examples of homogeneous lists could be the achievements matched with famous individuals, historical events matched with dates, definitions matched with words, etc. What should be avoided is including heterogeneous material in your lists.

2. **In the directions, indicate the basis for matching premises and responses.** Clearly state in the directions the basis for matching responses to premises. If you have difficulty specifying the basis for matching all the items in your lists, it is likely that your lists are too heterogeneous.

3. **Include more responses than premises.** By including more responses than premises you reduce the chance that an uninformed examinee can narrow down options and successfully match items by guessing.

4. **Indicate that responses may be used once, more than once, or not at all.** By adding this statement to your directions and writing responses that are occasionally used more than once or not at all, you also reduce the impact of guessing.

5. **Keep the list fairly brief.** For several reasons, it is desirable to keep the list of items fairly brief. It is easier for the person writing the test to ensure that the lists are homogeneous when the lists are brief. For the examinee taking the test it is easier to read and respond to a shorter list of items without the introduction of

Table 6.6 Checklist for the development of matching items

1. Is the material homogeneous and appropriate for the matching format?	_____
2. Do the directions indicate the basis for matching premises and responses?	_____
3. Are there more responses than premises?	_____
4. Do the directions indicate that responses may be used once, more than once, or not at all?	_____
5. Are the lists relatively short to facilitate scanning (e.g., less than 10)?	_____
6. Are the responses brief and arranged in a logical order?	_____

confounding factors such as short-term memory and attention skills. While there is not universal agreement regarding the number of items to include in a matching list, a maximum of 10 appears reasonable with lists between 5 and 8 items generally recommended.

6. **Ensure that the responses are brief and arrange them in a logical order.** Examinees should be able to read the longer premises and then scan the briefer responses in an efficient manner. To facilitate this process, keep the responses as

brief as possible and arrange them in a logical order when appropriate (e.g., alphabetical, numerically).

Matching items can be scored in an objective and reliable manner, can be completed in a fairly efficient manner, and are relatively easy to develop. Their major limitations include a rather limited scope and the possibility of promoting rote memorization of material by your examinees. Nevertheless, when carefully developed, matching items can effectively assess some constructs. Table 6.6 provides a checklist for developing matching items.

6.3.4 Essay Items

An *essay item* is a test item that poses a question or problem for the examinee to respond to in an open-ended written format. Being a constructed-response item, the examinees must respond by constructing a response, not by selecting among alternatives. While essay items

> An essay item is a test item that poses a question or problem for the examinee to respond to in an open-ended written format.

vary in the degree of structure they impose on the examinee's response, they generally provide to the examinee a considerable freedom in composing a response. Good essay items challenge the examinee to organize, analyze, integrate, and synthesize information. At their best, essay items elicit novel and creative cognitive processes. At their worst, they present an ambiguous task that is difficult, if not impossible, to score in a reliable manner.

Essay items are often classified as either *restricted-response* or *extended-response*. Restricted-response items are highly structured and clearly specify the form and scope of the examinee's response. Restricted-response items typically require examinees to list, define, describe, or give reasons. Extended-response items provide more latitude and flexibility in how examinees can respond to the item. There is little or no limit on the form and scope of the response. When limitations are provided, they are usually held to a minimum (e.g., page and time limits). Extended-response items provide less structure and this promotes greater creativity, integration, and organization of material.

As you might expect, restricted-response and extended-response essay items have their own strengths and limitations. Restricted-response essay items can be answered in a timely fashion and are easier to score in a reliable manner than extended-response items. However, by their very nature, there are some objectives that simply cannot be measured in a restricted format (e.g., ability to write an essay explaining the reasons for the Civil War). In contrast, extended-response items give examinees more latitude in responding. However, they are more difficult to score in a reliable manner and, since they take considerable time to complete (as does scoring), tests typically are limited to relatively few items, which results in limited sampling of the content domain. Below are our guidelines for developing essay items.

1. **Clearly specify the assessment task.** The most important criterion for a good essay item is that it clearly specifies the assessment task. The assessment task is simply what you want the examinee to do. We recommend that you provide enough information in your essay item that there is no doubt about what you expect. If you want the examinee to list reasons, specify that you want a list. If you want them to make an evaluative judgment, clearly state it. If you want a restricted-response, specify that. If you want an extended response, make that clear. We are not suggesting that your essay item stems be unnecessarily lengthy. In fact, we recommend that they be as brief as possible. That is, as brief as possible while still clearly specifying the assessment task.

2. **Use more restricted-response items in place of a smaller number of extended-response items.** Restricted-response items have measurement characteristics that may make them preferable over extended-response items. First, they are easier to score in a reliable manner. They are not as easy to score in a reliable manner as selected-response items, but they are easier than extended-response essays. Second, since examinees can respond to a larger number of items in a given amount of time, they can provide superior sampling of content domain. While some objectives simply require the use of extended-response items, when you have a choice we recommend using multiple restricted-response items.

3. **Develop and use a scoring rubric.** The major limitation of essay items is they are notoriously difficult to score in a reliable manner without a carefully designed scoring rubric (and scoring problems may still occur even with a carefully designed scoring rubric). A scoring rubric is a written guide that provides clear guidance for scoring a constructed response. For restricted-response essay items, the scoring rubric is often a sample answer or listing of necessary response elements. However, extended-response items typically require more complex rubrics because of the lack of restriction on the examinee's response. With this lack of restriction, it is usually not possible to provide one sample item that takes into consideration all possible "good" responses (as was the case for restricted-response items) because one cannot anticipate the exact form and content of the response.

   As a result, scoring rubrics are often classified as either analytic or holistic. *Analytic scoring rubrics* identify different critical aspects or dimensions of the response and the grader scores each dimension separately. For example, an analytic scoring rubric might distinguish between response content, writing style, and grammar/mechanics. With this scoring rubric, the grader will score each response in terms of these three categories. An advantage of analytic scoring rubrics is that they provide specific feedback to examinees regarding the adequacy of their response in different areas. The major drawback of analytic rubrics is that their use can be fairly time-consuming, particularly when the rubric specifies many dimensions to be graded individually.

   With a *holistic scoring rubric*, the grader assigns a single score based on the overall quality of the examinee's response. Holistic rubrics are often less detailed than analytic rubrics. They are easier to develop and scoring usually proceeds faster. Their primary disadvantage is that they do not provide specific feedback to examinees about the strengths and weaknesses of their response. We will not go into detail about the development and application of scoring rubrics, but we do strongly encourage those of you interested in developing and using essay

Table 6.7 Checklist for the development of essay items

1. Have you clearly specified the assessment task?	_____
2. Have you used more restricted-response essays in place of a smaller number of extended-response essays?	_____
3. Have you developed a scoring rubric?	_____
4. Have you limited the use of essay items to objectives that cannot be measured using selected-response items?	_____

items to read textbooks that address this important topic in greater detail (e.g., Reynolds, Livingston, & Willson, 2009).

4. **Limit the use of essay items to objectives that cannot be measured using selected-response items.** Essays are extremely popular among many teachers and have their strengths; nevertheless, they do have significant limitations including unreliable scoring and reduced content sampling, as well as increased time required to do high-quality scoring. As a result, we recommend that you restrict the use of essay items to the measurement of objectives that cannot be measured adequately using selected-response items. For example, if you want to assess the examinee's ability to organize and present material in a written format, an essay item would be a natural choice.

While essay items vary in terms of the limits they place on examinee responses, most essay items give examinees considerable freedom in developing their responses. The most prominent weaknesses of essay items involve difficulty scoring in a reliable manner and limited content sampling. Both of these issues can result in reduced reliability and validity. On the positive side, essay items are well suited for measuring many complex objectives and are relatively easy to write. We provided numerous suggestions for writing and scoring essay items, but encouraged test developers to limit the use of essay items to the measurement of objectives that are not easily assessed using selected-response items (Table 6.7).

6.3.5   Short-Answer Items

Short-answer items are items that require the examinee to supply a word, phrase, number, or symbol in response to a direct question. Short-answer items can also be written as incomplete sentences instead of direct questions, a format which is sometimes referred to as a completion item. Relative to essay items, short-answer items place stricter limits on the nature and length of the response. Practically speaking, a short-answer item is like a restricted-response essay item because restricted-response essay items provide more structure and limit the form and scope of the examinee's response relative to an extended-response essay item. Short-answer items take this a step further by providing even more structure and limits on the examinee's response. Below are specific suggestions for writing short-answer items.

1. **Structure the item so that the response is as short as possible.** As the name implies, you should write short-answer items so that they require a short answer. This makes scoring easier, less time-consuming, and more reliable.

2. **Make sure there is only *one* correct response.** In addition to brevity, it is important that there only be one correct response. This is more difficult than you might imagine. When writing a short-answer item, ask yourself if the examinee can interpret it in more than one way. Consider Examples 13A and B:

Example 13A: Poor item—has more than one correct response
  1. John Adams was born in _____?
Example 13B: Better item—has one correct response
  1. *John Adams was born in what state?* _____

Example 13A is a poor item because it has more than one correct response. The correct response could be "Massachusetts." Or it could be "Braintree" or even the "United States of America." It could also be "1735" or even "the 18th century." All of these would be correct! Sample 13B is a much better item because the only correct response is Massachusetts. This highlights the need for specificity when writing short-answer items.

3. **As a general rule, the direct-question format is preferable to the incomplete-sentence format.** There is usually less chance of examinee confusion when the item is presented in the direct-question format. This is particularly true when writing tests for young examinees, but even older examinees may find direct questions more understandable than incomplete sentences. Most experts recommend only using the incomplete-sentence format when it results in a briefer item without any loss in clarity.

4. **When using the incomplete-sentence format it is best to have only one blank space, and this should generally be near the end of the sentence.** As we noted, unless incomplete-sentence items are carefully written, they may be confusing or unclear to examinees. Generally, the more blank spaces an item contains, the less clear the task becomes. Therefore, we recommend that you usually limit each incomplete sentence to one blank space. We also recommend that you locate the blank space near the end of the sentence. This arrangement tends to provide more clarity than if the blank appears early in the sentence.

5. **Make sure the blanks provide adequate space for the examinee's response.** You should ensure that each blank provides adequate space for the examinee to

Table 6.8 Checklist for the development of short-answer items

1. Does the item require a short response?	_____
2. Is there only one correct response?	_____
3. Did you use an incomplete sentence only when there was no loss of clarity relative to a direct question?	_____
4. Do incomplete sentences contain only one blank? Are blanks in incomplete sentences near the end of the sentences?	_____
5. Do the blanks provide adequate space for the answers?	_____
6. For questions requiring quantitative answers, have you indicated the degree of precision expected?	_____
7. Have you created a scoring rubric for each item?	_____

write their response. In order for space length not to serve as a possible cue to the answer, you should determine how much space is necessary for providing the longest response in a series of short-answer items, and use that length for all other items.

6. **For questions requiring quantitative answers, indicate the degree of precision expected.** For example, if you want your answer stated in inches, specify that. If you want all fractions reduced to their lowest terms or all numerical answers rounded to the second decimal point, specify these expectations.

7. **Create a scoring rubric and consistently apply it.** As with essay items, it is important to create and consistently use a scoring rubric when scoring short-answer items. When creating this rubric, take into consideration any answers beside the preferred or "best" response that you will receive full or partial credit.

Short-answer items, like essay items, require the examinee to provide a written response. However, instead of having a large degree of freedom in drafting their response, on short-answer items, the examinee is usually required to limit their response to a single word, a brief phrase, or a symbol/number. Similar to essay items, short-answer items are somewhat difficult to score in a reliable manner because correct answers are often expressed in a number of different ways. On the positive side, short-answer items are well suited for measuring certain learning objectives (e.g., math computations) and are relatively easy to write. As with essay items, short-answer items have distinct strengths, but should be used in a judicious manner. Table 6.8 provides a checklist for developing short-answer items.

6.4   Typical-Response Tests

Now that we have covered many of the common item formats used in maximum-performance tests, we will turn to the items commonly used in typical-response tests such as personality and attitude scales. We will first describe the different item formats commonly used with these tests and then provide some general guidelines for developing items. We believe the assessment of feelings, thoughts, self-talk, and other covert behaviors is best accomplished by self-report, and this will be the focus of our discussion. However, like maximum-performance tests, there are a number of item formats available when using self-report measures.

> We believe the assessment of feelings, thoughts, self-talk, and other covert behaviors is best accomplished by self-report.

6.4.1   Typical-Response Item Formats

The first format we will discuss is the true–false format. True–false items are common in both maximum-performance and typical-response tests. The second edition of the Minnesota Multiphasic Personality Inventory (MMPI-2; Butcher et al., 1989) is a typical-response test that uses the true–false format. On this and other similar tests, examinees are asked to describe their current thoughts, feelings, and behaviors based on whether the statement is true about them. Other tests that use binomial items ask if examinees agree with a statement using yes–no or agree/disagree response alternatives. Example 14 presents true–false items that might be used to assess depressive symptoms.

Example 14: True–false item example

Directions: Read the following statements and select True (**T**) if you agree with the statement and False (**F**) if you do not agree with the statement. There are no right or wrong answers. Please do your best to answer every item

1. I feel sad	T	F
2. I think about harming myself	T	F
3. I sleep well at night	T	F

These items focus primarily on the individual's current experiences. And based on the responses, your client is currently feeling sad, thinking about harming him or herself, and not sleeping well at night, suggesting a possible diagnosis of major depressive disorder.

6.4.1.1 Rating Scale Item Example

Another common item format used on self-reports is *rating scales*. The term "rating scale" is defined differently by different researchers and authors. Some authors use rating scales only when the individual completing the scale is rating another individual. An example would be students rating their professors on instructional effectiveness and course quality. In this text, we take a broader definition of rating scales, one that includes the rating of self or others. A major distinction between true–false items and ratings is the number of options. That is, true–false items only allow two choices while rating scales typically have four or five alternatives. Another difference is that rating scales of thoughts, feelings, and moods, as well as behaviors typically denote frequency (e.g., Never, Sometimes, Often, Almost always), while true–false and yes–no items force the respondent to make a more definitive or absolute judgment call. True–false items can of course be introduced with stems to mimic such frequencies (e.g., "I always have good manners" or "Often, my hands feel sweaty") but more items are typically required with such a series of binomial response items in order to obtain reliable scores. Consider examples of rating scale items in 15A and 15B. How do they compare to the previous true–false items?

Example 15A: Frequency rating scale item

Directions: Read the following sentences and circle the response that is most descriptive for you. There are no right or wrong answers. Please do your best to answer every item.

1. I feel sad	Never	Sometimes	Often	Almost always
2. I think about harming myself	Never	Sometimes	Often	Almost always
3. I sleep well at night	Never	Sometimes	Often	Almost always

Example 15B: More specific frequency rating scale item

Directions: Read the following sentences and circle the response that is most descriptive for you. There are no right or wrong answers. Please do your best to answer every item.

1. I feel sad	Daily	Weekly	Monthly	Once a year or less	Never
2. I think about harming myself	Daily	Weekly	Monthly	Once a year or less	Never
3. I sleep well at night	Daily	Weekly	Monthly	Once a year or less	Never

Special Interest Topic 6.3: Mixing Item Formats

It has been common practice for personality scales to contain only one item type. For example, The Minnesota Multiphasic Personality Inventory—2nd Edition (MMPI-2), like its predecessor the MMPI, contains all true–false items. Similarly, the Self-Report of Personality, a component of the Behavior Assessment System for Children (BASC) contained all true–false items. While this practice was based more on tradition than empirical research, it was assumed that respondents might have difficulty switching between item formats and this might result in reduced reliability and validity.

When developing the Behavior Assessment System for Children, 2nd Edition (BASC-2; Reynolds & Kamphaus, 2004), the authors considered ways of increasing the range and reliability of scores on the Self-Report of Personality (SRP). The authors noted that some items could be viewed best as reflecting a continuum and not the dichotomy implied by true–false response options. As a result they evaluated the utility of a response format based on frequency: Never, Sometimes, Often, and Almost Always or N/S/O/A (note that some researchers refer to such multiple point response scales on self-report instruments as a "fuzzy response scale" or a "fuzzy metric"). To do this they created and evaluated two parallel forms of the SRP that differed in terms of response format—true–false versus N/S/O/A. In some cases, this also involved minor modifications to the wordings of items. For example, the true–false item "I often have nightmares" was changed to "I have nightmares" for the N/S/O/A format. The study evaluated the formats with regard to test/retest reliability, internal-consistency reliability, and the size of the individual standardized item loadings in a form of factor analysis, contrasting the items under each response condition.

The authors examined coefficient alpha for different combinations including all true–false, all N/S/O/A, and a mixture of the two. For the mixture condition, the format was the one that seemed most appropriate based on both content and psychometric grounds. The results revealed that scales containing a mixture of formats consistently had higher coefficient alphas than scales containing only one format. Also, examinees found it easier to respond to certain types of questions in a binomial, absolute sense (true–false) while finding it easier to respond to other items using a more detailed scale, allowing the expression of a gradient of the behavior in question. Additionally, the inclusion of the N/S/O/A items increased the range of scores, therefore reducing potential floor and ceiling effects. Despite these authors' wealth of experience with test development, this result was unexpected—it had been anticipated that the 4-choice response option would be superior in nearly every case. These results demonstrate that at times it is useful to look beyond "traditional" practices and empirically evaluate novel approaches to test development, and that it is important to listen to the data and not assume what will work best.

It should be noted that the final tests do keep all of the true–false items and N/S/O/A items together or segregated from one another. For example, on the adolescent SRP form (ages 12–21) the first 69 items are true–false, while items 70 through 176 are N/S/O/A. This way respondents do not have to switch between response formats more than once, which could be confusing.

As you see, the items in Example 15A and 15B ask that the respondent indicate the frequency of the thoughts, feelings, or behaviors, but 15B is more specific in soliciting information about frequencies.

There are several factors to consider when deciding between the true–false format and rating scales with frequency ratings. As a general rule, frequency ratings have advantages over true–false items. First, frequency rating items provide more information than true–false items and so increase the range of scores, produce more reliable scores, and/or reduce overall scale length. Second, frequency ratings enhance measurement at the extremes because options such as *Never* and *Almost Always* are inherently extreme ratings. Finally, frequency ratings are better suited to the content of some items than the true–false format and make responding simpler. While these advantages argue for the use of rating scales over true–false items, true–false items are appropriate for use on some scales. In fact, Reynolds and Kamphaus (2004) found that self-report scales using a combination of true–false items and rating scales with four options produced the higher alpha reliabilities than scales containing only one format (see Special Interest Topic 6.3 for more on this topic).

As we noted, rating scales are often used to solicit ratings from individuals who are familiar with the person you are assessing. This is very common when completing assessments of children and adolescents. For example, the *Behavior Assessment System for Children, Third Edition* (Reynolds & Kamphaus, 2015) includes two rating scales for assessing children and adolescents, one completed by parents and one completed by teachers. The primary difference between these rating scales and those used on self-reports is the focus. Self-report rating scales are routinely applied to a wide range of feelings, thoughts, and behaviors. Self-report scales, being completed by the client, are able to assess the client's subjective experiences. On the other hand, rating scales completed by a third party typically focus on overt behaviors since they observe those behaviors. Because of this, some authors use the term "behavior rating scales" to describe these instruments. Like self-report items, these items have been shown to provide reliable and valid information when used appropriately. Example 16 provides items that might be used on a behavior rating scale designed to be completed by parents regarding their child.

Example 16: Behavior rating scale items

Directions: Below are some phrases that describe how children may act. Read the phrases and circle the response that is most descriptive of your child. Please do your best to answer every item.

1. Appears sad	Never	Sometimes	Often	Almost always
2. Harms self	Never	Sometimes	Often	Almost always
3. Sleeps well at night	Never	Sometimes	Often	Almost always

These types of behavioral rating scales have proven very useful in the assessment of children and adolescents. For example, school psychologists routinely collect behavioral ratings from both parents and several teachers when completing psychological assessments. This provides very useful information since it allows clinicians to identify behavioral problems that are observed by different raters in different settings, and identify settings where the behaviors are less problematic. We will discuss the use of these scales more in Chap. 11.

The assessment of attitudes, as opposed to feelings, thoughts, self-talk, and behaviors, often uses *Likert* items (Likert, 1932). Likert items are similar to rating

Special Interest Topic 6.4: Guttman Scales and Thurstone Scales

You have read about scales of measurement in this text and perhaps elsewhere and their importance to the use and interpretation of test scores as well as their importance for defining appropriate levels of mathematical analysis of numbers. It was Louis Guttman in 1944 who really explained in a most approachable way that all forms of measurement belong to one of four types of scales: categorical, ordinal, interval, and ratio. However, many actually attribute these scales of measurement to Stevens (1946), who referred to them as nominal, ordinal, interval, and ratio. The mathematical foundations of these scales have since been examined in detail in a variety of sources, and for the mathematically inclined we recommend some older presentations such as that by Hays (1994, pp. 81–91), but if this is not accessible, the Pedhazur and Schmelkin (1991) discussion is also strong.

Guttman is better known for his ideas about developing a deterministic (absolute) scale that carries his name (i.e., Guttman Scales) in this same 1944 paper. Guttman scaling is also sometimes known as *cumulative scaling*. The purpose of Guttman scaling is to establish a one-dimensional continuum for a concept you wish to measure. Items having binary (e.g., yes–no) answers form a Guttman scale if they can be ranked in some order so that, for a rational respondent, the response pattern can be captured by a single index on that ordered scale. On a Guttman scale, items are arranged in a perfect hierarchical order so that an individual who agrees with a particular item on a survey or attitudinal dimension also agrees with items of lower rank, or statements that are in some way subordinate to the last statement one answers in the affirmative. In aptitude or achievement testing, a Guttman scale would exist when all persons tested answered every question correctly until missing one, and then failed to answer any additional questions correctly. The strength of a Guttman scale, indeed, its purpose, is to enable us to predict item responses perfectly knowing only the total score for the respondent. For example, if we asked a person to solve arithmetic problems, and the test had 100 items, if the examinee earned a score of 51, we would know immediately the person answered items 1–51 correctly and missed items 52–100. There are many obvious advantages of such a scale, one being the great reduction in testing time—as soon as a person misses or responds differently to just 1 item, we can cease testing!

Guttman scales are very appealing from an intuitive perspective, and you may wonder why all tests are not constructed in this manner—indeed, one rarely (if ever) sees a test with a true Guttman scale. First, Guttman scales are highly impractical; and second, when they are developed, they are rather simplistic in the information they provide. Oddly enough, to develop a Guttman scale, one ends up having only ordinal data—that is, Guttman scales rank-order people by their responses, but give us little information about the distance they are apart in the distribution of the underlying trait or construct we seek to assess. In some areas such as math, Guttman scales are easy to derive and are also a good illustration of the simplicity of the information. Consider the following five-item test, which is extremely likely to produce a Guttman scale:

1. How much is $2 + 2$?
2. How much is $20 - 10$?
3. How much is $10 * 55$?
4. Solve for x: $x - 3 + 7 = 15$
5. Solve for x: $(x + 3)(x + 3) = 16$

A person who answers item 5 correctly will almost certainly have answered items 1–4 correctly, and a person who answers item 4 but misses item 5, will almost certainly have answered items 1–3 correctly, and so on. However, to develop such a scale, we sacrifice a great deal of precision in assessing real skill in mathematics. For example, there may be great differences in the skills of students who answer four items correctly compared to those who can answer all five items. For most purposes of psychological assessment, the Guttman scale, however, appealing intuitively, is illogical and does not fit our need for information. Guttman scales that are not highly simplistic are more difficult to develop than typical scales and aspire only to ordinal level data, whereas most other scales give us at least interval scale data.

Another approach to developing a cumulative scale was developed by Thurstone (e.g., 1928). Unlike Guttman scales which can be used with maximum-performance or typical-response tests, Thurstone scales are limited to typical-response assessments, usually attitude scales. In developing a Thurstone scale one begins by writing a large number of statements that reflect the full range of attitudes from very negative to very positive with reference to a specific topic or issue. It is important for these items to reflect the full range of attitudes, including neutral statements. These statements are then reviewed by judges who assign a scale value to each statement along a continuum ranging from extremely favorable to extremely unfavorable. When doing this the judges often use a scale with 11 equal-width intervals. For example, the most negative statements are assigned values of 1 while the most favorable statements are assigned values of 11. With this scale, neutral statements would be assigned values of 6.

To illustrate this, consider the development of a scale to measure attitudes about the use of cell phones while driving. Following are three items that might be assigned different scale values by the judges.

Item	Scale value
1. It should be illegal to drive while using a cell phone—period!	**1** (very negative)
2. I don't have a strong opinion about the use of cell phones while driving	**6** (neutral)
3. I believe we should be able to use our cell phones at any time and any place we desire	**11** (very positive)

Once the judges have rated all of the statements, their ratings are reviewed with the goal of selecting a final set of statements that will be included on the scale. There are two primary criteria considered in selecting items to retain on the final scale. First, it is important to select items that are evenly distributed across the whole continuum ranging from very positive to very negative. In other words, you want items that have ratings ranging from 1 to 11, with all 11 values represented. Second, it is desirable to select items that the judges rated in a consistent manner. If an item received inconsistent ratings (i.e., some positive ratings, some negative ratings), this suggests that the item may be ambiguous and should be dropped from further consideration. There are statistics that can be calculated to help determine which items received the most consistent ratings.

The result is a final scale where examinees indicate their attitudes by endorsing items using a binary format, typically indicating that they *agree* or *disagree* with the statements. The total score an examinee receives is the median of the scale values of the items they endorsed. If we use our example of an 11-point scale, with 1 indicating the most unfavorable statements and 11 indicating the most favorable statements, an individual with a low total score (i.e., the median value of the items they endorsed) would be expressing an unfavorable attitude toward the issue or topic. An examinee with a favorable attitude would be expected to receive a high total score, while someone receiving a total score of 6 would have expressed a neutral response pattern. While Thurstone scales were popular for many years (and still have their advocates), they are used less commonly today. This decrease in popularity is partly due to the rather complex process used in developing Thurstone scales and research showing that other item formats (e.g., Likert scales) can produce more reliable scores with the same number of items (Friedenberg, 1995).

For more information on this topic, we recommend the following references.

Guttman, L. (1944). A basis for scaling qualitative data. *American Sociological Review, 9*, 139–150.

Hays, W. (1973). *Statistics for the social sciences.* New York, NY: Holt, Rinehart, & Winston.

Pedhazur, E., & Schmelkin, L. (1991). *Measurement, design, and analysis.* Hillsdale, NJ: Erlbaum.

Stevens, S. S. (1951). Mathematics, measurement, and psychophysics. In S. S. Stevens, (Eds.), *Handbook of experimental psychology* (pp. 1–49). New York, NY: Wiley.

Thurstone, L. L. (1928). Attitudes can be measured. *American Journal of Sociology, 33*, 529–554.

scales, but instead of focusing on frequency, the focus is on degree of agreement. That is, does the respondent agree or disagree with a statement. These scales are also referred to as summative rating scales. Example 17 presents Likert items one could use to assess attitudes toward politicians.

Example 17: Likert Items

Directions: Read the following sentences and circle the response that best describes your position or belief. The responses are Strongly Agree = **SA**, Agree = **A**, Neutral = **N**, Disagree = **D**, and Strongly Disagree = **SD**

1. Politicians can be trusted	SD	D	N	D	SD
2. Politicians lose sight of those they serve	SD	D	N	D	SD
3. I would like to enter politics	SD	D	N	D	SD

Likert items have become the most popular item format for assessing attitudes. In the past, other formats were very popular, namely Thurstone and Guttman scales. These have lost some popularity in recent years, primarily because Likert items are easier to develop and tend to produce more reliable results. Nevertheless, you will likely come across examples of Thurstone and Guttman scales, and we briefly discuss these in Special Interest Topic 6.4.

> Likert items have become the most popular item format for assessing attitudes.

Many of the general guidelines we presented at the beginning of the chapter apply to the development of items for typical-response tests. Below are brief guidelines for developing items for self-report measures.

6.4.2 Typical-Response Item Guidelines

1. **Focus on thoughts, feelings, and behaviors—not facts**. With typical-response tests you are trying to assess the examinee's experiences—their typical thoughts, feelings, and behaviors. As a result, you should avoid statements based on factual information that can be scored as "correct" or "incorrect."

2. **Limit statements to a single thought, feeling, or behavior**. Each statement should focus on just one thought, feeling, behavior, or attitude. Don't make the mistake of combining more than one construct as illustrated in Example 18:

Example 18A: Poor item—item combines two constructs		
1. I feel sad and angry	T	F
Example 18B: Better—replaces the item with two separate items		
1. I feel sad	T	F
2. I feel angry	T	F

3. **Avoid statements that everyone will endorse in a specific manner**. To increase variance and enhance reliability, you should strive to write items that measure individual differences. If everyone or almost everyone responds to an item in the same way, it is not contributing to the measurement of the identified constructs.

4. **Include items that are worded in both "Positive/Favorable" and "Negative/ Unfavorable" directions**. As a general rule, use a combination of items worded in "positive" and "negative" directions. This may encourage examinees to avoid a response style where they are simply marking one response option on all items. This is most applicable on True–False items and Likert scales and less applicable to rating scales where you are trying to assess the frequency of problematic thoughts, feelings, and behaviors.

5. **Use an appropriate number of options**. For rating scales, either 4 or 5 response options seem to be optimal in developing reliability without unduly lengthening the time required by the person completing the ratings. Rating scales with more than 4 or 5 options rarely improve reliability or validity of test score interpretation and take longer for examinees to complete. For Likert items, the maximum number of options appears to be seven steps, with little increase in reliability after that.

6. **Weigh the benefits of using an odd or even number of options**. On Likert items, it is generally recommended that you use an odd number of choices with the middle choice being "Neutral" or "Undecided." This is not universally accepted as some authors support the use of an even number of choices with no neutral option. This is based on the fact that some respondents tend to overuse the neutral choice if it is available. This can result in reduced variance and reliability. The downside of eliminating the neutral choice is that some respondents might become frustrated and simply not complete items when they don't have a strong opinion. Missing data can be a significant problem in these cases. Our recommendation is to use an odd number of options with a neutral option. With frequency rating scales, this is less important since there is not a need for a "neutral" option.

7. **For rating scales and Likert items, clearly label each of the options.** Consider the formats for Examples 19A and B:

Example 19A: Poor response options—Each response option is not clearly labeled					
Strongly Agree	1 2	3		4	5 Strongly Disagree
Example 19B: Better response options—each response option is clearly labeled					
Strongly Agree	Agree	Neither Agree/Disagree	Disagree	Strongly Disagree	
1	2	3	4	5	

The format for 19A may leave the respondent wondering about the difference between a "2" and a "3." Example 19B resolves any uncertainty by providing labels for each of the response options.

8. **Minimize the use of specific determiners**. The use of specific determiners like *never*, *always*, *none*, and *all* should be used cautiously as they can complicate the response process.

9. **With young children, you may want to structure the scale as an interview.** For young children, consider using an interview format where the items are read to the child. This may help reduce construct-irrelevant variance that is introduced by eliminating the impact of reading skills.

Table 6.9 provides a checklist for the development of items for typical-response tests.

6.5 Summary

At the beginning of this chapter, we make a main distinction between test items as to whether they are selected-response items or constructed-response items and go on to consider their use for maximum-performance and typical-response tests. For maximum-performance tests, selected-response items include multiple-choice, true–false, and matching items while constructed-response items include short-answer items and essay items. Each of these item types has strengths and weaknesses which are summarized below.

- *Multiple-choice* items are the most popular selected-response format for maximum-performance tests. They have numerous strengths including versatility, objective and reliable scoring and efficient sampling of the content domain. The

Table 6.9 Checklist for the development of typical-response items

1. Do the items focus on thoughts, feelings, and behaviors—not facts?	_____
2. Is each item limited to a single thought, feeling, or behavior?	_____
3. Did you avoid statements that everyone will endorse in a specific manner?	_____
4. Did you include items that are worded in both "Positive/Favorable" and "Negative/Unfavorable" directions?	_____
5. Did you use an appropriate number of response options?	_____
6. Did you weigh the benefits of using an odd or even number of options?	_____
7. For rating scales and Likert items, did you clearly label each of the options?	_____
8. Did you minimize the use of specific determiners?	_____
9. For young children did you consider structuring the scale as an interview?	_____

only weaknesses are that multiple-choice items are not effective for measuring all objectives and they are not easy to develop. Testing experts generally support the use of multiple-choice items as they can contribute to the development of reliable and valid assessments.

- *True–false* items can be scored in an objective and reliable manner and examinees can answer many items in a short period of time. However, they have numerous weaknesses. They are limited to the assessment of fairly simple objectives and are very vulnerable to guessing. While true–false items have a place in maximum-performance assessment, before using them we recommend that you weigh their strengths and weaknesses and ensure that they are the most appropriate item format for assessing the specific learning objectives.

- *Matching items* can be scored in an objective and reliable manner, can be completed in a fairly efficient manner, and are relatively easy to develop. Their major limitations include a rather limited scope and the possibility of promoting rote memorization of material by your examinees. Nevertheless, when carefully developed, matching items can effectively assess many lower-level learning objectives.

- *Essay items* pose a question or problem that the examinee responds to in a written format. While essay items vary in terms of the limits they place on responses, most essay items give examinees considerable freedom in developing their responses. The most prominent weaknesses of essay items include difficulty scoring them in a reliable manner and limited content sampling. Both of these issues can result in reduced reliability and validity. On the positive side, essay items are well suited for measuring many complex objectives and are relatively easy to write.

- *Short-answer items*, like essay items, require examinees to respond by providing a written response. However, instead of having considerable freedom in drafting their responses, examinees are usually required to limit their responses to a single word, a brief phrase, or a symbol/number. Similar to essay items, short-answer items are somewhat difficult to score in a reliable manner. On the positive side, short-answer items are well suited for measuring certain learning objectives (e.g., math computations) and are relatively easy to write.

At this point, we discuss items for typical-response tests. We initially focus on the assessment of feelings, thoughts, self-talk, and other covert behaviors using self-report items. These are briefly described below.

- *True–false items* and other binomial items (e.g., yes–no, agree/disagree) are commonly used on typical-response tests. Typically these items focus on the examinee's current experiences. For example, is your client currently feeling sad, thinking about harming him or herself, and sleeping well at night?

- *Rating Scales.* Rating scales can be designed both for self-report measures and the rating of other individuals (typically referred to as Behavior Rating Scales). While true–false items only allow two choices, rating scales typically have four or five alternatives. Rating scales also typically denote frequency (e.g., Never,

Sometimes, Often, Almost always), while true–false and yes–no items ask the respondent to make a more definitive or absolute judgment call.

As a general rule, rating scales have advantages over true–false items since they a) provide more information per item and can increase the range of scores, b) can enhance measurement at the extremes because options such as *Never* and *Almost Always* are inherently extreme ratings, and c) are better suited to the content of some items so make responding simpler. Nevertheless, true–false items are appropriate, and even show better measurement properties for the content of some items.

In closing, we address the assessment of attitudes. Likert items are similar to rating scales, but instead of focusing on frequency, they focus on the degree of agreement. That is, does the respondent agree or disagree with a statement. These scales are also referred to as summative rating scales. In past, cumulative rating scales such as Guttman and Thurstone scales were popular, but Likert scales have proven to be easier to develop and to have equivalent if not superior psychometric properties. As a result, Likert scales have become the most popular.

This chapter presents fairly brief coverage of a very complicated and technical topic. For those of you interested in more information, we encourage you to read the more comprehensive coverage of this topic in *Measurement and Assessment in Education* (Reynolds, Livingston, & Willson, 2009).

References

American Educational Research Association, American Psychological Association, & National Council on Measurement in Education. (2014). *Standards for educational and psychological testing*. Washington, DC: American Educational Research Association.

Butcher, J. N., Dahlstrom, W. G., Graham, J. R., Tellegen, A., & Kaemmer, B. (1989). *MMPI-2: Manual for administration and scoring*. Minneapolis, MN: University of Minnesota Press.

Costin, F. (1970). The optimal number of alternatives in multiple-choice achievement tests: Some empirical evidence for a mathematical proof. *Educational & Psychological Measurement, 30*, 353–358.

Friedenberg, L. (1995). *Psychological testing: Design, analysis, and use*. Boston, MA: Allyn & Bacon.

Grier, J. (1975). The number of alternatives for optimum test reliability. *Journal of Educational Measurement, 12*(2), 109–113.

Guttman, L. A. (1944). A basis for scaling qualitative data. *American Sociological Review, 9*, 139–150.

Hays, W. (1994). *Statistics* (5th ed.). New York, NY: Harcourt Brace.

Likert, R. (1932). A technique for the measurement of attitudes. *Archives of Psychology, 22*(140), 1–55.

Pedhazur, E. J., & Schmelkin, L. (1991). *Measurement, design, and analysis*. Hillside, NJ: Erlbaum.

Pike, L. W. (1979). *Short-term instruction, testwiseness, and the Scholastic Aptitude Test: A literature review with research recommendations*. Princeton, NJ: Educational Testing Service.

Powers, D. E., & Kaufman, J. C. (2002). *Do standardized multiple-choice tests penalize deep-thinking or creative students? (RR- 02-15)*. Princeton, NJ: Educational Testing Service.

Reynolds, C. R., & Kamphaus, R. W. (2004). *Behavior assessment system for children* (2nd ed.). Circle Pines, MN: American Guidance Service.

Reynolds, C. R., & Kamphaus, R. W. (2015). *Behavior assessment system for children* (3rd ed.). Bloomington, MN: NCS Pearson.

Reynolds, C. R., Livingston, R. B., & Willson, V. (2009). *Measurement and assessment in education*. Boston, MA: Allyn & Bacon.

Sidick, J. T., Barrett, G. V., & Doverspike, D. (1994). Three-alternative multiple choice tests: An attractive option. *Personnel Psychology, 47*, 829–835.

Stevens, S. S. (1946). On the theory of scales of measurement. *Science, 103*, 677–680.

Suggested Reading and Internet Sites

Aiken, L. R. (1982). Writing multiple-choice items to measure higher-order educational objectives. *Educational & Psychological Measurement, 42*, 803–806. A respected author presents suggestions for writing multiple-choice items that assess higher-order learning objectives.

Ebel, R. L. (1970). The case for true/false items. *School Review, 78*, 373–389. While many assessment experts are opposed to the use of true/false items for the reasons cited in the text, Ebel comes to their defense in this article.

Edwards, A. (1957). *Techniques of attitude scale construction*. New York, NY: Appleton. A classic text on developing attitude scales.

Reynolds, L., & Willson. (2009). *Measurement and assessment in education*. Boston, MA: Allyn & Bacon.

Item Analysis: Methods for Fitting the Right Items to the Right Test

7

The better the items, the better the test.

Abstract

When developing a test, there are numerous procedures that are useful for assessing the quality and measurement characteristics of test items. Not all procedures are appropriate for all types of tests, and not all procedures will indicate the same level of quality about a particular item. Classical test theory characteristics such as item difficulty, item discrimination, and response distractors are useful, as are characteristics associated with qualitative analyses and the techniques associated with item response theory. The challenge for all test developers is to evaluate the results of these procedures against the intended use of the test and make item-selection decisions that will support and maximize the test's overall effectiveness in measuring what it intends to measure.

Supplementary Information The online version of this chapter (https://doi.org/10.1007/978-3-030-59455-8_7) contains supplementary material, which is available to authorized users.

Learning Objectives

After reading and studying this chapter, students should be able to:
1. Discuss the relationship between the reliability and validity of test scores and the quality of items on a test.
2. Describe importance of the item difficulty index and demonstrate its calculation and interpretation.
3. Describe importance of the item discrimination index and demonstrate its calculation and interpretation.
4. Describe the relationship between item difficulty and discrimination.
5. Describe how item-total correlations can be used to examine item discrimination.
6. Describe importance of the distracter analysis and demonstrate its calculation and interpretation.
7. Describe how the selection of distracters influences item difficulty and discrimination.
8. Show how item analysis statistics can be used to improve test items.
9. Describe qualitative approaches to improving test items.
10. Describe major concepts related to item characteristic curves and how to interpret them.
11. Explain major aspects of item response theory.
12. Identify major contemporary applications of item response theory.

As noted in the last chapter, the goodness of a test is determined by the goodness of its items. Fortunately, there are a number of quantitative item analysis procedures that are useful in assessing the quality and measurement characteristics of the individual items that make up tests. These procedures are collectively referred to as *item analysis statistics* or procedures. Unlike reliability and validity analyses that evaluate the measurement characteristics of a test as a whole, item analysis procedures examine individual items separately, not the overall test. Item analysis statistics are useful in helping test developers decide which items to keep on a test, which items to modify, and which items to eliminate.

The reliability of test scores and the validity of the interpretation of test scores are dependent on the quality of the items on the test. If you can improve the quality of the individual items, you will improve the overall quality of your test. When discussing reliability, we noted that one of the easiest ways to increase the reliability of test scores is to increase the number of items that go into making up the scores. This statement is generally true and is based on the assumption that when you lengthen a test, you add items of the same quality as the existing items. If you use item analysis to delete poor items and improve other items, it is actually possible to

> Reliability and validity of test scores are dependent on the quality of items on the test. If you can improve quality of the individual items, you will improve overall quality of your test.

end up with a test that is shorter than the original version but produces more reliable scores and results in more valid interpretations.

While in this chapter we focus on quantitative procedures for evaluating the quality of test items, there are qualitative procedures that may also prove useful when evaluating the quality of test items. These qualitative procedures typically involve an evaluation of validity evidence based on the content of the test and an examination of individual items to ensure that they are technically accurate and clearly stated. While these qualitative procedures have not received as much attention as their quantitative counterparts, it is often beneficial to use a combination of quantitative and qualitative procedures. In this chapter, we will also introduce item characteristic curves in the context of item response theory, a modern test theory that complements and extends classical test theory in a number of test development applications.

We will begin our discussion by describing the major quantitative item analysis procedures including Item Difficulty, Item Discrimination, and Distractor Analysis. First, however, it should be noted that different types of items and different types of tests require different types of item analysis procedures. Items that are scored dichotomously (i.e., either right or wrong) are handled differently than items that are scored on a continuum (e.g., an essay that can receive scores ranging from 0 to 10). Tests that are designed to maximize the variability of scores (e.g., norm--referenced) are handled differently than mastery tests (i.e., scored pass or fail). As we discuss the different item analysis procedures, we will specify what types of procedures are most appropriate for what types of items and tests.

7.1   Item Difficulty Index (or Item Difficulty Level)

> Item difficulty is defined as the percentage or proportion of test takers who correctly answer the item.

When evaluating items on maximum performance or ability tests, an important consideration is the difficulty level of the items. *Item difficulty* is defined as the percentage or proportion of test takers who correctly answer the item. The *item difficulty level or index* is abbreviated as p and calculated with the following formula:

$$p = \frac{\text{Number of Examinees Correctly Answering the Item}}{\text{Number of Examinees}}$$

For example, in a class of 30 students, if 20 students get the answer correct, the item difficulty index is 0.66. The calculation is illustrated below:

$$p = \frac{20}{30} = 0.66$$

In the same class, if 10 students get the answer correct, the item difficulty index is 0.33. The item difficulty index can range from 0.0 to 1.0 with easier items having larger decimal values and difficult items having lower decimal values. An item that is answered correctly by all students receives an item difficulty of 1.00 while an item that is answered incorrectly by all students receives an item difficulty of 0.00. Items with p values of either 1.0 or 0.00 provide no information about individual differences and are of no value from a measurement perspective. For example, a math item that all students pass (or fail) does not tell us anything about the differences in math knowledge between students who completed the item. Some test developers will include one or two items with p values of 1.0 at the beginning of a test to instill a sense of confidence in test takers. This is a defensible practice from a motivational perspective, but from a technical perspective, these items do not contribute to the measurement characteristics of the test. Another factor that should be considered about the inclusion of very easy or very difficult items is the issue of time efficiency. The time examinees spend answering ineffective items is largely wasted and could be better spent on items that enhance the measurement characteristics of the test.

For maximizing variability and reliability, the optimal item difficulty level is 0.50, indicating that 50% of the test takers answered the item correctly and 50% answered the item incorrectly. Based on this statement, you might conclude that it is desirable for all test items to have a difficulty level of 0.50,

> For maximizing variability among test takers, the optimal item difficulty level is 0.50, indicating that 50% of the test takers answered the item correctly and 50% answered the item incorrectly.

but this is not necessarily true for several reasons. One reason is that items on a test are often correlated with each other. When items on a test are correlated, the measurement process may be confounded if all the items have p values of 0.50. As a result, it is often desirable to select some items that have p values below 0.50 and some with values greater than 0.50, but with a mean of 0.50. Aiken (2000) recommends that there should be approximately a 0.20 range of these p values around the optimal value. For example, a test developer might select items with difficulty levels ranging from 0.40 to 0.60, with a mean of 0.50.

Another reason why 0.50 is not the optimal difficulty level for every testing situation involves the influence of guessing. On constructed-response items (e.g., essay and short-answer items) where guessing is not a major concern, 0.50 is typically considered

> While a mean p of 0.50 is optimal for maximizing variability and reliability, different levels are desirable depending on testing applications.

the optimal difficulty level. However, with selected-response items (e.g., multiple choice and true–false items) where test takers might answer the item correctly simply by guessing, the optimal difficulty level varies. To take into consideration the effects of guessing, the optimal item difficulty level is set higher than for constructed-response items. For example, for multiple-choice items with 4 options, the average p should be approximately 0.74 (Lord, 1952). That is, the test developer might select items with difficulty levels ranging from 0.64 to 0.84 with a mean of approximately 0.74. Table 7.1 provides information on the optimal mean p value for selected-response items with varying numbers of alternatives or choices.

Table 7.1 Optimal p values for items with varying numbers of choices

Number of choices	Optimal mean p value
2 (e.g., true–false)	0.85
3	0.77
4	0.74
5	0.69
Constructed response (e.g., essay)	0.50

Source: Based on Lord (1952)

7.1.1 Special Assessment Situations and Item Difficulty

Our discussion of item difficulty so far is most applicable to norm-referenced tests. For criterion-referenced tests, particularly mastery tests, item difficulty is evaluated differently. On mastery tests, the test taker typically either passes or fails and there is the expectation that most test takers will eventually be successful. As a result, on mastery tests it is common for items to have average p values as high as 0.90 (almost all examinees will pass almost all items). Other tests that are designed for special assessment purposes may vary in terms of what represents desirable item difficulty levels. For example, if a test were developed to help employers select the upper 25% of job applicants, it would be desirable to have items with p values that average around 0.25. If it is desirable for a test to be able to distinguish the highest performing examinees (e.g., in testing gifted and talented students), it may also be desirable to include at least some very difficult items. In summary, while a mean p of 0.50 is optimal for maximizing variability among test takers, different difficulty levels are desirable depending on the specific testing application (see Special Interest Topic 7.1 for another example).

It should be noted that p values are sample dependent. That is, it is possible for one to achieve different item p values from different samples. For example, it is expected that item difficulty values will differ according to grade level. A specific reading comprehension item would likely be more difficult (lave a lower p value) when administered to third-grade students compared to fourth-grade students.

Percent Endorsement. As we noted, the item difficulty index is only applicable to maximum performance tests where items are scored correct/incorrect—either right or wrong. However, there is a conceptually similar index referred to as the ***percent endorsement statistic*** that can be calculated for typical-response tests (Friedenberg, 1995). In brief, the percent endorsement statistic indicates the percentage of examinees that responded to an item in a given manner. For example, a possible item on a depression scale might be:

1. I often feel sad.	True	False

A percent endorsement analysis might reveal that 15% of the respondents endorsed the item "True." As with item difficulty, the endorsement

> The percent endorsement statistic indicates the percentages of examinees who responded to an item in a given manner.

Special Interest Topic 7.1: Item Difficulty Indexes and Power Tests

As a rule of thumb and for psychometric reasons explained in this chapter, we have noted that item difficulty indexes of 0.50 are desirable in most circumstances on standardized tests. However, it is also common to include some very easy items so all or most examinees get some questions correct, as well as some very hard items, so the test has enough ceiling. With a power test, such an IQ test, that covers a wide age range and whose underlying construct is developmental, item selection becomes much more complex. Items that work very well at some ages may be far too easy, too hard, or just developmentally inappropriate at other ages. If a test covers the age range of say 3 years up to 20 years, and the items all had a difficulty level of 0.5, you could be left with a situation where the 3-, 4-, 5-, and even 6-year-olds typically pass no items and perhaps the oldest individuals nearly always get every item correct. This would lead to very low-reliability estimates at the upper and lower ages and just poor measurement of the constructs generally, except near the middle of the intended age range. For such power tests covering a wide age span, item statistics such as the difficulty index and the discrimination index are examined at each age level and plotted across all age levels. In this way, items can be chosen that are effective in measuring the relevant construct at different ages. When the item difficulty indexes for such a test are examined across the entire age range, some will approach 0 and some will approach 1.00. However, within the age levels, e.g., for 6-year-olds, there will be many items that are close to 0.50. This affords better discrimination and gives each examinee a range of items upon which they can express their ability on the underlying trait.

rate is dependent on the sample. Using this example, one might find that 15% of the respondents in a community sample endorsed the item "True," but that a much higher percentage from a clinical sample composed of individuals with psychological disorders endorsed the item in a positive manner (e.g., 80%).

> Item discrimination refers to how well an item accurately discriminates between test takers who differ on the construct being measured.

Later, in this chapter, we will provide some examples of how test developers use information about item difficulty and other item analysis statistics to select items to retain, revise, or delete when developing new tests or revising existing ones. First, we will discuss another popular item analysis procedure—the item-discrimination index.

7.2 Item Discrimination

Item discrimination refers to how well an item can discriminate or differentiate among test takers who differ on the construct being measured by the test. For example, if a test is designed to measure reading, item discrimination reflects an item's ability to distinguish

> One popular method of calculating an index of item discrimination is based on the difference between those who score well on the overall test and those who score poorly.

between individuals with good reading skills and those with poor reading skills. Unlike item difficulty level where there is agreement on how to calculate the statistic, over 50 different indices of item discrimination have been developed over the years (Anastasi & Urbina, 1997). Luckily, most of these indices produce similar results (Engelhart, 1965; Oosterhof, 1976). We will focus our discussion on two of the most popular indices of item discrimination: the discrimination index and item-total correlations.

7.2.1 Discrimination Index

One popular method of calculating an index of item discrimination is based on the difference in performance between two groups. While there are different ways of selecting the two groups, they are typically defined in terms of total test performance. One common approach is to select the top and bottom 27% of test takers in terms of their overall performance on the test and exclude the middle 46% (Kelley, 1939). Some assessment experts have suggested using the top and bottom 25%, some the top and bottom 33%, and some the top and bottom halves. In practice, all of these are probably acceptable, but our recommendation is to use the traditional top and bottom 27%. The difficulty of the item is computed for each group separately, and these are labeled p_T and p_B ("T" for top, "B" for bottom). The difference between p_T and p_B is the *discrimination index,* designated as D. It is calculated with the following formula (e.g., Johnson, 1951):

$$D = p_T - p_B$$

where

D = Discrimination Index
p_T = Proportion of Examinees in the Top Group Getting the Item Correct
p_B = Proportion of Examinees in the Bottom Group Getting the Item Correct

To illustrate the logic behind this index, consider an achievement test designed to measure academic achievement in some specified area. If the item is discriminating between examinees who know the material and those who do not, then examinees

Table 7.2 Guidelines for
evaluating D values

Difficulty	Descriptor
0.40 and larger	Excellent
0.30–0.39	Good
0.11–0.29	Fair
0.00–0.10	Poor
Negative values	Miskeyed or another major flaw

Source: Based on Hopkins (1998)

who are more knowledgeable (i.e., those in the "top" group) should get the item correct more often than examinees who are less knowledgeable (i.e., those in the "bottom" group). For example, if $p_T = 0.80$ (indicating 80% of the examinees in the top group

> As a general rule, items with D values at or above 0.30 are acceptable, and items with D values below 0.30 should be carefully reviewed and possibly revised or deleted.

answered the item correctly) and $p_B = 0.30$ (indicating 30% of the examinees in the bottom group answered the item correctly), then:

$$D = 0.80 - 0.30 = 0.50$$

Hopkins (1998) provided guidelines for evaluating items in terms of their D values (see Table 7.2). According to these guidelines, D values of 0.40 and above are considered excellent, between 0.30 and 0.39 are good, between 0.11 and 0.29 are fair, and between 0.00 and 0.10 are poor. Items with negative D values are likely miskeyed or there are other serious problems. Other testing assessment experts have provided different guidelines, some more rigorous and some more lenient.

As a general rule, we suggest that items with D values over 0.30 are acceptable (the larger the better), and items with D values below 0.30 should be carefully reviewed, and possibly revised or deleted. However, this is only a general rule and there are exceptions. For example, most indices of item discrimination, including the item-discrimination index (D), are biased in favor of items with intermediate difficulty levels. That is, the maximum D value of an item is related to its p value (see Table 7.3). Items that all examinees either pass or fail (i.e., p values of either 0.00 or 1.0) cannot provide any information about individual differences and their D values will always be zero. If half of the examinees correctly answered an item and half failed (i.e., p value of 0.50), then it is possible for the item's D value to be 1.0. This does not mean that all items with p values of 0.50 will have D values of

Table 7.3 Maximum D values at different difficulty levels

Item difficulty index (p)	Maximum D value
1.00	0.00
0.90	0.20
0.80	0.40
0.70	0.60
0.60	0.70
0.50	1.00
0.40	0.70
0.30	0.60
0.20	0.40
0.10	0.20
0.00	0.00

Special Interest Topic 7.2: Item Analysis for Constructed-Response Items

Our discussion and examples of the calculation of the item difficulty index and discrimination index used examples that were dichotomously scored (i.e., scored right or wrong, 0 or 1). While this procedure works fine with selected-response items (e.g., true–false, multiple choice), you need a slightly different approach with constructed-response items that are scored in a more continuous manner (e.g., an essay item that can receive scores between 1 and 5 depending on quality). To calculate the item difficulty index for a continuously scored constructed-response item, you use the following formula (Nitko, 2001):

$$p = \frac{\text{Average Score on the Item}}{\text{Range of Possible Scores}}$$

The range of possible scores is calculated as the maximum possible score on the item minus the minimum possible score on the item. For example, if an item has an average score of 2.7 and is scored on a 1–5 scale, the calculation would be:

$$p = \frac{2.7}{5-1} = \frac{2.7}{4} = 0.675$$

Therefore, this item has an item difficulty index = 0.675. This value can be interpreted the same as the dichotomously scored items we discussed. To calculate the item-discrimination index for continuously scored constructed-response item, you use the following formula:

$$D = \frac{\text{Average Score for the Top Group} - \text{Average Score for the Bottom Group}}{\text{Range of Possible Scores}}$$

For example, if the average score for the top group is 4.3, the average score for the bottom group is 1.7, and the item is scored on a 1–5 scale, and the calculation would be:

$$D = \frac{4.3 - 1.7}{5 - 1} = \frac{2.6}{4} = 0.65$$

Therefore, this item has an item-discrimination index = 0.65. Again, this value can be interpreted the same as the dichotomously scored items we discussed.

1.0, just that the item can conceivably have a D value of 1.0. As a result of this relationship between p and D, items that have excellent discrimination power (i.e., D values of 0.40 and above) will necessarily have p values between 0.20 and 0.80. In testing situations where it is desirable to have either very easy or very difficult items, D values can be expected to be lower than those normally desired. Additionally, items that measure abilities or objectives that are not emphasized throughout the test may have poor discrimination due to their unique focus. In this situation, if the item measures an important ability or learning objective and is free of technical defects, it should be retained (e.g., Linn & Gronlund, 2000).

In summary, while low D values often indicate problems, the guidelines provided in Table 7.2 should be applied in a flexible, considered manner. Our

| Several different approaches have been suggested for determining item discrimination on mastery tests. |

discussion of the calculation of Item Difficulty and Discrimination Indices has used examples with items that are dichotomously scored (i.e., correct/incorrect, 1 or 0). Special Interest Topic 7.2 provides a discussion of the application of these statistics with constructed-response items that are not scored in a dichotomous manner.

7.2.2   Item Discrimination on Mastery Tests

As we noted previously, the item difficulty indexes on mastery tests tend to be higher (indicating easier items) than on tests designed primarily to produce norm-referenced scores. This is because with mastery testing it is usually assumed that most examinees will be successful. As a result, on mastery tests it is common for items to have average p values as high as 0.90. As a result, the standard approach to interpreting item difficulty levels needs to be modified to accommodate this tendency.

The interpretation of indexes of discrimination is also complicated on mastery tests. Since it is common to obtain high p values for both high- and low-scoring examinees, it is normal for traditional item-discrimination indexes to underestimate an item's true measurement characteristics. Several different approaches have been suggested for determining item discrimination on mastery tests (e.g., Aiken, 2000; Popham, 2000). One common approach involves administering the test to two groups of examinees; one group that has received instruction and one that has not received instruction. The formula is:

$$D = p_{\text{instruction}} - p_{\text{no instruction}}$$

where

$p_{\text{instruction}}$ = Proportion of Instructed Examinees Getting the Answer Correct

$p_{\text{no instruction}}$ = Proportion of Examinees Without Instruction Getting the Answer Correct

This approach is technically adequate, with the primary limitation being the potential difficulty obtaining access to an adequate group that has not received instruction or training on the relevant material. If one does have access to an adequate sample, this is a promising approach.

Another popular approach involves administering the test to the same sample twice, once before instruction and once after instruction. The formula is:

$$D = p_{\text{posttest}} - p_{\text{pretest}}$$

Where

p_{posttest} = Proportion of Examinees Getting the Answer Correct on Posttest

p_{pretest} = Proportion of Examinees Getting the Answer Correct on Pretest

There are some drawbacks associated with this approach. First, it requires that the test developers write the test, administer it as a pretest, wait while instruction is provided, administer it as a posttest, and then calculate the discrimination index. This can be an extended period of time in some situations and test developers often want feedback in a timely manner. A second limitation is the possibility of carry-over effects from the pre- to posttest. For example, examinees might remember items or concepts emphasized on the pretest, and this carry-over effect can influence how they respond to instruction, study, and subsequently prepare for the posttest.

> Another approach to examining item discrimination is correlating performance on the item with the total test score.

Aiken (2000) proposed another approach for calculating discrimination for mastery tests. Instead of using the top and bottom 27% of examinees (or the top and bottom 50%), he recommends using item difficulty values based on the test takers who reached the mastery cut-off score (i.e., mastery group) and those who did not reach mastery (i.e., non-mastery group). The formula is:

$$D = p_{\text{mastery}} - p_{\text{non-mastery}}$$

where

$p_{mastery}$ = Proportion of Mastery Examinees Getting the Answer Correct
$p_{non - mastery}$ = Proportion of Non-mastery Examinees Getting the Answer Correct

The advantage of this approach is that it can be calculated based on the data from one test administration with one sample. A potential problem is that since it is common for the majority of examinees to reach mastery, the p value of the non-mastery group might be based on a small number of examinees. As a result, the statistics might not be stable and lead to erroneous conclusions.

Item-Total Correlation Coefficients. Another approach to examining item discrimination is to correlate performance on the items (scored as either 0 or 1) with the total test score. This is referred to as an *item-total correlation*. The total test score is usually the total number of items answered correctly (unadjusted) or the total number of items answered correctly omitting the item being examined (adjusted). Either way, the item-total correlation is usually calculated using the point-biserial correlation. As you remember from our discussion of basic statistics, the point-biserial is used when one variable is a dichotomous nominal score and the other variable is measured on an interval or ratio scale. Here, the dichotomous variable is the score on a single item (e.g., right or wrong) and the variable measured on an interval scale is the total test score. A large item-total correlation is taken as evidence that an item is measuring the same construct as the overall test measures and that the item discriminates between individuals high on that construct and those low on the construct. An item-total correlation calculated on the adjusted total will be lower than that computed on the unadjusted total and is preferred since the item being examined does not "contaminate" or inflate the correlation. The results of an item-total correlation will be similar to those of an item-discrimination index and can be interpreted in a similar manner (Hopkins, 1998).

In the past, some test developers preferred the item-discrimination index over item-correlations since it was easier to calculate. However, as computers and statistical programs have become widely available, the item-total correlation has become easier to compute and is becoming the dominant approach for examining item discrimination.

7.2.3   Item Discrimination on Typical-Response Tests

Item-total correlations can also be used with typical-response tests. For example, consider a test designed to mea-

> On speed tests, measures of item difficulty and discrimination will largely reflect the position of the item in the test rather than the actual difficulty of the item or its discriminative ability.

sure "sensation-seeking" tendencies using true–false items. Below is an example of an item that might be on such a test:

1. I would like to go parachuting.	True	False

If all "True" responses are scored "1" and indicate a tendency to engage in sensation-seeking behaviors and all "False" responses are scored "0" and indicate a tendency to avoid sensation-seeking behaviors, high scores on the test would indicate that the respondent enjoys high-sensation behaviors. Accordingly, low scores would suggest that the respondent tends to avoid high-sensation behaviors. Calculating item-total correlations would allow the test developer to select items with high correlations, i.e., those items that discriminate between respondents that are high and low in sensation-seeking behaviors.

7.2.4 Difficulty and Discrimination on Speed Tests

Based on our discussion up to this point, it should be clear that there are situations where the interpretation of indices of item difficulty and discrimination are complicated. One situation where the interpretation of item analysis results is complicated is with "speed tests." On speed tests, performance depends primarily on the speed of performance. Items on speed tests are often fairly easy and could be completed by most test takers if there were no time limits. However, there are strict time limits and these limits are selected so that no test taker will be able to complete all of the items. The key factor is how many items the test taker is able to complete in the allotted time. On power tests, everyone is given sufficient time to attempt all the items, but the items vary in difficulty with some being so difficult that no test takers will answer them all correctly. In many situations, tests incorporate a combination of speed and power, so the speed/power distinction is actually one of degree.

On speed tests, measures of item difficulty and discrimination will largely reflect the location of the item in the test rather than the item's actual difficulty level or ability to discriminate. Items appearing late on a speed test will be passed by fewer individuals than items that appear earlier simply because the strict time limits prevent examinees from being able to attempt them. The items appearing later on the test are probably not actually more difficult than the earlier items, but their item difficulty index will suggest that they are more difficult.

Similar complications arise when interpreting indices of discrimination with speed tests. Since the individuals completing the later items also tend to be the most capable test takers, indices of discrimination may exaggerate the discriminating ability of these items. While different procedures have been developed to take into consideration these and related factors, they all have limitations and none have received widespread acceptance (e.g., Aiken, 2000; Anastasi & Urbina, 1997). Our recommendation is that you should be aware of these issues and take them into consideration when interpreting the item analyses of highly speeded tests.

7.2.5   Examples of Item Difficulty and Discrimination Indices

To illustrate the results of common item analyses, we will present a few examples based on items administered in our upper-division undergraduate Test and Measurement class. We will present three examples to illustrate some common patterns.

---

1. A test that measures what it is designed to measure is _____; a test that produces consistent/stable scores is _____.
   - (a) reliable; valid
   - (b) valid; reliable   ≪
   - (c) marginal; optimal
   - (d) optimal; marginal

   Item Difficulty (p): 0.97
   Discrimination Index: 0.00
   Item-Total Correlation: 0.05

This is an easy item that almost all students answer correctly. Since it is so easy, it does not discriminate between students who know the material and those that do not. We often use this (or a similar item) as the first item in a test to help relax students and ease them into the assessment process.

---

2. Approximately what percentage of scores falls below an IQ of 130 if the scores are normally distributed?
   - (a) 16%
   - (b) 34%
   - (c) 50%
   - (d) 84%
   - (e) 98%   ≪

   Item Difficulty (p): 0.78
   Discrimination Index: 0.53
   Item-Total Correlation: 0.59

This item is a fairly easy for a five-alternative multiple-choice item (remember the optimal Mean p value for selected-response items with five choices was 0.69), but it does discriminate well.

Distracter analysis allows you to examine how many examinees in the top and bottom groups selected each response option on a multiple-choice item.

---

3. Which of the following is an appropriate estimate of reliability when one is assessing the reliability of a highly speeded test?
   - (a) Coefficient alpha
   - (b) Kuder-Richardson (KR-20)
   - (c) Split-half reliability
   - (d) Test-retest reliability   ≪

(e) all of the above
Item Difficulty (p): 0.44
Discrimination Index: 0.82
Item-Total Correlation: 0.66

This is a fairly difficult multiple-choice item for one with five-alternatives. It shows excellent discrimination and can help identify high-achieving students.

7.3   Distracter Analysis

The final quantitative item analysis procedure we will discuss in this chapter involves the analysis of individual distracters. On multiple-choice items, the incorrect alternatives are referred to as distracters since they serve to "distract" examinees who don't actually know the correct response. *Distracter analysis* allows you to examine how many examinees in the top and bottom groups selected each option on a multiple-choice item. The key is to examine each distracter and ask two questions. First, did the distracter distract some examinees? If no examinees selected the distracter, it is not doing its job. An effective distracter must be selected by some examinees. If a distracter is so obviously incorrect that no examinees select it, it is ineffective and needs to be revised or replaced. The second question involves discrimination. Effective distracters should attract more examinees in the bottom group than in the top group. When looking at the correct response, we expect more examinees in the top group to select it than examinees in the bottom group (i.e., it demonstrates positive discrimination). With distracters, we expect the opposite. We expect more examinees in the bottom group to select a distracter than examinees in the top group. That is, distracters should demonstrate *negative* discrimination! Consider the following example:

Item #1	Response options			
	A[a]	B	C	D
Number in Top Group	22	3	2	3
Number in Bottom Group	9	7	8	6

[a]Correct Answer

For this item, $p = 0.52$ (moderate difficulty) and $D = 0.43$ (excellent discrimination). This item serves as an example of what might be expected with a "good" item. As reflected in the D value, more examinees in the top group than the bottom group selected the correct answer (i.e., option A). By examining the distracters (i.e., response options B, C, and D), you see that they were all selected by some examinees which indicates that they are serving their purpose (i.e., distracting examinees who don't know the correct response). Additionally, all three distracters were selected more by members of the bottom group than the top group. This is the desired outcome! While we want more "high-scoring" examinees to select the correct answer than "low-scoring" examinees (i.e., positive discrimination), we want more "low-scoring" examinees to select distracters than "high-scoring" examinees (i.e., negative discrimination). In summary, this is a good item and all of the distracters are performing well.

Now we will consider an example that illustrates some problems. Consider the following example:

Item #3	Response options			
	A	B[a]	C	D
Number in Top Group	9	17	0	4
Number in Bottom Group	6	13	0	11

[a]Correct Answer

For this item, $p = 0.50$ (moderate difficulty) and $D = 0.14$ (fair discrimination but further scrutiny suggested). One could decide to exclude this item entirely based on the value of D, but this may not be the best decision if revisions would improve its discrimination and it is otherwise a good item (e.g., a good sample of the content domain). Examining option A you will notice that more examinees in the top group than in the bottom group selected this distracter. This is not a desirable situation since it indicates that more "top performing" examinees selected this distracter than "poor performing" examinees. As a result, option A needs to be examined to determine why it is attracting top examinees. It is possible that the wording is ambiguous or that the option is similar in some way to the correct answer, and as a result, it is selected by top examinees. Examining option C you note that no one selected this distracter. It attracted no examinees, suggesting that it was obviously not the correct answer, and as a result needs to be replaced. To be effective, a distracter must "distract" some examinees. Finally, option D performed well. More "poor performing" examinees selected this option than "top performing" examinees (i.e., 11 versus 4). It is likely that if the test developer revises options B and C, this will be a more effective item that can be retained.

7.3.1   How Distracters Influence Item Difficulty and Discrimination

Before leaving our discussion of distracters, we want to highlight how the selection of distracters impacts both item difficulty and discrimination. Consider the following item:

1. What year did Albert Einstein first publish his full general theory of relativity?
   (a) 1910
   (b) 1912
   (c) 1914
   (d) 1916   ≪
   (e) 1918

Unless you are very familiar with Einstein's work, this is probably a fairly difficult question. Now consider this revision:

---

1. What year did Albert Einstein first publish his full general theory of relativity?
   (a) 1655
   (b) 1762
   (c) 1832
   (d) 1916   ≪
   (e) 2001

This is the same question but with different distracters. This revised item would likely be a much easier item in a typical high school science class. The point is that the selection of distracters can significantly impact the difficulty of the item and consequently the ability of the item to discriminate.

7.4 Qualitative Item Analysis

In addition to the quantitative item analysis procedures described to this point, test developers can also use *qualitative item analysis* procedures to improve their tests. Along these lines, Popham (2000) provides some useful suggestions. He recommends that after

> In addition to quantitative item analysis procedures, test developers can also use qualitative procedures to improve their tests.

writing the test, the developer set the test aside for a few days to gain some distance from it. We can tell you from our own experience this is good advice. Even though you carefully proof a test immediately after writing it, a review a few days later will often reveal a number of errors. This delayed review often reveals both clerical errors (e.g., spelling or grammar) and less obvious errors that might make an item unclear or inaccurate. After a "cooling off" period, we are often amazed that an "obvious" error evaded detection earlier. Somehow the introduction of a period of time provides distance that seems to make errors more easily detected. The time you spend proofing a test is well spent and can help you avoid problems once the test is administered and scored.

Popham (2000) also recommends that you have a colleague review the test. Ideally, this should be a colleague familiar with basic psychometric principles and the construct being assessed by the test. In addition to checking for

> We recommend the use of both qualitative and quantitative approaches to improve the quality of test items.

clerical errors, clarity, and accuracy, the reviewer should determine if the test is covering all aspects of the construct that it is designed to cover. This is akin to collecting validity evidence based on the content of the test. Finally, he recommends that you have the examinees provide feedback on the test. For example, after completing the test you might have the examinees complete a brief questionnaire asking if the directions were clear and if any of the questions were confusing.

Ideally, a test developer should use both quantitative and qualitative approaches to improve tests. We regularly provide a delayed review of our own tests and use colleagues as reviewers whenever possible. After administering a test and obtaining the quantitative item analyses, we typically question examinees about problematic items, particularly items where the basis of the problem is not obvious. Often a combination of qualitative and quantitative procedures will result in the optimal enhancement of your tests.

Popham (2000) notes that historically quantitative item analysis procedures have been applied primarily to tests using norm-referenced score interpretations and qualitative procedures have been used primarily with tests using criterion-referenced interpretations. This tendency can be attributed partly to some of the technical problems we described earlier about using item analysis statistics with mastery tests. Nevertheless, we recommend the use of both qualitative and quantitative approaches with both types of score interpretations. When developing tests, we believe the more information one has, the better!

7.5   Item Characteristic Curves and Item Response Theory

The item analysis procedures that we have described so far in this chapter have literally been around for close to a century and are related to classical test theory. While they are well established and are still useful, they have their limitations and are typically complemented with sophisticated relatively new techniques associated with *item response theory* (IRT). We have already mentioned IRT several times in this text, specifically when discussing test scores and reliability. In summary, IRT is a theory or model of mental measurement that holds that the responses to items on a test are accounted for by latent traits. A latent trait is an ability or characteristic of an individual that is inferred to exist based on theories of behavior as well as empirical evidence, but a latent trait cannot be assessed directly. Intelligence is an example of a latent trait. It is assumed that each examinee possesses a certain amount of any given latent trait and that its estimation is not dependent on any specific set of items or any assessment procedure. Central to IRT is a rather complex mathematical model that describes how examinees at different levels of ability (or whatever latent trait is being assessed) will respond to individual test items. IRT is also known by other names, including unidimensional scaling, latent trait theory, and item characteristic curve theory. At this point, it is helpful to elaborate on IRT and its

> Today traditional item analysis procedures such as the item difficulty and discrimination indexes typically complement sophisticated new techniques associated with item response theory (IRT).

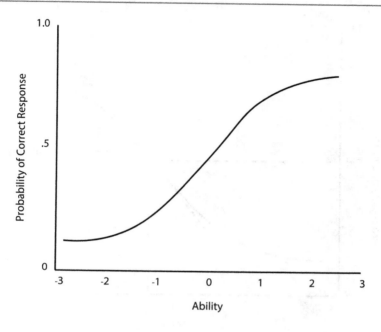

Fig. 7.1 Typical ICC

contribution to contemporary test development and analysis. A description of item characteristic curves is a good place to start our discussion.

7.5.1   Item Characteristic Curves

An item characteristic curve (ICC) is a graph with ability reflected on the horizontal axis and the probability of a correct response reflected on the vertical axis. It is important to recognize *that each item has its own specific ICC*. These ICCs are plotted from mathematically derived functions and usually involve iterative procedures (Anastasi & Urbina, 1997). Figure 7.1 presents a hypothetical, but typical, ICC for an item with good discrimination. The vertical axis represents the Probability of a Correct Response which ranges from 0% (0.0) to 100% (1.0). The horizontal axis represents Ability in z-score units, where 0 is equal to the mean ability level. Notice that this ICC takes a "Lazy S" shape and it is an asymptote (i.e., approaches but never intersects with 0 or 1.00). By examining this graph, you see that low levels of ability are associated with a low probability of a correct response. As the ability level increases, the probability of a correct response increases. In other words, test takers with greater ability have a better chance of answering the item correct than those with lower ability. This is what you expect with a good item!

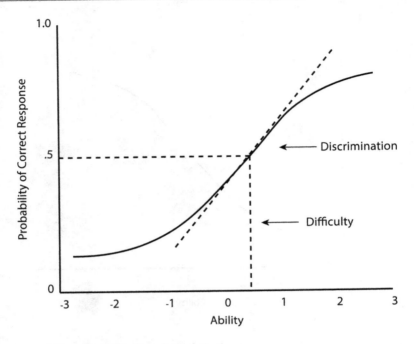

Fig. 7.2 ICC illustrating difficulty and discrimination

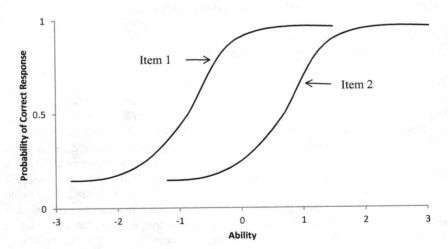

Fig. 7.3 Two ICCs with the same discrimination but different difficulties

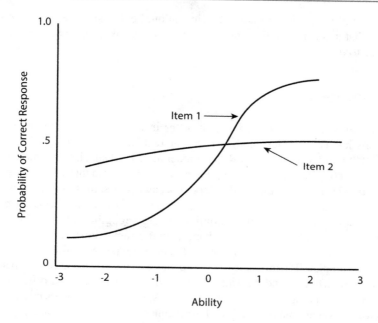

Fig. 7.4 Two ICCs with the same difficulty but different discrimination

ICCs incorporate information about item measurement characteristics that you are already familiar with: the item's difficulty and discrimination ability. In ICC terminology, the point half-way between the lower and upper asymptotes is referred to as the inflection point and represents the difficulty of the item

> Item characteristic curves (ICCs) incorporate information about item measurement characteristics that you are already familiar with: the item's difficulty and discrimination ability.

(i.e., the b parameter). That is, it pinpoints the ability level required for a test taker to have a 50% chance of getting the item correct. Discrimination (i.e., the a parameter) is reflected by the slope of the ICC at the inflection point. ICCs with steeper slopes demonstrate better discrimination than those with gentler slopes. Discrimination in this context refers to the ability of the item to differentiate or discriminate one level of ability or one level of the presence of the trait being assessed from another level. Figure 7.2 illustrates how both difficulty and discrimination are represented in an ICC. The vertical dotted line denoting "Difficulty" indicates that it requires an ability score (in z-score units) of approximately 0.25 to have a 50% chance of answering the item correctly. The dotted line representing "Discrimination" is at approximately 45° which suggests good discrimination. This is further illustrated in Figs. 7.3 and 7.4. Figure 7.3 depicts two items with equal slopes, but Item 2 is shifted to the right of Item 1. This shifting to the right indicates that relative to Item 1, Item 2 requires more ability to answer correctly—that is, it is more difficult. Figure 7.4 depicts two items that are of equal difficulty, but different discrimination. Item 1 has a steeper slope which indicates that it is better at discriminating between test takers low and high in ability compared to Item 2.

7.5.2   IRT Models

There are three major IRT models that differ in assumptions made about items' characteristics. The simplest model (if one can realistically use "simple" in the context of IRT) is referred to as the Rasch model after the Danish mathematician and statistician Georg Rasch who was a pioneer in the development of IRT. This model is referred to as a one-parameter IRT model because it assumes that items only differ in one parameter—difficulty (i.e., b parameter). That is, all items have equal discrimination or differences in discrimination are negligible. This implies that all items have ICCs with the same "S" shape with the same slope; they only differ in the location of their inflection point along the horizontal (i.e., Ability) axis.

A more complex IRT model is the two-parameter model that assumes that items differ in both difficulty and discrimination. In this model, the ICCs differ not only in their inflection points, but also in their slopes. While test developers might attempt to develop tests that contain items with the same degree of discrimination, in practice this is difficult if not impossible to accomplish. As a result, the two-parameter IRT model better reflects real-life test development applications than the one-parameter IRT model.

As you might have anticipated, the third model is the three-parameter IRT model. In both the one- and two-parameter IRT models, the ICCs asymptote toward a probability of 0, assuming essentially a 0% possibility of answering the items by chance. The three-parameter model assumes that even if the respondent essentially has no "ability," there is still a chance they may answer the item correctly simply by chance. Obviously, this occurs on selected-response items. For example, a multiple-choice item with four alternatives has a 25% chance of being answered correctly with random guessing. A true–false item has a 50% chance of being answered correctly with random guessing. The three-parameter model essentially adjusts the lower tail of the ICC to take into consideration the probability of answering an item correctly simply by chance (i.e., the c parameter). This model is mathematically very complex, and this complexity has prevented it from being widely applied.

7.5.3   Invariance of Item Parameters

The item statistics we discussed earlier in this chapter like item difficulty (i.e., p) and item discrimination (i.e., D) are based on classical test theory (CTT). These item statistics are dependent on the sample they are derived with. That is, one may obtain different p and D values in different samples. For example, if you calculated item difficulty for an item on a classroom psychology test in a sample of college freshmen psychology majors and in a sample of senior psychology majors, you might well get different p values. As a general rule, seniors will have more knowledge in their major area than freshmen so a higher percentage of seniors will answer the item correctly. Accordingly, traditional discrimination statistics may vary across samples.

In IRT, the parameters of items (e.g., difficulty and discrimination) are said to be "sample-free" or "sample-independent." That is, one should get the same results when using different samples. Going back to our example of freshmen and senior psychology students, when using IRT, one should

> In IRT, the parameters of items are said to be "sample-free" or "sample-independent"—that is, one should get the same results when using different samples.

obtain the same parameter estimates regardless of the sample used. Technically, this is referred to as "invariance of item parameters" and is an important aspect of IRT. As a result of this invariance, a fixed or uniform scale of measurement can be developed and used in different groups. Accordingly, examinees can be tested using different sets of items and their scores will be comparable (Anastasi & Urbina, 1997). These properties of IRT make it particularly useful in a number of special test development applications such as computer-based testing and developing equivalent or alternate forms of tests.

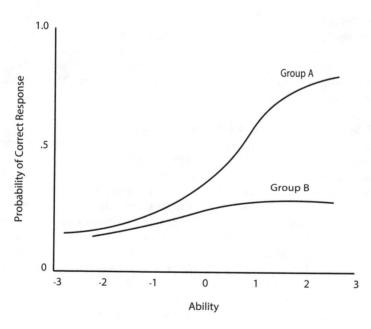

Fig. 7.5 ICCs for a biased item

7.5.4 Special Applications of IRT

As we discussed earlier, IRT is a modern psychometric theory that has extended, but not replaced classical test theory. Below are a few specific applications where IRT has made significant contributions to contemporary test development.

> IRT has made significant contributions to contemporary test development.

7.5.4.1 Computer Adaptive Testing

IRT is fundamental to the development and application of computer adaptive testing (CAT). In CAT, the test taker is initially given an item that is of medium difficulty. If the test taker correctly responds to that item, the computer selects and administers a slightly more difficult item. If the examinee misses the initial item, the computer selects a somewhat easier item. As the testing proceeds, the computer continues to select items on the basis of the test taker's performance on previous items. CAT continues until a specified level of precision is reached. Research has shown that CAT can produce the same levels of reliability and validity as conventional paper-and-pencil tests, but requires the administration of fewer test items, which means enhanced efficiency.

7.5.4.2 Detecting Biased Items

IRT has proved particularly useful in identifying biased test items. To this end, ICCs for different groups (e.g., males, females) are generated and statistically compared to determine the degree of differential item functioning (DIF). Figure 7.5 depicts an item with substantially different ICCs for two different groups. This application of IRT will be discussed in more detail in Chap. 15.

7.5.4.3 Scores Based on Item Response Theory

As we stated in Chap. 3, in addition to the norm-referenced and criterion-referenced score interpretations, IRT provides an additional approach for interpreting scores. Since we introduced IRT scores in Chap. 3, we will not go into great detail at this point. However, a brief review is warranted. In summary, the scores assigned to reflect an examinee's performance in IRT models are similar to raw scores on tests developed using classical test theory. For example, they can be transformed into either norm or criterion-referenced scores. However, they have an advantage in that unlike traditional raw scores, they are equal interval level scores (i.e., having equal intervals between values) and have stable standard deviations across age groups. These IRT scores go by different names, including W-scores, growth scores, change sensitive scores (CSS), or Rasch scores. The W-scores used on the Woodcock-Johnson IV (McGrew, LaForte, & Schrank, 2014) provide a good example of these scores. W-scores are set so a score of 500 reflects cognitive performance at the beginning fifth-grade ability level. W-scores have proven to be particularly useful in measuring changes in cognitive abilities. For example, they can help measure gains in achievement due to learning or declines in cognitive abilities due to dementia. In terms of measuring gains, if over time an examinee's W-score increases by 10 units (e.g., from 500 to 510), they can now complete tasks with 75% probability of success that they originally could only complete with a 50% probability of success. Conversely, if an examinee's W-score decreases by 10 W units (e.g., 500–490), they can now complete tasks with only 25% probability of success that originally could complete with 50% probability of success (Jaffe, 2009). While these IRT-based scores are not currently widely available, they will likely become more available in the future.

7.5.4.4 Reliability

In Chap. 4, we stated that IRT models information on the reliability of scores, reporting it as a test information function (TIF). A TIF illustrates the reliability of measurement at different points along the distribution. This implies that the reliability is not constant across the distribution of scores, an observation that is accurate in many testing situations. It is common to find that scores at both the high and low ends of a distribution have more measurement error. As a result, a test may provide more reliable measurement for examinees at one level of ability, and less reliable measurement for those at another level. While classical test theory provides only one estimate of reliability, IRT can provide information about reliability at different points along the distribution. TIFs can also be converted into an analog of the standard error of measurement for specific points in the distribution.

IRT models are most often used in the development of group achievement tests and in the various Woodcock cognitive and achievement scales. However, IRT models are becoming more widely applied in other assessments in psychology and their use will undoubtedly grow over the next decades.

7.6 Summary

Item analysis procedures are useful in helping test developers decide which items to keep on a test, which items to modify, and which items to eliminate. This chapter describes several these procedures including:

- *Item difficulty level.* The item difficulty level or index is defined as the percentage or proportion of examinees correctly answering the item. The item difficulty index (i.e., p) ranges from 0.0 to 1.0 with easier items having larger decimal values and difficult items having smaller values. For maximizing variability among examinees, the optimal item difficulty level is 0.50, indicating that half of the examinees answered the item correctly and half answered it incorrectly. While 0.50 is optimal for maximizing variability, there are many situations where other values are preferred. As a general rule, in most testing situations test developers will select items with p values between 0.20 and 0.80.
- *Item discrimination*: Item discrimination refers to the extent to which an item accurately discriminates between examinees that vary on the test's construct. For

example, on an achievement test the question is "Can the item distinguish between examinees who are high achievers and those who are poor achievers?" While there are a number of different approaches to assess item discrimination, we discuss the popular item-discrimination index (i.e., D). We provide guidelines for evaluating item-discrimination indexes, and as a general rule items with D values 0.30 and over are acceptable, and items with D values below 0.30 should be reviewed and possibly eliminated. However, this is only a general rule and we discussed a number of situations when smaller D values might be acceptable. Another approach to examining item discrimination is to correlate performance on individual items with the total test score. This is referred to as an item-total correlation. The results of an item-total correlation will be similar to those of an item-discrimination index and can be interpreted in a similar manner. In the past, some preferred the item-discrimination index over item-correlations since it was easier to calculate. However, the broad availability of computers has made calculating item-total correlations easy and they are becoming the dominant approach for examining item discrimination.

- *Distracter analysis*: The final quantitative item analysis procedure we describe is distracter analysis. In essence, distracter analysis allows the test developer to evaluate whether the distracters on multiple-choice items (i.e., incorrect alternatives) are functioning properly. This involves two primary questions. First, a properly functioning distracter should "distract" some examinees. If a distracter is so obviously wrong that no examinees selected it, it is useless and deserves deletion. The second question involves discrimination. Effective distracters should attract more examinees in the bottom group than in the top group. Distracter analysis allows you to answer these two questions.

- *Qualitative procedures*. In addition to quantitative item analysis procedures, test developers can also use qualitative procedures to improve their tests. For example, authors should carefully proof the test after setting it aside for a few days because this break allows them to gain some distance from the test which facilitates a more thorough review. Two other qualitative procedures involve getting a trusted colleague to review the test and soliciting feedback from examinees regarding the clarity of directions and ambiguous or otherwise problematic items. Test developers are probably best served by using a combination of quantitative and qualitative item analysis procedures.

- *Item characteristic curves and item response theory*. An item characteristic curve (ICC) is a graph with ability reflected on the horizontal axis and the probability of a correct response reflected on the vertical axis. ICCs incorporate information about an item's difficulty and discrimination ability and are a component of item response theory (IRT). IRT is a modern theory of mental measurement that holds that responses to items on a test are accounted for by latent traits. IRT assumes that each examinee possesses a certain amount of any given latent trait and that its estimation is not dependent on any specific set of items or any assessment procedure. IRT has significantly impacted contemporary test development, particularly in the development and application of computer adaptive testing.

Using item analysis procedures during the test development process will improve the reliability of test scores and the validity of their interpretation because reliability and validity are dependent on the quality of the test items. Using item analysis to delete poor items and improve other items may also result in a shorter more efficient test that produces more reliable scores and more valid interpretations.

References

Aiken, L. R. (2000). *Psychological testing and assessment.* Boston, MA: Allyn & Bacon.

Anastasi, A., & Urbina, S. (1997). *Psychological testing* (7th ed.). Upper Saddle River, NJ: Prentice Hall.

Engelhart, M. D. (1965). A comparison of several item discrimination indices. *Journal of Educational Measurement, 2,* 69–76.

Friedenberg, L. (1995). *Psychological testing: Design, analysis, and use.* Boston, MA: Allyn & Bacon.

Hopkins, K. D. (1998). *Educational and psychological measurement and evaluation* (8th ed.). Boston, MA: Allyn & Bacon.

Jaffe, L. E. (2009). *Development, interpretation, and application of the W score and the relative proficiency index (Woodcock-Johnson III Assessment Service Bulletin No. 11).* Rolling Meadows, IL: Riverside.

Johnson, A. P. (1951). Notes on a suggested index of item validity: The U-L index. *Journal of Educational Measurement, 42,* 499–504.

Kelley, T. L. (1939). The selection of upper and lower groups for the validation of test items. *Journal of Educational Psychology, 30,* 17–24.

Linn, R. L., & Gronlund, N. E. (2000). *Measurement and assessment in teaching* (8th ed.). Upper Saddle River, NJ: Prentice Hall.

Lord, F. M. (1952). The relation of the reliability of multiple-choice tests to the distribution of item difficulties. *Psychometrika, 17,* 181–194.

McGrew, K. S., LaForte, E. M., & Schrank, F. A. (2014). *Technical Manual. Woodcock-Johnson IV.* Rolling Meadows, IL: Riverside.

Nitko, A. J. (2001). Educational assessment of students. Upper Saddle River, NJ: Merrill Prentice Hall.

Oosterhof, A. C. (1976). Similarity of various item discrimination indices. *Journal of Educational Measurement, 13,* 145–150.

Popham, W. J. (2000). *Modern educational measurement: Practical guidelines for educational leaders.* Boston, MA: Allyn & Bacon.

Recommended Reading

Embretson, S., & Reise, S. (2000). *Item response theory for psychologists.* London, England: Taylor & Francis.

Johnson, A. P. (1951). Notes on a suggested index of item validity: The U-L index. *Journal of Educational Measurement, 42,* 499–504. This is a seminal article in the history of item analysis.

Kelley, T. L. (1939). The selection of upper and lower groups for the validation of test items. *Journal of Educational Psychology, 30,* 17–24. A real classic!

Achievement Tests in the Era of High-Stakes Assessment

8

Depending on your perspective, standardized achievement tests are either a bane or boon to public schools. Many politicians and citizens see them as a way of holding educators accountable and ensuring students are really learning. On the other hand, many educators feel standardized tests are often misused and detract from their primary job of educating students.

Abstract

Achievement tests assess a person's knowledge or skills in area where he or she has received instruction. Achievement tests are most often used in educational settings to track student achievement over time, make high-stakes decisions, identify specific strengths and weaknesses, evaluate the effectiveness of educational programs, and identify individuals with special learning needs. This chapter introduces several group- and individually-administered achievement tests. Best practices for preparing students to take standardized achievement tests are also reviewed, along with key steps teachers should follow when developing tests that are used to assign grades. The chapter concludes with a brief review of achievement tests used as part of licensure processes.

Supplementary Information The online version of this chapter (https://doi.org/10.1007/978-3-030-59455-8_8) contains supplementary material, which is available to authorized users.

© Springer Nature Switzerland AG 2021
C. R. Reynolds et al., *Mastering Modern Psychological Testing*,
https://doi.org/10.1007/978-3-030-59455-8_8

Learning Objectives

After reading and studying this chapter, students should be able to:

1. Describe characteristics of standardized tests and explain why standardization is important.
2. Describe major characteristics of achievement tests.
3. Describe major uses of standardized achievement tests in schools.
4. Explain what "high-stakes testing" means and trace the historical development of this phenomenon.
5. Compare and contrast group- and individually-administered achievement tests.
6. Describe strengths and weaknesses of group- and individually-administered achievement tests.
7. Identify major publishers of group achievement tests and their major tests.
8. Discuss major issues and controversies surrounding state and high-stakes testing programs.
9. Describe and evaluate common procedures to prepare students for standardized tests.
10. Describe and evaluate major individual achievement tests.
11. Describe and explain major factors to consider when selecting standardized achievement tests.
12. Describe and explain major factors to consider when developing a classroom achievement test.
13. Describe major factors to consider when assigning student grades.

This chapter focuses on standardized achievement tests, primarily as they are used in schools. As noted in Chap. 1, a *standardized test* is a test that is administered, scored, and interpreted in a standard manner. Most standardized tests are developed by testing professionals or test publishing companies. The goal of standardization is to ensure that testing conditions are as nearly the same as is possible for all individuals taking the test. If this is accomplished, no examinee will have an advantage over another due to variance in administration procedures, and assessment results will be comparable. An *achievement test* measures knowledge or skills that a person has acquired in formal or informal learning situations (American Educational Research Association, American Psychological Association, & National Council on Measurement in Education, 2014). Naturally, the vast majority of teacher-constructed classroom tests qualify as achievement tests, but they are not standardized. In this chapter, we will focus on *standardized achievement tests*, but later in this chapter, we briefly address *teacher-constructed achievement tests*, their development, and their application. In describing standardized achievement tests, Linn and Gronlund (2000) highlighted the following characteristics:

> Achievement tests are designed to assess students' knowledge in a skill or content domain in which they have received instruction.

- They typically contain high-quality items selected on the basis of both quantitative and qualitative item analysis procedures.
- They have explicit directions for administration and scoring so that examiners can follow consistent procedures in different settings.
- They often provide both norm-referenced and criterion-referenced interpretative guidelines. Norm-referenced guidelines enable comparisons to other examinees' performance, while criterion-referenced guidelines enable comparisons to an established criterion.
- They offer normative data based on large, representative samples.
- They offer equivalent or parallel forms of the test, enabling score comparisons between test administrations that are not confounded when the same items are used across administrations.
- They have professionally developed manuals and supporting materials that provide extensive information about the test (e.g., how to administer, score, and interpret it) and its measurement characteristics.

There are many different types of standardized achievement tests. Some are designed for group administration while others for individual administration. Individually-administered achievement tests are given to only one examinee at a time by a specially trained examiner. Some achievement tests focus on a single--subject area (e.g., reading) while others cover a broad range of academic skills and content areas (e.g., reading, language, and mathematics). Some use selection type items exclusively while others contain constructed-response and performance assessments.

Standardized achievement tests also have a number of different uses or applications. These include the following:

- Tracking student achievement over time or comparing group achievement across classes, schools, or districts.
- Using scores for decision making or placement in the public schools, commonly referred to as high-stakes testing. For example, administrators may determine which students are promoted or allowed to graduate based on achievement test scores. Government agencies may use achievement test scores to evaluate and rate teachers, administrators, schools, and school districts.
- Identifying strengths and weaknesses of individual examinees.
- Evaluating effectiveness of instructional programs or curricula to help educators identify areas of concern.
- Narrowing the pool of job applicants in employment settings to determine if an individual has the requisite knowledge needed for adequate job performance.
- Credentialing for licensing and certification requirements in a broad array of professions including psychology, medicine, electrical engineering, law, and even driving—the written test for a driver's license is an achievement test covering a prescribed area of content, i.e., the rules of the road and knowledge required to drive safely.

- Identifying students with special educational requirements; for example, school psychologists might use achievement tests to help determine if children qualify for special education services.

As is apparent from these applications, the most common use of achievement tests is by psychologists in public schools. However, community mental health clinics, private practitioners, and others who provide educational evaluations also use achievement tests. In the next section, we trace some of the historical factors influencing the use of achievement tests in today's schools.

8.1   The Impetus for Achievement Tests

Achievement tests have been in the American educational system since the mid--nineteenth century. According to a report commissioned by the U.S. Congress, the early use of tests was based on several main themes that are still applicable today (U.S. Congress, Office of Technology Assessment, 1992).

1. Formal written testing began to replace oral examinations administered by teachers around the same time schools changed their mission of servicing only the elite to education of the masses.
2. Although not designed to, early examinations were used to make comparisons among students and schools, motivated in part by a commitment to fairness in educational opportunities.
3. Early examinations focused on the basics (i.e., specific school subjects) of education, even though it was understood that the objectives of schooling were considerably broader than knowing just the basics.
4. Written tests were perceived as instruments of reform, intending to help advance the development of the school system.

Achievement tests were then, as they are today, often viewed as one way to ensure fairness in how educational resources are distributed and implemented. However, then, like today, their use has been somewhat contentious, as evidenced by the report to congress when discussing events occurring in Massachusetts during the late nineteenth century (U.S. Congress, Office of Technology Assessment, 1992):

> The fact that the first formal written examinations in the United States were intended as devices for sorting and classifying but were used also to monitor school effectiveness suggests how far back in American history one can go for evidence of test misuse. The ways in which these tests were used for monitoring was logical: to find out how students and their schools are performing ... But the motivation for the standardized examinations in Massachusetts was, in fact, more complicated and reveals a pattern that would become increasingly familiar. *The idea underlying the implementation of written examinations, that they could provide information about student learning, was born in the minds of individuals already convinced that education was substandard in quality.* This sequence—perception of failure followed by the collection of data designed to document failure (or success)—offers early evidence of what has become a tradition of school reform and a truism of student testing: tests are often administered not just to discover how well schools or kids are doing, but rather to obtain external *confirmation*—validation—of the hypothesis that they are not doing well at all. (p. 108).

Fast forward to the late twentieth century, where discontent in the American education system led to additional congressional study and action resulting in an increase in standardized testing. In 1983, the National Commission of Excellence in Education published *A Nation at Risk: The Imperative for Educational Reform*. This document reported that the United States was falling behind other nations in terms of childhood education. Parents increasingly began to question the quality of the education being provided and demanded evidence schools were actually educating their children. As a result, tests like the National Assessment of Educational Progress (NAEP) were developed to monitor academic progress across the nation (see Special Interest Topic 8.1).

Special Interest Topic 8.1: The "Nation's Report Card"

The National Assessment of Educational Progress (NAEP), also referred to as the "Nation's Report Card," is the only ongoing nationally administered assessment of academic achievement in the United States. NAEP provides a comprehensive assessment of our students' achievement at critical periods in their academic experience (i.e., Grades 4, 8, and 12). NAEP assesses performance in mathematics, science, reading, writing, world geography, U.S. history, civics, and the arts. New assessments in world history, economics, and foreign language are currently being developed. NAEP has been administered regularly since 1969. It does not provide information on the performance of individual students or schools, but presents aggregated data reflecting achievement in specific academic areas, instructional practices, and academic environments for broad samples of students and specific subgroups. The NAPE has an excellent website that can be accessed at: https://www.nationsreport-card.gov/. Of particular interest to teachers is the NAEP Sample Questions tab. This tool provides access to NAEP questions, student responses, and scoring guides that have been released to the public. The table below contains fourth-grade reading scores for the states, Department of Defense Education Agency, and the District of Columbia.

NAPE results: 2019 fourth-grade average reading scores

Jurisdiction		Score	Jurisdiction		Score
1	DoDEA	235	28	Washington	220
2	Massachusetts	231	29	New York	220
3	New Jersey	227	30	National public	219
4	Wyoming	227	31	Mississippi	219
5	Utah	225	32	Kansas	219
6	Colorado	225	33	Tennessee	219
7	Florida	225	34	Michigan	218
8	Connecticut	224	35	Illinois	218
9	New Hampshire	224	36	Missouri	218
10	Virginia	224	37	Georgia	218

(continued)

Jurisdiction		Score	Jurisdiction		Score
11	Pennsylvania	223	38	Oregon	218
12	Idaho	223	39	Delaware	218
13	Minnesota	222	40	Nevada	218
14	Nebraska	222	41	Hawaii	218
15	South Dakota	222	42	California	216
16	Ohio	222	43	Oklahoma	216
17	Vermont	222	44	Texas	216
18	Indiana	222	45	South Carolina	216
19	Montana	222	46	Arizona	216
20	North Carolina	221	47	Arkansas	215
21	Maine	221	48	District of Columbia	214
22	North Dakota	221	49	West Virginia	213
23	Kentucky	221	50	Alabama	212
24	Iowa	221	51	Louisiana	210
25	Rhode Island	220	52	New Mexico	208
26	Maryland	220	53	Alaska	204
27	Wisconsin	220	54	Puerto Rico	–

Note. Data retrieved from https://www.nationsreportcard.gov/profiles/statepr ofile?chort=1&sub=RED&sj=&sfj=NP&st=MN&year=2015R3+6%2F20 %2F2019

DoDEA Department of Defense Education Agency

More recently, the No Child Left Behind Act of 2001 (NCLB) required each state to develop high academic standards and implement annual assessments to monitor the performance of states, districts, and schools. It required state assessments to meet professional standards for reliability and validity and required that states achieve academic proficiency for all students within 12 years. In 2015, the NCLB was replaced by the Every Student Succeeds Act (ESSA), which maintained some annual testing requirements, but removed the requirement of adequate yearly progress and removed the use of assessment scores in evaluating teachers. Special Interest Topic 8.2 describes the ESSA, NCLB, and two other major federal laws that impact assessment practices in the public schools.

> The Every Student Succeeds Act, a reauthorization of the No Child Left Behind Act, requires annual assessments and the use of non-academic factors in determining school accountability.

With the purported need of achievement testing in educational settings well established over the last 150 years, we now turn to a discussion of some of the common achievement tests that are currently used.

Special Interest Topic 8.2: Federal Law and Achievement Assessment
There are numerous federal laws that have significantly impacted the assessment of students in public schools. Below are brief descriptions of three major statutes that significantly impact the way students are assessed.

Every Student Succeeds Act of 2015 (ESSA)
The Elementary and Secondary Education Act of 1965 (ESEA) was one of the first federal laws to focus on education. While the federal government recognizes that education is primarily the responsibility of the individual states, it holds that the federal government has a responsibility to ensure that an adequate level of educational services is being provided by all states (Jacob & Hartshorne, 2007). The ESEA has recently undergone a few reauthorizations: first in 2001 with the No Child Left Behind Act (detailed below) and in 2015 with the Every Student Succeeds Act. In general, the ESSA provides individual states with more decision-making opportunities within a Federal framework. Key highlights of the ESSA include the following:

1. States can set their own accountability goals, as long as the goals address test proficiency, English-language proficiency, and graduation rates, and that the goals aim at closing achievement and graduation gaps for groups that are furthest behind. In addition, states must measure a "non-academic" measure of accountability, such as student or educator engagement, post-secondary readiness, school climate/safety, or some other variable the state determines that is approved at the Federal level.
2. At least once every 3 years, individual states are required to identify the bottom 5% of performing schools, and intervene at those schools with the goal of improving their performance. In addition, states have to identify and intervene in schools where the graduation rate is 67% or less.
3. States are required to test students in reading and math in Grades 3 through 8, and at the high school-level test at least one time using a nationally recognized test (e.g., the SAT or the ACT).
4. States must adopt academic standards that are "challenging"; such standards could be the Common Core State Standards, but it doesn't have to be.
5. Teacher evaluations no longer have to incorporate student outcomes.

No Child Left Behind Act of 2001 (NCLB)
The No Child Left Behind Act of 2001 grew out of a concern that the American education system was falling behind other countries, and as such was no longer being competitive at the global level. It was passed with overwhelming bipartisan support and resulted in an increase in the Federal role for ensuring that states were held accountable for following the legislation. However, it quickly became widely criticized. For example, teachers and school administrators commonly complained about "teaching to the test" when discussing the impact of statewide assessment programs. While in retrospect many ultimately viewed the NCLB as forcing standardized testing at a massive scale, its intent was beyond testing. Major aspects of this act included:

(continued)

- *Increased State Accountability*. The NCLB Act requires that each state develops rigorous academic standards and implements annual assessments to monitor the performance of states, districts, and schools. It requires that these assessments meet professional standards for reliability and validity and requires that states achieve academic proficiency for all students within 12 years. To ensure that no group of children is neglected, the act requires that states and districts include all students in their assessment programs, including those with disabilities and limited English proficiency. However, the act does allow 3% of all students to be given alternative assessments. Alternative assessments are defined as instruments specifically designed for students with disabilities that preclude their assessment using the standard assessment.
- *More Parental Choice*. The act allows parents with children in schools that do not demonstrate adequate annual progress toward academic goals to move their children to another, better performing school.
- *Greater Flexibility for States*. A goal of the NCLB Act is to give states increased flexibility in the use of Federal funds in exchange for increased accountability for academic results.
- *Reading First Initiative*. A goal of the NCLB Act is to ensure that every student can read by the end of third grade. To this end, the Reading First initiative significantly increased Federal funding of empirically based reading instruction programs in the early grades.

The Individuals with Disabilities Education Improvement Act of 2004 (IDEA 2004)

The Education of All Handicapped Children Act of 1975 (EAHCA) was the original law that required that all children with disabilities be given a Free Appropriate Public Education (FAPE). At that time, it was estimated that there were more than eight million children with disabilities. Of these, over half were not receiving an appropriate public education and as many as one million were not receiving a public education at all (Jacob & Hartshorne, 2007). The Individuals with Disabilities Education Improvement Act of 2004 (commonly abbreviated as IDEA 2004 or simply IDEA) is the most current reauthorization of the EAHCA. IDEA designates 13 disability categories (e.g., mental retardation [referred to now as intellectual disability], visual or hearing impairment, specific learning disabilities, emotional disturbance) and provides funds to states and school districts that meet the requirements of the law. IDEA also provides guidelines for conducting evaluations for students suspected of having a disability. Students who qualify under IDEA have an Individualized Educational Program (IEP) developed specifically for them that designates the special services and modifications to instruction and assessment that they must receive. Possibly most important for regular education teachers is the move for students with disabilities to receive instruction in the "least restrictive environment," a movement referred to as "mainstreaming." In application, this means

(continued)

that most students with disabilities receive educational services in the regular education classroom. As a result, more regular education teachers are involved in the education of students with disabilities and are required to implement the educational modifications specified in their students' Individualized Educational Programs (IEP). These modifications can include modifications in both instructional strategies and assessment practices. For more information on IDEA 2004, go to the following site: http://idea.ed.gov

Rehabilitation Act of 1973 (Section 504)

This law mandates that any institution that receives federal funds must ensure that individuals with disabilities have equal access to all programs and services provided by the institution. More specifically, schools cannot exclude students with disabilities from any activities or programs based on their disability, and schools must make reasonable accommodations to ensure that students with disabilities have an equal opportunity to benefit from those activities or programs (Jacob & Hartshorne, 2007). Section 504 differs from IDEA in several important ways. First, it defines a handicap or disability very broadly, much broader than IDEA. Therefore, a child may not qualify for services under IDEA, but qualify under Section 504. Second, Section 504 is an antidiscrimination act, not a grant program like IDEA. While IDEA provides funds to provide the required services, Section 504 does not. In terms of the assessment of disabilities, Section 504 provides less specific guidance than IDEA. Similar to IDEA, students qualified under Section 504 may receive modifications to their instruction and assessments that are implemented in the classrooms. In recent years, there has been a rapid expansion in the number of students receiving accommodations under Section 504.

8.2   Group-Administered Achievement Tests

Achievement tests can be classified as either individual or group tests. *Individual tests* are administered in a one-to-one testing situation. One testing professional (i.e., the examiner) administers the test to one individual (i.e., the examinee) at a time. In contrast, *group tests* are those that can be administered to more than one examinee at a time. The main attraction of group administration is that it is an efficient way to collect information about students or other examinees. By efficient, we mean a large number of examinees can be assessed with a minimal time commitment from educational professionals. As you might expect, group-administered tests are very popular in school settings. For example, most teacher-constructed classroom tests are designed to be administered to the whole class at one time. Accordingly, if a school district wants to test all the students in Grades 3

> The main attractions of group-administered tests are that they are an efficient way to collect information about students' achievement.

through 8, it would probably be impossible to administer a lengthy test to each student on a one-to-one basis. There is simply not enough time or enough teachers (or other educational professionals) to accomplish such a task without significantly detracting from the time devoted to instruction. However, when you can have one professional administer a test to 20–30 examinees at a time, the task can be accomplished in a reasonably efficient manner.

Although efficiency is the most prominent advantage of group-administered tests, there are at least four other positive attributes of group testing that warrant mentioning. First, since the role of the individual administering the test is limited, group tests will typically involve more uniform testing conditions than individual tests. Second, unlike many individually-administered tests that have complicated administration procedures and require extensive administrator training to ensure standardized administration, group tests can be administered in a standardized manner with very little training. Third, group tests frequently involve items that can be scored objectively, often even by a computer (e.g., selected-response items). This reduces or eliminates the measurement error introduced by the scoring procedures that are more common in individual tests, many of which require the examiner to judge the adequacy of the response to open-ended questions. Finally, group tests often have very large standardization or normative samples. Normative samples for professionally developed group tests are often in the range of 100,000–200,000, while professionally developed individual tests will usually have normative samples ranging from 1000 to 8000 participants (Anastasi & Urbina, 1997).

Naturally, group tests have some limitations. For example, in a group-testing situation the individual administering the test has relatively little personal interaction with the individual examinees. As a result, there is little opportunity for the examiner to develop rapport with the examinees and closely monitor and observe their progress. Accordingly, they have limited opportunities to make qualitative behavioral observations about the performance of their examinees and how they approach and respond to the assessment tasks. Another concern involves the types of items typically included on group achievement tests. While some testing experts applaud group tests for often using objectively scored items, others criticize them since these items restrict the type of responses examinees can provide. This parallels the same argument for-and-against selected-response items we discussed in earlier chapters. Another limitation of group tests involves their lack of flexibility. For example, when administering individual tests, the examiner is usually able to select and administer only those test items matching the examinee's ability level. With group tests, however, all examinees are typically administered all the items. As a result, examinees might find some items too easy and others too difficult, resulting in boredom and/or frustration, while lengthening the actual testing time beyond what is necessary to assess the student's knowledge accurately (Anastasi & Urbina, 1997). It should be noted that publishers of major group achievement tests are taking steps to address these criticisms. For example, to address concerns about the extensive use of selected-response items, an increasing number of standardized achievement tests are being developed that incorporate more constructed-response items and performance tasks. To address concerns about limited flexibility in administration, online and computer-based assessments are becoming increasingly available.

In this section, we will be discussing a number of standardized group achievement tests. Many of these tests are developed by large test publishing companies and are commercially available to all qualified buyers (e.g., legitimate educational institutions). In addition to these commercially available tests, many states have started developing their own achievement tests that are specifically tailored to assess the state curriculum. These are often standards-based assessments that are used in high-stakes testing programs. We will start by briefly introducing some of the major commercially available achievement tests.

8.2.1 Commercial Standardized Achievement Test

Commercially developed *group achievement test batteries* are tests developed for use in public schools around the nation and are available for purchase by qualified professionals or institutions. The most popular tests are comprehensive batteries designed to assess achievement in multiple academic areas such as reading, language arts, mathematics, science, social studies, etc. These comprehensive tests are often referred to as survey batteries. As noted, many school districts use standardized achievement tests to track student achievement over time or to compare performance across classes, schools, or districts. These batteries typically contain multiple subtests that assess achievement in specific curricular areas (e.g., reading, language, mathematics, and science). These subtests are organized in a series of test levels that span different grades. For example, a subtest might have four levels with one level covering kindergarten through the second grade, the second level covering Grades 3 and 4, the third level covering 5 and 6, and the fourth level covering Grades 7 and 8 (Nitko, 2001). The most widely used standardized group achievement tests are produced and distributed by three publishers: Data Recognition Corporation, Pearson, and Houghton Mifflin Harcourt (HMH) Assessments.

> The most widely used standardized group achievement tests are produced by Data Recognition Corporation, Pearson, and Houghton Mifflin Harcourt Assessments.

8.2.1.1 Data Recognition Corporation (DRC)

DRC publishes the TerraNova, Third Edition, which offers a suite of products designed to meet a variety of user needs. All products offer updated norms and are based on items aligned to state curriculum standards. The national standardization process was completed in 2017/2018 for the final assessments.

- *TerraNova, Third Edition Complete Battery.* The Complete Battery is a traditional achievement battery that is designed for use with students from kindergarten through Grade 12, offering norm-referenced achievement scores, criterion-referenced objective mastery scores, and performance-level information. The Complete Battery assesses content in Reading, Mathematics, Language, Science, and Social Studies. Items are multiple choice; administration time ranges from approximately 2–4.5 h, depending on grade level. Also offered is a Survey edition, which is an abbreviated version of the Complete Battery that provides a general measure of achievement while minimizing testing time.

- *TerraNova, Third Edition, Multiple Assessments.* The TerraNova Third Edition Multiple Assessments achievement tests offer the same content areas as the Complete Battery. However, each content area offers a mixture of both multiple--choice responses and constructed response items, allowing for the additional measurement of higher-order thinking skills. The Multiple Assessments can be used with Grades 1 through 12. Administration times are generally longer than the administration of the Complete Battery, ranging from about 4 to 5.5 h.
- *SUPERA.* The SUPERA is the Spanish-language version of the TerraNova assessment series, providing assessment of reading/language and mathematics skills. It can be used in Grades 1 through 10, providing examinees with a mixture of multiple-choice and constructed-response items. Test scores are provided on the same scale as the English-language editions.

8.2.1.2 Pearson

Pearson publishes the Stanford Achievement Test Series, Tenth Edition (Stanford 10).

- *Stanford Achievement Test Series, Tenth Edition (Stanford 10).* Originally published in 1923, the Stanford Achievement Test Series has a long and rich history of use. The Stanford 10 can be used with students from kindergarten through Grade 12 and has year 2007 normative data. It assesses content in Reading, Mathematics, Language, Spelling, Listening, Science, and Social Science. The Stanford 10 is available in a variety of forms, including abbreviated and complete batteries. It can be completed online, or via the traditional paper-pencil format.

8.2.1.3 Houghton Mifflin Harcourt (HMH) Assessments

HMH Assessments publishes the Iowa series of achievement tests, which were initially developed over 80 years ago.

- *Iowa Tests of Basic Skills (ITBS).* The ITBS is designed for use with students from kindergarten through Grade 8, and as the name suggests, it is designed to provide a thorough assessment of basic academic skills. The most current ITBS form was published in 2007. The ITBS assesses content in Reading, Language Arts, Mathematics, Science, Social Studies, and Sources of Information. Various levels are provided, offering additional tests in the various core areas as the test--level increases. The ITBS is available in different formats for different applications (e.g., Complete Battery, Core Battery, Survey Battery).
- *Iowa Tests of Educational Development (ITED).* The ITED is designed for use with students from Grades 9 through 12 and was published in 2001. The ITED is designed to measure the long-term goals of secondary education. The ITED assesses content in Vocabulary, Reading Comprehension, Language: Revising Written Materials, Spelling, Mathematics: Concepts and Problem-Solving, Computation, Analysis of Science Materials, Analysis of Social Studies Materials, and Sources of Information. The ITED is available as both a complete battery and a core battery.
- *Iowa Assessments.* The Iowa Assessments are the latest in the series of Iowa tests. Offering parallel forms of the same content areas of the ITBS and ITED, the Iowa Assessments enable users to monitor academic growth from Grades 1

through 12, and starting at Grade 6, it offers an indicator of college and career readiness. Total testing time for the complete suite of tests ranges from 2.5 to 5 h, depending on the test level. Tests can be completed online, or via traditional paper and pencil answer forms.

8.2.1.4 Diagnostic Achievement Tests

The most widely used achievement tests have been the broad group achievement test batteries designed to assess the student's level of achievement across a number of broad academic areas. While these batteries do a good job in this context, they typically have too few items that measure specific skills and learning objectives to be useful to teachers when making instructional decisions. For example, the test results might suggest that a particular student's performance is low in mathematics, but the results will not pinpoint exactly what the student's strengths and weaknesses are. To address this limitation, many test publishers have developed *diagnostic achievement tests* that have online administration, scoring, and reporting solutions. These tests provide more diagnostic information in each achievement area that is linked to specific learning objectives. One such product, aimswebPlus (published by Pearson), provides reading and math measures that can be administered very quickly (4 min or less). Teachers can use the information provided in the reports to inform additional instruction that is needed at an individual or classroom level, helping to ensure that required state content standards are being adequately learned by students.

Obviously, here we provide only very brief descriptions of these major test batteries. These summaries were based on information current at the time of this writing. However, these tests are continuously being revised to reflect curricular changes and to update normative data. For the most current information, interested readers should access the Internet sites for the publishing companies (see Table 8.1) and/or refer to the current edition of the *Mental Measurements Yearbook* or other reference resources. See Special Interest Topic 8.3 for information on these resources.

Table 8.1 Major publishers of standardized group achievement tests

Data Recognition Corporation Website: http://datarecognitioncorp.com/
- TerraNova, Third Edition Complete Battery
- TerraNova, Third Edition Multiple Assessments
- SUPERA

Pearson Website: http://pearsonassessments.com/
- Stanford Achievement Test Series, Tenth Edition (Stanford 10)

Houghton Mifflin Harcourt (HMH) Assessments Website: http://www.hmhco.com/
- Iowa Tests of Basic Skills (ITBS)
- Iowa Tests of Educational Development (ITED)
- Iowa Assessments

Special Interest Topic 8.3: Finding Information on Standardized Tests

When you want to locate information on a standardized test, it is reasonable to begin by examining information provided by the test publishers. This can include their Internet sites, catalogs, test manuals, specimen test sets, score reports, and other supporting documentation. However, you should also seek out resources that provide independent evaluations and reviews of the tests you are researching. The Science Directorate of the American Psychological Association offers a helpful Frequently Asked Questions section that addresses finding information on psychological tests (see http://www.apa.org/science/programs/testing/find-tests.aspx). Here are descriptions of some of the most popular resources available for finding information on tests:

- *Mental Measurements Yearbook.* **Mental Measurements Yearbook** is published by the Buros Institute for Mental Measurements and lists tests alphabetically by title. Each listing provides basic descriptive information about the test (e.g., author, date of publication) plus information about test availability, technical information, and scoring and reporting services. Most listings also include one or more critical reviews.
- *Tests in Print.* **Tests in Print** is also published by the Buros Institute for Mental Measurements and is a bibliographic encyclopedia of information on practically every published test in psychology and education. Each listing provides basic descriptive information on tests, but does not contain critical reviews or psychometric information. After locating a test that meets your criteria, you can turn to the Mental Measurement Yearbook for more detailed information on the test.
- *Test Critiques.* **Test Critiques** is published by Pro-Ed, Inc. and contains a three-part listing for each test that includes an Introduction, Practical Applications/Uses, and Technical Aspects, followed by a critical review of the test.
- *Tests.* **Tests** is also published by Pro-Ed, Inc. and is a bibliographic encyclopedia covering thousands of assessments in psychology and education. It provides basic descriptive information on tests, but does not contain critical reviews or information on reliability, validity, or other technical aspects of the tests. It serves as a companion to *Test Critiques*.

These resources can be located in the reference section of most college and larger public libraries. In addition to these traditional references, "Test Reviews Online" is a web-based service of the Buros Institute of Mental Measurements (https://marketplace.unl.edu/buros/). This service makes test reviews available online to individuals precisely as they appear in the *Mental Measurements Yearbook*. For a relatively small fee, users can download information on any of more than 3500 commercially available tests.

8.2.2 State-Developed Achievement Tests

As we noted earlier, information obtained from standardized achievement tests continues to be used in making high-stakes decision at the state level (e.g., which students are promoted or graduate; evaluating school and school district performance). While all states now have testing

> Standardized achievement tests are increasingly being used in making high-stakes decisions at the state level.

programs, different states have adopted different approaches. Some states utilize commercially available achievement batteries like those described in the previous section (often referred to as off-the-shelf tests). An advantage of these commercial tests is that they provide normative data based on national samples. This allows one to compare a student's performance to that of students across the nation, not only students from one's state or school district. For example, one could find that Johnny's reading performance was at the 70th percentile relative to a national normative group. Using these commercial tests, it is also possible to compare state or local groups (e.g., a district, school, or class) to a national sample. For example, one might find that a school district's mean fourth-grade reading score was at the 55th percentile based on national normative data. These comparisons can provide useful information to school administrators, parents, and other stakeholders.

All states have developed educational standards that specify the academic knowledge and skills their students are expected to achieve (see Special Interest Topic 8.4 for information on state standards). One significant limitation of using a commercial off-the-shelf national test is that it might not closely match the state's curriculum standards. Boser (1999) notes that commercial achievement tests typically are not designed to measure the content standards of specific states, but instead reflect a blend of the content of major textbooks, state standards, and national standards. He described a study commissioned by the California education department that examined a number of commercially available achievement tests to see how they align with the state's math standards. These studies found that the off-the-shelf tests focused primarily on basic math skills and did not adequately assess if students had mastered the state's standards. This comes down to a question of test validity. If you are interested in assessing what is being taught in classrooms across the nation, the commercially available group achievement tests probably give you a good measure. However, *state-developed achievement tests* are preferable to off-the-shelf tests if you are more interested in determining if your students are mastering your state's content standards.

Special Interest Topic 8.4: Standards-Based Assessments

AERA et al. (2014) defines *standards-based assessments* as tests that are designed to measure an individual's standing with respect to systematically described content and performance standards. In this context, content standards are statements that specify what students are expected to achieve in a given subject matter at a specific grade (e.g., Mathematics, Grade 5). In other words, content standards specify the skills and knowledge we want our students to master. Performance standards indicate what constitutes acceptable performance by specifying a level of performance, typically in the form of a cut score or a range of scores that indicates achievement levels. National and state educational standards have been developed and can be easily accessed via the Internet. Below are a few examples of state educational Internet sites that specify the state standards.

- *California:* Content Standards for California Public Schools
  http://www.cde.ca.gov/re/cc/
- *Florida:* Standards for Florida Public Schools
  http://www.cpalms.org
- *New York:* Next Generation Learning Standards
  http://www.nysed.gov/aimhighny
- *Texas:* Texas Essential Knowledge and Skills
  http://tea.texas.gov/Academics/Curriculum

Education World provides a website that allows you to easily access state and national standards. Many states have adopted the Common Core Standards, which was a movement aimed at defining consistent learning goals across all states. More information about the Common Core Standards, and which states have adopted them, can be found at: http://www.corestandards.org/

To address this limitation, many states have developed their own achievement batteries that are designed to closely match the state's curriculum. In contrast to the commercial tests that typically report normative scores, state-developed achievement tests often emphasize criterion-referenced score interpretations. In Texas, there is a statewide program that includes the Texas Assessment of Knowledge and Skills (TAKS). The TAKS measures success of students in the state's curriculum in reading (Grades 3 through 9), mathematics (Grades 3 through 11), writing (Grades 4 and 7), English-language arts (Grades 10 and 11), science (Grades 5, 10, and 11), and social studies (Grades 8, 10, and 11). There is a Spanish TAKS that is administered in Grades 3 through 6. The decision to promote a student to the next grade may be based on passing the reading and math sections, and successful completion of the TAKS at Grade 11 is required for students to receive a high school diploma. The statewide assessment program contains two additional tests. There is a Reading Proficiency Test in English (RPTE) that is administered to limited English proficient students to assess annual growth in reading proficiency. Finally, there is the State-- Developed Alternative Assessment (SDAA) that can be used with special education students when it is determined that the standard TAKS is inappropriate. All of these tests are designed to measure the educational objectives specified in the state curriculum, the Texas Essential Knowledge and Skills curriculum (TEKS) (see http:// www.tea.texas.gov).

Some states have developed hybrid assessment strategies to assess student performance and meet accountability requirements. For example, some states use a combination of state-developed tests and commercial off-the-shelf tests, using different tests at different grade levels. Another approach, commonly referred to as *augmented testing*, involves the use of a commercial test that is administered along with test sections that address any misalignment between state standards and the content of the commercial test. Table 8.2 provides information of the assessment strategies used 2008 in state assessment programs (Education Week, 2017). A review of this table reveals that in 2008 (the latest year where data were available), the majority of states (i.e., 45) have state-developed tests that are specifically designed to align with their standards. Only one state (i.e., Iowa) reported exclusively using an off-the-shelf test. It should be noted that any report of state assessment practices is only a snapshot of an ever-changing picture. The best way to get information on your state's current assessment practices is to go to the website of the state's board of education and verify the current status.

There is considerable controversy concerning statewide testing programs. Proponents of high-stake testing programs see them as a way of increasing academic expectations and ensuring that all students are judged according to the same standards. They say these testing programs guarantee that students graduating from public schools have the skills necessary to be

> Proponents of high-stakes testing programs believe they increase academic expectations and ensure that all students are judged according to the same standards.

successful in life after high school. Critics of these testing programs argue that these tests emphasize rote learning and often neglect critical thinking, problem-solving, and communication skills. To exacerbate the problem, critics feel that too much instructional time is spent preparing students for the tests instead of teaching the really important skills teachers would like to focus on. Additionally, they argue that these tests are culturally biased and are not fair to minority students (Doherty, 2002). For additional information on the pros and cons of high-stakes testing programs, see Special Interest Topic 8.5. Special Interest Topic 8.6 provides an overview of a promising and sophisticated approach to high-stakes assessment referred to as *Value-Added Assessment*. This debate is likely to continue for the foreseeable future, but in the meantime, these tests will continue to play an important role in public schools.

Table 8.2 State assessment practices (2008)

State	State-developed tests (criterion referenced)	Augmented/ hybrid tests	Off-the-shelf tests (norm referenced)
Alabama	Yes	No	Yes
Alaska	Yes	No	Yes
Arizona	Yes	Yes	Yes
Arkansas	Yes	No	Yes
California	Yes	No	Yes
Colorado	Yes	No	Yes
Connecticut	Yes	No	No
Delaware	No	Yes	No
District of Columbia	Yes	No	No
Florida	Yes	No	Yes
Georgia	Yes	No	Yes
Hawaii	No	Yes	No
Idaho	Yes	No	No
Illinois	Yes	Yes	No
Indiana	Yes	No	No
Iowa	No	No	Yes
Kansas	Yes	No	No
Kentucky	Yes	No	Yes
Louisiana	Yes	Yes	No
Maine	Yes	No	Yes
Maryland	Yes	Yes	No
Massachusetts	Yes	No	No
Michigan	Yes	Yes	No
Minnesota	Yes	No	No
Mississippi	Yes	No	No
Missouri	No	Yes	No
Montana	Yes	No	Yes
Nebraska	Yes	No	No
Nevada	Yes	No	Yes
New Hampshire	Yes	No	No
New Jersey	Yes	No	No
New Mexico	Yes	No	Yes
New York	Yes	No	No
North Carolina	Yes	No	No
North Dakota	Yes	No	No
Ohio	Yes	No	No
Oklahoma	Yes	No	No
Oregon	Yes	No	No
Pennsylvania	Yes	No	No
Rhode Island	Yes	No	No
South Carolina	Yes	No	No
South Dakota	Yes	No	No
Tennessee	Yes	No	No
Texas	Yes	No	No

(continued)

Table 8.2   (continued)

State	State-developed tests (criterion referenced)	Augmented/ hybrid tests	Off-the-shelf tests (norm referenced)
Utah	Yes	No	Yes
Vermont	Yes	No	No
Virginia	Yes	No	No
Washington	Yes	No	No
West Virginia	Yes	No	Yes
Wisconsin	Yes	No	No
Wyoming	Yes	No	No
Totals	**47**	**8**	**16**

Note: Data provided by Edweek.org, accessed 6/21/2017 at http://www.edcounts.org/createtable/step1.php?clear=1. **State-Developed Test (Criterion Referenced):** defined as tests that are custom-made to correspond to state content standards. **Augmented/hybrid Test:** defined as tests that incorporate aspects of both commercially developed norm referenced and state-developed criterion-referenced tests (includes commercial tests augmented or customized to match state standards). **Off-the-Shelf Test (Norm Referenced):** defined as commercially developed norm-referenced tests that have not been modified to specifically reflect state standards

Special Interest Topic 8.5: American Educational Research Association (AERA) Position Statement on High-Stakes Testing

The American Educational Research Association (AERA) is a leading organization that studies educational issues. The AERA (2000) presented a position statement regarding "high-stakes" testing programs employed in many states and school districts. Their position is summarized in the following points:

1. Important decisions should not be based on a single test score. Ideally, information from multiple sources should be taken into consideration when making high-stake decisions. When tests are the basis of important decisions, students should be given multiple opportunities to take the test.
2. When students and teachers are going to be held responsible for new content or standards, they should be given adequate time and resources to prepare themselves before being tested.
3. Each test should be validated for each intended use. For example, if a test is going to be used for determining which students are promoted and for ranking schools based on educational effectiveness, both interpretations must be validated.
4. If there is the potential for adverse effects associated with a testing-- program, efforts should be made to make all involved parties aware on them.
5. There should be alignment between the assessments and the state content standards.
6. When specific "cut-scores" are used to denote achievement levels, the purpose, meaning, and validity of these passing scores should be established.

(continued)

7. Students who fail a high-stakes test should be given adequate opportunities to overcome any deficiencies.
8. Adequate consideration and accommodations should be given to students with language differences.
9. Adequate consideration and accommodations should be given to students with disabilities.
10. When districts, schools, or classes are to be compared, it is important to clearly specify which students are to be tested and which students are exempt, and ensure that these guidelines are followed.
11. Test scores must be reliable.
12. There should be an ongoing evaluation of both the intended and unintended effects of any high-stakes testing program.

These guidelines may be useful when trying to evaluate the testing programs employed in your state or school. For more information, the full text of this position statement can be accessed at: http://www.aera.net/About-AERA/AERA-Rules-Policies/Association-Policies/Position-Statement-on-High-Stakes-Testing

Special Interest Topic 8.6: Value-Added Assessment: A New Approach to Educational Accountability
Victor Willson, Ph.D.
Texas A&M University

The term *value-added* has been used in business and industry to mean the gain in economic occurring when material is changed through manufacturing or manipulation. In education, this has been interpreted as the change in a student's knowledge that occurs as the result of instruction. In many ways, it can be seen as determining the value of instruction in raising knowledge levels (however, the model does not attempt to determine many benefits of schooling that go beyond knowledge acquisition). One of the most complex models of value-added assessment has been developed in Tennessee (Ceperley & Reel, 1997; Sanders, Saxton, & Horn, 1997). This model also has been implemented in a form in Dallas (Webster & Mendro, 1997). This is a rather complex model, and the basic ideas are presented here in a hypothetical situation.

Consider students who attend Washington School in East Bunslip, New Jersey in Ms. Jones' third-grade class (all names are made up). These students may be typical or representative of third-grade students, or there may be a substantial proportion of excellent or poor students. Ms. Jones teaches in her style, and the students are given the state achievement test at the end of the year. For this example, let's assume that statewide testing begins in Grade 3.

(continued)

The results of the state test, student by student, are used to build a model of performance for each student, for Ms. Jones, for Washington School, and for the East Bunslip school district. One year's data are inadequate to do more than simply mark the levels of performance of each focus for achievement: student, teacher, school, and district.

The next year Ms. Jones's previous students have been dispersed to several fourth-grade classrooms. A few of her students move to different school districts, but most stay in East Bunslip and most stay at Washington School. All of this information will be included in the modeling of performance. Ms. Jones now has a new class of students who enter the value-added assessment system. At the end of this year, there are now data on each student who completed fourth grade, although some students may have been lost through attrition (e.g., missed the testing, left the state). The Tennessee model includes a procedure that accounts for all of these "errors." The performance of the fourth-grade students can now be evaluated in terms of their third-grade performance and the effect of their previous teacher, Ms. Jones, and the effect of their current teacher (assuming that teacher also taught last year and there was assessment data for the class taught). In addition, a school-level effect can be estimated. Thus, the value-added system attempts to explain achievement performance for each level in the school system by using information from each level. This is clearly a very complex undertaking for an entire state's data. As of 1997, Sanders et al. noted that over 4 million data points in the Tennessee system were used to estimate effects for each student, teacher, school, and district.

The actual value-added component is not estimated as a gain, but as the difference in performance from the expected performance based on the student's previous performance, current grade in school effect, sum of current and previous teacher effectiveness, and school effectiveness. When 3 or more years' data become available, longitudinal trend models can be developed to predict the performance in each year for the various sources discussed.

Student achievement is what it is. A student either passes or fails the state test according to criteria the state establishes. What is unique in the value--added model of accountability is that the focus is on teacher, school, and district effectiveness rather than on individual student performance. The system is intended to (1) guide instructional change through inspection of the teacher and grade-level estimates of average performance and (2) evaluate teachers and administrators by examining consistency of performance averages across years. The second purpose is certainly controversial and has its detractors. In particular, teacher evaluation based on state assessments has been criticized due to the limited coverage of the state tests. This, it is argued, has resulted in reduced coverage of content, focus on low-level conceptual understanding, and over-emphasis on "teaching to the test" at the expense of content instruction. Nevertheless, there is continued interest in the value-added models and their use will likely increase.

8.2.3   Best Practices in Preparing Students for Standardized Assessment

As you can see from our discussion of standardized achievement tests to this point, these tests have widespread applications in public education. As a result, educators are often asked to prepare students for these tests. Much has been written in recent years about the proper procedures or practices for preparing students to take standardized achievement tests. As we noted earlier, high-stakes testing programs are in place in every state and these tests are used to make important decisions such as which students graduate or get promoted, which teachers receive raises, and which administrators retain their jobs. As you might imagine, the pressure to ensure that students perform well on these tests has also increased. Legislators put pressure on state education officials to increase student performance, who in turn put pressure on local administrators, who in turn put pressure on teachers. An important question is what test preparation practices are legitimate and acceptable, and what practices are unethical or educationally contraindicated? This is a more complicated question than one might first imagine.

> Critics of high-stakes tests programs believe too much instructional time is spent preparing students for the tests instead of teaching the really important skills necessary for success in life.

A popular phrase currently being used in both the popular media and professional educational literature is *teaching to the test*. The phrase "teaching to the test" generally implies efforts by teachers to prepare students to perform better on a standardized achievement test.

> Teaching to the test has become a popular concept in both the popular media and professional literature.

Many writers use teaching to the test in a derogatory manner referencing unethical or inappropriate test preparation practices. Other writers use the phrase more broadly to reference any instruction that is designed to enhance performance on a test. As you will see, there is a wide range of test preparation practices that can be applied. Some of these practices are clearly appropriate while others are clearly inappropriate. As an extreme example, consider a teacher that shared the exact items from a standardized test that is to be administered to students. This practice is clearly a breach of test security and is tantamount to "cheating." It is unethical and educationally indefensible and most responsible educators would not even consider such a practice. In fact, such a breach of test security could be grounds for the dismissal of the educator, revocation of license, and possible legal charges (Kober, 2002).

Thankfully such flagrantly abusive practices are relatively rare, but they do occur. However, the appropriateness of some of the more common methods of preparing students for tests is less clear. *With one notable exception*, which we will describe below, it is generally accepted that *any test preparation practice that raises test scores without also increasing mastery of the underlying knowledge and skills is inappropriate*. In other words, if a practice *artificially* increases test performance while failing to increase mastery of the domain of knowledge or skills reflected on the test, the practice is inappropriate. You may recognize this involves the issue of test validity. Standardized achievement tests are meant to assess the academic achievement of students in specific areas. If test preparation practices increase test scores without increasing the level of achievement, the validity of the test is compromised. Consider the following examples of various test preparation procedures:

- *Instruction in generic test-taking skills.* This involves instruction in general test-taking skills such as completing answer sheets, establishing an appropriate pace, narrowing choices on selected-response items, and introductions to novel item formats (e.g., Kober, 2002). This is the "notable exception" to the general rule we noted above. While instruction in general test-taking skills does not increase mastery of the underlying knowledge and skills, it does make students more familiar and comfortable with standardized tests. As a result, their scores are more likely to reflect accurately their true academic abilities and not the influence of deficient test-taking skills (e.g., Linn & Gronlund, 2000; Popham, 1999; Stroud & Reynolds, 2006). This practice enhances the reliability and validity of the assessment. This type of instruction is also typically fairly brief and, as a result, not detrimental to other educational activities. Therefore, instruction in generic test-taking skills is an appropriate test preparation practice (see Table 8.3). Stroud and Reynolds (2006) in fact include a test-taking strategies scale on their School Motivation and Learning Strategies scale so that educators can assess the need to teach these skills to individual students or entire classes.
- *Preparation using practice forms of the test.* Many states and commercial test publishers release earlier versions of their exams as practice tests. Since these are released as practice tests, their use is not typically considered unethical. However, if these tests become the focus of instruction at the expense of other teaching activities, this practice can be harmful. Research suggests that direct instruction using practice tests may produce short-term increases in test scores without commensurate increases in performance on other measures of the test

Table 8.3 Important test-taking skills to teach students

1. Carefully listen to or read the instruction.
2. Carefully listen to or read the test items.
3. Establish an appropriate pace. Don't rush carelessly through the test, but don't proceed so slowly that you will not be able to finish.
4. If you find an item to be extremely difficult, don't spend an inordinate amount of time on it. Skip it and come back if time allows.
5. On selected-response items, make informed guesses by eliminating alternatives that are clearly wrong.
6. Unless there is a penalty for guessing, try to complete every item. It is better to try and guess the correct answer than simply leave it blank.
7. Ensure that you carefully mark the answer sheet. For example, on computer-scored answer sheets, make sure the entire space is darkened and avoid extraneous marks.
8. During the test, periodically verify that the item numbers and answer numbers match.
9. If time permits, go back and check your answers.

Based on Linn and Gronlund (2000) and Sarnacki (1979)

domain (Kober, 2002). Like instruction in generic test-taking skills, the limited use of practice tests may help familiarize students with the format of the test. However, practice tests should be used in a judicious manner to ensure that they do not become the focus of instruction.

- *Preparation emphasizing test-specific item formats.* Here, teachers provide instruction and assignments that prepare students to deal exclusively with the specific item formats that are used on the standardized test. For example, teachers might use classroom tests and homework assignments that resemble actual items on the test (Kober, 2002). If the writing section of a test requires single paragraph responses, teachers will restrict their writing assignments to a single paragraph. If a test uses only multiple-choice items, the teachers will limit their classroom tests to multiple-choice items. The key feature is that students are given instruction that only exposes them to the material as presented and measured on the test. With this approach, students will be limited in their ability to generalize acquired skills and knowledge to novel situations (Popham, 1999). Test scores may increase, but the students' mastery of the underlying domain is limited. As a result, this practice should be avoided.

- *Preparation emphasizing test content.* This practice is somewhat similar to the previous practice, but instead of providing extensive exposure to items resembling those on the test, the goal is to emphasize the skills and content most likely to be included on the standardized tests. Kober (2002) notes that this practice often has a "narrowing effect" on instruction. Since many standardized achievement tests emphasize basic skills and knowledge that can be easily measured with selected-response items, this practice may result in teachers neglecting more complex learning objectives such as the analysis and synthesis of information or development of complex problem-solving skills. While test scores may increase, the students' mastery of the underlying domain is restricted. This practice should be avoided.

- *Preparation using multiple instructional techniques.* With this approach, students are given instruction that exposes them to the material as conceptualized and measured on the test, but also presents the material in a variety of different formats. Instruction covers all salient knowledge and skills in the curriculum and addresses both basic and higher-order learning objectives (Kober, 2002). With this approach, increases in test scores are associated with increases in mastery of the underlying domain of skills and knowledge (Popham, 1999). As a result, this test preparation practice is recommended.

While this list of test preparation practices is not exhaustive, we have tried to address the most common forms. In summary, only preparation that introduces generic test-taking skills and uses multiple instructional techniques can be recommended enthusiastically. Teaching generic test-taking skills makes students more familiar and comfortable with the assessment process and as a result enhances the reliability and validity of the assessment. Since test-taking skills may vary greatly among students, teaching these skills to all students levels the playing field so to speak, so no one has an undue advantage simply by being a sophisticated test-taker.

The use of multiple instructional techniques results in enhanced test performance that reflects an increased mastery of the content domain. As a result, with both of these practices the validity of the score interpretation as reflecting domain-specific knowledge is preserved. Other test preparation practices generally fall short of this goal. For example, practice tests may be useful when they are used cautiously, but they are often overused and become the focus of instruction with detrimental results. Any procedures that emphasize test-specific content or test-specific item formats should be avoided since they may increase test scores without actually enhancing mastery of the underlying test domain. In addition to preparing students to take standardized achievement tests, educators are often expected to help administer these tests. Special Interest Topic 8.7 provides some guidelines for administering standardized group achievement tests.

Special Interest Topic 8.7: Administering Standardized Group Achievement Tests

When introducing this chapter, we noted that standardized tests are professionally developed and must be administered and scored in a standard manner. For standardized test scores to be meaningful and useful, it is imperative that these standard procedures be followed precisely. These procedures are explicitly specified so that the tests can be administered in a uniform manner in different settings. The administration of individual intelligence (e.g., Wechsler Intelligence Scales) or achievement tests (Woodcock-Johnson Tests of Achievement) requires extensive training at the graduate level. For example, every Master's or doctorate-level psychology and counseling program we are aware of has specific courses that prepare students to administer and interpret intelligence and other individualized tests.

The administration of group tests such as the Iowa Tests of Basic Skills (ITBS) or state-developed achievement tests requires less rigorous training. Teachers and other educational professionals are often responsible for administering group achievement tests to their students and as a result should understand the basics of standardized test administration. Below are a few guidelines to help teachers administer standardized tests to their students that are based on our own experience and a review of the literature (e.g., Kubiszyn & Borich, 2003; Linn & Gronlund, 2000; Popham, 1999, 2000).

- *Review the test administration manual before the day of the test.* Administering standardized tests is not an overly difficult process, but it is helpful to review the administration instructions carefully before the day of the test. This way you will be familiar with the procedures and there should be no surprises. This review will alert you to any devices (e.g., stopwatch) or supporting material (e.g., scratch paper) you may need during the administration. It is also beneficial to do a mock administration by reading the instructions for the test in private before administering it to the students. The more familiar you are with the administration instructions the

(continued)

better prepared you will be to administer the test. Additionally, you will find the actual testing session to be less stressful.

- *Encourage the students to do their best*. Standardized achievement tests (and most other standardized tests used in schools) are maximum performance tests and ideally students will put forth their best efforts. This is best achieved by explaining to the students how the test results will be used to their benefit. For example, with achievement tests you might explain to the students that the results can help them and their parents track their academic progress and identify any areas that need special attention. While it is important to motivate students to do their best, it is equally important to avoid unnecessarily raising their level of anxiety. For example, you would probably not want to focus on the negative consequences of poor performance immediately before administering the test. This presents a type of balancing act; you want to encourage the students to do their best without making them excessively anxious.
- *Closely follow instructions*. As we noted, the reliability and validity of the test results are dependent on the individual administering the test closely following the administration instructions. First, the instructions to students must be read word-for-word. You should not alter the instructions in any way, paraphrase them, or try to improvise. It is likely that some students will have questions, but you are limited in how you can respond. Most manuals indicate that you can clarify procedural questions (e.g., where do I sign my name?), but you cannot define words or in any other way provide hints to the answers.
- *Strictly adhere to time limits*. Bring a stopwatch and practice using it before the day of the test.
- *Avoid interruptions*. Avoid making announcements or any other types of interruptions during the examination. To help avoid outside interruptions you should post a "Testing in Session—Do Not Disturb" sign on the door.
- *Avoid distractions*. Don't check your email or voice-mail or engage in "texting" during the assessment. It is your professional responsibility to focus on the task at hand—proctoring the examination.
- *Be alert to cheating*. While you don't want to hover over the students to the extent that it makes them unnecessarily nervous, active surveillance is indicated and can help deter cheating. Stay alert and monitor the room from a position that provides a clear view of the entire room. Walk quietly around the room occasionally. If you note anything out of the ordinary, increase your surveillance of those students. Document any unusual events that might deserve further consideration or follow-up.

By following these suggestions, you should have a productive and uneventful testing session. Nevertheless, you should be prepared for unanticipated events to occur. Keep the instruction manual close so you can refer to it if needed. It is also helpful to remember you can rely on your professional educational training to guide you in case of unexpected events.

8.3 Individual Achievement Tests

As we noted, standardized achievement tests are also used in the identification, diagnosis, and classification of examinees with special learning needs. While some group-administered achievement tests might be used in identifying children with special needs, in many situations *individually-administered achievement tests* are used. For example, if a student is having learning difficulties and parents or teachers are concerned about the possibility of a learning disability, the student would likely be given a thorough assessment which would include an individual achievement test. A testing professional, with extensive training in psychometrics and test administration, administers these tests to one student at a time. Since these tests are administered individually, they can contain a wider variety of item formats. For example, the questions are often presented in different modalities, with some questions being presented orally and some in written format. Some questions may require oral responses while some require written responses. In assessing writing abilities, some of these tests elicit short passages while others require fairly lengthy essays. Relative to the group tests, individual achievement tests typically provide a more thorough assessment of the student's skills. Since they are administered in a one-to-one context, the examiner is able to observe the student closely and hopefully gain insight into the source of learning problems. Additionally, since these tests are scored individually they are more likely to incorporate open-ended item formats (e.g., essay items) requiring qualitative scoring procedures. In the following sections, we will briefly introduce you to some of the most popular individual achievement tests in use today.

> Relative to the group tests, individual achievement tests typically provide a more thorough assessment of the student's skills.

8.3.1 Wechsler Individual Achievement Test, Third Edition (WIAT-III)

The WIAT-III (Pearson, 2009) is a comprehensive individually-administered norm-referenced achievement test published by Pearson. By comprehensive we mean it covers a broad spectrum of academic skill areas in individuals from 4 to 50 years. It contains the following composites and subtests:

- *Total Reading Composite*: Composed of the Word Reading subtest (letter knowledge, phonological awareness, and decoding skills), Reading Comprehension subtest (comprehension of short passages varying in type of text, such as fictional text, informational text, etc.), Pseudoword Decoding (phonetic decoding skills using nonsense words), and Oral Reading Fluency (speed, accuracy, fluency, and prosody of oral reading).
- *Mathematics Composite*: Composed of the Numerical Operations subtest (number knowledge, ability to solve calculation problems, and simple equations) and Math Problem-Solving subtest (ability to reason mathematically including basic concepts, everyday applications, geometry, and algebra).

- *Written Expression Composite*: Composed of the Spelling subtest (ability to write dictated letters and words), Alphabet Writing Fluency subtest (measures automaticity in written letter formation and sequencing), Sentence Composition subtest (sentence formulation and syntactic maturity and syntactic ability), and Essay Completion Subtest (measures spontaneous, compositional writing skills).
- *Oral Language composite*: Composed of the Listening Comprehension subtest (ability to listen and comprehend verbal information) and Oral Expression subtest (verbal word fluency, repetition, story generation, and providing directions).

The WIAT-III produces a variety of derived scores, including standard scores and percentile ranks. The WIAT-III has excellent psychometric properties and documentation. Additionally, the WIAT-III has the distinct advantage of being statistically linked to the Wechsler intelligence scales. Linkage with these popular intelligence tests facilitates the **aptitude-achievement discrimination analyses** often used to diagnose learning disabilities (this will be discussed more in the next chapter on aptitude tests).

8.3.2   Woodcock-Johnson IV Tests of Achievement (WJ-IV ACH)

The WJ-IV ACH (Schrank, Mather, & McGrew, 2014a) is a comprehensive individually-administered norm-referenced achievement test distributed by Houghton Mifflin Harcourt. The standard battery includes 11 subtests, while the extended battery contains nine additional subtests. Fourteen cluster scores can be derived from the standard battery subtests, while an additional six cluster scores can be derived using the extended battery subtests. The domains for the cluster scores include the following:

- *Reading*: Includes cluster scores such as Basic Reading Skills, Reading Comprehension, and Reading Fluency.
- *Mathematics*: Includes cluster scores such as Broad Mathematics, Math Calculation Skills, and Math Problem-Solving.
- *Writing*: Includes cluster scores such as Written Language, Basic Writing Skills, and Written Expression.
- *Cross-Domain*: Includes cluster scores such as Academic Fluency, Academic Skills, and Academic Applications.

The WJ-IV ACH offers three parallel test forms, provides a variety of derived scores, and has excellent psychometric properties and documentation. The availability of different forms is an advantage when testing a student on more than one occasion since the use of different forms can help reduce carry-over effects. Additionally, the WJ-IV ACH, the Woodcock-Johnson IV Tests of Cognitive Abilities (WJ-IV COG: Schrank, McGrew, & Mather, 2014b), and the Woodcock-Johnson IV Tests of Oral Language (Schrank, Mather, & McGrew, 2014b) compose a comprehensive diagnostic system, the Woodcock-Johnson IV (WJ-IV: Schrank, McGrew, & Mather, 2014a). When administered together, they facilitate the aptitude-achievement discrimination analyses often used to help diagnose learning disabilities. An additional advantage of the WJ-IV ACH is that it covers all areas specified by Individuals with Disabilities Education Act (IDEA, 2004) for assessing learning disabilities.

8.3.3   Wide Range Achievement Test Fifth Edition (WRAT5)

The WRAT5 (2017) is brief achievement test that measures reading, spelling, arithmetic skills in individuals 5 through 95 years. It contains the following subtests:

- *Word Reading*: Assesses ability to recognize and name letters and pronounce printed words.
- *Sentence Comprehension*: Assesses ability to read and comprehend the meaning of sentences.
- *Spelling*: Assesses ability to write letters, names, and words that are presented orally.
- *Math Computation*: Assesses ability to recognize numbers, count, and perform written computations.

Word Reading and Sentence Comprehension are combined to form a Reading Composite score. The WRAT5 can be administered in 15–40 min and comes in two parallel forms. Relative to the WIAT-III and WJ-IV ACH, the WRAT5 measures a restricted range of skills. However, when only a quick estimate of achievement in reading, spelling, and math computation is needed, the WRAT5 can be useful instrument.

The individual achievement batteries described to this point measure skills in multiple academic areas. As with the group achievement batteries, there are also individual tests that focus on specific skill domains. In the following section, we will briefly describe two tests that are examples of individual achievement tests that focus on specific skill areas.

8.3.4   Individual Achievement Tests That Focus on Specific Skills

8.3.4.1 Gray Oral Reading Test: Fifth Edition (GORT-5)
The GORT-5 is a measure of oral reading fluency and comprehension and is often used in the diagnosis of reading problems. The GORT-5 contains 16 passages of increasing difficulty which a student reads aloud. The examiner records reading rate and reading errors (e.g., skipping or inserting words, mispronunciation). Additionally, each reading passage contains five questions to assess comprehension. There are two parallel forms available.

8.3.4.2 KeyMath-3 Diagnostic Assessment (KeyMath-3)
The KeyMath-3, published by Pearson, measures mathematics skills in the following areas: Basic Concepts (numeration, algebra, geometry, measurement, and data

analysis and probability), Operations (addition, subtraction, multiplication, division, and mental computations and estimation), and Applications (foundations of problem-solving and applied problem-solving). The KeyMath-3 is available in two parallel forms.

8.4   Selecting an Achievement Battery

There are numerous factors that should be considered when selecting a standardized achievement battery. If you are selecting a test for administration to a large number of students, you will more than likely need a group achievement test. Nitko (1990, 2001) provides some suggestions for selecting a group achievement battery. He notes that while most survey batteries assess the common educational objectives

> When selecting a standardized achievement test, many factors should be considered, including the content covered, its technical properties, and practical issues such as cost and time requirements.

that are covered in most curricula, there are some potentially important differences in the content covered. In some instructional areas such as reading and mathematics, there is considerable consistency in the curricula used in different schools. In other areas such as science and social study, there is more variability. As a result, potential users should examine closely any potential battery to determine if its content corresponds with the school, district, or state curriculum. Naturally, it is also important to evaluate the technical adequacy of a test. This includes issues such as the adequacy of the standardization sample, the reliability of test scores, and the availability of validity evidence supporting the intended use. This is best accomplished using some of the resources we discussed earlier in this chapter (Special Interest Topic 8.3). Finally, it is also useful to consider practical issues such as cost, testing time required, availability of scoring services, and the quality of support materials such as administration and interpretative guides.

Many of the same factors should be considered when selecting an individual achievement test. You should select a test that adequately assesses the specific content areas you are interested in. For example, while a test like the WRAT-5 might be sufficient for screening purposes, it is not adequate for in-depth diagnostic purposes. If one is testing a student to determine if they have a specific learning disability, it would be important to use a battery like the WJ-IV ACH that covers all recognized areas of learning disability under the IDEA.

8.5   Teacher-Constructed Achievement Tests and Student Evaluation

It is probably safe to say that you have literally taken hundreds of classroom achievement tests in your academic career—from kindergarten through college! It is also likely that most of these tests were developed by your teachers. It has been estimated that teachers devote at least one-third of their professional time to assessment-related activities (Stiggins & Conklin, 1992). Classroom assessments should provide relevant information that both enhance instruction and promote student learning. They should provide objective feedback about what the students have

> It has been estimated that teachers devote as least one--third of their professional time to assessment-related activities.

learned, how well they have learned it, how effective the instruction has been, and what information, concepts, and objectives require more attention. Another important feature is that course grades are often based on the results of these tests. The following quote from Stiggins and Conklin (1992) highlights the important role teacher-made tests play in the overall process of educational assessment.

> As a nation, we spend billions of dollars on educational assessment, including hundreds of millions for international and national assessments, and additional hundreds of millions for statewide testing programs. On top of these, the standardized tests that form the basis of district-wide testing programs represents a billion-dollar industry. If we total all of these expensive highly visible, politically important assessments, we still account for less than 1 percent of all the assessments conducted in America's schools. The other 99 percent are conducted by teachers in their classrooms on a moment-to-moment, day-to-day, and week--to-week basis (back cover).

Given your years of experience taking classroom tests, you have probably noticed that some of these tests were well-developed and seemed to clearly cover the material presented in class—that is, they had "face validity." You probably also noticed that some were poorly developed and seemed to have little to do with the material covered in class and your readings. In the following section, we will highlight some key steps teachers should follow when developing tests and using the results to assign grades.

- *Specify Educational Objectives.* The first step in developing a classroom achievement test should be to specify the educational objectives or goals a teacher has for their students. While we will not go into detail about developing educational objectives, some general guidelines include the following: (1) write objectives that cover a broad spectrum of knowledge and abilities, (2) identify behaviors that are observable and directly measurable, (3) state any special conditions (e.g., the use of calculators), and (4) when appropriate, specify an outcome criterion. For more information on writing educational objectives, refer to Reynolds, Livingston, and Willson (2009).
- *Develop A Test Blueprint.* The next step in developing a classroom test is to write a table of specifications. A table of specifications is essentially a blueprint for the test that helps one organize the educational objectives and make sure that the test content matches what was taught in class. A table of specifications also helps one include items of varying degrees of complexity. We will provide more information on test blueprints in Chap. 18.
- *Determine How the Scores Will be Interpreted.* Teachers must decide if they will use a norm-referenced or criterion-referenced score interpretation based on how

they will use the test results. If one needs to determine a student's standing relative to a specified norm group, a norm-referenced interpretation is indicated. If one needs to determine what the student knows or what tasks they can perform, a criterion-referenced interpretation is indicated. With classroom achievement tests, we are most interested with the student's level of mastery of the educational objectives and as a result criterion-referenced interpretations are usually most useful.

- *Select Item Formats.* Teachers must also decide which type of items to include in the test. We spent considerable time discussing different item formats and their development in Chap. 6. In that chapter, we noted that the overriding goal is to develop items that measure the specified constructs and contribute to psychometrically sound tests. Selected-response items have characteristics that can contribute to psychometrically sound tests (e.g., objective and reliable scoring, good sampling of content domain), but it is often necessary to use constructed-response items to adequately measure a student's knowledge or abilities. For example, if you want to determine if a student can write a poem, you need them to actually write a poem. After item formats are selected, it is important to follow best practices in actually developing the items.

- *Assignment of Grades.* As we noted, teacher-made classroom tests often serve as the basis for student evaluation and assigning course grades. Grading has a long and rich history and this is briefly described in Special

> The assignment of grades has both positive and negative aspects.

Interest Topic 8.8. Evaluation in the schools is often divided into formative and summative evaluation. ***Formative evaluation*** involves evaluative activities that are aimed at providing feedback to students. In this context, feedback implies the communication of information concerning a student's performance or achievement that is intended to have a corrective effect. ***Summative evaluation*** involves the determination of the worth, value, or quality of an outcome. In the classroom, summative evaluation typically involves the formal evaluation of performance or progress in a course, often in the form of a numerical or letter grade or mark.

The assignment of grades has both positive and negative aspects. On the positive side, grades can represent a fair system for comparing students that minimizes irrelevant characteristics such as gender or race. Additionally, since most people are familiar with grades and their meaning, grades provide an effective and efficient means of providing information about student achievement. On the downside, a grade is only a brief summary of a student's performance and does not convey detailed information about specific strengths and weaknesses. Additionally, while most people understand the general meaning of grades, there is variability in what grades actually mean in different classes and schools. For example, some schools are plagued with grade inflation where practically everyone receives good grades (e.g., As and Bs), while other schools are much more rigorous in assigning grades. Finally, student competition for grades may become more important than actual achievement and students may have difficulty separating their personal worth from

Special Interest Topic 8.8: A Brief History of Grading

Brookhart (2004) provides a discussion of the history of grading in the United States. Below are a few of the key developments she notes in this timeline.

- *Pre-1800:* Grading procedures were first developed in universities. Brookhart's research suggests that the first categorical grading scale was used at Yale in 1785 and classified students as *Optimi* (i.e., best), *Second Optimi* (i.e., second best), *Inferiores* (i.e., lesser), and *Pejores* (i.e., worse). In 1813, Yale adopted a numerical scale where students were assigned grades between 1 and 4 with decimals used to reflect intermediary levels. Some universities developed scales with more categories (e.g., 20) while others tried simple Pass/Fail grading.

- *1800s:* The common school movement of the 1800s saw the development of public schools designed to provide instruction to the nation's children. Initially, these early schools adopted grading scales similar to those in use at universities. Around 1840, schools started the practice of distributing report cards. Teachers at the time complained that assessment and grading were too burdensome and parents complained the information was difficult to interpret. These are complaints that are still with us today!

- *1900s:* Percentage grading was common in secondary schools and universities at the beginning of the twentieth century. By 1910, however, educators began to question the reliability and accuracy of using a scale with 100 different categories or scale points. By the 1920s, the use of letter grades (A, B, C, D, & F) was becoming the most common practice. During the remainder of the 1900s, a number of grading issues came to the forefront. For example, educators became increasingly aware that non-achievement factors (e.g., student attitudes and behaviors and teacher biases) were influencing the assignment of grades and recognized that this was not a desirable situation. Additionally, there was a debate regarding the merits of norm-referenced versus criterion-referenced grading systems. Finally, there were efforts to expand the purpose of grades so they not only served to document the students' level of academic achievement, but also served to enhance the learning of students. As you might expect, these are all issues that educators continue to struggle with to this day!

In some aspects, we have come a long way in refining the ways we evaluate the performance of our students. At the same time, we are still struggling with many of the same issues we struggled with more than a hundred years ago.

their grades, both undesirable situations. Nevertheless, grades are viewed as an essential component of our educational process and efforts should be made to assign them in an accurate and responsible manner. To this end, we have the following suggestions:

- *Basis of Grades.* We recommend that grades be assigned <u>solely</u> on the basis of academic achievement. Some teachers will penalize students for missing class or inappropriate behavior by lowering their grades. While factors such as class behavior and attitude are certainly important, if they are combined with achievement when assigning grades, they blur the meaning of grades.
- *Frame of Reference.* Once a teacher has decided what to base student grades on (hopefully academic achievement), they must decide what frame of reference to use. When assigning grades, it is common to use either a relative or absolute approach. These approaches are comparable to the norm-referenced (i.e., relative) and criterion-referenced (i.e., absolute) score interpretations we have discussed throughout this text. In a relative or norm-referenced approach, grades are assigned by comparing each student's performance to that of other students in the class. For example, the top 10% of the students might receive As; the next 20% might receive Bs, etc. In an absolute or criterion-referenced approach, grades are assigned by comparing each student's performance to a specified level of performance. One of the most common criterion-referenced grading systems is the traditional percentage-based system. Here, students with cumulative grades between 90% and 100% would receive As; those between 80% and 89% would receive Bs, etc. We believe that both relative (i.e., norm-referenced) and absolute (i.e., criterion-referenced) grading approaches can be used successfully. They both have advantages and limitations, but when used conscientiously, either approach can be effective. In contrast, some educators have suggested that grades should be based on effort or improvement. For example, if a student with very poor skills at the beginning of instruction achieves a moderate level of achievement, they should receive a better grade than a high achieving student who demonstrated a smaller gain, but a higher overall level of achievement. Another variation is to base grades on achievement relative to ability or aptitude. Here, a student with average intelligence who scores above average on tests of achievement is considered an overachiever and receives good grades. Accordingly, an underachiever is a student whose achievement is considered low in relation to their level of intelligence, and these students would receive lower grades (regardless of the absolute level of achievement). There are a number of technical and practical problems with these approaches and they should be avoided (see Reynolds et al., 2009 for more information).
- *Reporting Student Progress.* While a number of different approaches have been proposed, *letter grades* (i.e., A, B, C, D, and F) are the most popular method of reporting student progress and are used in the majority of schools and universities today. While there might be some variation in the meaning attached to them, letter grades are typically interpreted as:

A = Excellent/Superior Achievement
B = Above-Average Achievement
C = Average Achievement
D = Below-Average or Marginal Achievement
F = Failing/Poor Achievement

Students and parents generally understand letter grades and the evaluative judgment represented by letter grades is probably more widely accepted than any other system available.

- *Keep Grades Confidential.* Students and parents should be informed of their grades in a timely manner and this information should be conveyed in a confidential and protected manner. Grades or test scores should not be posted or otherwise displayed in any way that reveals a student's individual performance. A Federal law, the Family Educational Rights and Privacy Act (FERPA: also known as Public Law 93-380 or the Buckley Amendment) governs the maintenance and release of educational records, including grades, test scores, and related evaluative material.

This has been a very brief review of some important issues related to the development of classroom achievement tests and their use in assigning grades. There are a number of texts that cover these topics in more detail (e.g., Reynolds et al., 2009), and if you aspire to become a teacher or professor, we encourage you to study this topic further.

8.6   Achievement Tests: Not Only in the Public Schools!

Our discussion of achievement assessment to this point has focused on their application in public schools. While it is true that achievement tests are widely used in schools, that is not their only application. For example, most of you have taken a test to obtain a driver's license. This is an example of an achievement test being used outside of public schools. They are also used in personnel selection (i.e., discussed in Chap. 12) and in allowing

> It is true that achievement tests are widely used in schools, but that is not their only application.

students to gain college credit by examination (e.g., College-Level Examination Program; CLEP testing). Another major application of achievement assessment is in licensing and certification of a multitude of professions (e.g., psychologists, physicians, lawyers, plumbers, and electricians). Police and firefighters often take achievement tests for promotions to certain levels of authority or rank in their jobs. In the following sections, we will briefly discuss two achievement tests that are used for professional licensing.

8.6.1   Examination for Professional Practice in Psychology (EPPP)

Licensing of professionals is a state right, and each state has boards that are responsible for testing and licensing professionals in their state. The EPPP is administered by the Association of State and Provincial Psychology Boards and is used by individual state licensing boards to license psychologists. The EPPP contains 225 items,

175 of which are actual test items and 50 are pilot test items. The content areas of the test are outlined below:

- *Biological Basis of Behavior* (12%): knowledge of the biological and neural basis of behavior, psychopharmacology, and methodologies supporting this body of knowledge.
- *Cognitive-Affective Basis of Behavior* (13%): knowledge of cognition, theories and empirical research on learning, memory, motivation, affect, emotion, and executive function, and factors that influence cognitive performance.
- *Social and Cultural Basis of Behavior* (12%): knowledge of group processes, theories of personality, and diversity issues.
- *Growth and Lifespan Development* (13%): knowledge of development across the full lifespan, atypical patterns of development, and the protective and risk factors that impact developmental outcomes.
- *Assessment and Diagnosis* (14%): knowledge of psychometrics, assessment models and instruments, and diagnostic/classification systems and their limitations.
- *Treatment, Intervention, Prevention, and Supervision* (14%): knowledge of individual, couple, family, group, organization, or community interventions for specific problems/disorders in diverse populations, intervention and prevention theories, best practices, consultation and supervision models, and evidence supporting efficacy and effectiveness of interventions.
- *Research Methods and Statistics* (8%): knowledge of research design, methodology, and program evaluation, instrument selection and validation, statistical models, assumptions, and procedures, and dissemination methods.
- *Ethical/Legal/Professional Issues* (15%). Knowledge of codes of ethics, professional standards for practice, legal mandates and restrictions, guidelines for ethical decision making, and professional training and supervision.

Performance on the EPPP is reported in scaled scores which are conversions of raw scores. The recommended passing scaled score for independent practice is 500 (which reflects approximately 70% correct responses) and for supervised practice is 450 (approximately 65% correct responses). These cut scores are simply recommendations, and each state's licensing board typically establishes their own standards. More information about the EPPP can be found at www.asppb.net.

8.6.2   United States Medical Licensing Examination (USMLE)

The USMLE is a three-stage examination for licensing physicians for practice in the U.S. It is administered by the Federation of State Medical Boards (FSMB) and the National Board of Medical Examiners (NBME). It involves the three following steps.

- *Step 1*: This computer-based multiple-choice assessment is designed to determine if the applicant is knowledgeable about the essential scientific facts and concepts that are fundamental to the practice of medicine. In addition to assess-

Table 8.4 Sample of achievement test applications outside of public schools

Application	Examples
Personnel Selection and Promotion	• Wonderlic Personnel Test • Wide Range Achievement Test • Tests specific to the job, e.g., clerical knowledge, knowledge of policy and procedures, knowledge of law applicable to one job, etc.
College Credit by Examination	• College-Level Examination Program (CLEP) • ACT Proficiency Examination Program (PEP)
Professional Licenses	• Examination in the Professional Practice of Psychology (EPPP) • United States Medical Licensing Examination (USMLE) • *The Praxis Series*: Teacher Licensure and Certification
Non-Professional Licenses	• Driver's Licenses of all types including chauffeur's licenses

ing basic scientific knowledge, this assessment is designed to determine if the applicant understands the scientific principles needed to be a lifelong learner and maintain competence throughout their professional career.

- *Step 2*: This step contains two assessments: Step 2 Clinical Knowledge (CK) and Clinical Skills (CS). Step 2 CK is a computer-based multiple-choice test designed to determine if the applicant can apply medical knowledge and skills in a clinical setting under supervision. This goal of this assessment is to determine if the applicant can practice medicine in a safe and competent manner. Step 2 CS is a test of clinical skills that uses standardized patients to assess an applicant's clinical, cognitive, and communication skills. This assessment is only administered at five testing centers in the U.S.
- *Step 3*: This computer-based multiple-choice assessment is designed to determine if the applicant can apply medical knowledge and skills in an unsupervised setting. This step includes multiple-choice items and computer-based case simulations. The computer-based simulations present clinical vignettes and allow the applicant to select appropriate tests and interventions—and there are literally thousands of tests and interventions they can select from. This is the final assessment and is intended to ensure that applicants are prepared for the independent practice of medicine. More information on the USMLE is available at http://www.usmle.org.

We have only reviewed two of the many tests used by state boards for licensing professionals. Many, many such tests exist—for licensing lawyers, realtors, engineers, teachers, nurses, counselors, etc. Table 8.4 provides a brief listing on some of the many uses of achievement tests outside of our public schools.

8.7   Summary

This chapter discusses achievement tests and their applications in the schools. The bulk of the chapter focused on standardized achievement tests which are designed to be administered, scored, and interpreted in a standard manner. The goal of standardization is to ensure that testing conditions are the same for all individuals taking the test. If this is accomplished, no examinee will have an advantage over another, and test results will be comparable. These tests have different applications in the schools, including:

- Tracking student achievement over time
- High-stakes decision making (e.g., promotion decisions; teacher evaluations)
- Identifying individual strengths and weaknesses
- Evaluating the effectiveness of educational programs
- Identifying students with special learning needs

Of these uses, high-stakes testing programs are probably the most controversial. These programs use standardized achievement tests to make such important decisions as which students will be promoted and evaluating educational professionals and schools. Proponents of high-stake testing programs see them as a way of improving public education and ensuring that students are all judged according to the same standards. Critics of high-stakes testing programs argue that they encourage teachers to focus on low-level academic skills at the expense of higher-level skills such as problem-solving and critical thinking.

There are popular commercial group achievement tests. The chapter includes a discussion of the current trend toward increased high-stakes assessments in the public schools and how this is being implemented by states using a combination of commercial and state-developed assessments. Value-added assessment is a potentially useful approach for assessing and monitoring student achievement.

We also provide some guidelines to help teachers prepare their students for these tests. However, any test preparation procedure that raises test scores without also increasing the mastery of the underlying knowledge and skills is inappropriate. After evaluating different test preparation practices, we recommend two: preparation that introduces generic test-taking skills and use of multiple instructional techniques. These practices should result in improved performance on standardized tests that reflects increased mastery of the underlying content domains. Preparation practices that emphasize the use of practice tests or focus on test-specific content or test-specific item formats should be avoided since they may increase test scores, but not increase mastery of the underlying test domain.

Individual achievement tests are also used in schools. These individually-administered tests are used by professionals with specialized training in assessment for a variety of purposes, including assessment of learning disabilities under the Individuals with Disabilities Education Act (IDEA). We provide suggestions regarding the selection of achievement tests for different applications.

In closing, we discuss teacher-constructed classroom achievement tests and their use in assigning grades. These tests are administered in great numbers and have significant impact on students. When developing classroom tests, it is imperative to (1) clearly specify student learning objectives, (2) develop and follow a test blueprint, (3) select a score interpretation approach based on how the results will be used, and (4) include items that measure the specified constructs and contribute to the reliability and validity of test results. In terms of grading, assign grades based solely on academic achievement not contaminated with factors such as behavior, attendance, or attitude. Both relative (i.e., norm-referenced) and absolute (i.e., criterion-referenced) grading approaches can be used successfully, but teachers should avoid basing grades on effort, improvement, or achievement relative to aptitude. Letter grades are the most popular method of reporting student progress and they are typically well understood by both students and parents. In closing, it is important to keep grades confidential, which is mandated by the Family Educational Rights and Privacy Act (FERPA).

References

American Educational Research Association. (2000). *AERA position statement concerning high-stakes testing in PreK-12 education*. Retrieved March 1, 2020, from http://www.aera.net/About-AERA/AERA-Rules-Policies/Association-Policies/Position-Statement-on-High-Stakes-Testing

American Educational Research Association, American Psychological Association, & National Council on Measurement in Education. (2014). *Standards for educational and psychological testing*. Washington, DC: American Educational Research Association.

Anastasi, A., & Urbina, S. (1997). *Psychological testing* (7th ed.). Upper Saddle River, NJ: Prentice Hall.

Boser, U. (1999). Study finds mismatch between California standards and assessments. *Education Week, 18*, 10.

Brookhart, S. M. (2004). *Grading*. Upper Saddle River, NJ: Pearson Merrill Prentice Hall.

Ceperley, P. E., & Reel, K. (1997). The impetus for the Tennessee value-added accountability system. In J. Millman (Ed.), *Grading teachers, grading schools* (pp. 133–136). Thousand Oaks, CA: Corwin Press.

Doherty, K. M. (2002). Education issues: Assessment. *Education Week*. Retrieved from http://www.edweek.org/context/topics/issuespage.cfm?id=41

Education Week. (2017). Data provided by Edweek.org. Retrieved June 21, 2017, from http://www.edcounts.org/createtable/step1.php?clear=1

Jacob, S., & Hartshorne, T. (2007). *Ethics and law for school psychologists* (5th ed.). Hoboken, NJ: Wiley.

Kober, N. (2002). *Teaching to the test: The good, the bad, and who's responsible. Test talk for leaders* (Issue 1). Washington, DC: Center on Education Policy. Retrieved from http://www.cep-dc.org/testing/testtalkjune2002.htm

Kubiszyn, T., & Borich, G. (2003). *Educational testing and measurement: Classroom application and practice* (7th ed.). New York, NY: Wiley.

Linn, R. L., & Gronlund, N. E. (2000). *Measurement and assessment in teaching* (8th ed.). Upper Saddle River, NJ: Prentice Hall.

Nitko, A. J. (1990). Educational measurement. *Issues and Practice, 9*(4), 3–32.

Nitko, A. J. (2001). *Educational assessment of students*. Upper Saddle River, NJ: Merrill Prentice Hall.

Pearson. (2009). *WIAT-III: Examiners manual*. San Antonio, TX: Author.

Popham, W. J. (1999). *Classroom assessment: What teachers need to know*. Boston, MA: Allyn & Bacon.

Popham, W. J. (2000). *Modern educational measurement: Practical guidelines for educational leaders*. Boston, MA: Allyn & Bacon.

Reynolds, C. R., Livingston, R. B., & Willson, V. (2009). *Measurement and assessment in education*. Boston, MA: Allyn & Bacon.

Sanders, W. L., Saxton, A. M., & Horn, S. P. (1997). The Tennessee value-added assessment system: A quantitative, outcomes based approach to educational assessment. In J. Millman (Ed.), *Grading teachers, grading schools* (pp. 137–162). Thousand Oaks, CA: Corwin Press.

Sarnacki, R. E. (1979, Spring). An examination of test-wiseness in the cognitive domain. *Review of Educational Research, 49,* 252–279.

Schrank, F. A., Mather, N., & McGrew, K. S. (2014a). *Woodcock-Johnson IV tests of achievement.* Rolling Meadows, IL: Riverside.

Schrank, F. A., Mather, N., & McGrew, K. S. (2014b). *Woodcock-Johnson IV tests of oral language.* Rolling Meadows, IL: Riverside.

Schrank, F. A., McGrew, K. S., & Mather, N. (2014a). *Woodcock-Johnson IV.* Rolling Meadows, IL: Riverside.

Schrank, F. A., McGrew, K. S., & Mather, N. (2014b). *Woodcock-Johnson IV tests of cognitive abilities.* Rolling Meadows, IL: Riverside.

Stiggins, R. J., & Conklin, N. F. (1992). *In teachers' hands: Investigating the practices of classroom assessment.* Albany, NY: State University of New York Press.

Stroud, K. C., & Reynolds, C. R. (2006). *School motivation and learning strategies inventory (SMALSI).* Los Angeles, CA: Western Psychological Services.

U.S. Congress, Office of Technology Assessment. (1992). *Testing in American schools: Asking the right questions, OTA-SET-519.* Washington, DC: U.S. Government Printing Office.

Webster, W. J., & Mendro, R. L. (1997). The Dallas value-added accountability system. In J. Millman (Ed.), *Grading teachers, grading schools* (pp. 81–99). Thousand Oaks, CA: Corwin Press.

Wilkinson, G. S. & Robertson G. J. (2017). *Wide Range Achievement Test, Fifth Edition* (WRAT5). Bloomington, MN: Pearson Inc.

Suggested Reading

Reynolds, C. R., Livingstion, R. B., & Willson, V. L. (2009). *Measurement and assessment in education.* Boston, MA: Allyn & Bacon.

Assessment of Intelligence

9

Conventional intelligence tests and even the entire concept of intelligence testing are perennially the focus of considerable controversy and strong emotion.

—Reynolds and Kaufman (1990)

Abstract

Intelligence tests and other aptitude tests are designed to measure cognitive skills, abilities, and knowledge that are accumulated as the result of overall life experiences including those at school, home, work, and all other settings. As a result, general intelligence tests are not linked to a specific academic curriculum or knowledge domain and so are much broader in scope than achievement tests. General intelligence tests assess abilities such as problem-solving, abstract reasoning, and the ability to acquire knowledge. This chapter highlights some of the important and interesting historical milestones for intelligence testing, major applications of intelligence tests in school and clinical settings, and commonly used intelligence and aptitude tests. Practical guidelines are also presented for selecting aptitude tests and understanding the elements of the formal psychological report which is used to communicate assessment findings.

Supplementary Information The online version of this chapter (https://doi.org/10.1007/978-3-030-59455-8_9) contains supplementary material, which is available to authorized users.

Learning Objectives

After reading and studying this chapter, students should be able to:
1. Compare and contrast the constructs of achievement and intelligence/ aptitude.
2. Explain how achievement and aptitude can be conceptualized as different aspects of a continuum and provide examples to illustrate this continuum.
3. Discuss the major milestones in the history of intelligence assessment.
4. Describe the major uses of aptitude and intelligence tests.
5. Describe and evaluate the major individually administered intelligence tests.
6. Understand the central concepts of neuropsychological testing.
7. Understand the central concepts of memory testing.
8. Describe and evaluate the major individually administered memory tests.
9. Understand a report of an intellectual assessment.
10. Identify the major college admission tests and describe their use.

In Chap. 1, when describing maximum performance tests we noted that they are often classified as either achievement tests or aptitude tests. (In some professional sources, the term *aptitude* is being replaced with *ability*. For historical purposes, we will use *aptitude* to designate this type of test in this chapter, but we do want to alert readers to this variability in terminology.)

> Aptitude tests are designed to measure the cognitive skills, abilities, and knowledge that individuals have accumulated as the result of their overall life experiences.

We defined ***achievement tests*** as those designed to assess students' knowledge or skills in a content domain in which they have received instruction (American Educational Research Association, American Psychological Association, & National Council on Measurement in Education, 2014). In contrast, ***aptitude tests*** are designed to measure the cognitive skills, abilities, and knowledge that individuals have accumulated as the result of their overall life experiences. In some instances, such as with measures of general intelligence, aptitude measures are much broader than achievement measures, but some aptitude measures can be very narrow and focus on something as distinctive as visual attention or psychomotor speed. Whereas achievement tests are tied to a specific program of instruction, aptitude tests reflect the cumulative impact of life experiences as a whole in concert with an individual's underlying or latent ability to use information. Aptitude tests are more likely to focus on cognitive processes as opposed to content of knowledge domains as well. Some interpret the use of the term aptitude to denote the maximum level at which a person can perform now and in the future—we do not ascribe immutability to any aptitude assessed by psychological tests. Rather, aptitude scores as used here reflect how well a person performed on a task at that point in time, which we understand will predict future levels of performance, but far from perfectly. Also, because a person's cognitive skills, abilities, and knowledge are likely to change as a result of life experience, aptitude scores and the aptitude underlying performance are also likely to change over time.

These introductory comments might lead you to believe there is a clear and universally accepted distinction between achievement and aptitude tests. However, in actual practice this is not the case and the distinction is actually a matter of degree. Many, if not most, testing experts conceptualize both achievement and aptitude tests as tests of developed cognitive abilities that can be ordered along a continuum in terms of how closely linked the assessed abilities are to specific learning experiences. This continuum is illustrated in Fig. 9.1. At one end of the continuum, you have teacher-constructed classroom tests that are tied directly to the instruction provided in a specific classroom or course. For example, a classroom mathematics test should assess specifically the learning objectives covered in the class during a specific instructional period. This is an example of a test that is linked clearly and directly to specific academic experiences (i.e., the result of curriculum and instruction).

Next along the continuum are the survey achievement batteries that measure a fairly broad range of knowledge, skills, and abilities. Although there should be alignment between the learning objectives measured by these tests and the academic curriculum, the scope of a survey battery is considerably broader and more comprehensive than that of a teacher-constructed classroom test. The group-administered survey batteries described in an earlier chapter are dependent on direct school experiences, but there is variability in how direct the linkage is. For example, the achievement tests developed by states specifically to assess the state's core curriculum are more directly linked to instruction through the state's specified curriculum than the commercially developed achievement tests that assess a more generic curriculum.

Next are intelligence and other aptitude tests that emphasize verbal, quantitative, and visual-spatial abilities. Many traditional intelligence tests can be placed in this category, and even though they are not linked to a specific academic curriculum, they do assess many skills that are commonly associated with academic success. The Otis-Lennon School Ability Test, Eighth Edition (OLSAT 8), Stanford-Binet Intelligence Scales, Fifth Edition (SB-5), Wechsler Intelligence Scale for Children, Fifth Edition (WISC-V), and Reynolds Intellectual Assessment Scales, Second Edition (RIAS-2) are all examples of tests that fit in this category (some of these will be discussed later in this chapter). In developing these tests, the authors attempt to measure abilities that are acquired through common, everyday experiences; not

Very Specific	Moderate Specificity		Very General
Teacher-Constructed Classroom tests	Broad Survey Achievement Batteries	Verbal Intelligence and Aptitude Tests	Cross-Cultural Intelligence Tests

Fig. 9.1 A continuum of general abilities. *Note.* Modeled after Anastasi and Urbina (1997), Cronbach (1990), and others

only those acquired through formal educational experiences. For example, a quantitative section of one of these tests will typically emphasize mental computations and quantitative reasoning as opposed to the developed mathematics skills traditionally emphasized on achievement tests. Novel problem-solving skills are emphasized on many portions of these tests as well. Modern intelligence tests are not just measures of knowledge or how much you know, but also how well you think and can manipulate information.

Finally, at the most "general" end of the continuum are the nonverbal and cross-cultural intelligence or aptitude tests. These instruments attempt to minimize the influence of language, culture, and educational experiences on test performance. They typically emphasize the use of nonverbal performance items and often completely avoid

> Both achievement and aptitude tests measure developed abilities and can be arranged along a continuum according to how dependent the abilities are on direct school experiences.

language-based content (e.g., reading, writing, etc.). The Naglieri Nonverbal Ability Test, Third Edition (NNAT3), is an example of a test that belongs in this category. The NNAT3 is a nonverbal measure of general ability that is thought to be relatively independent of educational experiences, language, and cultural background (however, no test is truly culture-free or independent of all of one's life experiences). The NNAT3 employs items in which the test taker must find the missing pattern in a series of designs or figures. The matrices in the NNAT3 are arranged in order of difficulty and contain designs and shapes that are not specific to any one culture but appear across most cultures or are novel to nearly all test takers. Promoters of the test suggest that this test may be particularly useful for students with limited English proficiency, minorities, or those with hearing impairments.

In summary, both achievement and aptitude tests measure developed cognitive abilities and can be arranged along a continuum according to how dependent the abilities are on direct school experience. As we progress from the specific to the general end of the continuum, test performance becomes less and less dependent on specific learning experiences. The abilities measured by achievement tests are specifically linked to academic instruction or training. In contrast, the abilities measured by aptitude tests are acquired through a broad range of life experiences, including those at school, home, work, and all other settings.

Although we feel it is important to recognize that the distinction between achievement and aptitude tests is not absolute, we also feel the aptitude-achievement distinction is useful. In schools and other settings (e.g., clinical, employment), aptitude and achievement tests traditionally have been used for different purposes, and these labels help us identify their intended applications. For example, achievement tests typically are used to measure what has been learned or "achieved" at a specific point in time. In contrast, aptitude tests usually are used to predict future performance (e.g., academic or job performance). Even college quarterbacks who are trying out for the National Football League routinely take a specialized aptitude test to gauge their ability to learn complex offensive schemes and to recognize defensive alignments and make adjustments quickly and effectively. Because some aptitude tests are excellent predictors of academic and occupational performance, some *mistakenly* interpret this to mean that these tests measure potential. Special Interest Topic 9.1 provides a brief discussion differentiating between "predicting performance" and "measuring potential."

Special Interest Topic 9.1: Do Intelligence Tests Reveal Your Potential for Learning or Other Achievements?

The short answer is an emphatic "No!"

Intelligence tests are among the very best predictors of performance in school as well as on the job, especially in vocational training programs or nearly anything related to academic achievement. This fact is often misconstrued and interpreted to mean that an intelligence test measures your potential to acquire knowledge and skills.

Intelligence tests do predict very, very well compared to most other indicators of what you will most likely achieve in these domains. However, the predictions made by an IQ about your future performance are actually the mean levels of performance by others at the same IQ point who have the average level of motivation, spend the same average amount of time studying, have the same average level of study and learning skills and strategies, have the same average level of opportunity to learn or develop these skills, have the same average level of quality of instruction, have the same average level of attentional skills, and so on.

This means that if any one of these assumptions is untrue for you, you will most likely not perform at the predicted level. In fact, around each predicted level of achievement or performance, there is a normal distribution of actual performance. So, if you study harder than others with the same IQ as you, you will perform at a higher level than predicted by the IQ you obtained—if you have a higher level of motivation than others who have the same IQ as you, you will most likely perform at a higher level over time. On the other hand, if you spend less time studying than the average person with the same IQ as you, you will most likely perform at a lower level than others at this IQ point.

An IQ then is not a determinant or indicator of your potential, it is only a very good predictor of what you are most likely to achieve. You have a great deal of control over the accuracy of this prediction. Work harder, study harder and smarter, and attend better, and you will perform at a higher level than most people with your IQ, thus beating the prediction. Do less than others with the same IQ, and you will perform at a lower level. You get to choose on which side of the predicted level of performance you will actually fall.

Although many sources use the terms *aptitude* and *intelligence* interchangeably, general intelligence tests are not the only type of aptitude test in use today. In addition to intelligence tests, special aptitude tests and multiple-aptitude batteries frequently are used in many educational, clinical, and employment settings. Special aptitude tests were developed originally in the context of employment settings to help employers select job applicants based on their aptitudes in specific areas such as mechanical or clerical ability. Subsequently, test developers developed multiple-aptitude batteries to measure a number of distinct abilities.

General intelligence tests historically have been the most popular and widely used aptitude tests in psychology whether in clinical practice, school settings, or even in employment environments. Intelligence tests are the most advanced, psychometri-

> General intelligence tests historically have been the most popular and widely used aptitude tests in school settings.

cally, of all tests in the armamentarium of psychologists, yet psychology as a discipline as well as the media and lay public seem to have a "love-hate" relationship with intelligence and intelligence testing in particular. It is not uncommon for parents of a child, when reviewing the results of an intellectual assessment of the child with a psychologist, to dismiss the idea of IQ in one breath and inquire as to the results of the child's IQ testing in the next! Intelligence testing research spawns strong emotions. As one example, consider the following. In the 1980s when the American Psychological Association (APA) held its annual convention in Anaheim, California, Arthur Jensen, who became famous following a 1969 article in *Harvard Educational Review* ("How Much Can We Boost IQ and Scholastic Achievement?"), was scheduled to deliver an invited address on his research on intelligence. One of the authors of this text (CRR) had been asked by the APA to introduce Jensen, whose conclusions on racial differences in intelligence based on his research were often seen as controversial by many (and led to the coining of the term Jensenism). Several weeks before the convention, CRR was contacted by the Anaheim police and told they had received what they considered a credible threat that if Jensen were to speak, he would be assassinated during his address. Despite this threat, Jensen spoke and CRR did introduce him, but the police patrolled the venue of the invited address that day quite heavily (with canines in attendance as well) and screened the audience as they entered the convention center hall, a hall that was completely filled for Jensen's address. Few topics in psychology can engender such strong and polemic responses. (More detailed consideration of historical and ongoing debates regarding IQ is provided in Special Interest Topics 9.2 and 9.3 as well as Chap. 15 of this text on cultural bias in testing.)

9.1   A Brief History of Intelligence Tests

While practically everyone is familiar with the concept of ***intelligence*** and uses the term in everyday conversations, it is not easy to develop a definition of intelligence on which everyone agrees. Although practically all psychologists and psychometricians have their own personal definition of intelligence, most of these definitions will incorporate abilities such as problem-solving, abstract reasoning, and the ability to acquire knowledge—how well can you think and problem solve (e.g., Gray, 1999; Reynolds & Kamphaus, 2003).

> Most definitions of intelligence incorporate abilities such as problem-solving, abstract reasoning, and the ability to acquire knowledge.

Beyond this point, developing a consensus about the definition of intelligence and other critical issues is more difficult. Psychologists continue to debate important issues regarding IQ including the contributing role of genetics, environment, nutrition, race, and other matters (see Special Interest Topic 9.2 for more on the controversial state of intelligence), as well as the appropriate application of intelligence tests, particularly in school settings (see Special Interest Topic 9.3 for additional discussion). For our present purpose, instead of pursuing a philosophical discussion of the meaning of intelligence, we will focus only on intelligence as measured by contemporary intelligence tests. These tests typically produce an overall score referred to as an ***intelligence quotient*** (**IQ**), and this is the most common operational definition of intelligence in research on intelligence.

Special Interest Topic 9.2: The Controversial IQ: Knowns and Unknowns

A task force established by the American Psychological Association produced a report titled "Intelligence: Knowns and Unknowns" (Neisser et al., 1996). Its authors summarize the state of knowledge about intelligence and conclude by identifying seven critical questions about intelligence that have yet to be answered. These issues are summarized here:

1. It is widely accepted that there is a substantial genetic contribution to the development of intelligence, but the pathway by which genetic differences are expressed is not known.

2. It is also accepted that environmental factors contribute significantly to the development of intelligence, but no one really knows the mechanism by which they express their influence.

3. The role of nutrition in the development of intelligence is unclear. It is clear that profound early malnutrition is detrimental, but the effects of more subtle nutritional differences in populations that are "adequately fed" are not well understood.

4. Research has revealed significant correlations between information-processing speed and intelligence, but these findings have not resulted in clear theoretical models.

5. The "Flynn Effect" is real! That is, mean IQs are increasing worldwide. No one is really sure what factors are driving these gains. (See Chap. 3 for more on this topic.)

6. Mean IQ differences between races cannot be attributed to obvious test bias or simply to differences in socioeconomic status. There is also no

support for genetic explanations. Simply put, no one really knows the basis of these differences.

7. It is widely accepted that standardized intelligence tests do not measure all aspects of intelligence such as creativity, common sense, and interpersonal finesse. However, we do not know very much about these abilities such as how they relate to more traditional aspects of intelligence or how they develop.

In concluding their report, Neisser et al. (1996) noted:

> In a field where so many issues are unresolved and so many questions unanswered, the confident tone that has characterized most of the debate on these topics is clearly out of place. The study of intelligence does not need politicized assertions and recriminations; it needs self-restraint, reflection, and a great deal more research. The questions that remain are socially as well as scientifically important. There is no reason to think them unanswerable, but finding the answers will require a shared and sustained effort as well as the commitment of substantial scientific resources. Just such a commitment is what we strongly recommend. (p. 97)

Special Interest Topic 9.3: The Controversial IQ: Schools and IQ Tests

Although IQ tests had their origin in the schools, they have been the source of considerable controversy essentially since their introduction. Opponents of IQ tests often argue IQ tests should be banned from schools altogether whereas proponents can hardly envision the schools without them. Many enduring issues contribute to this controversy, and we will mention only the most prominent ones. These include the following:

Mean IQ Differences among Ethnic Groups

There is considerable research that documents mean IQ differences among various ethnic groups, and this has often been the source of considerable controversy. Although the basis for these differences has not been identified, there is ample evidence the differences cannot be attributed merely to test bias (something we address in more detail in Chap. 15). Nevertheless, because mean group differences in IQ may result in differential educational treatment and placement, there continues to be the *appearance* of test bias, and this *appearance* promulgates the controversy regarding the use of IQ tests in schools (Canter, 1997). For example, because of the perception of test bias, the state of California has prohibited the use of a number of popular IQ tests for making placement decisions with certain ethnic minorities. This is not based on the psychometric properties of the IQ tests, but on public perception and legal cases. Other states have examined the same tests and concluded that the tests are not biased and supported their use with minorities.

Can IQ Be Increased?

Given the importance society places on intelligence and a desire to help children excel, it is reasonable to ask how much IQ can be improved. Hereditarians, those who see genetics as playing the primary role in influencing IQ, hold that efforts to improve it are doomed to failure. In contrast, environmentalists, who see environmental influences as primary, see IQ as being highly malleable. So who is right? In summary, the research suggests that IQ can be improved to some degree, but the improvement is rather limited. For example, adoption studies indicate that lasting gains of approximately 10–12 IQ points are the most that can be accomplished through even the most pervasive environmental interventions. The results of preschool intervention programs such as Head Start are much less impressive. These programs may result in modest increases in IQ, but even these gains are typically lost in a few years (Kranzler, 1997). These programs do have other benefits to children, however, and should not be judged only on their impact on IQ.

Do We Really Need IQ Tests in Schools?

Although public debate over the use of IQ tests in schools typically has focused on ethnic differences and the malleability of intelligence, professional educators and psychologists also have debated the usefulness of IQ tests in educational settings. Different terms have been applied to this question over the years. For example, Wigdor and Garner (1982) framed it as the *instructional validity* of IQ test results, Hilliard (1989) referred to it as the *pedagogical utility question,* and Gresham and Witt (1997) indicated it was essentially an issue of *treatment validity.* Whatever label you use, the question is "Does the use of IQ tests result in educational benefits for students?" Proponents of IQ tests highlight evidence that intelligence plays a key role in success in many areas of life, including school achievement. As an extension, they argue that information garnered from IQ tests allows educators to tailor instruction so that it meets the specific needs of their students. As a result, more students are able to succeed academically. Opponents of IQ tests argue that there is little evidence that the use of IQ tests results in any real improvement in the education of students. A contemporary debate involves the use of IQ tests in the identification of students with learning disabilities. Historically, the diagnosis of learning disabilities has been based on a discrepancy model in which students' level of achievement is compared to their overall level of intelligence. If students' achievement in reading, mathematics, or some other specific achievement area is significantly below that expected based on their IQ, they may be diagnosed as having a learning disability (actually the diagnosis of learning disabilities is more complicated than this, but this explanation is sufficient in this context). Some researchers have argued that IQs need not play a role in the diagnosis of learning disabilities and are calling for dropping the use of a discrepancy model. Recent Federal laws (e.g., Individuals with Disabilities Education Act,

Every Student Succeeds Act) no longer require such a discrepancy, but they do permit its use in diagnosing disabilities.

So what does the future hold for IQ testing in the schools? We believe that when used appropriately, IQ tests can make a significant contribution to the education of students. Braden (1997) noted that:

> ....eliminating IQ is different from eliminating intelligence. We can slay the messenger, but the message that children differ in their learning rate, efficiency, and ability to generalize knowledge to new situations (despite similar instruction) remains. (p. 244)

At the same time, we recognize that on occasion IQ tests (and other tests) have been used in inappropriate ways that are harmful to students. The key is to be an informed user of assessment results. To this end, a professional educator should have a good understanding of the topics covered in this text, including basic psychometric principles and the ethical use of test results.

Intelligence tests had their beginning in the schools. In the early 1900s, France initiated a compulsory education program. Recognizing that not all children had the cognitive abilities necessary to benefit from regular education classes, the minister of education wanted to develop special educational programs to meet the particular needs of these children. To accomplish this, he needed a way of identifying children who needed special services. *Alfred Binet* and his colleague *Theodore Simon* had been attempting to develop a measure of intelligence for some years, and the French government commissioned them to develop a test that could predict academic performance accurately. The result of their efforts was the first *Binet-Simon Scale,* released in 1905. This test contained problems arranged in the order of their difficulty and assessed a wide range of abilities. The test contained some sensory-perceptual tests, but emphasized verbal items assessing comprehension, reasoning, judgment, and short-term memory. Subsequent revisions of the Binet-Simon Scale were released in 1908 and 1911. These scales gained wide acceptance in France and were soon translated and standardized in the United States, most successfully by *Louis Terman* at Stanford University. This resulted in the *Stanford-Binet Intelligence Scale*, which has been revised numerous times (the fifth revision, *SB5,* remains in use today). Ironically, Terman's version of the Binet-Simon Scale became even more popular in France and other parts of Europe than the Binet-Simon Scale!

The development and success of the Binet-Simon Scale, and subsequently the Stanford-Binet Intelligence Scale, ushered in the era of widespread intelligence testing in the United States. Following Terman's lead, other assessment experts

> The development and success of the Binet-Simon Scale, and subsequently the Stanford-Binet, ushered in the era of widespread intelligence testing in the United States.

developed and released their own intelligence tests. Some of the tests were designed for individual administration (like the Stanford-Binet Intelligence Test) whereas others were designed for group administration. Some of these tests placed more emphasis on verbal and quantitative abilities whereas others focused more on visual-spatial and abstract problem-solving abilities. As a general rule, research has shown with considerable consistency that contemporary intelligence tests are good predictors of academic success. This is to be expected considering this was the precise purpose for which they were initially developed over 100 years ago. In addition to being good predictors of school performance, research has shown that IQs are fairly stable over time. Nevertheless, these tests have become controversial themselves as a result of the often emotional debate over the meaning of intelligence. To try and avoid this association and possible misinterpretations, many test publishers have adopted more neutral names such as *academic potential, scholastic ability, school ability, mental ability,* and simply *ability* to designate essentially the same construct.

The concept of ability testing received a major boost in the United States in the 1915–1920 period as a result of World War I. The U.S. Army needed a way to determine whether thousands of recruits were suitable for military service and to classify them for jobs in the military. The APA and one of its Presidents, Robert M. Yerkes, identified a group of experts in the field who devised a series of aptitude tests that could be administered in a group format. These tests came to be known as the Army Alpha and Army Beta—one was verbal (Alpha) and one nonverbal (Beta). As with the Binet-Simon scale, the collaboration between APA and the Army to develop group aptitude tests was driven by practical considerations and advanced intelligence testing in a number of ways. For example, it was not practical to assess thousands of recruits using individually administered aptitude/intelligence tests so the Army Alpha and Beta were designed for group administration, which established the basis for ongoing development of group aptitude/intelligence testing. Also, through these screening efforts literally millions of Americans became familiar with the concept of intelligence or ability testing. Subsequently, in 1925, the **College Entrance Examination Board (CEEB)** commissioned the development of what is now the **Scholastic Aptitude Test (SAT)**, and the first version was administered in 1926. The SAT was important because it assisted development of objective criteria for college admissions. Prior to use of the SAT, admission to colleges and universities was largely determined by legacy systems and who was willing to recommend you—not by what we consider today to be academic credentials or successes.

Intelligence testing received another boost in the next decade, the 1930s, when David Wechsler developed an intelligence test that included measures of verbal ability and nonverbal (or so-called performance) abilities on the same test. The first version of this test was the Wechsler-Bellevue I, so named because Wechsler was chief of psychology at the famous Bellevue Hospital in New York. (It was common in this era for authors to name tests after where they were employed, hence the Stanford-Binet, named after Terman's place of employment, the Hiskey-Nebraska Test of Learning Aptitude, etc.) Prior to Wechsler's test, intelligence tests typically assessed verbal or nonverbal intelligence, not both. Wechsler saw

342   9 Assessment of Intelligence

the clinical value in having an assessment that provided separate scores for verbal and nonverbal intelligence on the same person with a common standardization sample used to calculate the scores. Wechsler broke ranks with Binet whose test yielded a score for general intelligence only and other intelligence test authors who calculated IQ based on mental and chronological age. The Binet-Simon scale and many other tests computed IQs based upon age curves as well as computing IQs using the old formula of 100 × (Mental Age/Chronological Age), which produces an ordinal scale of measurement at best. It is an odd scale we know as it mixes ratio scales like chronological age with ordinal measurement (e.g., Mental Age) and manipulates them in statistically inappropriate ways (see Chap. 2). Wechsler instead created age-corrected deviation scaled scores for his tests, which are interval scales of measurement and quite likely rise to the level of equal interval scaling in most cases. With only a few psychometric improvements in their derivation, these are the same types of scores yielded by nearly every intelligence test in use today.

Wechsler subsequently developed versions of his Wechsler-Bellevue for different age groups, including preschoolers (Wechsler Preschool and Primary Scale of Intelligence, WPPSI), school aged-children (Wechsler Intelligence Scale for Children, WISC), and adults (Wechsler Adult Intelligence Scale, WAIS). These tests were revised multiple times, mostly occurring after Wechsler's death in the early 1980s, and are the most frequently used individually administered intelligence tests by school and clinical psychologists today. Until the 1980s, the various Wechsler Scales and the Stanford-Binet truly dominated the individual intelligence testing market. However, with the success of Alan and Nadeen Kaufman's Kaufman Assessment Battery for Children (KABC), published in 1983, numerous other competitors emerged over the next 20 years. Although the Wechsler Scales remain the most frequently used measure of intelligence, many clinicians also now use other individually administered intelligence tests to meet current demands of practice including most commonly such scales as the Universal Nonverbal Intelligence Test (UNIT), Reynolds Intellectual Assessment Scales (RIAS), Cognitive Assessment System (CAS), Woodcock-Johnson Tests of Cognitive Abilities (WJ), and the Differential Ability Scales (DAS).

9.2 The Use of Aptitude and Intelligence Tests in School Settings

As you can see from the previous discussion, aptitude and intelligence tests have a long history of use in the school settings. Their widespread use continues to this day, with major applications including:

- Providing alternative measures of cognitive abilities that reflect information not captured by standard achievement tests or school grades
- Helping educators tailor instruction to meet a student's unique pattern of cognitive strengths and weaknesses

- Assessing how well students are prepared to profit from school experiences
- Identifying clients who are underachieving and may need further assessment to rule out learning disabilities or other cognitive disorders, including intellectual disability, as well as disability determination
- Identifying students for gifted and talented programs
- Providing a baseline against which other client characteristics may be compared
- Helping guide students and parents with educational and vocational planning

Although we have identified the most common uses of aptitude/intelligence tests in the public schools, the list clearly is not exhaustive. Today's educators need to be familiar with these tests and their interpretations. Classroom teachers are involved to varying degrees with these applications. For example, teachers are frequently called on to administer and interpret many of the group aptitude tests for their own students. School psychologists and other professionals with specific training in administering and interpreting clinical and diagnostic tests typically administer and interpret the individual intelligence and aptitude tests. Even though they are not directly involved in administering individual intelligence tests, it is important for teachers to be familiar with these individual tests. Teachers frequently need to read and understand psychological reports describing student performances on these tests. Additionally, teachers are often on committees that plan and develop educational programs for students with disabilities based on information derived from these tests.

9.2.1   Aptitude-Achievement Discrepancies

One common assessment practice employed in schools and in clinical settings since the mid-1970s is referred to as aptitude-achievement discrepancy analysis. This involves comparing a student's performance on an aptitude test with performance on an achievement test. The basic rationale behind this practice is that normally, students'

> One common assessment practice employed in schools and in clinical settings in determining a specific learning disability is referred to as aptitude-achievement discrepancy analysis.

achievement scores should be commensurate with their aptitude scores. In other words, performance on an aptitude test (ability to learn) serves as a type of baseline from which to compare performance on an achievement test (amount of information learned) with the expectation that they will be similar. In the majority of cases, this is what you will discover when you compare aptitude and achievement scores. This is not to suggest that the scores will be identical, but that they will be similar, i.e., there will not be a statistically significant discrepancy between aptitude and achievement. If students' achievement scores are significantly higher than their aptitude scores, they are considered academic overachievers. This may be attributed to a number of factors such as strong motivation and/or an enriched learning environment. This may not necessarily be a reason for concern, but may suggest that while they perform well with the specific skills that are emphasized in school, they have more difficulty solving novel problems and generalizing their skills to new situations. These students may benefit from instructional activities that emphasize transfer of learning, generalization, and creativity (Riverside Publishing, 2002).

If students' achievement scores are significantly lower than their aptitude scores, they may be considered academic underachievers, which may be cause for concern. Academic underachievement may be the result of a number of factors. The student may not be motivated to perform well in school or may have had inadequate opportunities to learn. This could include limited exposure to instruction or an impoverished home environment. It could also reflect cultural or language differences that impact academic achievement. Naturally, a number of medical factors could also be involved, such as impaired hearing or vision, or chronic illnesses that cause children to have high rates of absenteeism or that affect them in other ways (e.g., creating fatigue, causing attentional problems, or some chronic illnesses even degrade new learning skills). Additionally, a number of psychological disorders or factors could be implicated. For example, children with an attention-deficit/hyperactivity disorder (ADHD) experience attentional problems that interfere with achievement. Emotional disorders such as depression or anxiety can be detrimental to academic performance. Finally, learning disabilities are typically characterized by significant discrepancies between aptitude and achievement. In fact, many contemporary definitions of learning disabilities incorporate a significant discrepancy between aptitude and achievement as a diagnostic criterion for the disorder. Although reliance on aptitude-achievement discrepancies to diagnose learning disabilities is currently the focus of considerable debate (e.g., Fletcher et al., 2002; Reynolds & Shaywitz, 2009), many psychologists continue to use it when evaluating and treating learning disabilities, in an effort to inform intervention and treatment plans.

In practice, there are a number of methods for determining whether there is a significant discrepancy between aptitude and achievement scores. Reynolds (1985, 1990) chaired a Federal task force that developed criteria for conducting aptitude-achievement discrepancy analyses. These included the requirement that correlation and regression analyses, which are used in predicting achievement levels and establishing statistical significance, must be based on representative samples. To help meet this requirement, many of the popular aptitude/intelligence tests are either co-normed (i.e., their normative data were based on the exact same sample of children), linked with a standardized achievement test (i.e., there is some overlap in the standardization sample so that a proportion of the sample received both tests), or specific studies are conducted to establish the mathematical relationship between an IQ and an achievement measure (e.g., Reynolds & Kamphaus, 2007). This is a desirable situation and whenever possible one should use co-normed or linked aptitude-achievement tests when performing aptitude-achievement analyses. When aptitude-achievement discrepancy analyses are conducted using tests that are not co-normed or linked, or when studies to establish the relationship between the measures are poorly constructed, the results should be interpreted with caution (Psychological Corporation, 2002; Reynolds, 1985).

Some of the popular individual intelligence tests have been co-normed with a standardized achievement test to facilitate the calculation of aptitude-achievement comparisons. These comparisons typically involve the identification of a statistically significant discrepancy between ability and achievement. Although approaches differ, the simple-difference method and predicted-achievement method are most commonly used (Psychological Corporation, 2002; Reynolds, 1985). In the brief descriptions of major aptitude/intelligence tests that follow, we will indicate which instruments have been co-normed or linked to achievement tests and which tests they have been paired with.

Before proceeding, we should note that although it is common for educators and clinicians to make ability-achievement comparisons, many testing experts criticize this practice. Critics of this approach argue that ability-achievement discrepancies can usually be attributed simply to measurement error, differences in the content covered, and variations in student attitude and motivation on the different tests (Anastasi & Urbina, 1997; Linn & Gronlund, 2000). Reynolds (1985) provides methods to overcome the psychometric problems, but non-cognitive factors are more difficult to control. Also, as we noted, there is considerable debate about relying on ability-achievement discrepancies to diagnose learning disabilities. Our position can probably be best described as middle of the road. Analysis of ability-achievement discrepancies may help identify children who are experiencing some academic problems, but they should be interpreted cautiously. That is, interpret such discrepancies in the context of other information you have about the student (e.g., observations, school grades, classroom behavior), and if there is reason for concern, pursue additional assessment.

> Although it is common for educators and clinicians to make aptitude-achievement comparisons, many testing experts criticize the practice.

9.2.2   A New Assessment Strategy for Specific Learning Disabilities: Response to Intervention (RTI)

As we noted, there has been growing criticism of reliance on aptitude-achievement discrepancies for diagnosing learning disabilities. If the profession is going to move away from the use of aptitude-achievement discrepancies, the natural question is "What is the best way to identify students with learning disabilities?" The approach that has garnered the most attention and enthusiasm in recent years is referred to as response to intervention (RTI). RTI has been defined and applied in a number of different ways, but Fuchs, Mock, Morgan, and Young (2003) provided a broad but succinct definition:

1. Students are provided with "generally effective" instruction by their classroom teacher
2. Their progress is monitored
3. Those who do not respond get something else, or something more, from a teacher or someone else

4. Again, their progress is monitored
5. Those who still do not respond either qualify for special education or for special
   education evaluation (p. 159)

Additionally, Fuchs et al. (2003) outline the perceived benefits of RTI relative to
the aptitude-achievement discrepancy approach. For example, RTI is purported to
provide help to struggling students sooner. That is, RTI will help identify students
with learning disabilities in a timely manner, not waiting for them to fail before
providing assistance. Additionally, proponents hold that RTI effectively distin-
guishes between students with actual disabilities and students that simply have not
received adequate instruction. With RTI, different instructional strategies of increasing intensity are implemented as part of the process. It is also believed by some that
RTI will result in a reduced number of students receiving special education services
with an accompanying reduction in costs.

While RTI appears to hold promise in the identification of students with learning
disabilities (LD), a number of concerns remain. The RTI process has been defined
and applied in different ways, by different professionals, in different settings (e.g.,
Christ, Burns, & Ysseldyke, 2005; Fuchs et al., 2003). For example, some professionals envision RTI as part of a behavioral problem-solving model while others
feel it should involve the consistent application of empirically validated protocols
for students with specific learning problems. Even when there is agreement on the
basic strategy (e.g., a problem-solving model), differences exist in the number of
levels (or tiers) involved, who provides the interventions, and if RTI is a precursor
to a formal assessment or if the RTI process replaces a formal assessment in identifying students with disabilities (Fuchs et al., 2003).

While some argue in favor of RTI as a stand-alone method of disability determination, many (e.g., Reynolds & Shaywitz, 2009) see it as substantially flawed as a
means of diagnosis. However, even among those who propose using it for diagnosis,
there is little agreement and many problems from a testing and measurement standpoint in determining just how to assess whether a student has responded (the R in
RTI) to an intervention or not (see Reynolds, 2009, and Reynolds & Shaywitz,
2009, for detailed discussions). This is a crucial point because different methods of
determining whether a response has occurred will identify different children as disabled! These inconsistencies present a substantial problem since they make it difficult to establish empirically the utility of the RTI process. Currently, the RTI model
has been evaluated primarily in the context of reading disabilities with children in
the early grades, and this research is generally promising. However, much less
research is available supporting the application of RTI with other learning disorders
and with older children (Feifer & Toffalo, 2007; Reynolds, 2005; Reynolds &
Shaywitz, 2009). In summary, there is much to be learned!

At this point, we view RTI as a useful process that can help identify struggling
students and ensure that they receive early attention and more intensive instructional
interventions. We also feel that students that do not respond to more intensive instruction should receive a formal psychological assessment that includes, among other
techniques, standardized cognitive tests (i.e., aptitude, achievement, and possibly
neuropsychological tests). We do not agree with those that support RTI as a

"stand-alone" process for identifying students with LD. This position excludes the use of standardized tests and essentially ignores 100 years of empirical research supporting the use of psychometric procedures in identifying and treating psychological and learning problems. A more moderate and measured approach that incorporates the best

> A more moderate and measured approach that incorporates the best of Response to Intervention (RTI) and psychometric assessment practices seems most reasonable at this time.

of RTI and psychometric assessment practices seems most reasonable at this time. If future research demonstrates that RTI can be used independently to identify and develop interventions for students with learning disabilities, we will re-evaluate our position.

9.2.3 Diagnosing Intellectual Disability

The diagnosis of intellectual disability (formerly referred to as mental retardation) is made in many settings, but the most common is in public school settings. This occurs in part because mild levels of intellectual disability, which are the most frequently occurring, might not be evident until a child begins the formal schooling process and experiences broad failures to learn at a pace near that of peers. An intellectual disability diagnosis is based on an evaluation of both

> IQs that are two or more standard deviations below the mean on an individually administered intelligence test are a necessary but insufficient condition for a diagnosis of intellectual disability; also required is a deficit in adaptive functioning determined by a formal evaluation of adaptive functioning.

IQ and adaptive functioning. According to the DSM-V, an intellectual disability diagnosis can be made when an IQ score is two or more standard deviations below the mean, and when there are deficits in adaptive functioning. The severity level of an intellectual disability diagnosis (i.e., mild, moderate, severe, or profound) is determined by a person's level of adaptive functioning across a variety of skill areas (e.g., conceptual, social, and practical life skills). The purpose of this is to help ensure that clinicians base their diagnosis on the impact made on a person's general life functioning; information gleaned from this can positively impact the development of comprehensive and effective treatment plans.

9.3 The Use of Aptitude and Intelligence Tests in Clinical Settings

Psychologists involved in various health care settings including private clinical practice use intelligence tests for many purposes, both with children and with adults. Clinical child and pediatric psychologists may use intelligence tests for all of the same reasons they are useful in schools in addition to other reasons. Clinical neuropsychologists who specialize in pediatrics will do likewise. In addition to common school applications, intelligence tests might be used in such clinical settings to evaluate a patient's suitability for certain types of psychological interventions, to monitor recovery following a brain injury, to assess the appropriateness of different levels of care when intellectual decline is seen to exist, and to determine disability status for government programs. For example, neuropsychologists in the Veterans Administration health system may assess the intelligence of a soldier exposed to a nearby explosion that caused no apparent external injury but caused a concussive injury to the brain serious enough to cause him or her to be unable to work in a competitive setting in civilian life. In medical settings, neuropsychologists may assess intelligence to identify undesirable side effects of treatments for medical conditions; e.g., leukemia treatments and other forms of chemotherapy may lessen intellectual function, as may prolonged surgery under general anesthesia requiring a heart-lung machine; long-term treatment on moderate to high doses of corticosteroids may denigrate intellectual skills. In legal settings, intellectual assessment may be used to assist in determining whether a juvenile offender is suitable to be tried as an adult. They may also be used to make recommendations regarding appropriate vocational training programs for adults with other disabilities. Intelligence tests can even be used to monitor dietary compliance in children with certain metabolic disorders such as phenylketonuria, where the failure to maintain a strict diet (in this instance, free of all phenylalanine) causes a drop in intelligence that can be measured via repeat administrations of intelligence tests! This long list represents but a few of the many purposes for which intelligence tests may be applied in clinical settings. Intelligence tests also are used in personnel selection (which is addressed in Chap. 12) and in a variety of other settings where selection or sorting as a function of intellectual level may be an issue of importance.

9.4   Major Aptitude/Intelligence Tests

9.4.1   Group Aptitude/Intelligence Tests

As with the standardized achievement tests discussed in the previous chapter, schools routinely administer standardized aptitude/intelligence tests to a large number of students. Also, as with standardized achievement tests, the most commonly used aptitude tests are also group-administered, largely due to the efficiency of these tests. In contrast to individually administered intelligence tests, teachers are often called on to help administer and interpret the results of these tests. Other large institutions such as prisons and juvenile facilities also use group intelligence or aptitude measures on a large scale, for screening and classification purposes, and these are often conducted by intake counselors or related staff. The guidelines presented in the previous chapter for administering and interpreting standardized tests apply equally well to both achievement and aptitude tests however, and even group measures need to interpreted by appropriately trained professionals. Currently, the most widely used group aptitude/intelligence tests used in school and clinical settings are produced and distributed by two publishers: Pearson and Houghton Mifflin Harcourt.

9.4.1.1 K-12 Tests

9.4.1.1.1   Otis-Lennon School Ability Test, 8th Edition (OLSAT-8)

The OLSAT-8, published by Pearson, is designed for use with students from kindergarten through Grade 12. It is designed to measure verbal processes and nonverbal processes that are related to success in school. This includes tasks such as detecting similarities and differences, defining words, following directions, recalling words/numbers, classifying, sequencing, completing analogies, and solving mathematics problems. The OLSAT-8 produces Total, Verbal, and Nonverbal School Ability Indexes (SAIs). The publishers note that although the total score is the best predictor of success in school, academic success is dependent on both verbal and nonverbal abilities, and the Verbal and Nonverbal SAIs can provide potentially important information. When administered with the Stanford Achievement Test Series, Tenth Edition (Stanford 10), one can obtain aptitude-achievement comparisons (Achievement/Ability Comparisons, or AACs).

9.4.1.1.2   Naglieri Nonverbal Ability Test, Third Edition (NNAT3)

The NNAT3, published by Pearson, is a nonverbal measure of general ability that can be used in identifying students in grades K-12 with the potential for advanced scholastic achievement; it is commonly used within schools for evaluating students for gifted and talented services. It is described by its publisher as a culturally neutral assessment of general ability that is appropriate for use in a diverse student population. It consists of 48 multiple-choice items that present various figures where the student chooses which option belongs in the corresponding matrix. It uses pictorial directions, so it can be administered using no written or spoken language.

9.4.1.1.3   Cognitive Abilities Test (CogAT), Form 7

The CogAT, distributed by Houghton Mifflin Harcourt, is designed for use with students from kindergarten through Grade 12. It provides information about the development of verbal, quantitative, and nonverbal reasoning abilities that are related to school success. Students in kindergarten through Grade 2 are given the following subtests: Picture Analogies, Picture Classification, Sentence Completion, Number Analogies, Number Series, Number Puzzles, Figure Matrices, Figure Classification, and Paper Folding. All items in these subtests are picture based. Students in grades 3–12 undergo the following subtests: Verbal Analogies, Verbal Classification, Sentence Completion, Number Analogies, Number Series, Number Puzzles, Figure Matrices, Figure Classification, and Paper Folding. Verbal, quantitative, and nonverbal battery scores are provided along with an overall composite score. The publishers encourage educators to focus on an analysis of the profile of the three battery scores rather than the overall composite score. They feel this approach provides the most useful information to teachers regarding how they can tailor instruction to meet the specific needs of students (see Special Interest Topic 9.4 for examples). Table 9.1 illustrates the organization of the major group aptitude/intelligence tests.

Special Interest Topic 9.4: Ability Profiles on the *Cog*AT

The Cognitive Abilities Test (*Cog*AT) is an aptitude test that measures the level and pattern of a student's cognitive abilities. When interpreting the *Cog*AT, the publisher encourages teachers to focus on the student's performance profile on the three CogAt batteries: Verbal Reasoning, Quantitative Reasoning, and Nonverbal Reasoning. To facilitate interpretation of scores, the profiles are classified as **A**, **B**, **C**, or **E** profiles. These are described below:

- *"A" Profiles*: Students with **A** Profiles perform at approximately the s*A*me level on verbal, quantitative, and nonverbal reasoning tasks. That is, they don't have any relative strengths or weaknesses. Approximately 1/3 of students receive this profile designation.
- *"B" Profiles*: Students with **B** Profiles have one battery score that significantly a*B*ove or *B*elow the other two scores. That is, they have either a relative strength or a relative weakness on one subtest. "B" Profiles are designated with symbols to specify the student's relative strength or weakness. For example, **B (Q+)** indicates that a student has a relative strength on the Quantitative Reasoning battery, while a **B(V−)** indicates that a student has a relative weakness on the Verbal Reasoning Battery. Approximately 40% of students have this type of profile.
- *"C" Profiles:* Students with **C** Profiles have *both* a relative strength and a relative weakness. Here, the **C** stands for *C*ontrast. For example, **C (V+N−)** indicates that a student has a relative strength in Verbal Reasoning and a relative weakness in Nonverbal Reasoning. Approximately 14% of the students demonstrate this profile type.
- *"E" Profiles:* Some students with **B** or **C** profiles demonstrate strengths and/or weaknesses that are so extreme they deserve special attention. With the *Cog*AT, score differences of 24 points or more (on a scale with a mean of 100 and SD of 16) are designated as **"E" Profiles** ("E" stands for *E*xtreme). For example, **E (Q−)** indicates that a student has an extreme or severe weakness in Quantitative Reasoning. Approximately 14% of students have this type of profile.
- *Level of Performance:* In addition to the pattern of performance, it is also important to consider the level of performance. To reflect the level of performance, the letter code is preceded by a number indicating their middle stanine score. For example, if a student received stanines of 4, 5, and 6 on the Verbal, Quantitative, and Nonverbal Reasoning batteries their middle stanine is 5. In classifying stanine scores, they classify Stanine 1 as Very Low, Stanines 2–3 as Below Average, Stanines 4–6 as Average, Stanines 7–8 as Above Average, and Stanine 9 as Very High.

As an example of a complete profile, the profile **8A** would indicate a student with relative evenly developed Verbal, Quantitative, and Nonverbal Reasoning abilities with their general level of performance in the Above Average Range.

Table 9.1 Organization of major group intelligence/aptitude tests

Aptitude test	Subtests	Composite scores
Otis-Lennon School Ability Test, 8th Edition	Verbal Comprehension Verbal Reasoning	Verbal School Ability Index
	Pictorial Reasoning Figural Reasoning Quantitative Reasoning	Nonverbal School Ability Index
		Total School Ability Index
Naglieri Nonverbal Ability Test, Third Edition	Matrices	Naglieri Ability Index
Cognitive Abilities Test (CogAT), Form 7 (Levels 5–8)	Picture Analogies Picture Classification Sentence Completion	Verbal Battery Score
	Number Analogies Number Series Number Puzzles	Quantitative Score
	Figure Matrices Figure Classification Paper Folding	Nonverbal Score
		Overall Composite Score
Cognitive Abilities Test (CogAT), Form 7 (Levels 9–18: Grades 3–12)	Verbal Classification Sentence Completion Verbal Analogies	Verbal Battery Score
	Quantitative Relations Number Series Equation Building	Quantitative Score
	Figure Classification Figure Analogies Figure Analysis	Nonverbal Score
		Overall Composite Score

9.4.1.2 Personnel and Vocational Assessment

In the personnel and vocational arena, you are likely to encounter the use of the Miller Analogies Test (MAT), an entirely verbal measure that relies heavily on vocabulary development in addition to reasoning skills. The Wonderlic Personnel Test, which is really an IQ measure from our perspective, is also used in this arena. The Wonderlic samples a broad range of reasoning and knowledge capacities in a short period of time—it is one of the few speeded measures of intelligence available and has rigid time limits set such that few make it to the last item on the test. In large institutional settings where individuals with below average intelligence levels are more common, such as in the prison system, the use of group nonverbal intelligence tests such as the Beta-IV Test is more common. The Beta-IV is a current incarnation of what was once known as the Army Beta, a nonverbal measure of intelligence devised to screen recruits in WWI.

9.4.1.3 College Admission Tests

A final type of aptitude test includes those used to make admission decisions at colleges and universities. College admission tests were specifically designed to predict academic performance in college, and although they are less clearly linked to a specific educational curriculum than most standard achievement tests, they do focus on abilities and skills that are highly academic in nature. Higher education admission decisions are typically based on a number of factors including high school GPA, letters of recommendation, personal interviews, written statements, and extracurricular activities, but in many situations, scores on standardized admission tests are a prominent factor. The two most widely used admission assessment tests are the Scholastic Assessment Test (SAT) and the American College Test (ACT). Prior to the advent of these tests, admissions decisions were highly subjective and strongly influenced by family background and status, so another purpose for the development of these instruments was to make the selection process increasingly objective.

> College admission tests were specifically designed to predict academic achievement in college.

9.4.1.3.1 Scholastic Assessment Test

The College Entrance Examination Board (CEEB), commonly referred to as the College Board, was originally formed to provide colleges and universities with a valid measure of students' academic abilities. Its efforts resulted in the development of the first Scholastic Aptitude Test in 1926. The test has undergone numerous revisions, and in 1994, the title was changed to Scholastic Assessment Test (SAT). The newest version of the SAT was administered for the first time in Spring of 2016. Changes to the SAT included a focus on areas of math that matter the most, an increased emphasis on vocabulary words more relevant to the college classroom, no more penalty for guessing, and the completion of an optional essay. Thus, the SAT currently includes a reading test, a writing and language test, a math test, and an optional essay. Students typically take the SAT in their junior or senior year of high school. The College Board also produces the Preliminary SAT (PSAT), which is designed to provide practice for the SAT. The PSAT helps students identify their academic strengths and weaknesses so they can better prepare for the SAT. Students typically take the PSAT during their sophomore or junior year. Several programs, e.g., the Duke Talent Search, also use these measures with younger students to locate highly capable students for early participation in advanced programs. More information about the SAT can be found at the College Board's website: www.collegeboard.org.

9.4.1.3.2 American College Test

The American College Testing Program was initiated in 1959 and is the major competitor of the SAT. The American College Test (ACT) is designed to assess the academic development of high school students and predict their ability to complete college work. The test includes 215 multiple-choice questions that cover four skill areas—English, Mathematics, Reading, and Science. The test publisher's description of the ACT emphasizes that it is not an aptitude or IQ test, but an achievement test that reflects the typical high school curriculum in English, mathematics, and science. To assist in developing appropriate content, every other year the ACT reviews and assesses the curriculum trends in the public schools of the USA. In addition to the four skill areas, the ACT incorporates an interest inventory that provides information that may be useful for educational and career planning. Beginning in the 2004–2005 academic year, the ACT included an optional 30-min writing test that assesses an actual sample of students' writing. More information about the ACT can be found at the ACT's website: www.act.org.

9.4.2 Individual Aptitude/Intelligence Tests

As with achievement tests, both group and individual intelligence tests are commonly used by psychologists in different areas of practice. The measures discussed below are the most commonly used individually administered tests of intelligence in various settings. We would caution our readers, however, that intelligence tests are constantly being revised and updated. We present below information on the most recent versions of these tests at the time of preparation of this textbook, but those who may use such tests need to be vigilant for revisions!

9.4.2.1 Wechsler Intelligence Scale for Children-Fifth Edition (WISC-V)

The Wechsler Intelligence Scale for Children (currently in its fifth edition) is the most popular individual test of intellectual ability for children used in clinical and school settings (e.g., Livingston, Eglsaer, Dickson, & Harvey-Livingston, 2003). The first version, known simply as the WISC, was published in 1949, and the first revision was not until 1974. Wechsler scales now are revised approximately every 10–12 years.

> Surveys of psychologists and other assessment personnel have consistently shown that the Wechsler intelligence scales are the most popular individual intelligence tests used in clinical and school settings with children and adults.

WISC-V administration time varies depending on how many of its 16 subtests are administered, but the 10 core subtests needed to calculate Primary Index Scale scores and Full Scale IQ can be administered in approximately 65 min. The WISC-V must be administered by professionals with extensive graduate-level training and supervised experience in psychological assessment. It is normed for use with children ages 6–16 years of age. For younger and older individuals, different versions of the Wechsler Scales must be used. Here are brief descriptions of the subtests of the WISC-V (Wechsler, 2014):

- *Arithmetic.* The client is presented a set of arithmetic problems to solve mentally (i.e., no pencil and paper) and answer orally. This subtest involves numerical reasoning ability, mental manipulation, concentration, and auditory memory.
- *Block Design.* The client reproduces a series of geometric patterns using red-and-white blocks. This subtest measures the ability to analyze and synthesize abstract visual stimuli, nonverbal concept formation, and perceptual organization.

- *Cancellation.* The client scans sequences of visual stimuli and marks target forms. This subtest involves processing speed, visual attention, and vigilance.
- *Coding.* The client matches and copies symbols that are associated with either objects (i.e., Coding A) or numbers (Coding B). This subtest is a measure of processing speed, short-term visual memory, mental flexibility, attention, and motivation.
- *Comprehension.* The client responds to questions presented orally involving everyday problems or social situations. This subtest is a measure of verbal comprehension and reasoning as well as the ability to apply practical information.
- *Digit Span.* The client is presented sequences of numbers orally to repeat verbatim (i.e., Digits Forward) or in reverse order (i.e., Digits Backwards). This subtest involves short-term auditory memory, attention, and on Digits Backwards, mental manipulation.
- *Figure Weights.* The client reviews pictures of shapes on a scale, with one side of the scale empty. The client then selects a choice that will balance the scale. This subtest measures quantitative and analogical fluid reasoning.
- *Information.* The client responds to questions that are presented orally involving a broad range of knowledge (e.g., science, history, geography). This subtest measures the student's general fund of knowledge.
- *Letter-Number Sequencing.* The client reads a list of letters and numbers and then recalls the letters in alphabetical order and the numbers in numerical order. This subtest involves short-term memory, sequencing, mental manipulation, and attention.
- *Matrix Reasoning.* The client examines an incomplete matrix and then selects the item that correctly completes the matrix. This subtest is a measure of fluid intelligence and is considered a largely language-free and culture-fair measure of intelligence.
- *Picture Concepts.* The client examines rows of objects and then selects objects that go together based on an underlying concept. This subtest involves nonverbal abstract reasoning and categorization.
- *Picture Span.* The client views pictures in a stimulus book, and the selects from pictures that the client saw.
- *Similarities.* Two words are presented orally to the client, who must identify how they are similar. This subtest measures verbal comprehension, reasoning, and concept formation.
- *Symbol Search.* The client scans groups of symbols and indicates whether a target symbol is present. This subtest is a measure of processing speed, visual scanning, and concentration.
- *Visual Puzzles.* The client views a completed puzzle in a stimulus book, and then reviews pictures of puzzle pieces and chooses which three pieces can be used to construct the puzzle. This subtest assesses the ability to analyze and synthesize abstract information.
- *Vocabulary.* The client is presented a series of words orally to define. This subtest is primarily a measure of word knowledge and verbal conceptualization.

Ten of these subtests are core subtests and the remaining six are supplemental. The core subtests are combined to produce five Primary Index Scores, brief descriptions of which follow (Wechsler, 2003):

- *Verbal Comprehension Index (VCI)*. The VCI includes the Similarities and Vocabulary subtests. It reflects the ability to access and apply acquired knowledge. The application of knowledge involves verbal concept formation, reasoning, and expression.
- *Visual-Spatial Index (VSI)*. The VSI includes the Block Design and Visual Puzzles subtests. It reflects an ability to evaluate visual details and understand visual-spatial relationships to construct geometric designs from a model.
- *Fluid Reasoning Index (FRI)*. The FRI includes the Matrix Reasoning and Figure Weights subtests. It reflects an ability to detect important elements among visual objects, to understand the underlying conceptual relationship, and the ability to apply the knowledge in order to identify another object that best represents the concept.
- *Working Memory Index (WMI)*. The WMI includes Digit Span and Picture Span subtests. It is a measure of verbal and visual working memory; it also measures the ability to resist proactive interference. Working memory involves attention, concentration, mental control, and reasoning.
- *Processing Speed Index (PSI)*. The PSI is a composite of the Coding and Symbol Search subtests. The PSI reflects the student's ability to quickly process nonverbal material as well as attention and visual-motor coordination.

This five-index framework is based on factor analytic and clinical research (Wechsler, 2014). Similar index scores have a rich history of clinical use and have been found to provide reliable information about the student's abilities in specific areas (Kaufman, 1994; Kaufman & Lichtenberger, 1999; Wechsler, 2003). In addition to the five Primary Index Scores, the WISC-V provides a Full Scale IQ score as well as Ancillary Index Scales (Quantitative Reasoning, Auditory Working Memory Index, Nonverbal Index, General Ability Index, and a Cognitive Proficiency Index) that can be used to further enhance the clinical utility of the WISC-V. The organization of the WISC-V is depicted in Table 9.2. To facilitate the calculation of aptitude--achievement discrepancies, the WISC-V is statistically linked to the Wechsler Individual Achievement Test-Third Edition (WIAT-III), which was described in the previous chapter on standardized achievement tests.

The WISC-V was designed for use with children between the ages of 6 and 16. For early childhood assessment, the Wechsler Preschool and Primary Scale of Intelligence-Fourth Edition (WPPSI-IV) is available and is appropriate for children between 2 years 6 months and 7 years 7 months. It shares many features in common with the WISC-V, including:

- Similar subtests (Vocabulary, Information, Block Design, Matrix Reasoning, Picture Concepts, Similarities, Comprehension, Cancellation)
- General IQ score (Full Scale IQ)
- Primary Index Scales (Verbal Comprehension, Visual-Spatial, Working Memory, Fluid Reasoning, Processing Speed)

Table 9.2 Organization of the Wechsler Intelligence Scale for Children-Fifth Edition (WISC-V)

Subtests	Primary index scores	IQ
Similarities (c)[a] Vocabulary (c)[a] Information (s) Comprehension (s)	Verbal Comprehension	Full Scale IQ
Block Design (c)[a] Visual Puzzles (c)	Visual-Spatial	
Matrix Reasoning (c)[a] Figure Weights (c)[a] Picture Concepts (s) Arithmetic (s)	Fluid Reasoning	
Digit Span (c)[a] Picture Span (c) Letter-Number Sequencing (s)	Working Memory	
Coding (c)[a] Symbol Search (c) Cancellation (s)	Processing Speed	

Note. (C) core subtest, *(S)* supplemental subtest; "a" indicates scales contributing to the WISC-V Full Scale Index

- Ancillary Index Scales (Vocabulary Acquisition, Nonverbal, General Ability, Cognitive Proficiency)

However, there are some notable differences from the WISC-V as one might expect, given differences in cognitive abilities between very young and older children. For very young children, between the ages of 2 years 6 months and 3 years 11 months, the WPPSI-IV has only 3 Primary Index Scales (Verbal Comprehension, Visual-Spatial, Working Memory) and 3 Ancillary Index Scales (Vocabulary Acquisition, Nonverbal, General Ability). For children between the ages of 4 years 0 months and 7 years 7 months, there are 5 Primary Index Scales (Verbal Comprehension, Visual-Spatial, Working Memory, Fluid Reasoning, Processing Speed) and 4 Ancillary Index Scales (Vocabulary Acquisition, Nonverbal, General Ability, Cognitive Proficiency). Different subtests from the WISC-V are included on the WPPSI-IV to provide age-appropriate assessment of ability areas (Picture Naming, Receptive Vocabulary, Picture Memory, Zoo Locations, Object Assembly, Bug Search, Animal Coding). The WPSSI has its own normative sample and the test materials and instruction are designed to be appropriate for younger children.

The Wechsler Adult Intelligence Scale-Fourth Edition (WAIS-IV) is available for assessment of intelligence in adults between the ages of 16 and 89 years of age. You will recall from the brief history of intelligence testing that we presented earlier in this chapter, David Wechsler published a new intelligence test named the Wechsler-Bellevue I (WBI) in the 1930s that incorporated a number of appealing features (e.g., Verbal and Nonverbal IQs). Wechsler revised the WBI to become the original Wechsler Adult Intelligence Scale (WAIS) which was published in 1955 and served as the model for subsequent test versions. Today, the WAIS-IV and WISC-V share many common features. The 15

WAIS-IV subtests are all contained on the WISC-V—the only non-overlapping subtest is Picture Span, which is included as a working memory measure on the WISC-V but not on the WAIS-IV. The WAIS-IV subtests are used to calculate scores for Primary Index Scales (Verbal Comprehension, Perceptual Reasoning, Working Memory, Processing Speed), a Full Scale IQ (FSIQ), and a General Ability Index (GAI). The FSIQ reflects combined performance across all of the Primary Index Scales, while the GAI reflects combined performance across Verbal Comprehension and Perceptual Reasoning Index Scales. Because the WAIS-IV is used to assess adults, it has its own normative sample, difficulty level of items on the subtests is generally increased, and the test materials and instructions are appropriate for adults.

9.4.2.2 Stanford-Binet Intelligence Scales, Fifth Edition (SB5)

As we noted, the Stanford-Binet Intelligence Test was the first intelligence test to gain widespread acceptance in the United States. While the Wechsler scales have become the most popular and widely used intelligence tests in schools and clinical practice, the Stanford-Binet scales have continued to have a strong following. The most recent edition of these scales is the

> An appealing aspect of the Stanford-Binet Intelligence Scales, Fifth Edition is the availability of an Expanded IQ scale that allows the calculations of IQs higher than 160.

Stanford-Binet Intelligence Scales, Fifth Edition (SB5), released in 2003. The SB5 is designed for use with individuals from 2 to 85 years of age. It contains ten subtests, which are combined to produce five-factor indexes (Fluid Reasoning, Knowledge, Quantitative Reasoning, Visual-Spatial Processing, and Working Memory), two domain scores (Verbal IQ and Nonverbal IQ), and a Full Scale IQ reflecting overall intellectual ability. The organization of the SB5 is depicted in Table 9.3 (Riverside Publishing, 2003). A potentially appealing aspect of the SB5 is the availability of an Extended IQ scale that allows the calculation of FSIQs higher than 160. This can be useful in the assessment of extremely gifted individuals.

9.4.2.3 Woodcock-Johnson IV (WJ IV) Tests of Cognitive Abilities

The Woodcock-Johnson IV (WJ IV) Tests of Cognitive Abilities has gained a loyal following and has some unique qualities that warrant mentioning. The battery is designed for use with individuals 2–90 years of age. The WJ IV Tests of Cognitive Abilities is based on the Cattell-Horn-Carroll (CHC) theory of cognitive abilities, which incorporates Cattell's and Horn's *Gf-Gc* theory and Carroll's three-

> The WJ IV Tests of Cognitive Abilities is based on the Cattell-Horn-Carroll (CHC) theory of cognitive abilities, which incorporates Cattell's and Horn's Gf-GC theory and Carroll's three-stratum theory.

stratum theory. Special Interest Topic 9.5 presents a brief description of the CHC Theory of Intelligence. The CHC theory provides a comprehensive model for

Table 9.3 Organization of the Stanford-Binet Intelligence Scales, 5th Edition (SB5)

Subtests	Factor scores	IQs
Verbal Fluid Reasoning (v) Nonverbal Fluid Reasoning (n)	Fluid Reasoning (FR)	Verbal IQ (composite of 5 verbal subtests)
Verbal Knowledge (v) Nonverbal Knowledge (n)	Knowledge (KN)	Nonverbal IQ (composite of 5 nonverbal subtests)
Verbal Quantitative Reasoning (v) Nonverbal Quantitative Reasoning (n)	Quantitative Reasoning (QR)	Full Scale IQ (composite of all 10 subtests)
Verbal Visual-Spatial Processing (v) Nonverbal Visual-Spatial Processing (n)	Visual-Spatial Processing (VS)	
Verbal Working Memory (v) Nonverbal Working Memory (n)	Working Memory (WM)	

Note. (v) verbal subtest, *(n)* nonverbal subtest

Special Interest Topic 9.5: The Cattell-Horn-Carroll (CHC) Theory of Intelligence and Its Impact on Contemporary Intelligence Test Batteries

Kevin S. McGrew

Woodcock-Muñoz Foundation

University of Minnesota

Each mind has its own method
(Emerson, 1841)

Since the beginning of our existence, humans have searched for order in their world. Part of this search has focused on observed individual differences between and among different individuals and groups. This search has been propelled by the only universal proven law of human behavior—the law of individual differences. People differ on many characteristics and are more different than they are alike.

1. *Psychometric theories of intelligence.* The concept of *intelligence*, which has long attracted the interests of scholars and laypersons alike, has been the result of people observing that "individuals differ from one another in their ability to understand complex ideas, to adapt effectively to the environment, to learn from experience, to engage in various forms of reasoning, to overcome obstacles by taking thought" (Neisser et al., 1996, p. 77). "Though rarely appreciated outside academe, the breakthrough in objectively gauging the nature and range of mental abilities is a pivotal development in the behavioral sciences" (Lamb, 1994, p. 386). The objective measurement of mental abilities is referred to as the *psychometric* approach

to intelligence. To date, of the different approaches to conceptualizing intelligence, the psychometric approach has been the most influential, has generated the most systematic research, and, more importantly, has facilitated the development of the reliable, valid, and practical intelligence test batteries (Neisser et al., 1996).

2. *CHC theory has narrowed the intelligence theory-testing gap.* Since the recognition of CHC theory as the first consensus-based, comprehensive, empirically validated working taxonomy (or table) of human cognitive elements (McGrew, 1997, 2005) in the early 1990s, it "has formed the foundation for most contemporary IQ tests" (Kaufman, 2009, p. 91). CHC theory has served, either explicitly or implicitly, as the main test blueprint for most all contemporary, comprehensive, individually administered intelligence test batteries (Differential Abilities Scales-2nd Edition, DAS-II; Stanford-Binet Intelligence Scale-5th Edition, SB5; Kaufman Assessment Battery for Children-2nd Edition, KABC-II; Woodcock-Johnson Battery-3rd Edition, WJ III). CHC influence can also be seen in recent revisions of the Wechsler intelligence battery trilogy (WPPSI-III; WISC-IV; WAIS-IV; Kaufman, 2009) and has been acknowledged as a design influence for entirely new batteries (e.g., the Reynolds Intellectual Assessment Scales, RIAS; Reynolds & Kamphaus, 2003).

3. *Broad strokes of CHC theory.* The birth of psychometric efforts to measure, describe, and catalog human intelligence is typically associated with Spearman (1904). The psychometric study of human intelligence has since been lengthy and extensive and recently converged on a generally accepted psychometric-based consensus taxonomy of human cognitive abilities namely, the *Cattell-Horn-Carroll (CHC)* theory of cognitive abilities (see McGrew, 2005, 2009). CHC theory is a hierarchical model of intelligence that combines the Cattell-Horn Gf-Gc (Horn, 1989) and Carroll (1993) tri-stratum models of cognitive abilities (see McGrew, 2005, 2009; also see Kaufman, 2009). CHC theory is a three-stratum model that includes over 70 narrow abilities at stratum I, eight broad abilities at stratum II, and an overall g (general intelligence) ability at the apex of the hierarchy (stratum III).[1] The model is the result of decades of psychometric research by many intelligence scholars, primarily via factor analytic (structural evidence)

---

[1] John Horn (no g) and John Carroll (g exists) where in sharp disagreement regarding the validity of the construct of g. Horn felt it was a statistical artifact of the positive manifold of correlation matrices while Carroll believed it did represent some form of essential mental energy. This author had the privilege to participate in small private meetings (during the development of the WJ III and SB5 intelligence test batteries) with both Horn and Carroll and can attest to many "spirited" exchanges regarding the "g or not to g" disagreement between these two giants in the field of human intelligence.

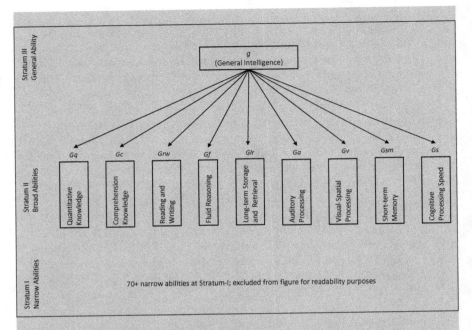

Fig. 9.2 Cattell-Horn-Carroll (CHC) hierarchical model of intelligence

research. Support for the CHC structure is also based on neurocognitive, heritability (genetic), developmental, and prediction of differential outcomes evidence (Horn & Noll, 1997). His model is depicted in Fig. 9.2.

4. *Broad CHC ability domains.* Nine broad (stratum II) CHC ability domains are generally accepted as the hallmark feature of CHC theory, of which typically five to seven broad abilities are represented by tests in contemporary intelligence batteries.[2] Brief definitions of the nine primary broad CHC abilities follow below:[3]

(a) *Fluid reasoning (Gf)*: The use of deliberate and controlled mental operations to solve novel problems that cannot be performed automatically. Inductive and deductive reasoning and logic are generally con-

---

[2] Other broad domains that are relatively new to the CHC model, or which have not been deemed relevant to practical intelligence batteries, include decision and reaction speed (Gt), general (domain-specific) knowledge (Gkn), tactile abilities (Gh), kinesthetic abilities (Gk), olfactory abilities (Go), psychomotor abilities (Gp), and psychomotor speed (Gps). See McGrew (2009).

[3] Space does not allow for a list (with definitions) of the 70+ narrow abilities that are subsumed under the broad CHC domains. See McGrew (2005) for the names and definitions of the various narrow CHC abilities.

sidered the hallmark indicators of Gf. Gf has been linked to the ability to handle greater degrees of cognitive complexity which is typically defined as more efficiency in processing a wider and diverse array of elementary cognitive processes (in active working memory) during cognitive performance.

(b) *Comprehension-knowledge (Gc)*: A person's breadth and depth of acquired knowledge of the language, information and concepts of a culture, and/or the application of this knowledge. Gc is primarily a store of verbal or language-based declarative (knowing *what*) and procedural (knowing *how*) knowledge acquired through the investment of other abilities during formal and informal educational and general life experiences.

(c) *Short-term memory (Gsm):* The ability to apprehend and maintain awareness of a limited number of elements of information in the immediate situation (events that occurred in the last minute or so). A limited resource-capacity system that loses information quickly through the decay of memory traces, unless an individual activates other cognitive resources to maintain the information in immediate awareness.

(d) *Visual-spatial processing (Gv)*: The ability to generate, store, retrieve, and transform visual images and sensations in the "mind's eye." Gv abilities are typically measured by tasks (viz., figural or geometric stimuli) that require the perception and transformation of visual shapes, forms, or images or tasks that require maintaining spatial orientation with regard to objects that may change or move through space.

(e) *Auditory processing (Ga)*: Abilities that depend on sound as input and on the functioning of hearing. A key characteristic of Ga is the extent an individual can cognitively control (i.e., handle the competition between signal and noise) the perception of auditory information. The Ga domain circumscribes a wide range of abilities involved in the interpretation and organization of sounds, such as discriminating patterns in sounds and musical structure (often under background noise and/or distorting conditions) and the ability to analyze, manipulate, comprehend and synthesize sound elements, groups of sounds, or sound patterns.

(f) *Long-term storage and retrieval (Glr)*: The ability to store and consolidate new information in long-term memory and later fluently retrieve the stored information (e.g., concepts, ideas, items, names) through association. Memory consolidation and retrieval can be measured in terms of information stored for minutes, hours, weeks, or longer. Some Glr narrow abilities have been prominent in creativity research (e.g., production, ideational fluency, or associative fluency).

(g) *Cognitive processing speed (Gs)*: The ability to automatically and fluently perform relatively easy or over-learned elementary cognitive tasks, especially when high mental efficiency (i.e., attention and focused concentration) is required over a sustained period of time. Typically measured by timed tasks.

(h) *Reading and writing (Grw)*: The breadth and depth of a person's acquired store of declarative and procedural reading and writing skills and knowledge. Grw includes both basic skills (e.g., reading and spelling of single words) and the ability to read and write complex connected discourse (e.g., reading comprehension and the ability to write a story).

(i) *Quantitative knowledge (Gq)*: The breadth and depth of a person's acquired store of declarative and procedural quantitative or numerical knowledge. Gq is largely acquired through the investment of other abilities primarily during formal educational experiences. Gq represents an individual's store of acquired mathematical knowledge, not reasoning with this knowledge.

5. *Concluding comments and caveats:* The connection between intelligence theorists and applied test developers has resulted in a small revolution in the field of applied intelligence testing. Most of all comprehensive intelligence batteries implicitly or explicitly acknowledge the role of the CHC framework during test design. Yet, CHC theory should not be viewed as static. One should not succumb to the "hardening of the CHC categories" (McGrew, 2005) as new factor analytic research has already suggested possible modifications and revisions in the model. More importantly, a number of contemporary researchers are examining causal or dynamic CHC models (i.e., causal relations between CHC broad abilities), models that place the CHC structure within the framework of information-processing theories, and research that seeks to understand the relations between CHC abilities and neurocognitive constructs and functioning. The CHC human ability taxonomy, although relatively new on the psychometric scene, should be considered just one major landmark accomplishment on the road to mapping the complete terrain of human cognitive performance. CHC has provided researchers and intelligence testing practitioners with a common nomenclature around which to frame and investigate research questions and issues. At this time, the CHC taxonomy should be considered the first accurate starting point from which scholars of human intelligence can finally ground their research with an eye on refining, extending, and/or fundamentally revising the CHC framework to eventually better describe and explain human cognitive performance.

assessing a broad range of cognitive abilities, and many clinicians like the WJ IV because it allows coverage of this broad range of abilities. The organization of the WJ IV Tests of Cognitive Abilities is depicted in Table 9.4 (Riverside Publishing, 2003). The WJ IV Tests of Cognitive Abilities is co-normed with the WJ IV Tests of Achievement described in the chapter on standardized achievement tests.

Table 9.4 Organization of the Woodcock-Johnson IV (WJ IV) Tests of Cognitive Abilities

Subtests	CHC factor scores	IQ
Oral Vocabulary[a] General Information	Comprehension/Knowledge (Gc)	General Intellectual Ability (GIA) score
Number Series[a] Concept Formation Analysis-Synthesis	Fluid Reasoning (Gf)	
Verbal Attention[a] Numbers Reversed Object-Number Sequencing	Short-Term Working Memory (Gwm)	
Letter-Pattern Matching[a] Pair Cancellation	Cognitive Processing Speed (Gs)	
Phonological Processing[a] Non-word Repetition	Auditory Processing (Ga)	
Story Recall[a] Visual-Auditory Learning	Long-Term Retrieval (Glr)	
Visualization[a] Picture Recognition	Visual Processing (Gv)	

[a]Denotes subtest is a part of General Intellectual Ability (GIA) score

9.4.2.4 Reynolds Intellectual Assessment Scales, Second Edition (RIAS-2)

The Reynolds Intellectual Assessment Scales, Second Edition (RIAS-2; Reynolds & Kamphaus, 2015), is a relative newcomer to the clinician's collection of intelligence tests rapidly growing in popularity in schools and in clinical settings. It is designed for use with individuals between 3 and 94 years of age and incorporates a co-normed supplemental memory scale, as well as a processing speed scale. One particularly desirable aspect of the RIAS is the ability to obtain a reliable, valid measure of intellectual ability that incorporates both verbal and nonverbal abilities in a relatively brief period (i.e., 20–25 min). Most other tests that assess verbal and nonverbal cognitive abilities require considerably more time. The supplemental memory tests require about 10 min for administration, and the processing speed subtests require about 5 min for administration. Thus, a clinician can assess both intelligence, memory, and processing speed in approximately 35–45 min. The organization of the RIAS-2 is depicted in Table 9.5.

> One particularly desirable aspect of the Reynolds Intellectual Assessment Scales Second Edition (RIAS-2) is the ability to obtain a reliable, valid measure of intellectual ability that incorporates both verbal and nonverbal abilities in a relatively brief period (20–25 min).

Table 9.5 Organization of the Reynolds Intellectual Assessment Scales, Second Edition

Subtests	Factor scores	IQs
Verbal Reasoning	Verbal Intelligence Index (VIX)	Composite Intelligence Index (CIX)
Guess What		
Odd-Item Out	Nonverbal Intelligence Index (NIX)	
What's Missing		
Verbal Memory	Composite Memory Index (CMX)	
Nonverbal Memory		
Speeded Naming Task	Speeded Processing Index (SPI)	
Speeded Picture Search		

9.5   Selecting Aptitude/Intelligence Tests

A natural question at this point is "Which of these tests should I use?" There are numerous factors to consider when selecting an aptitude or intelligence test. An initial consideration involves the decision to use a group or individual test. As is the case with standardized achievement tests, group apti-

> When selecting an intelligence or aptitude test, it is important to consider factors such as how the information will be used and how much time is available for testing.

tude tests are used almost exclusively for mass testing applications because of their efficiency. Even a relatively brief individual intelligence test typically requires approximately 20–30 min per person to administer. Additionally, assessment professionals with special training in test administration are needed to administer these individual tests. A limited amount of time to devote to testing and a limited number of assessment personnel combine to make it impractical to administer individual tests to large numbers of individuals, especially when screening procedures can be applied to cull individuals for more expensive, time-consuming, comprehensive assessment procedures. However, some situations demand the use of an individual intelligence test. This is often the case when disability determination is an issue or more complex diagnostic questions are to be addressed.

The first question to ask in deciding what measure to use is "What information do I really need about this person's level of intellectual function?" The answer to this question is usually based on the reason for the assessment or the "referral question." If the reason for the assessment is to obtain a general estimate of IQ for personnel screening and job selection from a large pool of job applicants, then information provided by a brief group-administered test is usually sufficient. If the reason for assessment is to determine a diagnosis of intellectual disability, then a more comprehensive assessment with an individually administered IQ test that provides more detailed information is usually warranted. The guiding principle is to select a test that will provide information needed to directly answer the referral question in the most efficient and cost-effective manner.

When selecting an intelligence or aptitude test, it is also important to consider how the information will be used. Are you primarily interested in predicting performance in school or a vocational training program, or do you need a test that provides multiple scores reflecting different sets of cognitive abilities? As we noted, as a general rule intelligence tests are good at predicting academic success. Therefore, if you are simply interested in predicting school success, practically any of these tests will meet your needs. If you want to identify the cognitive strengths and weaknesses of your students, you should look at the type of scores provided by the different test batteries and select one that meets your needs from either a theoretical or practical perspective. For example, a clinician who has embraced the Cattell-Horn-Carroll (CHC) theory of cognitive abilities would be well served using the RIAS-2, SB5, or the Woodcock-Johnson IV Tests of Cognitive Abilities because they are based to different degrees on that model of cognitive abilities. The key is to select a test that provides the specific type of information you need for your application. Look at the type of factor and intelligence scores the test produces and select a test that provides meaningful and practical information for your application.

If you are interested in making aptitude-achievement comparisons, ideally you should select an aptitude test that is co-normed with an achievement test that also meets your specific needs. All of the major group aptitude tests we discussed are co-normed or linked to a major group achievement test. When selecting a combination aptitude-achievement battery, you should examine both the achievement test and the aptitude test to determine which set best meets your specific assessment needs. In reference to the individual intelligence tests we discussed, only the WISC-V and WJ IV Tests of Cognitive Abilities have been co-normed with or linked to an individual achievement test battery. While it is optimal to use co-normed instruments when aptitude-achievement comparisons are important, in actual practice many clinicians rely on aptitude and achievement tests that are not co-normed or linked. In this situation, it is important that the norms for both tests be based on samples that are as nearly identical as possible. For example, both tests should be normed on samples with similar characteristics (e.g., age, race, geographic region) and obtained at approximately the same time (Reynolds, 1990).

Another important question involves the population you will use the test with. For example, if you will be working with children with speech, language, or hearing impairments or diverse cultural/language backgrounds, you may want to select a test that emphasizes nonverbal abilities and minimizes cultural influences. Finally, when selecting any test, you want to examine the psychometric properties of the test. You should select a test that produces reliable scores and has been validated for your specific purposes. All of the aptitude/intelligence tests we have discussed have good psychometric properties, but it is the test user's responsibility to ensure that the selected test has been validated for the intended purposes.

9.6   Understanding the Report of an Intellectual Assessment

Once testing is completed, the examiner will often present the results of the examination in a formal psychological report that is sent to the referral source. The format of these reports varies based on a number of different factors. For example, a report for an assessment conducted to determine the presence of a learning disability in a fourth-grade student will most likely include recommendations about classroom teaching strategies to help the child learn. A forensic mental health evaluation completed during the sentencing phase of a capital case to help decide between a sentence of life without parole or the death penalty will devote substantial time to discussing risk factors and protective factors that affected the defendant's life course and should be considered when sentencing. Some reports may be quite long and others relatively brief. Despite these differences, psychological reports do share some common features. For example, most contain sections for client background information, reporting of test results, interpretation of test results, diagnostic impressions, and specific recommendations.

With the advancement of technology, computers are playing a greater role in the reporting process. Special Interest Topic 9.6 presents an unedited computer--generated report of the intellectual assessment of a fictional client, John Smith, who is 68 years old and referred for a psychological evaluation because of memory complaints. Typically, you will not encounter an unedited computer-generated report. Such reports are, however, used by a school, clinical, and other psychologists as the foundation for their own individualized reporting on clients. We thought it would be instructive for you to have the opportunity to read such a report in its raw state.

Special Interest Topic 9.6: Example of a Computerized Report of an Intellectual Assessment of an Adult

RIAS-2 Score Report

by Cecil R. Reynolds, PhD, and Randy W. Kamphaus, PhD

Client name: John Smith (Fictitious Client)

Client ID: JS

Gender: Male

Age: 68:1

Ethnicity: Caucasian

Grade/highest level of education: 16 years

Test date: 02/29/2016

Date of birth: 01/09/1948

Examiner: P Smith

Reason for referral: Memory loss

Referral source: Dr Jennings

This report is intended for use by qualified professionals only and is not to be shared with the examinee or any other unqualified persons.

Background Information

John Smith is a 68-year-old man. John has completed 16 years of education and is currently not attending school.

Caveat and Descriptive Text

The test scores, descriptions of performance, and other interpretive information provided in this computer report are predicated on the following assumptions. First, it is assumed that the various subtests were administered and scored correctly in adherence with the general and specific administration and scoring guidelines provided in Chap. 2 of the RIAS-2/RIST-2 Professional Manual (Reynolds & Kamphaus, 2015). Second, it also is assumed that the examinee was determined to be appropriately eligible for testing by the examiner according to the guidelines for testing eligibility provided in Chap. 2 of the RIAS-2 Professional Manual and that the examiner was appropriately qualified to administer and score the RIAS-2/RIST-2. This report is intended for evaluation, transmission to, and use only by individuals appropriately qualified and credentialed to interpret the RIAS-2/RIST-2 under the laws and regulations of their local jurisdiction and meeting the guidelines for use of the RIAS-2/RIST-2 as stated in the RIAS-2 Professional Manual (Reynolds & Kamphaus, 2015; see Chap. 2).

John was administered the Reynolds Intellectual Assessment Scales--Second Edition (RIAS-2). The RIAS-2 is an individually administered measure of intellectual functioning normed for individuals between the ages of 3 and 94 years. The RIAS-2 contains several individual tests of intellectual problem-solving and reasoning ability that are combined to form a Verbal Intelligence Index (VIX) and a Nonverbal Intelligence Index (NIX). The subtests that compose the VIX assess verbal reasoning ability along with the ability to access and apply prior learning in solving language-related tasks. Although labeled the Verbal Intelligence Index, the VIX also is a reasonable approximation of crystallized intelligence. The NIX comprises subtests that assess nonverbal reasoning and spatial ability. Although labeled the Nonverbal Intelligence Index, the NIX also provides a reasonable approximation of fluid intelligence. These two indexes of intellectual functioning are then combined to form an overall Composite Intelligence Index (CIX). By combining the VIX and NIX to form the CIX, a stronger, more reliable assessment of general intelligence (g) is obtained. The CIX measures the two most important aspects of general intelligence according to widely accepted theories and research findings: reasoning or fluid abilities and verbal or crystallized abilities. Each of these indexes is expressed as an age-corrected standard score that is scaled to a mean of 100 and a standard deviation of 15. These scores are essentially normally distributed and can be converted to a variety of other metrics if desired.

The RIAS-2 also contains subtests designed to assess verbal memory and nonverbal memory. Depending on the age of the individual being evaluated, the verbal memory subtest consists of a series of sentences, age-appropriate stories, or both, read aloud to the examinee. The examinee is then asked to recall these sentences or stories as precisely as possible. The nonverbal memory subtest consists of the presentation of pictures of various objects or abstract designs for a period of 5 s. The examinee is then shown a page containing six similar objects or figures and must discern which object or figure was previously shown. The scores from the verbal memory and nonverbal memory subtests are combined to form a Composite Memory Index (CMX), which provides a reliable assessment of working memory and also may provide indications as to whether or not a more detailed assessment of memory functions may be required. In addition, the high reliability of the verbal and nonverbal memory subtests allows them to be compared directly to each other.

Moreover, the RIAS-2 contains subtests designed to assess verbal and nonverbal speeded processing. Depending on the age of the individual being evaluated, the speeded naming task (i.e., verbal speeded processing) consists of rapidly naming a series of common objects (i.e., dogs, cats, tree, cars) or geometric shapes (i.e., triangle, circle, square, star). Also depending on the age of the individual being evaluated, the speeded picture search subtest (i.e., nonverbal speeded processing) consists of the ability to find target faces in an array of faces or finding target pictures (i.e., houses and geometric designs) in an array of similar pictures. The scores from the speeded naming and speeded picture search subtests are combined to form a Speeded Processing Index (SPI), which provides a reliable assessment of speeded processing and also may provide indications as to whether or not a more detailed assessment of speeded processing may be required. In addition, the high reliability of the verbal and nonverbal speeded processing subtests allows them to be compared directly to each other.

For reasons described in the RIAS-2/RIST-2 Professional Manual (Reynolds & Kamphaus, 2015), it is recommended that the RIAS-2 subtests be assigned to the indices described above (e.g., VIX, NIX, CIX, CMX, and SPI). For those who do not wish to consider the memory or speeded processing scales as a separate entity and prefer to apportion the subtests strictly according to verbal and nonverbal domains, the RIAS-2 subtests can be combined to form a Total Verbal Battery (TVB) score and a Total Nonverbal Battery (TNB) score. The subtests that compose the Total Verbal Battery score assess verbal reasoning ability, verbal memory, verbal speeded processing, and the ability to access and apply prior learning in solving language-- related tasks. Although labeled the Total Verbal Battery score, the TVB also is a reasonable approximation of crystallized intelligence. The TNB comprises subtests that assess nonverbal reasoning, spatial ability, nonverbal memory, and nonverbal speeded processing. Although labeled the Total Nonverbal Battery score, the TNB also provides a reasonable approximation of fluid intelligence. These two indexes of intellectual functioning are then combined to form an overall Total Test Battery (TTB) score. By combining the TVB and the TNB to form the TTB, a stronger, more reliable assessment of general intelligence (g) is obtained. The TTB measures the two most important aspects of general intelligence according to recent theories and research findings: reasoning, or fluid, abilities and verbal, or crystallized, abilities. Each of these scores is expressed as an age-corrected standard score that is scaled to a mean of 100 and a standard deviation of 15. These scores are essentially normally distributed and can be converted to a variety of other metrics if desired.

Composite Norm-Referenced Interpretations

On testing with the RIAS-2, John earned a Composite Intelligence Index or CIX of 144. On the RIAS-2, this level of performance falls within the range of scores designated as significantly above average and exceeds the performance of more than 99% of individuals at John's age. The chances are 95 out of 100 that John's true CIX falls within the range of scores from 139 to 147.

John earned a Verbal Intelligence Index (VIX) of 136, which falls within the significantly above average range of verbal intelligence skills and exceeds the performance of more than 99% of individuals John's age. The chances are 95 out of 100 that John's true VIX falls within the range of scores from 131 to 139.

John earned a Nonverbal Intelligence Index (NIX) of 142, which falls within the significantly above average range of nonverbal intelligence skills and exceeds the performance of more than 99% of individuals John's age. The chances are 95 out of 100 that John's true NIX falls within the range of scores from 135 to 146.

John earned a Composite Memory Index (CMX) of 99, which falls within the average range of working memory skills. This exceeds the performance of 47% of individuals John's age. The chances are 95 out of 100 that John's true CMX falls within the range of scores from 93 to 105.

John earned a Speeded Processing Index (SPI) of 87, which falls within the below average range of speeded processing skills. This exceeds the performance of 19% of individuals John's age. The chances are 95 out of 100 that John's true SPI falls within the range of scores from 84 to 90 (Fig. 9.3).

On testing with the RIAS-2, John earned a Total Test Battery or TTB score of 125. This level of performance on the RIAS-2 falls within the range of scores designated as moderately above average and exceeds the performance of 95% of individuals at John's age. The chances are 95 out of 100 that John's true TTB falls within the range of scores from 121 to 128.

John's Total Verbal Battery (TVB) score of 123 falls within the range of scores designated as moderately above average and exceeds the performance of 94% of individuals his age. The chances are 95 out of 100 that John's true TVB falls within the range of scores from 118 to 127.

John's Total Nonverbal Battery (TNB) score of 120 falls within the range of scores designated as moderately above average and exceeds the performance of 91% of individuals his age. The chances are 95 out of 100 that John's true TNB falls within the range of scores from 115 to 124.

Subtest Norm-Referenced Interpretations

The Guess What subtest measures vocabulary knowledge in combination with reasoning skills that are predicated on language development and acquired knowledge. On testing with the RIAS-2, John earned a T score of 77 on Guess What.

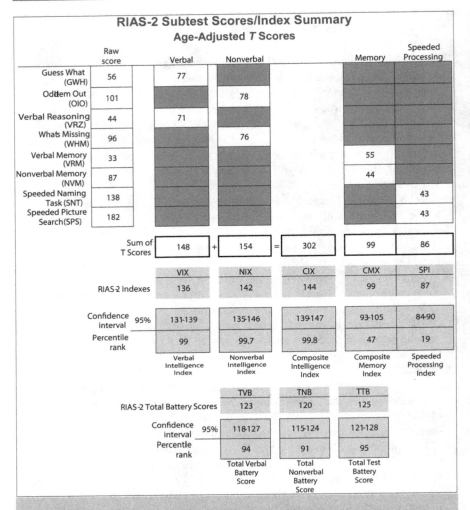

Fig. 9.3 RIAS-2 subtest scores, index scores, and age-adjusted *T* scores

Odd-Item Out measures analytical reasoning abilities within the nonverbal domain. On testing with the RIAS-2, John earned a T score of 78 on Odd-Item Out.

Verbal Reasoning measures analytical reasoning abilities within the verbal domain. English vocabulary knowledge is also required. On testing with the RIAS-2, John earned a *T* score of 71 on Verbal Reasoning.

What's Missing measures spatial and visualization abilities. On testing with the RIAS-2, John earned a *T* score of 76 on What's Missing.

Verbal Memory measures the ability to encode, briefly store, and recall information in the verbal domain. English vocabulary knowledge also is required. On testing with the RIAS-2, John earned a *T* score of 55 on Verbal Memory.

Nonverbal Memory measures the ability to encode, briefly store, and recall information in the nonverbal and spatial domains. On testing with the RIAS-2, John earned a T score of 44 on Nonverbal Memory.

Speeded Naming measures the ability to differentiate and recognize simple stimuli verbally under time constraints. On testing with the RIAS-2, John earned a T score of 43 on the Speeded Naming Task.

Speeded Picture Search measures the ability to differentiate simple stimuli visually under time constraints. On testing with the RIAS-2, John earned a T score of 43 on Speeded Picture Search.

Discrepancy Norm-Referenced Interpretations

John's VIX of 136 and NIX of 142 are consistent with his CIX noted previously and indicate that John's verbal and nonverbal abilities are similarly developed. When compared to John's measured level of general intelligence as reflected in John's CIX, it can be seen that his CMX falls significantly below his CIX. This result indicates that John is able to engage in intellectual problem-solving and general reasoning tasks at a level that significantly exceeds his ability to use immediate recall and working memory functions. The magnitude of the difference seen in this instance may take on special diagnostic significance due to its relative infrequency in the general population. A difference between CIX and CMX of this magnitude occurs in less than 1% of the population (Fig. 9.4).

Discrepancy Score	Score Difference	Statistically Significant?	Prevalence in Standardization Sample
VIX < NIX	6	no	>20%
CIX > CMX	45	yes (.01)	<= 1%
VRM > NVM	11	yes (.05)	>20%
CIX > SPI	57	yes (.01)	<= 1%
SNT = SPS	0	no	>20%
TVB > TNB	3	no	>20%

VIX is the Verbal Intelligence Index, NIX is the Nonverbal Intelligence Index, CIX is the Composite Intelligence Index, CMX is the Composite Memory Index, VRM is the Verbal Memory Subtest, NVM is the Nonverbal Memory Subtest, CIX is the Composite Intellige nce Index, SPI is the Speeded Processing Index, SNT is the Speeded Naming Task, SPS is the Speeded Picture Search Subtest, TVB is the Total Verbal Battery Index, and TNB is the Total Nonverbal Battery Index.

Fig. 9.4 RIAS-2 discrepancy score summary table

Within the subtests making up the CMX, John's performance in the verbal memory domain significantly exceeded his level of performance within the nonverbal memory domain. This difference is reliable and indicates that John functions at a significantly higher level when asked to recall or engage in working memory tasks that are easily adapted to verbal linguistic strategies, as opposed to tasks relying on visual-spatial cues and other nonverbal memory features. Although most likely representing a real difference in John's abilities in these two areas, the magnitude of this difference is relatively common, occurring in more than 20% of the population at John's age.

Within the subtests making up the SPI, John's performance was substantially equivalent on verbal and nonverbal speeded processing tasks. This result indicates that John functions about equally well when called on to differentiate simple stimuli verbally or nonverbally under time constraints.

John's TVB of 123 and TNB of 120 are consistent with his TTB noted previously and indicate that John's verbal and nonverbal abilities are similarly developed (Figs. 9.5 and 9.6).

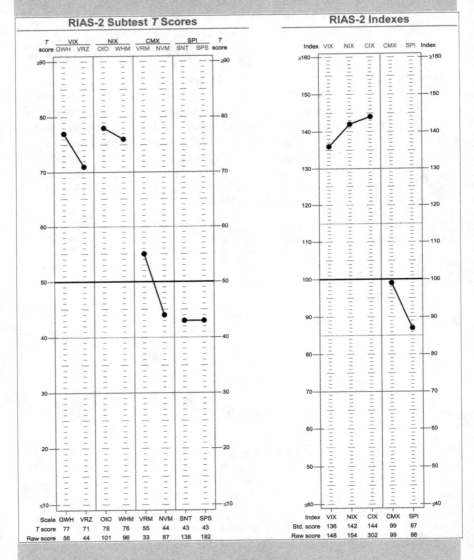

Fig. 9.5 RIAS-2 profiles

Fig. 9.6 RIAS-2 total battery profiles

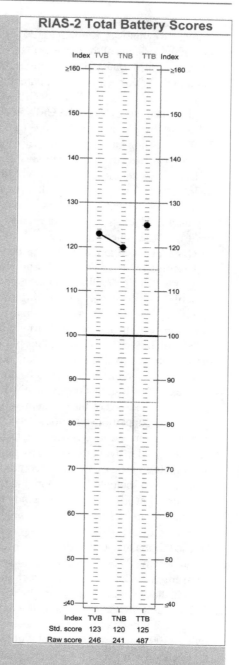

If interested in comparing the TTB and CIX scores, the TTB and CMX scores, or the TTB and SPI scores, it is better to compare the CIX and CMX or the CIX and SPI directly. As noted in the RIAS-2/RIST-2 Professional

Manual (Reynolds & Kamphaus, 2015), the TTB is simply a reflection of the sum of the T scores of the subtests that compose the CIX, CMX, and SPI. Thus, it is more appropriate to make a direct comparison of the CMX and CIX or the SPI and the CIX because any apparent discrepancy between the TTB and the CIX or the TTB and the CMX or SPI will in fact be a reflection of discrepancies between the CIX and the CMX or between the CIX and the SPI, so these values are best examined directly. To compare the CMX, SPI, or CIX to the TTB may exaggerate some differences inappropriately.

General Interpretive Caveats

Examiners should be familiar with the cultural and linguistic background of John (which may radically alter the suggestions contained herein) and be certain to consider these factors before arriving at a final decision regarding any diagnosis, classification, or related decision and before making any form of further assessment or treatment recommendations.

General Feedback and Recommendations

Composite Score Feedback and Recommendations

John's SPI of 87 falls within the below average range and indicates mild difficulties with speeded processing of verbal and visual/spatial information relative to others John's age. This may cause mild problems and some frustration in the acquisition of new learning or academic or training material when faced with the specialized demands placed by learning under time constraints, but is unlikely to disturb most functions of day-to-day living. Test taking under timed conditions may also be adversely affected and John may benefit from extended testing times wherein John can demonstrate more accurately what he has learned or his problem-solving skills under untimed conditions.

Various adaptations are often recommended for individuals who perform in this range on speeded processing tasks. For example, day-to-day tasks may be redesigned to avoid the necessity of decision making under speeded conditions including tasks in work, community, and home environments. Other adaptations of potential benefit include vocational, academic, and social planning aimed at lessening the demands for accurate speeded decisions. When adaptations are not possible, technological aids (e.g., digital calculators, digital cueing of explicit decision rules related to work performances, etc.) may be used to make speeded decisions necessary for daily functioning. Test taking under timed conditions may also be adversely affected and John may benefit from extended testing times wherein John can demonstrate more accurately what he has learned or his problem-solving skills under untimed conditions.

Discrepancy Feedback and Recommendations

The magnitude of discrepancy between John's CIX score of 144 and CMX score of 99 is relatively unusual within the normative population, suggesting that general intellectual skills are relatively more intact than memory function. Prognostically, this finding suggests that overall functioning can improve if the effects of memory difficulties can be mitigated.

The use of multiple modalities is typically recommended to increase recall, such as routinely pairing visual/spatial stimuli with verbal stimuli in order to enhance recall. The use of lists, oral language and written language directions, signs, and verbal reminders may be especially helpful. Yet another example would involve adding verbal instructions to directions given via a map, graph, or picture. Frequent verbal and visual/spatial directions and reminders are recommended in most circumstances where recall needs to be enhanced.

The use of tools such as personal digital devices (e.g., smartphones, tablet computers, personal computers, or other technologies) or hard copies of reminders may all be used to mitigate the effects of verbal memory problems.

The magnitude of discrepancy between John's CIX score of 144 and SPI score of 87 is relatively unusual within the normative population, suggesting that general intellectual skills are relatively more intact than speeded processing of information. Prognostically, this finding suggests that overall functioning may be improved when speeded processing of information is not required by school, community, or work demands. Various adaptations are often recommended for individuals who perform in this range on speeded processing tasks. For example, day-to-day tasks may be redesigned to avoid the necessity of decision making under speeded conditions including tasks in work, community, and home environments. Other adaptations of potential benefit include vocational, academic, and social planning aimed at lessening the demands for accurate speeded decisions. When adaptations are not possible, technological aids (e.g., digital calculators, digital cueing of explicit decision rules related to work performances, etc.) may be used to make speeded decisions necessary for daily functioning. Test taking under timed conditions may also be adversely affected and John may benefit from extended testing times wherein John can demonstrate more accurately what he has learned or his problem-solving skills under untimed conditions.

Recommendations for Additional Testing

John's CIX score of 144 is significantly higher than his CMX score of 99. As such, follow-up evaluation may be warranted. Additional testing with the Child and Adolescent Memory Profile (Sherman & Brooks, 2015), TOMAL-2 (Reynolds & Voress, 2007), or similar measure is suggested to determine if John's memory difficulties are modality-specific in that it is localized to either verbal or visual/spatial information, or if the impairment exists in short-term acquisition or long-term retrieval of previously learned material. A thorough history, supplemented by questions about qualitative aspects of memory, should be used as well. It also may be helpful to inquire about the individual's perception of memory problems and have him describe the onset, duration, and environmental contexts that are affected.

John's CIX score of 144 is significantly higher than his SPI score of 87. As such, follow-up evaluation may be warranted. Additional testing is suggested to determine if John's speeded processing of information difficulties is modality-specific in that it is localized to either verbal or nonverbal information, or if the impairment is exacerbated by other problems, such as memory. A thorough history, supplemented by questions about qualitative aspects of daily functioning under speeded decision-making conditions should be used as well. It also may be helpful to inquire about the individual's perception of speeded information-processing problems and have him describe the onset, duration, and environmental contexts that are affected (Fig. 9.7).

Subtest	Raw score	T score (Mean = 50, SD = 10)	z score (Mean = 0, SD = 1)	Scaled score (Mean = 10, SD = 3)
GWH	56	77	2.70	18
OIO	101	78	2.80	18
VRZ	44	71	2.10	16
WHM	96	76	2.60	18
VRM	33	55	0.50	12
NVM	87	44	-0.60	8
SNT	138	43	-0.70	8
SPS	182	43	-0.70	8

Index	Sum of subtest T scores	T score (Mean = 50, SD = 10)	z score (Mean = 0, SD = 1)	Index score (Mean = 100, SD = 15)	Percentile rank	95% confidence interval	90% confidence interval	NCE (Mean = 50, SD = 21.06)	Stanine (Mean = 5, SD = 2)
VIX	148	74	2.40	136	99	131-139	132-139	>99	9
NIX	154	78	2.80	142	99.7	135-146	136-145	>99	9
CIX	302	79	2.93	144	99.8	139-147	140-146	>99	9
CMX	99	49	-0.07	99	47	93-105	94-104	49	5
SPI	86	41	-0.87	87	19	84-90	85-90	32	3
TVB	246	65	1.53	123	94	118-127	119-126	82	8
TNB	241	63	1.33	120	91	115-124	116-123	78	8
TTB	487	67	1.67	125	95	121-128	122-128	85	8

Fig. 9.7 RIAS-2 extended score summary table

Source. From Reynolds, C. R., & Kamphaus, R. W. (2015). *Reynolds Intellectual Assessment Scales, Second Edition.* Lutz, FL: Psychological Assessment Resources. Reprinted with permission of PAR.

The report begins with a review of all of the data gathered as a result of the administration and scoring of the intelligence test. You will see a number of terms employed that you have already learned throughout this text. You will see, for example, that confidence intervals based on the standard errors of measurement are applied to the various intelligence indexes and that not only standard scores but percentile ranks are provided to assist in the interpretation. The report continues by providing brief background information on why John was being evaluated accompanied by several behavioral observations considered important by the person administering the test.

The next section of the report provides some caveats regarding proper administration and use of the results of the intellectual assessment. This section will clue the reader into the assumptions that underlie the interpretation of the results that follow later in the report. A computer-generated report cannot currently take into account extraneous factors that may necessitate altering standard interpretations of test performance such as the behavior of the examinee or the capabilities of the professional examiner.

The next section of the report provides a narrative summary of John's scores on this intellectual assessment and provides norm-referenced interpretations. ***Norm-referenced interpretations*** are those that compare John's performance to other individuals of the same chronological age and who belong to the population sampled for development of the norms for this particular test. You will also see references within this section to the practical application of a confidence interval as well as estimates of true scores, all terms you have become acquainted with earlier in this text.

Once the more global indexes of intellectual function have been reviewed, the report provides information on more specific intellectual tasks John completed. This is followed by a section where the pattern of John's intellectual development is discussed by the use of norm-referenced discrepancy interpretations. Essentially, this section presents an actuarial analysis of the differences among John's scores across the different subdomains of intelligence evaluated during this assessment. Such an analysis logically leads to recommendations for understanding John's particular pattern of intellectual development and ways that it may be relevant to altering instructional methods or making other changes in how material is presented to him in an educational setting. Because tests like the RIAS-2 are commonly used in educational settings, the next major section of the report deals precisely with school feedback and recommendations. Here, the reader is provided with a general understanding of the implications of these findings for John's academic development and alternative methods of instruction are recommended. These are based on various studies of the implications of intelligence test results for student learning over many decades. In particular, the actuarial analyses of discrepancies in John's various areas of intellectual development have led to recommendations for some additional assessment as well as changes in teaching methods.

The purpose of all of the commentary in this report is ultimately to achieve an understanding of John's intellectual development and how it may be related to furthering his academic development in the best way possible.

The sample report is restricted to recommendations for school or other formal instructional settings. Other specialized reports can be generated separately for specialized clinical settings that make quite different recommendations and even provide provisional diagnoses that should be considered by the professional psychologist administering and interpreting the intellectual assessment. In John's case, given that he is no longer of school age and was referred for evaluation because of memory complaints, his specialized report would probably focus on the diagnosis and treatment of dementia or another brain disorder. The reader should be aware that it is rare for a report to be based only on an intellectual assessment, and we doubt you will ever see such a report based on a singular instrument. Typically, reports of the assessment of a student conducted by a diagnostic professional will include not only a thorough assessment of intellectual functions, such as reported in Special Interest Topic 9.5, but also will include evaluations of academic skills and status, personality, and behavior that may affect academic performance, specialized areas of development such as auditory perceptual skills, visual perceptual skills, visual-motor integration, attention, concentration, and memory skills, among other important aspects of the student's development, that are dictated by the nature of the referral and information gathered during the ongoing assessment process.

9.7   Summary

Standardized intelligence and aptitude tests are used in many settings. Aptitude/intelligence tests are designed to assess the cognitive skills, abilities, and knowledge that are acquired as the result of broad, cumulative life experiences. In contrast, achievement tests are designed to assess skills and knowledge in areas in which specific instruction has been provided. Both aptitude and achievement tests measure developed cognitive abilities and the distinction them is not absolute. However, there is a distinction that lies with the degree to which the cognitive abilities are dependent on or linked to formal learning experiences. Achievement tests are intended to measure abilities that are developed as the direct result of formal instruction and training whereas aptitude tests assess abilities acquired from all life experiences, not only formal schooling. In addition to this distinction, achievement tests are usually used to measure knowledge learned or achieved at a fixed point in time, whereas aptitude tests are often used to predict future performance. Although the distinction between aptitude and achievement tests is not as clear as one might expect, the two types of tests do differ in their focus and are used for different purposes.

The most popular type of aptitude tests used by psychologists today is the general intelligence test. Intelligence tests actually had their origin in the public schools approximately 100 years ago when Alfred Binet and Theodore Simon developed the Binet-Simon Scale to identify children who needed special educational services to be successful in French schools. The test was well received in France and was subsequently translated and standardized in the United States to produce the Stanford--Binet Intelligence Test. Subsequently, other test developers developed their own intelligence tests and the age of intelligence testing had arrived. Some of these tests were designed for group administration and others for individual administration. Some of these tests focused primarily on verbal and quantitative abilities whereas others placed more emphasis on visual-spatial and abstract problem-solving skills. Some of these tests even avoided verbal content altogether. Research suggests that, true to their initial purpose, intelligence tests are fairly good predictors of academic success. Nevertheless, the concept of intelligence has taken on different meanings for different people, and the use of general intelligence tests has been the focus of controversy and emotional debate for many years. This debate is likely to continue for the foreseeable future. In an attempt to avoid negative connotations and misinterpretations, many test publishers have switched to more neutral titles such as *school ability* or simply *ability* to designate the same basic construct.

Contemporary intelligence tests have numerous applications in today's practice of psychology. These include providing a broader measure of cognitive abilities than traditional achievement tests, helping teachers tailor instruction to meet students' unique patterns of cognitive strengths and weaknesses, determining whether students are prepared for educational experiences, identifying students who are underachieving and may have learning or other cognitive disabilities, identifying students for gifted and talented programs, helping students and parents make educational and career decisions, monitoring a variety of changes in mental functions in medical disorders, Alzheimer's Disease and other dementias, and many other clinical applications. For example, intelligence tests play a key role in the diagnosis of intellectual disability, with performance two or more standard deviations below the mean on an individually administered test of intelligence being a necessary but insufficient condition for such a diagnosis.

One common practice when interpreting intelligence tests is referred to as aptitude-achievement discrepancy analysis and is often used when a learning disability is expected. This simply involves comparing a student's performance on an aptitude test with performance on an achievement test. The expectation is that achievement will be commensurate with aptitude. Students with achievement scores significantly greater than ability scores may be considered academic overachievers whereas those with achievement scores significantly below ability scores may be considered underachievers. There are a number of possible causes for academic underachievement ranging from poor student motivation to specific learning disabilities. We noted that there are different methods for determining whether a significant discrepancy between ability and achievement scores exists and that standards have been developed for performing these analyses. To meet these standards, many of the popular aptitude and achievement tests have been co-normed or statistically linked to permit comparisons. We cautioned that while ability-achievement discrepancy analysis is a common practice, not all assessment experts support the practice. As we have emphasized throughout this text, test results should be interpreted in addition to other sources of information when making important decisions. This suggestion applies when making ability-achievement comparisons.

An alternative to the use of ability-achievement discrepancies for diagnosing learning disabilities is referred to as Response to Intervention (RTI). Currently, RTI appears to be a useful process that can help identify struggling students and ensure that they receive early attention and intervention. However, current research does not support the use of RTI as a "stand-alone" process for identifying students with LD. We believe the best approach for identifying students with LD is one that incorporates the best of RTI and psychometric assessment practices (e.g., intelligence tests).

In the next sections, we examine a number of the popular group and individual intelligence tests, including a brief review of college admissions testing where we note their original purpose was to enhance the objectivity of college admissions procedures. In closing, we provide some guidelines for selecting intelligence and provide an extended example of a report of an intellectual assessment.

References

American Educational Research Association, American Psychological Association, & National Council on Measurement in Education. (2014). *Standards for educational and psychological testing*. Washington, DC: American Educational Research Association.

Anastasi, A., & Urbina, S. (1997). *Psychological testing* (7th ed.). Upper Saddle River, NJ: Prentice Hall.

Braden, J. P. (1997). The practical impact of intellectual assessment issues. *School Psychology Review, 26*, 242–248.

Canter, A. S. (1997). The future of intelligence testing in the schools. *School Psychology Review, 26*, 255–261.

Carroll, J. B. (1993). *Human cognitive abilities: A survey of factor-analytic studies*. New York, NY: Cambridge University Press.

Christ, T. J., Burns, M. K., & Ysseldyke, J. E. (2005). Conceptual confusion within response-to-intervention vernacular: Clarifying meaningful differences. *Communique, 34*(3), 1–2.

Cronbach, L. J. (1990). *Essentials of psychological testing (5th ed.)*. New York: HarperCollins.

Emerson, R. W. (1841). Self-Reliance. Boston, Massachusetts. Project Gutenberg. November, 2019 from www.gutenberg.org/ebooks/16643.

Feifer, S. G., & Della Toffalo, D. (2007). *Integrating RT/with cognitive neuropsychology: A scientific approach to reading*. Middletown, MD: School Neuropsych Press.

Fletcher, J. M., Foorman, B. R., Boudousquie, A., Barnes, M. A., Schatschneider, C., & Francis, D. J. (2002). Assessment of reading and learning disabilities: A research based intervention oriented approach. *Journal of School Psychology, 40*, 27–63.

Fuchs, D., Mock, D., Morgan, P., & Young, C. (2003). Responsiveness-to-intervention: Definitions, evidence, and implications for the learning disabilities construct. *Learning Disabilities Research & Practice (Black well Publishing Limited), 18*(3), 157–171.

Gray, P. (1999). *Psychology*. New York, NY: Worth.

Gresham, F. M., & Witt, J. C. (1997). Utility of intelligence tests for treatment planning, classification, and placement decisions. Recent empirical findings and future directions. *School Psychology Quarterly, 12*, 146–154.

Hilliard, A. G. (1989). Back to Binet: The case against the use of IQ tests in the schools. *Diagnostique, 14*, 125–135.

Horn, J. L. (1989). Measurement of intellectual capabilities: A review of theory. In K. S. McGrew, J. K. Werder, & R. W. Woodcock (Eds.), *WJ-R technical manual* (pp. 197–245). Chicago, IL: Riverside.

Horn, J. L., & Noll, J. (1997). Human cognitive capabilities: Gf-Gc theory. In D. P. Flanagan, J. L. Genshaft, & P. L. Harrison (Eds.), *Contemporary intellectual assessment: Theories, tests and issues* (pp. 53–91). New York, NY: Guilford Press.

Kaufman, A. S. (1994). *Intelligent testing with the WISC-III*. New York, NY: Wiley.

Kaufman, A. S. (2009). *IQ testing 101*. New York, NY: Springer.

Kaufman, A. S., & Lichtenberger, E. O. (1999). *Essentials of WAIS-III assessment*. New York, NY: Wiley.

Kranzler, J. H. (1997). Educational and policy issues related to the use and interpretation of intelligence tests in the schools. *School Psychology Review, 26*, 50–63.

Lamb, K. (1994). Genetics and Spearman's "g" factor. *Mankind Quarterly, 34*(4), 379–391.

Linn, R. L., & Gronlund, N. E. (2000). *Measurement and assessment in teaching* (8th ed.). Upper Saddle River, NJ: Prentice Hall.

Livingston, R. B., Eglsaer, R., Dickson, T., & Harvey-Livingston, K. (2003). *Psychological assessment practices with children and adolescents*. Presentation at the 23rd Annual National Academy of Neuropsychology Conference, Dallas, TX.

McGrew, K. (2009). Editorial: CHC theory and the human cognitive abilities project: Standing on the shoulders of the giants of psychometric intelligence research. *Intelligence, 37*, 1–10.

McGrew, K. S. (1997). Analysis of the major intelligence batteries according to a proposed comprehensive Gf-Gc framework. In D. P. Flanagan, J. L. Genshaft, & P. L. Harrison (Eds.), *Contemporary intellectual assessment: Theories, tests, and issues* (pp. 151–179). New York, NY: Guilford Press.

McGrew, K. S. (2005). The Cattell-Horn-Carroll theory of cognitive abilities. In D. P. Flanagan & P. L. Harrison (Eds.), *Contemporary intellectual assessment: Theories, tests, and issues* (2nd ed., pp. 136–181). New York, NY: Guilford Press.

Neisser, U., BooDoo, G., Bouchard, T., Boykin, A., Brody, N., Ceci, S., ... Urbina, S. (1996). Intelligence: Knowns and unknowns. *American Psychologist, 51*, 77–101.

Psychological Corporation. (2002). *WIAT-II: Examiners manual.* San Antonio, TX: Author.

Reynolds, C. R., & Kaufman, A. S. (1990). Assessment of children's intelligence with the Wechsler Intelligence Scale for ChildrenRevised (WISC-R). In C. R. Reynolds & R. W. Kamphaus (Eds.), *Handbook of psychological and educational assessment of children: Intelligence and achievement* (pp. 127–165). New York: Guilford Press.

Reynolds, C., & Shaywitz, S. (2009). Response to intervention: Ready or not? Or, from wait-to-fail to watch-them-fail. *School Psychology Quarterly, 24*(2), 130–145.

Reynolds, C. R. (1985). Critical measurement issues in learning disabilities. *Journal of Special Education, 18*, 451–476.

Reynolds, C. R. (1990). Conceptual and technical problems in learning disability diagnosis. In C. R. Reynolds & R. W. Kamphaus (Eds.), *Handbook of psychological and educational assessment of children: Intelligence and achievement* (pp. 571–592). New York, NY: Guilford Press.

Reynolds, C. R. (2005, August). *Considerations in RTI as a method of diagnosis of learning disabilities.* Paper presented to the Annual Institute for Psychology in the Schools of the American Psychological Association, Washington, DC.

Reynolds, C. R. (2009). *Determining the R in RTI: Which score is the best score?* Miniskills workshop presented at the annual meeting of the National Association of School Psychologists, February, Boston.

Reynolds, C. R., & Kamphaus, R. W. (2003). *Reynolds Intellectual Assessment Scales.* Lutz, FL: Psychological Assessment Resources.

Reynolds, C. R., & Kamphaus, R. W. (2007). *Reynolds Intellectual Assessment Scales/Wide Range Achievement Test 4 Discrepancy Interpretive Report professional manual supplement.* Lutz, FL: Psychological Assessment Resources.

Reynolds, C. R., & Kamphaus, R. W. (2015). *Reynolds Intellectual Assessment Scales, Second Edition.* Lutz, FL: Psychological Assessment Resources.

Reynolds, C. R., & Voress, J. (2007). *Test of memory and learning-second edition (TOMAL-2).* Austin, TX: Pro-Ed.

Riverside Publishing. (2002). *Cognitive abilities test, form 6: A short guide for teachers.* Itasca, IL: Author.

Riverside Publishing. (2003). *Clinical and special needs assessment catalog .* Itasca, IL: Author.

Sherman, E., & Brooks, B. (2015). *Child and adolescent memory profile.* Lutz, FL: PAR.

Sheslow, D., & Adams, W. (2003). *Wide range assessment of memory and learning* (2nd ed.). Wilmington, DE: Jastak Associates.

Spearman, C. (1904). "General intelligence," objectively determined and measured. *The American Journal of Psychology, 15*(2), 201–293.

Wechsler, D. (2014). *Wechsler intelligence scale for children* (5th ed.). Bloomington, MN: NCS Pearson.

Wechsler, D. W. (2003). *Wechsler Intelligence Scale for Children-Fourth Edition: Technical and interpretive manual.* San Antonio, TX: Psychological Corporation.

Wigdor, A. K., & Garner, W. K. (1982). *Ability testing: Uses, consequences, and controversy.* Washington, DC: National Academy Press.

Recommended Reading

Cronbach, L. J. (1975). Five decades of public controversy over mental testing. *American Psychologist, 36*, 1–14. An interesting and readable chronicle of the controversy surrounding mental testing during much of the twentieth century.

Fletcher-Janzen, E., & Reynolds, C. R. (Eds.). (2009). *Neuroscientific and clinical perspectives on the RTI initiative in learning disabilities diagnosis and intervention.* New York, NY: John Wiley and Sons. This text provides a review of the use of RTI in the identification of learning disabilities.

Kamphaus, R. W. (2001). *Clinical assessment of child and adolescent intelligence.* Boston, MA: Allyn & Bacon. This text provides an excellent discussion of the assessment of intelligence and related issues.

Assessment of Personality

10

Once studied solely by introspection, assessment of personality is now an objective science.

Abstract

Personality assessments are designed to identify relatively stable patterns of thinking, feeling, and behaving, which differentiate one individual from another. Results from personality assessments are used by psychologists and other professionals to help facilitate diagnosis and treatment of mental-health problems, help enhance an individual's self-understanding and awareness, identify emotional and behavioral disorders that interfere with an individual's ability to learn, identify job candidates who are best matched for a particular job, answer questions relevant to legal proceedings, and measure constructs that are important in a wide range of psychological research. This chapter describes two broad categories of personality measures: objective self-report measures and projective techniques. A review of major personality tests is provided, highlighting different approaches used in their development.

Supplementary Information The online version of this chapter (https://doi.org/10.1007/978-3-030-59455-8_10) contains supplementary material, which is available to authorized users.

Learning Objectives

After reading and studying this chapter, students should be able to:
1. Compare and contrast maximum performance tests and typical response tests.
2. Define and give examples of response sets.
3. Explain how test validity scales can be used to guard against response sets and give examples.
4. Explain factors that make the assessment of personality more challenging in terms of reliability and validity.
5. Distinguish between objective and projective personality tests and give examples of each.
6. Describe the major approaches to developing objective personality scales and give an example of each.
7. Describe the major features of the MMPI-2-RF, its prominent applications, and its psychometric properties.
8. Describe the five-factor model of personality.
9. Describe special considerations related to the assessment of personality in children and adolescents and give examples of scales used with this population.
10. Define and give an example of a narrow-band personality scale.
11. Explain the central hypothesis of projective techniques and give examples of popular projective techniques.
12. Discuss the debate over the use of projective techniques.

In Chap. 1, when describing the different types of tests, we noted that tests typically can be classified as measures of either maximum performance or typical response. Maximum performance tests are often referred to as ability tests. On these tests, items are usually scored as either correct or incorrect, and examinees are encouraged to demonstrate the best performance possible. Achievement and aptitude tests are common examples of maximum performance tests. In contrast, typical response tests attempt to measure the typical behavior and characteristics of examinees. Typical response tests typically assess constructs such as personality, behavior, attitudes, or interests (Cronbach, 1990). In this chapter, we will focus on the assessment of ***personality***, but in other chapters, we will present other instruments that focus on assessment of behavior (Chap. 11) and career interests (Chap. 12: Employment and Vocational Assessment). Although there is no single agreed definition of personality, Gray (1999) defines personality as "the relatively consistent patterns of thought, feeling, and behavior that characterize each person as a unique individual" (p. G12). This definition probably captures most people's concept of personality. In conventional assessment terminology, personality is defined in a similar manner, incorporating a host of emotional, motivational, interpersonal, and attitudinal characteristics (Anastasi & Urbina, 1997; Cronbach, 1990). Many of the tests that we address are broad measures of personality. However, in this chapter, we also introduce some tests that measure narrow constructs such as depression or anxiety. It is common for both broad and narrow measures of personality to be referred to as inventories, but other terms are also used (e.g., questionnaire and scale).

10.1 Assessing Personality

Even though we might not consciously be aware of it, we all engage in the assessment of personality on a regular basis. When you note that "Kylo has a good personality," "Niabi is trustworthy," or "Meaghan is extroverted," you are making a judgment about personality. We often use these informal evaluations to make

> Even though we might not consciously be aware of it, we all engage in the assessment of personality on a regular basis.

important decisions, like who we want to associate with and who we want to avoid, and so improving the accuracy of our evaluations has real consequences. The goal of personality testing is to do just that—improve our evaluations of individuals in order to improve the decisions we make about them, whether they might be a good choice for a life partner, successful employee, honorable police officer or FBI agent, and the like.

The development of the first formal instrument for assessing personality typically is traced to the efforts of Robert Woodworth. In 1918, he developed the **Woodworth Personal Data Sheet**, which was designed to help collect personal information about military recruits. Much as the development of the Binet scales ushered in the era of individual intelligence testing and the Army Alpha and Beta tests popularized group aptitude testing, the introduction of the Woodworth Personal Data Sheet, developed during World War I, ushered in the era of personality assessment. Subsequent instruments for assessing personality took on a variety of forms, but they all had the same basic purpose of helping us to understand the personal characteristics of ourselves and others. Special Interest Topic 10.1 provides a brief description of an early informal test of personality.

Special Interest Topic 10.1: The Handsome and the Deformed Leg

Sir Francis Galton (1884) related a tale attributed to Benjamin Franklin about a crude test of personality. Franklin describes two basic types of people, those who are optimistic and focus on the positive and those who are pessimistic and focus on the negative. Franklin reported that one of his philosophical friends desired a test to help him identify and avoid people who were pessimistic, offensive, and prone to acrimony.

In order to discover a pessimist at first sight, he cast about for an instrument. He of course possessed a thermometer to test heat and a barometer to tell the air pressure, but he had no instrument to test the characteristic of

(continued)

which we are speaking. After much pondering, he hit upon a happy idea. He chanced to have one remarkably handsome leg and one that by some accident was crooked and deformed, and he used these for the purpose. If a stranger regarded his ugly leg more than his handsome one, he doubted him. If he spoke of it and took no notice of the handsome leg, the philosopher determined to avoid his further acquaintance. Franklin sums up by saying that everyone does not have this two-legged instrument, but everyone with little attention may observe the signs of a carping and fault-finding disposition (pp. 9–10).

Source: This tale was originally reported by Sir Francis Galton (1884). Galton's paper was reproduced in Goodstein and Lanyon (1971).

Psychologists use personality inventories in different settings to answer different questions. Any attempt to list all of these applications would inevitably be incomplete, but we will highlight some major uses below.

- Psychologists and other mental-health professionals use personality inventories to facilitate diagnosis and help plan treatment. It is often apparent from clinical interviews and observations that a client is experiencing some form of psychopathology, but identifying the specific disorder(s) can often be quite challenging. A review of *DSM-V* reveals that many disorders present with overlapping symptoms, and the process of identifying the correct disorder and ruling out competing diagnosis is referred to as differential diagnosis. Personality inventories can help with this process.
- Repeated assessments are also used in clinical practice to monitor the client's progress, such as whether depression is increasing as a result of treatment. This applies to both psychopharmacological and psychological treatments. That is, repeated assessments can reveal what is working to help the client and what is not.
- Psychologists frequently use personality inventories to enhance their client's self-understanding and self-actualization. While some personality measures are designed to facilitate clinical diagnosis and others to determine the effectiveness of treatment, still others are designed to assess normal personality functioning and enhance the individual's functioning in a number of spheres (e.g., personal, social, and marital adjustment). Special Interest Topic 10.2 describes Therapeutic Assessment, a novel approach that uses assessment as the centerpiece of a clinical intervention.
- Psychologists routinely use measures of personality to identify children with emotional and behavioral disorders that interfere with their ability to learn in schools. Some of these children may receive special education services under the Individuals with Disabilities Education Act (IDEA) under the designation of Emotional Disturbance. In these cases, test results may also assist in arriving at the appropriate intervention for the emotional issues present.

Special Interest Topic 10.2: Therapeutic Assessment

Hale Martin, Ph.D., Assistant Clinical Professor, University of Denver

Can psychological assessment change someone's life? Some psychologists believe that it can and have research to back it up. Stephen E. Finn at the Center for Therapeutic Assessment in Austin, Texas, has led the way in developing an empirically grounded approach to assessment that research suggests works as a brief therapy. Time-honored psychological tests can yield insights into people's persistent problems and difficulties. Finn and others contend that if these insights are offered back to clients in a supportive, sensitive, and clinically astute way, it will have a positive impact on clients' lives. This argument is a far cry from previous concerns that explaining the results of testing to a client could damage him or her. The accumulating evidence is on the side of Finn and others who are working to develop strategies for using testing to help clients overcome problems, grow emotionally, and improve relationships.

Collaboration is a central aspect of the semistructured approach developed by Dr. Finn, which he calls Therapeutic Assessment. Finn built on the seminal work of Dr. Constance Fischer at Duquesne University who first advanced the value of collaborative assessments in the 1970s. Her sensible approach began the movement of assessment from esoteric—and often unhelpful—understanding to practical, helpful interventions that had a positive impact on the client. Fischer focuses on the practical. For example, for an assessment of a waitress with organizational problems, Fischer might begin by visiting the coffee shop where the waitress worked to watch how she functioned in that setting. Then, when they met in the office, Fischer might ask her to copy a set of geometric figures on paper (the Bender Gestalt Test) and talk about the disorganization that appeared in those drawings. Fischer might then ask if the woman could think of a better way to approach the drawings, have her try that way out, and assess the success of that strategy. If it worked, Fischer would talk with the woman about how to export that new approach back to the coffee shop. If it did not work, Fischer would guide the woman to a solution that might work and then try that solution out. This approach can be more helpful than a feedback session and traditional report written to the referring professional focusing on a diagnosis, such as ADHD.

In Therapeutic Assessment, collaboration between assessor and client begins from the start with clients identifying what questions they need to answer to better deal with their current struggles in life. Typically, clients ask such questions as "Why do I have so much trouble keeping relationships?", "Where does all my anger come from?", or "Am I depressed?" The assessor then directs the assessment in search of those answers and helps the client understand the assessment findings in useful ways. Finn believes that psychological assessment can produce longstanding change if it helps clients improve

(continued)

the accuracy and quality of their "story" about themselves and the world. This can't be done recklessly because our stories about ourselves and the world are central props that we all use to feel safe in the world. However, by using clients' motivation, which is often high when they come in for assessment, and their active involvement in examining and revising their story, a new story can emerge that better explains the clients' behaviors and the world around them. This new story coauthored by the client can produce changes that last long after an assessment is completed.

Helping the client feel safe and emotionally supported is essential. The empathy that the assessor can develop through the tests and the resulting relationship between assessor and client provide a powerful basis for decreasing shame and increasing self-esteem. Research has demonstrated that increases in self-esteem, elusive in even some long courses of therapy, can be realized quickly as a result of the Therapeutic Assessment process. With increases in self-compassion, clients are able to make meaningful changes in their lives.

Furthermore, Therapeutic Assessment applies our growing understanding that experience, not just intellectual insight, is important for change to occur. One of the last steps in a Therapeutic Assessment, called the assessment intervention session, creates an in vivo experience related to the main struggles that clients face and works to help clients have a different experience with their problems. For example, an assessor might use a picture story technique like the Thematic Apperception Test to put a client face-to-face with her issues. When working with a client who the testing suggests avoids emotions, the assessor might select cards that pull for strong emotions. By noting the client's characteristic responses and eliciting the client's curiosity about them, the assessor guides the client to greater self-insight.

It doesn't stop there. Recognizing the importance of felt experience, the assessor devises ways for the client to handle the challenging situation in a new way that offers hope of new solutions to old problems. The assessor and client explore the resistances, fears, and obstacles as well as the excitement and hope the new experience offers. This experiential learning is carefully built from the insights derived from the empirical testing results. It can be a pivotal experience for the client and paves the way for deeper and more meaningful discussion of testing results. Therapeutic Assessment can have a powerful impact on assessors as well, as they closely attune to the lives of others and learn how others change their life trajectories.

An example comes from Finn's book *In Our Clients' Shoes*, in which he reports a Therapeutic Assessment with David, a 28-year-old man whose therapy was floundering. David had been in treatment for several years with a therapist named Elizabeth focusing, on being more successful at work and in relationships. As a child, David had been diagnosed with ADD, which he believed explained his lack of attention, poor memory, disorganization, and perhaps the meandering course of therapy. However, Elizabeth had come to wonder whether bipolar or dissociative disorder might better explain the

(continued)

problems. David readily agreed to the assessment, and the journey to new understanding began.

Through a careful initial interview, Dr. Finn helped David frame his own questions for the assessment: (1) Do I really have ADD, and if not, why do I have trouble concentrating and remembering things? (2) Why can't I break up with girlfriends when they're treating me badly? What in me is too weak to do this? (3) Why is it so hard for me to be alone? Subsequent testing sessions were designed to collaboratively answer these questions, the results of which were shared along the way. The results revealed an unrecognized, severe, chronic depression that David had coped with since childhood by attempting to screen out distressing emotions that threatened to push him into an abyss. David reported a childhood with divorced parents who were absorbed in their own problems and clearly were unable to meet his emotional needs. He was left to cope with the world as best as he could.

The assessment intervention session alternated stimulating strong feelings through telling stories to highly emotional pictures and measuring David's ability to remember numbers. This tactic clearly demonstrated that when his emotions were high, David's memory suffered—which illustrated in vivo an important answer. His struggle to manage difficult emotions impaired his attention and memory. Furthermore, it became apparent that David was easily overwhelmed and disorganized by emotions, especially anger. Additionally, his early relationship experiences led him to expect that his emotional needs would not be met, while at the same time, he held on to whatever hope of being nurtured he found. Finally, in this session, through telling stories to the carefully selected pictures, David had a breakthrough emotional experience and was able to feel how overwhelmed and lonely he had been as a child. Dr. Finn handled this feared vulnerability gently, which helped David assimilate it.

In the final session with David and Elizabeth, David himself explained "how 'old feelings' were causing his 'brain to melt down.'" Dr. Finn added that those old feelings also made it difficult for David to be alone and kept him in bad relationships. Dr. Finn stressed the importance of having people in our lives, beginning with parents, who can keep us from being too overwhelmed and help us become increasingly competent in managing emotions. He outlined a way that David could grow in this regard. Through the assessment process, the answers to the initial questions had become clear. David's struggles were not rooted in ADHD, bipolar, or dissociative disorder but rather in the limitations of his early adaptation to difficult emotions.

The impact of the assessment was substantial. Six years later as Dr. Finn wrote about the case, Elizabeth reported that David had worked in treatment for 5 years and that his emotional facility had grown. He had married a loving woman about a year previously, and they were expecting their first child, which if a female, he would name Elizabeth. He had received the help that he

(continued)

needed to get his life unstuck. Elizabeth also had grown from the experience, recognizing her own need to reach out for help when she felt overwhelmed.

The Therapeutic Assessment approach can be applied to a range of assessments. Most research to this point has been with individuals, but Finn has used variations of Therapeutic Assessment with couples and to help families change the inaccuracies in the stories they have about their children. A couple's assessment strives not only to help each member understand themselves better but also to see their contribution to problems that the couple has. The couple is videotaped to highlight problematic patterns in their interactions, and this often has a powerful effect in changing those interactions. A child/family assessment involves the parents throughout the assessment process with the child. Research that Finn and Dr. Deborah Tharinger are spearheading at the University of Texas at Austin shows powerful outcomes that result from addressing the all-important system in which the child grows up. The child/family assessor also gives the child a new perspective by writing and presenting an age-appropriate fable or story that captures the child's dilemma and offers alternatives. Others are working to adapt the Therapeutic Assessment approach to neuropsychological assessment and even as an alternative to some forensic assessments.

How far can Therapeutic Assessment go in changing the way that assessors work with their clients? Could this therapeutic approach have utility for managed care, which is constantly looking for short-term, effective, interventions? The future will tell, but with the accumulating supporting research and the increasing prominence of Therapeutic Assessment in the psychology community, the answers are on the way.

- Psychologists use a variety of personality measures to help determine which job applicants will become successful employees. Likewise, they use personality measures to help current employees better understand themselves and their colleagues, thus enhancing the workplace environment.
- Psychologists use measures of personality to answer questions relevant to legal proceedings such as competency to stand trial or future dangerousness.
- Psychologists in academic and research settings use personality tests to measure a multitude of constructs in a wide range of psychological research.

Personality is a complex, multidimensional construct. As such, it cannot be summarized in one omnibus score, and so personality tests typically attempt to measure multiple dimensions or aspects of personality. This is accomplished through the use of multiple scale or factor scores. The scales on a personality test vary greatly from test to test depending on the purpose of the instrument. For example, personality tests that are designed to be used in clinical settings to facilitate the diagnosis of mental disorders often contain scales reflecting constructs such as depression, anxiety, psychosis, and aggressiveness. Personality tests that are designed to be used in a general population will typically have reflecting dimensions such as introversion/ extroversion, agreeableness, and dependability. As you will see, there are different approaches to developing these scales. However, before we describe these approaches, we will introduce the concept of response sets, an important topic when considering the use of personality tests.

10.1.1 Response Sets and Dissimulation

Response sets and ***dissimulation*** are patterns of test responses that misrepresent a person's true characteristics. When a person unconsciously responds in either a negative or positive manner, they are evidencing a response set;

> Response sets and dissimulation are test responses that misrepresent a person's true characteristics.

when they purposefully misrepresent themselves, it is dissimulation. In both cases, the respondent's true characteristics are distorted or misrepresented. For example, an individual completing an employment-screening test might attempt to present an overly positive image by answering all of the questions in the most socially appropriate manner possible, even though the responses do not accurately represent the person. On the other hand, an individual who is hoping to win a large settlement in a court case might exaggerate the mental distress they are experiencing as a result of a traumatic event. In both these situations, the individual completing the test or scale, consciously or unconsciously, responded in a manner that distorted reality, and so the results of the test cannot be interpreted in a valid manner, i.e., the results are not useful for understanding the true characteristics of the individual.

Response sets and dissimulation can also be present when completing maximum performance tests. For example, an individual with a pending court case claiming neurological damage resulting from an accident might dissimulate on an intelligence test by giving a suboptimal or "*fake bad*" performance in an effort to substantiate the presence of brain damage and enhance his or her legal case. However, they are even a bigger problem on typical performance tests. Since many of the constructs measured by typical performance tests (e.g., personality, behavior, attitudes, and beliefs) have dimensions that may be seen as either socially "desirable" or "undesirable," the tendency to employ a response set is heightened. When response sets or dissimulation are present, the interpretability of the test results may be compromised because they introduce construct-irrelevant error to test scores (e.g., American Educational Research Association, American Psychological Association, & National Council on Measurement in Education, 2014). That is, the test results do not accurately reflect the construct that the test was designed to measure.

To combat this, many typical performance tests incorporate some types of ***validity scales*** designed to detect the presence of response sets and dissimulation. Validity scales take different forms, but the general principle is that they are designed to detect individuals who are not responding in an accurate manner.

> Validity scales take different forms, but the general principle is that they are designed to detect individuals who are not responding in an accurate manner.

To illustrate some different types of validity scales, we will briefly review some of the validity scales included in the Behavior Assessment System for Children, Third Edition—Self-Report of Personality (SRP: Reynolds & Kamphaus, 2015). Three validity scales included on the SRP are the *F* index, *L* Index, and *V* Index. These scales are grounded in a long psychometric tradition for personality inventories such as the Minnesota Multiphasic Personality Inventory (MMPI) and other similar measures. That have accrued substantial validity evidence supporting their use. The **F index** is composed of items that have response options that are "infrequently" endorsed in a specific manner in a normal population. For example, very few children or adolescents indicate that they are never "a good friend" or respond true to a statement that indicates that they "often cheat on tests." This type of validity scale is often referred to as an infrequency index. If an examinee chooses enough of these response options, his or her *F* Index will be elevated. High scores on the *F* Index can be the result of numerous factors, ranging from reading difficulties, to random responding to test items, to an intentional desire to "fake bad" in order to look more disturbed or pathological. In rare cases, it could also indicate a "cry for help" where severe problems are present that require immediate attention. Another SRP validity scale is the **L Index**, which also contains items that are rarely endorsed in a specific manner in a normal population. Unlike the *F* Index, items on the *L* Index are intended to identify individuals with a "social desirability" response set (i.e., examinees that are trying to "fake good"). For example, few adolescents who are responding honestly will indicate that "their life is perfect" or that "their teachers are always right." High scores on the *L* Index may indicate a psychological *naïveté* and below average insight into one's thoughts or feelings, or it can indicate a defensiveness or unwillingness to share personal information. Such response patterns can indicate that the SRP clinical scale scores might underestimate any existing emotional or behavioral problems. The **V Index** is composed of nonsensical items that may be endorsed due to carelessness, reading difficulty, or simply a refusal to cooperate. An example of an item that might be included in the *V* Index is "Batman is my best friend." Special Interest Topic 10.3 provides an example of a fake good response set and how the use of the SRP *L* Index helps identify this response set.

> The development and use of personality assessments are plagued with challenges above and beyond those present in other areas of psychological assessment.

Special Interest Topic 10.3: An Example of a "Fake Good" Response Set
Self-report inventories, despite the efforts of test developers, always remain susceptible to response sets. The following case is based on a real-life example. In this case, the Behavior Assessment System for Children, Third Edition Self-Report of Personality (BASC-3 SRP) was utilized.

Maury was admitted to the inpatient psychiatric unit of a general hospital with the diagnoses of impulse control disorder and major depression. She is

(continued)

repeating the seventh grade this school year because she failed to attend school regularly last year. When skipping school, she spent time roaming the local shopping mall or engaging in other relatively unstructured activities. She was suspended from school for lying, cheating, and arguing with teachers. She failed all of her classes in both semesters of the past school year.

Maury's responses to a diagnostic interview suggested that she was trying to portray herself in a favorable light and not convey the severity of her problems. When asked about hobbies, for example, she said that she liked to read. When questioned further, however, she could not name a book that she had read.

Maury's father reported that he has been arrested many times. Similarly, Maury and her sisters have been arrested for shoplifting. Maury's father expressed concern about her education. He said that Maury was recently placed in an alternative education program designed for youth offenders.

Maury's SRP results show evidence of a social desirability or a fake good response set. All of her clinical scale scores were lower than the normative T-score mean of 50, and all of her adaptive scale scores were above the normative mean of 50. In other words, the BASC-3 SRP results suggest that Maury is optimally adjusted, which is in stark contrast to the background information obtained.

Maury's response set, however, was identified by the L Index of the SRP, where she obtained a score of 12, which is on the border of the caution and extreme caution ranges. The following table shows her full complement of SRP scores.

Scale	T-score
Clinical scales	
Attitude to school	41
Attitude to teachers	39
Sensation seeking	41
Atypicality	38
Locus of control	38
Somatization	39
Social stress	38
Anxiety	34
Depression	43
Sense of inadequacy	41
Attention problems	48
Hyperactivity	44
Adaptive scales	
Relations with parents	53
Interpersonal relations	57
Self-esteem	54
Self-reliance	52

10.1.2 Factors Affecting Reliability and Validity

Anastasi and Urbina (1997) note that the development and use of personality assessments are plagued with challenges above and beyond those present in other areas of psychological assessment. For example, as just discussed, response sets are often present in personality assessment and may compromise the interpretation of the results. While response biases may influence performance on maximum performance tests, they are far more problematic on personality assessments. Additionally, the constructs measured by personality tests (e.g., sadness) may be less stable than the constructs measured by maximum performance tests such as aptitude tests (e.g., intelligence). In this context, it is useful to distinguish between *psychological traits* and *psychological states*. A trait is a stable internal characteristic that is manifested as a tendency for an individual to behave in a particular manner. For example, introversion/extraversion is often considered a trait that is fairly stable over time. In support of the stability or personality traits, Cronbach (1990) noted that 6-year test-retest reliability coefficients of approximately 0.80 have been reported for broad personality traits and that these correlations can exceed 0.90 when correcting for short-term fluctuations. In contrast, psychological states are transient emotional states that fluctuate over time. Test-retest reliability coefficients will naturally be lower when measuring state-related constructs compared to constructs reflecting broad traits, and as Cronbach noted, these transient emotional states may influence attempts to measure more stable constructs.

We also have to be careful when talking about or considering the test-retest reliability of all measures, but especially personality test scores. For some reason, the field continues to confuse the accuracy of measurement at one point in time with the stability of the underlying attribute. Often, when measuring unstable variables, psychologists will refer to the test-retest reliability of the score as poor or as having poor accuracy when, in fact, the test has measured the variable quite well on both occasions. If you had a piece of wood and measured it under extremely dry conditions and it was 100 mm long and you then soaked it in water overnight and measured it the next day and it was 103 mm long—would you say your ruler was unreliable? Probably not—the measuring device measured it with a very high degree of accuracy both times, but the length of the board actually changed.

Special Interest Topic 10.4 presents a discussion of the "Forer Effect." The discovery of this effect significantly influenced the way that validity evidence for personality tests was collected.

Special Interest Topic 10.4: The Forer Effect—or, You and Your Aunt Fanny!
Before reading beyond the following paragraph, read it carefully, stop immediately, and ask yourself this question: *How accurately does this describe me and my personality in general?* Then, answer it to yourself, before reading the text below the paragraph.

(continued)

You have a need for other people to like and admire you, and yet you tend to be critical of yourself. While you have some personality weaknesses, you are generally able to compensate for them. You have considerable unused capacity that you have not turned to your advantage. Disciplined and self-controlled on the outside, you tend to be worrisome and insecure on the inside. At times, you have serious doubts as to whether you have made the right decision or done the right thing. You prefer a certain amount of change and variety and become dissatisfied when hemmed in by restrictions and limitations. You also pride yourself as an independent thinker; and do not accept others' statements without satisfactory proof. But you have found it unwise to be too frank in revealing yourself to others. At times, you are extroverted, affable, and sociable, while at other times, you are introverted, wary, and reserved. Some of your aspirations tend to be rather unrealistic.

Our bet is that this statement describes you reasonably well—how did we know that? Are we just impossibly psychic???

In the early days of personality assessment, one approach to the validation of the interpretation of personality test scores that was quite popular was to have people take the test and then a psychologist familiar with the test in question would write a description of the examinee's personality structure. This description would be given to the examinee, with the interpretation based upon the examinee's own scores. The examinee would then complete a rating scale, indicating to what extent the examinee agreed with the description and its overall level of accuracy as applied to the individual examinee. Not surprisingly, this approach to validating the interpretations of personality test scores usually turned out well for the test and its interpretation.

However, the level of agreement was dependent on a variety of factors beyond the actual personality test profile. Clinicians tend to want to include things they know about people in general in such interpretations, and one can easily devise descriptions that most people will agree, which are consistent with how they view themselves.

In 1949, Bertram Forer (Forer, 1949) conducted a study in which he had a group of college students take a personality test. A short time later, he provided each with an interpretation of the results and description of their personality. Each student was then asked to read the description privately and complete a rating scale, indicating how well the interpretation matches their own views of their personality characteristics. Unbeknownst to the students, they were all given not individualized interpretations but a common interpretation. It was in fact the interpretation that you read above. As a group, the students rated the personality description and interpretation given to them as being highly consistent with their view of themselves. Since the publication of Forer's study, the use of such validation procedures has diminished greatly, as it should. Still, however, one finds occasionally just such an approach or a variation on this method where clinicians interview examinees and then are asked to rate the agreement between an interpretation based on a personality test and their own view of the examinee from the interview. Such approaches remain subject to the Forer effect. Interpretations such as that given above are

(continued)

also referred to often as "Aunt Fanny" personality descriptions, because it seems to fit everyone and their Aunt Fanny!

The same basic principles that go into creating these Aunt Fanny descriptions are often used in the writing of horoscopes as well as results of nonstandardized personality surveys often published in the lay press, in books, as well as in popular magazines. These are reasonably easy to create. You might even consider writing one of these yourself and having four or five of your friends each read it independently and ask how well they think it describes them. They may be amazed at your insights.

10.2 Objective Personality Tests: An Overview

A search of the *Mental Measurements Yearbook* results in the identification of over 600 tests listed in the category on personality tests. Obviously, we will not be discussing all of these tests, but we will introduce a few major contemporary personality measures in this chapter. We will describe two broad categories of personality measures: objective self-report measures and projective techniques. *Objective personality measures* are those where respondents endorse selected-response items to reflect their characteristic ways of behaving, feeling, thinking, etc. On an objective self-report measure, an examinee might answer True or False to a statement like "I am usually outgoing." *Projective personality measures* are closely associated with psychodynamic theory and involve the presentation of unstructured or ambiguous stimuli, which allows an almost infinite range of responses from the respondent. For example, the clinician shows the examinee an inkblot and asks: "What might this be?" With projective measures, the stimuli are thought to serve as a blank screen on which examinees "project" their thoughts, desires, fears, needs, and conflicts, i.e., project their personality.

We will first focus on objective self-report measures of personality. Two of the most popular item types with these objective self-report measures are True–False items and self-rating scales (e.g., Never, Sometimes, Often, Almost Always). Some personality instruments have also used forced-choice item formats. An example of a forced-choice item is one that presents two phrases that are of equal acceptability in terms of social desirability. For example, "I enjoy reading novels" and "I enjoy watching sports." The respondent must select the one that best describes them. In the past, it was believed that forced-choice items might help reduce response biases, but research has shown that these items were not very effective in reducing response biases and also introduced other technical problems (e.g., Anastasi & Urbina, 1997). As a result, forced-choice items are not very common in contemporary typical response tests, but on occasion, you will still see tests that use this item type.

To facilitate our presentation, we will organize our discussion around the major approaches to scale development. That is, the way test developers select and group the items on their personality tests. We discuss four major approaches including content/rational, empirical keying, factor analytic, and theoretical. While we discuss these approaches separately, but in actual practice test, development is a process that typically combines these procedures. For example, an author might initially develop items based on the content/rational approach, but retain items and develop scales based on factor analytic procedures.

10.2.1 Content/Rational Approach

The *content/rational approach* is the earliest approach to developing personality scales because it develops items based on their apparent relevance to the construct being measured. For example, in developing items to measure anxiety, you might include items addressing apprehension, worry, muscle tension, and fear. The inclusion of these items is based on your understanding of the construct you want to measure (i.e., anxiety). The Woodworth Personal Data Sheet, which we

> The earliest approach to developing objective personality scales was to develop items based on their apparent relevance to the construct being measured.

noted was the first formal instrument for assessing personality, was developed primarily using a content-based approach. While there are some more contemporary personality measures that have used this approach (e.g., Symptom Checklist—90—Revised: Derogatis, 1994), this approach has largely fallen out of favor as a standalone approach to scale development. One major limitation of this approach is that the scales are transparent to the extent that examinees can easily manipulate the results in order to present themselves in a specific way (e.g., Anastasi & Urbina, 1997). For example, if one wants to appear depressed, endorsing items reflecting feelings of sadness, hopelessness, isolation, and inferiority will result in a "high" depression score. Likewise, avoiding the endorsement of such items will result in a "low" depression score. Another limitation of the content/rational approach is that it assumes an item that measures a specific construct, which is not always correct. While we might believe that individuals with Generalized Anxiety Disorder will endorse the item "My muscles are tense" in a positive direction more than those without the diagnosis, this might not be the case! What an item actually measures is an empirical question that can only be answered through careful statistical analysis (e.g., Friedenberg, 1995). Most test authors on some occasions have been surprised to discover that one of their favorite items developed using content analysis failed to holdup under empirical scrutiny.

While contemporary test developers rarely rely exclusively on a content/rational approach to scale development, it is common to start with this approach when writing items for personality tests. Once items have been written based on their content, empirical studies can reveal which items are actually measuring the constructs of interest.

10.2.2 Empirical Criterion Keying

Empirical criterion keying is a process in which a large pool of items is administered to two groups, one typically a clinical group composed of individuals with a specific diagnosis and the other a control or normal group representative of the general population. The items are then statistically examined with the goal of identifying and retaining items that discriminate between the two groups. With this approach, it is not necessary that the items have logical appeal or content relevance. For example, if the item "I like classical music" discriminates well between depressed and nondepressed individuals, it might be retained even though its content does not appear to be relevant to depression. (Don't worry—this is just an example and enjoying classical music is not indicative of depression!)

The *Minnesota Multiphasic Personality Inventory* (MMPI®) is a prime example of a test developed using the empirical criterion keying approach. The original MMPI was published in the early 1940s (Hathaway & McKinley, 1940, 1943) to aid in the diagnosis of psychiatric disorders. By the 1960s, the MMPI was the most widely used and thoroughly researched personality test. It was used not only in clinical settings to facilitate diagnosis but also in nonclinical settings to assess examinees in employment, military,

> The Minnesota Multiphasic Personality Inventory (MMPI) is a prime example of a test developed using the empirical criterion keying approach.

medical, forensic, and other settings. By the 1980s, there was increased criticism of the MMPI with detractors noting that advances in personality theory, our understanding of psychopathology, and psychometrics all called for a revision of the original MMPI (Anastasi & Urbina, 1997). The revision, the *Minnesota Multiphasic Personality Inventory-2*, was published in 1989 (Butcher, Dahlstrom, Graham, Tellegen, & Kaemmer, 1989). To allow continuity with its predecessor, the MMPI-2 retained many of the items and the overall structure of the original MMPI. However, it did incorporate changes intended to modernize and improve the instrument including the development of contemporary norms using a national standardization sample and removal or revision of outdated and objectionable items.

The MMPI-2 consists of 567 true–false items that are used to calculate more than 70 different scales. Scale scores are reported in T-scores (mean = 50; sd = 10) based on the normative sample, and T-scores greater than 65 are considered clinically relevant. Ten of these scales, the Clinical Scales, are typically the focus of clinical interpretation, and they are summarized in Table 10.1 (based on information provided by Hathaway & McKinley, 1989; Graham, 1993). Eight of these scales were originally developed using empirical criterion keying; the Masculinity-Femininity and Social Introversion scales were added after the publication of the original MMPI and were developed using content-based procedures (Graham, 1993). In clinical practice, most psychologists utilize a configural approach to interpreting MMPI-2 scores. That is, instead of examining single scales in isolation, they examine scores as a profile or in relation to each other. The most popular approach is to examine the highest two scores in a client's profile that are clinically elevated

Table 10.1 MMPI-2 Clinical scales

#	Name	Symbol	Items	High scores
1	Hypochondriasis	Hs	32	High scores are associated with somatic complaints and excessive concern about health issues.
2	Depression	D	57	High scores are associated with depressive symptoms such as pessimism, hopelessness, and discouragement.
3	Hysteria	Hy	60	High scores are associated with the development of physical symptoms in response to stress and to avoid responsibility.
4	Psychopathic deviate	Pd	50	High scores are associated with difficulty in incorporating societal standards and values.
5	Masculinity--femininity	Mf	56	High scores are associated with tendency to reject stereotypical gender roles.
6	Paranoia	Pa	40	High scores are associated with behaviors ranging from general over-sensitivity to paranoid delusions.
7	Psychasthenia	Pt	48	High scores are associated with anxiety, agitation, and discomfort.
8	Schizophrenia	Sc	78	High scores may be associated with psychotic symptoms, confusion, or disorientation.
9	Hypomania	Ma	46	High scores are associated with high energy levels, narcissism, and possibly mania.
0	Social introversion	Si	69	High scores are associated with social introversion.

($T > 65$). With this approach, the highest two clinical scales produce a two-point code. For example, consider a profile with the highest score being scale 4 (Psychopathic Deviate) followed by scale 9 (Hypomania). This would be coded as a 4–9 two-point code. Considerable research has been completed regarding the behavioral correlates of MMPI-2 code types, and this information is condensed in a number of interpretive clinical guides. For example, consider these excerpted descriptive comments regarding a 4–9 (or 9–4) code type. Figure 10.1 depicts a completed MMPI-2 profile with a 4–9 code type. Graham offers the following interpretive information about this code type.

> The most salient characteristic of 49/94 individuals is a marked disregard for social standards and values. They frequently get into trouble with the authorities because of antisocial behavior. They have poorly developed conscience, easy morals, and fluctuating ethical values. Alcoholism, fighting, marital problems, sexual acting out, and a wide array of delinquent acts are among the difficulties in which they may be involved. (Graham, 1993, p. 95)

In addition to the original 10 clinical scales, a number of additional scales are available. In fact, close to 60 additional scales are listed in the MMPI-2 manual (Hathaway & McKinley, 1989). Some of these supplementary scales have received considerable research and clinical attention. For example, the MacAndrew Alcoholism Scale-Revised (MAC-R) is a 49-item scale that research indicates may be sensitive in detecting substance-abuse problems. Another example is the Negative Treatment Indicators scale. Elevated scores on this scale may reflect client attitudes

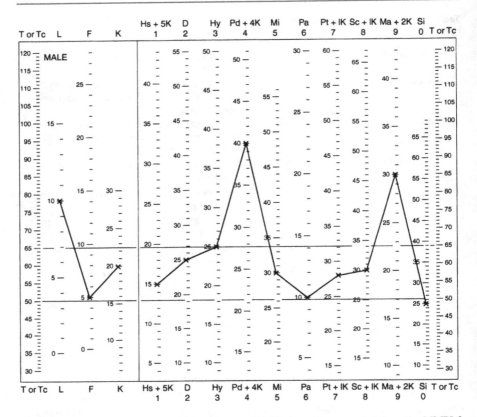

Fig. 10.1 MMPI-2 profile with a 4–9 code type. MMPI-2 profile: excerpted from the MMPI-2 (Minnesota Multiphasic Personality Inventory-2) Manual for Administration, Scoring, and Interpretation, Revised Edition. Copyright © 2001 by the Regents of the University of Minnesota. (Used with permission of the University of Minnesota Press. All rights reserved. "MMPI®" and "Minnesota Multiphasic Personality Inventory®" are trademarks owned by the Regents of the University of Minnesota)

that interfere with psychological treatment such as resistance to change or the belief that change is simply not possible (Butcher et al., 1989).

One of the most impressive features of the MMPI and its revision is the development and application of *validity scales*. These scales are designed to detect response sets (e.g., faking good or bad), resistance, carelessness, random responding, or errors due to misunderstanding or poor reading ability. The original MMPI included four validity scales that are listed in Table 10.2. The MMPI-2 includes three new validity scales, the Back F Scale (FB), Variable Response Inconsistency Scale (VRIN), and the True Response Inconsistency Scale (TRIN). These will not be described here, but interested readers can find more

Table 10.2 Original MMPI-2 validity scales

Name	Symbol	High scores
Cannot say	?	Number of items not answered for any of a number of reasons such as defiance, confusion, depression, poor reading, and suspiciousness.
Lie scale	L	High scores may indicate a tendency to present oneself in a favorable way. While it may indicate deliberate attempt to "fake good," it might simply reflect a strong moral and virtuous self-image. Very low scores may reflect an attempt to "fake bad."
Infrequency scale	F	High scores may indicate random responding, faking bad, or a cry for help.
Correction scale	K	High scores are often associated with a subtle defensiveness. May be a blatant attempt to fake good or a just guarded approach to the test. Very low scores may reflect an attempt to fake bad or a cry for help.

information in a number of resources (e.g., Graham, 1993). Interpretation strategies for the validity scales vary from the simple to the complex. One simple strategy is to consider any protocol with an excessive number of omitted items as invalid. However, the authors disagree about what constitutes an excessive number, with some suggesting a "Cannot Say (?)" score greater than 10 as the cutoff, with others setting the cutoff as high as 30. Likewise, some clinicians will discount any protocol with a validity scale score greater than 65, while others utilize a more complex configural approach that considers the pattern formed by the validity scales as a whole (Graham, 1993).

In addition to the MMPI-2, there is also the **Minnesota Multiphasic Personality Inventory – Adolescents** (MMPI-A) and the more recently released **MMPI-A Restructured Form** (RF). These instruments are designed for adolescents between the ages of 14 and 18 and contain the basic clinical and validity scales from the original MMPI and an assortment of supplementary and content-based scales.

The reliability of the MMPI-2 can generally be described as adequate. For example, 1 week test-retest data for the basic validity and clinical scales ranged from 0.67 to 0.92 in a sample of 82 males and 0.58 to 0.91 in a sample of females (Butcher et al., 1989). Granted this is not impressive compared to the reliability of many intelligence and other cognitive tests, but it is in line with scores produced by many personality measures. There is another aspect of reliability that is often overlooked when evaluating the MMPI-2. Since many MMPI-2 interpretive strategies emphasize configural analysis, it is also important to evaluate the stability of profile configurations. Graham (2000) noted that many clinicians assume that if individual scales have adequate reliability, profiles or configurations using multiple scores will also be reliable. However, the evidence supporting this belief is meager at best. The most common approach to examine the stability of MMPI-2 profile configurations has been to examine code type congruence. That is, what percentage of subjects obtains the same MMPI-2 code type on two separate administrations of the test? Graham (2000) reviewed the research on the stability of one, two, and three-point codes for the MMPI and MMPI-2 and noted that approximately one-fourth to one--half will have the same two-point code type on two administrations and only about one-fourth will have the same three-point code type. These results are found in fairly short test-retest intervals (e.g., 1–2 weeks). This does not mean that these configural approaches to interpretation should be abandoned, but it does mean that these interpretive strategies should be used with an appropriate degree of caution (something that can be said for all interpretive approaches).

In terms of validity evidence, it is safe to say that a very large amount of validity evidence accumulated over 50 years of research with the original MMPI. Since the MMPI-2 retained the overall structure of the original MMPI, much of the existing validity evidence can also be used to support the MMPI-2. The downside of retaining the original structure is that the MMPI-2 inherited many problems from its predecessor. These problems include

- The MMPI was developed in the 1930s and was based on a taxonomy of psychopathology that is clearly outdated in the twenty-first Century. For example, consider use of the term Psychasthenia to describe one of the clinical scales. Instead of using this outdated terminology, many clinicians simply refer to the scales using their scale number, and so rather than Psychasthenia, the scale is simply referred to as scale 7.
- The "normal" group used in the original empirical analysis was composed of people visiting a hospital in Minnesota. This presents obvious problems as the group is clearly not representative of the national population. To exacerbate the problem, most were visiting patients at the hospital and were likely experiencing some degree of distress as a result of the illness of a relative or friend when they completed the instrument (e.g., Thorndike, 2005).
- Reliance on what has been described as "flawed" application of empirical criterion keying resulted in numerous psychometric problems (e.g., Anastasi & Urbina, 1997). For example, there is a high degree of overlap in items across the clinical scales, and this results in high scale intercorrelations.

To address these problems, a new version MMPI-2 referred to as the ***MMPI-2 Restructured Form*** (MMPI-2-RF™) was released in 2008. In Special Interest Topic 10.5, one of the authors of the MMPI-2-RF describes its development, along with the development of the next evolution of the MMPI tests, the ***MMPI-3***.

Special Interest Topic 10.5: The MMPI-3: The Next Step in the Evolution of an Instrument

Yossef S. Ben-Porath
Kent State University

The original MMPI was developed in the late 1930s by psychologist Starke Hathaway and psychiatrist Charnley McKinley. These authors did not view the MMPI as the final word on personality assessment. Commenting on the state of the MMPI some 20 years after its completion, Hathaway (1960) observed: "That the MMPI will be a steppingstone to a higher level of validity, I still sincerely hope… In the meantime I see it as a steppingstone that permits useful communication at its own level even though the stone is rather wobbly."

(continued)

Returning to this topic on the 30th anniversary of its publication, Hathaway (1972) commented:

> If another twelve years were to go by without our having gone on to a better instrument or better procedure for the practical needs, I fear that the MMPI, like some other tests, might have changed from a hopeful innovation to an aged obstacle. Do not misunderstand me. I am not agreeing with a few critics who have already called for the funeral and written the epitaph. They have not yet identified what is better. We cannot lay down even a stone-age axe if we have no better one to hew with. (p. xiv)

As reflected in these quotes, Hathaway perceived some significant limitations in the original MMPI, but doubted whether the science of personality assessment had, 30 years later, yielded a more solid foundation upon which a better instrument could be built. Although his reference to stone-age technology was undoubtedly an exaggeration designed for effect, the original MMPI Clinical Scales targeted an increasingly outdated nosological system, and the methodology used in their development, empirical keying, is no longer preferentially employed by contemporary test constructors.

In the early 1980s, a team of psychologists assembled by the test publisher, the University of Minnesota Press, began a project to update the MMPI. Their effort yielded the MMPI-2. Consistent with Hathaway's view that the field of assessment psychology had yet to produce a better framework upon which to construct measures of psychopathology, the test's original Clinical Scales were essentially left unchanged in the revision. The primary change offered by the MMPI-2 was a much-needed update of the test's norms. However, shortly after it was completed, a member of the team that restandardized the test, Professor Auke Tellegen, of the University of Minnesota, embarked on a project that initially yielded restructured versions of the original MMPI Clinical Scales and eventually produced the MMPI-2-RF.

Two primary shortcomings of the original MMPI Clinical Scales motivated Tellegen's efforts: Their heterogeneous and over-inclusive content and its result: the considerable overlap and higher than clinically and theoretically expected correlations between the scales. Over the years, MMPI researchers and users developed a number of effective, albeit cumbersome ways to overcome these challenges (e.g., interpretation of patterns of scores on the scales [code types] and various subscales and supplementary scales designed to guide and clarify further their interpretation). Tellegen sought to address these difficulties directly and parsimoniously by developing a set of Restructured Clinical (RC) Scales, each designed to measure a major distinctive core component of an original Clinical Scale. In developing the RC Scales, Tellegen employed modern test-construction techniques. This meant conducting hundreds of factor analyses, any one of which would have literally taken Hathaway and McKinley several months to complete using the technology at their disposal at the time that the MMPI was developed.

(continued)

In the closing paragraphs of monograph introducing the RC Scales (Tellegen et al., 2003), the authors commented that the methodology used to develop these measures could be applied further and perhaps yield a set of new scales that captures all of the core constructs represented by the MMPI-2 item pool in a more transparent and effective manner. That was the authors' goal in using the RC Scales as a starting point for construction of the MMPI-2-RF, to develop a modern assessment device linked to current concepts and models of personality and psychopathology, by applying contemporary scale construction techniques to the highly diverse item pool assembled by Hathaway and McKinley for the original MMPI and augmented by Butcher et al. (1989) for the MMPI-2. A substantial body of more than 450 peer reviewed studies (https://www.upress.umn.edu/test-division/MMPI-2-RF/mmpi-2-rf-references) indicates that this objective was largely achieved.

The MMPI-3 represents the next step in the evolution of the MMPI instruments. Two primary goals guided its development: to expand the item pool and update the 30-year-old test norms. Data used to construct the MMPI-3 were collected with an expanded version of the MMPI-2-RF, the MMPI-2-RF-EX, which included the 338 MMPI-2-RF items followed by 95 trial items that were candidates for inclusion in the revised inventory. Of the 338 MMPI-2-RF items, 39 were rewritten to correct awkward language or simplify content. Placing the 338 MMPI-2-RF items first in the MMPI-2-RF-EX booklet made it possible to administer the expanded booklet in applied settings, score the MMPI-2-RF, and use the obtained results in actual assessments.

Field data were obtained with these materials from over 14,000 individuals who were administered the MMPI-2-RF-EX as part of assessments representing the broad range of settings and populations within which the test is used. These included evaluations conducted in various mental-health, medical, forensic, and public safety agencies and practices. As detailed in the *MMPI-3 Technical Manual*, field data were used for three purposes: scale development, scale score validation (using data not used for scale development), and assembling MMPI-3 comparison groups. Validation data, available for subsets of field data participants, included clinician ratings and extensive record reviews in mental-health settings; clinical ratings and postsurgical outcome data in medical settings; standardized test scores and available outcomes in forensic settings; and job performance outcomes, psychosocial history data, and standardized test results in public safety settings.

The MMPI-2-RF-EX was also administered by several researchers to over 8000 students at colleges and universities. These data were collected for research purposes. Students were administered a broad range of collateral measures selected to examine in detail the empirical correlates of revised and new MMPI-3 scale scores. Limitations imposed by the relatively restricted range of psychopathology among college students were offset by the opportunity to administer comprehensive test batteries that facilitated detailed, fine-grained validity analyses of MMPI-3 scores and by the broad range of field data just described.

(continued)

The MMPI-2-RF-EX was also used to collect data for the development of two new MMPI-3 normative samples. The publisher enlisted the services of a social science and market research firm experienced in nationwide data collection and with expertise in recruiting members of difficult-to-reach populations, including collecting data with Hispanic and Spanish-speaking populations, to collect the data used to develop English- and Spanish-language norms for the MMPI-3. Data were collected between September 2017 and December 2018 from 3400 individuals throughout the United States. The MMPI-3 English-language normative sample is made up of 810 men and 810 women, selected to target Census Bureau race/ethnicity, education, and age projections for the U.S. adult population in 2020. The Spanish-language MMPI-3 normative sample is composed of 275 men and 275 women.

As mentioned earlier, the MMPI-3 authors sought to expand content coverage of the MMPI-2-RF while retaining the length of the test. Toward this end, some MMPI-2-RF scales were removed (e.g., MMPI-2-RF Aesthetic-Literary and Mechanical-Physical Interest Scales) and the length of others was reduced to not more than the number of items necessary for maintaining reliability and validity. This ultimately resulted in the MMPI-3 consisting of 335 items with 52 validity and substantive scales.

MMPI-3 scale development began with the Restructured Clinical (RC) Scales. Empirical analyses were conducted to identify existing items that could be removed from the RC Scales without loss of reliability and validity and trial items that could be added to the remaining RC Scale items to expand content coverage. In general, item composition changes of the RC Scales led to comparable convergent and discriminant validities for most scales and improvements for RC Scales targeted for expansion of coverage. Similar analyses guided changes to the Specific Problem (SP) Scales, which map onto constructs related to somatic/cognitive, internalizing, externalizing, and interpersonal problems. Four new SP Scales were developed, labeled Eating Concerns (EAT), Compulsivity (CMP), Impulsivity (IMP), and Self-Importance (SFI). The MMPI-2-RF Anxiety (AXY) scale was expanded substantially and is now labeled Anxiety-Related Experiences (ARX). The MMPI-2-RF Stress/Worry (STW) was divided into two scales—Stress (STR) and Worry (WRY). The Higher-Order (H-O) and Personality Psychopathology-5 (PSY-5) Scales were also updated by using remaining items available for each scale following the deletion of RC and Scale items and addition of trial items. Item analyses were conducted to ensure robust item consistency of the scales.

Development of the MMPI-3 Validity Scales also began with their MMPI-2-RF counterparts. Updated versions of the Variable Response Inconsistency (VRIN) and True Response Inconsistency (TRIN) scales—replacing deleted items and incorporating items added to the MMPI-3—were developed along with a new Combined Response Inconsistency (CRIN) scale, consisting of 86 inconsistent response composites that make up VRIN and

(continued)

TRIN. For the MMPI-3 overreporting scales, Infrequent Responses (F), Infrequent Psychopathology Responses (Fp), and Infrequent Somatic Responses (Fs), the three MMPI-2-RF infrequency indicators were updated incorporating new items and item response frequencies. The remaining two MMPI-2-RF overreporting scales—Symptom Validity Scale (FBS) and the Response Bias Scale (RBS)—were carried over unchanged. The MMPI-3 underreporting scales—Uncommon Virtues (L) and Adjustment Validity (K)—were updated with new items as well.

Following, is a brief description of the 52 MMPI-3 Scales.

Validity scales	
CRIN	Combined response inconsistency—combination of random and fixed inconsistent responding
VRIN	Variable response inconsistency—random responding
TRIN	True response inconsistency—fixed responding
F	Infrequent responses—responses infrequent in the general population
Fp	Infrequent psychopathology responses—responses infrequent in psychiatric populations
Fs	Infrequent somatic responses—somatic complaints infrequent in medical patient populations
FBS	Symptom validity scale—noncredible somatic and cognitive complaints
RBS	Response bias scale—exaggerated memory complaints
L	Uncommon virtues—rarely claimed moral attributes or activities
K	Adjustment validity—claims of uncommonly high level of psychological adjustment
Higher-order (H-O) scales	
EID	Emotional/internalizing dysfunction—problems associated with mood and affect
THD	Thought dysfunction—problems associated with disordered thinking
BXD	Behavioral/externalizing dysfunction—problems associated with under-controlled behavior
Restructured clinical (RC) scales	
RCd	Demoralization—general unhappiness and dissatisfaction
RC1	Somatic complaints—diffuse physical health complaints
RC2	Low positive emotions—lack of positive emotional responsiveness

(continued)

RC4	Antisocial behavior—rule breaking and irresponsible behavior
RC6	Ideas of persecution—self-referential beliefs that others pose a threat
RC7	Dysfunctional negative emotions—maladaptive anxiety, anger, and irritability
RC8	Aberrant experiences—unusual perceptions or thoughts associated with thought dysfunction
RC9	Hypomanic activation—overactivation, aggression, impulsivity, and grandiosity

Specific problem (SP) scales
 Somatic/cognitive scales

MLS	Malaise—overall sense of physical debilitation and poor health
NUC	Neurological complaints—dizziness, weakness, paralysis, loss of balance, etc.
EAT	Eating concerns—problematic eating behaviors
COG	Cognitive complaints—memory problems and difficulties in concentrating

 Internalizing scales

SUI	Suicidal/death ideation—direct reports of suicidal ideation and recent attempts
HLP	Helplessness/hopelessness—belief that goals cannot be reached or problems solved
SFD	Self-doubt—lack of self-confidence and feelings of uselessness
NFC	Inefficacy—belief that one is indecisive and inefficacious
STR	Stress—problems involving stress and nervousness
WRY	Worry—excessive worry and preoccupation
CMP	Compulsivity—engaging in compulsive behaviors
ARX	Anxiety-related experiences—multiple anxiety-related experiences such as catastrophizing, panic, dread, and intrusive ideation
ANP	Anger proneness—becoming easily angered and impatient with others
BRF	Behavior-restricting fears—fears that significantly inhibit normal behavior

 Externalizing scales

FML	Family problems—conflictual family relationships
JCP	Juvenile conduct problems—difficulties at school and at home and stealing
SUB	Substance abuse—current and past misuse of alcohol and drugs

(continued)

IMP	Impulsivity—poor impulse control and nonplanful behavior
ACT	Activation—heightened excitation and energy level
AGG	Aggression—physically aggressive and violent behavior
CYN	Cynicism—nonself-referential beliefs that others are bad and not to be trusted
Interpersonal scales	
SFI	Self-importance—beliefs related to having special talents and abilities
DOM	Dominance—being domineering in relationships with others
DSF	Disaffiliativeness—disliking people and being around them
SAV	Social avoidance—not enjoying and avoiding social events
SHY	Shyness—feeling uncomfortable and anxious in the presence of others
Personality psychopathology-five scales	
AGGR	Aggressiveness—instrumental, goal-directed aggression
PSYC	Psychoticism—disconnection from reality
DISC	Disconstraint—under-controlled behavior
NEGE	Negative emotionality/neuroticism—anxiety, insecurity, worry, and fear
INTR	Introversion/low positive emotionality—social disengagement and anhedonia

10.2.3 Factor Analysis

We initially discussed factor analysis in Chap. 5 as it plays a prominent role in test validation. It also plays a prominent role in the development of personality and other tests. To refresh your memory, Reynolds and Kamphaus (2003) described factor analysis as a statistical approach that allows one to evaluate the pres-

> Factor analysis also plays a prominent role in the development of personality and other tests.

ence and structure of latent constructs existing among a set of variables. Factor analysis plays a long and important role in identifying the structure of personality with models including from as few as three to several dozen factors (see Goldberg, 1993 for a readable summary). Raymond Cattell is typically credited with being a leader in the use of factor analysis to understand the structure of the normal personality. He published the original *16 Personality Factor Questionnaire* (16 PF) in

1949, and the most recent fifth edition was released in 1993. It is a 185 item inventory that, as the name suggests, is based on a 16 factor model of personality. The 16 Primary Factors are Warmth, Reasoning, Emotional Stability, Dominance, Liveliness, Rule Consciousness, Social Boldness, Sensitivity, Vigilance, Abstractedness, Privateness, Apprehension, Openness-to-Change, Self-Reliance, Perfectionism, and Tension. The 16 PF adopts a hierarchical model that contains second order factors obtained by factor analyzing the 16 primary factors. These five Global Factors are Extraversion, Anxiety, Tough-Mindedness, Independence, and Self-Control. The 16 PF 5th Edition is more psychometrically sound than earlier editions; however, problems remain. Possibly, the most problematic issue is that the 16 Primary Factors are not statistically independent. Accordingly, other researchers have not been able to reproduce the 16 factor structure when examining Cattell's data (e.g., Anastasi & Urbina, 1997). Nevertheless, the 16 PF has a fairly strong following and is a popular measure of normal personality functioning, particularly in counseling, school, and industrial/organizational settings.

In recent years, a Five Factor Model of personality has received widespread (but not universal) acceptance. This model holds that five major factors or dimensions underlie the construct of personality. Some have suggested that Cattell was actually the father of the contemporary Five Factor Model citing the five global factors in the 16 PF as evidence.

> The five-factor model of personality has received widespread acceptance.

However, Cattell never accepted this recognition or embraced the Five Factor Model (he maintained that there were more than five factors underlying personality). It appears that Fiske's research (1949) attempting to reproduce Cattell's 16 factors actually resulted in a five-factor solution, and he is usually credited as the first in identifying the five factors contained in the FFM. Ironically, Fisk never followed up on his findings and left the development of the Five Factor Model to others (Goldberg, 1993). The five factors included in the contemporary Five Factor Model are as follows:

- *Neuroticism*: Individuals who score high on this factor tend to experience high levels of negative effects (e.g., depression, anxiety, and anger). In contrast, individuals who score low tend to be emotionally stable.
- *Extraversion*: Individuals with high scores on this factor tend to be gregarious, active, and enjoy group activities, while those with low scores tend to be more reserved and enjoy solitary activities.
- *Openness to Experience*: Individuals with high scores tend to be curious and value adventure and novel experiences, while those with low scores prefer familiar and conventional behavior.
- *Agreeableness*: Individuals with high scores tend to be courteous, tolerant, and compassionate, while those with low scores tend to be disagreeable, egocentric, and antagonistic.
- *Conscientiousness*: Individuals with high scores tend to be self-disciplined, responsible, and dependable, while those with low scores tend to be unreliable and display less self-control.

Table 10.3 Domain and Facet scales for the NEO PI-3

Domain	Facet scales
Neuroticism	• Anxiety • Hostility • Depression • Self-consciousness • Impulsiveness • Vulnerability
Extraversion	• Warmth • Gregariousness • Assertiveness • Activity • Excitement seeking • Positive emotions
Openness	• Fantasy • Aesthetics • Feelings • Actions • Ideas • Values
Agreeableness	• Trust • Straightforwardness • Altruism • Compliance • Modesty • Tender-mindedness
Conscientiousness	• Competence • Order • Dutifulness • Achievement striving • Self-discipline • Deliberation

The test that most exemplifies the Five Factor Model is the **_NEO Personality Inventory-3_** (NEO-PI-3: McCrae & Costa, 2010). The NEO PI-3 is a 240-item inventory based largely on the results of factor analytic studies. It produces five domain scores reflecting Neuroticism, Extraversion, Openness to Experience, Agreeableness, and Conscientious. Each of the five domain scores have six subordinate facet scores that are listed in Table 10.3. There are two forms available, one for self-report and the other for completion by an observer (i.e., a third party such as a spouse or friend). The NEO-PI-3 contains one item that is intended to serve as a validity check, but it has no formal validity scales.

The NEO PI-3 scale scores have good reliability, and there is reasonable evidence of the validity of the score interpretations found using its predecessor, the NEO PI-R. Given similarity between the versions, it is reasonable to expect that studies with the new version will result in similar findings. The primary limitation of the NEO PI tests involves their somewhat limited range of applications. The NEO PI tests clearly play a role in basic research on personality, but they have not proven particularly effective in predicting performance or facilitating decision-making in clinical settings (e.g., Thorndike, 2005). As a result, it is a good measure of normal personality development, but additional research is warranted for further establishing its usefulness in clinical or other applied settings.

10.2.4 Theoretical Approach

A number of tests have been developed based on a specific theory of personality. For example, the *Myers-Briggs Type Indicator* (MBTI: Myers & McCaulley, 1985) was based on the theory of psychological types proposed by C.G. Jung postulating the existence of dichoto-

> A number of objective personality scales have been developed based on a specific theory of personality.

mies reflecting psychological dispositions or personal preferences. The dichotomies measured by the MBTI are described below.

- *Extraversion (E)–Introversion (I)*: Extraversion reflects a preference to focus on the external world of people and objects. Introversion reflects an individual's preference to focus on the inner world of thoughts and ideas.
- *Sensing (N)–Intuition (N)*: Sensing suggests a preference to focus on what can be perceived by the five senses, while Intuition indicates a preference for focusing on complex relationships and patterns.
- *Thinking (T)–Feeling (F)*: Thinking reflects a preference for basing decisions on a logical analysis of the facts, while Feeling reflects a preference for basing decisions on personal values and situational features.
- *Judging (J)–Perceiving (P)*: In dealing with the external world, Judging indicates a preference for structure and decisiveness, while Perceiving reflects a preference for flexibility and adaptability.

The first three dichotomies were postulated by Jung, while the Judging-Perceiving dichotomy was later added by Isabel Briggs Myers and Katherine Briggs when developing the MBTI.

The scores on these four dimensions are used to assign people to 1 of the 16 personality types that are designated by letters reflecting the individual's preference. For example, the code type ISTJ indicates a person with preferences reflecting Introversion, Sensing, Thinking, and Judging. The test manual (Myers, McCaulley, Quenk, & Hammer, 1998) provides interpretive guides describing characteristics of each personality code type. For example, the ISTJ type is described as quite, serious, and dependable. They are practical, realistic, and responsible. Their lives are organized, and they value traditions and loyalty.

> The Myers-Briggs Type Indicator and the Millon Clinical Multiaxial Inventory-IV are examples of theoretically based contemporary objective personality tests.

The MBTI is one of the most widely used psychological tests today. As might be expected, it has both supporters and detractors. There are many psychologists and professional counselors that find the instrument useful in their clinical practice. In contrast, many psychometricians have criticized the MBTI with regard to its psychometric properties. An often-cited criticism is that it is possible for examinees to be assigned the same four letter code type while differing greatly in their actual response patterns. For example, two people classified as an ISTJ may vary greatly in the strength of their preferences. One examinee may demonstrate strong preferences on one or more dimensions (e.g., extremely introverted), and the other might demonstrate only moderate or weak preferences (e.g., mild preference for introversion). The MBTI actually does provide scores reflecting the strength of the preferences, but over reliance of categorical code types without considering the strength of the preferences is probably a common interpretive error. The stability of the MBTI code types has also been criticized. For example, the MBTI manual reports that after 4 weeks, 65% of the examinees obtain the same four-letter code type, while 35% change (most on only one dichotomy). This is often cited as a significant weakness of the MBTI. However, when compared to the stability of MMPI-2 two-point code types (i.e., 25–50% will obtain the same code type), this criticism appears somewhat overstated.

Another example of a theoretically based personality inventory is the *Millon Clinical Multiaxial Inventory-IV* (MCMI-IV: Millon, Grossman, & Millon, 2015). This inventory is based on Theodore Millon's theory of personality (Millon & Davis, 1996), and like the MMPI-2, this was designed to facilitate the assessment and diagnosis of clients with psychological disorders. Many clinicians find the MCMI-IV particularly useful in the assessment of individuals with personality disorders. It is a self-report measure containing 195 statements that are marked as true or false. The inventory's scales include 12 Clinical Personality Pattern scales, 3 Severe Personality Pathology scales, 7 Clinical Syndrome scales, and 3 Severe Clinical Syndrome scales. The personality and clinical syndrome scales parallel DSM-V diagnostic categories and are grouped into two levels of severity. There are also three Modifying Indices that can be used to modify clinical scale scores to take into consideration the client's response style and two Validity Indices that help detect potentially invalid protocols. These scales are listed in Table 10.4.

The MCMI-IV scores have adequate reliability and validity evidence. One innovative feature of the test is the use of Base Rate Scores. Instead of using the normalized standard scores like most other personality measures, these scores are based on actuarial base rate information. As a result, they take into account the base or prevalence rate of different disorders in different settings, which can enhance the diagnostic accuracy of the scales. A limitation of the MCMI-IV is that, like the MMPI-2, it has high intercorrelations between the scale scores (albeit the intercorrelations are lower in the fourth edition compared to the third edition), and this complicates the instruments' use for differential diagnosis (e.g., Thorndike, 2005).

Before ending our discussion of the MCMI-IV, we must note that while we use this as an example of a personality measure developed from a theoretical perspective, like many contemporary personality scales, it also incorporated empirical/

Table 10.4 MCMI-IV scales

Category	Diagnostic scales
Clinical personality patterns	• Schizoid • Avoidant • Melancholic • Dependent • Histrionic • Turbulent • Narcissistic • Antisocial • Sadistic • Compulsive • Negativistic • Masochistic
Severe personality pathology	• Schizotypal • Borderline • Paranoid
Clinical syndromes	• Generalized anxiety • Somatic symptom • Bipolar spectrum • Persistent depression • Alcohol use • Drug use • Post-traumatic stress
Severe clinical syndromes	• Schizophrenic spectrum • Major depression • Delusional
Modifying indices	• Disclosure •Desirability • Debasement
Validity indices	• Invalidity

statistical methods. The author's website (www.millonpersonality.com) notes that item and scale development involved the following three steps:

- *Theoretical-Substantive.* In this stage, items were developed based on Million's theory of personality and to align with DSM-IV criteria.
- *Internal-Structural.* In this stage, the internal consistency of the scales was examined. Items that did not behave as expected were modified or removed.
- *External-Criterion.* In this final stage, the items were examined to determine if they facilitated discrimination between diagnostic groups. In these analyses, the authors examined the ability of the items to discriminate between clinical groups (e.g., depression versus anxiety) rather than simply between clinical groups and a control or normal group. This was done to enhance the ability of the test to not only identify those with psychopathology but also help the clinician differentiate between different psychological disorders (i.e., differential diagnosis).

The authors note that items had to clear each developmental stage successfully to proceed to the following stage. As you see, this is essentially an amalgamation of what we described as the Content/Rational and Empirical Criterion Keying approaches, with internal consistency analysis used to enhance the psychometric properties of the scales. This is characteristic of the modern trend in personality measure development. That is, most contemporary personality measures use multiple approaches to scale development.

10.3   Assessment of Personality in Children and Adolescents

In the context of child and adolescent assessment, the term personality is appropriately used cautiously. Measures of personality in children demonstrate that the personality characteristics of children show less stability than comparable characteristics in adults. This is not particularly surprising given the rapid developmental changes characteristic of children and adolescents. As a result, when using the term personality in the context of child and adolescent assessment, it is best to interpret it cautiously and understand that it does not necessarily reflect a fixed construct, but one that is subject to development and change. Although the use of objective personality measures has a long and rich history with adults, their use with children is a relatively new development because it was long believed that children did not have the personal insights necessary to understand and accurately report their subjective experiences. To further complicate the situation, skeptics noted that young children typically do not have the reading skills necessary to complete written self-report tests (e.g., Kamphaus & Frick, 2002). However, numerous self-report measures have been developed and used successfully with children and adolescents. Although insufficient reading skills do make these instruments impractical with very young children, these new self-report measures are being used with older children (e.g., >7 years) and adolescents with considerable success. Objective measures have proven to be particularly useful in the assessment of internalizing disorders such as depression and anxiety that have symptoms that are not always readily apparent to observers. The development and use of self-report measures with children are still at a relatively early stage, but several instruments are gaining widespread acceptance. We will now briefly describe one of the most popular child and adolescent self-report personality measures.

> In the context of child and adolescent assessment, the term personality is used cautiously.

10.3.1 Behavior Assessment System for Children, Third Edition: Self-Report of Personality (SRP)

The *Behavior Assessment System for Children, Third Edition, Self-Report of Personality* (SRP) (Reynolds & Kamphaus, 2015), is a component of the Behavior Assessment System for Children (BASC-3), and research suggests that preceding editions have been the most popular self-report measure among school psychologists (Livingston, Eglsaer, Dickson, & Harvey-Livingston, 2003). There are four levels of the SRP, one for children 8–11 years, one for adolescents 12–18 years, and one for college students 18–25 years. A fourth version, the SRP-I (for interview), is standardized as an interview version for ages 6 and 7 years. The SRP has an estimated second-grade reading level, and if there is concern about the student's ability to read and comprehend the material, the instructions and items can be presented using audio. The SRP contains brief descriptive statements that children or adolescents mark as true or false to some questions, or never, sometimes, often, or almost always to other questions, as it applies to them. Reynolds and Kamphaus (2015) describe the subscales as follows:

- *Anxiety*: feelings of nervousness, worry, and fear and a tendency to be overwhelmed by problems
- *Attention Problems*: being easily distracted and unable to concentrate
- *Attitude to School*: feelings of alienation and dissatisfaction with school
- *Attitude to Teachers*: feelings of resentment and dissatisfaction with teachers
- *Atypicality*: having bizarre or "odd" thoughts or behaviors
- *Depression*: feelings of rejection, unhappiness, and sadness
- *Hyperactivity*: being overly active, impulsive, and rushing through work
- *Interpersonal Relations*: positive social relationships
- *Locus of Control*: perception that events in one's life are externally controlled
- *Relations with Parents*: positive attitude toward parents and feeling of being important in the family
- *Self-Esteem*: positive self-esteem characterized by self-respect and acceptance
- *Self-Reliance*: self-confidence and ability to solve problems
- *Sensation Seeking*: tendency to take risks and seek excitement
- *Sense of Inadequacy*: feeling unsuccessful in school and unable to achieve goals
- *Social Stress*: stress and tension related to social relationships
- *Somatization*: tendency to experience and complain about physical discomforts and problems

The SRP produces five composite scores. The most global composite is the Emotional Symptom Index (ESI) composed of the Anxiety, Depression, Self-Esteem, Self-Reliance, Sense of Inadequacy, and Social Stress scales. The ESI is an index of global psychopathology, and high scores usually indicate serious emotional problems. The four lower-order composite scales are

- *Inattention/Hyperactivity*. This scale combines the Attention Problems and the Hyperactivity scales to form a composite reflecting difficulties with the self-regulation of behavior and ability to attend and concentrate in many different settings.
- *Internalizing Problems*. This is a combination of the Anxiety, Atypicality, Depression, Locus of Control, Sense of Inadequacy, Social Stress, and Somatization scales. This scale reflects the magnitude of internalizing problems, and clinically significant scores (i.e., T-scores > 70) suggest significant problems.
- *School Problems*: This is composed of the Attitude to School, Attitude to Teachers, and Sensation Seeking scales. High scores on this scale suggest a general pattern of dissatisfaction with schools and teachers. Clinically significant scores suggest pervasive school problems, and adolescents with high scores might be at risk for dropping out.

- *Personal Adjustment*: This is composed of the Interpersonal Relationships, Relations with Parents, Self-Esteem, and Self-Reliance scales. High scores are associated with positive adjustment, whereas low scores suggest deficits in interpersonal relationships and identity formation.

High scores on the SRP Clinical Composites and Scales reflect abnormality or pathology. The authors provide the following classifications: *T*-score 70 or higher is Clinically Significant; 60–69 is At-Risk; 41–59 is Average; 31–40 is Low; and 30 or less is Very Low. Scores on the Adaptive Composite and Scales are interpreted differently, with high scores reflecting adaptive or positive behaviors. The authors provide the following classifications to facilitate diagnosis: *T*-score 70 or higher is Very High; 60–69 is High; 41–59 is Average; 31–40 is At-Risk; and 30 or less is Clinically Significant. An example of a completed SRP profile is depicted in Fig. 10.2.

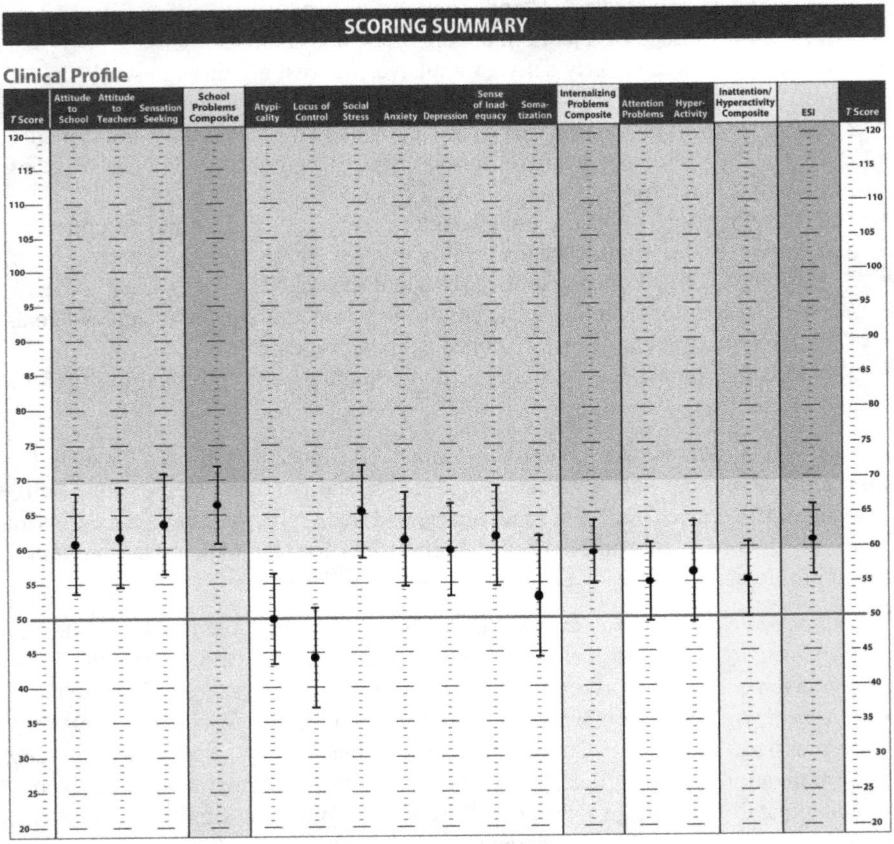

Fig. 10.2 BASC-3 Self-Report of Personality Profile. Behavior Assessment System for Children, Third Edition Copyright ©2015 NCS Pearson, Inc. (Reproduced with permission. All rights reserved)

10.3.2 Single-Domain Self-Report Measures

The personality inventories that we have reviewed to this point have been omnibus or broadband scales. That is, they are designed to measure personality broadly and to cover many aspects of personality and behavior. There are also a number of briefer more focused scales that are designed to measure narrow aspects of personality or to focus on a single clinical syndrome (often referred to as syndrome-specific). It is common practice in psychological assessment to start with a broadband instrument like the MMPI-2-RF or BASC-3 to get a comprehensive view of your client. This helps the clinician identify problematic areas and narrow the focus of subsequent assessment. For example, the results of the MMPI-2-RF might suggest a potential depressive or anxiety disorder, and the clinician can then follow-up with syndrome-specific anxiety and depression scales to develop a more refined understanding of presenting problem. Even within one disorder, there is typically considerable variation in symptom presentation. One person with major depression may have symptoms including depressed mood, weight gain, insomnia, fatigue, and suicidal ideations, while another person with the same diagnosis may present with anhedonia (loss of pleasure from activities that once brought pleasure), loss of appetite, psychomotor agitation, and difficulty in concentrating. While they are both depressed, they have distinctive patterns of symptoms and would likely benefit from different interventions. A targeted assessment using a combination of broad and narrow personality measures can help identify each client's unique pattern of symptoms, which can then help the psychologist tailor treatment to best meet the needs of each client.

> In addition to broad measures of personality and behavior, there are also brief, more focused scales designed to measure narrow aspects of personality or to focus on a single clinical syndrome.

An example of a single-domain (or syndrome-specific) self-report measure is the **Beck Depression Inventory, Second Edition** (BDI-2: Beck, Steer, & Brown, 1996). As the name suggests, the BDI-2 is designed to assess severity of depression in individuals between 13 and 80 years old. It is aligned with the diagnostic criteria for major depression in the *Diagnostic and Statistical Manual of Mental Disorders-IV (DSM-IV)*. The BDI-2 contains 21-items reflecting a depressive symptom. Each item includes four statements of increasing severity, which describe a specific depressive symptom (0 indicates that the symptom is not present, and 3 indicates that the symptom is severe). The BDI-2 produces a total score that is interpreted with the use of specific cut scores that delineate ranges reflecting the severity of depressive symptoms (minimal, mild, moderate, or severe depression). The BDI-2 score has good reliability, including good test-retest reliability with a 1-week interval (i.e., $r_{xx} = 93$). Different versions of the BDI have been in use for over 30 years, and it continues to be one of the most widely used self-report measures of depression.

An example of a single-domain self-report measure used with children is the *Children's Depression Inventory - Second Edition* (CDI-2; Kovacs & MHS Staff, 2011). The CDI is a 27-item self-report inventory designed for use with children between 7 and 17 years (it parallels the BDI-2 in format) that can be completed by adolescents, parents, or teachers. The CDI-2 presents a total score as well as five factor scores: Negative Mood, Interpersonal Problems, Ineffectiveness, Anhedonia, and Negative Self-Esteem. The CDI-2 is easily administered and scored, is time efficient and inexpensive, and has a fairly extensive research database. As with other single-domain measures, the BDI-2 and CDI-2 do not provide coverage of a broad range of psychological disorders or personality characteristics, but they do give a fairly in-depth assessment of depressive symptoms in their targeted populations.

10.4 Projective Personality Tests: An Overview

Projective techniques involve the presentation of unstructured or ambiguous materials, which allows an almost infinite range of responses from the examinee. For example, the clinician shows the examinee an inkblot and asks: "What might this be?" The central hypothesis of projective techniques is that examinees will interpret the ambiguous material in a manner that reveals important and often unconscious aspects of their

> Projective techniques involve the presentation of unstructured or ambiguous materials that allows an almost infinite range of responses from the examinee.

psychological functioning or personality. In other words, the ambiguous material serves as a blank screen on which the examinees "project" their most intimate thoughts, desires, fears, needs, and conflicts (Anastasi & Urbina, 1997; Finch & Belter, 1993). Although extremely popular in clinical settings, the use of projective techniques in the assessment of personality has a controversial history. In fact, Chandler (1990) noted that projective techniques have been the focus of controversy practically since they were initially introduced. Proponents claim that they are the richest source of clinical information available and are necessary in order to gain a thorough understanding of the individual. They suggest that self-report personality measures reflect only what the examinee wants to reveal and so are susceptible to response sets. In contrast, projective techniques are thought to be relatively free of response sets because the examinee has little idea of what types of responses are expected or are socially appropriate.

Critics of the use of projective techniques note that these procedures typically do not meet even minimum psychometric standards (e.g., having appropriate evidence to support the reliability of their scores and validity of score interpretations), and as a result, their use cannot be justified from an ethical or technical perspective. To justify their use, advocates often argue that they don't use projective techniques in a psychometric or diagnostic manner, but simply use them to supplement their objective instruments and gain insight that may be treated as clinical hypotheses. The critics argue that even if projective techniques are used simply to supplement a psychometrically sound battery of objective measures, their questionable reliability and validity will still detract from the technical soundness of the overall assessment process (Kamphaus & Frick, 2002). Psychodynamic theory (which is a theory of Freudian origin), which forms the foundation of the projective hypothesis, is also controversial and not nearly as popular today as it was in the early twentieth century.

The debate over the use of projective techniques has been going on for decades. Although there is evidence of diminished use of projective techniques in assessment, these techniques are still popular and used in clinical and educational settings (Livingston et al., 2003). This debate is apt to continue, but it is highly likely that projective techniques will continue to play a prominent role in psychological assessments for the foreseeable future. Next, we will briefly describe a few of the major projective techniques.

10.4.1 Projective Drawings

Some of the most popular projective techniques in contemporary use, especially with children and adolescents, involve the interpretation of *projective drawings*. This popularity is usually attributed to two factors. First, young children with limited verbal abilities are hampered in their ability to respond to clinical interviews, objective self-report measures, and even most other projective techniques. However, these young children can produce drawings because this activity is largely nonverbal. Second, because children are usually familiar with and enjoy drawing, this technique provides a nonthreatening "child-friendly" approach to assessment (Finch & Belter, 1993; Kamphaus & Frick, 2002). There are several different projective drawing techniques in use today.

10.4.1.1   Draw-A-Person (DAP) Test

The *Draw-A-Person* (DAP) *Test* is the most widely used projective drawing technique. The client is given a blank sheet of paper and a pencil and asked to draw a whole person. Although different scoring systems have been developed for the DAP test, no system has received universal approval. The figure in the drawing is often interpreted as a representation of the "self." That is, the figure reflects how examinees feel about themselves and how they feel as they interact with their environment (Handler, 1985).

10.4.1.2   House-Tree-Person (H-T-P)

With the *House-Tree-Person* (H-T-P), the examinee is given paper and a pencil and asked to draw a house, a tree, and a person of each gender, all on separate sheets. The clinician then typically asks a standard set of questions for each picture. After these drawings are completed, the examinee is then given a set of crayons and the process is repeated. The House is typically interpreted as reflecting feelings associated with home life and family relationships. The Tree and Person are thought to reflect aspects of the self, with the Tree representing deep unconscious feelings about the self and the Person reflecting a closer-to-conscious view of self (Hammer, 1985).

10.4.1.3   Kinetic Family Drawing (KFD)

With the *Kinetic Family Drawing* (KFD), examinees are given paper and pencil and asked to draw a picture of everyone in their family, including themselves, doing something (hence the term kinetic). After completing the drawing, the examinees are asked to identify each figure and describe what each one is doing. The KFD is thought to provide information regarding the examinee's view of their family and their interactions (Finch & Belter, 1993).

Despite their popularity and appeal to clinicians, little empirical data support the use of projective drawings as a means of predicting behavior or classifying examinees by diagnostic type (e.g., depressed, anxious, etc.). These techniques may provide a nonthreatening way to initiate the assessment process and an opportunity to develop rapport, but, otherwise, they should be used with considerable caution and an understanding of their technical limitations (Finch & Belter, 1993; Kamphaus & Frick, 2002).

10.4.2 Sentence Completion Tests

Sentence completion tests are another popular projective approach. These tests typically present incomplete-sentence stems that are completed by the examinee. The sentence completion forms either can be given to the examinee to complete independently or can be read aloud, and the responses are recorded. Examples of possible incomplete sentence stems include "I really enjoy _____." and "My greatest fear is _____." Numerous sentence completion forms are available, and as with the projective drawings, there are different ways of interpreting the results. Because incomplete-sentence stems provide more structure than most projective tasks (e.g., drawings or inkblots), some have argued that they are not actually "projective" in nature, but are more or less a type of structured interview. As a result, some prefer the term semiprojective to characterize these tests. Regardless of the classification, relatively little empirical evidence documents the psychometric properties of these tests (Kamphaus & Frick, 2002). Nevertheless, they remain popular, are nonthreatening to examinees, and, in the hands of skilled clinicians, may enhance rapport and provide an opportunity to enhance their understanding of their clients.

10.4.3 Apperception Tests

Another type of projective technique is an *apperception test*. With this technique, the examinee is given a picture and asked to make up a story about it. These techniques are also sometimes referred to as thematic, pictorial, or storytelling techniques. The *Thematic Apperception Test* (TAT: Murray & Harvard University, 1943) is the most widely used apperception test and has a long history of clinical use. It is composed of 19 black and white cards (pictures and drawings) and 1 blank card (for the blank card, the examinee is asked to imagine a picture, describe it, and then tell a story about it). The examinee is typically presented ten cards, and their stories are analyzed in a qualitative manner intended to identify personal factors such as needs for achievement, affiliation, etc. Like most other projective techniques, limited empirical evidence supports the use of the TAT.

A more recently developed apperception test is the **Roberts Apperception Test for Children**, which is now titled the Roberts-2 (Roberts & Gruber, 2005). It is designed for children and adolescents who are 6–18 years old and includes a standardized scoring system and normative data. The standardized scoring approach results in increased reliability relative to other apperception tests. While there are still concerns about the technical adequacy of this instrument in terms of contemporary psychometric standards (e.g., Valleley, 2009), the Roberts-2 is a step in the right direction in terms of enhancing the psychometric qualities of projective techniques.

10.4.4 Inkblot Techniques

The final projective approach that we will discuss is the **inkblot technique**. With this technique, the examinee is presented an ambiguous inkblot and asked to interpret it in some manner, typically by asking "What might this be?" Figure 10.3 presents an example of an inkblot similar to those used on inkblot tests. Of all the inkblot techniques, the **Rorschach** is the most widely used. Hermann Rorschach developed the Rorschach inkblots in the 1920s (1921/1942) and died soon after publishing the test. In his absence, a number of different researchers developed distinctive systems for administering, scoring, and interpreting the instrument. By the 1960s, there were five major Rorschach systems in use and this division resulted in a piecemeal approach to establishing the psychometric properties of the technique (Anastasi & Urbina, 1997). John E. Exner, Jr. undertook the task of developing a comprehensive system that integrated the most empirically supported features of the existing systems. The Exner Comprehensive System (1974, 1991, 1993; Exner & Weiner, 1995) provides a complex standardized scoring system that produces approximately 90 possible scores. Relative to other Rorschach interpretive systems, the Exner system produces more reliable measurement and has adequate normative data. However, validity evidence is somewhat limited (Kamphaus & Frick, 2002). For example, Anastasi and Urbina (1997) note that meta-analytic research suggests that convergent validity evidence for the Rorschach is comparable to that of the MMPI, but in terms of facilitating diagnosis and predicting behavior, the results are not as impressive. Nevertheless,

> In light of the paucity of empirical evidence supporting the utility of projective techniques, we recommend that they can be used cautiously.

Exner's efforts to produce a more psychometrically sound approach to administering, scoring, and interpreting the Rorschach are clearly a step in the right direction.

Fig. 10.3 Inkblots similar to those used in the Rorschach

In summary, in spite of relatively little empirical evidence supporting their util-ity, projective techniques continue to be popular among psychologists and other clinicians. Our recommendation is to use these instruments cautiously. They should not be used for making important clinical and diagnostic decisions, but they may have merit in introducing the examinee to the assessment process, establishing rap-port, and developing hypotheses that can be pursued with more technically adequate assessment techniques.

10.5   Summary

This chapter focuses on the assessment of personality. Personality is generally defined as relatively stable patterns of thinking, feeling, and behaving that differen-tiate one individual from another. In assessment terminology, this definition is expanded to incorporate a host of emotional, motivational, interpersonal, and attitu-dinal characteristics. Psychologists use personality measures in a number of ways including:

- Psychologists and other mental-health professionals use personality inventories to facilitate diagnosis and help plan treatment.
- Psychologists frequently use personality inventories to enhance their client's self-understanding and self-actualization.
- Psychologists use measures of personality to identify children with emotional and behavioral disorders that interfere with the ability to learn in schools.
- Psychologists use a variety of personality measures to help determine which job applicants will become successful employees.
- Psychologists use measures of personality to answer questions relevant to legal proceedings such as competency to stand trial or future dangerousness.
- Psychologists in academic and research settings use personality tests to measure a multitude of constructs in a wide range of psychological research.

Response biases can impact personality assessment. Response biases or response sets are test responses that misrepresent an examinee's true characteristics. For example, examinees may answer questions in a way that makes them appear more socially appropriate, even if their responses are not truthful or accurate. When response sets are present, the validity of the test results may be compromised because they introduce construct-irrelevant error into test scores. To combat this, many personality tests incorporate validity scales designed to detect the presence of response sets.

Most of the chapter describes two broad categories of personality measures: objective self-report measures and projective techniques. Objective self-report measures are those where respondents endorse selected-response items to reflect their characteristic ways of behaving, feeling, thinking, etc. Projective techniques involve the presentation of unstructured or ambiguous stimuli that allow an almost infinite range of responses from the respondent. Major approaches employed in developing objective person tests include:

- *Content/Rational Approach.* In the content/rational approach, items are selected based on their apparent relevance to the construct being measured. The Woodworth Personal Data Sheet is a notable example of a personality measure developed primarily using a content-based approach. While contemporary test developers rarely rely exclusively on a content/rational approach to scale development, it is common to start with this approach when writing items for personality tests.

- *Empirical Criterion Keying.* Empirical criterion keying is a process in which a large pool of items is administered to two groups, one typically a clinical group composed of individuals with a specific diagnosis and the other a control or normal group representative of the general population. The items are then statistically examined with the goal of identifying and retaining items that discriminate between the two groups. The Minnesota Multiphasic Personality Inventory (MMPI) is a prime example of a test developed using the empirical criterion keying approach. The MMPI was revised in 1989 (MMPI-2) and retained much of the overall structure of the original MMPI. While this allowed continuity between the two inventories, it also meant that the MMPI-2 inherited many of the limitations of its predecessor. To address these problems, a new version MMPI referred to as the MMPI Restructured Form (MMPI-2-RF) has been developed.

- *Factor Analysis.* Factor analysis has played a prominent role in identifying the structure of personality with models ranging from three to several dozen factors. Raymond Cattell has been a leader in the use of factor analysis to understand the structure of the normal personality. He published the original *16 Personality Factor Questionnaire* (16 PF) in 1949, and the most recent edition was released in 1993. As the name suggests, the 16 PF is based on a sixteen factor model of personality. In recent years, a Five Factor Model of personality has received widespread acceptance. The test that most exemplifies the Five Factor Model is the NEO Personality Inventory – Revised.

- *Theoretical Approach.* A number of tests have been designed largely based on a specific theory of personality. We described two examples of personality tests based on theories of personality. The Myers-Briggs Type Indicator (MBTI) is based on the theory of psychological types proposed by C.G. Jung and is a broad measure of normal personality development. The Millon Clinical Multiaxial Inventory-IV (MCMI-IV) is based on Theodore Millon's theory of personality and is designed to facilitate the assessment and diagnosis of clients with psychological disorders.

The contemporary trend in developing personality assessments is to employ multiple strategies in developing items and scales (and this was actually evident in many of the inventories we described). For example, a test author might initially develop items based on their apparent relevance to the construct being measured and then use multiple statistical techniques to select items and refine the scales.

In child and adolescent assessment, the term personality is used cautiously due to the rapid developmental changes characteristic of children and adolescents. When using the term personality in the context of child and adolescent assessment, it does not necessarily reflect a fixed construct, but one that is subject to development and change. The Behavior Assessment System for Children, Third Edition Self-Report of Personality (SRP) was described as an example of an objective personality measure used with children and adolescents.

Projective techniques involve the presentation of an ambiguous task that places little structure or limitation on the examinee's response. A classic example is the presentation of an inkblot followed by the question: "What might this be?" In addition to inkblot tests, projective techniques include projective drawings, sentence completion tests, and apperception (or storytelling) tests. The hypothesis behind the use of projective techniques is that the examinees will respond to the ambiguous stimuli in a manner that reveals basic, often unconscious aspects of their personality. There is considerable controversy over the use of projective techniques. Proponents of their use claim that projective techniques represent the richest source of information about the subjective experience of the examinee. Supporters also hold that behavior rating scales and self-report measures are vulnerable to the distorting effects of response sets, whereas projective techniques are relatively free from these effects because it is not obvious what type of response is expected or socially appropriate. In contrast, critics claim that most projective techniques do not meet even minimal psychometric standards and their use cannot be ethically or technically justified. While the use of these projective techniques is vigorously debated in the professional literature, they continue to be among the most popular approaches to assessing personality. Our position is that although projective techniques should not be used as the basis for making important educational, clinical, or diagnostic decisions, they may have merit in developing rapport with clients and in generating hypotheses that can be pursued using technically superior assessment techniques.

References

American Educational Research Association, American Psychological Association, & National Council on Measurement in Education. (2014). *Standards for educational and psychological testing*. Washington, DC: American Educational Research Association.

Anastasi, A., & Urbina, S. (1997). *Psychological testing* (7th ed.). Upper Saddle River, NJ: Prentice Hall.

Beck, A. T., Steer, R. A., & Brown, G. K. (1996). *Manual for the beck depression inventory— Second edition*. San Antonio, TX: Psychological Corporation.

Butcher, J. N., Dahlstrom, W. G., Graham, J. R., Tellegen, A., & Kaemmer, B. (1989). *MMPI-2: Manual for administration and scoring*. Minneapolis, MN: University of Minnesota Press.

Chandler, L. A. (1990). The projective hypothesis and the development of projective techniques for children. In C. R. Reynolds & R. Kamphaus (Eds.), *Handbook of psychological and educational assessment of children: Personality, behavior; & context* (pp. 55–69). New York, NY: Guilford Press.

Cronbach, L. J. (1990). *Essentials of psychological testing* (5th ed.). New York, NY: HarperCollins.

Derogatis, L. R. (1994). *Symptom Checklist-90-R: Administration, scoring, and procedures manual* (3rd ed.). Minneapolis, MN: National Computer Systems.

Exner, J. E. (1974). *The Rorschach: A comprehensive system I*. New York, NY: Wiley.

Exner, J. E., Jr. (1991). *The Rorschach: A comprehensive system: Vol. 2. Interpretation* (2nd ed.). New York, NY: Wiley.

Exner, J. E., Jr. (1993). *The Rorschach: A comprehensive system: Vol. 1. Basic foundations* (3rd ed.). New York, NY: Wiley.

Exner, J. E., Jr., & Weiner, I. B. (1995). *The Rorschach: A comprehensive system: Vol. 3. Assessment of children and adolescents* (2nd ed.). New York, NY: Wiley.

Finch, A. J., & Belter, R. W. (1993). Projective techniques. In T. H. Ollendick & M. Hersen (Eds.), *Handbook of child and adolescent assessment* (pp. 224–238). Boston, MA: Allyn & Bacon.

Fiske, D. (1949). Consistency of the factorial structures of personality ratings from different sources. *Journal of Abnormal and Social Psychology, 44*(3), 329–344.

Forer, B. (1949). The fallacy of personal validation: A classroom demonstration of gullibility. *Journal of Abnormal and Social Psychology, 44*, 118–123.

Friedenberg, L. (1995). *Psychological testing: Design, analysis, and use*. Boston, MA: Allyn & Bacon.

Galton, F. (1884). Measurement of character. *Fortnightly Review, 42*, 179–185. (Reprinted in L. D. Goodstein & R. I. Lanyon [Eds.], *Readings in personality assessment*. New York, NY: Wiley.).

Goldberg, L. (1993). The structure of phenotypic personality traits. *American Psychologist, 48*(1), 26–34.

Goodstein, L. D., & Lanyon, R. I. (1971). *Readings in personality assessment*. New York: NY: Wiley.

Graham, J. R. (1993). *MMPI-2: Assessing personality and psychopathology* (2nd ed.). New York, NY: Oxford University Press.

Graham, J. R. (2000). *MMPI-2: Assessing personality and psychopathology* (3rd ed.). New York, NY: Oxford University Press.

Gray, P. (1999). *Psychology*. New York, NY: Worth.

Hammer, E. (1985). The house-tree-person test. In C. Newmark (Ed.), *Major psychological assessment instruments* (pp. 135–164). Boston, MA: Allyn & Bacon.

Handler, L. (1985). The clinical use of the DrawA-Person (DAP) test. In C. Newmark (Ed.), *Major psychological assessment instruments* (pp. 165–216). Boston, MA: Allyn & Bacon.

Hathaway, S. R. (1960). Forward. In W. G. Dahlstrom & G. S. Welsh (Eds.), *An MMPI handbook: A guide to use in clinical practice and research*. Minneapolis, MN: University of Minnesota Press.

Hathaway, S. R. (1972). Forward. In W. G. Dahlstrom, G. S. Welsh, & L. E. Dahlstrom (Eds.), *An MMPI handbook: Vol. 1. Clinical interpretation*. Minneapolis, MN: University of Minnesota Press.

Hathaway, S. R., & McKinley, J. C. (1940). A multiphasic personality schedule: I. Construction of the schedule. *Journal of Psychology, 10*, 249–254.

Hathaway, S. R., & McKinley, J. C. (1943). *The Minnesota Multiphasic Personality Inventory* (Rev. ed.). Minneapolis, MN: University of Minnesota Press.

Hathaway, S. R., & McKinley, J. C. (1989). *Manual for the Minnesota Multiphasic Personality Inventory-2 (MMPI-2)*. Minneapolis, MN: University of Minnesota Press.

Kamphaus, R. W., & Frick, P. J. (2002). *Clinical assessment of child and adolescent personality and behavior*. Boston, MA: Allyn & Bacon.

Kovacs, M., & MHS Staff. (2011). *Children's Depression Inventory, Second Edition (CDI 2). Technical manual*. Toronto, Canada: Multi-Health Systems.

Livingston, R. B., Eglsaer, R., Dickson, T., & Harvey-Livingston, K. (2003). *Psychological assessment practices with children and adolescents*. Presentation at the 23rd Annual National Academy of Neuropsychology Conference, Dallas, TX.

McCrae, R. R., & Costa, P. T., Jr. (2010). *NEO inventories professional manual for the NEO Personality Inventory-3, NEO Five-Factor Inventory-3, and NEO Personality Inventory-Revised*. Lutz, FL: PAR.

Millon, T., & Davis, R. (1996). An evolutionary theory of personality disorders. In J. F. Clarkin & M. F. Lenzenweger (Eds.), *Major theories of personality disorder* (pp. 221–346). New York, NY: Guilford Press.

Millon, T., Grossman, S., & Millon, C. (2015). *Manual for the Millon Clinical Multiaxial Inventory-IV (MCMI-IV)*. Minneapolis, MN: NCS Pearson.

Murray, H. A., & Harvard University. (1943). *Thematic apperception test: Manual*. Cambridge, MA: Harvard University Press.

Myers, I. B., & McCaulley, M. H. (1985). *Manual: A guide to the development and use of the Myers-Briggs Type Indicator*. Palo Alto, CA: Consulting Psychologists Press.

Myers, I. B., Mccaulley, M. H., Quenk, N. L., & Hammer, A. L. (1998). *MBTI manual: A guide to the development and use of the Myers Briggs Type Indicator* (3rd ed.). Palo Alto, CA: Consulting Psychologists Press.

Reynolds, C. R., & Kamphaus, R. W. (2003). *Reynolds Intellectual Assessment Scales*. Lutz, FL: Psychological Assessment Resources.

Reynolds, C. R., & Kamphaus, R. W. (2015). *Behavior Assessment System for Children* (3rd ed.). Bloomington, MN: NCS Pearson.

Roberts, G. E., & Gruber, C. (2005). *Roberts-2*. Los Angeles, CA: Western Psychological Services.

Tellegen, A., Ben-Porath, Y. S., McNulty, J. L., Arbisi, P. A., Graham, J. R., & Kaemmer, B. (2003). *MMPI-2 Restructured Clinical (RC) Scales: Development, validation, and interpretation*. Minneapolis, MN: University of Minnesota Press.

Thorndike, R. M. (2005). *Measurement and evaluation in psychology and education*. Upper Saddle River, NJ: Pearson.

Valleley, R. J. (2009). Review of the Roberts-2. In *Mental Measurements Yearbook* (Vol. 18). Lincoln, NE: Buros Institute of Mental Measurement.

Recommended Reading

Dawes, R. M., Faust, D., & Meehl, P. E. (1989). Clinical versus actuarial judgments. *Science, 243*, 1168–1674. An interesting article that compares clinical versus actuarial approaches to decision-making (e.g., diagnosis, treatment planning), with the actuarial approach coming out on top!

McCord, D. M. (2018). *Assessment using the MMPI–2–RF*. Washington, DC: American Psychological Association. A great resource for learning about how to use the MMPI-2-RF.

Behavioral Assessment

The study of behavior is the raison d'être of psychology as a science and objective assessment of behavior is a necessity.

Abstract

Behavioral assessment focuses on observable acts or behaviors to describe how a person behaves on a day-to-day basis. Early conceptualizations of behavioral assessment dealt only with overtly observable behavior and often involved counting the occurrence of specific behaviors of concern in highly specific settings. Over the past 90 years, behavior assessment has evolved to include use of standardized self- or other-report behavior rating scales to produce objective findings about the behavior of individuals and determine the degree to which behaviors cluster together to reflect broader behavioral dimensions. This chapter provides information relevant to behavioral assessment including assessment of behaviors in schools, fundamentals of behavioral interviewing, descriptions of popular omnibus and specific behavioral rating scales, and usefulness of direct observation. Special consideration is given to adaptive behavior scales in the diagnosis of intellectual disability as well as psychophysiological assessment as a method of behavioral assessment.

Supplementary Information The online version of this chapter (https://doi.org/10.1007/978-3-030-59455-8_11) contains supplementary material, which is available to authorized users.

Learning Objectives

After reading and studying this chapter, students should be able to:

1. Compare and contrast maximum performance tests and typical response tests.
2. Explain how behavioral assessment is similar to as well as different from other forms of assessment, especially personality testing.
3. Explain the difference between behavioral interviewing and traditional clinical interviews.
4. Explain how test validity scales can be used to guard against response sets and give an example.
5. Describe the strengths and limitations of behavior rating scales.
6. Describe and evaluate the major behavior rating scales.

Behavioral assessment has a storied history in psychology and has evolved from a simple counting of behavioral occurrences to more sophisticated rating scales and observational schemes. Although professional psychologists traditionally have focused primarily on assessment of cognitive abilities and personality characteristics, the drive for less inferential measures of behavior as well as a movement toward establishing diagnoses based upon observable behavior has led to a renewal of interest and use of behavioral assessment methods. Additionally, Federal laws mandate that schools provide special education and related services to students with emotional disorders. Before these services can be provided, the schools must be able to identify children with these disorders. The process of identifying these children often involves a psychological evaluation completed by a school psychologist or other clinician wherein behaviors consistent with the Federal definition of emotionally disturbed must be documented clearly. This has also led to the derivation of increasingly sophisticated measures of actual behavior.

In several places in this book, we have noted that tests typically can be classified as measures of either maximum performance or typical response. Maximum performance tests are often referred to as ability tests. On these tests, items are usually scored as either correct or incorrect, and examinees are encouraged to demonstrate the best performance possible. Achievement and aptitude tests are common examples of maximum performance tests. In contrast, typical response tests attempt to measure the typical behavior and characteristics of examinees. Typical response tests typically assess constructs such as personality, behavior, attitudes, or interests (Cronbach, 1990). Behavioral assessment as most commonly conducted is a measure of typical responding (i.e., what a person does on a regular basis) as are personality scales. Behavioral assessments can be constructed, which measure maximum levels of performance, but tests that are designed to measure maximum performance levels are better conceptualized as aptitude, ability, or achievement measures.

> Behavioral assessment emphasizes what a person does. Most methods of personality assessment emphasize what a person has (e.g., attributes, character, or other latent traits such as anxiety).

While both personality and behavioral assessments can be classified as typical response tests, they differ in several ways. Behavioral assessment emphasizes what a person does and, in this context, emphasizes observable behavior as opposed to covert thoughts and feelings. Behavioral assessment attempts then to define how a person behaves overtly on a day-to-day basis using observable expression and acts as the primary means of evaluating behavior. Most methods of personality assessment emphasize what a person has, e.g., their character, attributes, or reported feelings and thoughts. How we say what we think and feel is not always congruent with what we do. Behavioral assessment is generally seen as more objective than personality assessment as well, since most behavioral assessment scales do not ask for interpretations of behavior, only observations of the presence and frequency of a specified behavior. Thus, many see behavioral assessment as having a lower level of inference for its interpretations than traditional personality assessment, where the level of inference between scores and predictions of behavior can be quite high.

Early conceptualizations of behavioral assessment dealt only with overtly observable behavior. Typically, behavioral assessment in its formative years (from the 1930s into the late 1970s) relied upon observation and counting of specific behaviors of concern. For example, in the 1960s and the early 1970s, many school psychologists were issued behavior counters (often referred to as clickers because of the

> Early conceptualizations of behavioral assessment relied on observation and counting of specific behaviors of concern in highly specific settings.

clicking sound they made each time a behavior was "counted") along with other standardized test materials. School psychologists would use these materials to document specific behaviors, such as the number of times a child got out of her seat during an hour of classroom instruction. Behavior was also seen as being highly contextually or setting specific—this perception is still characteristic of behavioral assessment, but is viewed with less rigidity today. For example, there are clear tendencies for children to behave similarly in the presence of their father and their mother, but it is not unusual for some clear differences to emerge in how a child behaves when alone with each parent. The same is true across classrooms with different teachers—a child will have a tendency to respond in similar ways in all classrooms, but there will be clear differences depending upon the teacher present and the teacher's personality, approach to classroom management, and experience in working with children. As the field of behavioral assessment has matured, practitioners of behavioral assessment have come to recognize the importance of chronic characteristics such as anxiety and depression, locus of control, impulsivity, and other latent traits that do generalize across many settings to a significant extent, though far from being perfect. However, in assessing these traits, behavioral assessment scales ask about observable behaviors that are related to anxiety or depression as opposed to asking a student about thoughts and feelings. Examples might be "Says, I have no friends" and "Says, no one likes to be with me" on a behavioral assessment scale that a parent completes on her child's behavior, whereas on a self-report personality scale, an item asking about a similar construct might be worded "I feel lonely much of the time."

Many traditional scales of personality assessment (though certainly not all) have come to be used in conjunction with behavioral assessment. However, these scales, such as the BASC-3 Self-Report of Personality (Reynolds & Kamphaus, 2015) discussed in the preceding chapter, do rely less upon high inference items and constructs and instead focus on more behavioral questions (e.g., "My parents blame me for things I do not do" as opposed to an item stem such as "People are out to get me"). While this distinction may seem subtle, behavioral assessment professionals argue in favor of the use of terms and items that describe actual behavior as opposed to states.

Thus, the lines between behavioral assessment and some forms of traditional personality assessment do blur at points. The key difference in our minds is the level of inference involved in the interpretations of the test scores obtained under these two approaches. They are also quite complementary—it is important to know both how people typically behave *and* how they think and feel about themselves and others. Behavioral assessment is also not a specific or entirely unique set of measuring devices, but rather more of a paradigm, a way of thinking about and obtaining assessment information. Even responses to projective tests, which most psychologists would view as the antithesis of behavioral assessment, can be reconceptualized and interpreted as behavioral in nature (e.g., see the very interesting chapter by Teglasi, 1998) by altering the method of interpretation, i.e., moving toward low inference interpretations of responses as samples of actual behavior. It is now common practice for clinicians to use a multimethod multimodal approach to behavioral assessment. Practitioners will collect data or assessment information via behavioral interviewing, direct observation, and impressionistic behavior rating scales, as well as self-report "personality scales" designed to reduce the level of inference involved in their interpretation.

11.1 Assessing Behavior

Just as we noted about personality in the preceding chapter, while we might not consciously be aware of it, we all engage in the assessment and interpretation of behavior on a regular basis. When you note that "Tommy is a difficult child" or "Tamiqua is extroverted," you are making an assessment (albeit a crude and general one) and then forming a judgment about their behavior. We use these informal evaluations as one of the many ways to determine who we want to associate with and who we want to avoid. Clinicians use behavioral assessment to produce far more objective determinations about the behavior of individuals. By using standardized behavioral assessment methods such as behavior rating scales, practitioners can also determine the degree to which behaviors cluster together to reflect broader behavioral dimensions. For example, most behavior rating scales produce scores that reflect dimensions such as distractibility, aggression, hyperactivity, depression, or anxiety. In addition to telling us if clients behave in particular ways, behavior rating scales also indicate how common or rare these behaviors are in the general population. In other words, is the strength of the exhibited tendency to behave in particular ways strong enough or severe enough to warrant clinical interventions, or are these tendencies of a similar level to other people? With clients referred for an evaluation, this information is important in helping the clinician determine if there are real behavioral problems requiring psychological interventions or if the behavior is within normal limits. At times, one determines that the problem is one of a caregiver or teacher who simply has a very low tolerance level for what is a common, normal set of behaviors, and thus, a different intervention is required—with a different target! Additionally, through repeated behavioral assessments, which are quite efficient and also have no so-called practice effect, one can monitor treatment effects regularly and accurately when behavioral change is the goal of intervention.

11.2 Response Sets

We discussed response sets in more detail in the preceding chapter and will refer to them again in Chap. 18. However, response sets occur in behavioral assessments as well. As you recall, response biases or *response sets* are test responses

> Response sets also occur in behavioral assessments.

that misrepresent a person's true characteristics. For example, an individual completing an employment-screening assessment that asks about behaviors on the job might attempt to present an overly positive image by answering all of the questions in the most socially appropriate manner possible, even if these responses do not accurately represent the person. On the other hand, a teacher who is hoping to have a disruptive student transferred from his or her class might be inclined to exaggerate the student's misbehavior when completing a behavior rating scale in order to hasten that student's removal. A parent may be completing a rating scale of his/her child's behavior and not want to be seen as a poorly skilled parent and so may deny common behavior problems that are present with the child being rated. In each of these situations, the individual completing the test or scale responded in a manner that systematically distorted reality. This is often referred to as *dissimulation*—that is, making yourself or another person appear dissimilar from how they really are or how they really behave. When response sets are present, the validity of the interpretation of test results may be compromised because they introduce construct-irrelevant error to test scores (e.g., American Educational Research Association, American Psychological Association, & National Council on Measurement in Education, 2014). That is, the test results do not accurately reflect the construct that the test was designed to measure. To combat this, many behavioral assessment scales incorporate several types of *validity scales* designed to detect the presence of response sets. Validity scales take different forms, but the general principle is that they are designed to detect individuals who are not responding in an accurate manner. Special Interest Topic 11.1 provides an example of a "fake bad" response set that might appear on a behavior rating scale completed by parents about their child. Why would parents want the behavior ratings on their child to represent behavior that is worse than what actually is occurring? There are many reasons, but the two most common are a plea for immediate help with the child, and so overwrought ratings are provided to get the clinician's attention to the desperate plight of the parents. The second is to obtain a diagnosis for which services or disability payments might be received. We will talk more about detecting response sets when we look at behavior rating scales below and also in our later chapter giving practical guidance in test development.

Special Interest Topic 11.1: An Example of a "Fake Bad" Response Set on a Parent Behavior Rating Scale

Typical response measures, despite the efforts of test developers, always remain susceptible to response sets. The following case is an authentic example of a response set identified by the Parent Rating Scale from the Behavior Assessment System for Children, Second Edition (BASC-2).

Susan was brought to a private psychologist's office on referral from the State Department of Rehabilitation Services. Her mother was applying for disability benefits for Susan and reported that Susan has Bipolar Disorder. Susan is 14 years old and repeating the seventh grade this school year because she failed to attend school regularly last year. When skipping school, Susan spent time roaming the local shopping mall or engaging in other relatively unstructured activities. She failed all of her classes in both semesters of the past school year. Her mother says that this is because she is totally out of control behaviorally and "has Bipolar Disorder." Susan's father expressed concern about her education, especially her lack of interest and unwillingness to do homework, but did not describe the hyperirritability and depressive attributes that are common with Pediatric Bipolar Disorder (PBD).

Susan's responses to a diagnostic interview suggested that she was not interested in school and wanted to spend time with friends and engaged in social activities. She complained about having trouble keeping up in school as well, noting that reading was especially difficult for her. She acknowledged some attentional problems that she attributed to lack of interest in academic work, but did not note any other behavioral issues commonly associated with PBD.

Susan's mother completed the BASC–2 Parent Rating Scale, Adolescent (PRS-A). The PRS-A results indicate evidence of a "fake bad" response set. All Clinical Scale scores were above the normative T-score mean of 50, and all Adaptive Scale scores were below the normative mean of 50. In other words, the PRS-A results suggest that Susan is severely maladjusted in all behavioral domains, which, although possible, is not likely.

The mother's response set, however, was identified by F-Index, a measure of infrequency indicating inordinately negative ratings. She obtained a score of 16, which is in the Extreme Caution range, indicating a high probability that the overall ratings provide a far more negative picture of the Susan's behavior than that might actually be the case. The following table shows Susan's full complement of PRS-A scores based upon the mother's ratings.

Scale	T-score
Clinical scales	
Aggression	81
Anxiety	73
Attention problems	70
Atypicality	66
Conduct problems	65
Depression	91
Hyperactivity	67
Somatization	85
Withdrawal	59
Adaptive scales	
Activities of daily living	44
Adaptability	35
Functional communication	28
Leadership	39
Social skills	49

11.3   Assessment of Behavior in the Schools

Federal laws (e.g., Public Law 94-142 [IDEA], Individuals with Disabilities Education Act of 2004, and Every Student Succeeds Act [ESSA]) mandate that schools provide special education and related services to students with emotional disorders. These laws compel schools to identify students with emotional disorders, and as a result, school assessment practices that were previously focused primarily on cognitive abilities have been expanded to now include the

> Public Law 94-142 and its most current reauthorization, the Every Student Succeeds Act, mandate that schools provide special education services to students with emotional disorders.

evaluation of personality, behavior, and related constructs. We emphasize schools as a setting and children as a group in this chapter, because that is the location and the population with whom behavioral assessments are most common, although behavioral assessments are also often used in clinics, private psychology practices, and other settings. A small number of behavioral assessment devices are also available for assessment of adults.

The instruments used to assess behavior and personality in the schools can usually be classified as behavior rating scales, self-report measures, or projective techniques. The results of a national survey of school psychologists indicated that five of the top ten instruments were behavior rating scales, four were projective techniques, and one was a self-report measure (Livingston, Eglsaer, Dickson, & Harvey-Livingston, 2003; see Table 11.1 for a listing of these assessment instruments). These are representative of the

Table 11.1 Ten most popular tests of child personality and behavior

Rank	Name of test	Type of test
1	BASC Teacher Rating Scale	Behavior rating scale
2	BASC Parent Rating Scale	Behavior rating scale
3	BASC Self-Report of Personality	Self-report measure
4	Draw-A-Person	Projective technique
5	Conners Rating Scales—Revised	Behavior rating scale
6	Sentence Completion Tests	Projective technique
7	House-Tree-Person	Projective technique
8	Kinetic Family Drawing	Projective technique
9	Teacher Report Form (Achenbach)	Behavior rating scale
10	Child Behavior Checklist (Achenbach)	Behavior rating scale

Note. *BASC* Behavior Rating System for Children. The Conners Rating Scales—Revised and Sentence Completion Tests—actually were tied, based on a national sample of school psychologists (Livingston et al., 2003)

instruments that school psychologists use to assess children suspected of having an emotional, behavioral, or other type of disorder. The distribution is quite interesting to observe. The field of psychology has moved strongly, as has medicine and some other fields, to what is often termed *evidence-based practice*, referring to engagement in professional practices that have clear support in the science that underlies the profession. Traditionally, stemming from work from the late 1800s into the 1960s, projective assessment dominated assessment and diagnosis of emotional and behavioral disorders. We reviewed in Chap. 10 the polemic, staunch emotional controversy surrounding projective testing. Nowhere is the division of opinion more evident than in these survey results—about half of the most frequently used tests in this assessment area in the schools are behavior rating scales—the most objective of behavior assessments and those with the strongest scientific evidence to support their use—while 40% are projective tests, clearly the most subjective of our assessment devices and the class of assessments with the least scientific support!

When behavioral assessments are conducted in schools, psychologists or other behavior specialists will often conduct an observational assessment in a classroom or perhaps even on the playground, counting the frequency of specified behaviors. However, teachers are often called on to provide relevant information on students' behavior. Classroom teachers are often asked to help with the assessment of students in their classrooms, for example, by completing behavior rating scales on students in their class. This practice provides invaluable data to school psychologists and other clinicians because teachers have a unique opportunity to observe children in their classrooms. Teachers can provide information on how the child behaves in different contexts, both academic and social. Those who do behavioral assessments understand the need for information on how children behave in different settings, with school, home, and community being the most important, and are interested in consistencies as well as inconsistencies in behavior across settings.

> Those who do behavioral assessments understand the need for information on how children behave in different contexts and are interested in the consistencies as well as inconsistencies in behavior across settings.

11.4   Behavioral Interviewing

Most assessments begin with a review of the referral information and statement of the referral questions. Next comes a form of interview with the person to be evaluated, or in the case of a child or adolescent, an interview with a parent or caregiver may occur first. The traditional clinical interview usually begins with broad sweeping questions such as why are you here, how can I help you, or perhaps with a child, why do you think you were asked to come here. The clinician brings out the presenting problem in this way, then solicits a detailed history, attempts to understand the current mood states of the interviewee as well as any relevant traits of interest, and seeks to understand the psychodynamics of the behaviors or states of concern. Behavioral interviewing has a different emphasis.

A behavioral interview tends to focus on the antecedents and consequences of behaviors of concern as well as what attempts at change have been made. An attempt to look at the relevant reinforcement history is made as well.

When conducting a behavioral interview, once the clinician establishes the issue to be addressed, the clinician then focuses on the antecedents and consequences of behaviors of concern as well as what attempts at change have been made. An attempt to look at the relevant reinforcement history is made as well, i.e., what has sustained the behavior and why has it not responded to efforts to create change. Problem-solving strategies are then introduced that are intended to lead to an intervention. Ramsay, Reynolds, and Kamphaus (2002) describe six steps in behavioral interviewing that can be summarized as follows:

1. Identify the presenting problem and define it in behavioral terms.
2. Identify and evaluate environmental contingencies supporting the behaviors.
3. Develop a plan to alter these contingencies and reinforcers to modify the behavior.
4. Implement the plan.
5. Evaluate the outcomes of treatment or intervention. (This often involves having done a behavioral assessment using standardized rating scales for example to establish a baseline rate of behaviors of concern and then reassessing with the same scales later to look for changes from baseline.)
6. Modify the intervention plan if the behavior is not responding and evaluate the outcome of these changes.

The first three of these steps are the heart of the interview process in a behavioral interview, while the follow-up steps are conducted on a continuing basis in a behavioral paradigm. One of the key goals of the behavioral interview, contrasted with a traditional clinical interview, is to minimize the levels of inference used to obtain and interpret information. By stressing behavior as opposed to subjective states, a more definitive plan can be derived, clear goals can be set, and the progress of the individual is monitored more clearly.

11.5   Behavior Rating Scales

A *behavior rating scale* is essentially an inventory that asks a knowledgeable informant to rate an individual on a number of dimensions. When working with children
and adolescents, the informants are typically parents or teachers. On behavior rating
scales designed for adults, the informants might be a spouse, adult child, or health-
care worker. The instructions of the behavior rating scale typically ask an informant
to rate a person by indicating whether they observe the behavior described as
occurring:

0 = rarely or never
1 = occasionally
2 = often
3 = almost always

The scale will then present a series of item stems for which the informant rates
the individual. For example,

Reacts to minor noises from outside the classroom.	0	1	2	3
Tell lies.	0	1	2	3
Interacts well with peers.	0	1	2	3
Is irritable.	0	1	2	3

As we have noted, behavior rating scales have been used most often with children and adolescents, but there is growing interest in using behavior rating scales
with adults. The following discussion will initially focus on some major behavior
rating scales used with children and adolescents, but we will also provide an example of a scale used with adults.

Behavior rating scales have a number of
positive characteristics (e.g., Kamphaus &
Frick, 2002; Piacentini, 1993; Ramsay et al.,
2002; Witt, Heffer, & Pfeiffer, 1990). For
example, children may have difficulty in accurately reporting their own feelings and behaviors due to a number of factors such as limited

> Behavior rating scales have
> been used most often with
> children and adolescents, but
> there is growing interest in
> using them with adults.

insight or verbal abilities or, in the context of self-report tests, limited reading ability. However, when using behavior rating scales, information is solicited from the
important adults in a child's life. Ideally, these adult informants will have had adequate opportunities to observe the child in a variety of settings over an extended
period of time. Behavior rating scales also represent a cost-effective and time-
efficient method of collecting assessment information. For example, a clinician may
be able to collect information from both parents and one or more teachers with a
minimal investment of time or money. Most popular child behavior rating scales
have separate inventories for parents and teachers. This allows the clinician to collect information from multiple informants who observe the child from different

perspectives and in various settings. Behavior rating scales can also help clinicians assess the presence of rare behaviors. Although any responsible clinician will interview the client and other people close to the client, it is still possible to miss important indicators of behavioral problems. The use of well-designed behavior rating scales may help detect the presence of rare behaviors, such as fire setting and animal cruelty that might be missed in a clinical interview.

There are some limitations associated with the use of behavior rating scales. Even though the use of adult informants to rate children provides some degree of objectivity, as we noted these scales are still subject to response sets that may distort the true characteristics of the child. For example, as a "cry for help" a teacher may exaggerate the degree of a student's problematic behavior in hopes of hastening a referral for special education services or even in the hope that the child will be removed from the classroom to a different placement. Some parents might not be willing or able to acknowledge that their child has significant emotional or behavioral problems and so tend to underrate the degree and nature of problem behaviors. Although behavior rating scales are particularly useful in diagnosing "externalizing" problems such as aggression and hyperactivity, which are easily observed by adults, they may be less helpful when assessing "internalizing" problems such as depression and anxiety, which are not apparent to observers.

Ratings of behavior on such omnibus behavior rating scales are impressionistic (i.e., based on the impressions of the person completing the scale) to a large extent. Test authors do not ask or expect the person completing the rating to count behaviors, and typically, items that ask for a specific count are avoided (e. g., one would rarely see an item such as "Gets out of seat without permission or at an inappropriate time 1 time per day"). Rather, behavior rating scales ask "Gets out of seat without permission or at an inappropriate time" with a range of responses such as rarely, sometimes, often, and

> Behavior rating scale scores, despite their impressionistic basis, predict diagnoses accurately, predict future behavior and learning problems, help detect changes in behavior, and can even predict what types of interventions are most likely to work to change a behavior.

almost always. Not everyone will interpret such terms as rarely, sometimes, often, etc. in the same way, and this does introduce some error into the ratings. However, the research on carefully developed behavior rating scales generally demonstrates their scores to be very reliable. Research also shows them to differentiate better among various groups of diagnostic conditions in the emotional and behavioral domain than any other single form of assessment available to us. Behavior rating scale scores, despite their impressionistic basis, predict diagnosis accurately, predict future behavior and learning problems, help us detect changes in behavior, and can even predict what types of interventions are most likely to work to change a behavior (e.g., see Vannest, Reynolds, & Kamphaus, 2009).

It is no surprise then that over the past several decades, behavior rating scales have gained popularity and become increasingly important in the psychological assessment of children and adolescents (Livingston et al., 2003). It is common for a clinician to have both parents and teachers complete behavior rating scales for one child. This is desirable because parents and teachers have the opportunity to observe the child in different settings and can contribute unique yet complementary information to the assessment process. The consistencies as well as inconsistencies of a child's behavior in different settings and with different adults are also quite informative. Next, we will briefly review some of the most popular scales.

11.5.1 Behavior Assessment System for Children, Third Edition: Teacher Rating Scales and Parent Rating Scales (TRSs and PRSs)

The *Behavior Assessment System for Children* (BASC) is a comprehensive, coordinated system for assessing and remediating behavioral and emotional problems in children and adolescents. In addition to wide-scale behavioral screening, behavioral evidence-based intervention techniques, and targeted behavioral monitoring, the Behavior Assessment System for Children, Third Edition (BASC–3; Reynolds & Kamphaus, 2015) includes an integrated set of instruments designed to enable a comprehensive assessment of behavioral and emotional problems including the *Teacher Rating Scales (TRSs),* the *Parent Rating Scales (PRSs),* the Self-Report of Personality (SRP, discussed previously), a classroom observation system, a scale that assesses the parent child relationship (the *Parenting Relationship Questionnaire*), and a structured developmental history (Reynolds & Kamphaus, 1992). Although the BASC scales are a relatively new set of instruments, a 2003 national survey of school psychologists indicates that the TRS and PRS are the most frequently used behavior rating scales in the public schools today (Livingston et al., 2003). Information obtained from the publisher estimates that the BASC instruments were used with more than one million children in the United States alone in 2003. By 2006, following the release of its second edition (BASC-2), this estimate had grown to upward of 2 million children per year. The TRS and PRS are appropriate for children from 2 to 21 years. Both the TRS and PRS provide item stems describing a behavior to which the informant responds *Never, Sometimes, Often,* or *Almost Always.* The TRS is designed to provide a thorough examination of school-related behavior, whereas the PRS is aimed at the home and community environment (Ramsay et al., 2002). Now, in its third edition, the BASC-3 offers a variety of composite scales, clinical and adaptive scales, content scales, clinical indexes, and executive functioning scales on the TRS and PRS forms (see Table 11.2). Reynolds and Kamphaus (2015) describe the individual clinical and adaptive scales of the TRS and PRS as follows:

- *Adaptability:* ability to adapt to changes in one's environment
- *Activities of Daily Living:* skills associated with performing basic everyday tasks
- *Aggression:* acting in a verbally or physically hostile manner that threatens others
- *Anxiety:* being nervous or fearful about actual or imagined problems or situations

Table 11.2 BASC-3 composites, primary scales, and content scales in the TRS and PRS

BASC-3 scales	TRS			PRS		
	P	C	A	P	C	A
Composite						
Behavioral symptoms index	x	x	x	x	x	x
Internalizing problems	x	x	x	x	x	x
Externalizing problems	x	x	x	x	x	x
School problems		x	x			
Adaptive skills	x	x	x	x	x	x
Clinical and adaptive scales						
Activities of daily living				x	x	x
Adaptability	x	x	x	x	x	x
Aggression	x	x	x	x	x	x
Anxiety	x	x	x	x	x	x
Attention problems	x	x	x	x	x	x
Atypicality	x	x	x	x	x	x
Conduct problems		x	x		x	x
Depression	x	x	x	x	x	x
Functional communication	x	x	x	x	x	x
Hyperactivity	x	x	x	x	x	x
Leadership		x	x		x	x
Learning problems		x	x			
Social skills	x	x	x	x	x	x
Somatization	x	x	x	x	x	x
Study skills		x	x			
Withdrawal	x	x	x	x	x	x
Content scale						
Anger control	x	x	x	x	x	x
Bullying	x	x	x	x	x	x
Developmental social disorders	x	x	x	x	x	x
Emotional self-control	x	x	x	x	x	x
Executive functioning	x	x	x	x	x	x
Negative emotionality	x	x	x	x	x	x
Resiliency	x	x	x	x	x	x
Clinical index						
ADHD probability index		x	x		x	x
Autism probability index		x	x		x	x
Clinical probability index	x			x		
EBD probability index		x	x		x	x
Functional impairment index	x	x	x	x	x	x
Executive functioning index	x	x	x	x	x	x
Attentional control index	x	x	x	x	x	x
Behavioral control index	x	x	x	x	x	x
Emotional control index	x	x	x	x	x	x
Overall executive functioning index	x	x	x	x	x	x
Problem-solving index		x	x		x	x

Note. *BASC-3* Behavior Rating System for Children, Third Edition; *TRS* Teacher Rating Scale; *PRS* Parent Rating Scale; *P* preschool; *C* child; *A* adolescent

- *Attention Problems:* inclination to be easily distracted or have difficulty in concentrating
- *Atypicality:* behaviors that are considered odd or commonly associated with psychosis
- *Conduct Problems:* inclination to display antisocial behavior and rule-breaking behavior (e.g., cruelty and destructiveness)
- *Depression:* reflects feelings of sadness and unhappiness
- *Functional Communication:* expression of ideas and communication in any way others can understand
- *Hyperactivity:* inclination to be overactive and impulsive
- *Leadership:* reflects ability to achieve academic and social goals, particularly the ability to work with others
- *Learning Problems:* reflects the presence of academic difficulties (only on the TRS)
- *Social Skills:* reflects the ability to interact well with peers and adults in a variety of settings
- *Somatization:* reflects the tendency to complain about minor physical problems
- *Study Skills:* reflects skills that are associated with academic success, for example, study habits and organization skills (only on the TRS)
- *Withdrawal:* the inclination to avoid social contact

The content scales, clinical indexes, and executive functioning scales are designed to provide important supplementary information to the clinical and adaptive scales, enabling clinicians to evaluate targeted areas that can be particularly informative when trying to make specific treatment recommendations. In addition, they can also serve as aids in making clinical diagnoses and/or educational classification decisions.

In addition to these individual scales, the TRS and PRS provide several different composite scale scores. The composite scales serve to summarize generalized areas of behavioral and emotional functioning (e.g., externalizing problems), which can be helpful for understanding the pervasiveness of behavioral and emotional functioning problems, as well as provide a way of classifying and organizing scales in a hierarchical, more meaningful fashion.

The authors recommend that interpretation follows a "top-down" approach, by which the clinician starts at the most global level and progresses to more specific levels (e.g., Reynolds & Kamphaus, 2015). The most global measure is the Behavioral Symptoms Index (BSI), which is a composite of the Aggression, Attention Problems, Atypicality, Depression, Hyperactivity, and Withdrawal scales. The BSI reflects the overall level of behavioral problems and provides the clinician with a reliable but nonspecific index of pathology. For more

> The authors of the Behavior Assessment System for Children, Third Edition (BASC-3) recommend that interpretation follow a "top-down" approach, by which the clinician starts at the most global level and progresses to more specific levels.

specific information about the nature of the problem behavior, the clinician proceeds to the four lower-order BASC-3 composite scores:

- *Internalizing Problems:* This is a composite of the Anxiety, Depression, and Somatization scales. Some authors refer to internalizing problems as "overcontrolled" behavior. Students with internalizing problems experience subjective or internal discomfort or distress, but they do not typically display severe acting-out or disruptive behaviors (e.g., aggression and impulsiveness). As a result, these children may go unnoticed by teachers and school-based clinicians. There are some notable exceptions. Children with depression, especially boys, are often irritable, have attentional difficulties, and can be misdiagnosed as having attention-deficit/hyperactivity disorder if one looks only at these symptoms and does not obtain a full picture of the child's behavior.
- *Externalizing Problems:* This is a composite of the Aggression, Conduct Problems, and Hyperactivity scales. Relative to the behaviors and symptoms associated with internalizing problems, the behaviors associated with externalizing problems are clearly apparent to observers. Children with high scores on this composite are typically disruptive to both peers and adults and usually will be noticed by teachers and other adults.
- *School Problems:* This TRS composite consists of the Attention Problem and Learning Problem scales. High scores on this scale suggest academic motivation, attention, and learning difficulties that are likely to hamper academic progress.
- *Adaptive Skills.* This is a composite of the Activities of Daily Living, Adaptability, Leadership, Social Skills, and Study Skills scales. It reflects a combination of social, academic, and other positive skills (Reynolds & Kamphaus, 2015).

The third level of analysis involves examining the clinical scales (e.g., Hyperactivity and Depression) and adaptive scales (e.g., Leadership and Social Skills), as well as the content scales, clinical indexes, and the executive functioning scale scores. Finally, clinicians will often examine the individual items. Although individual items are often unreliable, when interpreted cautiously, they may provide clinically important information. This is particularly true of what is often referred to as "critical items." Critical items, when coded in a certain way, suggest possible danger to self or others or reflect an unusual behavior that may be innocuous, but also may not, and require questioning by the clinician for clarification. For example, if a parent or teacher reports that a child often "threatens to harm self or others," the clinician would want to determine whether these statements indicate imminent danger to the child or others.

When interpreting the Clinical Composites and Scale scores, high scores reflect abnormality or pathology. The authors provide the following classifications: *T*-score ≥70 is Clinically Significant; 60–69 is At-Risk; 41–59 is Average; 31–40 is Low; and ≤30 is Very Low. Scores on the Adaptive Composite and Scales are interpreted differently, with high scores reflecting adaptive or positive behaviors. The authors provide the following classifications: *T*-score ≥70 is Very High; 60–69 is High; 41–59 is Average; 31–40 is At-Risk; and ≤30 is Clinically Significant. Computer software is available to facilitate scoring and interpretation, and the use of this software is recommended because hand scoring can be challenging for new users. An example of a completed TRS profile is depicted in Fig. 11.1.

The TRS and PRS have several unique features that promote their use. First, they contain a validity scale that helps the clinician detect the presence of response sets. As noted previously, validity scales are especially developed and incorporated in the test for the purpose of detecting response sets. Both the parent and teacher scales contain a "fake bad" (F) index that is elevated when an informant excessively rates maladaptive items as *Almost always* and adaptive items as *Never*. If this index is elevated, the clinician should consider the possibility that a negative response set has skewed the results. Another unique feature of these scales is that they assess both negative and adaptive behaviors. Before the advent of the BASC, behavior

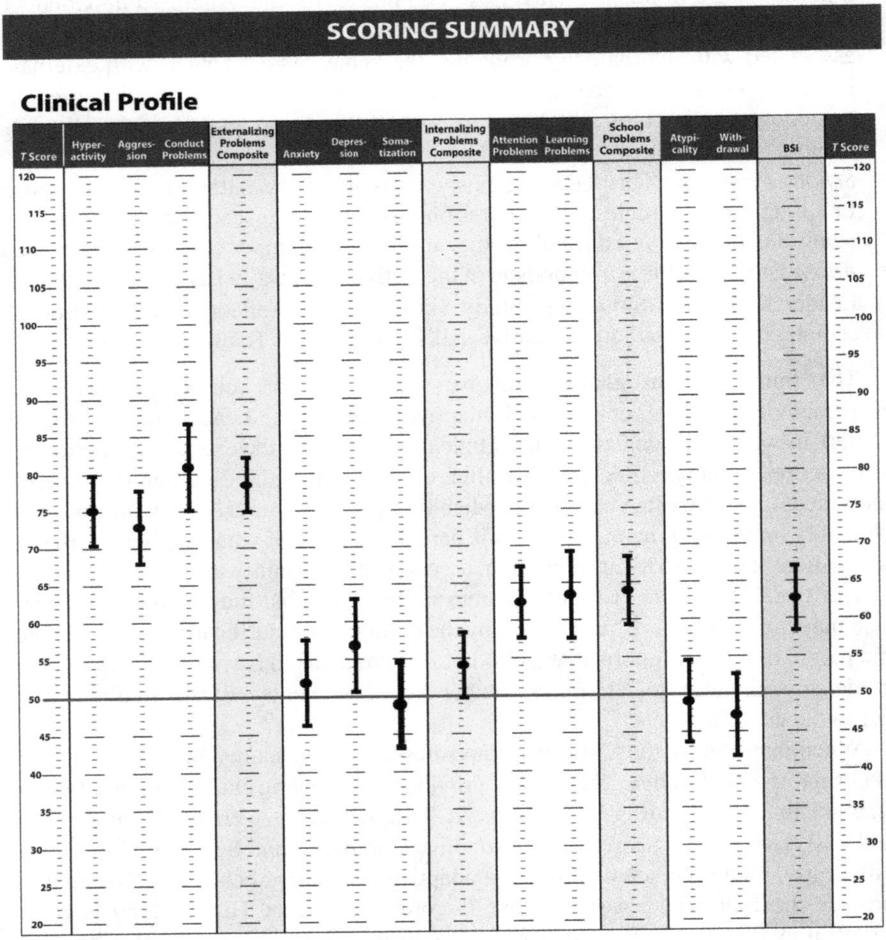

Fig. 11.1   An example of a completed TRS profile

rating scales were often criticized for focusing only on negative behaviors and pathology. Both the TRS and PRS address this criticism by assessing a broad spectrum of behaviors, both positive and negative. The identification of positive characteristics can facilitate treatment by helping identify strengths to build on. Still, another unique feature is that the TRS and PRS provide three norm-referenced comparisons that can be selected depending on the clinical focus. The child's ratings can be compared with a general national sample, a gender-specific national sample, or a national clinical sample composed of children who have a clinical diagnosis and are receiving treatment. In summary, the BASC-3 TRS and BASC-3 PRS are psychometrically sound instruments that have gained considerable support since the release of the original BASC.

Currently, there is an interesting discussion underway regarding the relative merits of categorical diagnostic systems (such as that employed in the DSM-V) versus dimensional models of diagnosis. Special Interest Topic 11.2 presents a brief introduction to this topic.

Special Interest Topic 11.2: Categorical Versus Dimensional Diagnosis

There are many approaches to grouping individuals as well as objects. Whenever we engage in diagnosis, we are engaged in grouping via the assignment of a label or designation to a person as having or not having a disorder or disease—and, having a disorder or not having a disorder typically are mutually exclusive decisions. In the traditional medical approach to diagnosis, categorical systems and methods are used. Typically, categorical approaches to diagnosis of mental and developmental disorders rely heavily on observation and interview methods designed to detect the presence of particular symptoms or behaviors, both overt and covert. The degree or severity of the symptom is rarely considered except that it must interfere with normal functioning in some aspect of one's life, i.e., it must have a negative impact on the patient. A symptom is then either present or absent. A dichotomous decision is then reached on a diagnosis based on a declaration of the presence or absence of a set of symptoms known to cluster into a pattern designated as a disorder or syndrome.

In dimensional approaches to diagnosis, the clinician recognizes that many traits and states exist that contribute to a diagnosis and that all of these exist at all times to some greater or lesser extent, i.e., they are present on a continuum. Psychologists, the primary practitioners of dimensional diagnosis, then measure each of the relevant constructs using psychological tests of various types. The relative relationship of each of these constructs to one another is used to derive a diagnosis or classification. Typically, in order to arrive at a correct diagnosis or classification, a mathematical algorithm is used such as discriminant analysis, cluster analysis, latent profile analysis, configural frequency analysis, logistic regression, or some other multivariate classification approach. More often than not, psychologists will refer to a diagnosis made using such a dimensional and actuarial approach as a classification as opposed to traditional diagnosis, which assists in making a distinction between the methods applied.

(continued)

Dimensional approaches can at times blur the lines between "normality" and "psychopathology"; however, this is not necessarily a negative outcome. Dimensional approaches can allow individuals who may not meet a strict symptom count to receive services when the combination of behavioral and emotional issues that they are experiencing results in clear impairment, even when a simple symptom count might deny a diagnosis. There is also considerable evidence to show that mathematical or actuarial models of diagnosis and classification tend to be more accurate and objective overall than are traditional methods. The math algorithms are not swayed by subjective impression—however, some see this as a criticism as well, arguing that diagnosis is as much or more an art than a science and that good clinicians should be swayed by subjective information. For this reason, dimensional classification and diagnosis have been very slow to catch on and are particularly resisted by the medical community. However, the current trend toward the practice of evidence-based medicine that has moved into many professional health-care fields invited greater acceptance of dimensional approaches to diagnosis and classification.

The use of dimensional models continues to grow more so in psychology than elsewhere, but we see growth in other areas of health care as well. The issues are complex, but the data are compelling. If you want to know more about these approaches, we suggest the following two sources:

Grove, W. M., & Meehl, P. E. (1996). Comparative efficiency of informal (subjective, impressionistic) and formal (mechanical, algorithmic) prediction procedures: The clinical-statistical controversy. Psychology, Public Policy, and Law, 2, 293–323.

Kamphaus, R., & Campbell, J. (Eds.) (2006). Psychodiagnostic assessment of children: Dimensional and categorical approaches. New York: Wiley.

11.5.2 Achenbach System of Empirically Based Assessment: Child Behavior Checklist and Teacher Report Form (CBCL and TRF)

The *Child Behavior Checklist (CBCL)* and the *Teacher Report Form (TRF)* (Achenbach, 1991a, 1991b) are two components of the *Achenbach System of Empirically Based Assessment* (ASEBA) that also includes a self-report scale and a direct observation system. There are two forms of the CBCL, one for children 2–3 years and the other for children 4–18 years. The TRF is appropriate for children from 5 to 18 years. The CBCL and TRF have long played an important role in the assessment of children and adolescents and continue to be among the most frequently used psychological tests in schools today. The scales contain two basic sections. The first section collects information about the child's activities and competencies in areas such as recreation (e.g., hobbies and sports), social functioning (e.g., clubs and organizations), and schooling (e.g., grades). The second section assesses problem behaviors and contains item stems describing problem behaviors. On these items, the informant records a response of *Not true, Somewhat true/ Sometimes true,* or *Very true/Often true.* The clinical subscales of the CBCL and TRF are:

- *Withdrawn/Depressed:* reflects withdrawn behavior, shyness, and a preference to be alone
- *Somatic Complaints:* a tendency to report numerous physical complaints (e.g., headaches and fatigue)
- *Anxious/Depressed:* reflects a combination of depressive (e.g., lonely, crying, and unhappy) and anxious (nervous, fearful, and worried) symptoms
- *Social Problems:* reflects peer problems and feelings of rejection
- *Thought Problems:* evidence of obsessions/compulsions, hallucinations, or other "strange" behaviors
- *Attention Problems:* reflects difficulty in concentrating and attention problems
- *Delinquent Rule-Breaking Behavior:* evidence of behaviors such as stealing, lying, vandalism, and arson
- *Aggressive Behavior:* reflects destructive, aggressive, and disruptive behaviors

The CBCL and TRF provide three composite scores:

- *Total Problems:* overall level of behavioral problems
- *Externalizing Problems:* a combination of the Delinquent Behavior and Aggressive Behavior scales
- *Internalizing:* a combination of the Withdrawn, Somatic Complaints, and Anxious/Depressed scales.

Computer-scoring software is available for the CBCL and TRF and is recommended because hand scoring is a fairly laborious and time-consuming process. The CBCL and TRF have numerous strengths that continue to make them popular among school psychologists and other clinicians. They are relatively easy to use, are time efficient (when using the computer-scoring program), and have a rich history of clinical and research applications (Kamphaus & Frick, 2002).

The BASC-3 TRS and PRS, the CBCL and TRF, and similar rating scales are typically referred to as *omnibus rating scales.* This indicates that they measure a wide range of symptoms and behaviors that are associated with different emotional and behavioral disorders. Ideally, an omnibus rating scale should be sensitive to symptoms of both internalizing (e.g., anxiety and depression) and externalizing (e.g., ADHD and Oppositional Defiant Disorder) disorders to ensure that the clinician is not missing important indicators of psychopathology. This is particularly important when assessing children and adolescents because there is a high

> Omnibus rating scales measure a wide range of symptoms and behaviors that are associated with different emotional and behavioral disorders.

degree of comorbidity with this population. Comorbidity refers to the presence of two or more disorders occurring simultaneously in the same individual. For example, a child might meet the criteria for both an externalizing disorder (e.g., conduct disorder) and an internalizing disorder (e.g., depressive disorder). However, if a clinician did not adequately screen for internalizing symptoms, the more obvious externalizing symptoms might mask the internalizing symptoms and result in an inaccurate or incomplete diagnosis. Inaccurate diagnosis typically leads to inadequate treatment.

11.5.3 Single-Domain or Syndrome-Specific Rating Scales

Although omnibus rating scales play a central role in the assessment of psychopathology, there are also a number of *single-domain* or *syndrome-specific* rating scales. These single-domain rating scales resemble the omnibus scales in format, but they focus on a single disorder (e.g., ADHD) or behavioral dimension (e.g., social skills). Although they are narrow in scope, they often provide a more thorough assessment of the specific domain they are

> Single-domain (syndrome-specific) rating scales often provide a more thorough assessment of the specific domain that they are designed to assess than the omnibus scales.

designed to assess than the omnibus scales. As a result, they can be useful in supplementing more comprehensive assessment techniques (e.g., Kamphaus & Frick, 2002). Common examples of single domain scales include measures limited to Attention-Deficit/Hyperactivity Disorder, depression, or obsessive-compulsive disorder. Below are some brief descriptions of some contemporary syndrome-specific behavior rating scale.

11.5.3.1 Childhood Autism Rating Scale, Second Edition (CARS-2)

The CARS-2 (Schopler, Van Bourgondien, Wellman, & Love, 2010) is a 15-item scale that is designed to help identify autism in children over 2 years. The individual items are summed to form a total score that is used to rate a child on a continuum from nonautistic, to mild-to-moderate autism, to severe autism. The CARS-2 can be completed by a professional such as a psychologist, pediatrician, or teacher, based on observations performed in a variety of settings (e.g., classrooms and clinics). In the manual, the authors report results of psychometric studies that suggest adequate reliability and validity and a training video is available that shows how to use and score the instrument.

11.5.3.2 Reynolds Adolescent Depression Scale, Second Edition (RADS-2)

The RADS-2 (Reynolds, 2002) is a 30-item self-report scale that is designed to measure four areas of depression in children and young adults 11–20 years of age: Dysphoric Mood, Anhedonia/Negative effect, Negative Self-Evaluation, and Somatic Complaints. It provides scale scores for each of these areas, as well as a total depression score that indicates the overall severity of depression. The test manual provides information on the stratified standardization sample, as well as provides information on the reliability and validity of the scores and their interpretations.

11.5.3.3 Pediatric Behavior Rating Scale (PBRS)

The PBRS (Marshall & Wilkinson, 2008) contains two rating scales, one for teachers (95 items) and the other for parents (102 items). This instrument is for children and adolescents between 3 and 18 years and is intended to help identify early onset bipolar disorder and help distinguish it from other disorders with similar presentations. Both forms produce nine scales: Atypical, Irritability, Grandiosity, Hyperactivity/Impulsivity, Aggression, Inattention, Affect, Social Interactions, and a Total Bipolar Index. The authors report results of preliminary psychometric studies that indicate adequate reliability and validity.

These are just a few examples of the many single-domain and syndrome-specific behavior rating scales. There are many of these available for a number of psychological disorders and behavioral dimensions. These are particularly helpful in the assessment of externalizing disorders such as ADHD and Conduct Disorder in children and adolescents. It should be noted that they are intended to supplement the omnibus scales such as the BASC-3 and the CBCL, which should always be used over single domain scales for initial screening and assessment.

> Omnibus scales such as the BASC-3 and CBCL should always be used over single-domain scales for initial diagnosis.

11.5.4 Adaptive Behavior Scales

A special type of syndrome specific scale is the one designed to assess adaptive behavior. The American Association on Intellectual and Developmental Disabilities, an influential organization that advocates for the rights of individuals with disabilities, describes adaptive behavior as a collection of skills in three broad areas:

- *Conceptual skills*—which includes literacy, quantitative skills such as telling time and using money, and the ability for self-direction.
- *Practical skills*—which includes activities of daily living (e.g., getting dressed and adequate hygiene), health care, using transportation, preparing meals, and house cleaning.
- *Social skills*—which includes general interpersonal and social skills and the ability to follow rules and obey laws.

The measurement of adaptive behaviors is particularly important in the assessment of individuals with developmental and intellectual disabilities. For example, when diagnosing Intellectual Disability, it is necessary to document deficits in adaptive skills in addition to deficits in intellectual functioning. The assessment of adaptive behaviors can also facilitate treatment planning for individuals with a wide range of disabilities.

11.5.4.1 Vineland Adaptive Behavior Scales, Third Edition (Vineland-3)

The Vineland-3 (Sparrow, Cicchetti, & Saulnier, 2016) is an example of a scale designed to assess adaptive behavior. There are a number of forms available for the Vineland-3. These are:

- *Interview Form:* The comprehensive or domain-level form is administered to a parent or other caregiver as a semistructured interview. That is, the survey provides a set of questions that the clinician presents to the respondent. It includes open-ended questions that may allow the clinician to gather more in-depth and accurate information than that acquired using standard behavior rating scales. According to the authors, the format allows the administrator to probe for the true frequency and independent application of such behaviors, which is critical when evaluating individuals on their ability to function and perhaps live independently, or for determining the amount of assistance that an individual might need to maximize their independence.

- *Parent/Caregiver Rating Form:* This behavior rating scale covers the same content as the Interview form, but does so using different wording that makes it easier for those responding to the questions. This form is recommended when time limitations prevent the use of the Interview form and can also be used for periodic monitoring of client progress during treatment.

> The measurement of adaptive behaviors is particularly important in the assessment of individuals with developmental and intellectual disabilities.

- *Teacher Rating Form:* This behavioral questionnaire is designed to be completed by a teacher who has experience with a child in a school or preschool setting. It also covers the same content as the Interview and Parent/Caregiver forms, but focuses more on behaviors likely to be observed in a classroom or structured daycare setting.

11.5.5 Adult Behavior Rating Scales

We have thus far emphasized behavior rating scales that are used with children and adolescents. Behavior rating scales at these ages are far more common in clinical and school practice than in the adult age range. Nevertheless, there are behavior rating scales for adults and we expect that their use will grow in the future. The **Clinical Assessment Scales for the Elderly** (CASE; Reynolds & Bigler, 2001) is an example of such a scale. It is an omnibus behavior rating scale for persons from ages 55 years through 90 years designed to be completed by a knowledgeable caregiver, such as a spouse, adult child, or a health-care worker who has nearly daily contact with the examinee. The CASE also has a separate self-report scale for cognitively intact seniors to complete, but here we will focus on the behavior rating scale. The various clinical scales of the CASE focus on diagnosis and evaluation of the presence primarily of DSM clinical disorders in this age group. The complete self-report scale and the behavior rating scale of the CASE contain 13 scales each, 10 clinical scales, and 3 validity scales. Table 11.3 lists and describes the scales of the CASE. As you can see, there is much overlap with rating scales designed for children and

Table 11.3 Clinical Assessment Scales for the Elderly—clinical scales and descriptions

	Description
Clinical scales	
Anxiety (ANX)	Items assess a generalized sense of apprehension and fears that tend toward being irrational and nonspecific, including observable and subjective symptoms and worry states.
Cognitive Competence (COG)	Items assess impaired thought processes commonly associated with higher cognitive deficits in areas such as attention, memory, reason, and logical thought.
Depression (DEP)	Items assess indications of depressed mood, general dysthymia, sadness, fatigue, melancholy, and some cognitive symptoms associated with major depressive episodes.
Fear of Aging (FOA)	Items assess a sense of apprehension about aging and over-concern with the natural processes of aging and its effects on oneself and one's family.
Mania (MAN)	Items assess characteristics of manic states including pressured speech, grandiose thought, agitation, distractibility, flight of ideas, and related phenomena.
Obsessive--Compulsive (OCD)	Items assess nonproductive, ruminative thought patterns and excessive, targeted worry, and related phenomena.
Paranoia (PAR)	Items assess the presence of ideas of reference, nonbizarre delusions, suspicions of others' motives, and a preoccupation with doubts about others, and related ideas.
Psychoticism (PSY)	Items assess disorders of thought, bizarre delusions, confusion, negative symptoms, and associated problems.
Somatization (SOM)	Items assess hypersensitivity to health concerns and physical symptoms not fully explained by medical problems or excessive numbers of physical complaints.
Substance Abuse (SUB)	Items assess overuse of mood altering substances of a variety of forms, including common consumer products such as coffee/caffeine, alcohol, and illicit substances, and the tendency toward dependency upon such substances.
Validity scales	
Infrequency (F)	Items assess a tendency to overreport symptoms across a broad range of disorders not commonly endorsed in concert and potentially reflecting acute stress, frank psychosis, malingering, or a very negative response set.
Lie (L)	Items assess the tendency to deny common problems or difficulties, to respond in a socially desirable manner, or an attempt to present oneself in an overly positive light.
Validity (V)	Items on this scale reflect highly unrealistic responses typically endorsed at high levels only by a failure to read and comprehend the items, a failure to take the test seriously, or by random responding.

adolescents in terms of the constructs being assessed, but there are some key differences as well. For example, the CASE contains a Fear of Aging scale that is often useful in evaluating the source of anxieties as well as depressive symptoms in this age group. A Cognitive Competency screening scale is included to alert clinicians when a more careful or thorough evaluation of intelligence and related neuropsychological skills might be advised. A Substance Abuse scale is included to alert clinicians about issues in this domain as well—abuse of common substances and prescription medications are included on this scale because they are far more common in this population than many clinicians perceive and are thus often overlooked. You might here wonder why most behavior rating scales for adolescents do not include a substance abuse scale. While this information is certainly valuable and no one denies that substance abuse is a problem in the 13–18 year old group, most behavior rating scales do not include this for several practical reasons. Most adolescents abuse psychoactive substances in a secretive fashion, and so raters are most likely unaware of the issues, and even if aware or suspicious, they have no opportunity to observe the use. Further, if these scales come up within the normal range or indicate "no problem," clinicians may be overconfident that they have effectively ruled this out. More importantly, however, most of these scales are commonly used in the public schools, which often have prohibitions against psychologists asking students about substance abuse issues. The 10 CASE clinical scales were designed to assist in the process of differential diagnosis of the primary DSM clinical disorders that occur in the population over 55 years of age. Scales as study skills, conduct problems, and hyperactivity have limited if any value in this age group, and so they were not included.

Three validity scales are provided with the full-length scales, a Lie (L) or social desirability scale, an Infrequency (F) scale, and a Validity (V) scale composed of nonsensical items designed to detect random or insincere marking. Screening versions of the CASE are also available and are significantly shortened versions of the same scales noted in Table 11.3, including two of the three validity scales. The Infrequency (F) Scale does not appear on the CASE screening scales. Otherwise, the clinical and validity scales are common across the CASE versions, although individual items that make up the scales vary somewhat from scale-to-scale. The full-length CASE rating scales are typically completed in 30 minutes or less and are easy to use in a clinician's office, nursing homes, and rehabilitation settings, as well as in a general or gerontological medical practice. The CASE screening versions are half or less of the length of the full scales and require proportionately less time. The four forms of the CASE (the self-report, the rating form, and the corresponding short versions of each) are designed to be used independently or in combination.

11.6 Direct Observation

Direct observation and recording of behavior counts is the oldest method of behavioral assessment and is still widely used. As Ramsay

> Direct observation of behavior is the oldest form of behavioral assessment and remains useful.

et al. (2002) note, some believe this approach to be the true hallmark of what constitutes a behavioral assessment. In direct observation, an observer travels to some natural environment of the individual (a school, a nursing home, etc.) and observes the subject, typically without the person knowing that they are the target of the observation, although the latter is not always possible or even ethical. In reality, it is very difficult to get an accurate sample of typical behavior from a person who knows they are being observed—observing the behavior will nearly always change it—this is in some ways analogous to the Heisenberg Principle of Uncertainty in physics; we can never observe something in its unobserved state, i.e., observing something changes it!

In a direct observation, a set of behaviors is specified, then recorded, and counted as they occur. In such an instance, it is crucial that the observer/recorder is as impartial and objective as possible and that the behaviors to be recorded are described in clear, crisp terms, and so there is a least amount of inference possible for the observer. Direct observation adds another dimension to the behavioral assessment—rather than being impressionistic, as are behavior ratings, it provides true ratio scale data that are actual counts of behavior. It also adds another dimension by being a different method of assessment that allows triangulation or checking of results from other methods and allowing the observer to note antecedent events as well as consequences assigned to the observed behaviors.

This form of traditional behavioral assessment can occur with or without a standardized recording scheme. Often, observers will develop a form to aid them in coding and counting behaviors that are specific to the individual circumstance of any one observation period or simply devise one that they are comfortable using with all of their observations. However, this can introduce a variety of biases and increase the subjectivity of the observations. It can also enhance the error rates of recording behaviors due to the cognitive demand on the observer. Standardized observation forms are available for many different settings and enhance observer training, objectivity, consistency, and accuracy, but do limit the flexibility of direct observation, which is one of its key strengths. Nevertheless, we view the advantages of using a standardized observational or recording system as outweighing the limitations of such systems.

The most widely used such system is the Student Observation System (SOS), which is a component of the BASC-3. The SOS is a standardized, objective observational recording system that allows for the observation of 15 dimensions of behavior (some positive dimensions and some negative dimensions) and is designed to be useful in any structured setting that has educational goals. It is most commonly used in classrooms. The 15 categories of behavior assessed are listed in Table 11.4. Each of these categories or behavioral dimensions is defined specifically and clearly for the observer, and research indicates high levels of interobserver agreement on the ratings with a few as two in vivo training sessions (Reynolds & Kamphaus, 2015). The SOS uses a momentary time sampling (MTS) procedure to ensure that it adequately samples the full range of a child's behavior in the classroom (Reynolds & Kamphaus, 1992). Several characteristics of the SOS exemplify this effort including:

Table 11.4 Behavioral categories of the BASC-3 student observation system (SOS)

Category/definition	Specific behavior examples
1. *Response to Teacher/Lesson:* Used to describe appropriate academic behaviors or responses with the teacher or class	Raising hand to ask/answer a question; contributing to class discussion; waiting when asking for help
2. *Peer Interaction:* Used to assess positive or appropriate interactions with other students	Conversing with others in small group or class discussion; lightly touching another student in a friendly or encouraging manner (e.g., a pat on the back)
3. *Work on School Subjects:* Used to record appropriate academic behaviors that the student engages in alone (i.e., not when interacting with others)	Independently working on a school subject while seated
4. *Transition Movement:* Used to record transition movements that are appropriate and nondisruptive	Walking to the blackboard; getting a book; sharpening a pencil; lining up
5. *Inappropriate Interactions:* Used to record interactions with others that are disruptive or perceived by others as negative.	Preventing others from working; ignoring appropriate requests from others; invading one's personal space
6. *Inappropriate Movement:* Used to record inappropriate motor behaviors that are unrelated to classroom work	Being asked to leave the room, hitting others with a classroom-related object; refusing to leave a teacher's side to participate in school activities
7. *Inattention:* Used to record inattentive behaviors that are not disruptive.	Scribbling on paper or desks; staring at an object without paying attention
8. *Inappropriate Vocalization:* Used to record disruptive vocal behaviors	Criticizing another harshly; picking on another student; making disruptive noises; talking out of turn
9. *Somatization:* Use to record physical complaints or behaviors, regardless of inferred reason (e.g., a student falls asleep because of medication, boredom, etc.)	Complaints of stomach hurting, head hurting
10. *Repetitive Motor Movement:* Used to record repetitive behaviors (both disruptive and nondisruptive) that appear to have no external reward	Finger/foot tapping, swinging foot, and twirling/spinning a pencil
11. *Aggression:* Used to record harmful behaviors directed at another student, the teacher, or property. The student must attempt to hurt another or destroy property for the behavior to be checked in this category; aggressive play is not included here	Intentionally breaking own or another's work, belongings, or property
12. *Self-Injurious Behavior:* Used to record severe behaviors that attempt to injure one's self. These behaviors should not be confused with self-stimulatory behaviors. This category is intended to capture behaviors of children with severe disabilities who are being served in special classes in schools and institutions	Pulling own hair with enough force to pull it out; slapping or punching self with enough force to cause a bruise or laceration; banging head on a wall, floor, or object with enough force to bruise or injure

(continued)

Table 11.4 (continued)

Category/definition	Specific behavior examples
13. *Inappropriate Sexual Behavior:* Used to record behaviors that are explicitly sexual in nature. The student could be seeking sexual gratification	"Petting" self or others, any form of sexual touching (not a simple hug when saying hello or goodbye)
14. *Bowel/Bladder Problems:* Used to record urination and defecation	Urinating in his or her pants; having a bowel movement outside the toilet
15. *Other:* Used to record behaviors that do not seem to fit in any other categories (such behaviors are infrequent)	

- Both adaptive and maladaptive behaviors are observed (see Table 11.4).
- Multiple methods are used including clinician rating, time sampling, and qualitative recording of classroom functional contingencies.
- A generous time interval is allocated for recording the results of each time sampling interval (27 seconds to record observations after a 3-seconds observation period).
- Operational definitions of behaviors and time sampling categories are included in the BASC-3 manual (Reynolds & Kamphaus, 2015).
- Inter-rater reliabilities for the time sampling portion are high, which lends confidence that independent observers are likely to observe the same trends in a child's classroom behavior.

These characteristics of the SOS have contributed to its popularity as a functional behavioral assessment tool. It is crucial, for example, to have adequate operational definitions of behaviors that, in turn, contribute to good inter-rater reliability. Without such reliability, clinicians will never know if their observations are unique and potentially influenced by their own biases or idiosyncratic definitions of behavior. Momentary time sampling (MTS) is also important in making direct observation practical as well as accurate. In MTS, the observer watches the target individual for a specified period of time and then looks at the recording sheet, marks the relevant behaviors seen, and again does this in a specified period of time, and then observes the target individual again. The BASC-3 SOS MTS is set to be a total of 15 minutes. With this time frame, an observer can target multiple children in a classroom or efficaciously observe the same target in multiple settings to assess the generalizability of the behavioral occurrences.

Data from the direct observation of behavior is useful in initial diagnosis, treatment planning, and monitoring changes and treatment effectiveness. It gives the clinician a unique look at the immediate antecedents and consequences of behavior in a relevant context in a way that no other method can document. An electronic version of the BASC-3 SOS is available that may be used on a smartphone or a laptop computer.

11.7 Continuous Performance Tests

Continuous performance tests (known commonly as CPTs) are a specific type of behavioral test originally designed to measure vigilance, sustained and selective attention, and, more generally, executive control. There are many different CPT paradigms that have been devised since the original CPT of Rosvold, Mirsky, Sarason, Bransome, and Beck in 1956, but the basic CPT

> Continuous performance tests are a specific type of behavioral test originally designed to measure vigilance, attention, and more generally, executive control.

paradigms have remained similar until just recently. Typically, a CPT requires an examinee to view a computer screen and respond when a specific, but highly simple, stimulus or sequence of stimuli appears on the screen and to inhibit responding at all other times. For example, in the first CPT, the examinee pressed a lever whenever the letter X appeared on a screen but was to resist pressing the lever whenever any other letter or a number appeared. Gradually, CPTs became more complex and an examinee might be required to respond only when the letter "X" is preceded by the letter "A" but inhibit responding whenever the "X" appears (or any other letter appears) but it has not been immediately preceded by the letter "A." CPTs can be made more complex by using sequences that mix color, numbers, letters, and even geometric or nonsense figures. CPTs can also be auditory wherein examinees respond to a target sound but only when preceded by a designated or preparatory sound. The patterns used have always been kept simple in order to minimize the effects of short-term memory and maximize attention and inhibition as the key variables being assessed. While the tasks seem simple enough, and indeed, they are intended to be simple so that factors like general intelligence are minimized, they do require intense levels of concentration, and over a period of 15 or 20 min, many people will make mistakes on these simple tasks.

CPTs have been found highly sensitive over decades of research in detecting disorders of self-regulation in which attention, concentration, and response inhibition systems are impaired. These are often key indicators of disorders such as attention-deficit/hyperactivity disorder, and are frequently appearing symptoms following traumatic brain injury and many central nervous system diseases, and attempts have been made to use CPT results as the so-called gold standard for diagnosis of attention-deficit/hyperactivity disorder. However, disturbances of attention, concentration, and response inhibition apparent on CPTs are not specific to even a small subset of disorders. In fact, not only do individuals with attention-deficit/hyperactivity disorder show abnormal results on CPTs, but also do individuals with bipolar disorder, borderline personality disorder, chronic fatigue syndrome, nearly all forms of dementia, intellectual disability, schizophrenia, seizure disorder, and a host of neurodevelopmental disorders that are genetic in origin. Nevertheless, CPTs remain widely used and are in fact highly sensitive to symptoms associated with abnormalities of the self-regulatory and executive control systems of the brain.

Based on research indicating that working memory is also associated with the executive control systems of the brain, a recent CPT has been devised to assess the executive system of the brain more broadly and has added working memory assessment to the standard CPT paradigms that also assess inhibitory control, sustained attention, and vigilance (Isquith, Roth, & Gioia, 2010). Known as the Tasks of Executive Control (TEC), the TEC consists of a set of six different tasks that manipulate working memory load as a component of attention, vigilance, and response inhibition. It yields a wide range of scores associated with each of these tasks, some of which are common to the traditional CPT paradigms and some of which are relatively new. It is too early to determine how well these new approaches to the traditional CPT paradigm, particularly the addition of working memory demands, will fare in the clinical and research communities.

CPTs in general do not correlate highly with behavior rating scale data based upon observations of children and adolescents in routine aspects of daily life or when performing academic tasks. It seems clear that CPTs do provide unique forms of performance-based information about the executive control systems of the brain and their continuous evolution should provide additional insights into brain function as well as diagnostic issues related to central nervous system problems.

11.8 Psychophysiological Assessments

Psychophysiological assessment is another powerful method of behavioral assessment that typically involves recording physical changes in the body during some specific event. The so-called Lie Detector or polygraph is perhaps the best-known example. It records a variety of changes in the body of a person while answering yes–no questions, some of which are relevant to what the examiner wants to know and

> Psychophysiological assessment is another powerful method of behavioral assessment that typically involves recording physical changes in the body during some specific event.

some of which are not. Heart rate, respiration, and the galvanic skin response (the ability of the skin to conduct an electric charge—which changes if you start to sweat even a little bit) are commonly monitored by such devices. There are many examples of psychophysiological assessment including the use of electroencephalographs (EEGs), which monitor brain wave activity, electromyographs, which monitor activation of muscle tissue, and one of the most controversial, the penile plethysmograph, which monitors blood flow changes in the penis during exposure to different stimuli. The latter devices have been used to conduct evaluations of male sex offenders for some years, and their proponents claim to be able to diagnose pedophilia and other sexual disorders involving fetishes with high degrees of accuracy—having looked at this literature, we remain skeptical of many of these claims.

All devices in the psychophysiological assessment domain are highly sensitive and require careful calibration along with standardized protocols for their use. Too many of them do not however have adequate standardization or reference samples to make them as useful in clinical diagnosis—however, others such as the EEG are very common, well-validated applications that are immensely useful in the right hands. We believe that this form of assessment holds great promise for the future of psychological assessment.

11.9   Summary

Behavioral assessment is not simply a specific set of measuring devices, but more of a paradigm, a way of thinking about and obtaining assessment information. Behavioral assessment differs from traditional personality assessment in that behavioral assessments emphasize what an individual actually does, while most personality assessments emphasize characteristics or traits of the individual. Many contemporary clinicians use a multimethod multimodal approach to assessment. That is, they collect data or assessment information using multiple techniques, including behavioral interviewing, direct observation, and impressionistic behavior rating scales, as well as traditional self-report "personality scales." This approach is designed to reduce the level of inference involved in interpretation.

While a behavioral approach to assessment is best considered a broad paradigm, it does typically involve common techniques. For example, it is common for the clinician to conduct a behavioral interview. In a behavioral interview, the clinician focuses on the antecedents and consequences of behaviors of concern as well as what interventions have been used. In contrast to traditional clinical interviews, a key goal of the behavioral interview is to minimize the level of inference used to obtain and interpret information. By stressing behavior as opposed to subjective states, a more definitive plan can be derived, clear goals can be set, and the progress of the individual is monitored more clearly.

Another popular behavioral approach is the use of behavior rating scales. A behavioral rating scale is an objective inventory that asks a knowledgeable informant to rate an individual on a number of dimensions. These ratings of behavior are largely impressionistic in nature (i.e., based on the informant's impression rather than actually counting behaviors), but research has shown that they predict diagnosis accurately, predict future behavioral and learning problems, help us detect changes in behavior, and can even predict what types of interventions are most likely to work to change a behavior. As a result, behavior rating scales have gained considerable popularity in recent years. Many of the most popular behavioral rating scales are referred to as omnibus rating scales because they measure a wide range of symptoms and behaviors that are associated with different emotional and behavioral disorders. Ideally, an omnibus rating scale is sensitive to symptoms of both internalizing (e.g., anxiety and depression) and externalizing (e.g., ADHD and Oppositional Defiant Disorder) disorders to ensure that the clinician is not missing important indicators of psychopathology. We provided detailed descriptions of two popular omnibus behavioral rating scales, the Behavior Assessment System for Children (BASC), which includes a Teacher Rating Scale (TRS) and a Parent Rating Scale (PRS), and the Achenbach System of Empirically Based Assessment (ASEBA), which includes the Child Behavior Checklist (CBCL) and the Teacher Report Form (TRF).

While omnibus rating scales play a central role in the assessment of psychopathology, there are also a number of *single-domain* or *syndrome-specific* rating scales. These single-domain rating scales resemble the omnibus scales in format, but focus on a single disorder or behavioral dimension. Although they are narrow in scope, they often provide a more thorough assessment of the specific domain that they are designed to assess than the omnibus scales. As a result, they can be useful in supplementing more comprehensive assessment techniques.

Behavior rating scales have been used most often with children and adolescents, but there are behavior rating scales for adults. As an example, we discuss the *Clinical Assessment Scales for the Elderly*, which is an omnibus behavior rating scale for individuals from ages 55 years through 90 years. It is designed to be completed by a knowledgeable caregiver, such as a spouse, adult child, or a health-care worker who has frequent contact with the examinee. It is our impression that in the future, there will be an increase in the development and use of behavioral rating scales for adults.

The direct observation and recording of behavior constitutes one of the oldest approaches to behavioral assessment and is still commonly used. In direct observation, an observer travels to some natural environment of the individual and observes the subject, typically without the person knowing they are the target of the observation. Direct observation adds another dimension to the behavioral assessment—rather than being impressionistic, as are behavior ratings, it provides true ratio scale data that are actual counts of behavior. It also adds another dimension by being a different method of assessment that allows triangulation or checking of results from other methods and allowing the observer to note antecedent events as well as consequences assigned to the observed behaviors. As an example of an approach to direct observation, we described the Student Observation System (SOS), which is a component of the BASC-3.

Continuous performance tests (i.e., CPTs) are another type of behavioral assessment designed to measure vigilance, sustained and selective attention, and executive control. They have been found to be highly sensitive in detecting disorders of self--regulation in which attention, concentration, and response inhibition systems are impaired. While often considered essential techniques in the assessment of attention--deficit/hyperactivity disorder, the constructs that they measure are also commonly impaired in individuals with a number of other psychological and neurological disorders. Research indicates that CPTs provide performance-based information about executive control systems of the brain and can facilitate both diagnosis and treatment.

The final behavioral approach that we discuss is psychophysiological assessment. Psychophysiological assessments typically involve recording physical changes in the body during specific events. The polygraph or so-called Lie Detector is perhaps the best known example of psychophysiological assessment. It records a variety of changes in the body of a person while answering yes–no questions, some of which are relevant to what the examiner wants to know and some of which are not. Psychophysiological assessment devices are highly sensitive and require careful calibration along with standardized protocols to produce valid and reliable results. While many of these instruments have inadequate standardization and normative data to make them clinically useful, this approach holds considerable potential.

References

Achenbach, T. M. (1991a). *Manual for the child behavior checklists/4-18 and 1991 profile.* Burlington, VT: University of Vermont, Department of Psychiatry.

Achenbach, T. M. (1991b). *Manual for the Teacher's Report Form1 and 1991 profile.* Burlington, VT: University of Vermont, Department of Psychiatry.

American Educational Research Association, American Psychological Association, & National Council on Measurement in Education. (2014). *Standards for educational and psychological testing.* Washington, DC: American Educational Research Association.

Cronbach, L. J. (1990). *Essentials of psychological testing* (5th ed.). New York, NY: HarperCollins.

Isquith, P., Roth, R., & Gioia, G. (2010). *Tasks of executive control: Professional manual.* Lutz, FL: Psychological Assessment Resources.

Kamphaus, R. W., & Frick, P. J. (2002). *Clinical assessment of child and adolescent personality and behavior.* Boston, MA: Allyn & Bacon.

Livingston, R. B., Eglsaer, R., Dickson, T., & Harvey-Livingston, K. (2003). *Psychological assessment practices with children and adolescents.* Presentation at the 23rd Annual National Academy of Neuropsychology Conference, Dallas, TX.

Marshall, R., & Wilkinson, B. (2008). *Pediatric Behavior Rating Scale.* Lutz, FL: Psychological Assessment Services.

Piacentini, J. (1993). Checklists and rating scales. In T. H. Ollendick & M. Hersen (Eds.), *Handbook of child and adolescent assessment* (pp. 82–97). Boston, MA: Allyn & Bacon.

Ramsay, M., Reynolds, C., & Kamphaus, R. (2002). *Essentials of behavioral assessment.* New York, NY: Wiley.

Reynolds, C. R., & Bigler, E. D. (2001). *Clinical Assessment Scales for the elderly.* Odessa, FL: Psychological Assessment Resources.

Reynolds, C. R., & Kamphaus, R. W. (1992). *Behavior Assessment System for children: Manual.* Circle Pines, MN: American Guidance Service.

Reynolds, C. R., & Kamphaus, R. W. (2015). *Behavior Assessment System for children* (3rd ed.). Bloomington, MN: NCS Pearson.

Reynolds, W. M. (2002). *Reynolds Adolescent Depression Scale–2nd Edition: Professional manual.* Lutz, FL: Psychological Assessment Resources.

Rosvold, H., Mirsky, A., Sarason, I., Bransome, E., & Beck, L. (1956). A continuous performance test of brain damage. *Journal of Consulting Psychology, 20*(5), 343–350.

Schopler, E., Van Bourgondien, M. E., Wellman, G. J., & Love, S. R. (2010). *Childhood Autism Rating Scale, Second Edition [Manual].* Torrance, CA: Western Psychological Services.

Sparrow, S. S., Cicchetti, D. V., & Saulnier, C. A. (2016). *Vineland Adaptive Behavior Scales, Third Edition (Vineland-3).* San Antonio, TX: Pearson.

Teglasi, H. (1998). Assessment of schema and problem-solving strategies with projective techniques. In C. R. Reynolds (Ed.), *Assessment, Vol. 4 of A. Bellack & M. Hersen (Eds.), Comprehensive clinical psychology* (pp. 459–500). Oxford, England: Elsevier Science.

Vannest, K., Reynolds, C. R., & Kamphaus, R. W. (2009). *Intervention guide for behavioral and emotional issues.* Bloomington, MN: Pearson Assessments.

Witt, J., Heffer, R., & Pfeiffer, J. (1990). Structured rating scales: A review of self-report and informant rating processes, procedures, and issues. In C. R. Reynolds & R. Kamphaus (Eds.), *Handbook of psychological and educational assessment of children: Personality, behavior, and context* (pp. 364–394). New York, NY: Guilford Press.

Recommended Reading

Kamphaus, R. W., & Frick, P. J. (2002). *Clinical assessment of child and adolescent personality and behavior.* Boston, MA: Allyn & Bacon. This text provides comprehensive coverage of the major personality and behavioral assessment techniques used with children and adolescents. It also provides a good discussion of the history and current use of projective techniques..

Reynolds, C. R., & Kamphaus, R. W. (2003). *Handbook of psychological and educational assessment of children: Personality, behavior, and context.* New York, NY: Guilford Press. This is another excellent source providing thorough coverage of the major behavioral and personality assessment techniques used with children. Particularly good for those interested in a more advanced discussion of these instruments and techniques..

Riccio, C., Reynolds, C. R., & Lowe, P. A. (2001). *Clinical applications of continuous performance tests: Measuring attention and impulse of responding in children and adolescents.* New York, NY: John Wiley & Sons. A good source on CPTs..

Employment and Vocational Testing

12

> *What business does testing have in business? Turns out, a pretty big one...*

Abstract

Tests have been used in employment settings for over a century. Perhaps the biggest initial influence that introduced testing in employment setting was the development and use of the Army Alpha and Beta tests to help select Army recruits best qualified to become officers during World War I. Development of these tests provided the groundwork for subsequent expansion of testing in education, industry, and government for employee selection purposes. Today, tests are used in work settings for many purposes. This chapter reviews a variety of measurement tools used in employment and vocational settings. For personnel selection, this includes cognitive ability tests, interviews, personality tests, integrity tests, assessment centers, and work sample tests. Recommendations for choosing a personnel selection approach are provided, as well as discussion on how assessments are used to evaluate job performance. This chapter concludes with an overview of some common career assessment inventories that are used by individuals interested in obtaining career guidance.

Supplementary Information The online version of this chapter (https://doi.org/10.1007/978-3-030-59455-8_12) contains supplementary material, which is available to authorized users.

Learning Objectives

After reading this chapter, students should be able to:

1. Describe the origins of testing in employment settings.
2. Identify and describe the major types of personnel selection strategies.
3. Summarize the major findings associated with the use of cognitive ability tests in employment settings and how to minimize unintended outcomes.
4. Describe some of the major findings of using personality tests for selecting employees, and summarize the current state of the research.
5. Describe the strengths and weaknesses of each major personnel selection strategy.
6. Provide an example of how meta-analysis is used in employment settings.
7. Define job analysis, identify why it is important in personnel selection, and describe some common techniques for completing a job analysis.
8. Describe some common methods for evaluating job performance.
9. Define some common sources of errors found when rating performance.
10. Identify and define key terms found in the Guidelines on Employee Selection Procedures.
11. Provide some key points from the Principles for the Validation and Use of Personnel Selection.
12. Describe some common surveys used in career assessment.

As discussed throughout this book, psychological measurement is used successfully across a variety of applications; thus, it should be no surprise that testing has a rich and successful track record when used in employment and vocational settings. In employment and vocational applications, "tests" are often considered in a broader sense than simply a collection of items with correct and incorrect responses. While such "tests" do exist in such settings (e.g., cognitive ability tests), a collection of other instruments is often included in this category, including surveys, inventories, and questionnaires. These instruments commonly purport to measure abilities, attitudes, knowledge, opinions, interests, or skills that are deemed important for a variety of outcomes, such as successful job performance, productivity, tenure, or absenteeism. When used for personnel selection, tests are also heavily regulated, principally through the *Equal Employment Opportunity Commission* (EEOC), a Federal agency responsible for coordinating the Federal government's employment nondiscrimination effort. Their regulations require that tests used in this way are demonstrably job-related. You can view their regulations at www.eeoc.gov.

This chapter reviews a variety of measurement tools commonly used in employment and vocational settings. A brief overview of the history of Industrial/Organizational (I/O) psychology will be given, to provide a context for the origins of personnel selection tests. After a detailed discussion of employee selection tools is presented, a number of related topics are discussed, including applicant reactions to testing, job analysis, evaluation of job performance, and vocational testing.

12.1 Historical View of I/O Psychology

Industrial-Organizational (I/O) psychology origins can be traced back to the early 1900s, when psychology was applied to the problems experienced by businesses, particularly with respect to the skills needed to perform a job task successfully (Katzell & Austin, 1992; Landy, 1997). Notable psychologists applying general psychological principles to work settings during this time included Hugo Munsterberg, James McKeen Cattell, Walter Dill Scott, and Walter VanDyke Bingham. The growth of all new things requires a catalyst, and in the case of I/O psychology, growth seemed to be sparked by an economic environment of capitalism and industrialization, as well as the American emphasis on the importance of individual differences (a direct contrast from the European structuralist paradigm). Perhaps the largest contributor to the growth of I/O psychology was World War I. A group of psychologists led by Scott and Bingham helped the United States Army in the selection of officers (Katzell & Austin, 1992; Landy, 1997). The results of this effort helped establish the potential of applied applications of psychology in the business world.

> Perhaps the largest contributor to the growth of I/O psychology was World War I.

After World War I, several notable organizations were founded, including The Scott Company (1919), The Psychological Corporation (1921), and the Association of Consulting Psychologists (1932), in an effort to advance the applied applications of psychology. While The Scott Company went out of business a few years after it started, it was largely a victim of its own success; key members of the organization left the company for more attractive offers (Katzell & Austin, 1992). The *Psychological Corporation*, founded by J. McKeen Cattell, included involvement by almost 200 psychologists who either held positions in the company or who owned company stock (Katzell & Austin, 1992). While some of the services it offered have changed, The Psychological Corporation brand (now called PsychCorp) still exists today as part of the Pearson publishing group. The *Association of Consulting Psychologists* was formed to protect the reputation of I/O psychology from challenges by other professional psychologists who remained resistant to industrial psychology applications and from individuals taking advantage of new found prosperity without having any psychological training (Benjamin, 1997). The Association of Consulting Psychologists was later called the American Association for Applied Psychology and eventually (post World War II) formed the basis of what is now known as the Society for Industrial-Organizational Psychology, a division of the American Psychological Association (APA). Special Interest Topic 12.1 highlights some of the early contributions of female psychologists in the development of I/O Psychology.

In addition to these organizations, I/O psychology was involved in several well--known studies that advanced the scientific field of research. One group of studies, commonly known as the *Hawthorne Studies*, began in the late 1920s and involved a team of psychologists who intend on improving the operating efficiency of a plant owned by the Western Electric Company. These studies are often referenced when highlighting the importance of human variables (e.g., social relationships) in worker

Special Interest Topic 12.1: Contributions of Female Psychologists in Early I/O Psychology

In many accounts of the early days of I/O psychology, there is little if any mention of the contributions of female psychologists. However, Koppes (1997) provides a detailed look at four prominent female psychologists during this period. Each of these psychologists was born in the late 1800s and received their PhDs in psychology from high-quality institutions (Bryn Mawr College, Columbia University, Brown University, and University of Chicago) during the first quarter of the twentieth century. A selective summary of their work is provided below.

1. Marion A. Bills—Among her many accomplishments, Dr. Bills worked as a research assistant for the Bureau of Personnel Research where she consulted with businesses on selection, training, and supervision issues. She developed expertise in personnel selection and studied selection techniques for clerical and sales positions. She conducted predictive validity studies between tests and criteria, including productivity and withdrawal, and was one of the first to note the potential advantages of using a battery of tests, rather than a single test. She also worked for Aetna Life Insurance Company, where she specialized in personnel issues such as wage incentives, job classification, and consultation with top management. She published several of her works in leading scientific journals.

2. Elsie Oschrin Bregman—Initially hired by R.H. Macy and Company in New York, Dr. Bregman was charged with examining the company's personnel processes. While there, she focused on research examining procedures for recruitment, selection, training, and management. In an effort to examine the effectiveness of the selection procedures, she computed correlations using the Spearman formula between 13 selection tests and sales ability. After R.H. Macy and Company, she was hired by The Psychological Corporation to develop and publish revisions of the Army Alpha General Intelligence Examinations. Eventually, she received royalties for revised versions of the tests that she helped develop for use in private businesses. Because of these royalties, she was considered as one of the only individuals to profit from The Psychological Corporation during its early years. In addition, she also published several books with E. L. Thorndike on intelligence and learning and authored 12 articles in leading scientific journals during the first half of the twentieth century.

3. Lillian Moller Gilbreth—Dr. Gilbreth established an industrial management and engineering consulting business with her husband and used time and motion studies to determine how worker efficiency could be enhanced and productivity improved. She continued to run the company after her husband's death and worked with a variety of companies including Eastman Kodak, Remington Typewriter, U.S. Rubber, and Sears, Roebuck,

(continued)

and Company. Over the course of her career, she published several books and scholarly articles. Her work emphasized ways to reduce employee fatigue and increase job satisfaction as well as the application of psychological principles to scientific management as a way to compensate for a lack of consideration of human aspects of the job. She also noted the value of observing workers in the workplace, and she described the utility of a questionnaire that today would be referred to as a biodata form. One of her books, *The Psychology of Management*, was considered one of the most influential textbooks on industrial relations.

4. Mary H.S. Hayes—Dr. Hayes was one of the few women who were directly involved in studies during World War I. She worked as a laboratory technician and civilian expert in the U.S. Army Medical School and Surgeon General's Office and was associated with a committee that conducted research on personnel problems with the likes of E .L. Thorndike, W. V. Bingham, R. M. Yerkes, E. K. Strong, L. M. Terman, and J. B. Watson. She was one of the original employees of The Scott Company, where she coauthored a book entitled *Science and Common Sense in Working with Men* and also helped develop a graphic rating scale method. Dr. Hayes was also employed by the U.S. Department of Labor to conduct a study on the problems of unemployed youth and later helped to make decisions on how to prepare youth for national defense jobs.

performance and when discussing variables that can confound the results of a study. While the findings of the Hawthorne studies are often maligned and criticized, these studies consisted of controlled, scientific field-based research that is consistent with the scientific philosophy that underlies I/O research; this fact is often forgotten or omitted from discussion (Katzell & Austin, 1992; Olson, Verley, Santos, & Salas, 2004).

World War II led to the further growth of I/O psychology, as hundreds of psychologists were employed by the United States armed services or civilian agencies (Katzell & Austin, 1992). Within the armed services, there were a number of tests designed to place recruits in optimal positions. In addition, a number of other variables common to I/O psychology were studied, including procedures for appraisals, team development, attitude change methods, and equipment design (Katzell & Austin, 1992). Upon completion of the war, educational programs across the country expanded their programs to include the study of I/O psychology, which was met by companies' increased demands for such services. Numerous consulting companies currently exist that provide a number of off-the-shelf or customized selection or talent assessments, as well as a host of other employee or organizational services and trainings. I/O psychology has continued to grow at a fast pace; according to the Occupational Outlook Handbook, the need for I/O psychologists is expected to increase 19% from 2014 to 2024 (Bureau of Labor Statistics, 2016).

12.2   Personnel Selection Approaches

Over the last century, there have been a number of employee selection tests that have been developed in an effort to hire workers who will be successful in the job. The primary goal of these methods or tests is to save organizations' money and effort by helping them hire employees who will be able to perform the required duties of the job and who will be satisfied in the organization's work environment, thereby reducing the costs associated with poor performance, turnover, or counter-productive work behaviors. Detailed below are the methods most widely used by today's organizations.

12.2.1 Cognitive Ability

Cognitive ability tests have a long history in employment settings, dating back to the end of World War I (Schmidt & Hunter, 2004). Their use has been described as one of the most discussed and controversial topics in applied psychology (Murphy, Cronin, & Tam, 2003), even though there is an extensive body of research showing that cognitive ability scores can predict a variety of job performance variables. Cognitive ability tests measure a variety of mental abilities, such as reasoning, verbal and/or math ability, perception, or problem-solving. In employment settings, in contrast to clinical settings, items from these tests are most often multiple-choice or short answer response formats.

According to Wagner (1997), advances in statistical methods such as meta--analysis (i.e., a technique used to aggregate previously completed research in an attempt to statistically identify trends or patterns in the results of the previous studies) and the availability of large-scale datasets from military applications brought cognitive ability assessment in employment settings into a new era. The ability to summarize large numbers of studies and the application of cognitive ability tests across a variety of applications and performance criteria helped to establish the general predictive ability of cognitive ability tests. These tests were shown to be highly reliable, practical, and easily administered to applicants just entering the job market.

Numerous studies document the effective-ness of cognitive ability in predicting job per-formance. Perhaps the most well-known researchers in this area over the last several decades are John Hunter and Frank Schmidt. A series of meta-analyses and summary research has documented the results of numerous studies incorporating the results of tens of thousands of job applicants. A selection of their findings is included below.

> Numerous studies document the effectiveness of cognitive ability in predicting job performance.

1. A corrected validity coefficient between cognitive ability and job performance $r = 0.53$, with higher validity coefficients for professional jobs and lower coefficient for jobs requiring lesser skills (Hunter & Hunter, 1984); thus, cognitive ability is generally a strong predictor of job performance.

2. Multiple R values from multiple regression analyses of cognitive ability and one of the several other predictors at levels in 0.60s, such as integrity (0.65), work sample tests (0.63), structured interviews (0.63), and conscientiousness (0.60; Schmidt & Hunter, 1998); thus, combing cognitive abilities with several other variables increases prediction of job performance.
3. Cognitive ability test scores predict occupational level attained (in both cross--sectional studies and longitudinal studies) as well as job performance across a variety of job families; the relationship between cognitive ability and job performance is mediated by job knowledge (Schmidt & Hunter, 2004).
4. When estimating the relative economic value of using cognitive ability tests (in terms of the value of increased productivity resulting from increased job performance), they determined that in 1984, the economic impact resulting from the use of cognitive ability tests for hiring entry-level jobs in the Federal government for a single year was over $15 billion.

One of the primary concerns with cognitive ability tests is known performance differences across racial and ethnic groups, with minority groups performing up to one standard deviation below white applicants (Hunter & Hunter, 1984; Sackett, Schmitt, Ellingson, & Kabin, 2001); the effects of their use can lead to adverse impact on minority group members (Gottfredson, 1986). Sackett et al. (2001) reviewed a number of strategies for reducing the performance differences that are commonly found in cognitive ability tests. A review of these strategies and their findings is presented below.

1. *Strategy:* Combine cognitive ability tests with other noncognitive predictors that are valid predictors of job performance and that have smaller subgroup differences. *Findings*: While subgroup differences can be reduced when combining multiple predictors, such reductions do not necessarily eliminate adverse impact. A reduction in adverse impact is a function of many factors, including the validities of each predictor, the relationships between predictors, the size of the subgroup differences in each predictor, the ratio of the number of applicants tested and selected for the job, and the way in which the tests are used (also see Pulakos & Schmitt, 1996; Sackett & Ellingson, 1997).
2. *Strategy*: Identify and remove test items that are culturally biased. *Findings*: Studies that have attempted to remove items that are biased toward a certain subgroup (i.e., items that display differential item functioning or DIF) have shown a negligible impact on differences between the performance of subgroups, although the removal of such items is still recommended.
3. *Strategy*: Present test items in a way that reduces the demands of verbal or written skills, for example, using an auditory or visual presentation of items. *Findings*: Studies have shown that such presentation strategies can reduce subgroup differences, but such reductions do not necessarily eliminate adverse impact. Findings have been inconsistent, and much research is needed to draw more firm conclusions.
4. *Strategy*: Manipulate instructional sets in order to increase applicants' motivation to complete preemployment tests. *Findings*: The observed effects on sub-

group differences have been small and have been mainly done in laboratory settings. However, additional research is recommended.

5. *Strategy*: Directly measure aspects of the job of interest, using portfolios, accomplishment records, or performance assessments (e.g., work sample tests). *Findings*: Studies have shown some reduction in subgroup differences, although findings have been mixed, which is likely the result of differences in the amount of cognitive load contained in each measure. Results will likely mirror those found in the first strategy discussed.

6. *Strategy*: Provide coaching and study and practice materials. *Findings*: Results of studies indicate a negligible impact on reducing subgroup differences. However, applicants generally feel positive about such programs, which might lead to fewer complaints about a test and less litigation.

Overall, cognitive ability tests can cause considerable tension for organizations that choose to use them for employment decisions (Sackett et al., 2001). The tension stems from the potential conflict between maximizing performance (by selecting those that are most likely to succeed on the job based on their performance on preemployment tests) and maximizing diversity. It appears that there is growing consensus by I/O psychologists and researchers that cognitive ability tests are both valid and fair, as evidenced by the extensive meta-analytic studies conducted to date and a survey of members of the Society for Industrial and Organizational Psychology (Murphy et al., 2003). However, it is also clear that research will continue in areas aimed at reducing the subgroup differences commonly associated with cognitive ability measures. As an example, recent employee selection research has utilized the Cattell-Horn-Carroll (CHC) model (discussed earlier in Chap. 9). When second-stratum cognitive ability factors were used in evaluating job applicants (rather than overall ability or "g"), minority hiring rates were improved by increasing the number of job offers made to minority candidates and by reducing adverse impact rates (Wee, Newman, & Joseph, 2014).

One of the most widely used cognitive ability tests is the ***Wonderlic Personnel Test***. Revised in 2007, the Wonderlic Personnel Test consists of 50 multiple-choice questions covering a wide variety of topics, including math problems, vocabulary words, analogies, problem-solving, and other types of problems. Examinees have 12 minutes to complete the test. While used in a variety of different professions, the Wonderlic is perhaps best known for its use when evaluating college football players for their potential to be successful players in the National Football League.

12.2.2 Interviews

Employment interviews are one of the most frequently used approaches to evaluating job candidates (Wilk & Cappelli, 2003).
Interviewers typically use either an unstructured or structured approach when collecting information from job applicants. Unstructured approaches generally rely on the ability of the interviewer to generate questions that are relevant to the applicant being questioned or the

> Employment interviews are one of the most frequently used approaches to evaluating job candidates.

content that is being discussed at a given point in time. The results of such interviews are often subjective and can be very hard to compare across applicants due to the potential uniqueness of each interview session. Structured approaches, on the other hand, require the development of questions prior to the interview. Applicants who are competing for the same job are presented the same questions, and their responses are typically "scored" using a predetermined scoring key. Campion, Pursell, and Brown (1988) provide a number of suggestions for developing effective structured interviews, which are summarized in Table 12.1.

While employment interviews are generally considered to be related to job performance, the level or extent to which they can predict job performance has been unclear. Hunter and Hunter (1984) indicated that interviews had a mean validity of only $r = 0.14$ for predicting job performance. However, much recent research has indicated stronger relationships with job performance. For example, McDaniel, Whetzel, Schmidt, and Maurer (1994) found higher relationships for both

Table 12.1   Steps for developing effective structured interviews

Steps	Benefits
1. Develop questions based on a job analysis to determine characteristics that will lead to job success	Follows recommendations given in the Uniform Guidelines on Employee Selections Procedures, is important in court decisions, and potentially reduces bias
2. Ask the same questions to each job candidate	Consistency across candidates provides a more uniform application of the selection process and enables a more direct comparison of the results
3. Develop rating scales for scoring answers using examples and illustrations	Helps to make scoring system explicit, which is essential for justifying the validity evidence based on the content of the assessment procedure
4. Use a panel of interviewers	Reduces the impact of idiosyncratic bias that can result when only a single interviewer is used
5. Be consistent when administering the process to all candidates (e.g., have each interviewer asked the same question(s) across job candidates)	Consistency across candidates provides a more uniform application of the selection process
6. Document the process used to develop the interview questions and scoring procedures	This can serve as a written summary of the events that took place and is helpful for providing to others as needed later down the road (e.g., in the event of a legal challenge)

unstructured ($r = 0.33$) and structured ($r = 0.44$) interviews. Similarly, Huffcutt and Arthur (1994) derived a mean validity coefficient between interviews and job performance of $r = 0.37$ that is directly comparable to the Hunter and Hunter (1984) estimate. In addition, Huffcutt and Arthur delineated the amount of structure used during the interview and found that the mean validity estimate for interviews with the least amount of structure was $r = 0.20$, while the mean validity estimate for interviews classified as having the second highest amount of structure was $r = 0.56$ (the mean estimate for interviews with the highest amount of structure was essentially the same, $r = 0.57$). A common explanation given for the differences in predictive validity of unstructured and structured interviews is that the latter method demonstrates higher levels of reliability. However, while such an explanation is intuitive, Schmidt and Zimmerman (2004) present only limited support for this belief; higher reliabilities were not always associated with higher validity coefficients. Further, they demonstrated that averaging scores from 3 to 4 independent unstructured interviews provided the same level of predictive validity as that of a structured interview conducted by a single interviewer, a finding that is somewhat contradictory to Campion, Pursell, and Brown (1998). Schmidt and Zimmerman called for additional research in this area before definitive recommendations could be given.

Perhaps the most spirited line of research in personnel selection over the last two decades has been conducted using personality tests to select job candidates. Morgeson et al. (2007) indicated that from 1990 to 2005, there was a ninefold increase in articles published in some of the most popular I/O psychology journals (*Journal of Applied Psychology* and *Personnel Psychology*) and presentations at the annual conferences of the Society for Industrial and Organizational Psychology. Unfortunately, it is unclear whether the surge in research has led to a consensus among researchers or an advancement of the field.

Personality, as discussed in this section, refers to the unique characteristics that define an individual and are used by the individual when interacting with others. Such characteristics might include traits such as conscientiousness, agreeableness, flexibility, intuition, or aggression. In employment settings, personality is most often assessed by self-report questionnaires or inventories that are generally easy for applicants to complete. It is important to note that within employment settings, use of personality tests requires special consideration with respect to legal issues. Personality tests that are used by mental-health professionals to diagnose mental-health deficiencies are deemed as medical examinations and as such are restricted for use only after a job offer has been made (e.g., the Minnesota Multiphasic Personality Inventory-2 [MMPI-2; Butcher, Dahlstrom, Graham, Tellegen, & Kaemmer, 1989]). Personality tests that do not provide information on mental health (i.e., "normal" personality measures) are generally considered appropriate for use prior to the tender of a job offer (provided that they do not "invade" a person's privacy by asking a person's inner most thoughts

> Personality, as discussed in this section, refers to the unique characteristics that define an individual and are used by the individual when interacting with others.

Table 12.2 Big 5 personality dimensions

Personality dimension	Common traits associated with each dimension
Extraversion	Sociable, gregarious, assertive, talkative, and active
Emotional stability	Anxious, depressed, angry, embarrassed, emotional, worrisome, and insecure
Agreeableness	Courteous, flexible, trusting, good-natured, cooperative, forgiving, and tolerant
Conscientiousness	Dependable, careful, thorough, responsible, and organized
Openness to experience	Imaginative, cultured, curious, broadminded, and artistically sensitive

and feelings) and are the basis for much of the research conducted over the past two decades. The remainder of this section focuses on this research.

A seminal and often-cited paper on the use of personality testing in selection contexts is Guion and Gottier (1965), who generally concluded that personality tests were of limited utility for making preemployment decisions about applicants. However, the use of personality tests in employment settings continued over the next several decades, the results of which were summarized in two separate studies in the early 1990s. The first study, Barrick and Mount (1991), examined the relationship between personality traits (as categorized into the Big 5 personality dimensions of Extraversion, Emotional Stability, Agreeableness, Conscientiousness, and Openness to Experience) and job performance. Table 12.2 provides a summary of each of these dimensions.

Based on their meta-analytic findings, Barrick and Mount (1991) concluded that Conscientiousness was found to be a consistently valid predictor across a variety of occupational groups and across a variety of criterion types, meaning that persons who tend to be dependable, responsible, organized, etc. tend to be better job performers than those who are not. In addition, they concluded that Extraversion was also a valid predictor across criterion types for two occupations: managers and sales. Openness to Experience was a significant predictor of performance in job-training exercises, while Emotional Stability and Agreeableness did not appear to be valid predictors of job performance.

Tett, Jackson, and Rothstein (1991) also used meta-analytic techniques to examine the relationship between personality and job performance. While similar to the Barrick and Mount (1991) study, the Tett et al. study also investigated a number of variables that were proposed to moderate the relationship between personality and job performance and used some slightly different methodological techniques when conducting the analyses. Tett et al. found even stronger relationships between personality and job performance (purportedly in part due to a methodological process of using absolute values when averaging validity coefficients within a study). They also found several significant moderating variables, including

1. *The type of study*. Mean validities from confirmatory studies are considerably greater than mean validities from exploratory studies.

2. *The use of job analysis.* Personality dimensions that were selected as a result of a job analysis were more strongly related to job performance than personality dimensions that were not selected as a result of a job analysis.
3. *Job tenure.* Personality dimensions were a stronger predictor of performance for employees with longer job tenure than for employees with less job tenure.

While the 1990s saw a resurgence of personality testing within I/O psychology, the last several years have witnessed a marked split among researchers interpreting the results of these studies. Morgeson et al. (2007) discuss several perceived problems with the research examining personality and personnel selection. These authors, all former editors of leading I/O psychology journals, focus on three key problem areas: low validity coefficients, the reliance on meta-analyses that may overestimate the true relationship to performance due to the number of statistical corrections being made to both predictor and outcome variables, and the uncertain effects that applicant "faking" may have on the ability of personality test results to accurately predict job performance.

In response to Morgeson et al. (2007), Tett and Christiansen (2007) and Ones, Dilchert, Viswesvaran, and Judge (2007) provided a more positive view on the existing state of preemployment personality testing, arguing for its continuous use and expanding lines of research. The true relationship between personality and work outcomes is likely underestimated for a variety of reasons, including an over-reliance on exploratory strategies, ignoring personality-oriented job analysis, and ignoring the value of narrow-band personality traits and criterion measures. Table 12.3 presents a summary of these authors' reviews of the current state of personality testing in employment settings, focusing on the interpretation of the existing validity evidence, the impact of faking on the results of personality tests and subsequent validities, and recommendations for future research in this area.

A nonclinical personality inventory commonly used in employment settings is the *Hogan Personality Inventory, Revised* (Hogan & Hogan, 1995). Based on the five-factor personality model, it consists of 206 true and false items that are designed to be nonintrusive and noninvasive and is estimated to take about 15–20 min to complete. The HPI-R provides scores for each of the following dimensions: Adjustment (degree to which a person is steady in the face of pressure), Ambition (degree to which a person seems leader-like and values achievement), Sociability (degree to which a person needs or enjoys social interaction), Interpersonal Sensitivity (tact, sensitivity, and perceptiveness), Prudence (self-control and conscientiousness), Inquisitive (degree to which a person seems to be creative and analytical), and Learning Approach (degree to which a person enjoys academic activities and value education), along with each of their subdimensions. In addition to scale scores and graphs, the software reports provide a candidates' strengths and shortcomings, identifies characteristics that are relevant for success in most work environments, and identifies the suitability of the candidate for the position.

Table 12.3 Summary of contemporary views regarding personality testing in job settings

Authors	Test-criterion validity evidence	Impact of faking	Recommendations
Morgeson et al. (2007)	• Levels of validity are disappointingly low, but they might offer some incremental validity over cognitive ability tests (although they should not be used as a substitute for cognitive ability tests) • Meta-analyses may be overestimating true relationship due to the number of corrections for statistical artifacts such as range restriction and unreliability of both the predictor and outcome	• Faking on personality tests should be expected, and probably cannot be avoided • It is currently unclear if faking is even problematic when personality tests are used in actual employment settings • Faking does not distort the criterion-related validity of personality tests • Attempts to create "faking" scales and adjusting personality scores will have at best minimal effects on criterion-related validities	• Establish direct links between personality measures being used and measures of job performance • Avoid published personality measures in most instances, and construct custom measures that are directly linked to job tasks • Group items according to scales or similar content (rather than using the item sequence as a way to get more truthful or unguarded responding) • Improve methods for obtaining data by either improving self-report or simply abandoning it
Tett and Christiansen (2007)	• Meta-analytic data suggests that personality tests' validities reach useful levels under some conditions • Confirmatory strategies are preferred over exploratory strategies • The validity of personality is underestimated for many reasons (e.g., variability in estimates is ignored, the value of narrow trait dimensions and criterion measures is ignored, incremental validity when combining scores from multiple trait measures is ignored)	• Past research on faking is inadequate and uninformative due to an overreliance on social desirability measures and statistical partialing techniques • Faking appears to attenuate personality test validity but enough personality trait variance remains to be useful for predicting job performance	• Contemporary personality tests have been shown to be psychometrically sound • Theory-guided predictions between traits and performance are needed • Greater attention should be given to delineating the conditions under which personality testing is most valid, rather than simply dismissing them

(continued)

Table 12.3 (continued)

Authors	Test-criterion validity evidence	Impact of faking	Recommendations
Ones et al. (2007)	• Based on the evidence to date, the Big Five personality variables are predictive of job performance and its facets, leadership, and other work-related criteria • Personality validity coefficients are at levels similar to that of other selection and assessment techniques	• Faking does not ruin the validity of personality scores • Faking studies conducted in lab settings may not be the same phenomenon as faking that might occur in applicant settings	• Different sets of personality variables are useful in predicting job performance for different occupational groups • Customized tests are not necessarily superior to off-the-shelf tests, and there is no reason to believe that homegrown scales would necessarily have superior validity than off-the-shelf tests • In addition to predicting job performance, personality variables are also useful in understanding and predicting work attitudes (e.g., job satisfaction) and organizational behavior (e.g., motivation and effort)

12.2.3 Integrity

Often considered a form of personality testing, ***integrity testing*** typically refers to self-report tests that are designed to identify persons inclined to be dishonest. Developed as an alternative to polygraph tests (which are no longer legal in preemployment situations), self-report integrity testing was met with skepticism (e.g., Guion, 1991). However, attitudes toward integrity testing began to change based on research that established a link between integrity and job performance (Ones, Viswesvaran, & Schmidt, 1993; Schmidt & Hunter, 1998). In Schmidt and Hunter's seminal work on the validity and utility of employee selection procedures, integrity tests were shown to have a corrected validity coefficient of 0.41 with job performance and were shown to provide the greatest incremental validity in predicting job performance over cognitive ability test scores.

> In Schmidt and Hunter's seminal work on the validity and utility of employee selection procedures, integrity tests were shown to have a corrected validity coefficient of 0.41 with job performance and were shown to provide the greatest incremental validity in predicting job performance over cognitive ability tests.

Integrity tests are commonly divided into two groups: "overt" and "personality oriented" (Sackett, Burris, & Callahan, 1989). Overt tests typically consist of questions pertaining to general beliefs about or attitudes toward theft, as well as admissions about previous theft or wrongdoing. Personality-oriented tests focus primarily on personality traits or areas that may be related to theft, such as conscientiousness (or the lack thereof) and sensation or thrill seeking, among others.

Sackett and colleagues have monitored the status of integrity testing in preemployment settings since the late 1970s, providing an interesting and comprehensive analysis of integrity research (Berry, Sackett, & Wiemann, 2007; Sackett et al., 1989; Sackett & Decker, 1979; Sackett & Wanek, 1996). Some of the main conclusions from their most recent summary are provided below.

1. Integrity seems to reflect in part a complex mix of some of the Big 5 personality dimensions, including conscientiousness, agreeableness, and emotional stability, although a substantial amount of variance in integrity still remains.
2. While integrity was previously thought to be unrelated to cognitive ability (Ones et al., 1993), recent research that has avoided combining positive and negative personality facets together has resulted in stronger correlations with cognitive ability (combining personality facets that had negative and positive correlations with cognitive ability in effect canceled each other out, resulting in a near zero correlation).
3. Criterion-related validation studies continue to show positive (yet modest) correlations between integrity test scores and job performance as well as a number of counterproductive work behaviors.
4. While integrity test scores are subject to change based on coaching or faking, it remains unclear whether applicants do fake on such tests and what effect this faking has on the validity of the test scores.
5. When used for the purpose for which they are intended, integrity tests continue to be consistent with EEOC guidelines with respect to legal use in preemployment settings.

Although there are a number of integrity preemployment tests that are commercially available, one of the more well-established tests is the ***Personnel Selection Inventory*** (PSI; available from General Dynamics Information Technology at: https://www.gdit.com/humancapital), which consists of between 60 and 140 items and can be completed in about 30 min (depending on the specific PSI version). Similar to other integrity tests, the PSI consists of a series of questions that are rated on a multipoint rating scale (often ranging from 5 to 7 rating scale points), which cover a wide number of work-related domains (see Table 12.4 for a sample of domains covered by the PSI). Oftentimes, questions related to the honesty or integrity tests or scales are indirect (e.g., It is OK to bend the rules. Never, Seldom, Sometimes, Often, and Almost always) or direct (e.g., During your previous job, please estimate the following value of merchandise you took for personal use: $0, $5, $15, $25, $100, $500, $1000, $2000, or more). Each of these items is assigned a value, and the values across items are summed to form a total honesty scale score. While the last types of questions (i.e., the direct questions) might be surprising to

Table 12.4 Dimensions from the Personnel Selection Inventory

Dimension	Description
Honesty	Assesses how likely a person will steal from an employer
Tenure	Assesses how likely a person will be to stay at a job for an extended period of time
Nonviolence	Assesses how likely a person will be to refrain from violence in the workplace
Employee/customer relations	Assesses a person's tendency to be courteous and cooperative with customers and coworkers
Customer service aptitude	Assesses an applicant's understanding of effective methods of dealing with customers
Sales aptitude	Assesses an applicant's understanding of effective methods of selling and sales interest
Stress tolerance	Assesses an applicant's ability to tolerate stress
Risk avoidance	Assesses an applicant's willingness or desire to engage in high-risk or dangerous behaviors
Safety	Assesses an applicant's attitude toward safety and practicing safe behaviors
Supervision attitude	Assesses an applicant's attitude toward completing assigned work and appropriately responding to work directives
Work values	Assesses an applicant's attitude to productive work habits
Responsibility	Assesses an applicant's attitude toward engaging in counterproductive or careless workplace behavior
Candidness	Assesses an applicant's tendency to present him/herself in a socially desirable manner
Accuracy	Assesses whether the applicant understood and carefully completed the test

some readers (e.g., you might be asking yourself "Why would someone admit to previously taking anything from a previous worksite?"), the explanation that is commonly offered by selection professionals is related to the state of mind of the job applicant. When completing tests, job applicants are told to be honest and forthright when providing answers to each item. When reading such questions, oftentimes, applicants who have no problem taking company property for their personal use tend to be more willing to admit to at least a small level of theft, believing that it is the "norm" to engage in such behavior and fearing that if they do not admit to at least some theft, they believe that those administering the tests will think or know that they are lying.

12.2.4 Assessment Centers

An assessment center typically refers to a collection of tasks or exercises that are designed to simulate a variety of situations that are experienced in a work environment. Assessment centers are often used in selection and career development/training situations. Small groups of participants or employees participate in a series of tasks over an extended period (usually 1–3 days), including activities such as in-- basket exercises, simulated interviews, group discussions, fact-finding exercises, and oral-presentation exercises (Byham, 1970). Assessors observe each participant and rate their performance across a variety of dimensions, such as communication, drive, consideration of others, organizing/planning, stress tolerance, and a variety of personality dimensions (Meriac, Hoffman, Woehr, & Fleisher, 2008). Recent guidelines have been established describing defining characteristics and components of an assessment center, including the use of job analysis to identify critical job-related tasks, classification of candidate behaviors into meaningful dimensions, use of multiple assessment techniques that measure critical behaviors, use of multiple assessors who are trained in rating participants' performance, and systematic procedures for evaluating participants (International Task Force on Assessment Center Guidelines, 2000).

> An assessment center typically refers to a collection of tasks or exercises that are designed to simulate a variety of situations that are experienced in a work environment.

There is a sizable amount of research demonstrating the predictive validity of assessment center results. Gaugler, Resenthal, Thornton, and Bentson (1987), in their meta-analysis of assessment centers, reported a test-criterion validity coefficient for an overall assessment center rating of 0.37, while an updated review of similar studies has produced a slightly lower result (0.28; Hermelin, Lievens, & Robertson, 2007). Arthur, Day, McNelly, and Edens (2003), focusing on the predictive validity of individual dimensions assessed in assessment centers rather than an overall composite score, found that individual dimensions of problem-solving, influencing others, and organizing and planning met or exceeded the test-criterion validity coefficient of the overall composite found by Gaugler et al. and that individual dimensions could be used to account for significantly more total variance in performance compared to an overall score. This line of research was extended by Meriac et al. (2008), who used meta-analytic techniques to examine the relationship between assessment center scores, cognitive ability, and personality and examined the potential incremental validity of assessment centers. They found that the relationships between assessment center dimensions and cognitive ability and personality were somewhat surprisingly low (uncorrected $r = 0.30$ or less) and that assessment center dimensions are able to predict job performance ratings above and beyond cognitive ability and personality, accounting for an additional 10% of explained variance. While taken together, these studies appear to clearly demonstrate the predictive validity of assessment center ratings, there is less optimism about the level of construct-related validity evidence across assessment center dimensions. Lance (2008) provides a comprehensive review of the problem and suggests a paradigm shift from assessing dimensions to focusing on candidate behavior that is more directly tied to roles or tasks performed in various exercises. It is likely that such research will further the contributions provided by assessment centers.

12.2.5 Work Sample Tests

Work sample tests, also referred to as performance-based tests or simulations, have been used to select employees for decades (e.g., see Asher & Sciarrino, 1974). As the name suggests, work sample tests require applicants to perform tasks related to the job being applied for; such tasks can be actual work samples (e.g., answering phone calls and operating a drill press) or can be contrived examples of various tasks (e.g., writing a letter to respond to hypothetical customer's complaints). Work sample tests are thought to provide direct evidence of the applicant's ability to work on a job, are believed to be some of the most effective methods for predicting future job performance (Hunter & Hunter, 1984), and are often considered to have strong face validity. However, their use has not been as widespread as one might expect, for a variety of reasons. Gatewood and Field (1998) offer three primary limitations of work sample tests: (1) great care must be taken when constructing work sample tests in order to ensure that a representative sample of tasks is selected; (2) they assume that applicants already have the knowledge, skills, and ability to perform the job behavior; and (3) they are expensive, relative to other selection methods, with respect to both test development and the time it takes to administer and score them.

> Work sample tests are thought to provide direct evidence of the applicant's ability to work on a job, are believed to be some of the most effective methods for predicting future job performance (Hunter & Hunter, 1984), and are often considered to have strong face validity.

Roth, Bobko, and McFarland (2005) conducted a meta-analysis on work sample tests, reexamining some of the previous work sample research. While their results demonstrated that work sample tests are generally found to be predictive of job performance, the magnitude of the relationship is somewhat lower than what was previously thought (a corrected mean r of 0.33, compared to 0.54 found in previous studies). In addition, Roth and colleagues have suggested that scores on work sample tests may produce larger than previously thought differences between groups of applicants (Roth, Bobko, McFarland, & Buster, 2008). For example, mean scores between black and white applicants have been shown to differ almost three-fourths of a standard deviation ($d = 0.73$), a value that is similar to what is often found on cognitive ability tests and is almost twice as high as had been previously reported. These results should not necessarily rule out the use of work sample tests; rather, as noted by Roth et al., these results will allow decision makers to more accurately compare the adverse impact potential of various selection devices.

12.2.6 Biodata

In psychology, it is often said that the best predictor of future behavior is past behavior. The use of biographical data (i.e., biodata) for selecting applicants is steeped in this belief (Farmer, 2006; Guion, 1998). Biodata refers to an applicant's personal experiences and background and can be collected in many ways, such as structured interviews or self-report questionnaires. While biodata questions often center on previous educational and work experiences, they can also expand to areas such as hobbies, interests, and attitudes. There is generally overlap between the content found in biodata surveys and personality tests; however, biodata is generally

Table 12.5 Examples of dimensions assessed on biodata questionnaires

Dimension	Description
Historical	Pertains to past behavior or general questions on what typical past behavior has been
External	Refers to behaviors that actually have occurred, rather than simply thoughts or attitudes
Objective	Refers to behaviors that can be objectively or factually recalled, considered by some as first-hand knowledge
Discrete actions	Refers to single events or unique behaviors, rather than a summary or average of behaviors
Verifiable	Refers to a behavior that can be corroborated from an independent source, such as a transcript, written document, or testimony by another person
Controllable	Refers to actions or behaviors that are controlled by the respondent (e.g., how many times have you taken a college entrance exam), rather than events that simply "happened" to the respondent (e.g., what is the greatest number of coworkers have you had in your team)
Equally accessible	Refers to including only questions that are related to skills and experiences that are equally accessible to all applicants (e.g., opportunity to become a class president might be considered as equal access vs. opportunity to be captain of a volleyball team)
Visibly job relevant	Refers to questions demonstrating a face-valid relationship to the job
Noninvasive	Refers to items that do not invade a person's privacy or contradict federal, state, or local privacy laws (e.g., a question about religious affiliation would be inconsistent with federal law)

considered to measure broader domains than that of personality tests. Table 12.5 presents a summary developed by Mael (1991) of the dimensions or attributes of biodata item types that commonly appear on biodata forms.

Biodata surveys have been shown to be predictive of job performance in a variety of studies. Hunter and Hunter (1984) reported a corrected correlation between biodata and job performance of $r = 0.37$. Schmidt and Hunter (1998) reported a corrected correlation of $r = 0.35$, along with a small increase in predictive validity when combined with a measure of cognitive ability. In addition, biodata has been shown to be a valid predictor of job performance across a variety of settings and organizations (Rothstein, Schmidt, Erwin, Owens, & Sparks, 1990).

12.3 Choosing a Personnel Selection Approach

12.3.1 Advantages and Disadvantages of Different Approaches

There are a number of factors to consider when choosing a personnel selection approach. Effectiveness, cost, appropriateness to the job, time, and legal considerations are only some of these factors. The Society for Industrial and Organizational Psychology, the division of the American Psychological Association that studies human well-being and performance in organizational and work settings, offers an overview of advantages and disadvantages of each approach discussed above. This overview is summarized in Table 12.6.

Table 12.6 Summary of advantages and disadvantages of personnel selection approaches

Method	Advantages	Disadvantages
Cognitive ability tests	• Shown to be valid across a variety of organizational outcomes and job types • Easy to administer, in both paper--pencil and computerized formats • Cost effective • Little training needed for administration • Are not subject to attempts to manage impressions or fake responses	• Costly and labor intensive to develop custom versions • Subject to differences between races and sexes
Interviews	• Viewed as favorable by applicants (most expect to be interviewed) • Provides opportunity for communication from both the interviewer and applicant • Can serve as a measure of verbal communication (in contrast to tests or surveys) • Typically less likely to result in differences by race or gender	• Subject to a variety of rating errors and/or biases • Time-consuming, particularly if there are a large number of applicants and available positions • Can be costly to train interviewers • May lead to applicants responding in socially desirable ways
Personality tests	• Shown to be valid across a variety of organizational outcomes • Typically less likely to result in differences by race or gender • Easy to administer in both paper--pencil and computerized formats	• May be less favorable to applicants, especially if viewed as unrelated to the job or intrusive • May lead to applicants responding in socially desirable ways • May lead to legal challenges if test is used to diagnose a medical condition rather than to assess work-related dimensions
Integrity	• Shown to be valid across a variety of organizational outcomes • Can reduce business costs by hiring employees who are less likely to engage in counterproductive work behaviors • Suggests to applicants that integrity is important • Typically less likely to result in differences by race or gender • Easy to administer in both paper--pencil and computerized formats	• May lead to applicants responding in socially desirable ways • May be less favorable to applicants, especially if viewed as unrelated to the job or intrusive
Assessment centers	• Shown to be valid across a variety of organizational outcomes • Positively viewed by applicants because of job relevance • Can provide useful feedback regarding training needs • Typically less likely to result in differences by race or gender	• Costly and labor intensive to develop • Longer administration time

(continued)

Table 12.6 (continued)

Method	Advantages	Disadvantages
Work sample tests	• Typically less likely to result in differences by race or gender • Positively viewed by applicants because of job relevance • Can provide useful feedback regarding training needs	• Does not assess aptitude to perform complex tasks • Administration and keeping content up to date can be costly • Not conducive to group administration • May be inappropriate for jobs that only require a short period of training to perform the job well
Biodata	• Easy to administer and cost effective • Shown to be valid across a number of outcomes • Typically less likely to result in differences by race or gender • Does not required skilled administrators	• Can encourage applicants to present themselves in an overly positive light • Provides little insight into additional areas for development (only shows information about one's past) • Customized versions can be expensive

12.3.2 Applicant Reactions

Another factor to consider when choosing a selection method is how applicants will react to the chosen method. Hausknecht, Day, and Thomas (2004) offer five reasons why employee reactions to the selection method are important: (1) applicants who view the method as invasive may view a company as a less attractive option, which could result in loss of top candidates; (2) applicants with a negative reaction to the selection method might dissuade other persons from seeking employment in that organization; (3) applicants may be less likely to accept a job offer from a company that is considered to have unfavorable selection practices; (4) negative reactions can lead to increased filings of legal complaints and court challenges; and (5) negative reactions can lead to a lower likelihood of reapplying to a company or buying a company's product.

In general, research has indicated that individuals do not view various selection methods equally. For example, Hausknecht et al. (2004) report that interviews and work sample tests were perceived relatively favorably, cognitive ability tests, personality tests, and biodata instruments were perceived as moderately favorable, and honesty tests were perceived as less favorable. Interestingly, the general patterns of preferences seem to hold up internationally in places such as the Netherlands, France, Spain, Portugal, and Singapore (Anderson & Witvliet, 2008). It is important to note that many studies reporting on selection method preferences often are conducted using students in university settings and not just actual employment scenarios that raise concerns about whether the results will generalize to actual employment scenarios. However, upon graduation, college students make up a large percentage of the job applicant pool, and so their opinions about selection methods are of concern to organizations seeking employees.

> In general, research has indicated that individuals do not view various selection methods equally.

12.3.3 Job Analysis

Before choosing a method to select an employee, one must have a firm understanding of the knowledge, skills, and abilities (often referred to as KSAs) needed to successfully perform a job. The process used to define a job is known as *job analysis*; a more formal definition of a job analysis is offered by Harvey (1991; p. 74):

Before choosing a method to select an employee, one must have a firm understanding of the knowledge, skills, and abilities (often referred to as KSAs) needed to successfully perform a job.

...the collection of data describing (a) observable (or otherwise verifiable) job behaviors performed by workers, including both what is accomplished as well as what technologies are employed to accomplish the end results and (b) verifiable characteristics of the job environment with which workers interact, including physical, mechanical, social, and informational elements.

Harvey (1991) suggests that there are three primary characteristics of a job analysis: (1) describe observables; (2) describe work behavior that is independent of personal characteristics or attributes of those that perform a job; and (3) include only observations that are verifiable and replicable. Job analysis is central and necessary for choosing a valid employee selection method, for both intuitive and legal reasons. While it is beyond the scope of this chapter to describe job analysis methodologies in full, a brief overview of some of the most common ways to gather information about jobs is described below.

- *Interview*. The interview is one of the most common techniques for collecting information about a particular job (Cascio, 1991). A trained interviewer meets with incumbents and supervisors who are very familiar with the job being studied and records the tasks deemed most important to the job, the KSAs required for the job, the physical activities associated with the job, and the environmental conditions in which the job is performed. Interviews are generally considered to be a relatively inexpensive way to collect information about a job. However, the skills of the interviewer and the distortion of information by the interviewee impact quality of the data collected (Cascio, 1991).
- *Direct Observation*. Simply observing workers perform their jobs is another method for collecting information about the job. This method is best used for jobs that include a lot of manual labor and activities that can be completed in a relatively short amount of time. Jobs such as an assembly specialist or a retail employee might be good candidates for this approach, while jobs such as an electrical engineer or a screen writer might be poor candidates for this approach. While this approach can also be an inexpensive way of collecting job-related information, the observer must maintain a background presence in order to not influence or interfere with work performance.
- *Subject Matter Expert Panels*. Employees who are considered experts in their jobs (i.e., subject matter experts or SMEs) can be assembled into groups of about 5–10 to perform a job analysis. Typically, these employees are led by a trained facilitator who engages them in exercises and discussions that include rating

both job tasks and their corresponding KSAs (Gatewood & Field, 1998). An advantage of this approach is that relevant information for the job analysis is not based on the interpretation of an interviewer or observer because the SMEs are directly providing the information. However, this approach can be more costly to implement, and its success can rest on both the expertise levels of those forming the panel.

- *Questionnaires.* There are a number of commercially available questionnaires used to perform a job analysis (e.g., the Position Analysis Questionnaire and the Work Profiling System). These questionnaires typically consist of many items covering a variety of job tasks. Job incumbents are asked to rate the relevance of each task to their job and may also be asked to supply importance ratings to each task. Typically, items that are ranked the highest and/or are rated as most important are then used to define the KSAs needed for a job.

12.4 Evaluating Job Performance

Up to this point, we have focused primarily on how employees have been selected for vacant job positions. We have compared these strategies by highlighting their usefulness in predicting organizational outcomes, with the most important outcome being job performance. We have taken for granted the concept of job performance and perhaps have even assumed that job performance is comparable across strategies and various lines of research. However, research on job performance criteria has existed for about as long as personnel selection research, and the corresponding issues and debates are just as complex and challenging. In fact, Austin and Villanova (1992) provide a historical summary of the "*criterion problem*" that dates back to 1917. In general, the criterion problem refers to the difficulty in conceptualizing and measuring performance criteria that are multidimensional and dependent on specific organizations or situations. While it is beyond the scope of this chapter to provide a detailed review of the history of the criterion problem (and to increase the likelihood that you might continue to read this chapter), presented below are some of the most common ways of measuring job performance, along with some of their common pitfalls.

> In general, the criterion problem refers to the difficulty in conceptualizing and measuring performance criteria that are multidimensional and dependent on specific organizations or situations.

Once job tasks have been identified and applicants have been selected to fill vacant job positions, managers in organizations need a way to evaluate the performances of their employees. Borman (1991) identifies four major types of measures used to assess performance: (1) performance ratings; (2) objective measures (e.g., sales volume, turnover, and absenteeism); (3) performance tests or job simulations; and (4) written job knowledge tests. In this chapter, we focus on the first measure—performance ratings.

12.4.1 Approaches to Performance Ratings

There are four primary sources used for gathering performance ratings: supervisor, peer, subordinate, and self. Arguably, the most common approach is ratings made by a supervisor. Most of us who have had jobs have been rated at some point by a boss or supervisor. The logic behind supervisor ratings is pretty straightforward. Supervisors are often considered to know the job requirements, the most about an individual's performance at work, and are typically responsible for the success or failure of their subordinates. Supervisors often act as the link between an employee and the organization, providing feedback to management concerning the performance levels of their employees and providing feedback to subordinates on how their actions and behaviors are benefiting or working against an organization's goal. Research has shown that such feedback is important and is more highly related to performance than information obtained from any other source (Becker & Klimoski, 1989).

> There are four primary sources used for gathering performance ratings: supervisor, peer, subordinate, and self.

Peer ratings generally refer to performance ratings made by persons who hold a position similar to the position of the person being rated. Perhaps surprisingly, peer performance evaluations exhibit a number of favorable properties that include (1) acceptable reliabilities and above average predictive validities; (2) stability over time; (3) differentiation between effort and performance; and (4) relatively high accuracy (McEvoy & Buller, 1987). However, there are a number of concerns about peer appraisal systems including friendship bias, the tendency to inflate ratings for those in the same subgroup as the raters, an overreliance on the use of stereotypes, and the possibility of retaliation in subsequent ratings by those rated low during a previous rating period (DeNisi & Mitchell, 1978). In addition, employees' have a negative perception of peer rating programs in general (Cederblom & Lounsbury, 1980; Love, 1981), although they have more favorable perceptions of ratings used for developmental purposes rather than evaluative purposes (McEvoy & Buller, 1987).

Subordinate ratings refer to performance ratings of one's direct supervisor. Subordinate ratings of supervisors are perhaps most commonly used in multisource performance evaluation systems (aka 360-degree feedback programs). For these evaluation systems, a supervisor's evaluation is based on feedback from subordinates, equals, superiors, and other relevant sources (e.g., self, customers, and stakeholders). In general, there exists a substantial amount of support for the effectiveness of subordinate ratings. For example, they increase the likelihood that relevant information will be included in a performance evaluation (beyond that of supervisor ratings), and they can serve to increase the reliability of ratings because subordinates are often in a better position to rate supervisors on certain performance dimensions, such as delegation, work direction, and communication (Mount, 1984). In addition, there can be a number of other positive benefits of implementing subordinate ratings, including (1) increased formal and informal feedback of supervisor performance, (2) increased management learning (i.e., the learning by those the supervisor reports to), and (3) improvement of supervisor behavior and effectiveness (Morgeson, Mumford, & Campion, 2005).

The final type of performance rating discussed here is self-ratings, in which individual employees typically rate themselves on a variety of performance dimensions. Rarely are self-ratings of performance gathered in isolation, and oftentimes, they use the same rating form used by supervisors in their ratings of performance. While self-ratings of performance are desirable because of their relatively low cost to obtain and their potential value to inform discussions about job performance (e.g., in comparing differences found between supervisor and subordinate ratings), they are often considered to be biased in some fashion, leading to inflated ratings. Cascio (1991) suggests several strategies to improve the effectiveness of self-ratings:

1. Ask individuals to rate themselves relative to others rather than in absolute terms (e.g., on the dimension of communication, ask individuals to rate themselves on how well they communicate with others in the organization, rather than asking individuals how good of a communicator they are)
2. Provide multiple opportunities for self-appraisal; it is a skill that may well improve with practice
3. Ensure confidentiality of ratings

12.4.2 Comparison of Rating Approaches

As you might imagine, researchers are particularly interested in understanding the relationship between these rating approaches and the differences they may exhibit when evaluating job performance. Harris and Schaubroeck (1988), in their meta-analysis of self, supervisor, and peer ratings, indicated that using multiple raters leads to a number of advantages, including enhanced ability to observe and measure numerous job facets, greater reliability, fairness, and ratee acceptance, as well as improved defensibility when addressing legal concerns. Results from their study found moderate agreement between self- and peer ratings and self- and supervisor ratings, but much higher agreement between peer and supervisor ratings. Putting another way, although significant correlations were found between rating formats, a relatively low amount of overall variance between scores was found. In the case of the self-peer and self-supervisor ratings, only about 12% of the variance was shared; for the peer-supervisor ratings, the amount of shared variance was markedly higher, but still only about 38%. Thus, each rating format appears to provide a substantial amount of unique information.

> Putting it another way, although significant correlations were found between rating formats, a relatively low amount of overall variance between scores was found.

One specific performance criterion area that has received considerable attention is the criteria used when validating selection methods and tools. This area is of key interest to researchers and practitioners alike;

both have a keen interest in maximizing the chances of finding a relationship between the variable being studied (e.g., a selection test) and job performance criteria. Nathan and Alexander (1988) examined studies of tests used to predict a variety of job performance measures for clerical positions (e.g., supervisor ratings, supervisor rankings, production data, and work samples, among others) and found similar validity coefficients across objective and subjective criteria, regardless of the type of test being used to predict job performance. Hoffman, Nathan, and Holden (1991) came to similar conclusions in a study of mechanical, maintenance, and field service jobs in a gas utility company; both objective and subjective criteria resulted in similar levels of validity. However, they also found that one type of subjective performance rating—self-appraisals—showed validity levels around zero. They concluded "While the use of self-appraisal may have merit for other performance appraisal purposes…, its use in test validation research may be problematic" (p. 615). Although these results suggest that both subjective and objective performance result in similar levels of validity, this does not imply that they are measuring the same thing. A meta-analysis conducted by Bommer, Johnson, Rich, Podsakoff, and Mackenzie (1995) found a corrected average correlation between these measures of 0.39, suggesting that they are not interchangeable.

12.4.3 Types of Rating Methods

When making performance ratings, the rater often will use a rating system that is either relative or absolute (Cascio, 1991). *Relative performance rating* methods involve directly comparing the performance of the ratee with those of other persons performing similar jobs. For example, five customer service representatives might be evaluated by a rater who simply lists their names on a sheet of paper according to their performance level, with the best performer in the group listed first and the worst performer in the group listed last. A variation of this approach is the one in which paired comparisons are made between all employees within a group. For example, if five employees from a single group were being evaluated, the rater would compare each employee with all other employees and indicate which employee is the better performer. After all employees are compared, the rater sums the number of times that each employee was rated the better performer, and employees are then ranked according to the total number of times he or she was ranked superior. A final relative rating method is the one that mandates the rater to assign employees a rating based on predetermined percentages (e.g., 20% of employees must receive a "needs improvement" rating, and 5% of employees must receive an "outstanding" rating).

Absolute performance rating methods do not involve making direct comparisons with other employees. Rather, the rater focuses on comparing an individual employee's behavior with a defined (formally or informally) measure of performance. One such method is a narrative essay, in which the rater describes an employee's strengths, weaknesses, and areas of improvement. Another method is behavioral checklists, in which the rater evaluates the employee based on a series of statements about job-related behaviors. Oftentimes, the rater is asked to rate these behaviors using a Likert-type scale that has a variety of response options (e.g., never, sometimes, often, and almost always). Such ratings are then summed across behavioral dimensions, providing a total performance score for an employee. A rating format that has received a lot of research attention is **behaviorally anchored rating scales** (BARS; Smith & Kendall, 1963). Using the notion of critical incidents, different effectiveness levels of job performance are used to anchor a rating scale. When making a rating, the rater reads through the descriptions of each rating point on the corresponding scale and selects the level of performance that is best reflected by the ratee. While originally BARS was thought to hold promise for reducing some of the common problems associated with ratings scales (e.g., various forms of error, reliability, and validity), research has shown that BARS is not substantially better than a variety of other rating formats (Borman, 1991; Cascio, 1991).

12.4.4 Sources of Error

In many settings, a substantial amount of effort goes into developing effective measures of job performance. Human resource professionals can use employee interviews, subject-matter expert reviews, literature reviews, and job analysis techniques to help create rating forms. However, all ratings will be subject to a variety of sources of error. These errors are considered to be the result of systematic errors in judgment that leads to *rater drift*. Rater drift, or differential rater function over time, refers to changes in rater behavior | These error types are considered to be the result of systematic errors in judgment. |

across rating administrations that occur because of contextual factors and differences in the values and background experiences of individual raters. Some of the most common types of error that result from rater drift are provided in Table 12.7.

Table 12.7 Common error types when evaluating job performance

Common types of errors	Description
Leniency	Employee is rated more favorably than his/her job performance warrants
Severity	Employee is rated more negatively or harshly than his/her job performance warrants
Recency	Raters assign lower scores to employees rated early in the day and higher scores to those rated late in the day
Primacy	Raters assign higher scores to employees rated early in the day and lower scores to those rated late in the day
Central tendency	Raters avoid using the low and high extremes of the rating scale but simply use the middle values in the scale, resulting in all employees being rated in the "average" range
Halo or horns	Rater uses a global impression of an employee when rating performance, resulting in either overly positive (halo) or negative (horns) ratings

At times, raters are too lenient and so tend to rate an employee more favorably than the employee's performance warrants. Other times, raters are too harsh or severe and rate the employee at a lower level than what is warranted. In situations where ratings are conducted over the course of a day, some raters may assign lower scores to employees rated early in the day and higher scores to those rated later (recency), while other raters may exhibit the opposite pattern (primacy). Raters can also fall into a pattern in which their ratings are subject to a central tendency bias in which all employees are rated as "average." Finally, raters can introduce a halo or horn bias, in which a general impression of an employee influences ratings on specific dimensions in either a positive (halo) or negative (horns) manner (Cooper, 1981; Thorndike, 1920). We focus on job performance ratings in this chapter, but it is worth noting that these errors can impact any type of rating (e.g., child personality ratings using measures such as the BASC-3, ratings/grading of constructed-response items such as essay questions, etc.). Of course, when completing ratings, there are steps that raters can take to minimize the errors introduced into the rating process. For example, many biases can be minimized by trying to reduce ambiguity that might be present in the rating scales themselves or by using a type of forced distribution in which ratees are apportioned according to an approximately normal distribution. Additionally, informing raters about how to use the rating instruments and convincing them of the value and uses of the ratings that they provide can also help to minimize these biases (Cascio, 1991).

12.5   Legal Issues

Up to this point, this chapter has focused on a number of issues related to selecting employees and measuring how well employees perform on the job. Enormous amounts of time, effort, and energy are devoted to maximizing the efficiency and effectiveness of these methods. However, all of these expenditures are pointless if human resource professionals ignore federal, state, and local laws that affect their hiring, promotion, compensation, and retention practices.

There is a substantial literature based on employment law and personnel selection. While there are a number of classic books and articles (e.g., *Fairness in Selecting Employees*, Arvey & Faley, 1992), there are two source documents that anyone working in this field should be familiar with. Each of these documents is discussed below.

Table 12.8 Key Concepts from the Uniform Guidelines on Employee Selection Procedures

Concept	Definition
Adverse impact	A substantially different rate of selection… that works to the disadvantage of members of a race, sex, or ethnic group.
Unfairness of a selection measure	A condition in which members of one race, sex, or ethnic group characteristically obtain lower scores on a selection procedure than members of another group, and the differences are not reflected in measures of job performance
Four-fifths rule	A selection rate for any race, sex, or ethnic group, which is less than 4/5 (or 80%) of the rate for the group with the highest rate, will generally be regarded by the Federal enforcement agencies as evidence of adverse impact
Discrimination	The use of any selection procedure, which has an adverse impact…of members of any race, sex, or ethnic group, will be considered to be discriminatory…, unless the procedure has been validated in accordance with these guidelines…

12.5.1 The Uniform Guidelines on Employee Selection Procedures (1978)

The *Uniform Guidelines on Employee Selection Procedures* (1978) present guidelines describing characteristics of acceptable selection procedures, adopted by a number of federal agencies, including the Equal Employment Opportunity Commission, the Civil Service Commission, the Department of Labor, and the Department of Justice. In addition to hiring procedures, these guidelines apply to any selection procedure that is used as a basis for any employment decision, such as hiring, promotion, retention, or referral. Definitions of some key concepts discussed in the Guidelines are provided in Table 12.8.

The Uniform Guidelines on Employee Selection Procedures (1978) present guidelines describing characteristics of acceptable selection procedures, adopted by a number of federal agencies, including the Equal Employment Opportunity Commission, the Civil Service Commission, the Department of Labor, and the Department of Justice.

In addition to defining key terms, the Guidelines also provide details on establishing validity evidence for selection procedures, both in terms of the type of studies that can be conducted and parameters for establishing validity when it is not technically feasible to implement a predictive validity study at a given location. The Guidelines also define parameters for documenting selection rate and validation data.

12.5.2 Principles for the Validation and Use of Personnel Selection Procedures, Fifth Edition (2018)

The *Principles for the Validation and Use of Personnel Selection Procedures* was developed by a task force from the Society of Industrial and Organizational Psychology (Society of Industrial and Organizational Psychology, 2018), in an effort to document scientific findings and generally accepted practices for using personnel selection procedures and conducting personnel selection research. In addition to providing an overview of the validation process and describing generally accepted sources of validity evidence, these principles also describe operational considerations in personnel selection and propose guidelines for documenting the results of validation studies. Table 12.9 provides a selected summary of key points from several of these areas.

Table 12.9 Key Points from the Principles for the Validation and Use of Personnel Selection Procedures

Key points	
Sources of validity evidence	• Empirical relationship of predictor scores to external variables • Content-related evidence that documents relationship between predictor and job outcomes • Attributes of the internal structure of a test, with respect to how the items are related to each other and/or to the construct being measured • Attributes related to the processes an individual goes through to perform job task or generate a response • Consequences of personnel decisions, with respect to whether differences found in a predictor are also found in measures of job outcomes
Key steps in planning a validation effort	• Identify existing validation research that is relevant • Design the study in a way that is consistent with how the predictor will be used • Ensure the adequacy of the methods of analysis used in the study, along with the skills of those performing the analysis • Ensure that the study is feasible, given the situation in which the predictor is being used
Strategies for generalizing existing validity evidence to local situations	• Transportability, in which attributes from a job setting in an existing research study are directly comparable to a local situation • Synthetic validity, in which the relationship between the selection procedure and one or more work domains is clearly delineated and documented • Meta-analysis, in which the results of predictor-criterion relationships in existing research across a large number of settings are summarized and analyzed

Fairness	• As a social rather than psychometric concept, fairness can be viewed as:
	  – Equal group performance on a predictor
	  – Equal treatment of all examinees
	  – A lack of predictive bias, in which a common regression line can describe the predictor-criterion relationship for all subgroups

Bias	• Any construct-irrelevant source of variance that influences predictor scores

While the Principles are likely to provide an abundance of relevant information to those working in the personnel selection field, it is only intended to provide helpful information; it is not intended to interpret or supplant federal, state, or local laws or regulations. In addition, it is not a "how to" document that can be used by a novice who wants to go into this field. Individuals with formal training in personnel selection must use their own knowledge to determine which portions of the Principles are most applicable to the situation at hand.

12.6 Career Assessment

Although not a personnel selection method, a related field is that of *career assessment*, which is commonly used to provide information about attitudes and interests of a person interested in entering the workforce. While traditional use of career assessments has often been through a counselor, career assessments are readily found on the Internet and can be taken at one's convenience, without the involvement of a counselor (although such use is better suited for those who simply want to better understand some of their occupational and job-related interests, rather than those who are about to spend a significant amount of time and money pursuing a career path). This section provides a summary of several of the more popular career assessments that are in use today.

12.6.1 Strong Interest Inventory, Revised Edition

The *Strong Interest Inventory* is one of the most well-known career assessment inventories available. It was originally developed by E. K. Strong, Jr. (1926, 1927a, 1927b) and substantially revised in 2004 and 2012 (Donnay, Morris, Schaubhut, & Thompson, 2004; Herk, & Thompson, 2012). Designed for high-school students through adults, the revised version contains 291 items covering 6 interest areas: Occupations, Subject Areas, Activities, Leisure Activities, People, and Your Characteristics. Items are answered using a five-point rating scale, and take between 30 and 45 min to complete.

The Strong Interest Inventory consists of four primary categories of scales:

1. *General Occupational Themes*: Six scales representing level of interest in occupational themes from Holland's RIASEC theory of careers and vocational choice (see Table 12.10).

Table 12.10 Holland's RIASEC personality type categories

Personality type	Characteristics
Realistic	Practical, to the point, brief
Investigative	Analytical and intellectual
Artistic	Creative and innovative
Social	Nurturing and agreeable
Enterprising	Energetic and persuasive
Conventional	Dependable and careful

Note. *RIASEC*: realistic, investigative, artistic, social, enterprising, and conventional

2. *Basic Interest Scales*: 30 scales reflecting clusters of interests related to the occupational themes, such as athletics, science, performing arts, public speaking, and sales.
3. *Personal Style Scales*: Five scales including work style, learning environment, leadership style, risk taking, and team orientation.
4. *Occupational Scales*: 122 separate scales for males and females that measure the extent to which a person's interests are similar to person of the same sex working in 122 diverse occupations.

After completing the survey, a variety of computerized report options are available. For each examinee, reports include top RIASC interest areas (e.g., Investigative might include medical science, research, and mathematics), top 10 occupational matches from the 122 occupational scales, and ratings for all occupational groups. In addition, a summary of the examinee's personal style scale ratings is provided, describing preferences across each of the personal style groupings. As noted in Case and Blackwell (2008), "The Strong's qualitative features…and its psychometric characteristics continue to distinguish this instrument as a standard of excellence…and represent another significant step in the continuing evolution of this extremely valuable tool."

12.6.2 Career Decision-Making System, Revised

The *Career Decision-Making System, Revised* (CDM-R; Harrington & O'Shea, 2000) is a self-score assessment that helps identify the occupational interests and abilities of middle- and high-school students. There are two versions of levels. Level one has 96 items and is designed for junior high/middle school students or those with less developed reading abilities. Level 2 has 120 items and is designed for high-school students, college students, and adults who have higher level reading abilities. Like the Strong Interest Inventory, the CDM-R is based on Holland's RIASEC personality type, although uses slightly different names that are designed to be more occupationally relevant (Holland's Realistic is denoted as Crafts, Investigative as Scientific, Artistic as The Arts, Enterprising as Business, and Conventional as Office Operations; Social remained the same). The CDM-R can be hand or computer administered and scored. When completing the inventory, students proceed through the following steps:

1. *Identify career choices.* Using a list of 18 career clusters, each with detailed samples of careers within a cluster, students choose their top 2 career cluster choices.
2. *Identify school subjects.* Using a list of 15 school subject areas, students choose the 4 school subjects they like the most.
3. *Identify work values.* Using a list of 14 work values (e.g., creativity, good salary, and outdoor work), students choose 4 work values that they feel are most important.

4. *Identify abilities*. Using a list of 14 abilities (e.g., clerical, manual, and spatial), students identify their top 4 abilities.
5. *Identify future plans*. Using a list of 10 possible plans for additional training or schooling (e.g., 4-year college degree, military service, and 1-year business school), students indicate their current plan for continuing their education.
6. *Identify interests*. Students read a series of activities and indicate whether they like or dislike an activity (or if they can't make up their mind).

Upon completion of the survey, students' responses are scored, possible matches between their responses, and careers are presented. The CDM-R provides an Internet-based job exploration tool that includes both text-based descriptions about a given job and video clips showing someone performing the job. In addition, the CDM-R updates its job listings based on the biennial release of the ***Occupational Outlook Handbook*** by the Bureau of Labor Statistics. The Handbook is the U.S. government's primary source for career guidance and provides vital statistics on hundreds of occupations for those seeking employment or investigating career opportunities. The website has a number of very useful features, including options to select potential occupations based on median pay, entry-level education, number of projected new jobs, and projected growth rate, among other important considerations (https://www.bls.gov/ooh/home.htm). The Handbook is no longer available in print but is available for *iOS* and for *Android* devices at https://www.bls.gov/ooh/. Linking CDM-R scores with current and prospective occupational opportunities makes the CDM-R especially useful for providing career guidance to middle- and high-school students who are considering future employment opportunities.

12.6.3 Self-Directed Search

The Self-Directed Search (SDS; Holland, 1997) is a vocational interest inventory that can be used by vocational counselors or can be self-administered. Also based on Holland's RIASEC model, the SDS provides a description of the congruence between a person's personality type and various occupational codes. Two forms of the SDS are offered, one for those with typical reading skills (Form R) and the other for those with limited reading skills or lower educational levels (Form E). Similar to other vocational instruments, the SDS offers a tool designed to link occupations and a person's personality type. Interestingly, a leisure activity finder is also offered (e.g., for retired persons), which is designed to identify leisure activities that are most suitable for a given personality type.

12.7 Summary

When used in employment settings, tests are considered more than simply a collection of items with correct and incorrect responses. They refer more broadly to a collection of instruments that measure a variety of factors related to job performance, such as general ability, job-related attitudes, job knowledge, opinions, interests, and specific skills. With origins dating back to World War I, the use of psychological tests for predicting job performance and other work-related outcomes has continued to grow and has resulted in one of the fastest growing areas in psychology over the last few decades.

In this chapter, we discuss a number of personnel selection approaches. Cognitive ability tests have a long history of use in employment settings and are consistently one of the best predictors of job performance, even though there are some significant drawbacks and challenges to their use. Interviews not only are one of the most widely used selection strategies but are also among the most subjective; development of structured questions and standardized approaches will go a long way toward improving their effectiveness. Over the past 50 years, personality tests come in and out of vogue and remain a point of contention in I/O psychology. Use of integrity tests (sometimes considered a close cousin of personality tests) for making selection decisions continues, and these tests show some of the highest levels of incremental validity beyond what is predicted by cognitive ability tests. Assessment centers, work sample tests, and biodata forms are still used for making employment decisions, although to a somewhat lesser degree than the other selection approaches discussed in this chapter.

When using selection tools, we learned that a number of related areas are important to their success. Using methods that result in favorable reactions by applicants can have a positive outcome for a company. Conducting a thorough job analysis can increase the likelihood of assessing skills and abilities that are truly related to the job.

In addition, we review some common methods for evaluating and obtaining measures of job performance. This area is directly related to the evaluation of selection methods and necessitates the same care and consideration. We review relevant legal considerations for employment settings, highlighting some of the most important concepts, and note that failure to comply with federal, state, and local regulations will potentially nullify any positive contributions of psychological testing to employee selection and performance evaluation. We end the chapter with a discussion of career or vocational assessment and describe some of the most common assessment tools, including the Strong Interest Inventory, the Career Decision-Making System, and the Self-Directed Search.

References

Anderson, N., & Witvliet, C. (2008). Fairness reactions to personnel selection methods: An international comparison between the Netherlands, the United States, France, Spain, Portugal, and Singapore. *International Journal of Selection and Assessment, 16(1)*, 1–13.

Arthur, W., Day, E. A., McNelly, T. L., & Edens, P. S. (2003). A meta-analysis of the criterion-related validity of assessment center dimensions. *Personnel Psychology, 56*, 125–154.

Arvey, R. D., & Faley, R. H. (1992). *Fairness in selecting employees*. New York, NY: Addison-Wesley.

Asher, J. J., & Sciarrino, J. A. (1974). Realistic work sample tests: A review. *Personnel Psychology, 27*, 519–533.

Austin, J. T., & Villanova, P. (1992). The criterion problem: 1917-1992. *Journal of Applied Psychology, 77(6),* 836–874.

Barrick, M. R., & Mount, M. K. (1991). The big five personality dimensions and job performance: A meta-analysis. *Personnel Psychology, 44,* 1–26.

Becker, T. E., & Klimoski, R. J. (1989). A field study of the relationship between the organizational feedback environment and performance. *Personnel Psychology, 42,* 343–358.

Benjamin, L. T. (1997). Organized industrial psychology before division 14: The ACP and the AAAP (1930–1945). *Journal of Applied Psychology, 82(4),* 459–466.

Berry, C. M., Sackett, P. R., & Wiemann, S. (2007). A review of recent developments in integrity test research. *Personnel Psychology, 60,* 271–301.

Bommer, W. H., Johnson, J. L., Rich, G. A., Podsakoff, P. M., & Mackenzie, S. B. (1995). On the interchangeability of objective and subjective measures of employee performance: A meta-analysis. *Personnel Psychology, 48,* 587–605.

Borman, W. C. (1991). Job behavior, performance, and effectiveness. In M. D. Dunnette & L. M. Hough (Eds.), *Handbook of industrial and organizational psychology* (pp. 271–326). Palo Alto, CA: Consulting Psychologists Press.

Bureau of Labor Statistics. (2016). U.S. Department of Labor, Occupational Outlook Handbook, 2016-17 Edition, Psychologists, on the Internet at https://www.bls.gov/ooh/life-physical-and-social-science/psychologists.htm (visited September 10, 2017).

Butcher, J. N., Dahlstrom, W. G., Graham, J. R., Tellegen, A., & Kaemmer, B. (1989). *MMPI-2: Manual for administration and scoring.* Minneapolis, MN: University of Minnesota Press.

Byham, W. C. (1970). Assessment center for spotting future managers. *Harvard Business Review, 48,* 150–160.

Campion, M., Pursell, E., & Brown, B. (1988). Structured interviewing: Raising the psychometric properties of the employment interview. *Personnel Psychology, 41,* 25–42.

Cascio, W. F. (1991). *Applied psychology in personnel management.* Upper Saddle River, NJ: Prentice Hall.

Case, J. C., & Blackwell, T. L. (2008). Test review: Strong Interest Inventory, Revised Edition. *Rehabilitation Counseling Bulletin, 51(2),* 122–126.

Cederblom, D., & Lounsbury, J. W. (1980). An investigation of user acceptance of peer evaluations. *Personnel Psychology, 33,* 567–579.

Cooper, W. H. (1981). Ubiquitous halo. *Psychological Bulletin, 90(2),* 218–244.

DeNisi, A. S., & Mitchell, J. L. (1978). An analysis of peer ratings as predictors & criterion measures and a proposed new application. *Academy of Management Review, 3,* 369–374.

Donnay, D., Morris, M., Schaubhut, N., & Thompson, R. (2004). *Strong Interest Inventory* (Rev. ed.). Mountain View, CA: Consulting Psychologists Press.

Farmer, W. L. (2006). *A brief review of biodata history, research, and applications.* Retrieved from https://apps.dtic.mil/dtic/tr/fulltext/u2/a460872.pdf.

Gatewood, R. D., & Field, H. S. (1998). *Human resource selection.* Fort Worth, TX: Dryden Press.

Gaugler, B. B., Rosenthal, D. B., Thornton, G. C., & Bentson, C. (1987). Meta-analysis of assessment center validity. *Journal of Applied Psychology, 72(3),* 493–511.

Gottfredson, L. (1986). Societal consequences of the g factor in employment. *Journal of Vocational Behavior, 29,* 379–410.

Guion, R. (1998). Some virtues of dissatisfaction in the science and practice of personnel selection. *Human Resource Management Review, 8(4),* 351–365.

Guion, R. M. (1991). Personnel assessment, selection, and placement. In M. D. Dunnette & L. M. Hough (Eds.), *Handbook of industrial and organizational psychology* (pp. 327–397). Palo Alto, CA: Consulting Psychologists Press.

Guion, R. M., & Gottier, R. F. (1965). Validity of personality measures in personnel selection. *Personnel Psychology, 8,* 135–164.

Harrington, T. F., & O'Shea, A. J. (2000). *Career Decision-Making System—Revised.* Circle Pines, MN: American Guidance Service.

Harris, M. M., & Schaubroeck, J. (1988). A meta-analysis of self-supervisor, self-peer, and peer-supervisor ratings. *Personnel Psychology, 41,* 43–62.

Harvey, R. J. (1991). Job analysis. In M. D. Dunnette & L. M. Hough (Eds.), *Handbook of industrial and organizational psychology* (pp. 71–163). Palo Alto, CA: Consulting Psychologists Press.

Hausknecht, J. P., Day, D. V., & Thomas, S. C. (2004). Applicant reactions to selection procedures: An updated model and meta-analysis. *Personnel Psychology, 57,* 639–683.

Herk, N. A., & Thompson, R. C. (2012). *Strong Interest Inventory Manual Supplement.* Mountain View, CA: CPPI.

Hermelin, E., Lievens, F., & Robertson, I. T. (2007). The validity of assessment centres for the prediction of supervisory performance ratings: A meta-analysis. *International Journal of Selection and Assessment, 15(4),* 405–411.

Hoffman, C. C., Nathan, B. R., & Holden, L. M. (1991). A comparison of validation criteria: Objective versus subjective performance measures and self-versus supervisor ratings. *Personnel Psychology, 44,* 601–619.

Hogan, R., & Hogan, J. (1995). *Hogan Personality Inventory manual.* Tulsa, OK: Hogan Assessment Systems.

Holland, J. L. (1997). *Self-directed search* (4th ed.). Tampa Bay, FL: Psychological Assessment Resources.

Huffcutt, A. I., & Arthur, W., Jr. (1994). Hunter and Hunter (1984) revisited: Interview validity for entry-level jobs. *Journal of Applied Psychology, 79,* 184–190.

Hunter, J. E., & Hunter, R. F. (1984). Validity and utility of alternative predictors of job performance. *Psychological Bulletin, 96,* 72–98.

International Task Force on Assessment Center Guidelines. (2000). *Guidelines and ethical considerations for assessment center operations.* Retrieved from http://www.assessmentcenters.org/pdf/00guidelines.pdf.

Katzell, R. A., & Austin, J. T. (1992). From then to now: The development of industrialorganizational psychology in the United States. *Journal of Applied Psychology, 77(6),* 803–835.

Koppes, L. L. (1997). American female pioneers of industrial and organizational psychology during the early years. *Journal of Applied Psychology, 82(4),* 500–515.

Lance, C. (2008). Why assessment centers do not work the way they are supposed to. *Industrial and Organizational Psychology: Perspectives on Science and Practice, 1(1),* 84–97.

Landy, F. J. (1997). Early influences on the development of I/O psychology. *Journal of Applied Psychology, 82(4),* 467–477.

Love, K. G. (1981). Comparison of peer assessment methods: Reliability, validity, friendship bias, and user reaction. *Journal of Applied Psychology, 66,* 451–457.

Mael, F. A. (1991). A conceptual rationale for the domain and attributes of biodata items. *Personnel Psychology, 44,* 763–792.

McDaniel, M. A., Whetzel, D. L., Schmidt, F. L., & Maurer, S. D. (1994). The validity of employment interviews: A comprehensive review and meta-analysis. *Journal of Applied Psychology, 79(4),* 599–616.

McEvoy, G. M., & Buller, P. F. (1987). User acceptance of peer appraisals in an industrial setting. *Personnel Psychology, 40,* 785–797.

Meriac, J. P., Hoffman, B. J., Woehr, D. J., & Fleisher, M. S. (2008). Further evidence for the validity of assessment center dimensions: A meta-analysis of the incremental criterion-related validity of dimension ratings. *Journal of Applied Psychology, 93(5),* 1042–1052.

Morgeson, F. P., Campion, M. A., Dipboye, R. L., Hollenbeck, J. R., Murphy, K., & Schmitt, N. (2007). Reconsidering the use of personality tests in personnel selection contexts. *Personnel Psychology, 60,* 683–729.

Morgeson, F. P., Mumford, T. V., & Campion, M. A. (2005). Coming full circle using research and practice to address 27 questions about 360-degree feedback programs. *Consulting Psychology Journal: Practice and Research, 57(3),* 196–209.

Mount, M. K. (1984). Psychometric properties of subordinate ratings of managerial performance. *Personnel Psychology, 37,* 687–701.

Murphy, K. R., Cronin, B. E., & Tam, A. P. (2003). Controversy and consensus regarding the use of cognitive ability testing in organizations. *Journal of Applied Psychology, 88(4),* 660–671.

Nathan, B. R., & Alexander, R. A. (1988). A comparison of criteria for test validation: A meta-analytic investigation. *Personnel Psychology, 41*, 517–535.

Olson, R., Verley, J., Santos, L., & Salas, C. (2004). What we teach students about the Hawthorne studies: A review of content within a sample of introductory I-O and OB textbooks. *The Industrial-Organizational Psychologist, 41(3)*, 23–39.

Ones, D. S., Dilchert, S., Viswesvaran, C., & Judge, T. A. (2007). In support of personality assessment in organizational settings. *Personnel Psychology, 60*, 995–1027.

Ones, D. S., Viswesvaran, C., & Schmidt, F. L. (1993). Comprehensive meta-analysis of integrity test validities: Findings and implications for personnel selection and theories of job performance. *Journal of Applied Psychology, 78(4)*, 679–703.

Pulakos, E. D., & Schmitt, N. (1996). An evaluation of two strategies for reducing adverse impact and their effects on criterion-related validity. *Human Performance, 9*, 241–258.

Roth, P. L., Bobko, P., & McFarland, L. A. (2005). A meta-analysis of work sample test validity: Updating and integrating some classic literature. *Personnel Psychology, 58*, 1009–1037.

Roth, P. L., Bobko, P., McFarland, L. A., & Buster, M. (2008). Work sample tests in personnel selection: A meta-analysis of BlackWhite differences in overall and exercise scores. *Personnel Psychology, 61*, 637–662.

Rothstein, H. R., Schmidt, F. L., Erwin, F. W., Owens, W. A., & Sparks, C. P. (1990). Biographical data in employment selection: Can validities be made generalizable? *Journal of Applied Psychology, 75(2)*, 175–184.

Sackett, P. R., Burris, L. R., & Callahan, C. (1989). Integrity testing for personnel selection: An update. *Personnel Psychology, 42*, 491–529.

Sackett, P. R., & Ellingson, J. E. (1997). The effects of forming multi-predictor composites on group differences and adverse impact. *Personnel Psychology, 50*, 707–722.

Sackett, P. R., Schmitt, N., Ellingson, J. E., & Kabin, M. B. (2001). High stakes testing in employment, credentialing, and higher education: Prospects in a post-affirmative action world. *American Psychologist, 56*, 302–318.

Sackett, P. R., & Wanek, J. E. (1996). New developments in the use of measures of honesty, integrity, conscientiousness, dependability, trustworthiness, and reliability for personnel selection. *Personnel Psychology, 49*, 787–829.

Sackett, R. R., & Decker, P. J. (1979). Detection of deception in the employment context: A review and critique. *Personnel Psychology, 32*, 487–506.

Schmidt, F., & Hunter, J. (2004). General mental ability in the world of work: Occupational attainment and job performance. *Journal of Personality and Social Psychology, 86(1)*, 162–173.

Schmidt, F. L., & Hunter, J. (1998). The validity and utility of selection methods in personnel psychology: Practical and theoretical implications of 85 years of research findings. *Psychological Bulletin, 124(2)*, 262–274.

Schmidt, F. L., & Zimmerman, R. D. (2004). A counterintuitive hypothesis about employment interview validity and some supporting evidence. *Journal of Applied Psychology, 89(3)*, 553–561.

Smith, P. C., & Kendall, L. M. (1963). Retranslation of expectations: An approach to the construction of unambiguous anchors for rating scales. *Journal of Applied Psychology, 47*, 149–155.

Society for Industrial-Organizational Psychology. (2018). *Principles for the validation and use of personnel selection procedures* (5th ed.). Washington, DC: American Psychological Association.

Strong, E. K., Jr. (1926). An interest test for personnel managers. *Journal of Personnel Research, 5*, 194–203.

Strong, E. K., Jr. (1927a). *Vocational interest blank*. Palo Alto, CA: Stanford University Press.

Strong, E. K., Jr. (1927b). A vocational interest test. *Educational Record, 8*, 107–121.

Tett, R. P., & Christiansen, N. D. (2007). Personality tests at the crossroads: A response to Morgeson, Campion, Dipboye, Hollenbeck, Murphy, and Schmitt. *Personnel Psychology, 60*, 967–993.

Tett, R. P., Jackson, D. N., & Rothstein, M. (1991). Personality measures as predictors of job performance: A meta-analytic review. *Personnel Psychology, 44*, 703–742.

Thorndike, E. L. (1920). A constant error in psychological ratings. *Journal of Applied Psychology, 4*(1), 25–29.

Wagner, R. K. (1997). Intelligence, training, and employment. *American Psychologist, 52*(10), 1059–1069.

Wee, S., Newman, D. A., & Joseph, D. L. (2014). More than g: Selection quality and adverse impact implications of considering second-stratum cognitive abilities. *Journal of Applied Psychology, 99*(4), 547–563.

Wilk, S., & Cappelli, P. (2003). Determinants and outcomes of employee selection procedures. *Personnel Psychology, 56*(1), 103–125.

Recommended Reading

Berry, C. M., Sackett, P. R., & Wiemann, S. (2007). A review of recent developments in integrity test research. *Personnel Psychology, 60*, 271–301.

Campion, M., Pursell, E., & Brown, B. (1988). Structured interviewing: Raising the psychometric properties of the employment interview. *Personnel Psychology, 41*, 25–42.

Hunter, J. E., & Hunter, R. F. (1984). Validity and utility of alternative predictors of job performance. *Psychological Bulletin, 96*, 72–98.

Schmidt, F. L., & Hunter, J. (1998). The validity and utility of selection methods in personnel psychology: Practical and theoretical implications of 85 years of research findings. *Psychological Bulletin, 124*(2), 262–274.

Society for Industrial-Organizational Psychology. (2018). *Principles for the validation and use of personnel selection procedures* (5th ed.). Washington, DC: American Psychological Association.

Tett, R. P., Jackson, D. N., & Rothstein, M. (1991). Personality measures as predictors of job performance: A meta-analytic review. *Personnel Psychology, 44*, 703–742.

Uniform Guidelines on Employee Selection Procedures, Federal Register, Friday, August 25, 1978, 38290–38315..

Neuropsychological Testing

13

The brain is in charge of all behavior, and assessment of its functional integrity is important for understanding behavior, cognition, and emotion.

Abstract

Neuropsychological assessment utilizes standardized psychological tests designed to study brain-behavior relationships. These standardized tests are referred to as neuropsychological tests because they assess specific domains of cognitive functioning such as memory, attention, and problem-solving. Neuropsychological tests are used in research and clinical settings. Clinical neuropsychologists use these tests to inform patient care. Test results are often used to diagnose the cause of brain dysfunction, quantify its impact on cognitive abilities, prescribe or monitor the effects of treatment, or predict long-term functional outcomes. This chapter describes the components of neuropsychological evaluation, major assessment approaches and their associated tests, assessment of memory function, and major processes guiding the neuropsychological evaluation. Test interpretation based on two primary approaches (deficit and normative) is also discussed, including important procedures for establishing level of cognitive abilities prior to the onset of cognitive dysfunction.

Supplementary Information The online version of this chapter (https://doi.org/10.1007/978-3-030-59455-8_13) contains supplementary material, which is available to authorized users.

Learning Objectives

After reading and studying this chapter, students should be able to:

1. Explain the basic role of clinical neuropsychological assessment.
2. Identify and describe the two most commonly employed fixed battery approaches to neuropsychological assessment.
3. Describe the Boston Process Approach to neuropsychological assessment.
4. Compare and contrast the relative strengths and weaknesses of the fixed battery and flexible battery approaches.
5. Explain the unique importance of memory assessment.
6. Describe the development and the basic structure of the Test of Memory and Learning.
7. Explain the eight principal components of a neuropsychological evaluation.
8. Describe some of the common brain injuries often prompting a neuropsychological evaluation.
9. Outline the major procedures that are common to most neuropsychological evaluations.
10. Describe the primary elements that influence the selection of tests in a neuropsychological exam.
11. Explain the principal concepts and approaches to deficit measurement.
12. Define premorbid ability and its importance in the measurement of change.
13. Describe the Reliable Change Index and its importance in the measurement of change.
14. Explain the concepts that undergird *effort measurement* and why this is important for neuropsychologists to assess.

Neuropsychology is the study of brain-behavior relationships. *Clinical neuropsychology* is the application of this knowledge to patient care. *Neuropsychological testing* is the application of a set of standardized procedures designed to assess and quantify brain function as expressed in overt behavior to draw inferences about

> Clinical neuropsychology is the application of the knowledge gleaned from the study of brain-behavior relationships to patient care.

covert processes of the brain. Neuropsychological testing may include, for example, assessing the ability of the patient to solve novel problems; to learn new tasks; to execute well-defined simple and complex motor tasks; to deduce relationships using formal logic; to engage in recall, recognition, and related memory tasks; to recognize and/or interpret speech sounds, nonspeech sounds, and visual and tactile stimuli; to pay attention; and to develop and execute plans for behavior. Neuropsychological testing requires maximum effort from the patient in order to obtain accurate scores used to make valid inferences regarding brain function—more so than any other, neuropsychological tests are truly maximum performance tests.

Neuropsychological testing remains the premier method of assessing brain-behavior relationships even as neuroimaging methods advance. While SPECT, PET, rsfMRI, QEEG, MEG, and other imaging techniques do tell us if areas of the brain are functioning at normal levels (typically from a metabolic viewpoint), they cannot tell us if abnormal brain function causes a patient to be unable to read, add numbers, or learn a new job skill, or predict how well the patient may perform at any given cognitive task—they only tell us whether brain structures and circuits are functioning properly. Often after viewing a functional neuroimage, we can be reasonably certain that particular skills will be impaired based on brain regions that are abnormal, but the specific nature of the impairment and its severity cannot be established even with the most advanced neuroimaging technologies. At times, behavior functions will even be normal in the face of abnormal neuroimaging studies, and vice versa, with actual neuropsychological testing and quantification of the results remaining the gold standard to determine functioning.

Neuropsychological assessment examines the relationship between brain functioning and behavior through tests that tap specific domains of functioning. The use of intelligence tests like those described in Chap. 9 is a necessary component of comprehensive neuropsychological examination, but neuropsychological assessments emphasize much more specific cognitive domains such as attention, memory, forgetting, sensory functions, constructional praxis, and motor skills (Reitan & Wolfson, 1985; Reynolds & Mayfield, 2005). Clinical neuropsychologists examine the functioning of the brain based on behavioral expression and are able to determine whether a brain dysfunction exists or whether atypical patterns of functional neocortical development are present.

> Neuropsychological tests tend to be more highly specific in what they measure relative to general intelligence measures.

Although closely related disciplines, there are a number of important differences between neuropsychology and neurology. A neurologist examines the anatomical structure of the brain as well as the electrochemical systems of the *central nervous system* (CNS) to diagnose and prescribe treatment for CNS disorders. Working in conjunction with neurologists, neuropsychologists are able to determine the behavioral sequelae of CNS dysfunction regardless of etiology. Neurologists use advanced neuroimaging techniques such as those noted above. Neuropsychologists focus on behavior and cognition in order to offer remediation strategies to schools, family members, vocational specialists, and counselors. Clinical neuropsychologists deal with a variety of issues as family members seek to understand the cognitive and psychological needs of children and adults who are coping with neurological deficits. Family members frequently want to know what they can do to provide the optimal environment to help their loved one reach the maximum level of functioning and enjoy life to the fullest extent possible. They seek to understand the specific deficits and strengths, as well as possible compensatory strategies that may help improve functioning.

Although this chapter discusses examples of specific neuropsychological tests and batteries of tests, neuropsychology as practiced correctly is not a set of techniques. Rather, it is a way of thinking about behavior, often expressed as test scores. In essence, it is a paradigm for understanding behavior. Since the brain determines and controls our behavior, ultimately, all tests might be considered neuropsychological tests. However, most tests carrying this classification assess very specific cognitive functions and are concerned with understanding how they can be tied to very specific brain systems.

13.1 Components of a Neuropsychological Evaluation

When designing a thorough neuropsychological assessment, choosing a predesigned battery is often insufficient. Depending on the reason for the neuropsychological evaluation (i.e., the referral question), the most common neuropsychological batteries and approaches will often be supplemented in specific ways. In addition, choice of assessment procedures will be influenced by a person's medical, family, and developmental history, as well as specific behavioral and vocational concerns. The following eight general guidelines are useful for designing the neuropsychological assessment. These guidelines are derived from a variety of sources including our own practices, the general teachings of Lawrence C. Hartlage, and other specific sources—in particular, Rourke, Bakker, Fisk, and Strang (1983) and Reynolds and Mayfield (2005).

1. *All (or at least a significant majority) of a patient's relevant cognitive skills or higher-order information-processing skills should be assessed.* This will often involve an assessment of general intellectual level or *"g"* via an IQ test that includes both the verbal and nonverbal domains. Tests such as the Wechsler Intelligence Scales or the Reynolds Intellectual Assessment Scales are used for this purpose. Determining the efficiency of mental processing as assessed by strong measures of *g* is essential for providing a baseline for interpreting all other aspects of the assessment process. Assessment of basic academic skills (including reading, writing, spelling, and math) will be necessary, and so the assessment will often include components of individually administered achievement tests, some of which we describe in Chap. 8. Problems with memory, attention/concentration, and new learning are the most common of all complaints following CNS compromise resulting from chronic neurodevelopmental disorders (e.g., learning disability and attention-deficit/hyperactivity disorder [ADHD]) and various other forms of brain injury. Assessment of memory is accomplished with tests such as the *Test of Memory and Learning-2* (TOMAL-2; Reynolds & Voress, 2007), some of which also have the advantage of including performance-based measures of attention and concentration.

2. *Testing should sample the relative efficiency of the **right and left hemispheres of the brain***. One powerful tool that neuropsychologists use to detect brain dysfunction involves separate testing of the right and left sides of the body, noting unusual discrepancies or ***asymmetries*** of performance, which may indicate dysfunction in one brain hemisphere or the other. For example, we expect that an individual who is right handed will be able to perform speeded tasks (e.g., writing one's name) more quickly with the right hand than the left hand. When the right hand is slower than expected, i.e., there is no difference between the hands or the left hand is faster than the right, this would provide evidence for dysfunction in the left hemisphere of the brain. (Remember from your physiological psychology course that the right side of the body is controlled by the left hemisphere of the brain.) Because different brain systems are involved in each hemisphere, asymmetries, when present, have implications for treatment planning. Asymmetries are typically most pronounced when brain dysfunction is localized, that is, its affects are limited to a discrete brain region. However, even when more diffuse or generalized brain dysfunction is present, there may still be greater impact on one hemisphere relative to the other. For example, the genetic disorder ***Double Y Syndrome*** (in which male offspring has an XYY instead of XY chromosomal feature) often produces greater relative suppression in left hemisphere functioning and related language skill deficits compared to right hemisphere functioning and associated spatial abilities and related skills. Even in cases of ***anoxia*** where there is diffuse brain injury, it is possible to find greater impairment in one brain hemisphere than in the other. Tests of sensory-perceptual abilities and motor speed in the ***Halstead-Reitan Neuropsychological Test Battery*** (HRNB) are useful for identifying asymmetries, as are measures of verbal and nonverbal memory processes, among others.

> Neuropsychological testing should sample the relative efficiency of the right and left hemispheres of the brain.

3. *Testing should sample both anterior and posterior regions of cortical function.* The anterior portion of the brain is generative, expressive, and regulatory, whereas the posterior region is principally receptive. The ***anterior region*** of the brain includes the left and right frontal lobes, while the ***posterior region*** includes temporal, parietal, and occipital lobes. As with hemisphere differences, anterior and posterior brain regions involve different brain systems, and so the region affected will have a great impact on treatment choices. Many common tests, such as tests of receptive (posterior) and expressive (anterior) vocabulary, may be applied here, along with a systematic and thorough sensory-perceptual examination and certain specific tests of motor function. Combining tests examining anterior and posterior brain regions with those that examine integrity of the right and left hemispheres (described in point 2) allows for evaluation of the integrity of the four major quadrants of the neocortex: right anterior, right posterior, left anterior, and left posterior.

4. *Testing should determine the presence of specific deficits.* Any specific functional problem that a patient is experiencing must be determined and assessed. Neuropsychological tests tend to be less *g*-loaded as a group and have greater specificity of measurement than many common psychological tests and so are well-suited for identifying specific deficits. Noting areas of specific deficits is important in both diagnosis and treatment planning for many if not all neurological disorders. Neurodevelopmental disorders, traumatic brain injury (TBI), stroke, and even some toxins can produce very specific changes in neocortical function. As they age, people with neurodevelopmental and genetic disorders are also more vulnerable to CNS insults, which may have more profound effects because of their already compromised CNS and produce additional specific deficits. Similarly, certain patients who receive organ transplants will display specific patterns of deficits. Specific cognitive deficits that occur in these and other disorders are best investigated using neuropsychological assessment.

5. *Testing should determine the acuteness versus the chronicity of any problems or weaknesses found.* Determining the "age" of the neurological problem is important for diagnosis and treatment planning. When a thorough history is combined with neuropsychological test results, it is possible, with reasonable accuracy, to distinguish chronic neurodevelopmental disorders such as dyslexia or ADHD from new, acute problems resulting from trauma, stroke, neoplasm, or other disease. Particular care must be taken in developing a thorough, documented history when such a determination is made. Acuteness or chronicity of the brain dysfunction will affect the design of intervention strategies and often guide whether rehabilitation and habilitation approaches are needed. **Rehabilitation** helps an individual regain lost function or skills, as happens when an individual experiences a stroke and loses the ability to speak. **Habilitation** services address skills or functions that have not developed, as in the case of a child with a reading disorder who has never learned to read. It is also important to recognize that a person with a chronic neurological problem may develop new acute problems due to a number of factors (e.g., aging, onset of new disease), and distinguishing new from old symptoms is important when treatment recommendations are made.

6. *Testing should locate intact complex functional systems.* The brain functions as a series of interdependent, systemic networks often referred to as "complex functional systems." As neuroscience advances, it seems that the connectivity of all regions of

> Neuropsychological tests should locate intact complex functional systems.

the brain with one another becomes increasingly important to understand if we are to know just how the brain works. Multiple systems are affected by CNS problems, but some systems are almost always spared except in the most extreme cases. It is imperative in the assessment process to identify cognitive and functional strengths associated with these intact systems, which may be used to overcome functional deficits that result from the CNS dysfunction. Treatment following CNS compromise may involve habilitation or rehabilitation, with the understanding that some systems will remain permanently impaired but that intact systems may be used in the treatment process to help reestablish lost skills or establish new compensatory mechanisms. Identification of intact systems also suggests the potential for a positive outcome to patients and their families, which stands in contrast to fatalistic perspectives that sometimes occur following brain damage and create low expectations for recovery and future functioning.

7. *Testing should assess affect, personality, and behavior.* CNS compromise will result in deviations from normal affect and personality, and so personality is often assessed in the neuropsychological evaluation. Some personality changes will be transient, i.e., present only in the acute stage of brain injury, while others will continue into the chronic phases of the illness. Mechanisms underlying these changes may be direct or indirect. Direct effects result from CNS compromise at the cellular and systemic levels, as is the case where neurological damage to brain regions that regulate emotion causes the onset of depression or mania. Indirect effects that contribute to abnormal affect and personality include negative reactions to loss or changes in function by the patient, inappropriate responses from others to the patients' loss of function or disability, stressors associated with loss of employment, as well as a number of other factors. In these instances, environmental influences that occur in reaction to the CNS compromise further compound emotional distress and functional impairment. A thorough history is necessary, which includes information about when the problem behaviors started, since this may help determine whether they are the result of direct versus indirect effects of CNS dysfunction or are premorbid in nature, existing prior to the onset of CNS dysfunction. These abnormalities will also require intervention, and interventions may differ markedly if the affect, personality, and associated functional changes are caused by direct versus indirect effects of CNS damage, or if they are premorbid in nature.

8. *Test results should be presented in ways that are useful in a school or work environment, to acute care or intensive rehabilitation facilities, or to physicians (i.e., they should be responsive to the referral question and consider context of the patient's life).* Presentation of findings and recommendations from neuropsychological assessments should answer the referral question and be relevant to the individual and so often vary from setting-to-setting and from patient-to-patient. The report provided to a physician, for example, who requested neuropsychological testing to help establish a diagnosis of dementia, would be quite different from the report provided to a vocational rehabilitation specialist to help develop a training program for workforce reentry. We cannot consider here all of the possible uses for neuropsychological testing results, but consider the case where neuropsychological assessment is requested to help answer questions about readiness for entry into higher education or the work force. This situation is common since the majority of individuals with developmental disabilities, brain injury, or neurodevelopmental and genetic disorders will continue into higher education and join the adult workforce. They are assisted in such pursuits by various Federal laws such as the Individuals with Disabilities Education Act (IDEA), Americans with Disabilities Act (ADA), and Section 504 of the Vocational Rehabilitation Amendment of 1973. It is important to establish the

learning and vocational skills of these patients, and so they may be directed toward proper education, training, and employment, and to determine any reasonable accommodations that would be required to make them successful. Neuropsychological test results are often used by vocational rehabilitation specialists to determine appropriate guidance. For those individuals with more serious disorders and for whom postsecondary education and placement in a competitive work environment are not reasonable expectations, neuropsychological examinations are required to document the presence and extent of the disability that has resulted from CNS disorders. Not all CNS disorders result in disability, and, especially given the concepts of variable expressivity and modern treatments, disability determination must be made one case at a time. This determination is crucial for establishing eligibility for life-changing programs such as supplemental security income (SSI) and other government funded programs (e.g., Medicaid and Medicare) for workers who are permanently disabled.

13.2 Neuropsychological Assessment Approaches and Instruments

While the major theoretical premise of any neuropsychological assessment is the proposition that behavior has an organic basis (i.e., the brain controls behavior), and thus performance on behavioral measures, in this case, neuropsychological tests, can be used to assess brain functioning (Cullum, 1998) and the two major conceptual approaches to neuropsychological assessment are quite different from each other. In the first approach, a standard battery of tasks designed to identify brain impairment is used (the *fixed battery approach*). In the strictest sense, this approach administers the same tests to everyone assessed, regardless of the presenting concern, referral question, or type of CNS disorder. The Halstead-Reitan Neuropsychological Test Battery for Adults (Reitan & Wolfson, 1985) remains the most commonly used fixed battery, followed by the Luria Nebraska Neuropsychological Battery (Golden, Purisch, & Hammeke, 1991). The second approach to neuropsychological assessment favors the use of a *flexible battery approach* to a combination of traditional psychological, educational, and neuropsychological tests. Factors including history, functional level, CNS disorder, and presenting problem guide the selection of tests, and so, in the strictest sense, each assessment is specifically tailored to address the unique concerns and needs of each patient. This historical distinction has caused much debate in the field of clinical neuropsychology over the years, because there are strong advocates for each approach and each approach has significant limitations. In practice, most neuropsychologists (even strong advocates on different sides of the

> The major theoretical premise of any neuropsychological battery is the proposition that behavior has an organic basis, and thus, performance on behavioral measures can be used to assess brain functioning, i.e., every behavior has an anatomy.

issue) favor what might be best described as a combination of the two approaches, where a common set of neuropsychological tests is given to all patients to ensure that the major cognitive domains are assessed, with additional tests selected to address issues unique to each patient, such as the referral question, CNS disorder, history, etc. In the following sections, we provide some additional information about these approaches and the tests used to accomplish them.

13.2.1 The Halstead-Reitan Neuropsychological Test Battery (HRNB)

The HRNB was designed to assess the key behavioral correlation of brain function (Reitan & Wolfson, 1985). The HRNB consists of measures in six categories: (1) input, (2) attention, concentration, and memory, (3) verbal abilities, (4) spatial, sequential, and manipulatory abilities, (5) abstraction, reasoning, logical analysis, and concept formation, and (6) output (Reitan & Wolfson, 1993). Raw scores from four main components of the battery (level of test performance, patterns of test performance, right-left differences/asymmetries, and ***pathognomonic signs***) are weighted as

> As of this writing, there is no set of neuropsychological assessment devices with as much clinical history and empirical support as the Halstead-Reitan Neuropsychological Test Battery.

"perfectly normal" (score = 0), "normal" (score = 1), "mildly impaired" (score = 2), or "significantly impaired" (score = 3) based on cutoff scores associated with absolute levels of performance that differentiate normal from brain-damaged adults. These scores are then used to calculate the General Neuropsychological Deficit Scale, which reflects the person's overall level of neuropsychological functioning. Scores for various brain systems and right versus left hemisphere differences can also be derived. Evidence-based interpretations based on patterns of performance are also undertaken to gain more insight into potential causes of the dysfunction, brain regions that are most affected, and possible implications for daily function and treatment. Table 13.1 lists the components of the HRNB most appropriate for adults. Versions for children and adolescents are available as well.

The HRNB has a rich clinical history and has substantial empirical support for its use in neuropsychological settings. Among clinicians who prefer the strong scientific base of support for a fixed battery approach, the HRNB is the most common choice. However, the HRNB, done correctly, is quite lengthy and can require 8–10 h for administration and scoring, too much for some patients and an examination time infrequently supported by third party payers. Even so, many of its core tests are among those most commonly used by present day neuropsychologists. The HRNB, although derived initially from Halstead's (1947) biological theory of intelligence, evolved from a more purely actuarial or empirical perspective. That is, since the same tests were administered in the same standardized manner to thousands of individuals with CNS dysfunction, it was possible to identify patterns of performance

Table 13.1 Halstead-Reitan Neuropsychological Test Battery

Test	Function or skills assessed	Hypothesized localization
Lateral Dominance Test	• Determine dominance	• None
Aphasia Screening Test	• Language • Construction	• Language items related to left hemisphere • Constructional items related to right hemisphere
Finger Tapping Test	• Motor	• Frontal lobe
Grip Strength	• Motor	• Frontal lobe
Finger Localization Test	• Sensory-perceptual	• Unilateral errors implicate contralateral parietal lobe • Can also occur with bilateral errors
Rhythm Test	• Alertness • Concentration	• Global
Speech Sounds Perception Test	• Alertness • Concentration	• Global • Anterior left hemisphere
Category Test	• Reasoning	• Global
Trail Making Test Parts A & B	• Visual-spatial reasoning	• Global
Tactual Performance Test		
Total time score	• Motor	• Frontal lobe
Memory score	• Immediate memory	• Global
Localization score	• Immediate memory	• Global
Category Test	• Reasoning	• Global
Sensory-Perceptual Examination		
Tactile Perception Test	• Sensory-perceptual	• Contralateral parietal lobe
Auditory Perception Test	• Sensory-perceptual	• Temporal lobe
Visual Perception Test	• Sensory-perceptual	• Visual pathway • Visual fields
Finger-tip Number Writing	• Sensory-perceptual	• Peripheral nervous system • Parietal lobe
Tactile Form Recognition	• Sensory-perceptual	• Parietal lobe

across the battery, which were highly accurate in identifying certain CNS disorders and the location of CNS dysfunction. In fact, prior to the advent of modern neuro-imaging techniques such as the CT scan, studies demonstrated the HRNB was superior to other available medical procedures used to localize and diagnose brain dysfunction. The capability of the HRNB and other early tests to localize brain injury had two more general and significant influences: (1) it provided a strong empirical basis for the clinical application of neuropsychological tests as measures of brain-behavior relationships and (2) it made a major contribution in establishing clinical neuropsychology as an evidence-based discipline. Even so, the HRNB is criticized for short changing such important functions as memory, assessing only a few aspects of memory and doing so briefly. Some also point out that since the battery has existed in one form or another for more than 60 years, it has not allowed updating testing procedures to reflect substantial advances in our understanding of the CNS. During this time, the theoretical models of Alexander Luria were gaining influence (e.g., Luria, 1966) in Western neuropsychology, all of these factors eventually leading to the development of a second, popular fixed battery based upon Luria's model of the working brain.

13.2.2 The Luria-Nebraska Neuropsychological Battery (LNNB) for Adults

The LNNB was developed in the late 1970s and 1980, by Charles Golden and colleagues (see Golden et al., 1991) as a means of standardizing and quantifying the clinical assessment procedures of the famed Russian neuropsychologist, Alexander Luria. The LNNB was designed not only to diagnose cognitive deficits that are general in their manifestation but also to provide information on the lateralization and localization of any focal CNS deficiencies. Golden et al. (1991) argue that the LNNB detects very specific problems that might go unnoticed in less detailed examinations or interpretations of global scores. The LNNB is administered from the age of 12. There are 12 clinical scales on the LNNB. As Golden (1997; Golden et al., 1991) describes, the LNNB lends itself to three levels of interpretation: scale, item, and qualitative. Each of the LNNB scales yields a T score, and the resulting profile has been the subject of significant empirical work. However, the items within these scales vary in modality and other demand characteristics (i.e., are quite heterogeneous compared, for example, to items within subtests of the HRNB), and an analysis of item scores is also used. Finally, Luria was a renowned clinician and approached patients individually. Golden et al. (1991) thus designed the LNNB to allow qualitative analysis as a supplement to the typical Western psychological approach of quantitative analysis of performance on the various scales.

The LNNB has some scales and items where process is the dominant feature, but others where content and learned behavior predominate. Careful review of LNNB performance at all three levels (scale, item, and qualitative) is not just possible but necessary. In a qualitative analysis, the examiner is more concerned with wrong answers than with correct ones and analyzes the nature of the errors committed by the examinee. For example, was the inability to write to dictation caused by a visual--motor problem, a visual-perceptive deficit, a failure of comprehension, or a planning, attention, or execution problem? Only through careful observation and a review of successful tasks can these questions be answered. Examiners must have extensive experience with normal individuals, however, to avoid overinterpretation of such item-level performance and behavioral observations on the LNNB or any other scale for that matter.

13.2.3 The Boston Process Approach

Another, newer effort at evaluating processes using neuropsychological assessment is known as the Boston Process Approach (BPA) and is described in detail in Kaplan (1988, 1990). In contrast to the use of standard batteries, the BPA takes a flexible battery approach to select

> The strength of the Boston Process Approach lies in its flexibility, which enables a neuropsychologist to tailor the assessment to the referral problem.

developmental, psychological, and neuropsychological tests, which permits the clinician to select tasks appropriate for the specific referral question, functioning levels, and response limitations of the client. Client variables such as "age, gender, handedness, familial handedness, educational and occupational background, premorbid talents, patient's and family's medical, neurological, and psychiatric history, drug or alcohol abuse, use of medications (past and present), etiology of the CNS dysfunction, and laterality and focus of the lesion" (Kaplan, 1990, p. 72) all provide valuable information in developing the assessment. Furthermore, the BPA provides an analysis of the person's neuropsychological assets, rather than focusing on a diagnosis or a specific localization of brain impairment, for which the standardized batteries have been noted to be especially useful. The flexible battery approach purportedly translates more directly into educational and vocational interventions, and one major goal of conducting a neuropsychological assessment is to aid in the planning of such interventions. This model also tries to integrate quantitative and qualitative approaches to interpretation and analysis of performance on various cognitive tasks. The BPA alters the format of items on traditional tests such as the various Wechsler scales, and BPA versions of the Wechsler Intelligence Scale for Children-IV and the Wechsler Adult Intelligence Scale-IV are available. Additionally, supplementary tests have been devised specifically for the BPA over many years, including the Boston Naming Test, the Boston Diagnostic Aphasia Examination, and the California Verbal Learning Test, along with others. As with other methods of assessment, examiners are advised to use BPA assessments in conjunction with history and interview data and observations of the patient. However, clinicians are also free to pick and choose among a myriad of available neuropsychological measures. Table 13.2 lists a number of neuropsychological instruments that are commonly employed in a flexible battery approach.

The strength of the BPA lies in its flexibility, which enables a neuropsychologist to tailor the assessment to the referral problem. There is quite a bit of research on individual aspects of the BPA (e.g., see White & Rose, 1997), but research on the BPA as a whole is lacking—and this is a major weakness of the approach. The modifications made to well-designed, carefully standardized tests such as the Wechsler scales also have unpredictable and at times counterintuitive outcomes in patient examination (e.g., Slick et al., 1996; Lee, Reynolds, & Willson, 2003). Slick et al. (1996) found that changes made to the BPA version of the Wechsler Adult Intelligence Scale-Revised caused a substantial number of individuals to earn lower scores on the modified items than on the corresponding standardized versions of the items, even though the intent of the modification was in part to make the items

Table 13.2 Neuropsychological instruments commonly employed in a flexible battery

Premorbid ability
- National Adult Reading Test, Second Edition (NART; Nelson & Willison 1991)
- Wechsler Test of Adult Reading (WTAR; Wechsler, 2001)

General ability
- Reynolds Intellectual Assessment Scales, Second Edition (RIAS-2; Reynolds & Kamphaus 2015)
- Stanford-Binet Intelligence Scales-Fifth Edition (SB5; Roid 2003)
- Wechsler Adult Intelligence Scale-Fourth Edition (WAIS-IV; Wechsler 2008)

Achievement
- Wide Range Achievement Test-5 (WRAT-5; Wilkinson & Robertson 2017)
- Woodcock-Johnson IV Test of Achievement (WJ IV ACH; Schrank, Mather, & McGrew, 2014)

Executive functions
- Comprehensive Trail Making Test-2 (Reynolds 2019)
- Stroop Test (Golden 1978)
- Tower of London (Culbertson & Zillmer 2001)

Attention
- Conner's Continuous Performance Test-III (CPT-III; Conners 2014)
- Paced Auditory Serial Addition Test (PASAT; Gronwall 1977)
- Trail Making Test (Reitan & Wolfson 1985)

Memory
- California Verbal Learning Test-II (CVLT-II; Delis, Kramer, Kaplan, & Ober 2000)
- Rey Complex Figure Test (ROCF; Meyers & Meyers 1995)
- Test of Memory and Learning Second Edition (TOMAL-2; Reynolds & Voress 2007)
- Wide Range Assessment of Memory and Learning Second Edition (WRAML-2: Sheslow & Adams 2003)

Language tests
- Boston Diagnostic Aphasia Examination Third Edition (BDAE-3; Goodglass, Kaplan, & Barresi 2001)
- Boston Naming Test Second Edition (BNT-2; Kaplan, Goodglass, & Weintraub, 2001)
- Vocabulary subtest (WAIS-IV; Wechsler 2008)

Construction
- Clock Drawing Test (Goodglass & Kaplan 1983)
- Block Design subtest (WAIS-IV; Wechsler 2008)
- Free Drawing (Bicycle; Piaget 1930)

Concept formation and reasoning
- Category Test (Halstead 1947)
- Matrix Reasoning subtest (WAIS-IV; Wechsler 2008)
- Raven's Progressive Matrices (RPM; Raven, Raven, & Court 1998)
- Similarities subtest (WAIS-IV; Wechsler 2008)

Motor function
- Finger Tapping Test (FTT; Reitan 1969)
- Grip Strength (Reitan & Wolfson 1985)
- Grooved Pegboard (Klove 1963)

easier. This could easily draw a clinician into overinterpretation and overdiagnosis of pathology. Slick et al. (1996) correctly conclude that whenever changes are made to standardized instruments, comprehensive norms are required under the new testing conditions. They also conclude that clinical interpretation of such modified procedures prior to the development and purveyance of the norms is questionable from an ethical standpoint.

The lack of good normative or reference data has been a long-term problem for neuropsychological assessment (e.g., see Reynolds, 2008). This causes a variety of problems related to test interpretation, not the least of which is understanding the relationship of status variables such as gender, ethnicity, and socioeconomic status to test performance. The BPA, because of its principal strengths, also makes inordinate cognitive demands on the examiner. Another major concern about the process approach is the difficulty in establishing validity for the innumerable versions of batteries used, as interpretations may not be uniform or reliable. This issue has been addressed inadequately thus far. Base rates for the number of scores from a BPA approach that fall in the "impaired" range for normal and clinical samples are also absent in the literature, causing much consternation in determining whether low scores are a common or unusual occurrence. In contrast, base rates for such levels of performance on the HRNB are well established.

The issue of the reliability and validity of conclusions drawn from fixed versus flexible battery approaches has been a matter of controversy regarding the admittance of testimony in a variety of court cases. Thus far, fixed battery data (e.g., HRNB) have been more readily accepted in court, but data and conclusions from flexible batteries are also accepted more often than not, but not in all cases. The legal issues surrounding the use of the flexible approach in forensic settings are thus as yet unresolved, and so neuropsychologists should carefully consider its use and, in some situations, avoid it altogether (e.g., modifications to standardized items and administration procedures to allow qualitative interpretations should never be made when IQ tests are used to estimate intelligence in a capital murder case).

13.3 Assessment of Memory Functions

Memory complaints seem to be ubiquitous in nearly all cognitive disorders. Nearly every CNS disorder associated with disturbances of higher cognitive functions has memory disturbance in some form noted as a common complaint. In cases of traumatic brain injury (TBI), memory disturbances are the most common of all patient complaints. Three age groups account for a majority of cases of TBI—birth to 5, 15–24, and over 75, with males outnumbering females by about 2–1. Motor vehicle accidents are the most common cause of TBI; falls and violence are second and third, respectively (Rutland-Brown, Langlois, Thomas, & Xi, 2006). TBI produces the least predictable forms of memory loss with the exception of increased forgetting curves.

> Memory complaints seem to be ubiquitous in nearly all neurocognitive disorders.

Persons with learning disabilities of various forms, but especially reading-related learning disabilities, commonly are found to have memory problems, especially with sequential recall. Memory disturbances accompanied by other cognitive deficits are the hallmark of dementias although the cause of memory loss varies from one dementia to another. For example, a key feature of memory loss in dementia caused by Alzheimer's Disease (which is the most common cause of dementia) is the failure to encode new information, whereas memory loss in dementia caused by vascular disease is more often associated with breakdown in retrieval processes. Because each of the diseases that cause dementia affects the brain in different ways, one would anticipate differences in memory and other cognitive deficits. Table 13.3 compares the distinguishing characteristics of the most common forms of dementia. As research becomes more sophisticated, disturbances of memory and learning are being discovered in other disorders as well. In many medical disorders as well as in a variety of neuropsychiatric disturbances, retrieval of information is often compromised along with acquisition of new material.

Memory is almost always one focus of cognitive rehabilitation or retraining with TBI patients of all ages because problems with memory are some of the most persistent sequelae of TBI. Recovery of memory functions post-TBI is less predictable than improvements in more general aspects of intellectual function, which is at least in part due to disturbances of attention and concentration that typically accompany TBI. While some forms of memory tasks (e.g., immediate recall) are suppressed in functional and organic disorders, other memory tasks (e.g., delayed recall or forgetting) provide very good discrimination between psychiatric disorders such as depression, TBI, and other CNS disorders. Some form of memory assessment is nearly always included in comprehensive evaluations of cognitive functions whether conducted by school, clinical, or neuropsychologists, although neuropsychologists more commonly assess memory skills in greater depth than do other psychologists.

Given the ubiquitous nature of memory in daily affairs, particularly during the school-age years, and the importance of memory in evaluating the functional and the physiological integrity of the brain, it is surprising that comprehensive assessment of memory in children and adolescents is a recent phenomenon. This seems particularly odd given the plethora of such tasks available for adults dating from at least the 1930s. To some extent, memory assessment with children and adolescents must have been viewed as important since the earliest of modern intelligence tests (e.g., the 1907 Binet) and even the Wechsler Scales, in their various children's versions, all included one or two brief assessments of immediate recall. Still, the major texts on child neuropsychology of the 1970s and 1980s (e.g., Bakker, Fisk, and Strang 1983; Hynd & Obrzut, 1981) do not discuss assessment of memory despite the finding that 80% of a sample of various clinicians who perform testing noted memory as an important aspect of the assessment of cognitive and intellectual functions (Snyderman & Rothman, 1987). By 1995, assessment of memory function in children was discussed in key textbooks (e.g., Reynolds & Fletcher-Janzen, 1997) and its relation to various medical (e.g., Baron, Fennell, & Voeller, 1995) and neuropsychiatric disorders (e.g., Gillberg, 1995) was routinely included in major works on child neuropsychology.

Table 13.3 Symptom presentations in subtypes of dementia

Clinical Characteristic	Dementia type						
	Alzheimer's disease	Vascular dementia	Frontal lobe dementia	Lewy body dementia	Alcoholic dementia	Parkinson's dementia	Huntington's dementia
Genetic risk	Moderate	Moderate	High	Moderate	Low	Low	Very high
Cortical or subcortical features	Cortical	Both cortical and subcortical	Cortical	Both cortical and subcortical	Both cortical and subcortical	Subcortical	Subcortical
Environmental risk factors	Unknown	Hypertension Hyperlipidemia Smoking Obesity Strokes Diabetes	Unknown	Unknown	Alcohol abuse	Possibly environmental toxins	Little environmental influence
Mean age of onset	60–70	60–70	50–60	60–70	60–70	40–60	30–40
Prominent physiological changes	Neurofibrillary plaques and tangles. Cholinergic cell depletion. Atrophy in hippocampus and temporal lobe	Neuroimaging evidence of multiple strokes diffusely throughout the brain	Temporal and frontal lobe atrophy with reduced blood flow and metabolism	Lewy body deposits. Atrophy in cortex, limbic system, and substantia nigra	Cortical atrophy in temporal and frontal lobes and subcortical atrophy	Loss of dopaminergic cells in substantia nigra	Atrophy of caudate nucleus and putamen
Distinguishing neuropsychological features	Prominent memory problems in encoding, storage, and retrieval early in the disease	Low verbal and motoric output; executive function impaired	Social and personality changes precede cognitive changes	Visual hallucinations and delusions; fluctuating cognitive function; visuospatial deficits	Memory, behavioral and frontal lobe pathology; visuospatial deficits	Frontal and prefrontal problems; executive function impairment; significant motor disturbance	Early memory impairment with similar symptoms to Parkinson's dementia

Dorothea McCarthy, the noted psycholinguist, was aware of the importance of memory and included a memory index on the then-innovative McCarthy Scales of Children's Abilities (McCarthy, 1972). Koppitz (1977), another pioneer in assessment of children, noted the need for a more detailed evaluation of children's memory functions and devised the four-subtest Visual–Aural Digit Span Test (VADS; Koppitz, 1977). The VADS quickly became popular with school psychologists, among whom Koppitz was well known because of her work in childhood assessment with the Bender–Gestalt Test (which was updated only recently; Reynolds, 2007) and human figure drawings. The VADS is relatively narrow, assessing only sequential memory for digits but altering modality of input and output. No real attempt at developing a comprehensive assessment of children's memory appears until the introduction of the Wide Range Assessment of Memory and Learning (WRAML) for ages 5–17 by Sheslow and Adams (1990).

The WRAML was born of the frustration and dissatisfaction of its authors in not having a sound, comprehensive measure of memory functioning in children (Sheslow & Adams, 1990). The WRAML consists of nine subtests divided equally into three scales—Verbal Memory, Visual Memory, and Learning—followed by a brief delayed recall test to assess decay of information in long-term memory (i.e., forgetting). The WRAML was a substantial improvement over existing measures of memory for children but still provided a limited sample of memory and learning tasks. To increase the breadth and depth of analysis of memory function from the preschool years through the high school years (ages 5–20), Reynolds and Bigler (1994) developed the Test of Memory and Learning (TOMAL). The second edition of the TOMAL, the TOMAL-2 (Reynolds & Voress, 2007), continues to provide professionals with a standardized measure of different memory functions for children and adolescents but was also extended to incorporate assessment of adults. In the adult arena, the various incarnations of the Wechsler Memory Scale (now the WMS-IV), developed by David Wechsler of intelligence test fame, have been available since the 1940s.

13.3.1 TOMAL-2: An Example of a Contemporary Comprehensive Memory Assessment

The TOMAL-2 is arguably the most comprehensive of memory batteries available and provides subtests that assess most aspects of memory required for a comprehensive review of a patient's memory skills, and so we will describe it here as an example of a memory test.

The TOMAL-2 is a comprehensive battery of 14 memory and learning tasks (8 core subtests and 6 supplementary subtests) normed for use from ages 5 years 0 months 0 days through 59 years 11 months 30 days. The eight core subtests are divided into the content domains of verbal memory and nonverbal memory that can be combined to derive a Composite Memory Index. A Verbal Delayed Recall Index that requires recall of two of the verbal subtests' stimuli 30 minutes after their first administration is also available. Learning tasks of scales like the TOMAL-2 are those where the same stimuli are repeated over multiple trials until an examinee has recalled all of the stimuli or has reached a maximum number of trials allowed. These types of procedures also allow the plotting of learning curves for the individual relative to the average learning rate or curve of others with the same age.

As noted above, memory may be affected in many different ways by CNS disorders, and so traditional content approaches to memory may not be useful in all cases. The TOMAL-2 thus provides alternative groupings of the subtests into the Supplementary Indexes of Sequential Recall, Free Recall, Associative Recall, Learning, and Attention and Concentration.

Table 13.4 summarizes the names of the subtests and summary scores, along with their metric. The TOMAL-2 subtests are scaled to the familiar metric of mean equaling 10 and a standard deviation of 3 (range of 1–20). Composite or summary scores are scaled to a mean of 100 and standard deviation of 15.

Table 13.4 Core and supplementary subtests and indexes available for the TOMAL-2

Core subtests
Verbal
  • Memory for stories
  • Word selective reminding
  • Object recall
  • Paired recall
Nonverbal
  • Facial memory
  • Abstract visual memory
  • Visual sequential memory
  • Memory for location
Supplementary subtests
Verbal
  • Digits forward
  • Letters forward
  • Digits backward
  • Letters backward
Nonverbal
  • Visual selective reminding
  • Manual imitation
Summary Scores
Core indexes
  • Verbal Memory Index (VMI)
  • Nonverbal Memory Index (NMI)
  • Composite Memory Index (CMI)
Supplementary indexes
  • Verbal Delayed Recall Index (VDRI)
  • Attention/Concentration Index (ACI)
  • Sequential Recall Index (SRI)
  • Free Recall Index (FRI)
  • Associative Recall Index (ARI)
  • Learning Index (LI)

Table 13.5   Description of TOMAL-2 subtests

Core subtests

- *Memory for stories*. A verbal subtest requiring recall of a short story read to the examinee. It provides a measure of meaningful and semantic recall and is also related to sequential recall in some instances.
- *Facial memory*. A nonverbal subtest requiring recognition and identification from a set of distractors: black-and-white photos of various ages, males and females, and various ethnic backgrounds. It assesses nonverbal meaningful memory in a practical fashion and has been extensively researched. Sequencing of responses is unimportant.
- *Word selective reminding*. A verbal free-recall task in which the examinee learns a word list and repeats it only to be reminded of words left out in each trial: test learning and immediate recall functions in verbal memory. Trials continue until mastery is achieved or until six trials have been attempted. Sequence of recall is unimportant.
- *Abstract visual memory*. A nonverbal task assessing immediate recall for meaningless figures where order is unimportant. The examinee is presented with a standard stimulus and required to recognize the standard from any of six distractors.
- *Object recall*. The examiner presents a series of pictures, names them, has the examinee recall them, and repeats this process until mastery is achieved or until five trials have been attempted. Verbal and nonverbal stimuli are thus paired and recall is entirely verbal, creating a situation found to interfere with recall for many individuals with learning disabilities but to be neutral or facilitative for individuals without disabilities.
- *Visual sequential memory*. A nonverbal task requiring recall of the sequence of a series of meaningless geometric designs. The ordered designs are shown followed by a presentation of a standard order of the stimuli, and the examinee indicates the order in which they originally appeared.
- *Paired recall*. A verbal paired-associative task on which the examinee is required to recall a list of word pairs when the first word of each pair is provided by the examiner. Both easy and hard pairs are used.
- *Memory for location*. A nonverbal task that assesses spatial memory. The examinee is presented with a set of large dots distributed on a page and asked to recall the locations of the dots in any order.

Supplementary subtests

- *Digits forward*. A standard verbal number recall task. It measures low-level rote recall of a sequence of numbers.
- *Visual selective reminding*. A nonverbal analogue to Word Selective Reminding where examinees point to specified dots on a card, following a demonstration by the examiner, and are reminded only of dots recalled incorrectly. Trials continue until mastery is achieved or until five trials have been attempted.
- *Letters forward*. A language-related analogue to common digit span tasks using letters as the stimuli in place of numbers.
- *Manual imitation*. A psychomotor, visually based assessment of sequential memory where the examinee is required to reproduce a set of ordered hand movements in the same sequence as presented by the examiner.
- *Digits backward*. This is the same basic task as Digits Forward except that the examinee recalls the numbers in reverse order.
- *Letters backward*. A language-related analogue to the Digits Backward task using letters as the stimuli instead of numbers.

TOMAL-2 Subtests: The 8 core, 6 supplementary, and delayed recall TOMAL-2 subtests require about 45 minutes for a skilled examiner. The subtests were chosen to provide a comprehensive view of memory functions and, when used in toto, provide the most thorough assessment of memory available. The subtests are named and briefly described in Table 13.5.

The TOMAL-2 subtests systematically vary the mode of presentation and response so as to sample verbal, visual, motoric, and combinations of these modalities in presentation and in response formats. Multiple trials to a criterion are provided on several subtests, including selective reminding, so that learning or acquisition curves may be derived. Multiple trials (at least five are necessary) are provided on the selective reminding subtests to allow an analysis of the depth of processing. In the selective reminding format (wherein examinees are reminded only of stimuli "forgotten" or unrecalled), when items once recalled are unrecalled by the examinee on later trials, problems are revealed in the transference of stimuli from working memory and immediate memory to more long-term storage. Cueing is also provided at the end of Word Selective Reminding Delayed to add to the examiner's ability to probe depth of processing.

Subtests are included that sample sequential recall (which tends strongly to be mediated by the left hemisphere, especially temporal regions) and free recall in both verbal and visual formats allow localization; purely spatial memory tasks are included that are very difficult to confound via verbal mediation to assess more purely right hemisphere functions.

Well-established memory tasks (e.g., recalling stories) that also correlate well with school learning are included along with tasks more common to experimental neuropsychology that have high (e.g., Facial Memory) and low (e.g., Visual Selective Reminding) ecological salience; some subtests employ highly meaningful material (e.g., Memory for Stories), while some use highly abstract stimuli (e.g., Abstract Visual Memory).

Aside from allowing a comprehensive review of memory function, the purpose for including such a factorial array of tasks across multiple dimensions is to allow a thorough, detailed analysis of memory function and the source of any memory deficits that may be discovered. Delayed recall tasks are routinely included in many clinical assessments of memory to evaluate forgetting as well as to distinguish organic from functional deficits in memory. Unlike many other memory tests that employ sequential recall of digits and letters in forward and backward formats, the TOMAL-2 provides separate scores for forward and backward recall since the neural substrates underlying these tasks are different in many respects (Ramsey & Reynolds, 1995) and should not be combined for clinical analyses (Reynolds, 1997). To solve the complex puzzle of dysfunctional memory, neuropsychologists require a memory test like the TOMAL-2, which samples all relevant brain functions with subtests that have great specificity and variability of presentation and response.

13.4 The Process of Neuropsychological Assessment

As the field of clinical neuropsychology began to emerge from a predominantly research-oriented endeavor in the 1950s and 1960s, neuropsychologists were increasingly called upon to assist in determining the presence or absence of brain damage. At that time, brain pathology was generally viewed as a unitary concept, and the neuropsychologist's role was ostensibly to determine whether or not an individual had brain damage. Neuropsychologists were commonly asked to make the determination between "organic" pathology (having a structural basis) and "functional" pathology (having a psychological or other cause). This dichotomous conceptualization of pathology implied that abnormal presentations were either due to damaged neurological structures or due to other psychological, emotional, or behavioral factors. As neurology advanced, particularly with the advent and rapid progression of neuroimaging procedures, it was assumed by some that the neuropsychologist's role would inevitably be diminished and supplanted by neuroimaging. Instead, the field of clinical neuropsychology continued to expand as practitioners' scopes widened, gradually shifting away from diagnosis and toward a broader understanding of the functional implications of brain pathology. Even today, with relatively easy access to highly sophisticated and detailed neuroimaging, it is the neuropsychologist who is generally charged with making determinations regarding the functional ramifications of a brain injury or disease process. Depending on the purpose of the assessment, there may be some variations on the procedures involved in any given assessment. The next few sections will describe a general process of the assessment that is common to most purposes.

> Modern clinical neuropsychologists commonly serve as an integral member of a treatment team that includes other professionals in medical settings.

13.4.1 Referral

The neuropsychological assessment process inevitably begins with some referral question generated by a treatment team, agency, group, or individual. Most often, the question(s) revolves around suspected cognitive impairment or the functional ramifications of known brain damage, although neuropsychologists are increasingly being called upon for other purposes. Today, neuropsychologists receive referrals from an ever-increasing number of sources for a wide range of reasons. Although the bulk of referrals are due to known or suspected brain injury, evaluations are also requested for learning disabilities, vocational and occupational assessments, psychiatric and psychological disorders, treatment evaluation, disability determination, and habilitation or rehabilitation planning. Physicians, particularly neurologists, psychiatrists, and geriatricians, are often a primary referral source for neuropsychologists. Clinical neuropsychologists commonly serve as an integral member of a treatment team that includes other professionals in medical settings. Other referral sources include schools (elementary, secondary, and university-level), vocational and occupational service agencies, and attorneys and judges seeking evaluations for individuals involved in forensic cases. In the case of suspected memory problems associated with aging, it is often the patient's family members who first recognize potential symptoms, prompting the patient to seek an evaluation. Special Interest Topics 13.1 describes common referrals due to brain injury.

Special Interest Topic 13.1: Common Brain Injury Referrals

Neuropsychological evaluations are requested for a wide range of presenting complaints that have in common suspected or confirmed CNS dysfunction. The type of damage or dysfunction often influences the set of referral questions that neuropsychologist are asked to address. Communicating neuropsychological findings to medical professionals requires an understanding of the medical conditions for which patients are referred. Educational and practical training experiences provide neuropsychologists the requisite knowledge and clinical skills to understand these medical conditions, evaluate them, interpret evaluation findings, and communicate them to other medical professional for diagnostic and treatment planning purposes. Courses in neuropsychological assessment, neuroanatomy, cognitive, systems, behavioral neurosciences, psychopharmacology, and others are often part of this training as is research and supervised neuropsychological assessment of individuals suffering from CNS disorders. This section briefly presents some of the more common medical disorders referred to neuropsychologists for evaluation.

Traumatic Brain Injury

TBI can result from any number of injury sources including motor vehicle accidents, falls, direct blows to the head, and wounds from firearms or other projectiles and missiles. TBI is typically characterized as either a *closed head injury* (CHI) or *penetrating head injury* (PHI). In a CHI, the skull remains intact, whereas in a PHI, the skull and *dura mater* (the outermost layer of the protective tissues that cover the brain) is breached by skull fracture or penetrating head wound. TBI is classified by severity. TBI may be mild, moderate, or severe, depending on several variables to include the duration of the period of *loss of consciousness*, the degree of *Posttraumatic Amnesia*, the severity of the structural damage, and the patient's postinjury functional status.

Cerebrovascular Disorders

Cerebrovascular disorders are characterized by neuronal damage resulting from any disruption of proper vascular profusion to brain tissue. Blood carries oxygen and nutrients to neural tissue, and when blood supply is decreased or blocked, neural tissue is compromised. These disorders range from mild occlusive events known as *transient ischemic attacks* (TIAs) to the more severe completed *occlusive* or *hemorrhagic strokes* with a high mortality rate. Occlusive strokes prevent oxygen and nutrients from reaching neural tissue due to a blockage in a blood vessel. Hemorrhagic strokes are the result of a blood vessel bleeding into the brain, also preventing adequate oxygen and nutrients from reaching neuronal tissue. Neuropsychologists are often relied upon to measure functional capacity and preserved abilities after resolution of symptoms and stabilization of the patient.

Brain Tumors

Brain Tumors can arise as either primary brain tumors or secondary brain tumors. A primary brain tumor develops from cells within the brain tissue or *meninges* (membranes that form a covering over the brain). Brain tumors developing from *glial cells* (cells providing support and nutrition to neurons) are known as *gliomas*. Brain tumors developing from the meninges are known as *meningiomas*. Secondary brain tumors arise from cancer cells that have *metastasized* (spread) from tissues outside the CNS, e.g., cancer that starts in the lungs and later spreads to the brain.

If the tumor is treated through surgical intervention, radiation, or chemotherapy, the neuropsychologist is often involved in measuring posttreatment neuropsychological function. Like in the case of stroke, testing may be periodically repeated to measure progress over time. If the location of a small or slow-growing tumor prevents surgical removal, neuropsychological assessment can provide a measure of baseline function from which to periodically assess any changes of function that could be caused by growth of the tumor.

Dementia

Neuropsychologists play an important role in the diagnosis and subsequent treatment of dementia. Neuroimaging is often used to examine the brains of individuals with dementia but in some cases is not particularly helpful in identifying dementia type. More importantly, there is often little correlation between structural changes in the brain documented with neuroimaging and the functional status of the patient. As such, neuropsychologists are relied upon to quantify a patient's current functional status in various cognitive domains and to estimate the degree and type of losses from premorbid levels. Neuropsychological assessment can also provide evidence regarding the type of dementia that may be present. This type of distinction may be important with regard to treatment and prognosis. Some instruments have been found to be useful at distinguishing between the different types of dementia (e.g., the RBANS). Table 13.3 presents some of the differentiations between the various types of dementia.

Toxins

There are a wide range of substances that are neurotoxic, including alcohol, drugs, solvents, pesticides, and metals (Allen & Woods, 2014). Alcohol is the most common cause of brain injury due to toxins because of its wide availability and use. Heavy drinking over a period of years can result in significant damage that may result in serious CNS disorders like *alcoholic dementia* and *Korsakoff Syndrome*. Severe memory impairment is a key symptom of both disorders, and so neuropsychological assessment is used to assist in diagnosis and in characterizing the degree and extent of damage. Heavy alcohol consumption can also produce less severe cognitive deficits that interfere with functioning, and some will improve following cessation of alcohol use (Allen, Goldstein, & Seaton, 1997). Neuropsychological assessment is useful for tracking improvement in abilities following cessation of use that is spontaneous in nature or the result of rehabilitation efforts.

Pesticides, solvents, and metals often have subtle effects on cerebral white matter producing characteristic slowness, gait and balance disturbances, and problems with attention and concentration. In all cases of possible toxicity, it is important for the neuropsychologist to gather as much information as possible from the patient, family members, and medical reports regarding the source, duration, frequency, and levels of exposure.

13.4.2 Review of Records

Although we often think of a neuropsychological evaluation as an administration of a series of psychometric measures, it is important to remember that these tests only provide a behavioral measure at a given time, place, and circumstance. The scores obtained in any assessment gain relevancy only when interpreted within the context of the patient's history. Much historical information can be obtained during a detailed clinical interview with the examinee, but other germane information comes from historical records, including educational records, military records, legal records, records obtained from the referring agency, medical records, and previous evaluations including standardized test scores. These types of records can be critical in attempting to establish a baseline of function prior to injury. If there is a significant event that resulted in the functional change function (traumatic brain injury, stroke, toxicity, and medical condition), then medical records can be critical in determining the focus of the examination. For example, a patient with a localized gunshot wound to the left temporal lobe may require a different testing focus than a patient referred by a physician due to memory complaints. Records pertaining to either individual provide a documented written record of findings that will likely have an influence over the entire evaluation process. Typically, the neuropsychologist reviews these records prior to meeting with the examinee. The pertinence of each type of record may depend on the referral question. For example, in the case of moderate or severe traumatic brain injury (TBI), the recent history of the patient's medical condition and rehabilitation progress is typically more important than the patient's early developmental history in making determinations regarding rehabilitation and prognosis. Further, in the case of TBI, it is imperative to obtain detailed information about the cause of the TBI, extent and severity of the injury, duration of loss of consciousness, posttraumatic amnesia, etc. However, in such a case, we obviously do not have to ask the patient when his or her symptoms first occurred. In the case of a possible dementing illness, we would want to know when symptoms first appeared and obtain as much other historical information as possible regarding the genesis of early symptoms, family genetic history, substance abuse history, and family and patient reports regarding the progression of symptoms. At its core, the neuropsychological evaluation is ultimately concerned with some cognitive change and/or difference. Previous records provide one baseline from which to make inferences about current test data.

13.4.3 Clinical Interview

The clinical interview of the examinee remains a critical element of the evaluation process. The techniques and components of a general psychological clinical interview also apply within the neuropsychology context. As such, information is obtained in various domains about the person's history to include basic descriptive information, early developmental history, social history, educational, vocational, and avocational background, and psychological and psychiatric history. However, given the context of the referrals, neuropsychological interviews may be somewhat longer and more detailed, particularly in domains germane to cognitive function and/or change. For example, the examinee's apex of educational or vocational achievement provides the neuropsychologist with a gross estimate of the patient's previous or present level of functional capacity. Obtaining accurate information regarding these domains enables the neuropsychologist to make reasonable judgments regarding cognitive losses, preserved functions, and prognoses.

> Obtaining accurate information through clinical interviews enables the neuropsychologist to make judgments regarding cognitive losses, preserved functions, and prognoses.

Although it is difficult to outline all of the important historical domains of a clinical interview without knowing the specific referral question, most evaluations include aspects of the following:

1. *Information on injury/condition* (detailed accounts of accident, injury, or reason for the referral)
2. *Early developmental history* (birth and developmental milestones)
3. *Educational history* (elementary, secondary, university, grades, behavioral and/ or academic problems, learning disabilities, academic interests, General Educational Development Exam scores, standardized test scores, certifications, and awards)
4. *Vocational history* (present work status, work status prior to injury/condition, change in work status, highest level of vocational attainment, previous employment history, and terminations)
5. *Social history* (family history, marital status and history, children, and present and past residences)
6. *Medical history* (surgeries, hospitalizations, head injuries, current and past medications, chronic illnesses, and relevant medical history of first-degree relatives)
7. *Psychological and psychiatric history* (diagnoses, history of trauma, inpatient and outpatient treatment, and psychotherapy)
8. *Substance use and abuse* (duration, frequency, quantity, and patterns of use, periods of cessation, types of substances used including nicotine, caffeine, alcohol, marijuana, and illicit drugs)
9. *Legal history* (arrests, criminal history, incarcerations, and past and present litigation)

Although a clinical interview is always conducted with the patient, it is often helpful to obtain consent from the patient to also interview other individuals such as family members. Family members often provide valuable information about changes in function, including timelines and progression of the patient's functional capacity, which may be outside the patient's awareness. Special Interest Topic 13.2 discusses a condition where interviewing family members is important for determining its presence.

Special Interest Topic 13.2: Anosognosia

When interviewing patients known to have experienced a brain injury, clinicians have to be careful in relying upon the patient's rendition of their cognitive and behavioral changes postinjury. While some patients are acutely aware of changes to their behavior and thinking skills and are willing to discuss them in an effort to obtain the best possible rehabilitation plan, some engage in denial of such changes, even though being aware of them. However, there exists a third group of patients who have obvious deficits and changes to behavior on examination and in reports of family and friends who are adamant that they have not changed at all. In this group, aside from those who just are trying to hide any changes, we find patients with a disorder known as anosognosia, i.e., the inability to recognize deficits, injury, or behavioral changes associated with a brain injury due to the nature of the brain injury itself. Consequently, these patients genuinely do not know they have changed at all, and some become argumentative and quite agitated at attempts to explain how they have been affected. The presence of anosognosia, which is most commonly associated with injuries to the parietal lobe of the brain or significant disruption of the connectivity patterns of the frontotemporal-parietal regions, was first reported by Babinski (a neurologist best known for the "Babinski reflex") in 1918 and almost always complicates assessment and treatment planning for such patients as some can become extremely resistant to interventions and family involvement is critical to getting the right care for those so afflicted. This also points out the need for collateral interviews in detailing the day-to-day issues in the function of a brain injured patient.

13.4.4 Test Selection

As previously discussed, test selection is guided by a number of different factors, including the examiner's background and training, the referral question, and information obtained during interviews or observations. Typically,

> The purpose and intent of the assessment have great impact on the selection of tests.

the examiner starts with a battery of tests to consider, partly based on the referral question. Again, the battery that one uses for an 82 year-old examinee presenting with symptoms of dementia may differ significantly from a 35-year old physician with a mild TBI who is anticipating a return to full work status. The neuropsychologist can adjust and modify the battery as new information emerges from records or during the interview. If a particular deficit emerges during testing that elicits new concerns, supplemental measures can be added to further explore any particular domain. Some of the important variables that enter into the decision regarding test selection include the following:

1. *Time and cost.* Neuropsychological evaluations range in time from brief screening batteries (sometimes as short as 1 hour) to comprehensive batteries sometimes lasting more than 10 hours (usually conducted over 2 days). With a gradual increase in the influence of managed care, there has been a concomitant trajectory toward the development of shorter neuropsychological batteries. However, with continuous refinement of neuropsychological techniques and improved adherence to psychometric principles, neuropsychologists have been able to reduce battery length and time without decreasing the sensitivity and specificity of their evaluation. Moreover, neuropsychologists have become increasingly sensitive to the need to avoid unnecessary testing. For example, it may not be necessary to have a test battery longer than 2 hours in order to make a general assessment regarding the presence or absence of dementia. Time and cost are often the initial determinants of the extent of the battery in conjunction with the referral question and the age and degree of impairment of the patient.

2. *Examiner training.* Although neuropsychologists are broadly trained in a wide range of tests and routinely undertake training with new psychometric measures, each examiner inevitably develops a set of measures with which he or she is most familiar and comfortable. This is typically a set battery that is appropriate to the referral question and patient sequelae, supplemented with additional tests that may be particularly sensitive to the condition or injury. As previously discussed, some neuropsychologists are more apt to utilize a predominantly fixed battery approach, while others may use a flexible battery approach or process approach. However, all neuropsychologists have access to a variety of testing approaches and display some degree of flexibility in test choice.

3. *Assessment goals.* The purpose and intent of the assessment have great impact on the selection of tests. Sometimes, a neuropsychologist is asked to conduct a "screen" for a particular disorder. In such a case, he or she will select a short battery or a standardized screening instrument with a high sensitivity to the condition in question. This type of assessment can be very brief and focused. More often, a longer assessment will be required to adequately address the pending referral question. The injury site or specific cognitive function in question influences the battery's length and composition. For example, if there is a known injury to anterior left frontal areas, instruments that are sensitive measures of categorization and cognitive flexibility would be a necessary component to the battery (e.g,, Wisconsin Card Sorting Test and the Halstead Category Test). If the nature of the assessment involved a referral of a child with ADHD symptoms, a broad battery with a preponderance of attention measures (e.g., continuous performance tests, Comprehensive Trail Making Test, and Paced Auditory Serial Addition Task) would be more appropriate. In dementia assessments, the focus would center predominantly on learning and memory; instruments that are more sensitive to this cognitive domain would be required (e.g., Dementia Rating Scale [DRS]). If the purpose of the assessment involves litigation or serves some other forensic requirement, it is important to consider the inclusion of *validity measures.* These are special instruments or indexes designed to measure the patient's level of effort. This special type of testing is discussed in more detail in Special Interest Topic 13.3.

4. *Stage of testing*. Another aspect that has considerable impact on selection of test instruments involves the "stage" of testing, and whether previous or subsequent testing is or will be a factor. Sometimes, the goal is to test performance changes sequentially over time, and this must be considered when choosing the test battery. The model whereby the neuropsychologist conducts a single assessment to determine the extent and severity of impairment is gradually expanding into a model that is more attuned to the plasticity of functional cognitive changes. As such, the neuropsychologist must often consider the previous and/or subsequent assessment batteries when conducting the present assessment. In such cases, the neuropsychologist may be more interested in intraindividual change rather than a strict comparison to a set of norms and/or cutoff criteria. Areas of cognitive improvement are often the focus in rehabilitation settings or in serial evaluations during the implementation of school-based intervention programs. Some tests are more amenable to repeated administrations, and their test characteristics have been examined with this aspect in mind (e.g., RBANS; Randolph, Tierney, Mohr, & Chase, 1998).

5. *Psychometrics*. As with any assessment, the importance of adequate reliability and validity cannot be overstated. Neuropsychologists must take special effort to note the appropriateness of any test under the given circumstances. Thus, the patient characteristics (demographics, condition, and referral question) yield critical information about which test may be most appropriate. For example, the TOMAL-2 is established as an excellent measure of memory for a middle-aged individual, but it is not designed for measuring dementia in older adults. Likewise, other test characteristics (such as ceiling and floor effects, sensitivity and specificity, etc.) must be given high consideration when choosing a battery of tests. Understanding other test characteristics, such as the ***Flynn effect*** (see Chap. 9), can have enormous influence in flexible battery approaches due to the differing standardization samples used for each measure.

6. *Interview data and behavioral observations*. Information obtained by the examiner through the interview and observations of behavior may lead the neuropsychologist to augment the battery with supplemental measures or replace measures originally considered. For example, if the patient reports a motor weakness in her right hand, the neuropsychologist may consider additional measures designed to measure motor speed/dexterity that is more specific to left hemisphere frontal motor regions.

7. *Observations made during testing*. Neuropsychologists who are more comfortable with a process approach may sometimes consider adding additional measures to the battery as performance is observed during the assessment. This branching style of assessment in which compromised functions are given more specific attention enables the neuropsychologist to more fully investigate the observed area of deficit. Likewise, if the neuropsychologist discovers an unexpected finding that can impact the validity of some measures (e.g., a left-sided visual neglect in which the patient ignores spatial information from the left visual field), the neuropsychologist may need to give consideration to the impact of this deficit on subsequent tests as the testing proceeds.

Special Interest Topic 13.3: How Does a Neuropsychologist Measure Effort?

One of the most controversial issues in neuropsychological assessment is that of *effort*. Neuropsychological testing requires optimal performance in order to obtain test scores that will allow valid inferences regarding cognitive function. When given a good rationale for the purpose and goals of the assessment, most patients will engage the tasks with the effort necessary to obtain a valid and representative sample of their cognitive function. However, some patients, particularly those involved in litigation, perform at suboptimal levels in an attempt to obtain some **secondary gain**. Secondary gain may include some identifiable goal such as time off from work, financial compensation, or disability benefits. It may also include the perceived social and emotional advantages of assuming a sick role. At one extreme, a patient may deliberately exaggerate impairment or intentionally create neurological symptoms, known as **malingering**. Other causes of suboptimal effort with varying degrees of patient self-awareness include somatization, conversion, or factitious disorder. It is not incumbent upon the neuropsychologist to differentiate between the many possible presentations of suboptimal effort. However, it is critical that the examiner has a systematic and valid approach to measure effort.

Two types of measures have been validated for the measurement of effort. The first involves the use of an already existing neuropsychological measure. Indexes or cutoff scores are established on certain components of an existing neuropsychological test, which serve as measures of effort. An example of this would be the use of the Digit Span subtest from the Wechsler intelligence scales. In this subtest, the examinee is required to repeat a series of digits in order. He or she is asked to repeat digits forward in the first portion of the subtest, followed by a task of repeating digits backward. The relatively simple task of repeating digits forward has been found to be quite resistant to brain damage (Reynolds, 1997; Wilson and Kaszniak, 1986), but individuals feigning poor effort are usually unaware of this finding and may therefore produce unusually poor results. Griffenstein, Baker, and Gola (1994) have developed an effort index known as Reliable Digit Span that relies on the known expectations of Digit Span scores.

The second approach is to create a new instrument that is specifically designed as a validity test. Many of these tests appear challenging, but contain items or series of items that are rarely failed by individuals with most types of cognitive impairment. One example of this type of test is the Test of Memory Malingering (Tombaugh, 1996). Like many of these tests, it uses a forced-choice format in which the examinee is asked to choose between two items. Suboptimal effort may produce profiles with very low scores, sometimes even below chance performance. Below is a list of the various psychometric principles used in effort measures:

1. *Cutoff scores*: Some instruments and indexes utilize a performance cutoff score that is indicative of a high probability of suboptimal effort. This score is based on data regarding the known floor of a particular test or impairment condition, under which few scores are naturally obtained.

(continued)

2. *Atypical response patterns*: Some tests examine the within-test or across-test variability. This is based on the finding that it is difficult for patients to respond suboptimally in a consistent manner.
3. *Item analysis:* Some individual items within tests are rarely, if ever, failed by individuals giving good effort. As more of these items are failed, it becomes increasingly improbable that the examinee was performing optimally.
4. *Forced-choice format:* This format most often is composed of items that require examinees to choose between two answers and are rarely failed by cognitively normal individuals. Given the two-choice format, an index of statistical probability can be established to determine the likelihood of a valid response set.
5. *Repeated evaluation:* This format relies on the finding that it is difficult for examinees to demonstrate consistent suboptimal performance on similar tasks after a delay.
6. *Profile analysis:* Certain disorders have cognitive profiles that are fairly well established. As a simple example, it would be unlikely for an individual with pesticide exposure to consistently produce incorrect names for common objects, although this can occur in other types of brain injury. This *lack of fit* or inconsistency with expected findings can be used in making inferences regarding effort.

13.4.5 Test Conditions

As with any psychological evaluation, test conditions can influence the ability to obtain the optimal performance necessary in neuropsychological evaluations. As such, the neuropsychologist strives to maintain a quiet environment with ample lighting and comfortable seating. Lighting conditions may be particularly important when working with patients with low vision. Neuropsychologists are more inclined than most other psychologists to be working with individuals in wheelchairs or with other specific handicaps that might require special arrangements. When working with older adults, the examiner must be particularly attentive to possible hearing and visual deficits. It is unusual for an individual over the age of 50 to function optimally on some visually demanding tests without reading glasses, and this should be addressed prior to testing. Sometimes, a neuropsychologist is asked to conduct a "bed-side" examination, as he or she is often a member of a medical team that provides treatment to inpatients. In such cases, an optimal testing environment may not be obtainable. When this occurs, the conditions must be considered when interpreting testing results.

> Testing conditions can influence the ability to obtain the optimal performance necessary in neuropsychological evaluations.

Neuropsychologists sometimes have to consider other factors extrinsic to the test battery that can have a profound influence on test scores. Some individuals, particularly older adults, perform suboptimally when tested later in the day or evening. Inadequate sleep the night prior to testing can also have deleterious effects on test scores. Medications, particularly in older adults, can also impact the interpretation of test scores. Special Interest Topics 13.4 presents an interesting case study involving medication effects in an older adult.

Special Interest Topic 13.4: Case Study of Medication Effects on Neuropsychological Testing

The effects of medication on neuropsychological test data have yet to be fully investigated. This is of particular concerns in older adults. Many older patients are prescribed multiple medications, and there is increasing evidence that some of these medications can have negative effects on test performance in clinical settings.

The following case study presents scores obtained during an actual evaluation and reveal the effects of a lorazepam (a common anxiolytic) on neuropsychological performance in an 81 year old female. This patient was initially referred to a geriatrician by family members due to "short-term" memory loss that had been progressing for about 3 years. At the time the referral was made, the patient had been taking lorazepam for over 3 years at an approximate dose of 1 mg every 4–6 h, with an average daily intake of about 6 mg.

Results of the first neuropsychological assessment appeared to be consistent with a diagnosis of dementia; however, the potential effect of her relatively high dose of lorazepam generated concerns regarding diagnosis. Given this consideration, the physician decided to titrate the patient from lorazepam and have the patient retested after titration. The patient successfully titrated from lorazepam over a 5-month period with no reported or observed difficulty. The patient was rescheduled for a second neuropsychological assessment about 6 months after the first evaluation. Scores from the two separate assessments were compared. A Reliable Change Index (RCI) was calculated for each measure in order to analyze test-retest changes (see Special Interest Topic 13.5 for more information on RCI).

Table 13.6 presents scores for the patient's initial assessment and follow-up. Initial scores were consistent with significant cognitive impairment, although possible medication effects were considered problematic in making a clear determination. Most scores were below expectations based on estimated premorbid ability. Impaired scores were observed in the RBANS Immediate Memory Index, Delayed Memory Index, Language Index, and Total Score. Impaired scores were also observed in verbal fluency, Trails A and B, and the bicycle drawing task (raw score of 5). Most notable was her index score of 52 on Delayed Memory, a measure of verbal and nonverbal recall of previously rehearsed information.

(continued)

After titration, scores on some neuropsychological measures appeared to improve. Using a 90% confidence interval, RCI values show improvement in RBANS Total Scale score, Immediate Memory Index, Visuospatial/Constructional Index, and Language Index. Improvements were also observed in Similarities and Trail B. Despite these relative improvements, most scores remained below expected values. Most clinically notable was her equally impaired score in Delayed Memory on follow-up, which still reflected severe anterograde amnesia.

In this case study, some neuropsychological measures showed improvement after titration. This suggests the need for caution when interpreting neuropsychological profiles in older individuals taking certain medications. Nevertheless, despite some improvement after titration, the overall diagnostic picture remained similar, with the patient manifesting extremely impaired delayed recall under both conditions. This implies that neuropsychological assessment, with the RBANS as a core battery, may be robust enough to inform diagnosis, even in less than optimal test conditions.

Table 13.6 Test results showing medication effects on neuropsychological test performance

Test	Baseline	Follow-up	RCI
WTAR and RBANS (mean of 100 and SD of 15)			
WTAR IQ	106	106	0.00
RBANS Immediate Memory Index	57	83	3.46**
RBANS Visuospatial/Constructional Index	86	102	1.70*
RBANS Language Index	64	80	1.74*
RBANS Attention Index	97	94	0.36
RBANS Delayed Memory Index	52	52	0.00
RBANS Total Scale Score	64	78	2.58**
Supplemental measures (reported as T-scores)			
WAIS-III vocabulary	46	–	–
WAIS-III similarities	43	53	1.90*
WAIS-III block design	40	–	–
Letter fluency	30	34	0.69
Trail A	27	31	0.66
Trail B	24	46	3.17**
Grooved Pegboard-dominant	49	–	–
Grooved Pegboard-nondominant	40		–
Smell Identification Test	37	40	0.75

Note. For Wechsler subtests, the WTAR, and the RBANS, RCI values were calculated using SEMs reported in their respective manuals. For other measures, RCI values were calculated using published reliability coefficients to obtain SEMs. $* = p < .05$; $** = p < .01$

13.5   Measurement of Deficits and Strengths

As we noted, neuropsychologists are concerned with understanding the patient's current pattern of cognitive strengths and weaknesses. These patterns may have emerged acutely as a result of an injury or illness, or they may be the manifestation of longstanding cognitive patterns, such as in ADHD or a learning disability. In this sense, neuropsychological assessment is different from many other types of psychological assessment whose primary concern is to determine where the examinee stands in relation to some normative or reference group. These normative comparisons answer questions like "Does the 1st grade child read at a similar level to his peers?" or "How do the personality scores for this job applicant compare to those of current employees who are successful at the position?" or "Is the IQ of a college student with a learning disability in the normal or average range?" While neuropsychologists are interested in these normative comparisons, at its essence, neuropsychological assessment inevitably boils down to a process of deficit measurement where the individual, not a normative sample or reference group, serves as the point of comparison for test interpretation. Deficit measurement is used to answer questions like "How does this school teacher's current language ability compare to his language ability before he sustained a left hemisphere stroke?" or "Does the level of memory performance for this 65 year old female represent a decline from her prior level of memory functioning?" This is not to say that neuropsychologists are uninterested in intact neuropsychological processes, but most referrals are concerned with a deficit or decline in cognitive ability from some prior level of functioning. This deficit measurement process may seem relatively straightforward and is greatly facilitated when detailed previous test scores are available. Unfortunately, in most cases, previous test scores are not available, and so in their absence, how do we measure deficits? At some point, present test scores must be compared against a standard by which deficits or strengths are inferred. This can be done by using a normative approach or by using an idiographic approach.

13.5.1 Normative Approach

In the normative approach, neuropsychologists compare current performance against a normative standard. In the early days of neuropsychological assessment, there was an emphasis on comparing presently obtained scores with raw "cutoff" scores presumed, based on normative

> In the normative approach, neuropsychologists compare current performance against a normative standard.

databases, to indicate "brain damage." As the specialty of neuropsychology has progressed, an increased emphasis has been placed on calculating deviations from large population-based norms for any given test. For example, as with many behavioral measures, neuropsychological measures often produce scores with a normal distribution in the population. An individual's performance can be compared with population norms, thereby giving the person's scores a relative standing in the population regarding the given test domain. Clinical neuropsychologists using the normative approach typically convert raw scores to T-scores or z-scores using these population-based norms, thus providing a common metric when observing and analyzing a set of scores.

When using this approach, it is imperative that the neuropsychologist has a strong understanding of basic statistical variation. For example, in any given set of scores, a number of scores in a normal functioning individual will fall significantly below the population mean. In most cases, a preponderance of scores would have to fall below the population mean before accurate inferences can be made regarding possible damage. Additionally, these inferences must be made within the context of the individual's level of premorbid ability, a concept that is discussed in greater detail later in this chapter. For example, a prominent attorney with 18 years of education who is presently functioning in the average range on most verbal tests is more likely exhibiting signs of cognitive loss than a warehouse employee with a ninth grade education who obtains similar verbal test scores.

When using population norms, we must answer the question, to what population should the person's scores be compared? This seemingly simple question is not always so easily answered. While general population norms are often used, there has been an ever-increasing emphasis on demographically based norms. Demographic characteristics that typically have the most influence on neuropsychological tests include age, education, ethnicity, and gender. Some tests, for example, tests of motor speed/dexterity, are most influenced by age. Tests that tap verbal fluency tend to be more influenced by level of education. Increasingly, test manuals are offering raw-score transformations based on a more specifically defined demographic groups with these variables in mind. Additionally, there has been an increase in the development and the use of norms manuals that provide standardized demographic scores for a wide range of neuropsychological measures. One commonly used manual, the *Revised Comprehensive Norms for an Expanded Halstead-Reitan Battery* (Heaton, Miller, Taylor, & Grant, 2004), provides demographically corrected T-scores for over 50 neuropsychological parameters based on the demographics of sex, education, age, and race. Using this manual, examiners may compare an individual's test score with the general population norms or with the more specific demographic group to which an individual may belong.

13.5.2 Deficit Measurement Approach

In the deficit measurement or ideographic approach, the examiner uses previous scores or estimates of *premorbid ability* as the comparison measure against which current scores are compared. Premorbid ability refers to an individual's cognitive status prior to the injury or condition. When detailed premorbid neuropsychological scores are available, this greatly facilitates prepost injury comparisons. Such scores are seldom available since there

> In the idiographic approach, the examiner uses previous scores or estimates of premorbid ability as the comparison measure against which current scores are compared.

is no reason to administer neuropsychological tests to people prior to CNS dysfunction, just as there is no reason to perform a brain MRI scan on someone who has no medical symptoms. We will discuss a number of methods to estimate premorbid function later in this chapter, but before doing so, we point out that even when premorbid test scores are available, there are still some challenges to making inferences about change. One cannot simply look at the difference in scores in order to determine whether reliable and clinically important changes have occurred, primarily due to measurement error inherent to psychological tests, which may contribute to changes in test scores when no real change has occurred. Thus, determining if change has occurred between repeated assessments is a complex issue, whether they be pre- and postinjury assessments or serial assessment conducted to judge changes based on the progression of an illness-like dementia, estimate amount of recovery from a CNS disorder like TBI, or determine response to a cognitive rehabilitation intervention for memory disturbance. Although various statistical methods are available to measure change, many clinicians rely on clinical judgment in determining whether change has occurred. Psychometric formulas for evaluating change, such as the Reliable Change Index (RCI; Jacobson & Truax, 1991), are playing a greater role in making these decisions as neuropsychological techniques become more refined. Special Interest Topic 13.5 presents an interesting example of the use of the RCI in a clinical setting.

Special Interest Topic 13.5: How Does a Neuropsychologist Measure Change?
Neuropsychologists are sometimes asked to compare present scores with past scores and determine whether change has occurred. For example, in the case of various types of brain injury, serial assessments are often required. But how does a neuropsychologist determine when change has actually occurred? In any given dataset, there are going to be variations in scores that may not actually represent a statistical change. How do we know when sufficient change has occurred in any given measure to indicate a true change? This is complex question, and some of the statistical concepts involved are beyond the scope of this text. However, the following brief synopsis presents some of the basic ideas regarding the measurement of change.

Jacobson and Truax (1991) developed a measure known as the Reliable Change Index (RCI) that can be used to calculate whether change has occurred. Based on classical test theory, the RCI is an index of the probability that a change observed in an examinee's score on the same test is due to measurement error. When this value is exceeded, there is a high probability that real change has occurred on that particular measure. The RCI is calculated using the *Standard Error of the Difference* (SE$_D$). The formula for the (SE$_D$) is

$$SE_D = \sqrt{2 * (SEM)^2},$$

(continued)

where SEM is the Standard Error of Measurement. The RCI is calculated by dividing the observed amount of change by the SE_D as follows:

$$RCI = \frac{(S_2 - S_1)}{SE_D},$$

S_1 = an examinee's initial test score and
S_2 = an examinee's score at retest on the same measure.

As one can see from inspection of the formulas, the RCI score is critically dependent on the test's standard error of measure. As such, the test's reliability becomes paramount when giving consideration to the value of a nominal change in scores.

The examiner can choose any of several confidence intervals by which to evaluate change using the RCI, although a 95% confidence interval is routinely used. In this case, scores falling outside a range of −1.96 to 1.96 would be expected to occur less than 5% of the time as a result of measurement error alone; hence, reliable change has likely occurred. If the examiner chooses a less stringent confidence interval of 90%, scores falling outside the range of −1.64 to 1.64 would represent a reliable change.

Table 13.7 provides an example of the use of the RCI to determine the likelihood that change has occurred. The score set in the table represents theoretical scores of a patient with mild head injury. The first column contains the patient's scores 3 months postinjury. The second column contains scores obtained 3 months later using the same five tests. Using the SEM for each test (third column), an RCI is calculated.

An initial inspection of the scores from baseline to follow-up showed nominally improved scores in four of the five tests and a lower score in one test. However, a closer perusal of the data utilizing the RCI value indicates that significant improvement occurred in only two tests. This example illustrates the importance of the relationship between a test's SEM and the RCI and the resultant effect this can have on the inferences made about score changes.

Many neuropsychologists still rely solely on clinical judgment and experience to determine whether change has occurred. However, the use of the RCI and similar statistical analyses provides a more psychometrically sound approach to adequately answer questions regarding change of function across time. This approach has become more widely utilized as neuropsychological assessment continues to progress.

13.5.3 Premorbid Ability

In order to make inferences regarding loss and/or preserved functions, some understanding of the patient's function prior to the condition or injury must be obtained. This preinjury status is often referred to as premorbid ability or premorbid function,

Table 13.7 Determining change in test scores using the Reliable Change Index (RCI)

Test	Baseline	Follow-up	SEM	RCI
Test 1	81	93	3.2	2.65*
Test 2	77	85	3.8	1.49
Test 3	106	99	3.5	−1.41
Test 4	84	90	3.8	1.12
Test 5	91	101	2.8	2.53*

Note. * indicates a significant change at the 95% confidence interval based on the RCI value outside the range of −1.96 and 1.96

meaning that it is a state of function prior to onset of the disease or injury. While this may not be an especially useful concept in all neuropsychological evaluations (e.g., a learning disability evaluation), it is often a critical element when a significant change of cognitive status is suspected. Because previous neuropsychological scores are often unavailable, premorbid functioning must be inferred or estimated. While all neuropsychologists view an understanding of premorbid ability as critical for the evaluation process, there is no consensus regarding the best approach to ascertaining this. Most believe that a combination of methods probably provides the most accurate determination. In any case, any estimate of premorbid ability is primarily aimed at determining previous level of *global ability* and is less useful at determining an individual's previous level of function in more specific functional domains.

Demographic Estimation. One method used to estimate premorbid ability is to produce an estimate of global ability based on an examinee's demographics. For example, age, education, and race provide strong demographic predictions of intelligence quotient (IQ). Using these and other demographic predictors, regression equations and actuarial approaches can be used to give reasonable estimates of premorbid ability. This gives us some quantitative baseline from which to compare present scores. One example of this type of actuarial approach is the Barona Index (Barona, Reynolds, & Chastain, 1984). While this method provides a good baseline from which to draw inferences, there are two primary problems in relying too heavily on this method. The first problem entails the "fit" of the particular individual to the chosen demographic group. While actuarial data are very accurate in predicting group characteristics, there are a number of individuals whose scores would naturally fall toward the extremes of their group or who do not conform to the group characteristic for any number of reasons. For example, some highly intelligent people fail to graduate from high school for a wide variety of noncognitive reasons, and their premorbid ability would likely be significantly underestimated when utilizing this approach in isolation. The second problem of using a demographic approach is that the band of error it produces may be too wide to be useful. For example, knowing that an individual's premorbid IQ was likely between 85 and 105 may not be especially helpful in cases of mild traumatic brain injury. Still, this method provides a "yardstick" or general range of expectations that may be helpful in making inferences about present scores.

A second approach is to use current scores to estimate premorbid ability. One method is to utilize so-called "hold" tests (Wechsler, 1958) to obtain an estimate of previous level of function. "Hold" tests are those that are more resilient to brain damage and so may be helpful in providing an accurate estimate of function prior to injury. While Wechsler's original assumptions about the resiliency of some Wechsler subtests have been questioned (Crawford, Stewart, Cochrane, & Foulds, 1989; Russell, 1972), some cognitive tasks do seem to be relatively resistant to brain damage. For example, word reading tests have been employed to estimate premorbid global ability (National Adult Reading Test-Revised, NART-R; Wechsler Test of Adult Reading, WTAR) with some success. These tests are not designed to provide a comprehensive evaluation of reading. Rather, they test the examinee's capacity to pronounce a list of irregular words accurately. It has been found that the ability to pronounce irregular words is based on previous knowledge of the word and recognition of rules regarding their correct pronunciation. This ability is correlated with Full Scale IQ and is also usually well preserved after brain damage. These characteristics make this type of task an ideal hold measure that can be used to provide a reasonable estimate of premorbid ability.

13.5.4   Pattern Analysis

Another inferential model used in interpretation examines patterns of performance across tasks as a means of differentiating functional from dysfunctional neural systems. In this model, the neuropsychologist may examine intraindividual differences or asymmetry that is symptomatic of dysfunction. This type of approach enables the neuropsychologist to identify relative strengths as well as deficits; emphasis on a strength model for intervention planning is considered more efficacious than focusing only on deficits. Again, this is usually addressed in terms of anterior–posterior differences or left–right differences, rather than consideration of single scores, but it also may be done by comparison of abilities or domains of function that parallel the four quadrants.

13.5.5   Pathognomonic Signs

Another model of interpretation involves looking for, or identifying, what are called "*pathognomonic*" signs, from the Greek *pathos* "disease" and *gnomon* "indicator." In clinical neuropsychology, these signs may not be tied to

> A pathognomonic sign is the one that is highly indicative of brain damage or dysfunction.

a specific disorder, but rarely occur in the absence of brain dysfunction and so when present provide strong evidence for the presence of a cerebral dysfunction (Fennell & Bauer, 2009; Kaplan, 1988). A successful architect recovering from a TBI who can no longer draw an accurate copy of a simple figure exemplifies a pathognomonic sign of cognitive loss. Pathognomonic signs are not necessarily highly *sensitive* to the condition of interest but may have a very high *specificity* to the condition of interest. In other words, when the pathognomonic sign is present, the condition of interest may also exist. Another example of a pathognomonic sign for a specific disorder would be the relationship between the Trail Making Test and dementia. The Trail Making Test is one of the most commonly used neuropsychological tests. The second portion of the test, Trail B, consists of a connect-the-dot task whereby the patient alternatively connects numbers and letters in sequence. A vast majority of patients have no difficulty in completing this task, but the speed of completion usually provides some indication about cerebral integrity. However, individuals suffering from dementia often struggled to complete the task at all (Schmitt et al., 2010). For this population and others, task completion may serve as a highly specific pathognomonic sign for brain dysfunction.

13.6   Summary

In this chapter, we review key aspects and provide an introduction to neuropsychological assessment. Neuropsychology is the study of brain-behavior relationships, and clinical neuropsychology is the application of this knowledge to patient care. We note that even in light of recent advances in neuroimaging (e.g., SPECT, PET, and fMRI), neuropsychological testing remains the premier method of assessing brain-behavior relationships. We describe the issues in fixed versus flexible battery testing in clinical neuropsychology. The Halstead-Reitan Neuropsychological Battery and the Luria-Nebraska Neuropsychological Battery are the two most popular standardized neuropsychological batteries. In contrast, the Boston Process Approach (BPA) uses a flexible battery of neuropsychological, psychological, and developmental tests, which allows the clinician to select procedures appropriate for the specific referral question and client characteristics. We provide a review of memory assessment noting that memory complaints seem ubiquitous in nearly all cognitive disorders and use the TOMAL-2 as an example of a comprehensive measure of memory function, providing brief descriptions of the subtests.

We describe the process of neuropsychological assessment to include the referral process, review of records, clinical interviews, test selection, and test conditions. Referral sources for neuropsychologists continue to expand, and the types of different referrals were explored. The accumulation of data through a thorough review of previous records is a central aspect of assessment. The clinical interview provides the examiner with contextual information from which to draw accurate inferences. Common domains of an examinee's clinical history were presented. We explored the variables involved in test selection in detail. The importance of providing an appropriate environment for testing was discussed with a focus on the most commonly seen problems. We also present a case study of medication effects on neuropsychological assessment scores.

Clinical neuropsychological assessment is, at its essence, a process of deficit measurement in conjunction with the determination of normally functioning neuropsychological processes in the brain. Different approaches to the measurement of deficits are addressed. In the normative approach, a person's scores are compared with a normative population standard. In the idiographic approach, a person's scores are compared with some given expectation for that particular individual. This is most commonly seen when serial assessments are conducted with a patient, and change is observed over time. We present a model of change measurement known as the RCI (Jacobson & Truax, 1991). A patient's premorbid ability is a critical element in making determinations regarding change, and two different approaches to estimate premorbid ability are presented. We also discuss pattern analysis and the detection of pathognomonic signs as approaches to measure cognitive change.

References

Allen, D. N., Goldstein, G., & Seaton, B. E. (1997). Cognitive rehabilitation of chronic alcohol abusers. *Neuropsychology Review, 7*, 21–39.

Allen, D. N., & Woods, S. P. (Eds.). (2014). *Neuropsychological aspects of substance use disorders: Evidence based perspectives.* New York, NY: Oxford University Press.

Bakker, D. J., Fisk, J. L., & Strang, J. D. (1983). *Child neuropsychology.* New York, NY: Guilford Press.

Baron, I., Fennell, E., & Voeller, K. (1995). *Pediatric neuropsychology in the medical setting.* New York, NY: Oxford University Press.

Barona, A., Reynolds, C., & Chastain, R. (1984). A demographically based index of premorbid intelligence for the WAIS-R. *Journal of Consulting and Clinical Psychology, 52*(5), 885–887.

Conners, C. K. (2014). *Conners' continuous performance test* (3rd ed.). Toronto, Canada: Multi-Health Systems.

Crawford, J., Stewart, L., Cochrane, R., & Foulds, J. (1989). Estimating premorbid IQ from demographic variables: Regression equations derived from a UK sample. *British Journal of Clinical Psychology, 28*(3), 275–278.

Culbertson, W. C., & Zillmer, E. A. (2001). *Tower of London Drexel University.* Toronto, Canada: Multi-Health Systems.

Cullum, M. (1998). Neuropsychological assessment of adults. In C. R. Reynolds (Ed.), *Assessment, Vol. 4 of A. Bellack & M. Hersen (Eds.), Comprehensive clinical psychology* (pp. 303–348). Oxford, England: Elsevier Science.

Delis, D. C., Kramer, J. H., Kaplan, E., & Ober, B. A. (2000). *California verbal learning test* (2nd ed.). New York, NY: Psychological Corporation.

Fennell, E., & Bauer, R. (2009). Models of inference in evaluating brain-behavior relationships in children. In E. Fletcher-Janzen & C. R. Reynolds (Eds.), *Handbook of clinical child neuropsychology* (3rd ed., pp. 231–243). New York, NY: Springer Science + Business Media.

Gillberg, C. (1995). The prevalence of autism and autism spectrum disorders. In H. M. Koot & F. C. Verhulst (Eds.), *The epidemiology of child and adolescent psychopathology* (pp. 227–257). New York, NY: Oxford University Press.

Godwin-Austen, R., & Bendall, J. (1990). *The neurology of the elderly.* New York, NY: Springer-Verlag.

Golden, C. J. (1978). *Stroop color and word test: A manual for clinical and experimental uses.* Chicago, IL: Stoelting.

Golden, C. J. (1997). The Luria-Nebraska neuropsychological battery-children's revision. In C. R. Reynolds & E. Fletcher Janzen (Eds.), *Handbook of clinical child neuropsychology* (2nd ed., pp. 237–251). New York, NY: Plenum Press.

Golden, C. J., Purisch, A. D., & Hammeke, T. A. (1991). *Luria-Nebraska neuropsychological battery: Forms I and II (manual).* Los Angeles, CA: Western Psychological Services.

Goodglass, H., & Kaplan, E. (1983). *The assessment of aphasia and related disorders*. Philadelphia, PA: Lea and Febiger.

Goodglass, H., Kaplan, E., & Barresi, B. (2001). *Boston diagnostic aphasia examination* (3rd ed.). Philadelphia, PA: Lippincott Williams & Wilkins.

Greiffenstein, M., Baker, W., & Gola, T. (1994). Validation of malingered amnesia measures with a large clinical sample. *Psychological Assessment, 6(3)*, 218–224.

Gronwall, D. (1977). Paced auditory serial-addition task: A measure of recovery from concussion. *Perceptual and Motor Skills, 44*, 367–373.

Halstead, W. (1947). *Brain and intelligence: A quantitative study of the frontal lobes*. Chicago, IL: University of Chicago Press.

Heaton, R. K., Miller, S. W., Taylor, M. J., & Grant, I. (2004). *Revised comprehensive norms for an expanded Halstead-Reitan battery (norms, manual and computer program)*. Odessa, FL: Psychological Assessment Resources.

Hynd, G., & Obrzut, J. (1981). *Neuropsychological assessment of the school-aged child: Issues and procedures*. New York, NY: Grune & Stratton.

Jacobson, N., & Truax, P. (1991). Clinical significance: A statistical approach to defining meaningful change in psychotherapy research. *Journal of Consulting and Clinical Psychology, 59(1)*, 12–19.

Kaplan, E. (1988). A process approach to neuropsychological assessment. In T. Boll & B. K. Bryant (Eds.), *Clinical neuropsychology and brain function: Research, measurement, and practice*. Washington, DC: American Psychological Association.

Kaplan, E. (1990). The process approach to neuropsychological assessment of psychiatric patients. *Journal of Neuropsychiatry, 2(1)*, 72–87.

Kaplan, E., Goodglass, H., & Weintraub, S. (2001). *Boston naming test* (2nd ed.). Austin, TX: Pro-Ed.

Klove, H. (1963). Clinical neuropsychology. In E. M. Forster (Ed.), *The medical clinics of North America*. New York, NY: Saunders.

Koppitz, E. M. (1977). *The visual aural digit span test*. New York, NY: Grune & Stratton.

Lee, D., Reynolds, C., & Willson, V. (2003). Standardized test administration: Why bother? *Journal of Forensic Neuropsychology, 3(3)*, 55–81.

Luria, A. (1966). *Higher cortical functions in man* (B. Haigh, Trans.). New York, NY: Basic Books.

McCarthy, D. (1972). *McCarthy scales of children's abilities*. San Antonio, TX: Psychological Corporation.

Meyers, J. E., & Meyers, K. R. (1995). *Rey complex figure test and recognition trial*. Odessa, FL: Psychological Assessment Resources.

Nelson, H. E., & Willison, J. (1991). *National Adult Reading Test (Second Edition)*. London, England: GL Assessment.

Piaget, J. (1930). *The child's conception of physical causality*. New York, NY: Harcourt Brace.

Ramsay, M. C., & Reynolds, C. R. (1995). Separate digits tests: A brief history, a literature review, and re-examination of the factor structure of the Tests of Memory and Learning (TOMAL). *Neuropsychology Review, 5*, 151–171.

Randolph, C., Tierney, M. C., Mohr, E., & Chase, T. N. (1998). The Repeatable Battery for the Assessment of Neuropsychological Status (RBANS): Preliminary clinical validity. *Journal of Clinical and Experimental Neuropsychology, 20*, 310–319.

Raven, J., Raven, J. C., & Court, J. H. (1998). *Manual for Raven's Progressive Matrices and Vocabulary Scales. Section 1: General overview*. Oxford, England/San Antonio, TX: Oxford Psychologists Press/The Psychological Corporation.

Reitan, R. M. (1969). *Manual for administration of neuropsychological test batteries for adults and children*. Indianapolis, IN: Indiana University Medical Center.

Reitan, R. M., & Wolfson, D. (1985). *The Halstead-Reitan neuropsychological test battery*. Tucson, AZ: Neuropsychology Press.

Reitan, R. M., & Wolfson, D. (1993). *The Halstead-Reitan Neuropsychological Test Battery: Theory and clinical interpretation* (2nd ed.). Tucson, AZ: Neuropsychology Press.

Reynolds, C. (1997). Forward and backward memory span should not be combined for clinical analysis. *Archives of Clinical Neuropsychology, 12*, 29–40.

Reynolds, C., & Mayfield, J. (2005). Neuropsychological assessment in genetically linked neuro-developmental disorders. In S. Goldstein & C. R. Reynolds (Eds.), *Handbook of neurodevelopmental and genetic disorders in adults* (pp. 9–28). New York, NY: Guilford Press.

Reynolds, C. R. (2007). *Koppitz Developmental Scoring System for the Bender Gestalt Test (KOPPITZ-2)*. Austin, TX: Pro-Ed.

Reynolds, C. R. (2008). RTI, neuroscience, and sense: Chaos in the diagnosis and treatment of learning disabilities. In E. Fletcher-Janzen & C. R. Reynolds (Eds.), *Neuropsychological perspectives on learning disabilities in the era of RTI* (pp. 14–27). New York, NY: Wiley.

Reynolds, C. R. (2019). *Comprehensive Trail Making Test: Examiner's manual. (CTMT-2) Second Edition*. Austin, TX: Pro-Ed.

Reynolds, C. R., & Bigler, E. D. (1994). *Test of memory and learning*. Austin, TX: Pro-Ed.

Reynolds, C. R., & Fletcher-Janzen, E. (Eds.). (1997). *Handbook of clinical child neuropsychology* (2nd ed.). New York, NY: Plenum Press.

Reynolds, C. R., & Kamphaus, R. W. (2015). *Reynolds Intellectual Assessment Scales, Second Edition*. Lutz, FL: Psychological Assessment Resources.

Reynolds, C. R., & Voress, J. (2007). *Test of memory and learning-Second Edition (TOMAL-2)*. Austin, TX: Pro-Ed.

Roid, G. H. (2003). *Stanford-Binet Intelligence Scale-Fifth Edition*. Itasca, IL: Riverside.

Rourke, B. P., Bakker, D. I., Fisk, J. L., & Strang, J. D. (1983). *Child neuropsychology: An introduction to theory, research, and clinical practice*. New York, NY: Guilford Press.

Russell, E. (1972). WAIS factor analysis with brain-damaged subjects using criterion measures. *Journal of Consulting and Clinical Psychology, 39*(1), 133–139.

Rutland-Brown, W., Langlois, J. A., Thomas, K. E., & Xi, Y. L. (2006). Incidence of traumatic brain injury in the United States, 2003. *The Journal of Head Trauma Rehabilitation, 21*, 544–548.

Schmitt, A., Livingston, R., Smernoff, E., Reese, E., Hafer, D., & Harris, J. (2010). Factor analysis of the Repeatable Battery for the Assessment of Neuropsychological Status (RBANS) in a large sample of patients suspected of dementia. *Applied Neuropsychology, 17*(1), 8–17.

Schrank, F. A., Mather, N., & McGrew, K. S. (2014). *Woodcock-Johnson IV tests of achievement*. Rolling Meadows, IL: Riverside.

Sheslow, D., & Adams, W. (1990). *Wide range assessment of memory and learning*. Wilmington, DE: Jastak Associates.

Sheslow, D., & Adams, W. (2003). *Wide range assessment of memory and learning* (2nd ed.). Wilmington, DE: Jastak Associates.

Slick, D., Hopp, G., Strauss, E., & Fox, D. (1996). Effects of prior testing with the WAIS-R NI on subsequent retest with the WAIS-R. *Archives of Clinical Neuropsychology, 11*(2), 123–130.

Snyderman, M., & Rothman, S. (1987). Survey of expert opinion on intelligence and aptitude testing. *American Psychologist, 42*, 137–144.

Tombaugh, T. N. (1996). *The test of memory malingering*. Toronto, Canada: MultiHealth Systems.

Wechsler, D. (1958). *The measurement and appraisal of adult intelligence* (4th ed.). Baltimore, MD: Williams & Wilkins.

Wechsler, D. (2001). *Wechsler Test of Adult Reading: WTAR*. San Antonio, TX: The Psychological Corporation.

Wechsler, D. (2008). *Wechsler Adult Intelligence Scale* (4th ed.). San Antonio, TX: The Psychological Corporation.

White, R., & Rose, F. (1997). The Boston process approach: A brief history and current practice. In G. Goldstein & T. M. Incagnoli (Eds.), *Contemporary approaches to neuropsychological assessment* (pp. 171–211). New York, NY: Plenum Press.

Wilkinson, G. S., & Robertson, G. J. (2017). *Wide Range Achievement Test, Fifth Edition (WRAT5)*. Bloomington, MN: Pearson Inc.

Wilson, R. S., & Kaszniak, A. W. (1986). Longitudinal changes: Progressive idiopathic dementia. In L. W. Poon, T. Crook, K. L. Davis, C. Eisdorfer, & B. J. Gurland (Eds.), *Handbook for clinical memory assessment of older adults* (pp. 285–293). Washington, DC: American Psychological Association.

Recommended Reading

Lezak, M. D., Howieson, D. B., & Loring, D. W. (2004). *Neuropsychological assessment* (4th ed.). New York, NY: Oxford University Press.

Reynolds, C., & Fletcher-Janzen, E. (2009). *Handbook of clinical child neuropsychology* (3rd ed.). New York, NY: Springer Science + Business Media.

Reynolds, C. R. (1997). Postscripts on premorbid ability estimation: Conceptual addenda and a few words on alternative and conditional approaches. *Archives of Clinical Neuropsychology, 12*(8), 769–778.

Strauss, E., Sherman, E. M. S., & Spreen, O. (2006). *A compendium of neuropsychological tests: Administration, norms, and commentary* (3rd ed.). New York, NY: University of Oxford Press.

Forensic Applications of Psychological Assessment

14

The courts of our nation rely on science and the results of objective study. Psychology in the legal system has much to offer in understanding and evaluating states, traits, and extant behavior.

Abstract

A primary reason for the widespread use of psychological tests is the objectivity of the information they provide. When used and designed properly, tests provide objective standardized information about the skills, abilities, and competencies of individuals and so are important tools that help professionals make important decisions. An area where objectivity and fairness are of special importance is in the courtroom. Tests are used by forensic psychologists in a courtroom setting to help establish scientifically sound and objective opinions that can be used to inform a trial or legal hearing. This chapter provides an overview of psychological test use in criminal and civil forensic settings, including expert witness testimony, competency to stand trial, sentencing mitigation and severity, personal injury, divorce/custody, and other legal matters. It also discusses the use of third-party observers in forensic testing and the detection of malingering and other forms of dissimulation. A brief review of the *Daubert* standard is provided, which addresses the admissibility of testimony based on psychological testing.

Supplementary Information The online version of this chapter (https://doi.org/10.1007/978-3-030-59455-8_14) contains supplementary material, which is available to authorized users.

© Springer Nature Switzerland AG 2021
C. R. Reynolds et al., *Mastering Modern Psychological Testing*,
https://doi.org/10.1007/978-3-030-59455-8_14

Learning Objectives

After reading and studying this chapter, students should be able to:
1. Define forensic psychology and describe its major applications
2. Identify and define major terms and roles relevant to forensic psychology (e.g., expert witness, trier of fact)
3. Describe the role forensic assessments play in the court
4. Compare and contrast forensic with clinical assessment
5. Identify and describe major applications of forensic psychology in criminal cases
6. Discuss the special case of intellectual disability in capital sentencing
7. Identify and describe major applications of forensic psychology in civil cases
8. Describe and discuss the issue of third-party observers in forensic assessments
9. Describe the issue of malingering and other forms of dissimulation in forensic assessments
10. Discuss the issue of admissibility of testimony based on psychological tests results
11. Define and explain the importance of the *Daubert* challenge

Psychologists and others who use psychological tests are called into courtrooms to give expert testimony and their opinions are often based on the results of psychological tests. Since psychological tests provide objective, quantifiable data, results of psychological tests can be powerful and persuasive tools in adversarial legal proceeding. Hence, special rules apply to the forensic use of psychological tests not only within the profession of psychology but also in courtrooms themselves. There are federal and state rules that specify what constitutes admissible evidence in legal proceedings, as well as established case law including rulings from the United States Supreme Court that also speak directly to the admissibility of expert opinions based on quantifiable data such as the data obtained from psychological testing. In this chapter, we review the application of psychological tests to a variety of forensic issues and discuss the special rules of the profession as well as the laws regarding admissibility of opinions derived from psychological tests as evidence.

---

[1] Dr. Milam has evaluated defendants and testified at more than 30 Capital Murder Trials and numerous lesser crimes. She has performed more than 5000 evaluations for Child Protective Services and testifies often in these hearings. In addition, she provides risk assessments for sex offenders and performs competency to stand trial evaluations. She is a licensed psychologist and board certified in clinical neuropsychology.

14.1   What Is Forensic Psychology?

Broadly conceived, *forensic psychology* is the application of psychological principles, techniques, and procedures to the understanding of the law, legal proceedings, and legislative processes and the application of psychology to any ongoing legal proceeding such as a trial, administrative law hearing, and legal arbitration and mediation. Forensic psychology is not just

> Forensic psychology is the application of psychology to the understanding of the law and the application of psychological principles to a legal proceeding.

applicable for criminal matters (e.g., evaluating the psychological fitness of a defendant); it is equally if not more applicable to civil matters (e.g., in establishing the impact an adverse event has had on a plaintiff). Forensic psychology has a long history in the courts of the United States as well as in other countries. The American Psychology-Law Society, which is Division 41 of the American Psychological Association (APA), provides information for the public as well as psychologists, attorneys, and educators about forensic psychology generally as well as providing some guidelines for ethical practice in forensic psychology (e.g., see *Specialty Guidelines for Forensic Psychology*, 2013). Although many psychologists are involved in forensic activities at some time in their career, some psychologists specialize in forensic psychology. The American Board of Forensic Psychology (ABFP), on the basis of a psychologist's education, experience, and postdoctoral training as well as through a specialized examination, grants diplomate status in forensic psychology. The primary objective of the ABFP diplomate process is to recognize, certify, and promote competence in forensic psychology and to give notice to the public of practitioners who have passed such peer review and examination. Such a specialty certification is not required to practice forensic psychology, but does serve as additional evidence of one's qualifications as well as lending credibility to the existence of forensic psychology as a professional subspecialty in the broader discipline of psychology.

Psychological tests are used by forensic psychologists to assist them in forming scientifically sound and objective opinions. Therefore, in nearly all instances of courtroom and related proceedings, psychological testing becomes useful. Entire books, longer than this textbook, have been written just on the use of psychological tests in forensic psychology (e.g., Melton, Petrila, Poythress, & Slobogin, 2007). This chapter will be of necessity less than comprehensive but will introduce you to the world of psychological testing applications in forensic psychology. Special Interest Topic 14.1 presents one forensic psychologist's rational for using psychological tests in capital cases, divorce and child custody cases, and other areas of forensic practice.

> Psychological tests are used by forensic psychologists to assist them in forming scientifically sound and objective opinions.

Special Interest Topic 14.1: Why I Use Psychological and Neuropsychological Tests in Criminal Forensic Practice

Daneen Milam,[1] PhD, ABN

Forensic Psychology is a professional specialty within psychology that requires a strong ego willing to defend a position in a court of law, the willingness to spend hours with individuals who have done terrible things, and the ability to keep an open mind. At the end of the day, the third requirement is the hardest. Many professionals perform "evaluations" that are clearly just interviews. They review the facts of a crime, speak to a prisoner who "has an attitude problem" (e.g., is angry at the system that has incarcerated him, feels he is being treated unfairly or is being singled out for punishment), has a long history of skirmishes with the law, or has a radically different life experience and background from the examiner, or all of the above, and make a diagnosis or arrive at other life changing opinions regarding the defendant. Research shows that these decisions are as often wrong as they are right, but the mental-health professional is very confident of the opinion. In fact, extremely high levels of confidence and premature closure in diagnosis or the formation of opinions have been found to be predictive of high error rates in clinical diagnosis. As of this writing, over one hundred prisoners on death row have been exonerated using new DNA analyses and evidence. Each and every one was evaluated by a clinician who gave that prisoner a diagnosis and was very, very sure they were right—as was the sentencing jury. It is estimated that the incidence of Antisocial Personality Disorder (ASPD) occurs in a prison population 25% of the time, but it is diagnosed 80% of the time when the evaluation consists of a review of the records and a clinical interview. It all boils down to the concept that if the prisoner is scary looking, rude, and has a history of disrespect for the law or authority, they are ASPD and if a prisoner is ASPD, he is a lost cause, beyond redemption, and probably guilty and deserving of whatever punishment is forthcoming.

Standardized testing helps us side step this "very wrong but very sure" dilemma. Standardized tests give objective estimates of a variety of cognitive and affective factors that are important to the formation of supportable opinions. They quantify behavior and compare it with known base rates of responding in the general population—base rates often misconstrued and underestimated via clinical experience. After giving thousands of tests, I am often surprised. I find supposedly intellectually disabled individuals who are well within normal limits but are basically illiterate instead. I find intellectually disabled or brain injured defendants who can "pass for normal" using street skills. I find emotionally blunted, inarticulate individuals who have been diagnosed oppositional defiant disorder, and I find very bright, very articulate, and charming individuals who are genuinely ASPD. Stereotypes don't work; testing does. The clinicians who use "clinical experience" instead of hard data often mock extensive data gathering in forensic practice, but I live by the adage in the title to an article written by one of the authors of this text, Cecil Reynolds, and published in 1984: "In God we trust; all others must have data."

14.2   Expert Witnesses and Expert Testimony

There is much confusion in the lay public about an expert who testifies in court. Often, the public thinks of an expert as one who possesses very highly specialized knowledge above and beyond that of others in the same field of study or expertise—a person at the pinnacle of knowledge and skills in an area of science. This is a misconception—in fact, the ethical principles of psychologists prohibit them from making claims of specialized expertise that is unavailable to other psychologists or as having special knowledge or skills other psychologists cannot learn or master. The rules of evidence in federal and state courts define who is an expert. These rules will vary somewhat from one legal jurisdiction to another, but, in general, a person qualified as an *expert* in a legal proceeding (hereinafter just referred to as an expert) is a person who by reason of education, training, and experience possesses knowledge and expertise necessary to assist the *trier of fact* in a case in understanding some important issue before the court. Generally, this is an issue that requires more than common sense or logical reasoning to understand and relate to the case under consideration by the court. If it were a matter of common sense, no expert would be required. The burden of proving someone is an expert falls on the party that offers the testimony to the court. What is required then is that the offering party establishes that the expert has knowledge, skill, experience, training, or education regarding the specific issue before the court, which would qualify the expert to give an opinion on that specific subject. The trier of fact in a courtroom is the entity that makes the ultimate decision in a case and is either the judge (in a trial before the court, often referred to as a TBC) or a jury.

> An expert witness is a person who possesses knowledge and expertise necessary to assist the trier of fact in understanding some important issue before the court.

> A fact witness is a person with personal knowledge of the facts of a case.

> The trier of fact in a courtroom is the entity that makes the ultimate decision in a case (i.e., either the judge or a jury).

Expert witnesses play a unique role and are different from fact witnesses. Expert witnesses, regardless of who hires them, play their primary role in the objective presentation of information to the court to assist the court, not a predetermined party to the case. The expert should advocate for the objective interpretation and understanding of the data on which opinions are based. Given this role, it should be easy to see why psychological tests, which quantify behavior and constructs, commonly are used to provide a significant component of the expert's database and methods for reaching a particular conclusion. In practice, pure objectivity can be difficult to maintain due to client pressures and competing interests that occur during legal proceedings, which are adversarial by design. Forensic psychologists and those playing in such a role are held accountable for their testimony not just by the court but also by the profession. Most state licensing boards have rules of practice that deal with the practice of forensic psychology in a variety of ways. The ethical principles of psychologists espoused by state and national organizations such as the APA and the specialty guidelines for forensic psychologists noted above govern the behavior of forensic psychologists as well.

Later, we discuss some additional concepts that aid in understanding the role and applications of psychological tests in the courtroom such as credibility of experts and also the admissibility of their testimony—which are separate issues. Three important U.S. Supreme Court cases govern the admissibility of such testimony in the federal court system, and many states have similar rules.

14.3   Clinical Assessment Versus Forensic Assessment

Assessments conducted in clinical settings designed for purposes of diagnosis, clarification of a patient's condition, and the development of appropriate treatment plans are quite different in many respects from forensic assessments. Foremost is the circumstance of the assessment and conditions under which it is conducted. In the typical clinical assessment, participation is entirely voluntary. Someone has been referred to us or comes on their own to seek help with some life issue that involves a mental-health diagnosis—or to rule out such an issue. The assessment results are confidential and can be released to no one else without the written consent of the person (or if a minor, the parent, etc.) except in very special circumstances. As an example, one special circumstance would be if an assessment were to reveal the abuse of a child or an elderly person; in this scenario, most states have laws requiring psychologists to breach confidentiality and make a mandatory report to law enforcement. The clinical assessment is conducted in comfortable surroundings, in a quiet setting, and designed to elicit a person's best performance. The intent of the assessment is to assist the person in treatment of a condition or in resolving some important issue in their life.

In a forensic assessment, these circumstances can and most often do vary tremendously. While some assessments in civil proceedings can come close to mimicking those of the clinical assessment, there will always remain significant differences, and in criminal proceedings, the differences are substantial in all instances. This is because the purpose of a forensic assessment is to provide objective data and unbiased opinions to the court and to assist the court in understanding the issues before the court. As you can see, this is a very different purpose from a clinical assessment! Participation in the forensic assessment, while technically always voluntary, is not voluntary from a practical perspective in many instances. In a civil case related to a brain injury, for example, the plaintiffs may introduce evidence of neuropsychological injury based on a comprehensive assessment by their retained expert. One of the authors of this text (CRR) recalls vividly a suit for damage over an alleged brain injury that was dropped by the plaintiff when she learned that her prior psychiatric history had been

> In a forensic assessment, the purpose of the assessment is to provide objective data and unbiased opinions to the court and to assist the court in understanding the issues before the court.

ordered revealed by the judge, would be the subject of testimony to the jury, and could become part of the public record of the case if it went to trial. In nearly all cases, the defense will be allowed by the court to conduct their own examination with the expert of their choice. While the court lacks the authority to compel participation by the plaintiff in the defense examination, when the court orders such an examination and the plaintiff refuses, the court will often refuse to allow the plaintiff to introduce any evidence of the injury from their own expert. So while the plaintiff's participation can be seen as voluntary—is it really?

Consider a criminal proceeding where the defendant enters a plea of not guilty by reason of insanity and produces a report from a psychologist arguing in favor of such a finding. The prosecution is, in most states, allowed to obtain their own examination from an expert of its choosing to report to the court also. As in the civil case, the defendant may choose not to participate and the court cannot force participation, but the court may and in most cases would disallow any evidence from the defense examination to be heard by the jury. These issues of confidentiality and voluntariness hold true even in dire forensic examinations such as sentencing in death penalty cases. When the defense presents evidence of a lack of future dangerousness, for example, from an examination conducted by a defense mental-health expert, the state is entitled to its own examination from an expert of its choosing. It is difficult to conceptualize such examinations as voluntary, which greatly alters the dynamic of the assessment. Nor are the results subject to the customary rules of confidentiality. Results are presented in an open courtroom to a judge or jury and often become part of a public record available to anyone, with some exceptions (i.e., under special conditions, judges can seal such records and testimony).

In criminal cases, examinations may also be conducted in jails or prison settings where the conditions are less than optimal. In some settings, examinations are conducted through a glass partition with a telephone connection between the examiner and examinee. This precludes certain types of assessments altogether. Even contact examinations are often conducted in rooms poorly designed for such exams and at times with guards observing. In the sparse, steel, and concrete environment of some jail examination rooms, the echoes of test items spoken by the examiner can be distracting and confounding when memory testing is being conducted and when auditory tests of attention are used. This may require modifications of the examiner's choice of measures and lessen the usefulness of the assessment. We have encountered cases personally where it was necessary to obtain court orders to force prison wardens to remove handcuffs of examinees, and so they could adequately participate in neuropsychological examinations.

When an expert who is adverse to the position of the examinee in a forensic matter conducts an exam, it is not unusual to encounter an examinee that is hostile or curt, confrontational, guarded in responding, or who may practice dissimulation (i.e., a response set presenting a false picture of one's status). Even more insidious is the issue of attorney coaching of clients.

> It has been suspected that attorneys obtain access to various psychological tests and then coach their clients on how to answer or respond, and so the testing results favor their desired outcome.

While it is clearly unethical and perhaps even illegal, it has been suspected for decades by forensic psychologists that attorneys obtain access to various psychological tests and then coach their clients on how to answer or respond, and so the testing results favor the attorney's desired outcome. It is difficult to prove such nefarious deeds without the cooperation of the attorney's client (which is typically not in their best interest!), but nevertheless, there are clear confirmations of attorney coaching in forensic settings (e.g., see Youngjohn, 1995). In contrast, in a clinical assessment in the examiner's office where someone has come for help with a significant life issue, examinees are more likely to be forthcoming and desirous of the examiner achieving an accurate and full understanding of their life, personality structure, and cognitive skills. They partner with the examiner in achieving these goals rather than viewing the examiner as antagonistic to their goals, as often occurs in adverse forensic assessments.

Melton, Petrila, Poythress, and Slobogin (1997) have summarized the issues involved in clinical versus forensic assessments. Some of these issues include factors such as the scope of the assessment, the importance of the client's perspective, the voluntariness of the assessment, the autonomy of the assessment objectives and procedures, threats to the validity of assessment performance and interpretation, the relationship between the client and professional doing the testing, and the pace and setting of the assessment.

We have not reviewed all of the issues here nor attempted to explain all of the complexities. We do provide recommended readings at the end of this chapter for those interested in more detailed coverage of these matters.

14.4 Applications in Criminal Proceedings

Forensic psychology has many applications in criminal matters, and it is worth noting that the rules under which psychologists operate are different in some ways from those in civil proceedings, though there are more similarities than differences. There is both logical and technical overlap between criminal and civil proceedings. For example, a person accused of a criminal act may be evaluated to determine if they are competent to stand trial for the alleged crime. While technically such a competency proceeding is a civil matter, a mix of criminal and civil standards and rules ends up being applied to such cases. We will discuss such competencies where they seem to fit best overall. A list of examples of the many forms of competency that can be the subject of legal decisions is given in Table 14.1. We will not discuss all of these but will review some of the more common examples. We also cannot provide a review of all criminal forensic applications of psychological tests here, but will review the major applications.

Table 14.1 Examples of types of competency evaluations where psychological tests are often used

- Competency to manage one's affairs (e.g., managing finances, making day-to-day decisions, seeking treatment, etc.)
- Testamentary capacity (i.e., competency to make and execute a will)
- Competency to make medical decisions
- Competency to consent to research
- Competency of a juvenile to be tried as an adult
- Competency to stand trial (adult)
- Competency to waive counsel at trial
- Competency to enter a plea
- Competency to waive rights (including issues such as consent to search and seizure, right to remain silent, right to an attorney, etc.)
- Competency to confess
- Competency to give testimony
- Competency to waive appeals
- Competency to be executed

14.4.1 Not Guilty by Reason of Insanity: The NGRI Defense

One of the most widely known and likely the most controversial arenas wherein psychological tests are likely to be used in forensic settings is in the *not guilty by reason of insanity (NGRI) defense*. This defense is controversial not only among the general public but also among lawmakers, lawyers, judges, and many professionals. As we will note often in this chapter, the criteria for an NGRI verdict from a jury will differ from state-to-state, but the most

> One of the most widely known and likely the most controversial arenas wherein psychological tests are likely to be used in forensic settings is in the not guilty by reason of insanity (NGRI) defense.

common is that the jury must determine that at the time of the offense, the defendant, by reason of mental illness or mental defect, did not know his conduct was wrong. In some states, an additional clause may be added that allows such a finding if, for similar reasons, the defendant was unable to conform his conduct to the requirements of the law. The fundamental premise of public policy and jurisprudence on this issue is that a person who did not understand what he was doing or was unable to control his behavior because of reasons beyond his control should not be held culpable for a crime. Additionally, punishing such a person via criminal sanctions does not act as a deterrent to future criminal acts. It is also important to understand that the NGRI defense excludes what is commonly known as voluntary intoxication from consideration. So, if a defendant was heavily intoxicated from alcohol ingestion and committed a crime unknowingly and even has no recall of it, the state of intoxication cannot be used to form an NGRI defense.

The frequency with which this plea is entered by criminal defendants is grossly overestimated by the general public, and its success rate is overestimated as well. It is in fact a relatively infrequent plea, and most who enters it loses. Studies of public perception reviewed by Lilienfeld, Lynn, Ruscio, and Beyerstein (2010) indicate that the average member of the general public believes that this defense is used in 37% of felony criminal trials and is successful in nearly half (44%) of these cases. Legislators, who should be more informed, estimate poorly as well, believing that 21% of cases have an NGRI defense and of these, 40% are successful. The actual data show that the NGRI defense is used in less than 1% of felony criminal cases and is successful in only about 25% of these cases. Some quick math $(0.01 \times 0.25 = 0.0025)$ indicates then that less than 3 felony cases per thousand end in a verdict of NGRI. Most people also believe that following such a verdict, the person goes free. This is also a myth. Most are committed indefinitely to a mental-- health facility, and, in most states, if the crime involved violence, they must be committed to a forensic mental-health facility. This sometimes results in a person being housed in a mental-health facility longer than the maximum prison term for the original criminal charge that was the basis for the NGRI verdict!

Typically, when a defendant notifies the court of a plea of NGRI, the defense and the prosecution each obtain independent evaluations of the defendant's mental health and related issues in the case. These evaluations are most often done by a psychologist, a psychiatrist, or both. In addition to a clinical interview and a review of case records and the defendant's mental-health history, psychological testing is often used to obtain objective data regarding the defendant's cognitive and emotional state. Cognitive status can be important in such cases, and intelligence tests and neuropsychological measures of the integrity of brain functions may be useful in some cases. Personality scales are often administered, especially when defendants are thought to have a chronic mental illness such as schizophrenia that may have impaired their perceptions of reality.

14.4.2 Competency to Stand Trial

Competency to stand trial is one of the most common situations where a psychologist may use testing to assist in deriving an opinion within the criminal justice system. Although definitions and laws vary from state-to-state and in the federal system (this caveat is true in many aspects of our discussions and not always repeated), in general, a person is not competent to stand trial if by reason of mental illness or

> Competency to stand trial is one of the most common situations where a psychologist may assist in deriving an opinion within the criminal justice system.

mental defect, they do not have a rational and factual understanding of the charges and proceedings against them or are unable to assist their attorney in the preparation of a defense. Defendants are assumed competent when they appear in the criminal justice system. When it is claimed that defendants are incompetent to stand trial, the defendants and their counsels must raise the issue with court and then present enough evidence to convince the trier of the fact that they are in fact not competent to stand trial. The trier of fact in these situations varies based on state law. In some states, only a jury can find a person incompetent to stand trial, while in others, a judge or jury can be elected to make this determination.

As you can see, simple ignorance is insufficient to make a defendant incompetent to stand trial since the issue is determined in part by whether the defendant has mental illness or mental defect. Following an interview in which defendants are asked to explain the charges and proceedings against them and questioned about matters relevant to helping with their defense, a psychologist may have enough information to reasonably conclude a defendant is or is not competent to stand trial. In these cases, psychological testing may not be necessary or useful. It is not enough for defendants to remember the name and role of their attorney and have rote recall of the charges against them and the associated potential penalties—defendants must evidence a reasonable understanding of the charges and proceedings. For example, such an understanding might include knowing the charges and their implications for punishment, how a plea might be arranged and function, the roles of the judge, jury, and prosecutor, and the ability to understand and appraise legal advice as it applies to the specific case, to assist the attorney in choosing jurors, to follow testimony of witnesses at trial, to assess and notify defense counsel about errors in testimony and assist in developing questions, to tolerate the stress of a trial, and to maintain appropriate behavior in the courtroom. While this may require only minimal skills in some trials, in others, such as death penalty litigation, the requirements placed on the defendant's cognitive abilities may be far greater. A person competent to stand trial for shoplifting a $25.00 item from a store could be found incompetent to stand trial for the death penalty in a complex robbery/murder trial in which jury selection might last more than 2 weeks and a complex trial may take several more weeks.

If, however, the psychologist determines that the defendant does not possess the qualities of a person "competent to stand trial," then psychological testing is more likely and useful, since in a legal proceeding, the reason why the defendant cannot perform these functions is relevant to a legal finding of incompetency. In such determinations, psychologists often use intelligence tests or related measures of logic and reasoning, along with measures of verbal comprehension, listening comprehension, perceptual distortion, and attention and memory (among others) to examine cognitive factors that may impair the defendant's ability to understand the charges and proceedings as well as assist their attorney. Neuropsychological testing is common in such circumstances since defendants who are raising the issue of competency often have a history of central nervous system damage or illness (e.g., traumatic brain injury, stroke, seizure disorders, meningitis, or even dementias such as Alzheimer's or Korsakoff's Disease). When mental illnesses such as schizophrenia, schizoaffective disorder, bipolar disorder, or others are at issue, personality tests are often used as well. Clinical interviews are also used heavily, but are almost always supplemented by objective test data since the objective data can provide an unbiased quantitative perspective on the issues before the court.

14.4.3 Transfer of a Juvenile to Adult Criminal Court

There is also overlap between criminal and civil proceedings when a juvenile is tried in an adult criminal court. In many states, a juvenile who has been detained for committing an act that would be a crime for an adult is subjected to a *juvenile court*, which is technically a civil, not a criminal proceeding. The reasons for this are many but center around the lesser maturity, comprehension, and understanding of a juve-

> All states have means by which the state can petition the juvenile court to transfer the juvenile to the adult criminal court system.

nile versus an adult and the greater belief in rehabilitation at these younger ages. However, all states have means by which the state can petition the juvenile court to transfer the juvenile to the adult criminal court. If this transfer is approved, the juvenile is treated as would an adult in the criminal justice system. Juvenile judges have great latitude in making such decisions but nearly always request psychological evaluations to examine the cognitive, emotional, and moral maturity of the juvenile. While the nature of the crime is usually an important deciding factor, results of psychological testing are often critical in answering key questions required to make this decision. Does a juvenile possess an adequate understanding of the charges and the nature of the criminal justice system and have the ability to assist counsel in an adult criminal proceeding? Does the juvenile in question have greater or lesser intelligence and cognitive understanding in general than other juveniles? Is the juvenile in question amenable to treatments available in the community or in the juvenile justice system or are the programs available to the adult court more appropriate?

In addition to a review of the juvenile's life history, school performance, and any history of mental-health interventions, psychological testing can provide objective evidence of levels of intellectual functioning as well as emotional development. Responses to treatment can be predicted, though less well than many other variables, by psychological testing as well. These scores and predictions are unencumbered by the emotional pull of sympathy for adolescents that is natural to most of us and assist the court in reaching a decision that is in the best interest of the juvenile and in the best interests of society—interests that judges work hard to balance in such cases.

14.4.4 Mitigation in Sentencing

Many individuals who come before the courts for sentencing following a criminal conviction have had difficult life circumstances. In looking for factors that a jury or a judge might consider mitigating, psychologists are often involved in reviewing the life of the individual, prior mental-health records, and conducting objective examinations to determine their current mental-health

> In mitigation, the primary concern is whether circumstances exist in the individual's life that lessen his or her moral culpability for the crime committed.

status. In mitigation, the primary concern is whether circumstances exist in the individual's life that lessen their moral culpability for the crime committed. For example, an 18-year-old male with a frontal lobe injury that causes extremely impulsive behaviors and failure to consider its consequences commits a robbery on the spur of the moment. This individual might be viewed less harshly in punishment than a person who is neuropsychologically intact, who carefully planned and carried out a robbery, and perhaps even enlisted the aid of others to commit the crime. Or consider the real case of a Vietnam veteran who assaulted an employer that he thought cheated him on his wages. He was convicted of assault but during the punishment hearing, the court was presented with information from the veteran's medical records that clearly documented a brain injury suffered in combat and the results of a comprehensive neuropsychological examination revealed severe cognitive impairment consistent with the brain injury. Based on consideration of these mitigating factors, the court decided to impose the minimum sentence allowed for the assault charge. Finally, consider the case in Texas of a brain-injured teenaged girl whose drug dealer boyfriend took her with him to meet a customer. The drug dealer decided to rob the customer and but ended up killing him when the customer resisted. As an accomplice, she was indicted for capital murder along with her boyfriend. Her diminished mental state, documented through comprehensive psychological testing, was considered by the court and the prosecution, who subsequently charged her with a lesser crime and sentenced her to far fewer years in prison than the older boyfriend.

Nowhere in the criminal justice system is such evidence as important as in capital felony or death penalty cases. Although the criteria for imposing the death penalty on a person convicted of a capital felony differ across states, most require three findings from a jury in order to impose a death sentence, broadly stated here as: (1) there was an intent to do harm, (2) if not executed, the defendant will represent a continuing threat of violence or harm to society, and (3) when the defendant's life as a whole is considered, there are no circumstances that warrant mercy from the court. These criteria make the presentation of psychological expert testimony common in virtually all capital felony cases.

Psychological tests are used along with actuarial investigations to ascertain the probability of future violence. Predicting whether someone is a continuing threat or harm to society once imprisoned for life is a precarious enterprise at best. Nevertheless, measures of moral understanding, character, personality, neuropsychological status, as well as the history of prior violent acts and the context in which they occurred can be informative to the jury in reaching a difficult decision. Mitigation testimony is also presented in nearly all such cases.

Mitigation testimony in sentencing hearing for capital felonies essentially recounts the life story of the defendant to the jury and notes special circumstances (i.e., out of the ordinary features) of the person's life that can be related to the crime. Issues such as abuse and neglect of the defendant as a child, use of alcohol or drugs by the mother during the pregnancy, history of traumatic brain injury, and mental illness are all potentially relevant and common factors. Fetal alcohol spectrum disorders are not uncommon among capital felony defendants, but their effects on the brain and behavior are highly variable and must be determined and documented. It has been estimated that between 50% and 80% of death penalty defendants have a documented history of brain injury (Reynolds, Price, & Niland, 2004). Psychological testing is often used to document the effects of any potentially mitigating factors on the defendant's behavior. It is rarely enough that such factors are present—their effects on the defendant's behavior must be determined and these effects must then be shown to relate to the crime.

14.4.5 The Special Case of Intellectual Disability in Capital Sentencing

In a landmark decision in 2002 (Atkins v. Virginia, 122 S.Ct. 2242), the US Supreme Court outlawed the execution of persons with intellectual disability (referred to as *mental retardation* in the decision) as a violation of the U.S. Constitutional provisions against cruel and unusual punishment. This ruling essentially declared intellectual disability a mandatory mitigating factor that excludes a defendant from eligibility for the death penalty. This decision was lauded by the mental-health and intellectual disability communities. Although other factors were considered important, the crux of the decision relied upon the diminished moral culpability of persons with intellectual disability as related to their diminished mental capacities. Judge Stevens, writing for the majority of justices, indicated that individuals with intellectual disability have diminished mental capacity to:

> The U.S. Supreme Court outlawed the execution of persons with intellectual disability as a violation of constitutional provisions against cruel and unusual punishment.

1. understand and process information;
2. communicate;
3. abstract from mistakes and learn from experience;
4. engage in logical reasoning;
5. control impulses;
6. understand other's reactions.

This has resulted in much post hoc litigation concerning inmates on death row convicted prior to the *Atkins* decision who are now raising intellectual disability as a mitigating factor in their appeals. Accurate and objective psychological testing is especially crucial in *Atkins* intellectual disability claims.

Psychological and especially neuropsychological testing can assess the functional capacity or skill levels of individuals raising the *Atkins* defense in each of the areas listed by Judge Stevens. Moreover, the definition of intellectual disability that is most commonly applied in the United States is a psychometric one to a large extent. A diagnosis of intellectual disability requires that a person scores two or more standard deviations below the mean on an individually administered test of intelligence and evidence significant deficits in adaptive behavior, both of which must occur during the developmental period (defined somewhat arbitrarily as before 18 years of age). Not to be overly dramatic, but in this situation, accurate, objective psychological test results are in fact a life-and-death matter and should be strongly preferred over clinical experience or anecdotal evidence. Special Interest Topic 14.2 further considers the Supreme Court's decision in Atkins v. Virginia in the context of the Flynn effect.

Special Interest Topic 14.2: The Flynn Correction in Death Penalty Litigation: An Advocacy Perspective

Since the Supreme Court's decision in *Atkins v. Virginia* (536 US 304, 122 S.Ct. 2242, 2002) established that the execution of persons with an intellectual disability violates the Eighth Amendment's prohibition against cruel and unusual punishment, the importance of understanding and assessing intellectual disability in criminal defendants has become critical—literally a matter of life-and-death—in capital felony cases. Determining whether a defendant's intellectual functioning is severely limited is essential to a judgment as to whether that individual is able to act with the level of moral culpability that merits particular forms of punishment. As the most common measures of intellectual functioning, IQ tests are one of the two primary indicia of intellectual disability.

IQ tests are periodically revised and renormed to keep the content appropriate to current cultural contexts, ensure the representativeness of the normative or reference group (characteristics of the target population are constantly changing), and maintain an average IQ score of 100. The findings associated with these periodic revisions led researchers to observe that scores on standardized measures of intelligence have steadily risen over the last century, a phenomenon termed the Flynn Effect, which we discussed in Chap. 3. The Flynn Effect, whatever its cause, is as real as virtually any effect in the social sciences. Numerous studies report an increase of 0.3 IQ points per year on average; thus, in order for a test score to reflect accurately the examinee's intelligence, 0.3 points must be subtracted (the Flynn Correction) for each year since the test was standardized. Since the Flynn Effect's increased scientific acceptance in the 1990s, it has become one of the reasons why IQ tests have been revised and renormed more frequently than in the past, typically occurring on a 10–11 year schedule now as opposed to a 20 or more year schedule in the past. Even so, the Flynn Effect is observable in the years between revisions and is certainly relevant where outdated test versions are used—especially where even 2 or 3 IQ points may determine whether a defendant is allowed to live or is executed.

Because of the central role IQ tests play in determining an individual's level of intellectual disability and because of the importance of intellectual disability in determining a defendant's eligibility to be killed by the State, it is imperative that the Flynn Effect is taken into account in capital cases. IQ ranges that indicate intellectual disability are determined relative to the average score (which has been set by convention, albeit arbitrarily, at 100). The so-called average score is derived from a reference group, which is a snapshot of the population at one particular point in time. The determination of the intelligence component of the diagnosis of intellectual disability should be based on the person's standing relative to the target population at the time the person was actually tested, not the target population when the test was normed. (We do recognize that the actual diagnosis is far more complex than looking at an IQ score—but the IQ is a

(continued)

crucial component, and we deal only with it here.) Since it is at this time a practical impossibility to renorm tests annually to maintain a more appropriate reference group, to the extent corrections are available and valid, they should be applied to obtain scores, and so the most accurate IQ estimate is obtained. To do less is to do wrong—what possible justification could there be for issuing estimates of general intelligence in a death penalty case that are less than the most accurate estimates obtainable? The admonishments of the U. S. Supreme Court in multiple cases over many decades, where death penalty cases require special attention to accuracy, apply an even more profound legal argument to applying this correction.

In criminal proceedings, the law's primary concern is that justice is meted according to the procedures and guarantees contained in the federal and state constitutions. These constitutional concerns, as well as the need for accuracy, are at their highest when the death penalty is at issue. The highest court in this country has made the determination that executing persons with intellectual disability violates the Eighth Amendment's prohibition against cruel and unusual punishment. As a generally accepted scientific theory that could potentially make the difference between a constitutional and unconstitutional execution, the Flynn Correction must be applied in the legal context. Those who oppose the Flynn correction must dispute the scientific validity of the Flynn Effect, yet we see no such serious challenges—the remaining issue seems to be why the Flynn effect occurs, a debate that is irrelevant to whether it should be used to correct scores. If the Flynn Effect is real, and we believe it is, the failure to apply the Flynn Correction as we have described can have tragic outcomes. No one's life should depend upon when an IQ test was normed.

This view is in fact controversial. What are your views on the issue? Should the Flynn Correction be applied in death penalty cases or other criminal proceedings where level of cognitive functioning might be relevant to mitigation of punishment? Reynolds, Niland, Wright, and Rosenn (2010) provide an example of how the Flynn Correction would be applied in individual cases.

14.4.6 Competency to Be Executed

Most states have laws regarding punishment of individuals convicted of a crime and allow an exception for persons not deemed competent to receive punishment. This at first seems odd, but is consistent with the moral aspects of law. To be punished, most states require that the convicted understand the reason for the punishment and the nature of the punishment. This is

> To be punished, most states require that the convicted understand the reason for the punishment and the nature of the punishment.

rarely protested in most criminal cases; however, the issue is occasionally raised for individuals facing the death penalty. In 2009, for example, just hours before a death row inmate was to be executed in Texas, the Federal courts issued a stay of execution and sent the case back to a state court to hear evidence regarding whether the inmate understood why he was being punished and the nature of the death sentence. As with other forms of competency, psychologists look to psychological tests to provide objective evidence of the defendant's mental state.

14.5   Applications in Civil Proceedings

The list of applications of psychological tests in civil proceedings is even longer than in criminal proceedings. Here, different rules will often apply as to how and when examinations are conducted, and they are usually done in clinical settings or attorneys' offices as opposed to incarceration settings. In this section, we will review some of the more common applications to give you an understanding of what might be involved and why psychological tests are useful.

14.5.1 Personal Injury Litigation

Personal injury litigation typically is an attempt to seek recovery of damage from a responsible party for injuries suffered by a person or a class of persons as a result of an action or lack of action by the responsible party. If the action or lack thereof is especially egregious, then punitive as well as real damage may be sought. Physical injuries are the most obvious and first thought of in such circumstances, e.g., broken or lost limbs, being blinded, spinal injuries, etc. However, physical and emotional

> Personal injury litigation typically is an attempt to seek recovery of damage from a responsible party for injuries suffered.

pain and suffering caused by brain injuries and other physical injuries are also compensable under our laws. For example, consider the case of a woman who sustained brain damage and then developed posttraumatic stress disorder (PTSD) after being injured in a motor vehicle accident caused by an intoxicated driver. The PTSD symptoms cause great personal distress and result in a loss of her ability to carry out her job or care for herself and her family, including loss of consortium with her spouse. These and other negative consequences create huge financial burdens that require compensation for caregivers, immediate and ongoing medical expenses, life-care plans, and vocational education to prepare for a different line of work. The court may award her damage (monetary award) to defray these financial burdens and compensate her for pain and suffering as well.

In cases of central nervous system (CNS) damage, neuropsychologists are nearly always involved and use specialized tests to determine the degree of functional impairment to the brain. Degree of functional brain impairment is only reliably obtained by actual neuropsychological testing, since other methods to examine the brain such as neuroimaging studies can only document structural and metabolic changes to the brain, which may or may not result in functional impairment. Estimates of overall loss of intellectual function and how this affects one's future educational and vocational opportunities are obtained from specialized methods of psychological testing as well. Psychologists also use testing in personal injury litigation to develop rehabilitation plans and monitor progress in treatment. Using neuropsychological test data, economists and life-care planners can estimate future loss of income as well as special expenses that will be incurred over the person's lifetime that are a result of the injury. All of these are considered damage that has been suffered and are recoverable in such litigation.

In the case of emotional injuries and psychic suffering, juries compensate individuals as well. As illustrated before, the diagnosis of PTSD is often important in these cases and should be made on the basis of objective psychological testing as opposed to subjective impressions or complaints.

In both circumstances—physical and emotional injuries—psychological testing is important to quantify for the court the degree of injury and its implications for the individual's life. The implications vary tremendously across age, educational level, and occupation, and each circumstance must be considered on its own merits. Psychological tests are thus used to derive such objective estimates for the court and also to determine the extent to which the claimed injuries are real or possibly malingered—we discuss malingering later in this chapter.

14.5.2 Divorce and Child Custody

When a divorce involves individuals with children and there is no agreement on custody of the children, psychologists and psychological testing become involved in many (but fewer than most suspect) instances. In making decisions in contested custody cases, the courts are typically directed by law to consider the best interests of the children. When making this decision, the laws of various states differ in what they direct judges to consider, but primarily, judges are to consider the following matters:

> In making decisions in contested custody cases, the courts are typically directed by law to consider the best interests of the children.

1. The wishes of the parents or custodians,
2. The wishes of the children,
3. The interaction of the children with the caregivers as well as siblings and other close family members,
4. Continuity of care/who has been providing routine care for the child, e.g., who takes the child to the doctor when sick, attends school conferences, attends extracurricular activities, bathes, dresses, and feeds the child—all considering the age and maturity of the child,

5. Any special needs the child may have emotionally, physically, or education-ally, and

6. The mental and physical health of the parties involved.

You can see that many of these variables can be assessed via psychological tests although clearly, as with nearly all other matters, evaluating histories and interview-ing everyone are crucial for proper interpretation of the test results.

There are however many obstacles for the clinician in child custody proceedings. Some parents are distrustful of psychologists in this process and may be hostile. Dissimulation may be common since all parents want to appear their best emotionally and mentally at such a time, and emotions can run very high—what is more emotional to a loving, concerned parent than who will raise their child? Financial considerations may also act to restrict a clinician from performing as extensive an evaluation as may be required to do a thorough job in advising the court on these matters. Also in the back of every clinician's mind who is experienced in child custody evaluations is the fact that "misconduct or bias" in child custody evaluations is the most common of all ethical complaints filed with state licensing boards against psychologists.

In addressing these issues, parents are usually subjected to personality testing to ascertain their mental status and to determine if they have any mental-health issues that would interfere with parenting. Mental-health issues that do not affect parent-ing or the ability to build and maintain a relationship with the child are noted to be irrelevant and typically are not reported to the court. In addition to interviews with the parties, including the children, clinicians often assess the relationships of the children and the parents through the use of parenting scales such as the BASC-3 Parenting Relationship Questionnaire (BASC-3 PRQ: Kamphaus & Reynolds, 2015) as well as behavior rating scales such as the BASC-3 Teacher, Parent, and Self-Report of Personality Rating Scales, using methods described in Reynolds and Kamphaus (2002). Special Interest Topic 14.3 describes how the BASC-3 can be used in this context.

Special Interest Topic 14.3: Use of the BASC-3 in Custody Evaluations
Behavior rating scales have a variety of advantages in custody evaluations espe-cially when used along with self-report scales, interviews, and histories. The BASC-3 Teacher Rating Scales (TRS), Parent Rating Scales (PRS), and Self-Report of Personality (SRP) are especially useful instruments for evaluating many of the child and relationship variables in these cases. Aside from the excel-lent technical and psychometric characteristics of the scores provided on the BASC-3 rating scales, such scores are useful in determining the presence of emotional, behavioral, and some developmental disorders in the context of a custody dispute, just as in its general application to clinical practice. Its strong normative base also allows it to be interpreted as a measure of emotional and behavioral maturity, which interests courts in weighing not only the child's wishes but also the amount of care required relative to the child's age.

In considering various aspects of the common legal instructions to the courts on variables to consider in determining custody, it is apparent that the BASC-3

(continued)

rating scales offer some unique and efficacious contributions. For example, the *Uniform Marriage and Divorce Act* instructs the court to consider, "the interaction and interrelationship of the child with his [or her] parent or parents …" Commonly, this is considered by child custody evaluators, including psychologists, on a subjective basis, using interview and casual (or on occasion, more structured) observations. The BASC-3 SRP contains a Relations with Parents scale that provides an objective evaluation of the child's regard for the parents while also considering the child's feelings of being esteemed by the parents. A group of experienced clinical psychologists, during early research on the development of the BASC, recommended these items as measures of overall family adjustment as well (see Reynolds & Kamphaus, 1992, p. 166). Clinically significant scores on the Relations with Parents scale among adolescents are also associated with antisocial behavior and delinquency (see Reynolds & Kamphaus, 1992, Tables 14.17 and 14.19), which should be considered by the evaluator as well. The items on this scale provide an empirical measure of the relationship with the parents, and the individual items are useful in direct, follow-up interviews with the child that can segregate the responses by parent.

Additionally, the SRP-Child and SRP-Adolescent forms contain a Locus of Control (LOC) scale with many questions about how much control parents exert. A high score on LOC would alert the evaluator to query responses to questions such as "My parents blame too many of their problems on me," "My parents control my life," and "My parents expect too much from me." Melton et al. (1997) emphasize clinical inquiry into the "child's depictions and conceptualization of relationship with each parent" (p. 502). Certainly, results from the BASC-3 rating scales should not be the sole means of such inquiry (additional interviews with collateral sources, evaluating approaches to discipline, etc., also being useful), but it does provide some objective, quantifiable data and clear suggestions for follow-up queries.

The BASC-3 PRS also offers a somewhat unique opportunity to look quantitatively at how each parent views the behavior of a child and the concordance of the views with each other and with various collateral sources. During custody evaluations, as in other evaluations, it is useful to obtain behavior rating scale data independent of each parent and of other sources who know the child well (e.g., a teacher). Once these data have been obtained and analyzed, computer-generated profiles can be contrasted empirically for the ratings of each parent.

It is particularly noteworthy to the evaluator in a custody determination when parents show disagreement over the behavior of the child. In such instances, confirmation of any negative or positive biases will be important and often can be obtained by also comparing each parent's ratings with the ratings of one or more teachers. The multi-informant report allows the contrast of a PRS with another PRS, the PRS with a TRS, or a TRS with another TRS.

When children show large variations in their behavior with one parent versus the other, there are usually good reasons why and establishing why is nearly always important. Insights may be gleaned into the effectiveness of the parenting

(continued)

skills of each person, ability to discipline appropriately, or simply to be tolerant of the normal activity levels of children as the developmentally moving targets they represent. Overly negative views of children can be detrimental to their development and set up poor expectations, while overly positive views may lead a parent to ignore real problems of behavioral and emotional development, again to the detriment of the child. Purposive distortion is virtually always seen as a negative indicator in a custody evaluation. Parties should all put the child's best interest first, and this requires honest, cooperative interaction with the evaluator and with the court. Parents who are less knowledgeable about their children may present special problems as well. Often, a lack of knowledge reveals a lack of involvement in the daily care and routine of the child, another important consideration for the court. Comparisons between TRS and PRS results will be useful in this context as well.

We have provided this level of detail here to emphasize the complexity of child custody evaluations. As in other forensic contexts, the need for objectivity and a lack of bias are imperative in such evaluations. We have noted here some of the ways that personality scales can be used along with behavior rating scales in addressing some of these questions. Where children might have disabilities of various sorts and require specialized or more intensive care from a parent, many other types of psychological and even neuropsychological tests may be useful in determining specialized needs.

14.5.3 Determining Common Civil Competencies

In Table 14.2, we present examples of some of the more common civil competencies where psychologists may be called upon to assist the court. Each of these competencies involves specific statutory requirements that must be addressed. For example, testamentary capacity (the ability to execute a will and bequeath one's assets) typically requires that the person understands the "nature of their bounty" and has knowledge of their heirs and the ability to form intent. In some cases, this can be established by an interview, but at other times, psychological testing with measures of intelligence and neuropsychological function might be required. For example, an elderly stroke victim with limited or no language might have difficulty in communicating these factors, but neuropsychological testing could establish that the person has the intellectual wherewithal to understand and act competently in making or altering a will or to act on other financial documents. This could be true in other instances such as executing a power of attorney, agreeing to participate in medical research, or making treatment decisions in a medical setting. In order to be a witness in a trial, a person must understand the oath and be capable of narrating the facts they are to present to the court. Whether or not psychological testing has a contribution to make in determining such competencies is considered on an individual basis by the clinician involved, but testing is usually advisable and useful if the interview fails to provide clear evidence or impairments in communication exist.

Table 14.2 Summary of factors to consider under *Daubert* (1993) for admissibility of expert testimony in federal (and many state) courts

1. Is the scientific hypothesis testable?
2. Has the proposition been tested?
3. Is there a known error rate?
4. Has the hypothesis and/or technique been subjected to peer review and publication?
5. Is the theory upon which the hypotheses and/or technique is based generally accepted in the appropriate scientific community?
6. Are there nonjudicial uses which have been made of the theory or technique?

These six factors are *nonexclusive* and trial courts may consider other factors in a specific case.

Source: Daubert v. Merrell Dow Pharmaceuticals, 113 S.Ct. 2786 (1993)

14.5.4 Other Civil Matters

We hope that we have given you an overview of how psychological tests are used in major civil actions, but there are many more applications. In child abuse investigations, the court often finds psychological testing helpful when determining whether children should be removed from a home or whether parental rights should be terminated. Psychological tests are used in studies of the epidemiology of CNS injuries in large-scale toxic torts where exposure to neurotoxins is alleged in large members of a defined population. Virtually any time, the past, present, or predicted future cognitive or emotional status and behavior of an individual may be informative to the court in arriving at a legal decision, and objective opinions supported by psychological test results may be useful.

14.6   Third Party Observers in Forensic Psychological Testing

In forensic settings, it is not uncommon for attorneys to ask to be present when their clients are being examined, especially by an expert retained by the other side. These requests occur in both criminal and civil matters. Requests to have their own experts present during the examinations are also common. These requests

> Third-party observers alter the standardized procedures for most individually administered psychological tests.

are made for a variety of reasons ranging from the legitimate interest in protecting the client's rights to the nefarious desire to learn about the tests and their content for purposes of later coaching this or another client in how to respond. Some of the issues involving third party observers (TPOs) are resolved by having the expert attend in lieu of the attorney, but even this is problematic.

The presence of a third party in the examination of psychological function is different from an observer at a purely medical examination. Having a TPO in the room during psychological testing is inconsistent with the provisions of the *Standards for Educational and Psychological Testing* in several ways. If not a psychologist, the security of the tests is compromised since the observer may reveal the test content in a variety of sources to individuals not qualified to purchase and use such tests. The TPO also introduces a variable that was not present when most psychological tests are standardized, which involves individual test administration with only the examiner and examinee in the room. Thus, the presence of the TPO has the potential to: (1) disrupt standardized testing procedures, (2) compromise the reliability of the obtained scores, (3) affect accuracy of score interpretation in unknown ways, and (4) render normative data comparisons no longer appropriate as a reference standard, which precludes valid interpretation of the test results (McCaffrey, Fisher, Gold, & Lynch, 1996). Observer effects can result in a decline in performance of complex tasks yet enhance performance on overlearned tasks, again compromising our ability to interpret scores accurately (McCaffrey et al., 1996). TPOs are not disinterested parties and can be distracting to the examinee. Even experts in the same field can unintentionally convey approval or disapproval of answers and procedures during the exam and alter the examinee's natural responding. Having a person observe via video or one-way glass solves some but not all of the problems. The examinee's knowledge that they are being observed may change how they respond to emotionally laden questions or on performance tests where attention, concentration, problem-solving skills, and memory are required.

Recognizing the many issues involved, including the press by attorneys to be present when their clients are examined, the National Academy of Neuropsychology, the American Board of Clinical Neuropsychology, the Association of Test Publishers, and others have developed official position papers on the presence of TPOs in forensic examinations and all oppose such a presence. Forensic practitioners are aware of these issues and take appropriate steps to ensure the integrity of the examination process, while at the same time assuring the rights of the individual being examined. Special Interest Topic 14.4 highlights some additional historical developments and practical concerns pertaining to TPOs.

Special Interest Topic 14.4: Third Party Observers: Why You Ought Not to Watch

The realization that the presence of an observing audience altered the performance of the individual being observed was first reported in 1898 by Norman Triplett of Indiana University who is today considered the pioneer of sports social psychology. Triplett studied racing cyclists and found that racing against other cyclists produced better times than riding alone. In the years that followed, research provided inconsistent support for Triplett's original findings, most notably that sometimes an audience improved performance, while at other times, it hindered performance. It was the social psychologist Zajonc (1965) who discovered that the presence of an audience enhances performance if the performer is well acquainted with a task but decreases performance if the performer has limited or no talent for the task. Other social psychological studies found that an observer impacted an examinee's performance on tasks of interest to clinical psychologists such as word generation lists, paired-associate learning, concept attainment, maze learning, letter cancelation speed and accuracy, reaction time, as well as digit recall of numbers forward and backward (a standard component of many IQ tests).

This social psychological research provided a theoretical basis for studies of third party observers (TPOs) in forensic psychological evaluations, even though it was largely ignored until recently. Based on the research of Zajonc and others,

(continued)

one would expect that a TPO would actually decrease performance on neuropsychological tests because they are novel to examinees, i.e., since examinees are not skilled in completing neuropsychological tests, and audience (TPO) is predicted to decrease performance. This prediction was confirmed in a study that examined a child's performance on psychological tests when her mother was or was not present in the room (Binder & Johnson-Greene, 1995). When her mother was present, her performance declined, and when mother left the room, her performance improved. This report ignited clinical neuropsychologists' interest in the impact of TPO during neuropsychological testing, especially when conducted for forensic purposes.

A systematic series of research studies was subsequently carried out by Robert McCaffrey and colleagues at the University at Albany, State University of New York. McCaffrey and his colleagues systematically examined the impact of TPOs on neuropsychological test performance. Among other findings, TPOs negatively impact an examinee's performance on neuropsychological testing but especially on tests of memory. It did not matter whether the observer was present in the room where the testing was taking place or observing via a videotape or audiotape recorder. In one study (Yantz & McCaffrey, 2005), the examinee was instructed that the student examiner's *supervisor* was going to be present to observe and monitor how the student *examiner* administered memory tests. The *examinee's* memory performance was negatively impacted, despite being provided information that the TPO was there to observe and critique the student *examiner*, not the *examinee*. This study calls into question the assumption that a TPO has no impact on psychological assessment, which is especially relevant for forensic evaluations where TPOs are commonly requested.

The negative impact of a TPO during neuropsychological evaluations is considered to be of such importance that both the National Academy of Neuropsychology and the American Academy of Clinical Neuropsychology published position papers opposed to the presence of TPOs. However, in forensic clinical neuropsychological evaluations, lawyers and others continue to request TPOs be present despite evidence suggesting their presence may invalidate test results, which may have disastrous and unanticipated consequences for the examinee. In a capital murder case, the difference of a few IQ points could mean life or death. In a civil law suit, a plaintiff's performance on a symptom validity test could mean the difference between a life-changing financial verdict and being found to be malingering brain damage by a jury. Regarding the latter example, symptom validity tests are administered as part of neuropsychological evaluations to ensure that the examinee's level of effort during testing was adequate to produce meaningful test findings. The TPO effect reported in the Binder and Johnson-Greene (1995) case study occurred on the Portland Digit Recognition Test, which is a symptom validity test.

McCaffrey's findings may also have clinical applications. In some professions, such as medicine, students are trained by the principle of "See One, Do One, Teach One." In fact, historically, many of the skills acquired by clinical neuropsychologists involved this type of training. Recall that in the study by

(continued)

Yantz and McCaffrey (2005), the examinee's memory performance was negatively impacted when the supervisor was in the room. This study demonstrates that it can no longer be assumed in neuropsychological testing that the presence of a clinical supervisor as part of the "See One" style of training is benign.

Psychologists should avoid TPOs in order to ensure that their test results will provide them with the best possible data upon which to make decisions. This is true for clinically focused evaluations where, for example, the question might be to establish or rule out a diagnosis of dementia, and for forensic evaluations where the evaluation results are used to form an opinion within a reasonable degree of clinical neuropsychological certainty to assist the trier of fact. For all of these reasons, the presence of TPO during clinical or forensic neuropsychological testing should be avoided, as it is in no one's best interest, especially the examinees.

14.7   Detection of Malingering and Other Forms of Dissimulation

In forensic settings, individuals often have motivation to present themselves as different from how they really are—to appear dissimilar from their true selves. This can result in what is called *dissimulation*. When examinees intentionally dissimulate to look far worse off than they are in reality, it is termed *malingering*. For

> Malingering is the false presentation of injury or disability for the purposes of gain.

example, a person with a mild head injury who had deficits at first but has now largely recovered may feign severe memory and learning deficits, make too many mistakes on their job, and argue they are no longer able to work in order to receive disability benefits or obtain a larger settlement than is due them in a personal injury law suit. A person may claim to have PTSD from observing a wreck in which a child was killed when in fact they have recovered fully from their acute stress reaction and are only making the claim to obtain an insurance settlement. Malingering is in fact a substantial problem in personal injury litigation, with reasonable estimates ranging from 25% to 50% incidence levels in brain injury cases alone. In criminal cases, malingering may be even more of a problem as incarcerated individuals have great motivation to be seen as less culpable for their acts and to avoid long sentences and even the death penalty. Because of the strong incentive to dissimulate or malinger in personal injury and other forensic cases, psychologists include procedures to detect malingering and other forms of dissimulation in their psychological evaluations.

However, the diagnosis of malingering is fraught with conceptual, philosophical, and logistical difficulties. For example, if a psychologist conducts an evaluation and makes a determination of malingering, this infers that the examinee was not truthful and intentionally behaved in a deceptive way. Examinees may take issue with this determination asserting that the diagnosis is wrong, and they have been slandered by the psychologist (defamation of character) and, in cases of an unfavorable legal decision, claim that the psychologist harmed them and is liable for damage. For these and other reasons, malingering is a source of heated discussion among juries in NGRI cases, competency hearings, and intellectual disability claims in capital murder cases just to note a few examples. Considerable effort has been devoted to the evaluation of malingered responses, also sometimes referred to as effort testing, in the scientific literature. We are far from resolving the issues and developing a so-called gold standard indicator of malingering in clinical assessment. However, the nature and prevalence of the problem as well as its potential costs to society dictate that malingering is considered in forensic examinations. Organizations such as the National Academy of Neuropsychology have developed formal position papers noting the need for the inclusion of effort testing and assessment of malingered responses.

Assessment and diagnosis of malingering require extensive clinical knowledge as well as very specialized psychological tests. Reynolds and Horton (2010) discuss these methods and their difficulties in a book-length treatment, and there are many such books now available. In Chap. 18 of this volume, we discuss the development of scales designed to assess dissimulation. The key ideas to take from the current section is that the motivation to malinger is high in forensic settings, both civil and criminal, accurate detection of malingering is at times very difficult, specialized procedures are needed to assess malingering, and assessments of malingering should be included routinely in most forensic psychological testing batteries.

14.8   The Admissibility of Testimony Based on Psychological Testing Results

Experts render opinions and explanations to assist the trier of fact in a case. However, just because the court designates someone an expert, it does not mean their testimony will be allowed. The rules of evidence, guided by several US Supreme Court cases, dictate criteria the judge must consider in allowing an expert to render an opinion to the court. Many state courts have adopted the Federal standard, most often referred to as the Daubert standard after the name of the case (Daubert v. Merrill Dow. 509 U.S. 579, 113 S.Ct. 2786), which outlines the criteria for *admissibility* of scientific evidence into legal proceedings.

Admissibility of testimony is not the same as credibility. Admitting testimony requires a threshold finding by the court that the expert's methods and reasoning are reliable and logical. The federal rules of evidence tell us that for

> Admissibility of testimony is not the same as credibility.

purposes of determining whether expert testimony is sufficiently grounded on valid scientific principles so as to be admissible, the general acceptance of a scientific or technical theory in the scientific community is a factor to consider; however, it is not conclusive. For purposes of determining whether expert testimony is sufficiently grounded on valid scientific principles so as to be admissible, an opinion will not be admissible merely because some part of the methodology is scientifically valid; the entire reasoning process must be valid, and a credible link must be established between the reasoning and the conclusion. Once that is accomplished, inquiry changes from one of admissibility to credibility. Table 14.2 lists the factors to be considered as outlined in the Supreme Court's *Daubert* decision regarding the admissibility of scientific testimony. Admissibility then focuses on the expert's methods—not the opinions they have derived.

The ***credibility*** of the expert's testimony accrues to the weight that is given to the expert's opinions by the trier of fact. A judge or jury may listen to an expert and decide for a variety of reasons not to give much weigh to their opinions because of perceived biases of the expert, a lack of thoroughness, a failure to consider reasonable alternative interpretations of the data, and the like. Once an expert's testimony has been admitted, much of the focus of the opposing side turns to discrediting the expert's testimony in the eyes of the trier of fact by finding fault with the findings, reasoning, or conclusions.

The *Daubert* challenge to the admissibility of testimony essentially makes the assertion that there is no basis or an insufficient basis for the experts' opinions in the scientific discipline underlying their profession. As we have discussed on the scientific basis and methods for developing tests throughout this text, it is easy

> Expert testimony is often subject to the *Daubert* challenge.

to see that testimony is more likely to be admitted and believed when based on objective methods such as psychological tests that have thorough manuals that report extensively on the psychometric characteristics of the tests and the scores derived from them, particularly when compared to subjective judgments based on interviews and anecdotal data.

Nevertheless, a variety of problems can occur, which cause such testimony not to be admitted. For example, in our own work, we routinely rescore all tests administered by opposing experts and frequently find errors in scoring as well as in simple addition and in table lookups (e.g., reading down the wrong column, using the wrong age table, etc.). These errors render the underlying data unreliable. Changes in test administration procedures result in a nonstandardized administration that can cause errors in the test score derivations. Even seemingly "minor" departures from standardized procedures have been found to lead to significant alterations in an individual's test performance. Even more problematic is the difficulty in predicting the effects that these changes will have. Nonstandardized administration can significantly change the psychometric properties of the tasks. It could interact in unpredictable ways with various examinee characteristics including disability conditions, gender, and age, to cause changes in scores that are not uniform across examinees. The direction of these changes in scores is often counter intuitive, i.e., a change designed or thought to make a task easier may make it harder and vice versa (also see Chap. 16 of this text for discussions of how altered administrations may affect scores and their reliability and interpretation). Some clinicians use shortened versions of tests (referred to as short-forms) in order to decrease assessment time without investigating their psychometric characteristics. All of these issues and more may cause the results of psychological testing to be declared inadmissible. Various court decisions on the admissibility of testimony are clear in this regard; if the foundational data underlying opinion testimony are unreliable, an expert will not be permitted to present an opinion derived from the data because any opinion drawn from that data must also then be unreliable.

14.9   Summary

Frequently, psychologists and others who use psychological tests are called into courtrooms and other hearing locations to give expert testimony regarding opinions they have that are often derived from the use of psychological testing. Psychological tests provide objective, quantifiable data, and the results of psychological testing can be powerful and persuasive tools in an adversarial proceeding. In this chapter, we review the special rules that apply to the forensic use of psychological tests not only within the profession of psychology but also in courtrooms themselves. We describe a variety of areas of legal proceedings where psychological tests might be employed to give examples of the myriad of questions a forensic psychologist could be called upon to address using tests. The many pitfalls and challenges as well as the purposes of such testing in both criminal and civil proceedings are also discussed. In the context of criminal proceedings, we discuss the following applications:

- Not Guilty by Reason of Insanity: The NGRI Defense
- Competency to stand trial
- Transfer of a juvenile to adult criminal court
- Mitigation in sentencing
- The special case of Intellectual Disability in capital sentencing
- Competency to be executed.

In the context of civil proceedings, we describe the following applications:

- Personal injury litigation
- Divorce and child custody
- Determining common civil competencies
- Other civil matters (e.g., child abuse investigations; epidemiology of CNS injuries).

Other important topics in the context of forensic evaluations such as the use of third party observers in forensic examinations and the detection of dissimulation are addressed. In closing, we briefly discussed how federal and state rules as well as established case law provide guidelines regarding the admissibility of expert opinions based on quantifiable data such as those obtained from psychological testing.

References

American Psychological Association [APA]. (2013). Specialty guidelines for forensic psychology. *American Psychologist, 68*(1), 7–19.

Binder, L. M., & Johnson-Greene, D. (1995). Observer effects on neuropsychological performance: A case report. *The Clinical Neuropsychologist, 9*, 74–78.

Kamphaus, R. W., & Reynolds, C. R. (2015). *BASC-3 parenting relationship questionnaire.* Bloomington, MN: Pearson Assessments.

Lilienfeld, S., Lynn, S., Ruscio, J., & Beyerstein, B. (2010). *50 Great myths of popular psychology.* Oxford: Wiley.

McCaffrey, R. J., Fisher, J. M., Gold, B. A., & Lynch, J. K. (1996). Presence of third parties during neuropsychological evaluations: Who is evaluating whom? *The Clinical Neuropsychologist, 10*, 435–449.

Melton, G., Petrila, J., Poythress, N., & Slobogin, C. (1997). *Psychological evaluations for the courts: A handbook for mental health professionals and lawyers* (2nd ed.). New York, NY: Guilford Press.

Melton, G., Petrila, J., Poythress, N., & Slobogin, C. (2007). *Psychological evaluations for the courts: A handbook for mental health professionals and lawyers* (3rd ed.). New York, NY: Guilford Press.

Reynolds, C. R., & Horton, A. M. (2010). *Detection of malingering in head injury litigation* (2nd ed.). New York, NY: Springer.

Reynolds, C. R., & Kamphaus, R. W. (1992). *Behavior assessment system for children: Manual.* Circle Pines, MN: American Guidance Service.

Reynolds, C. R., & Kamphaus, R. W. (2002). *Clinical and research applications of the BASC.* New York, NY: Guilford Press.

Reynolds, C. R., Niland, J., Wright, J. E., & Rosenn, M. (2010). Failure to apply the Flynn correction in death penalty litigation: Standard practice of today maybe, but certainly malpractice of tomorrow. *Journal of Psychoeducational Assessment, 28*(5), 477–481.

Reynolds, C. R., Price, R. J., & Niland, J. (2004). Applications of neuropsychology in capital felony (death penalty) defense. *Journal of Forensic Neuropsychology, 3*, 89–123.

Yantz, C. L., & McCaffrey, R. J. (2005). Effects of a supervisor's observation on memory test performance of the examinee: Third party observer effect confirmed. *Journal of Forensic Neuropsychology, 4*, 27–38.

Youngjohn, J. R. (1995). Confirmed attorney coaching prior to a neuropsychological evaluation. *Assessment, 2*, 279–283.

Zajonc, R. B. (1965). Social facilitation. *Science, 149*, 269–274.

Additional Reading

Atkins v. Virginia 122 S.Ct. 2242 (June 20, 2002).

Daubert v. Merrill Dow 509 U.S. 579, 113 S.Ct. 2786 (1993).

Melton, G., Petrila, J., Poythress, N., & Slobogin, C. (2007). *Psychological evaluations for the courts, Third Edition: A handbook for mental health professionals and lawyers.* New York, NY: Guilford Publications.

Reynolds, C. R., Hays, J. R., & Ryan-Arredondo, K. (2001). When judges, laws, ethics, and rules of practice collide: A case study of assent and disclosure in assessment of a minor. *Journal of Forensic Neuropsychology, 2*, 41–52.

Reynolds, C. R., Price, R. J., & Niland, J. (2004). Applications of neuropsychology in capital felony (death penalty) defense. *Journal of Forensic Neuropsychology, 3*, 89–123.

Wiggins v. Smith 123 S.Ct. 2527 (2003).

Youngjohn, J. R. (1995). Confirmed attorney coaching prior to a neuropsychological evaluation. *Assessment, 2*, 279–283.

The Problem of Bias in Psychological Assessment

15

Test bias: In God we trust; all others must have data.

Reynolds (1983)

Abstract

Much the impetus for the current debate about bias in psychological testing is based on well-documented, consistent, and substantive differences between IQ scores of Whites, Hispanics, and Blacks in the U.S.A. Various explanations are offered for these differences including the idea that IQ tests are inherently biased against Blacks, Hispanics, and possibly other ethnics groups, or what is commonly known as the Cultural Test Bias Hypothesis (CTBH). Because tests are used to make many different and important decisions about people, lack of fairness in testing resulting from test bias is of grave concern. This chapter traces the historical roots of the CTBH to the present day, provides important distinctions regarding different definitions of test bias that are critical for empirical examination of the issue, presents common objections to the use of psychological testing, and describes how test authors and publishers detect bias in psychological tests. The chapter concludes by noting that while more research is necessary, the current evidence largely supports the proposition that most commercially developed widely use tests of achievement and aptitude are not culturally biased.

Supplementary Information The online version of this chapter (https://doi.org/10.1007/978-3-030-59455-8_15) contains supplementary material, which is available to authorized users.

Learning Objectives

After reading and studying this chapter, students should be able to:

1. Explain the cultural test bias hypothesis.
2. Describe alternative explanations for observed group differences in performance on aptitude and other standardized tests.
3. Describe the relationship between bias and reliability.
4. Describe the major objections regarding the use of standardized tests with minority students.
5. Describe what is meant by cultural loading, cultural bias, and culture-free tests.
6. Describe the mean difference definition of test bias and its current status.
7. Describe the results of research on the presence of bias in the content of educational and psychological tests.
8. Describe the results of research on the presence of bias in other internal features of educational and psychological tests.
9. Describe the results of research on bias in prediction and in relation to variables that are external to the test.
10. Explain what is implied by homogeneity of regression and describe the conditions that may result when it is not present.

Groups of people who can be defined based on descriptors such as gender or ethnicity do not always perform that same way on educational and psychological tests. For example, on tests of spatial skill, requiring visualization and imagery, men and boys tend to score higher than do women and girls. On tests that involve written language

Much effort has been expended to determine why group differences occur on standardized aptitude tests, but we do not know for certain why.

and tests of simple psychomotor speed, women and girls tend to score higher than men and boys (see Special Interest Topic 15.1 for additional information). Ethnic group differences in test performance also occur and are the most controversial and polemic of all group differences.

There is perhaps no more controversial finding in the field of psychology than the persistent one standard deviation difference between the intelligence test performance of Black and White students taken as a group, which is 15 standard score points on most IQ tests. There are many, many such group differences on various measures of specialized ability and achievement—and these differences go in

The cultural test bias hypothesis holds that differences in mean test scores across gender or ethnic groups are due to artifacts of the test or measurement process and do not reflect real differences among groups on the constructs or dimensions purported to be measured.

Special Interest Topic 15.1: Sex Differences in Intelligence

Research has shown that although there are no significant sex differences in overall intelligence scores, substantial differences exist with regard to specific cognitive abilities. Females typically score higher on a number of verbal abilities whereas males perform better on visual-spatial and (starting in middle childhood) mathematical skills. It is believed that sex hormone levels and social factors both influence the development of these differences. As is typical of group differences in intellectual abilities, the variability in performance within groups (i.e., males and females) is much larger than the mean difference between groups (Neisser et al., 1996). Diane Halpern (1997) has written extensively on gender differences in cognitive abilities. This table briefly summarizes some of her findings.

Selected abilities on which women obtain higher average scores

Type of ability	Examples
Rapid access and use of verbal and other information in long-term memory	Verbal fluency, synonym generation, associative memory, spelling, anagrams
Specific knowledge areas	Literature and foreign languages
Production and comprehension of prose	Writing and reading comprehension
Fine motor tasks	Matching and coding tasks, pegboard, mirror tracing
School performance	Most subjects

Selected abilities on which men obtain higher average scores

Type of ability	Examples
Transformations of visual working memory, moving objects, and aiming	Mental rotations, dynamic spatiotemporal tasks, accuracy in throwing
Specific knowledge areas	General knowledge, mathematics, science, and geography
Fluid reasoning	Proportional, mechanical, and scientific reasoning; SAT Math and GRE Quantitative

Source: This table was adapted from Halpern (1997, Appendix, p. 1102)

both directions. Much effort has been expended to determine why group differences occur but we do not know for certain why they exist. One major, carefully studied explanation is that the tests are biased in some way against certain groups. This is referred to as the ***CTBH*** (Cultural Test Bias Hypothesis).

The CTBH represents the contention that any gender, ethnic, racial, or other nominally determined groups who perform differently on mental tests are due to inherent, artifactual biases produced within the tests through flawed psychometric methodology. Group differences are believed then to stem from characteristics of the tests and to be unrelated to any actual differences in the psychological trait, skill, or ability in question. The resolution or evaluation of the validity of the CTBH is one of the most crucial scientific questions facing psychology today.

Bias in mental tests has many implications for individuals including the misplacement of students in educational programs, errors in assigning grades, unfair denial of admission to college, graduate, and professional degree programs, and the inappropriate denial of employment. The scientific implications are even more substantive. There would be dramatic implications for educational and psychological research and theory if the CTBH were correct: The principal research of the past 100 years in the study of the psychology of human differences would have to be dismissed as confounded and the results deemed largely artifactual because much of the work is based on standard psychometric theory and testing technology. This would in turn create major upheavals in professional psychology, because the foundations of clinical, counseling, educational, industrial, and school psychology are all strongly tied to the basic academic field of individual differences.

Each day psychologists in clinical practice use psychological tests to make diagnostic decisions that affect the lives of their patients in many ways, e.g., treatment approaches, types of psychopharmacological agents that may be applied, suitability for employment, and in forensic settings, even eligibility to receive the death penalty is affected by the results of intelligence tests. School psychologists arrive at diagnostic and eligibility decisions that determine school placements. Industrial and organizational psychologists design screening programs that test job applicants for employment skills and screen public safety officer applicants for various personality traits that predict success in law enforcement. Educational psychologists conduct research that assesses outcomes in learning environments using standardized tests in order to determine what methods and environments for learning are the most successful. These are examples of but a few of the many uses of psychological tests in the everyday practice of psychology. Typically, professionally designed tests used for such decision-making are subjected to lengthy development stages and tryout periods and are held up to stringent psychometric and statistical standards. If these methods turn out to be culturally biased when used with native-born American ethnic minorities, what about other alternative methods of making these decisions that are inherently more subjective, e.g., interviews, observation, review of references, performance, or portfolio assessments? Put another way, if well-constructed and properly standardized tests are biased, then less standardized, more subjective approaches are almost certain to be at least as biased and probably more so. As the reliability of a test or evaluation procedure goes down, the likelihood of bias goes up, the two being inversely related. A large reliability coefficient does not eliminate the possibility of bias, but as reliability is lowered, the probability that bias will be present increases.

> If well-constructed and properly standardized tests are biased, then interviews and other subjective evaluation procedures are almost certain to be at least as biased and probably more so.

The purpose of this chapter is to address the issues and findings surrounding the CTBH in a rational manner and evaluate the validity of the hypothesis, as far as possible, on the basis of existing empirical research. This will not be an easy task because of the controversial nature of the topic and its strong emotional overtones. Prior to turning to the reasons that test bias generates highly charged emotions and reviewing some of the history of these issues, it is proper to engage in a discussion of just what we mean by the term bias.

15.1   What Do We Mean by Bias?

Bias carries many different connotations for the lay public and for professionals in a number of disciplines. To the legal mind, bias denotes illegal discriminatory practices while to the lay mind it may conjure notions

> Bias carries many different connotations for the lay public and for professionals in a number of disciplines.

of prejudicial attitudes. Much of the rancor in psychology and education regarding proper definitions of *test bias* is due to the divergent uses of this term in general but especially by professionals in the same and related academic fields.

As presented in the *Standards* (American Educational Research Association, American Psychological Association, & National Council on Measurement in Education, 2014), bias is discussed within the overall context of fairness, a multi-faceted and complex concept that can include both subjective and objective arguments across a variety of both professional and casual discussions. Up to this point, we have directly or indirectly infused the notion of fairness throughout this book, whether it be in the context of:

- *Interpreting test scores*, e.g., use norm or criterion-referenced interpretations
- *Minimizing error in test scores*, e.g., follow standardized procedures for all examinees
- *Reducing threats to validity of score interpretations*, e.g., provide appropriate accommodations to those with disabilities
- *Writing appropriate test items*, e.g., conduct expert review to ensure cultural sensitivity and design to measure intended construct across a wide range of test-taker ability
- *Evaluating potential of job candidates*, e.g., use same standard criteria for all applicants
- *Disability evaluation*, e.g., establish diagnosis of intellectual disability using best assessment procedures

Fairness is fundamental to the development and use of psychological tests and the subsequent interpretation of scores. Fairness is required during the testing process so that all examinees are given a similar opportunity to demonstrate their true ability on the construct being assessed. Factors irrelevant to the construct are eliminated during assessment ensuring the construct is measured in a way that is impacted only by knowledge, skills, or abilities relevant to the construct itself. Standardized test materials, instructions, administration, and scoring also promote fairness, although there are some exceptions. For example, consider a parent of child being evaluated in school for a learning disability. The parent is an English-language learner who has a reasonable mastery of the language, but is unable to read effectively. As part of the child's evaluation, the parent is asked to complete a rating form designed to assess the behavioral-emotional functioning of the child. To ensure only the construct of interest is measured (i.e., child's functioning), the parent is allowed to complete the rating form by responding to an audio recording of the questions because being able to read the test item is not a requirement of assessing the behavioral-emotional functioning of the child.

Fairness can also be characterized by the extent to which the characteristics of the test itself are related to the construct being measured, and not to characteristics that are associated with attributes of a specific group. In the statistical sense, this is bias. The *Standards* defines bias as—a systematic error in a test score (AERA et al., 2014). A biased assessment is one that systematically underestimates or overestimates the value of the variable it is designed to measure. If the bias is a function of a nominal cultural variable (e.g., ethnicity or gender), then the test has a cultural bias. As an example, if an achievement test produces different mean scores for different ethnic groups, and there actually are true differences between the groups in terms of achievement, the test is not biased. However, if the observed differences in achievement scores are the result of the test underestimating the achievement of one group or overestimating the achievement of another, then the test is culturally biased.

> In terms of tests and measurements, bias is something systematic that distorts construct measurement or prediction by test scores of other important criteria.

Other definitions of the term bias in research on the CTBH or cross-group validity of tests are unacceptable from a scientific perspective for two reasons: (1) The imprecise nature of other uses of the term bias makes empirical investigation and rational inquiry exceedingly difficult, and (2) other uses of the term invoke specific moral value systems that are the subject of intense emotional debates that do not have a mechanism for rational resolution. It is imperative that the evaluation of bias in testing be undertaken from the standpoint of scholarly inquiry and debate. Emotional appeals, legal-adversarial approaches, and political remedies of scientific issues appear to us to be inherently unacceptable and unuseful.

15.2   Past and Present Concerns: A Brief Look

Concern about cultural bias in mental testing has been a recurring issue since the beginning of the use of assessment in education. From Alfred Binet in the 1800s to Arthur Jensen over the last 50 years, many scientists have addressed this controversial problem, with varying, inconsistent outcomes. In the last few decades, the issue of cultural bias has come forth as a major contemporary problem far exceeding the bounds of purely academic debate and professional rhetoric. The debate over the CTBH has become entangled and sometimes confused within the larger issues of individual liberties, civil rights, and social justice, becoming a focal point for psychologists, sociologists, educators, politicians, minority activists, and the lay public. The issues increasingly have become legal and political. Numerous court cases have been brought and New York state even passed "truth-in-testing" legislation that is being considered in other states and in the federal legislature. Such attempts at solutions are difficult. Take for example the legal response to the question "Are intelligence tests used to diagnose intellectual disability biased against cultural and ethnic minorities?" In California in 1979 (Larry P. v. Riles) the answer was "yes" but in Illinois, in 1980 (PASE v. Hannon), the response was "no." Thus two federal district courts of equivalent standing have heard nearly identical cases, with many of the same witnesses espousing much the same testimony, and reached precisely opposite conclusions. See Special Interest Topic 15.2 for more information on legal issues surrounding assessment bias.

Though current opinion on the CTBH is quite divergent, ranging from those who consider it to be for the most part unresearchable (e.g., Schoenfeld, 1974) to those who considered the issue settled decades ago (e.g., Jensen, 1980), it seems clear that empirical analysis of the hypothesis should continue to be undertaken. However difficult full objectivity may be in science, we must make every attempt to view all socially, politically, and emotionally charged issues from the perspective of rational scientific inquiry. We must also be prepared to accept scientifically valid findings as real, whether we like them or not.

15.3   The Controversy Over Bias in Testing: Its Origin, What It Is, and What It Is Not

Systematic group differences on standardized intelligence and aptitude tests may occur as a function of socioeconomic level, race or ethnic background, and other demographic variables. Black-White differences on IQ measures have received extensive investigation for more than 50 years. Although results occasionally differ slightly depending on the age groups under consideration, random samples of Blacks and Whites show a mean difference of about 1 standard deviation, with the mean score of the White groups consistently exceeding that of the Black groups. When a number of demographic variables are taken into account (most notably socioeconomic status, or SES), the size of the difference reduces to 0.5–0.7 standard deviation but remains robust. The differences have persisted at relatively constant levels for quite some time and under a variety of methods of investigation. Some research suggests these gaps are narrowing (Dickens & Flynn, 2006; Neisser et al., 1996; Nisbett, 2009), while other research disputes the narrowing of gaps (Rushton & Jensen, 2005, 2010).

Mean differences between ethnic groups are not limited to Black-White comparisons. Although not nearly as thoroughly researched as Black-White differences, Hispanic-White differences have also been documented, with Hispanic mean performance approximately 0.5 standard deviation below the mean of the White group. On average, Native Americans tend to perform lower on tests of verbal intelligence

Special Interest Topic 15.2: Courtroom Controversy Over IQ Testing in the Public Schools

Largely due to overall mean differences in the performance of various ethnic groups on IQ tests, the use of intelligence tests in the public schools has been the subject of courtroom battles around the United States. Typically such lawsuits argue that the use of intelligence tests as part of the determination of eligibility for special education programs leads to overidentification of certain minorities (traditionally African American and Hispanic children). A necessary corollary to this argument is that the resultant overidentification is inappropriate because the intelligence tests in use are biased, underestimating the intelligence of minority students, and that there is in fact no greater need for special education placement among these ethnic minorities than for other ethnic groups in the population.

Attempts to resolve the controversy over IQ testing in the public schools via the courtroom have not been particularly successful. Unfortunately, but not uncharacteristically, the answer to the legal question "Are IQ tests biased in a manner that results in unlawful discrimination against minorities when used as part of the process of determining eligibility for special education placements?" depends on where you live! There are four key court cases to consider when reviewing this question, two from California and one each from Illinois and Georgia.

The first case is Diana v. State Board of Education (C-70-37 RFP, N.D. Cal., 1970), heard by the same federal judge who would later hear the Larry P. case (see later discussion). Diana was filed on behalf of Hispanic (referred to as Chicano at that time and in court documents) children classified as EMR, or educable mentally retarded (a now archaic term that has been replaced with intellectual disability), based on IQ tests administered in English. However, the children involved in the suit were not native English speakers and when retested in their native language, all but one (of nine) scored above the range designated as EMR. Diana was resolved through multiple consent decrees (agreements by the adverse parties ordered into effect by the federal judge). Although quite detailed, the central component of interest here is that the various decrees ensured that children would be tested in their native language, that more than one measure would be used, and that adaptive behavior in nonschool settings would be assessed prior to a diagnosis of EMR.

It seems obvious to us now that whenever persons are assessed in other than their native language, the validity of the results as traditionally interpreted would not hold up, at least in the case of ability testing. This had been obvious to the measurement community for quite some time prior to Diana, but it had not found its way into practice. Occasionally one still encounters cases of a clinician evaluating children in other than their native language and making inferences about intellectual development—clearly this is inappropriate.

Three cases involving intelligence testing of Black children related to special education placement went to trial: Larry P. v. Riles (343 F. Supp. 306,

1972; 495 F. Supp. 976, 1979); PASE v. Hannon (506 F. Supp. 831, 1980); and Marshall v. Georgia (CV 482-233, S.D. of Georgia, 1984). Each of these cases involved allegations of bias in IQ tests that caused the underestimation of the intelligence of Black children and subsequently led to disproportionate placement of Black children in special education programs. All three cases presented testimony by experts in education, testing, measurement, and related fields, some professing the tests to be biased and others professing they were not. That a disproportionate number of Black children were in special education was conceded in all cases—what was litigated was the reason.

In California in Larry P. v. Riles (Wilson Riles being superintendent of the San Francisco Unified School District), Judge Peckham ruled that IQ tests were in fact biased against Black children and resulted in discriminatory placement in special education. A reading of Peckham's decision reveals a clear condemnation of special education, which is critical to Peckham's logic. He determined that because special education placement was harmful, not helpful, to children, the use of a test (i.e., IQ) that resulted in disproportionate placement was therefore discriminatory. He prohibited (or enjoined) the use of IQ tests with Black children in the California public schools.

In PASE v. Hannon (PASE being an abbreviation for Parents in Action on Special Education), a similar case to Larry P. was brought against the Chicago public schools. Many of the same witnesses testified about many of the same issues. At the conclusion of the case, Judge Grady ruled in favor of the Chicago public schools, finding that although a few IQ test items might be biased, the degree of bias in the items was inconsequential.

In Marshall v. Georgia, the NAACP brought suit against rural Georgia school districts alleging bias in the instructional grouping and special education placement associated with IQ testing. Although some of the same individuals testified in this case, several new opinions were offered. However, the judge in Marshall eventually ruled in favor of the schools, finding that IQ tests were not in fact biased, and that a greater actual need for special education existed in minority populations.

In the courtroom, we are no closer to resolution of these issues today than we were in 1984 when Marshall was decided. However, these cases and other societal factors did foster much research that has brought us closer to a scientific resolution of the issues. They also prompted the development of new, up-to-date IQ tests and more frequent revisions or updating of older tests. Many challenges remain, especially that of understanding the continued higher failure rates (relative to the majority ethnic population of the United States) of some ethnic minorities in the public schools (while other ethnic minorities have a success rate that exceeds the majority population) and the disproportionate referral rates by teachers of these children for special education placement. The IQ test seems to be only one of many messengers in this crucial educational issue, and bias in the tests does not appear to be the answer.

than Whites. Both Hispanics and Native Americans tend to perform better on visual-spatial tasks relative to verbal tasks. All studies of race/ethnic group differences on ability tests do not show higher levels of performance by Whites. Asian American groups have been shown consistently to perform as well as or better than White groups. Depending on the specific aspect of intelligence under investigation, other race/ethnic groups show performance at or above the performance level of White groups (for a readable review of this research, see Neisser et al., 1996).

It should always be kept in mind that the overlap among the distributions of intelligence test scores for different ethnic groups is much greater than the size of the differences between the various groups. Put another way, there is always more within-group variability in performance on mental tests than between-group variability. Neisser et al. (1996) frame it this way:

> Group means have no direct implications for individuals. What matters for the next person you meet (to the extent that test scores matter at all) is that person's own particular score, not the mean of some reference group to which he or she happens to belong. The commitment to evaluate people on their own individual merit is central to a democratic society. It also makes quantitative sense. The distributions of different groups inevitably overlap, with the range of scores within any one group always wider than the mean differences between any two groups. In the case of intelligence test scores, the variance attributable to individual differences far exceeds the variance related to group membership. (p. 90)

15.3.1 Explaining Mean Group Differences

Once mean group differences are identified, it is natural to attempt to explain them. Reynolds (2000) notes that the most common explanations for these differences have typically fallen into four categories:

1. The differences primarily have a genetic basis
2. The differences have an environmental basis (e.g., SES, education, culture)
3. The differences are due to the interactive effect of genes and environment
4. The tests are defective and systematically underestimate the knowledge and skills of minorities

The final explanation (i.e., Category 4) is embodied in the CTBH introduced earlier in this chapter. Restated, the CTBH represents the contention that any gender, ethnic, racial, or other nominally determined group differences on mental tests are due to inherent, artifactual biases produced within the tests through flawed psychometric methodology. Group differences are believed then to stem from characteristics of the tests and to be totally unrelated to any actual differences in the psychological trait, skill, or ability in question. Because mental tests are based largely on middle-class values and knowledge, their results are more valid for those groups and will be biased against other groups to the extent that they deviate from those values and knowledge bases. Thus, ethnic and other group differences result from flawed psychometric methodology and not from actual differences in aptitude. As will be discussed, this hypothesis reduces to one of *differential validity*; the hypothesis of differential validity being that tests measure intelligence and other constructs more accurately and make more valid predictions for individuals from the groups on which the tests are mainly based than for those from other groups. The practical implications of such bias have been pointed out previously and are the issues over which most of the court cases have been fought.

If the CTBH is incorrect, then group differences are not attributable to the tests and must be due to one of the other factors mentioned previously. The model emphasizing the interactive effect of genes and environment (category c, commonly referred to as the Environment × Genetic Interaction Model) is dominant among contemporary professionals who reject the argument that group differences are artifacts of test bias; however, there is much debate over the relative contributions of genetic and environmental factors (Reynolds, 2000; Suzuki & Valencia, 1997). In addition to the models noted, Williams (1970), Helms (1992), and Richardson (1993) proposed other models with regard to Black-White differences on aptitude tests, raising the possibility of qualitatively different cognitive structures that require different methods of measurement.

> The controversy over test bias should not be confused with that over etiology of any observed group differences.

15.3.2 Test Bias and Etiology

The controversy over test bias is distinct from the question of etiology. Reynolds and Ramsay (2003) note that the need to research etiology is only relevant once it has been determined that mean score differences are real, not simply artifacts of the assessment process. Unfortunately, measured differences themselves have often been inferred to indicate genetic differences and therefore the genetically based intellectual inferiority of some groups. This inference is not defensible from a scientific perspective.

15.3.3 Test Bias and Fairness

As mentioned previously, bias is considered a portion of the overall construct of fairness. As noted by Brown, Reynolds, and Whitaker (1999), fairness is a moral, philosophical, or legal issue on which reasonable people can disagree. On the other hand, bias is a statistical property of a test. Therefore, bias is a property empirically estimated from test data whereas fairness is a principle established through debate and opinion. Nevertheless, it is common to incorporate information about bias when considering the fairness of an assessment process. For example, a biased test would likely be considered unfair by essentially everyone. However, it is clearly possible that an unbiased test might be considered unfair by at least some. Special Interest Topic 15.3 summarizes the discussion of fairness in testing and test use from the *Standards* (AERA et al., 2014).

Special Interest Topic 15.3: Fairness and Bias: A Complex Relationship
The Standards (AERA et al., 2014) present four different ways that fairness is typically used in the context of assessment.

1. *Fairness in treatment during the testing process*: A primary goal of testing is to maximize the opportunity for test takers to demonstrate their knowledge or ability on the construct being measured. Carefully developed tests that follow standardized administration procedures in a controlled environment suitable for completing the test achieve this goal. Factors such as proper seating, adequate lighting, strictly controlled time limits, and test proctor responsibilities can be adequately controlled with minimal effort within a test setting, but for nationally based tests that occur (e.g., the SAT, the National Council Licensure Examination for nurses, etc.), it can be harder to control across multiple settings. Differences across settings can lead to inadvertent advantages for some test takers over others. Thus, to enable fairness across such settings, it is important to establish guidelines for use across multiple settings.

2. *Fairness as a lack of measurement bias*: When a test measures an attribute unrelated to the intended construct being measured or the manner in which the test is used, it can result test score differences across subgroups. Differential item functioning (DIF) occurs when test takers of equal ability do not have the same probability of answering a test item correctly. An indication of DIF must be accompanied by a suitable, substantial explanation for DIF to justify an item is biased. Differential test functioning (DTF) refers to differences in the functioning of tests between defined groups. DTF indicates that individuals from different groups who have the same standing on the construct being measured do not have the same expected test score. Items that indicate DIF or test scores that indicate DTF can lead to predictive bias, which is found when differences exist in the pattern of associations between test scores and other variables for different groups, causing concerns about bias in the inferences drawn from the use of test scores. Regression is used to determine differential prediction is present, which can be measured by slope and/or intercept differences in the regression analyses between targeted groups.

3. *Fairness in access to the construct as measured*: A goal of fairness in testing is to allow all test takers an opportunity to demonstrate their standing on the construct being measured. Accessible testing situations enable test takers to show their status on the construct without being unduly advantaged or disadvantaged by irrelevant individual characteristics (e.g., age, race, disability status, gender, etc.). Accessibility can be understood when contrasting the knowledge, skills, and abilities that reflect the construct being measured by the test with the knowledge, skills, and abilities that are required for test takers to respond to the test tasks or items. Factors related

to individual characteristics can restrict accessibility can interfere with measuring the construct. For example, presenting a personality test in Braille or large-print format makes it more accessible to a visually impaired person, increasing the changes for a valid measurement of a person's personality characteristics. When test-taker characteristics that impede accessibility are related to the construct being measured (e.g., dyslexia and a test of reading), then adaptation of the construct might be warranted, and might result in more accurate measurement of the construct for the test taker, even if it is not directly comparable to the measurement of the original construct.

4. *Fairness as validity of individual test score interpretations for the intended uses*: Fairness is concerned with the validity of interpreting individual scores for their intended uses. While treating all individuals as similarly as possible is an important aspect of fairness, it is also important to take into account the individual characteristics of the test taker and understand how these characteristics may interfere with contextual factors of the testing situation and the interpretation of test scores. Test professionals are tasked with developing an understanding of when standardized testing procedures can and should be modified to obtaining more accurate measurement for certain groups of test takers, and when modifications can lead to an unfair advantage over other test takers.

5. In concluding the discussion of fairness, the *Standards* notes that fairness should not be perceived as equality of testing outcomes for relevant population subgroups. While differences in subgroups scores should increase scrutiny that possible test bias exists, group differences alone do not indicate that a testing application is biased or unfair.

15.3.4 Test Bias and Offensiveness

There is also a distinction between test bias and item offensiveness. Test developers often use a minority review panel to examine each item for content that may be offensive or demeaning to one or more groups (e.g., see Reynolds & Kamphaus, 2003, for a practical example). This is a good procedure for identifying and eliminating offensive items, but it does not ensure that the items are not biased. Research has consistently found little evidence that one can identify, by personal inspection, which items are biased and which are not (for reviews, see Camilli & Shepard, 1994; Reynolds, Lowe, & Saenz, 1999).

15.3.5 Test Bias and Inappropriate Test Administration and Use

The controversy over test bias is also not about blatantly inappropriate administration and usage of mental tests. Administration of a test in English to an individual for whom English is a poor second language is inexcusable both ethically and legally, regardless of any bias in the tests themselves (unless of course, the purpose of the test is to assess English-language skills). It is of obvious importance that tests be administered by skilled and sensitive professionals who are aware of the factors that may artificially lower an individual's test scores. That should go without saying, but some court cases involve just such abuses. Considering the use of tests to assign pupils to special education classes or other programs, the question needs to be asked, "What would you use instead of a test?" Teacher recommendations alone are less reliable and valid than standardized test scores and are subject to many external influences. Whether special education programs are of adequate quality to meet the needs of children is an important educational question, but separate from the test bias question, a distinction sometimes confused.

15.3.6 Bias and Extraneous Factors

The controversy over the use of mental tests is complicated further by the fact that resolution of the cultural test bias question in either direction will not resolve the problem of the role of nonintellective factors that may influence the test scores of individuals from any group, minority, or majority. Regardless of any group differences, it is individuals who are tested and whose scores may or may not be accurate. Similarly, it is individuals who are assigned to classes and accepted or rejected for employment or college admission. Most assessment professionals acknowledge that a number of emotional and motivational factors may impact performance on intelligence tests. The extent to which these factors influence individual as opposed to group performance is difficult to determine.

15.4   Cultural Bias and the Nature of Psychological Testing

The question of cultural bias in testing arises from and is continuously fueled by the very nature of psychological and educational processes and how we measure those processes. Psychological processes are by definition internal to the organism and not subject to direct observation and measurement but must instead be inferred from behavior. It is difficult to determine one-to-one relationships between observable events in the environment, the behavior of an organism, and hypothesized underlying mediational processes. Many classic controversies over theories of learning revolved around constructs such as expectancy, habit, and inhibition. Disputes among different camps in learning were controversial and of long duration. Indeed, there are still disputes as to the nature and number of processes such as emotion and motivation. It should be expected that intelligence, as one of the most complex psychological processes, would involve definitional and measurement disputes that prove difficult to resolve.

In contrast, there are few charges of bias relating to physical measures that are on absolute scales, whether interval or ratio. Group differences in height, as an extreme example, are not attributed by anyone to any kind of cultural test bias. There is no question concerning the validity of measures of height or weight of anyone in any culture. Nor is there any question about one's ability to make cross-cultural comparisons of these absolute measures.

The issue of cultural bias arises because of the procedures involved in psychological testing. Psychological tests measure traits that are not directly observable, subject to differences in definition, and measurable only on a relative scale. From this perspective, the question of cultural bias in mental testing is a subset, obviously of major importance, of the problem of uncertainty and possible bias in psychological testing generally. Bias might exist not only in mental tests but in other types of psychological tests as well, including personality, vocational, and psychopathological. Making the problem of bias in mental testing even more complex, not all mental tests are of the same quality; some are certainly psychometrically superior to others. There is a tendency for critics and defenders alike to overgeneralize across tests, lumping virtually all tests together under the heading mental tests or intelligence tests. Professional opinions of mental tests vary considerably, and some of the most widely used tests are not well respected by psychometricians. Thus, unfortunately, the question of bias must eventually be answered on a virtually test-by-test basis.

> The question of bias must eventually be answered on a virtually test-by-test basis.

15.5   Objections to the Use of Educational and Psychological Tests with Minority Students

In 1969, the *Association of Black Psychologists* (ABPsi) adopted the following official policy on educational and psychological testing (Williams, Dotson, Dow, & Williams, 1980):

> The Association of Black Psychologists fully supports those parents who have chosen to defend their rights by refusing to allow their children and themselves to be subjected to achievement, intelligence, aptitude and performance tests which have been and are being used to (a) label Black people as uneducable; (b) place Black children in "special" classes and schools; (c) perpetuate inferior education in Blacks; (d) assign Black children to lower educational tracks than Whites; (e) deny Black students higher educational opportunities; and (f) destroy positive intellectual growth and development of Black people.

Since 1968 the ABPsi (a group with a current membership of about 1400) has sought a moratorium on the use of all psychological and educational tests with students from disadvantaged backgrounds. The ABPsi carried its call for a moratorium to other professional organizations in psychology and education. In direct response to the ABPsi call, the American Psychological Association's (APA) Board of Directors requested its Board of Scientific Affairs to appoint a group to study the use of psychological and educational tests with disadvantaged students. The committee report (Cleary, Humphreys, Kendrick, & Wesman, 1975) was subsequently published in the official journal of the APA, *American Psychologist*.

Subsequent to the ABPsi's policy statement, other groups adopted similarly stated policy statements on testing. These groups included the National Association for the Advancement of Colored People (NAACP), the National Education Association (NEA), the National Association of Elementary School Principals (NAESP), the American Personnel and Guidance Association (APGA), and others. The APGA called for the Association of Measurement and Evaluation in Guidance (AMEG), a sister organization, to "develop and disseminate a position paper stating the limitations of group intelligence tests particularly and generally of standardized psychological, educational, and employment testing for low socioeconomic and underprivileged and non-White individuals in educational, business, and industrial environments." It should be noted that the statements by these organizations assumed that psychological and educational tests are biased, and that what is needed is that the assumed bias be removed.

The request was timely and taken seriously by the profession of psychology. In 1969, there was actually very little research available to address the questions surrounding bias in psychological assessment. The efforts of ABPsi spurred the disciplines that develop and apply tests to create standards and conduct empirical inquiry into these issues. Today, we know a great deal about the problems of bias in psychological tests and assessments.

Many potentially legitimate objections to the use of educational and psychological tests with minorities have been raised by Black and other minority psychologists. Unfortunately, these objections are frequently stated, still, as facts, on rational rather than empirical grounds. The most frequently stated problems fall into one of the following categories (Reynolds, 2000; Reynolds et al., 1999; Reynolds & Ramsay, 2003).

15.5.1 Inappropriate Content

Black and other minority children have not been exposed to the material involved in the test questions or other stimulus materials. The tests are geared primarily toward White middle-class homes, vocabulary, knowledge, and values. As a result of inappropriate content, the tests are unsuitable for use with minority children.

15.5.2 Inappropriate Standardization Samples

Ethnic minorities are underrepresented in standardization samples used in the collection of normative reference data. As a result of the inappropriate standardization samples, the tests are unsuitable for use with minority children.

15.5.3 Examiner and Language Bias

Because most psychologists are White and speak only standard English, they may intimidate Black and other ethnic minorities and so examiner and language bias result. They are also unable accurately to communicate with minority children—to the point of being insensitive to ethnic pronunciation of words on the test. Lower test scores for minorities, then, may reflect only this intimidation and difficulty in the communication process, not lower ability.

15.5.4 Inequitable Social Consequences

As a result of bias in educational and psychological tests, minority group members, already at a disadvantage in the educational and vocational markets because of past discrimination, are thought to be unable to learn and are disproportionately assigned to dead-end educational tracks. This represents inequitable social consequences. Labeling effects also fall under this category.

15.5.5 Measurement of Different Constructs

Related to inappropriate test content mentioned earlier, this position asserts that the tests measure different constructs when used with children from other than the middle-class culture on which the tests are largely based, and thus do not measure minority intelligence validly.

15.5.6 Differential Predictive Validity

Although tests may accurately predict a variety of outcomes for middle-class children, they do not predict successfully any relevant behavior for minority group members. In other words, test usage might result in valid predictions for one group, but invalid predictions in another. This is referred to as differential predictive validity. Further, there are objections to the use of the standard criteria against which tests

> The hypothesis of differential validity suggests that tests measure constructs more accurately and make more valid predictions for individuals from the groups on which the tests are mainly based than for those from other groups.

are validated with minority cultural groups. For example, scholastic or academic attainment levels in White middle-class schools are themselves considered by a variety of Black psychologists to be biased as criteria for the validation of aptitude measures.

15.5.7 Qualitatively Distinct Aptitude and Personality

Minority and majority groups possess aptitude and personality characteristics that are qualitatively different, and as a result test development should begin with different definitions for different groups. For example, Richardson (1993) holds that researchers have not satisfactorily settled the debate over whether intelligence tests measure general intelligence or a European cognitive style. Similarly, Helms (1992) proposed a cognitive-difference model that emphasizes differences in "European-centered" and "African-centered" values and beliefs. Helms suggests that these different styles significantly impact the way examinees respond on intelligence tests, which would then require different item sets or at least different "correct answers" from individuals of different ethnic backgrounds. Special Interest Topic 15.4 provides an introduction to a unique explanation for group differences referred to as "stereotype threat."

Special Interest Topic 15.4: Stereotype Threat: An Emerging But Controversial Explanation of Group Differences on Various Tests of Mental Abilities

Steele and Aronson in 1995 posited a unique explanation for group differences on mental test scores. They argued that such differences were created by a variable they deemed "Stereotype Threat." More recently, they defined stereotype threat as follows:

> When a negative stereotype about a group that one is part of becomes relevant, usually as an interpretation of one's behavior or an experience one is having, stereotype threat is the resulting sense that one can then be judged or treated in terms of the stereotype or that one might do something that would inadvertently confirm it (Steele, Spencer, & Aronson, 2002, p. 389).

While we find this explanation somewhat vague and lacking specificity for research purposes, in experimental research regarding mental testing outcomes, stereotype threat is most often operationalized as being given a test that is described as diagnostic of one's ability and/or being asked to report one's race prior to testing. Therefore we see two components to the threat—being told one's ability is to be judged on a test of mental ability and secondly, being asked to report one's racial identification, or at least believing it to be relevant in some way to the evaluation of examination results (although some argue either component is sufficient to achieve the effect). Stereotype threat research then goes on to argue, as one example, that if one takes a test of mental ability, but the examinee is told it is not for evaluating the test taker, but to examine the test itself and no racial identifier is requested, then racial group differences in performance on the test will disappear.

Many studies now demonstrate this stereotype effect, but some incorporate controversial statistical procedures that might confound the results by equating the two groups (i.e., erasing the group differences) on the basis of variables irrelevant to the effect of the stereotype threat. Sackett and his colleagues (2004) have discussed this methodological problem in detail (noting additional violations of the assumptions that underlie such analyses), and we find ourselves in essential agreement with their observations. Nomura et al. (2007) stated it succinctly when they noted from their own findings:

"Equalizing the performance of racial groups in most Stereotype Threat Studies is not an effect of the manipulation of Stereotype Threat elicitors (task descriptions), but is a result of a statistical manipulation (covariance)" (p. 7). Additionally, some research that has taken a thorough look at the issue using multiple statistical approaches has argued that stereotype threat may have just the opposite effect at times from what was originally proposed by Steele and Aronson (e.g., see Nomura et al., 2007). That is, it may enhance the performance of the majority group as opposed to denigrating the performance of the minority.

We are also bothered by the theoretical vagaries of the actual mechanism by which stereotype threat might operate as a practical matter. Steele and Aronson essentially argue that it is a process of response inhibition; that is, when an individual encounters a circumstance, event, or activity in which a stereotype of a group to which the person belongs becomes salient, anxiety or concerns about being judged according to that stereotype arise and inhibit performance. Anxiety is not named specifically as the culprit by many stereotype threat researchers, but it seems the most likely moderator of the proclaimed effect. While the well-known inverted U-shaped anxiety-performance curve seems real enough, can this phenomenon really account for group differences in mental test scores? So far, we view the findings of racial equalization due to the neutralization of the so-called stereotype effect as a statistical artifact, but the concept remains interesting, is not yet fully understood, and we may indeed be proven wrong!

Some good readings on this issue for follow up include the following works:

Nomura, J. M., Stinnett, T., Castro, F., Atkins, M., Beason, S., Linden, S., ... Wiechmann, K. (2007, March). *Effects of stereotype threat on cognitive performance of African Americans*. Paper presented to the annual meeting of the National Association of School Psychologists, New York.
Sackett, P. R., Hardison, C. M., & Cullen, M. J. (2004). On interpreting stereotype threat as accounting for African-American differences on cognitive tests. *American Psychologist, 59*(1), 7–13.
Steele, C. M., & Aronson, J. (1995). Stereotype threat and the intellectual test performance of African Americans. *Journal of Personality and Social Psychology, 69*, 797–811.
Steele, C. M., Spencer, S. J., & Aronson, J. (2002). Contending with group image: The psychology of stereotype and social identity threat. In M. Zanna (Ed.), *Advances in experimental social psychology* (Vol. 23, pp. 379–440). New York, NY: Academic Press.

The early actions of the ABPsi were most instrumental in bringing forward these objections into greater public and professional awareness and subsequently prompted a considerable amount of research. When the objections were first raised, very little data existed to answer these charges. Contrary to the situation decades ago when the current controversy began, research now exists that examines many of these concerns and does so in great

> The early actions of the ABPsi brought these issues into public and professional awareness, which subsequently promoted a considerable amount of research.

detail. Test developers and publishers also routinely examine tests for potentially biasing factors as well, prior to making tests commercially available.

15.6   The Problem of Definition in Test Bias Research: Differential Validity

Arriving at a consensual definition of test bias has produced considerable as yet unresolved debate among many measurement professionals. Although the resulting debate has generated a number of models from which to examine bias, these models usually focus on the decision-making system and not on the test itself. The concept of test bias per se then comes down to a question of the validity of the proposed interpretation of performance on a test and the estimation of that performance level, that is, the test score. Test bias refers to systematic error in the estimation of some "true" value for a group of individuals, due to construct underrepresentation or due to construct-irrelevant components of test scores that differentially affect the performance of different groups of test takers (AERA et al., 2014). As we noted previously, differential validity is present when a test measures or estimates a construct differently for one group than for another.

As discussed in previous chapters, evidence for the validity of test score interpretations can come from sources both internal and external to the test. Bias in a test may be found to exist in any or all of these categories of validity evidence. Prior to examining the evidence on the CTBH, the concept of culture-free testing and the definition of mean differences in test scores as test bias merit attention (Special Interest Topic 15.5).

Special Interest Topic 15.5: Why Is the Cultural Test Bias Hypothesis So Robust in the Profession: And Why Do So Many Hold the Mean Differences Equals Bias Ideology?

Since the late 1960s, a substantial body of content and methodological research on bias has been conducted. Much of this research has been conducted by psychometricians and published in major psychometric journals not often read by those in other psychological specialties. However, much of what has been learned is summarized in book chapters and entire books easily accessible to mainstream psychologists and some of the empirical and methodological research has appeared in the most widely subscribed journals of the American Psychological Association. Nevertheless, certain myths persist in the writings and actions of many professional psychologists who are either unaware of this research or choose to ignore it. Below are some thoughts of this seeming conundrum.

With regard to the media, Herrnstein (1982) provided an account of his own media encounters that leads one to believe that bias in the media is responsible for their selective reporting (see also Brown et al., 1999, for additional examples). Perhaps this is the case, but with specific regard to race and ethnic differences on measures of IQ, aptitude, and achievement, a broader explanation—and one that captures the biases of psychologists—seems required. Whatever this explanation may be, it is likely related to the phenomenon that leads some in our profession to believe in miraculous cures for intellectual disability and the dramatic resistance to the discrediting of the Milwaukee Project (Reynolds, 1987). (The Milwaukee Project was discussed in Chap. 9. In summary, the project's initial results supported the hypothesis that early, intensive interventions with children at risk for intellectual disability could dramatically increase intelligence and future academic achievement. However, subsequent research found little or no support for the hypothesis that early interventions could result in lasting changes in IQ or achievement.)

Particularly for health providers, but for most of the lay public as well, it is our concern, our hope, and our belief in our fellow humans that leads to ready acceptance of the CTBH and to the idea that any mean difference in scores or performance levels on psychological tests confirms that tests are biased. We want everyone to be created equal not just in the sense of worth as a human being as acknowledged in our Constitution, but in the sense of level of aptitude or ability. We find it anathema that ethnic differences in aptitude or ability might be real; we simply do not want it to be so. So, we search for reasons for why these differences are not true. The CTBH seems far more palatable than the alternative, as it argues that racial and ethnic group differences on mental tests result from problems with the tests themselves—tests also being something for which we all have some, though varying degrees of dislike anyway. The emotional and political appeal of the hypothesis is strong but dangerous. It is also the appeal of the egalitarian fallacy.

Some who do read the psychometric research dismiss it in favor of political arguments. Gould (1995, 1996) has acknowledged that tests are not statistically biased and do not show differential predictive validity. He argues, however, that defining cultural bias statistically is confusing: The public is concerned not with statistical bias, but with whether minority-White IQ differences occur because society treats ethnic minorities unfairly. That is, the public considers tests biased if they record biases originating elsewhere in society (Gould, 1995). In this context we interpret the tests as the messengers—the Gould approach is the "kill the messenger" approach and does not lead to solutions; rather, it leads to ignorance.

A related issue that is also likely involved in the profession's reluctance to abandon the CTBH is a failure to separate the CTBH from questions of etiology. Data reflecting ethnic differences on aptitude measures have been interpreted as supporting the hypothesis of genetic differences in intelligence and implicating one group as superior to another. Such interpretations understandably call for an emotional response and are not defensible from a scientific perspective.

The task of science and rational inquiry is to understand the source of these differences, to pit alternative theories boldly against one another, to analyze and consider our data and its complexities again and again, and to do so without the emotional overpull of our compassion and our beliefs. Particularly with regard to such sensitive and polemic topics as racial and ethnic differences on mental tests, we must stay especially close to our empirical research, perhaps adopting an old but articulate rubric, the one with which we opened this chapter: In God we trust; all others must have data.

15.7 Cultural Loading, Cultural Bias, and Culture-Free Tests

Cultural loading and cultural bias are not synonymous terms, though the concepts are frequently confused even in the professional literature. A test or test item can be culturally loaded without being culturally biased. Cultural loading refers to the degree of cultural specificity present in the

> Cultural loading refers to the degree of cultural specificity present in the test or individual items of the test.

test or individual items of the test. Certainly, the greater the cultural specificity of a test item, the greater the likelihood of the item being biased when used with individuals from other cultures. Virtually all tests in current use are bound in some way by their cultural specificity. Culture loading must be viewed on a continuum from general (defining the culture in a broad, liberal sense) to specific (defining the culture in narrow, highly distinctive terms).

A number of attempts have been made to develop a culture-free (sometimes referred to as culture fair) intelligence test. However, *culture-free tests* are generally inadequate from a statistical or psychometric perspective (e.g., Anastasi & Urbina, 1997). It may be that because intelligence is often defined in large part on the basis of behavior judged to be of value to the survival and improvement of the culture and the individuals within that culture, a truly culture-free test would be a poor predictor of intelligent behavior within the cultural setting. Once a test has been developed within a culture (a culture-loaded test) its generalizability to other cultures or subcultures within the dominant societal framework becomes a matter for empirical investigation.

15.8   Inappropriate Indicators of Bias: Mean Differences and Equivalent Distributions

Differences in mean levels of performance on cognitive tasks between two groups historically (and mistakenly) are believed to constitute test bias by a number of writers (e.g., Alley & Foster, 1978; Chinn, 1979; Hilliard, 1979). Those who support mean differences as an indication of test bias state correctly that there is no valid a priori scientific reason to believe that intellectual or other cognitive performance levels should differ across race. It is the inference that tests demonstrating such differences are inherently biased that is faulty. Just as there is no a priori basis for deciding that differences exist, there is no a priori basis for deciding that differences do not exist. From the standpoint of the objective methods of science, a priori or premature acceptance of either hypothesis (differences exist versus differences do not exist) is untenable. As stated in the *Standards* (AERA et al., 2014):

> Certainly, most testing professionals agree that group differences in testing outcomes should trigger heightened scrutiny for possible sources of test bias … However, group differences in outcomes do not in themselves indicate that a testing application is biased or unfair. (p. 54)

Some adherents to the "mean differences as bias" position also require that the distribution of test scores in each population or subgroup be identical prior to assuming that the test is nonbiased, regardless of its validity. Portraying a test as biased regardless of its purpose or the validity of its interpretations conveys an inadequate understanding of the psychometric construct and issues of bias. The mean difference definition of test bias is the most uniformly rejected of all definitions of test bias by psychometricians involved in investigating the problems of bias in assessment (e.g., Camilli & Shepard, 1994; Cleary et al., 1975; Cole & Moss, 1989; Hunter, Schmidt, & Rauschenberger, 1984; Reynolds, 1982, 1995, 2000).

> The mean difference definition of test bias is the most uniformly rejected of all definitions of test bias by psychometricians involved in investigating the problems of bias in assessment.

Jensen (1980) discusses the mean differences as bias definition in terms of the egalitarian fallacy. The egalitarian fallacy contends that all human populations are in fact identical on all mental traits or abilities. Any differences with regard to any aspect of the distribution of mental test scores indicate that something is wrong with the test itself. As Jensen points out, such an assumption is scientifically unwarranted. There are simply too many examples of specific abilities and even sensory capacities that have been shown to differ unmistakably across human populations. The result of the egalitarian assumption then is to remove the investigation of population differences in ability from the realm of scientific inquiry, an unacceptable course of action (Reynolds, 1980).

The belief of many people in the mean differences as bias definition is quite likely related to the nature-nurture controversy at some level. Certainly data reflecting racial differences on various aptitude measures have been interpreted to indicate support for a hypothesis of genetic differences in intelligence and implicating one group as superior to another. Such interpretations understandably call for a strong emotional response and are not defensible from a scientific perspective. Although IQ and other aptitude test score differences undoubtedly occur, the differences do not indicate deficits or superiority by any group, especially in relation to the personal worth of any individual member of a given group or culture.

15.9   Bias in Test Content

Bias in the content of educational and psychological tests has been a popular topic of critics of testing. These criticisms typically take the form of reviewing the items, comparing them to the critics'

> Bias in the content of psychological and educational tests has been a popular topic of critics of testing.

views of minority and majority cultural environments, and then singling out specific items as biased or unfair because:

- The items ask for information that minority or disadvantaged individuals have not had equal opportunity to learn.
- The items require the child to use information in arriving at an answer that minority or disadvantaged individuals have not had equal opportunity to learn.
- The scoring of the items is improper, unfairly penalizing the minority child because the test author has a Caucasian middle-class orientation that is reflected in the scoring criterion. Thus minority children do not receive credit for answers that may be correct within their own cultures but do not conform to Anglocentric expectations—this occurs in personality tests wherein minorities may respond to various questions in ways seen as adaptive in their own subculture but as indicative of psychopathology in the mind of the test developer.
- The wording of the questions is unfamiliar to minorities and even though they may "know" the correct answer they are unable to respond because they do not understand the question.

These problems with test items cause the items to be more difficult than they should actually be when used to assess minority individuals. This, of course, results in lower test scores for minorities, a well-documented finding. Are these criticisms of test items accurate? Do problems such as these account for minority-majority group score differences on mental tests? These are questions for empirical resolution rather than armchair speculation, which is certainly abundant in the evaluation of test bias. Empirical evaluation first requires a working definition. We will define a *biased test item* as follows:

An item is considered to be biased when it is demonstrated to be significantly more difficult for one group than another item measuring the same ability or construct when the overall level of performance on the construct is held constant.

There are two concepts of special importance in this definition. First, the group of items must be unidimensional; that is, they must all be measuring the same factor or dimension of aptitude or personality. Second, the items identified as biased must be differentially more difficult for one group than another. The definition allows for score differences between groups of unequal standing on the dimension in question but requires that the difference be reflected on all items in the test and in an equivalent fashion across items. A number of empirical techniques are available to locate deviant test items under this definition. Many of these techniques are based on item-response theory (IRT) and designed to detect differential item functioning, or DIF. The relative merits of each method are the subject of substantial debate, but in actual practice, each method has led to similar general conclusions, though the specific findings of each method often differ.

With multiple-choice tests, another level of complexity can easily be added to the examination of content bias. With a multiple-choice question, typically three or four distracters are given in addition to the correct response. Distracters may be examined for their attractiveness (the relative frequency with which they are chosen) across groups. When distracters are found to be disproportionately attractive for members of any particular group, the item may be defined as biased.

Research that includes thousands of subjects and more than 100 published studies consistently finds very little bias in tests at the level of the individual item. Although some biased items are nearly always found, they seldom account for more than 2–5% of the variance in performance and often, for every item favoring one group, there is an item favoring the other group.

> Content bias in well-prepared standardized tests is irregular in its occurrence, and no common characteristics of items that are found to be biased can be ascertained by expert judges.

Earlier in the study of item bias, it was hoped that the empirical analysis of tests at the item level would result in the identification of a category of items having similar content as biased and that such items could then be avoided in future test development (Flaugher, 1978). Very little similarity among items determined to be biased has been found. No one has been able to identify those characteristics of an item that cause the item to be biased. It does seem that poorly written, sloppy, and ambiguous items tend to be identified as biased with greater frequency than those items typically encountered in a well-constructed, standardized instrument.

A common practice of test developers seeking to eliminate "bias" from their newly developed educational and psychological tests has been to arrange for a panel of expert minority group members to review all proposed test items. Any item identified as "culturally biased" by the panel of experts is then expurgated from the instrument. Because, as previously noted, no detectable pattern or common characteristic of individual items statistically shown to be biased has been observed (given reasonable care at the item writing stage), it seems reasonable to question the armchair or expert minority panel approach to determining biased items. Several researchers, using a variety of psychological and educational tests, have identified items as being disproportionately more difficult for minority group members than for members of the majority culture and subsequently compared their results with a panel of expert judges. Studies by Jensen (1976) and Sandoval and Mille (1979) are representative of the methodology and results of this line of inquiry.

After identifying the eight most racially discriminating and eight least racially discriminating items on the Wonderlic Personnel Test, Jensen (1976) asked panels of five Black psychologists and five Caucasian psychologists to sort out the eight most and eight least discriminating items when only these 16 items were presented to them. The judges sorted the items at a no better than chance level. Sandoval and Mille (1979) conducted a somewhat more extensive analysis using items from the WISC-R. These two researchers had 38 Black, 22 Hispanic, and 40 White university students from Spanish, history, and education classes identify items from the WISC-R that are more difficult for a minority child than a White child and items that are equally difficult for each group. A total of 45 WISC-R items was presented to each judge; these items included the 15 most difficult items for Blacks as compared to Whites, the 15 most difficult items for Hispanics as compared to Whites, and the 15 items showing the most nearly identical difficulty indexes for minority and White children. The judges were asked to read each question and determine whether they thought the item was (1) easier for minority than White children, (2) easier for White than minority children, or (3) of equal difficulty for White and minority children. Sandoval and Mille's (1979) results indicated that the judges were not able to differentiate between items that were more difficult for minorities and items that were of equal difficulty across groups. The effects of the judges' ethnic backgrounds on the accuracy of their item bias judgments were also considered. Minority and nonminority judges did not differ in their ability to identify accurately biased items nor did they differ with regard to the type of incorrect identification they tended to make. Sandoval and Mille's (1979) two major conclusions were that "1) judges are not able to detect items which are more difficult for a minority child than an Anglo child, and 2) the ethnic background of the judge makes no difference in accuracy of item selection for minority children" (p. 6). Research since that time has continued to produce similar results: minority judges seldom exceed chance expectations in designating biased versus nonbiased test items in aptitude and in personality domains. Even without empirical support for its validity, the use of expert panels of minorities continues but for a different purpose. Members of various ethnic, religious, or other groups that have a cultural system in some way unique may well be able to identify items that contain material that is offensive, and the elimination of such items is proper.

15.9.1 How Test Publishers Commonly Identify Biased Items

Today's most recommended method for detecting *item bias* arises from applications of item-response theory (IRT), followed by a thoughtful, logical analysis of item content (Reynolds, 2000). The goal in the use of these methods is to determine the degree of differential item functioning (DIF), that is, whether items function differently across groups, as indicated by model parameters associated with the items. Embretson and Reise (2000) present an excellent overview of the theory and

applications of item-response theory, including a highly readable chapter on detecting DIF. Statistically significant DIF, coupled with a logical analysis of item content
that suggests the item may measure construct-irrelevant differences across groups,
provides a basis for rejecting items from tests.

IRT is concerned fundamentally with creating a mathematical model of item difficulty— or more technically, the probability of occurrence of a particular response
to a test item as a function of an examinee's relative position on a latent trait. Such
models specify various parameters that describe the behavior of the item within the
model; most IRT models include one, two, or three parameters, which may be
graphically represented in an item characteristic curve (ICC). The three parameters
in the three-parameter (3P) model are (a) discrimination power of the item, or slope
of the ICC, (b) item difficulty, located at the point on the difficulty level of the latent
trait at which the examinee has a 50% chance of correctly answering the item, and
(c) guessing parameter. Figure 15.1 demonstrates an ICC that uses a one-parameter
(also known as the Rasch Model after its originator) unidimensional model which is
widely used in aptitude testing. Its appropriateness depends on the context so other
ICC models may be more appropriate, particularly for multiple-choice items. The
greater complexity that can be modeled with the 3P model comes with a price: one
generally requires a much larger sample to develop a valid and reliable 3P model.
Two computer programs widely used to estimate item and latent parameters are
LOGIST and BILOG, which use the joint maximum likelihood (JML) and marginal
maximum likelihood (MML) methods, respectively.

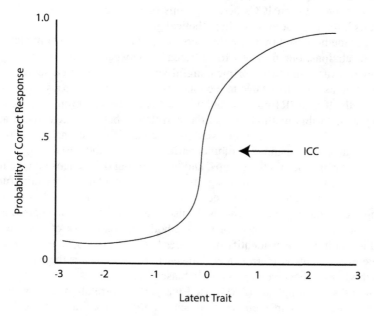

Fig. 15.1 An example of an item characteristic curve or ICC

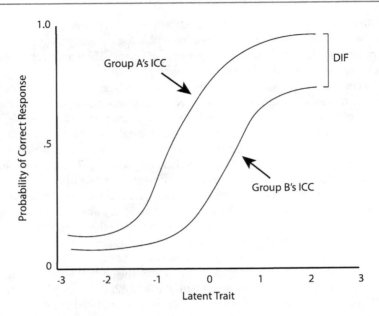

Fig. 15.2 A visual representation of DIF is the region between group A's and group B's item characteristic curves (ICCs)

In using IRT to determine DIF, one compares the ICCs of two different groups, yielding a DIF "index." Various statistical methods have been developed for measuring the gaps between ICCs across groups of examinees. Figure 15.2 demonstrates this DIF "gap" across two hypothetical groups.

Another method used by test publishers is a partial correlation approach. Using partial correlations, one may test for differences between groups on the degree to which there exists significant or meaningful variation in observed scores on individual test items not attributable to the total test score. It provides a simpler method than either the ICC or IRT models, and it is readily accessible through major statistical programs. In this method, the partial correlation between item score and the nominal variable of interest (e.g., sex) is calculated, partialling the correlation between total test score and the nominal variable. This method essentially holds the total score constant across the groups, and the resulting differences may be used to identify problematic items if it is significant and particularly if meaningful. This latter determination commonly based on effect size, which is easily obtained by squaring the partial r value. Reynolds, Willson, and Chatman (1984) provide more information on the development of this method. The main risk of the use of this method is that it may over-identify differences between groups, so it is necessary to calculate experiment-wise error rates. However, this also makes the partial correlation method more sensitive to potentially biased items.

Reynolds and Kamphaus (2003) used the partial correlation method to detect potentially bias items in their development of the first edition of the Reynolds

Intellectual Assessment Scales (RIAS). They computed the partial r of the item--subtest total score, partialling the total score correlation with each nominal variable of interest (gender and ethnicity) one variable at a time and separately by age group. One advantage of the partial correlation in such studies is that it can be used successfully with much smaller sample sizes than the ICC and most other techniques. Thus, analyses can be run at smaller age intervals and any developmental interaction can be detected more readily. The partial r and subsequently its effect size stabilize at smaller sample sizes compared to the IRT approach.

From a large number of studies employing a wide range of methodologies, a relatively clear picture emerges. Content bias in well-prepared standardized tests is irregular in its occurrence, and no common characteristics of items that are found to be biased can be ascertained by expert judges (minority or nonminority). The variance in group score differences on mental tests associated with ethnic group membership when content bias has been found is relatively small (typically ranging from 2% to 5%). Although the search for common biased item characteristics will continue, cultural bias in aptitude tests has found no consistent empirical support in a large number of actuarial studies contrasting the performance of a variety of ethnic and gender groups on items of the most widely employed intelligence scales in the United States. Most major test publishing companies do an adequate job of reviewing their assessments for the presence of content bias. Nevertheless, certain standardized tests have not been examined for the presence of content bias, and research with these tests should continue regarding potential content bias with different ethnic groups (Reynolds & Ramsay, 2003).

15.10   Bias in Other Internal Features of Tests

There is no single method for the accurate determination of the degree to which educational and psychological tests measure a distinct construct. The defining of bias in construct measurement, i.e., **construct bias**, then requires a general statement that can be researched from a variety of viewpoints with a broad range of methodology. The following rather parsimonious definition is proffered:

> Bias exists in regard to construct measurement when a test is shown to measure different hypothetical traits (psychological constructs) for one group than another or to measure the same trait but with differing degrees of accuracy. (Reynolds, 1982)

As is befitting the concept of construct measurement, many different methods have been employed to examine existing psychological tests and batteries of tests for potential bias. One of the more popular and necessary empirical approaches to investigating construct measurement is factor analysis. Factor analysis, as a procedure, identifies clusters of test items or clusters of subtests of psychological or educational tests that correlate highly with one another, and less so or not at all with other subtests or items. Factor analysis allows one to determine patterns of interrelationships of performance among groups of individuals. For example, if several subtests of an intelligence scale load highly on (are members of) the same factor, then if a group of individuals score high on one of these subtests, they would be expected to score at a high level on other subtests that load highly on that factor. Psychometricians attempt to determine through a review of the test content and correlates of performance on the factor in question what psychological trait underlies performance; or, in a more hypothesis testing approach, they will make predictions concerning the pattern of factor loadings. Hilliard (1979), one of the more vocal critics of IQ tests on the basis of cultural bias, pointed out early in test bias research that one of the potential ways of studying bias involves the comparison of factor analytic results of test studies across race.

If the IQ test is a valid and reliable test of "innate" ability or abilities, then the factors which emerge on a given test should be the same from one population to another, since "intelligence" is asserted to be a set of mental processes. Therefore, while the configuration of scores of a particular group on the factor profile would be expected to differ, logic would dictate that the factors themselves would remain the same (p. 53).

Although not agreeing that identical factor analyses of an instrument speak to the "innateness" of the abilities being measured, consistent factor analytic results across populations do provide strong evidence that whatever is being measured by the instrument is being measured in the same manner and is in fact the same construct within each group. The information derived from comparative factor analysis across populations is directly relevant to the use of educational and psychological tests in diagnosis and other decision-making functions. Psychologists, in order to make consistent interpretations of test score data, must be certain that the test(s) measures the same variable across populations.

A number of studies of factorial similarity of tests' latent structures have appeared over the past three decades, dealing with a number of different tasks. These studies have for the most part focused on aptitude or intelligence tests, the most controversial of all techniques of measurement. Numerous studies of the similarity of factor analysis outcomes for children of different ethnic groups, across gender, and even diagnostic groupings have been reported over the past 30 years. Results reported are highly consistent in revealing that the internal structure of most standardized tests varies quite little across groups. Comparisons of the factor structure of the Wechsler Intelligence Scales (e.g., various editions of the WISC and WAIS) and the Reynolds Intellectual Assessment Scales (Reynolds & Kamphaus, 2003) in particular and other intelligence tests find the tests to be highly factorially similar across gender and ethnicity for Blacks, Whites, and Hispanics. The structure of ability tests for other groups has been researched less extensively, but evidence thus far with Chinese, Japanese, and Native Americans does not show substantially different factor structures for these groups.

As is appropriate for studies of construct measurement, comparative factor analysis has not been the only method of determining whether bias exists. Another method of investigation involves the comparison of internal-consistency reliability estimates across groups. As described in Chap. 4, internal-consistency reliability is determined by the degree to which the items are all measuring a similar construct. The internal-consistency reliability coefficient reflects the accuracy of measurement of the construct. To be unbiased with regard to construct validity, internal-consistency estimates should be approximately equal across race. This characteristic of tests has been investigated for a number of popular aptitude tests for Blacks, Whites, and Hispanics with results similar to those already noted.

15.10.1 How Test Publishers Commonly Identify Bias in Construct Measurement

Factor analysis across groups is the most common method in use by various commercial test developers to assess for bias in construct measurement. However, many other methods of comparing construct measurement across groups have been used to investigate bias in tests. These methods include the correlation of raw scores with age, comparison of item-total correlations across groups, comparisons of alternate form and test-retest correlations, evaluation of kinship correlation and differences, and others (see Reynolds, 2002, for a discussion of these methods). A more recently proposed method for assessing test bias is comparative item selection (Reynolds, 1998). This method involves the use of the same method of selecting items for inclusion in a test repeated across the groups of interest; one is free to use item selection methods based on either classical test theory or IRT. Unbiased tests will generally obtain about a 90% rate of overlap between selected items. The technique will yield substantially lower rate of overlap with biased tests, as well as tests with poor item reliabilities. This method also requires large samples for stable results. Reynolds (1998) provides a full discussion of this approach and demonstrates its application to several personality measures. The general results of research with all of these methods have been supportive of the consistency of construct measurement of tests across ethnicity and gender.

Construct measurement of a large number of popular psychometric assessment instruments has been investigated across ethnicity and gender with a divergent set of methodologies. No consistent evidence of bias in construct measurement has been

> No consistent evidence of bias in construct measurement has been found in the many prominent standardized tests investigated.

found in the many prominent standardized tests investigated. This leads to the conclusion that these psychological tests function in essentially the same manner across ethnicity and gender, the test materials are perceived and reacted to in a similar manner, and the tests are measuring the same construct with equivalent accuracy for Blacks, Whites, Hispanic, and other American minorities for both sexes. Differential validity or single-group validity has not been found and likely is not an existing phenomenon with regard to well-constructed standardized psychological and educational tests. These tests appear to be reasonably unbiased for the groups investigated, and mean score differences do not appear to be an artifact of test bias (Reynolds & Ramsay, 2003).

15.11   Bias in Prediction and in Relation to Variables External to the Test

Internal analyses of bias (such as with item content and construct measurement) are less confounded than analyses of bias in prediction due to the potential problems of bias in the criterion measure. Prediction is also strongly influenced by the reliability of criterion measures, which frequently is poor. (The degree of relation between a predictor and a criterion is restricted as a function of the square root of the product of the reliabilities of the two variables.) Arriving at a consensual definition of bias in prediction is also a difficult task. Yet, from the standpoint of the traditional practical applications of aptitude and intelligence tests in forecasting probabilities of future performance levels, prediction is the most crucial use of test scores to examine. Looking directly at bias as a characteristic of a test and not a selection model, Cleary

> From the standpoint of traditional practical applications on aptitude and intelligence tests in forecasting probabilities of future performance levels, prediction is the most crucial use of test scores to examine.

et al.'s (1975) definition of test fairness, as restated here in modern times, is a clear direct statement of test bias with regard to *prediction bias*:

> A test is considered biased with respect to prediction when the inference drawn from the test score is not made with the smallest feasible random error or if there is constant error in an inference or prediction as a function of membership in a particular group. (Reynolds, 1982, p. 201)

The evaluation of bias in prediction under the Cleary et al. (1975) definition (known as the regression definition) is quite straightforward. With simple regressions, predictions take the form $Y = aX + b$ where a is the constant and b is the regression coefficient. When this equation is graphed (forming a regression line), a is the Y-intercept and b the slope of the regression line. Given our definition of bias in prediction validity, nonbias requires errors in prediction to be independent of group membership, and the regression line formed for any pair of variables must be the same for each group for whom predictions are to be made. Whenever the slope or the intercept differs significantly across groups, there is bias in prediction if one attempts to use a regression equation based on the combined groups. When the regression equations for two (or more) groups are equivalent, prediction is the same for those groups. This condition is referred to variously as homogeneity of regression across groups, simultaneous regression, or fairness in prediction. *Homogeneity of regression* is illustrated in Fig. 15.3, in which the regression line shown is equally appropriate for making predictions for all groups. Whenever homogeneity of regression across groups does not occur, then separate regression equations should be used for each group concerned.

> When the regression equations are the same for two or more groups, prediction is the same for those groups.

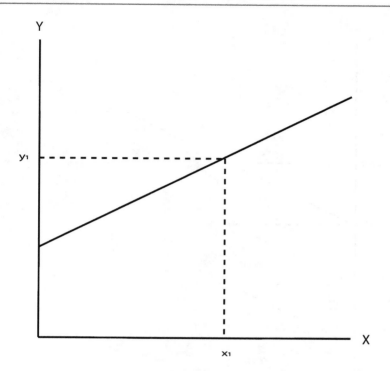

Fig. 15.3 Equal slopes and intercepts. Note: Equal slopes and intercepts result in homogeneity of regression where the regression lines for different groups are the same

In actual clinical practice, regression equations are seldom generated for the prediction of future performance. Rather, some arbitrary or perhaps statistically derived cutoff score is determined, below which failure is predicted. For school performance, a score of 2 or more standard deviations below the test mean is used to infer a high probability of failure in the regular classroom if special assistance is not provided for the student in question. Essentially then, clinicians are establishing prediction equations about mental aptitude that are assumed to be equivalent across race, sex, and so on. Although these mental equations cannot be readily tested across groups, the actual form of criterion prediction can be compared across groups in several ways. Errors in prediction must be independent of group membership. If regression equations are equal, this condition is met. To test the hypothesis of simultaneous regression, regression slopes and regression intercepts must both be compared.

When homogeneity of regression does not occur, three basic conditions can result: (1) Intercept constants differ, (2) regression coefficients (slopes) differ, or (3) slopes and intercepts differ. These conditions are illustrated in Figs. 15.4, 15.5, and 15.6, respectively.

When intercept constants differ, the resulting bias in prediction is constant across the range of scores. That is, regardless of the level of performance on the

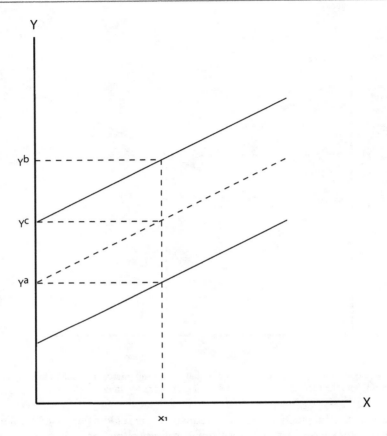

Fig. 15.4 Equal slopes with differing intercepts. Note: Equal slopes with differing intercepts result in parallel regression lines that produce a constant bias in prediction

independent variable, the direction and degree of error in the estimation of the criterion (systematic over- or underprediction) will remain the same. When regression coefficients differ and intercepts are equivalent, the direction of the bias in prediction will remain constant, but the amount of error in prediction will vary directly as a function of the distance of the score on the independent variable from the origin. With regression coefficient differences, then, the higher the score on the predictor variable, the greater the error of prediction for the criterion. When both slopes and intercepts differ, the situation becomes even more complex. Both the degree of error in prediction and the direction of the "bias" will vary as a function of level of performance on the independent variable.

A considerable body of literature has developed over the last 40 years regarding differential prediction of tests across ethnicity for employment selection, college admissions, and school or academic performance generally. In an impressive review of 866 Black-White prediction comparisons from 39 studies of test bias in personnel selection, Hunter, Schmidt, and Hunter (1979) concluded that there was no

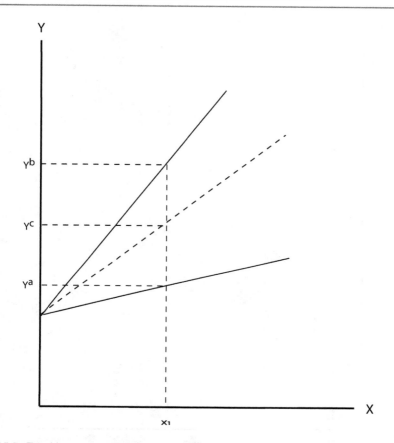

Fig. 15.5 Equal intercepts and differing slopes. Note: Equal intercepts and differing slopes result in nonparallel regression lines, with the degree of bias depending on the distance of the individual's score from the origin

evidence to substantiate hypotheses of differential or single-group validity with regard to the prediction of the job performance across race for Blacks and Whites. A similar conclusion has been reached by other independent researchers (e.g., Reynolds, 1995). A number of studies have also focused on differential validity of the Scholastic Aptitude Test (SAT) in the prediction of college performance (typically measured by grade point average). In general, these studies have found either no difference in the prediction of criterion performance for Blacks and Whites or a bias (underprediction of the criterion) against Whites. When bias against Whites has been found, the differences between actual and predicted criterion scores, while statistically significant, have generally been quite small.

Studies investigating bias in the prediction of future school performance based on IQ tests for children have covered a variety of populations including normal as well as referred children; high-poverty, inner-city children; rural Black; and Native American groups. Studies of preschool as well as school-age children have been

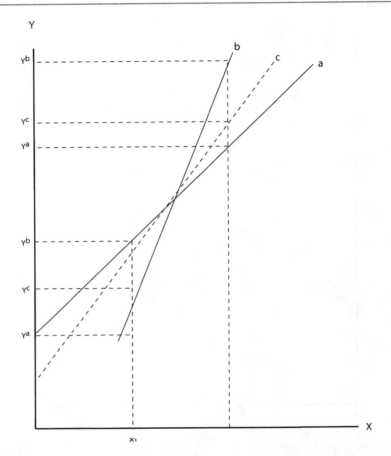

Fig. 15.6 Differing Slopes and Intercepts. Note: Differing slopes and intercepts result in a complex situation where the amount and the direction of the bias are a function of the distance of an individual's score from the origin

carried out. Almost without exception, those studies have produced results that can be adequately depicted by Fig. 15.1, that is, equivalent prediction for all groups. When this has not been found, intercepts have generally differed resulting in a constant bias in prediction. Yet, the resulting bias has not been in the popularly conceived direction. The bias identified has tended to overpredict how well minority children will perform in academic areas and to underpredict how well White children will perform. Reynolds (1995) provides a thorough review of studies investigating the prediction of school performance in children.

With regard to bias in prediction, the empirical evidence suggests conclusions similar to those regarding bias in test content and other internal characteristics. There is no strong evidence to support contentions of differential or single-group validity. Bias occurs infrequently and with no apparently observable pattern, except with regard to instruments of poor reliability and high specificity of test content.

When bias occurs, it usually takes the form of small overpredictions for low SES, disadvantaged ethnic minority children, or other low-scoring groups. These overpredictions are unlikely to account for adverse placement or diagnosis in these groups (Reynolds & Ramsay, 2003).

> Single-group or differential validity has not been found and likely is not an existing phenomenon with regard to well-constructed standardized psychological tests.

15.11.1 How Test Publishers Commonly Identify Bias in Prediction

Commercial test developers seldom demonstrate the presence or absence of bias in prediction prior to test publication. Unfortunately, the economics of the test development industry as well as that for researchers developing tools for specific research projects prohibit such desirable work prepublication. Most such work occurs post-publication and by independent researchers with interests in such questions.

15.12 Summary

A considerable body of literature currently exists failing to substantiate cultural bias against native-born American ethnic minorities with regard to the use of well-constructed, adequately standardized intelligence and aptitude tests. With respect to personality scales, the evidence is promising yet far more preliminary and thus considerably less conclusive. Despite the existing evidence, we do not expect the furor over the CTBH to be resolved soon. Bias in psychological testing will remain a polemic issue for some time. Psychologists and educators will need to keep abreast of new findings in the area. As new techniques and better methodology are developed and more specific populations examined, the findings of bias now seen as random and infrequent may become better understood and seen to indeed display a correctable pattern.

In the meantime, however, one cannot ethically fall prey to the sociopoliticolegal Zeitgeist of the times and infer bias where none exists (see Special Interest Topic 15.5 for further thoughts on this issue). Psychologists and educators cannot justifiably ignore the fact that low IQ, ethnic, disadvantaged children are just as likely to fail academically as are their low IQ, White, middle-class counterparts. Black adolescents with deviant personality scale scores and who exhibit aggressive behavior need treatment environments as much as their White peers with deviant personality scores and aggressive behaviors. The potential outcome for score interpretation (e.g., therapy versus prison, special education versus regular education) cannot dictate the psychological meaning of test performance. We must practice intelligent testing (Kaufman, 1994). We must remember that it is the purpose of the assessment process to beat the prediction made by the test, to provide insight into hypotheses for environmental interventions that prevent the predicted failure or subvert the occurrence of future maladaptive behavior.

Continued sensitivity by test developers to issues of bias is also necessary so that appropriate checks for bias are performed prior to test publication. Progress is being made in all of these areas. However, we must hold to the data even if we do not like them. At present, only scattered and inconsistent evidence for bias exists. The few findings of bias do suggest two guidelines to follow in order to ensure nonbiased assessment: (1) Assessment should be conducted with the most reliable instrumentation available, and (2) multiple abilities should be assessed. In other words, educators and psychologists need to view multiple sources of accurately derived data prior to making decisions concerning individuals. One hopes that this is what has actually been occurring in the practice of assessment, although one continues to hear isolated stories of grossly incompetent placement decisions being made. This is not to say educators or psychologists should be blind to an individual's cultural or environmental background. Information concerning the home, community, and school environment must all be evaluated in individual decisions. As we noted, it is the purpose of the assessment process to beat the prediction and to provide insight into hypotheses for environmental interventions that prevent the predicted failure.

Without question, scholars have not conducted all the research that needs to be done to test the CTBH and its alternatives. A number and variety of criteria need to be explored further before the question of bias is empirically resolved. Many different achievement tests and teacher-made, classroom-specific tests need to be employed in future studies of predictive bias. The entire area of differential validity of tests in the affective domain is in need of greater exploration. A variety of views toward bias have been expressed in many sources; many with differing opinions offer scholarly, nonpolemical attempts directed toward a resolution of the issue. Obviously, the fact that such different views are still held indicates resolution lies in the future. As far as the present situation is concerned, clearly all the evidence is not in. With regard to a resolution of bias, we believe that were a scholarly trial to be held, with a charge of cultural bias brought against mental tests, the jury would likely return the verdict other than guilty or not guilty that is allowed in British law—"not proven." Until such time as a true resolution of the issues can take place, we believe the evidence and positions taken in this chapter accurately reflect the state of our empirical knowledge concerning bias in mental tests.

References

Alley, G., & Foster, C. (1978). Nondiscriminatory testing of minority and exceptional children. *Focus on Exceptional Children, 9*, 1–14.

American Educational Research Association, American Psychological Association, & National Council on Measurement in Education. (2014). *Standards for educational and psychological testing*. Washington, DC: American Educational Research Association.

Anastasi, A., & Urbina, S. (1997). *Psychological testing* (7th ed.). Upper Saddle River, NJ: Prentice Hall.

Brown, R. T., Reynolds, C. R., & Whitaker, J. S. (1999). Bias in mental testing since "Bias in Mental Testing." *School Psychology Quarterly, 14*, 208–238.

Camilli, G., & Shepard, L. A. (1994). *Methods for identifying biased test items*. Thousand Oaks, CA: Sage.

Chinn, P. C. (1979). The exceptional minority child: Issues and some answers. *Exceptional Children, 46*, 532–536.

Cleary, T. A., Humphreys, L. G., Kendrick, S. A., & Wesman, A. (1975). Educational uses of tests with disadvantaged students. *American Psychologist, 30*, 15–41.

Cole, N. S., & Moss, P. A. (1989). Bias in test use. In R. L. Linn (Ed.), *Educational measurement* (3rd ed., pp. 201–219). New York, NY: Macmillan.

Dickens, W. T., & Flynn, J. R. (2006). Black Americans reduce the racial IQ gap: Evidence from standardization samples. *Psychological Science, 17*, 913–920.

Embretson, S., & Reise, S. (2000). *Item response theory for psychologists*. London: Taylor & Francis.

Flaugher, R. (1978). The many definitions of test bias. *American Psychologist, 33*(7), 671–679.

Gould, S. J. (1995). Curveball. In S. Fraser (Ed.), *The bell curve wars: Race, intelligence, and the future of America* (pp. 11–22). New York, NY: Basic Books.

Gould, S. J. (1996). *The mismeasure of man* (rev. ed.). New York, NY: Norton.

Halpern, D. F. (1997). Sex differences in intelligence: Implications for education. *American Psychologist, 52*, 1091–1102.

Helms, J. E. (1992). Why is there no study of cultural equivalence in standardized cognitive ability testing? *American Psychologist, 47*, 1083–1101.

Herrnstein, R. J. (1982, August). IQ testing and the media. *Atlantic Monthly, 250*, 68–74.

Hilliard, A. G. (1979). Standardization and cultural bias as impediments to the scientific study and validation of "intelligence". *Journal of Research and Development in Education, 12*, 47–58.

Hunter, J. E., Schmidt, F. L., & Hunter, R. (1979). Differential validity of employment tests by race: A comprehensive review and analysis. *Psychological Bulletin, 86*, 721–735.

Hunter, J. E., Schmidt, F. L., & Rauschenberger, L. (1984). Methodological, statistical, and ethical issues in the study of bias in psychological tests. In C. R. Reynolds & R. T. Brown (Eds.), *Perspectives on bias in mental testing* (pp. 41–100). New York, NY: Plenum Press.

Jensen, A. R. (1976). Test bias and construct validity. *Phi Delta Kappan, 58*, 340–346.

Jensen, A. R. (1980). *Bias in mental testing*. New York, NY: Free Press.

Kaufman, A. S. (1994). *Intelligent testing with the WISC-III*. New York, NY: Wiley.

Neisser, U., BooDoo, G., Bouchard, T., Boykin, A., Brody, N., Ceci, S., ... Urbina, S. (1996). Intelligence: Knowns and unknowns. *American Psychologist, 51*, 77–101.

Nisbett, R. E. (2009). *Intelligence and how to get it: Why schools and cultures count*. New York, NY: Norton.

Nomura, J. M., Stinnett, T., Castro, F., Atkins, M., Beason, S., Linden, S., ... Wiechmann, K. (2007, March). *Effects of stereotype threat on cognitive performance of African Americans*. Paper presented to the annual meeting of the National Association of School Psychologists, New York.

Reynolds, C., Willson, V., & Chatman, S. (1984). Item bias on the 1981 revision of the Peabody Picture Vocabulary Test using a new method of detecting bias. *Journal of Psychoeducational Assessment, 2*(3), 219–224.

Reynolds, C. R. (1980). In support of "Bias in Mental Testing" and scientific inquiry. *Behavioral and Brain Sciences, 3*, 352.

Reynolds, C. R. (1982). The problem of bias in psychological assessment. In C. R. Reynolds & T. B. Gutkin (Eds.), *The handbook of school psychology* (pp. 178–208). New York, NY: Wiley.

Reynolds, C.R. (1983). Test bias: In God we trust; all others must have data. *Journal of Special Education, 17*, 241–260.

Reynolds, C. R. (1987). Raising intelligence: Clever Hans, Candides, and the Miracle in Milwaukee. *Journal of School Psychology, 25*, 309–312.

Reynolds, C. R. (1995). Test bias in the assessment of intelligence and personality. In D. SakJofsky & M. Zeidner (Eds.), *International handbook of personality and intelligence* (pp. 545–576). New York, NY: Plenum Press.

Reynolds, C. R. (1998). Fundamentals of measurement and assessment in psychology. In A. Bellack & M. Hersen (Eds.), *Comprehensive clinical psychology* (pp. 33–55). New York, NY: Elsevier.

Reynolds, C. R. (2000). Why is psychometric research on bias in mental testing so often ignored? *Psychology, Public Policy, and Law, 6*, 144–150.

Reynolds, C. R. (2002). *Comprehensive trail-making test: Examiner's manual.* Austin, TX: Pro-Ed.

Reynolds, C. R., & Kamphaus, R. W. (2003). *Reynolds intellectual assessment scales.* Lutz, FL: Psychological Assessment Resources.

Reynolds, C. R., Lowe, P. A., & Saenz, A. (1999). The problem of bias in psychological assessment. In T. B. Gutkin & C. R. Reynolds (Eds.), *The handbook of school psychology* (3rd ed., pp. 549–595). New York, NY: Wiley.

Reynolds, C. R., & Ramsay, M. C. (2003). Bias in psychological assessment: An empirical review and recommendations. In J. R. Graham & J. A. Naglieri (Eds.), *Handbook of psychology: Assessment psychology* (pp. 67–93). New York, NY: Wiley.

Richardson, T. Q. (1993). Black cultural learning styles: Is it really a myth? *School Psychology Review, 22*(3), 562–567.

Rushton, J. P., & Jensen, A. R. (2005). Thirty years of research on group differences in cognitive ability. *Psychology, Public Policy, and Law, 11*, 235–294.

Rushton, J. P., & Jensen, A. R. (2010). Race and IQ: A theory-based review of the research in Richard Nisbett's intelligence and how to get it. *The Open Psychology Journal, 3*, 9–35.

Sackett, P. R., Hardison, C. M., & Cullen, M. J. (2004). On interpreting stereotype threat as accounting for african american-white differences on cognitive tests. *American Psychologist, 59*(1), 7–13.

Sandoval, J., & Mille, M. P. W. (1979). *Accuracy judgments of WISC-R item difficulty for minority groups.* Paper presented at the annual meeting of the American Psychological Association, New York.

Schoenfeld, W. N. (1974). Notes on a bit of psychological nonsense: "Race differences in intelligence". *Psychological Record, 24*, 17–32.

Steele, C. M., & Aronson, J. (1995). Stereotype threat and the intellectual test performance of African Americans. *Journal of Personality and Social Psychology, 69*(5), 797–811.

Steele, C. M., Spencer, S. J., & Aronson, J. (2002). Contending with group image: The psychology of stereotype and social identity threat. In M. P. Zanna (Ed.), *Advances in experimental social psychology* (Vol. 34, pp. 379–440). New York, NY: Academic Press.

Suzuki, L. A., & Valencia, R. R. (1997). Race-ethnicity and measured intelligence: Educational implications. *American Psychologist, 52*, 1103–1114.

Williams, R. L. (1970). Danger: Testing and dehumanizing Black children. *Clinical Child Psychology Newsletter, 9*, 5–6.

Williams, R. L., Dotson, W., Dow, P., & Williams, W. S. (1980). The war against testing: A current status report. *Journal of Negro Education, 49*, 263–273.

Recommended Reading

Cleary, T. A., Humphreys, L. G., Kendrick, S. A., & Wesman, A. (1975). *American Psychologist, 30*, 15–41 This is the report of a group appointed by the APA's Board of Scientific Affairs to study the use of psychological and educational tests with disadvantaged students--An early and influential article.

Embretson, S., & Reise, S. (2000). *Item response theory for psychologists.* London: Taylor & Francis An excellent overview of the theory and applications of IRT.

Halpern, D. F. (1997). Sex differences in intelligence: Implications for education. *American Psychologist, 52*, 1091–1102 A good article that summarizes the literature on sex differences with an emphasis on educational implications.

Neisser, U., BooDoo, G., Bouchard, T., Boykin, A., Brody, N., Ceci, S., … Urbina, S. (1996). Intelligence: Knowns and unknowns. *American Psychologist, 51*, 77–101 This report of an APA task force provides an excellent review of the research literature on intelligence.

Reynolds, C. R. (1995). Test bias in the assessment of intelligence and personality. In D. Saklofsky & M. Zeidner (Eds.), *International handbook of personality and intelligence* (pp. 545–573). New York, NY: Plenum Press This chapter provides a thorough review of the literature.

Reynolds, C. R. (2000). Why is psychometric research on bias in mental testing so often ignored? *Psychology, Public Policy, and Law, 6,* 144–150 This article provides a particularly good discussion of test bias in terms of public policy issues.

Reynolds, C. R., & Ramsay, M. C. (2003). Bias in psychological assessment: An empirical review and recommendations. In J. R. Graham & J. A. Naglieri (Eds.), *Handbook of psychology: Assessment psychology* (pp. 67–93). New York, NY: Wiley This chapter also provides an excellent review of the literature.

Suzuki, L. A., & Valencia, R. R. (1997). Race-ethnicity and measured intelligence: Educational implications. *American Psychologist, 52,* 1103–1114 A good discussion of the topic with special emphasis on educational implications and alternative assessment methods.

Assessment Accommodations

16

> *Assessment accommodations help students show what they*
> *know without being placed at a disadvantage by their disability.*
>
> United States Department of Education (2001, p. 8).

Abstract

A primary tenet of standardized testing is to strictly adhere to standard assessment procedures when administering tests and other assessments. However, accommodations to standardized procedures are often needed for people with disabilities. This chapter reviews the rationale for providing assessment accommodations to individuals with disabilities, including guidance to help determine whether accommodations are or are not appropriate. Various accommodation strategies are presented, such as modifications to test presentation and response format, adjusting time limits, providing adaptive devices/strategies and supports, and using modified or alternate assessments. Guidance for determining what accommodations should be provided is also reviewed, as well as guidance on how to report scores from test administrations where accommodations were provided. Special considerations for English Language Learners are also considered.

[1] Brookhart v. Illinois State Board of Education, 1983.
[2] Southeastern Community College v. Davis, 1979.

Supplementary Information The online version of this chapter (https://doi.org/10.1007/978-3-030-59455-8_16) contains supplementary material, which is available to authorized users.

© Springer Nature Switzerland AG 2021
C. R. Reynolds et al., *Mastering Modern Psychological Testing*,
https://doi.org/10.1007/978-3-030-59455-8_16

Learning Objectives

After reading and studying this chapter, students should be able to:
1. Explain the rationale for making modifications in assessment procedures for examinees with disabilities.
2. Distinguish between appropriate and inappropriate assessment accommodations and give examples of both.
3. Identify situations where assessment accommodations are inappropriate or unnecessary.
4. Identify major legislation that has impacted the provision of educational services to examinees with disabilities.
5. Identify and give examples of modifications of the presentation format that might be appropriate for examinees with disabilities.
6. Identify and give examples of modifications of the response format that might be appropriate for examinees with disabilities.
7. Identify and give examples of modifications of timing that might be appropriate for examinees with disabilities.
8. Identify and give examples of modifications of the setting that might be appropriate for examinees with disabilities.
9. Identify and give examples of adaptive devices and supports that might be appropriate for examinees with disabilities.
10. Describe and give examples illustrating the use of limited portions of an assessment or an alternate assessment with an examinee with a disability.
11. Identify and give examples of strategies for assessing examinees with limited English proficiency.

So far in this text we have emphasized the importance of strictly adhering to standard assessment procedures when administering tests and other assessments. This is necessary to maintain the reliability of test scores and the validity of score interpretations. However, there are times when it is appropriate to deviate from

> The goal of assessment accommodations is to provide the most valid and accurate measurement of the construct of interest for every examinee.

these standard procedures. Standard assessment procedures may not be appropriate for an examinee with a disability if the assessment requires them to use some ability (e.g., sensory, motor, language, etc.) that is affected by their disability, *but is irrelevant to the construct being measured*. To address this, psychologists and others involved in assessment may need to modify standard assessment procedures to accommodate the special needs of examinees with disabilities. In this context, changes in the standard assessment procedures are implemented in order to minimize the impact of examinee characteristics that are irrelevant to the construct being measured by the assessment but would alter obtained scores if the test was administered under standardized conditions. According to the *Standards* (American Educational Research Association, American Psychological Association, & National Council on

Measurement in Education, 2014), the term **accommodation** is used to denote changes to the procedure so that comparability of scores is retained. Such changes are considered relatively minor and occur in the presentation or format of the test, administration of the test, or the way in which the examinee responds to the test items.

The goal of accommodations is to provide the most valid and accurate measurement of the construct of interest for each examinee. An important consideration when selecting accommodations is that we want to implement only those accommodations that preserve the reliability of test scores and the validity of their interpretations. As an example, consider an achievement test designed to measure an examinee's knowledge of computer science. An examinee who is blind would not be able to read the material in its standard printed format but may read Braille. An appropriate accommodation would be to convert the test to Braille format. In this example, it is important to recognize that reading standard print is incidental to the construct being measured. That is, the test was designed to measure an examinee's knowledge of computer science not visual acuity, so to penalize her for an inability to see standard print makes the test a measure of visual acuity, not knowledge of computer science. In this example, one highly negative outcome resulting from failure to provide accommodations would be denying admission to a prestigious computer science doctoral program to an undergraduate student who was visually impaired but a brilliant computer scientist.

Understanding that negative consequences occur when appropriate accommodations are not made, there are instances when accommodations cannot be made. As an example, many commonly used cognitive psychological tests designed to measure processing speed are based on "digit symbol substitution," a procedure which was first reported more than a century ago. This paper-and-pencil test presents a key with matched words, numbers, or symbols (based on the test developers' preferences), like the one below.

CAT	SIP	OIL	NOT	GAB	PIN
1	2	3	4	5	6

The test presents a sheet of paper with key words only, and the examinee is required to fill in the corresponding numbers as quickly as possible. The total number of correct matches within a specified time limit (e.g., 60 seconds) is the typical score for these tests. Despite their simplicity, this type of testing procedure remains popular because of its clinical utility, i.e., it is brief to administer and produces scores that have impressive discriminant validity interpretations. However, appropriate accommodations are difficult to establish for tests methods like digit symbol substitution that rely on heterogeneous abilities such as processing speed, attention, concentration, visual scanning, and motor speed. Because this method of assessing processing speed relies heavily on rapid motor movements, it would be inappropriate for examinees with motor impairments since their score would reflect motor rather than processing speed deficits. However, accommodations that would make this assessment method appropriate for an examinee with motor impairment are difficult to imagine. So, in some cases, accommodations cannot be made and different methods altogether must be sought.

In addition to professional standards, there are laws that are related to the issue of assessment accommodations. For example, in our public schools the Every Student Succeeds Act (ESSA), the most recent amendment of the Individuals with Disabilities Education Act 2004 (IDEA 2004), requires that all students be included in state/district high-stakes assessments, and appropriate accommodations must be given to English Language Learners (ELLs) and children with disabilities. In addition, the ESSA requires, to the extent practicable, that assessments are developed using principles of universal design for learning. Universal design is aimed at reducing barriers to accurate assessment and improving flexibility in how students receive information or demonstrate knowledge. Special Interest Topic 16.1 provides more information on major laws that impact the assessment of students with disabilities. In forensic settings, there are legal guidelines (discussed in Chap. 14) that hold that if data used by an expert witness to form an opinion are unreliable or invalid, any opinions based on the data are not admissible. As a result, when assessment procedures are changed to accommodate an examinee's disability, this can call into question the reliability of the test data and result in it being inadmissible as evidence (Lee, Reynolds, & Willson, 2003).

Special Interest Topic 16.1: Major Legislation That Guides the Assessment of Students with Disabilities

A number of federal laws mandate assessment accommodations for students with disabilities in our public schools. The Every Student Succeeds Act (ESSA), the most recent amendment of the Individuals with Disabilities Education Act 2004 (IDEA 2004), and Section 504 of the Rehabilitation Act of 1973 are the laws most often applied in the schools. ESSA/IDEA requires that public schools provide students with disabilities a free appropriate public education (FAPE) and identifies a number of disability categories. These include learning disabilities, communication disorders, intellectual disability, emotional disturbance, other health impaired (OHI), hearing impairment, multiple disabilities, orthopedic impairments, autism, traumatic brain injury, and developmental delay. A key factor in the provision of services to students with disabilities is the individualized educational program (IEP). The IEP is a written document developed by a committee that specifies a number of factors, including the examinees' instructional arrangement, the special services they will receive, and any assessment accommodations they will receive.

Section 504 of the Rehabilitation Act of 1973, often referred to as Section 504 or simply 504, prohibits discrimination against individuals with disabilities in any agency or school that receives federal funds. In the public schools, Section 504 requires that schools provide examinees with disabilities reasonable accommodations to meet their educational needs. Section 504 provides a broad standard of eligibility, simply stating that an individual with a disability is anyone with a physical or mental disability that limits one or more life activities. Because Section 504 is broader than ESSA/IDEA, it is possible for an examinee to qualify under Section 504 and not qualify under ESSA/IDEA. This is sometimes referred to as "504 only."

The issue of assessment accommodations is relevant to practically all psychologists. For example, school psychologists often work with children and adolescents that have disabilities and are receiving special education services. Neuropsychologists frequently work with individuals that have experienced brain or other central nervous system injuries or have other disabilities that might limit their performance on standard assessments. In fact every psychologist that conducts assessments needs to be sensitive to the possibility that physical and mental disabilities might compromise the validity of their assessment results. Knowledge about assessment accommodations is not only important to psychologists and professional psychometrists, but others as well. For example, teachers in all grades regularly develop and administer tests in their classrooms, and these tests may also need to be modified to accommodate the needs of students with disabilities. In addition to disabilities, one must also be sensitive to the fact that examinees with limited English proficiency may also need assessment accommodations to ensure a valid assessment. In this chapter we will review a wide range of assessment accommodations that might facilitate the assessment of individuals with disabilities or limited English proficiency.

16.1   Accommodations Versus Modifications

The *Standards* (AERA et al., 2014) note that the terms accommodation and modification are used differently by different professionals. The *Standards* use ***accommodations*** to represent changes made to the administration of a test where the comparability of scores can be retained and use ***modifications*** to denote changes made to a test's administration that affect the underlying construct being measured. Other sources (e.g., the Americans with Disabilities Act) tend to use the terms accommodations and modifications more interchangeably, as we do in this text. Some researchers are skeptical of an actual distinction between the accommodations and modifications, believing such distinctions are dubious and can be harmful if leading to premature or overly general lists of accommodations (Lovett & Lewandowski, 2015). When reading other literature, it is important to note how the author(s) use these terms.

16.2   The Rationale for Assessment Accommodations

As we noted earlier, standard assessment procedures may not be appropriate for an examinee with a disability if the assessment requires use of an ability that is negatively affected by the disability and is irrelevant to the construct measured by the test. Assessment accommodations are modifications to standard assessment procedures that are granted in an effort to minimize the impact of examinee characteristics that are irrelevant to the construct being measured. The *Standards* refer to these types of changes as ***adaptations*** (AERA et al., 2014). If accomplished, these adaptations will provide a more valid and accurate measurement of an individual's true standing on the construct (AERA et al., 2014). The goal is not to simply allow an examinee to obtain a higher score; rather, the goal is to obtain more valid score interpretations. An assessment accommodation or adaptation made to an administration procedure should increase the validity of the score interpretations so they more accurately reflect the examinee's true standing on the construct being measured.

> Standard assessment procedures may not be appropriate for a client with a disability if the assessment requires the client to use some ability that is affected by the disability, but is irrelevant to the construct being measured.

While some physical, cognitive, sensory, or motor deficits may be readily apparent to professionals (e.g., vision impairment, hearing impairment, and physical impairment), other deficits that might undermine an examinee's performance are not as obvious. For example, an examinee with a learning disability might not appear outwardly to have any deficits that would impair performance on a test, but in fact have significant cognitive processing deficits that limit their ability to complete standard assessments. In some situations the examinee may have readily observable deficits, but have associated characteristics that also need to be taken into consideration. For example, an examinee with a physical disability (e.g., partial paralysis) may be easily fatigued when engaging in standard assessment activities. Since some tests require fairly lengthy testing sessions, the examinee's susceptibility to fatigue needs to be taken into consideration when planning assessment accommodations, not only the more obvious physical limitations.

Fairness to all parties is a central issue when considering assessment accommodations. For examinees with disabilities, fairness requires that they are not penalized as the result of disability related characteristics that are irrelevant

> Fairness to all parties is a central issue when considering assessment accommodations.

to the construct measured by the assessment. For examinees without disabilities, fairness requires that those receiving accommodations are not given an unjust advantage over those tested under standard conditions. As you can see, these are serious issues that deserve careful consideration.

16.3   When Are Accommodations _Not_ Appropriate or Necessary?

The *Standards* (AREA et al., 2014) specify three situations where accommodations should not be provided or are not necessary. These are:

- *Accommodations are not appropriate if the affected ability is directly relevant to the construct being measured.* For example, it would not be appropriate to give an examinee with a visual impairment a magnification device if the test is designed to measure visual acuity. Similarly, it would not be appropriate to give an examinee with a reading disability the use of a "reader" on a test designed to measure reading ability. Even if the test is designed as a measure of reading comprehension (as opposed to decoding or reading fluency), having someone else read the material turns the test into one of listening comprehension, not reading comprehension (Fuchs, 2002). In other words, if the testing accommodation changes the construct being measured, the accommodation is inappropriate. Again, the essential question is "Does the assessment require the use of some ability that is affected by the disability, but is *irrelevant* to the construct being measured?"

- *Accommodations are not appropriate for an assessment if the purpose of the test is to assess the presence and degree of the disability.* For example, it would not be appropriate to give an examinee with attention-deficit/hyperactivity disorder (ADHD) extra time on a test designed to diagnose the presence of attention problems. Likewise, it would not be appropriate to modify a test of dexterity for an examinee with impaired fine motor skills.

- *Accommodations are not necessary for all examinees with disabilities.* All examinees with disabilities do not need accommodations. Even when an examinee with a disability requires accommodations on one test, this does not necessarily mean accommodations will be needed on all tests. As we will discuss in more detail later, assessment accommodations should be individualized to meet the specific needs of each examinee with a disability. There is no specific accommodation that is appropriate, necessary, or adequate for all examinees with a given disability. As an example, consider examinees with learning disabilities. Learning disabilities are a heterogeneous group of disabilities that can impact an individual in a multitude of ways. One examinee with a learning disability may require extended time while this accommodation may not be necessary for another examinee with the same diagnosis.

> Assessment accommodations should be individualized to meet the specific needs of each examinee with a disability.

16.4 Strategies for Accommodations

A variety of assessment accommodations have been proposed and implemented to meet the needs of individuals with disabilities. Below is a brief description of some of the most widely used accommodations compiled from a number of sources (AERA, et al., 2014; King, Baker, & Jarrow, 1995; Mastergeorge & Miyoshi, 1999; Northeast Technical Assistance Center, 1999; Thurlow, Elliott, & Ysseldyke, 2003; US Department of Education, 2001). To facilitate our presentation we divided these accommodations into major categories. However, these categories are not mutually exclusive and some accommodations may be classified accurately into more than one category.

16.4.1 Modifications of Presentation Format

Accommodations in this category involve modifying or changing the medium or format used to present the directions, items, or tasks to the examinee. An example would be the use of Braille or large-print editions for examinees with visual handicaps (which can be supplemented with large-print or Braille figures). For computer administered tests, products like ZoomText Magnifier/Reader © (see www.zoomtext.com) enlarge images appearing on a computer screen and also read the text on the screen. In

> Modifications of presentation format involve modifying the medium or format used to present the directions, items, or tasks to the examinee.

some cases the use of oversized monitors may be appropriate. Reader services, which involve listening to the test being read aloud, may also be employed. Here the reader can read directions and questions and describe diagrams, graphs, and other visual material. Organizations such as the American Council of the Blind (see www.acb.org) provide a number of resources for persons with visual disabilities, and can be a good resource for keeping abreast of the latest available technologies. Other common modifications to the presentation format include (1) increasing the spacing between items, (2) reducing the number of items per page, (3) using raised line drawings, (4) using language simplified directions and questions, (5) changing from a written to oral format (or vice versa), (6) defining words, (7) providing additional examples, (8) helping examinees understand directions, questions, and tasks, and (9) providing verbal material through the use of sign communication or in writing (for persons with hearing impairments). Table 16.1 provides a listing of these and related accommodations.

Table 16.1 Accommodations involving modifications of presentation format

- Braille format
- Large-print editions
- Large-print figure supplements
- Braille figure supplement
- For computer administered tests, devices like ZoomText Magnifier/Reader © to magnify material on the screen or read text on the screen
- Reader services (read directions and questions, describe visual material)
- Sign language
- Audiotaped administration
- Videotaped administration
- Written exams converted to oral exams; oral exams converted to written format
- Alternative background and foreground colors
- Increasing the spacing between items
- Reducing the number of items per page
- Raised line drawings
- Language-simplified questions
- Defining words
- Additional examples
- Clarification and help for examinees to understand directions, questions, and tasks
- Highlighted key words or phrases
- Cues (e.g., bullets, stop signs) on test booklet
- Rephrased or restated directions and questions
- Simplified or clarified language
- Templates or colored overlays to limit amount of print visible at one time

16.4.2   Modifications of Response Format

Accommodations in this category allow examinees to respond with their preferred method of communication. For example, if examinees are unable to write due to a physical impairment you can allow them to take the exam orally or provide access to a scribe to write down responses (also referred to as dictation). In such cases, recorders should have training in verbatim transcription and write exactly what was said and not interpret what was said. An examinee whose preferred method of communication is sign language could respond in sign language and their responses could subsequently be translated for grading. However, interpreting the signs is a potential issue in standardized testing and specialized training is often required. Other common modifications to the response format include (1) allowing the examinee to point to the correct response, (2) having an aide mark the answers, (3) audio-recording verbal responses, (4) using a computer or Braillewriter to record responses, (5) using voice-activated computer software, (6) providing increased spacing between lines on the answer sheet, (7) using graph paper for math problems, and (8) allowing the examinee to mark responses in the test booklet rather than on a computer answer sheet. Table 16.2 provides a summary listing of these and related accommodations.

> Modifications of response format allow examinees to respond with their preferred method of communication.

16.4.3   Modifications of Timing

Extended time is the most frequent accommodation provided in educational testing situations (Lazarus, Thompson, & Thurlow, 2006). Extended time is appropriate for any examinee who is slowed down due to reduced processing speed, reading speed,

Table 16.2 Accommodations involving modifications of response format

- Oral examinations
- Scribe services (examinee dictates response to scribe who creates written response)
- Examinee allowed to respond in sign language
- Examinee allowed to point to the correct response
- Aide to mark the answers
- Tape-recorder to record responses
- Computer with read-back capability to record responses
- Braillewriter to record responses
- Voice-activated computer software
- Increased spacing between lines on the answer sheet
- Graph paper for math problems
- Examinee allowed to mark responses in the test booklet rather than on a computer answer sheet (e.g., Scantron forms)
- Ruler for visual tracking

Table 16.3 Accom-
modations involving
modifications of timing

- Extended time
- More frequent breaks
- Administration in sections
- Testing spread over several days
- Time of day when the test is administered

or writing speed. It is also appropriate for examinees that use other accommodations such as the use of a scribe or use of some form of adaptive equipment since these often require more time. Determining how much time to allow is a complex consideration; two of the most common allotments are 50% and 100% additional time (Lovett & Lewandowski, 2015). Research suggests that 50% additional time is adequate for most examinees with disabilities (Northeast Technical Assistance Center, 1999). While this is probably a good rule of thumb, be sensitive to special conditions that might demand extra time. Nevertheless, most assessment professionals do not recommend "unlimited time" as an accommodation. It is not necessary, can complicate the scheduling of assessments, and can be seen as "unreasonable," thus undermining the credibility of the accommodation process. Other time-related modifications include providing more frequent breaks, administering the test in sections and/or over several days, allowing time cues (e.g., a teacher alerts a student how much time has passed), and scheduling accommodations that specify a time of day or a day of the week for testing. Extra testing time is the most commonly requested accommodation on college and professional school admission tests such as the SAT and GRE, as well as professional licensing examinations. Various testing organizations and licensing boards have specific requirements for evaluating the need for additional testing time and other accommodations. You can read about these on their web sites. For some examinees it may be beneficial to change the time of day the test is administered to accommodate their medication schedule or fluctuations in their energy levels. Table 16.3 provides a summary listing of these and related accommodations.

16.4.4 Modifications of Setting

Accommodations in this category allow examinees to be tested in settings that will allow them to perform at their best. For example, on group administered tests examinees that are highly distractible may be given the test individually or in a small group setting. For other examinees, preferential seating in a standard assessment center may be sufficient. Some examinees have special needs based on space and accessibility requirements (e.g., a room that is wheelchair accessible). Some examinees need special accommodations such as a room free from extraneous noise/distractions, special lighting, special acoustics, or the use of a study carrel to minimize distractions. Table 16.4 provides a summary listing of these and related accommodations.

Table 16.4 Accom-modations involving modifications of setting

- Individual test administration
- Administration in a small-group setting
- Preferential seating
- Space or accessibility considerations
- Avoidance of extraneous noise/distractions
- Special lighting
- Special acoustics
- Study carrel to minimize distractions
- Alternate sitting and standing

16.4.5 Adaptive Devices and Supports

There is a multitude of adaptive devices and supports that are useful when testing examinees with disabilities. These range from sophisticated high-technology solutions to fairly simple low-technology supports. For individuals with visual impairments there are a number of companies that produce products ranging from hand-held magnification devices to systems that automatically enlarge the size of print viewed on a computer screen (e.g., ZoomText Magnifier/Reader ©). There are voice recognition computer programs that allow examinees to dictate their responses and printout a document containing their text (e.g., Dragon®). There are a number of adaptive computer keyboards available to accommodate persons with varying impairments (e.g., little-to-no arm movement, single hand movement). Auditory amplification devices as well as recording devices may be appropriate accommodations. On the low-tech side, some examinees benefit from special chairs and large surface desks, earplugs/earphones, colored templates, markers to maintain place, securing the paper to the desk with tape, dark/heavy/or raised lines, or pencil grips. It may be appropriate to provide an abacus, math tables, or calculators to facilitate math calculations. Accordingly, in some situations it may be appropriate to provide reference materials such as a dictionary or thesaurus. In many situations the use of aids like calculators, spell check, and reference materials have become so common they are being made available to examinees without disabilities. Table 16.5 provides a summary listing of these and related accommodations.

> A multitude of adaptive devices and supports exist that may be useful when testing examinees with disabilities.

16.4.6 Using Only Portions of a Test

Some situations require use of only limited portions of an assessment when an examinee has a disability. In clinical settings clinicians might delete certain subtests of a test battery that are deemed inappropriate for an individual with a disability. For example, when testing an examinee with a severe visual impairment a psychologist

Table 16.5 Accommodations involving adaptive devices and supports

- Hand-held magnification devices
- Systems that enlarge print or read text on the screen (e.g., ZoomText Magnifier/Reader ©)
- Voice recognition computer programs that allow examinees to dictate their responses and then print a document containing their text (e.g., Dragon®)
- Adaptive keyboards and trackball devices
- Auditory amplification devices
- Audiotape and videotape players and recorders
- Special chairs and large surface desks
- Earplugs/earphones
- Colored templates or transparencies
- Markers to maintain place, highlighters
- Paper secured to desk with tape
- Dark, heavy, or raised lines of pencil grips
- Abacus, math tables, or calculators (or talking calculators)
- Reference materials such as a dictionary or thesaurus, spell checkers
- Watches or clocks with reminder alarms

administering the WISC-V (see Chap. 9) might delete subtests that require vision (e.g., Block Design, Matrix Reasoning, Picture Concepts) and only use subtests that are presented and responded to orally (e.g., Vocabulary, Information, Similarities). The same principle can be applied to classroom achievement tests. That is, a teacher might decide to delete certain items that are deemed inappropriate for certain examinees with disabilities. Other situations may require deletion of items simply to reduce the length of the test (e.g., to accommodate an examinee who is easily fatigued). These may be acceptable accommodations in some situations, but it is also possible that using only portions of an assessment will significantly alter the nature of the construct being measured (AERA et al., 2014). As a result, this approach should be used with considerable caution.

16.4.7 Using Alternate Assessments

A final category of accommodations involves replacing the standard test with one that has been specifically developed for examinees with a disability (AERA et al., 2014). This accommodation is often appropriate for examinees with severe disabilities that prevent them from participating in the standard assessments, even with the use of more common accommodations.

> The use of alternate assessments may be an appealing accommodation because, with careful planning and development, they can produce reliable and valid results.

The use of alternative assessments may be an appealing accommodation since, with careful planning and development, they can produce reliable and valid results. One difficulty associated with use of alternative assessments is score comparability, in terms of aggregating scores obtained via regular or alternate assessments, and in comparing trend data for various subgroups (AERA et al., 2014).

16.5 Determining What Accommodations to Provide

Determining if an examinee needs assessment accommodations and which accommodations are appropriate is not an easy decision. The *Standards* (AREA et al., 2014) note that the goal of fairness in testing is to maximize the opportunity for examinees to demonstrate their standing on the construct being assessed. When administering tests, the *Standards* note that "… sometimes flexibility is needed to provide essentially equivalent opportunities for some test takers" (p. 51). Thus, professional judgment is needed when making the decision to provide accommodations for an examinee. Special Interest Topic 16.2 presents a summary of current testing accommodations practice.

Special Interest Topic 16.2: Understanding the Current State of Test Accommodation Implementation

In their comprehensive book on testing accommodations, Lovett and Lewandowski (2015) discuss the importance of ensuring that the accommodations being used for testing are informed by research-based practice. In their review of current testing accommodations, they provide the following findings, indicating a rather bleak view of the current state of practice:

1. *Teachers are often ignorant of which accommodations are even permissible on high-stakes tests.* In research studies separated by over a decade (Lazarus et al., 2006; Siskind, 1993), approximately one-half of teachers were unable to accurately identify common accommodations that were permitted or not based on their states' exams.
2. *Teachers' interpretations and implementation of accommodations vary.* A study by Byrnes (2008) indicated teachers were unable to correctly interpret several common accommodations (e.g., *extended time* meant unlimited time limits; *scribing* meant another student could scribe for a student receiving an accommodation).
3. *Teacher-recommended accommodations are less helpful and less efficient than accommodations suggested by objective testing.* In a series of studies (Fuchs, Fuchs, Eaton, Hamlett, Binkley, et al., 2000; Fuchs, Fuchs, Eaton, Hamlett, & Karns, 2000), comparisons were made between teacher judgments about appropriate accommodations compared to accommodations that were recommended based on a brief diagnostic test. Overall, accommodations recommended by the diagnostic test led to greater student ben-

(continued)

efits than teacher-recommended strategies. In addition, the studies showed that teachers tended to recommend more accommodations than did the diagnostic test.

4. *School-based teams make accommodations decisions on the basis of comfort and other affective factors, rather than on the basis of students' disability-related functional impairments.* A study by Rickey (2005) examined the testing process at three middle schools. Using observations and interviewers, the study concluded that the primary factor in making accommodation decisions was a student's affective state (e.g., self-esteem, anxiety, frustration level), rather than a student's ability to access a test.

5. *Diagnosticians are not sufficiently knowledgeable about standards for determining disability status and accommodations eligibility.* A study by Gordon, Lewandowski, Murphy, and Dempsey (2002) asked diagnosticians to complete an accommodations practice survey. Based on this survey, the researchers found that many diagnosticians believed their job as evaluators was to help clients secure testing accommodations, and the appropriateness of the accommodations depended in large part on their clients' ability to benefit from the accommodations.

Lovett and Lewandowski suggest that research-based practice when making testing accommodations is inhibited by the well-intentioned belief that accommodations are good because they offer the possibility that students with disabilities can demonstrate and reach their full potentials. They argue that there is a necessary tension between science and advocacy, and that focusing on only one can result in using (or not using) appropriate accommodations. In addition, the authors also suggest that research-based practices are not used because professionals are not exposed to these practices; therefore, they argue for improved professional development training opportunities.

Research on the topic of assessment accommodations has increased in the last decade (Christensen, Braam, Scullin, & Thurlow, 2011; Kettler, 2012; Thurlow, Christensen, & Lail, 2008). This increase is partially linked to the mandates included in Federal legislation (e.g., NCLB, ESSA) requiring states to include students with disabilities when conducting statewide assessments. Researchers have also provided guidance on best practices for providing accommodations with a variety of students

> The increase in the amount of research addressing the topic of assessment accommodations can be partially linked to the mandates included in Federal legislation requiring states to include students with disabilities when conducting statewide assessments.

(Bolt & Roach, 2009; Lovett & Lewandowski, 2015). Overall, there are a few principles that are generally accepted by experts working with examinees with disabilities. These are listed below:

• *Follow the recommended prescriptions as detailed in a student's individualized education program (IEP) or Section 504 plan.* IEP plans typically are written for students who qualify for special education services under state and federal laws, while Section 504 plans are written for students with temporary or chronic disabilities that substantially limit a major life activity. Such plans are created using input from the student and his/her family and a variety of educational professionals. The plans detail the services that are needed to ensure a student is receiving an appropriate education and need to be followed in order to comply with various laws and regulations. They typically will provide a listing of specific accommodations that are needed for a student.

- *Modifications should be tailored to meet the specific needs of the individual students.* Don't try to apply a "one-size-fits-all" set of accommodations to examinees with disabilities, even when they have the same disability. Not all examinees with any specific type of disability need the same set of accommodations. For example, examinees with learning disabilities are a heterogeneous group and vary in terms of the nature and severity of their disability. As a result, it is inappropriate to provide the same set of assessment accommodations to all examinees with learning disabilities. The *Standards* (AERA et al., 2014) give the example of providing a test in Braille format to all examinees with visual impairments. This might be an appropriate accommodation for some examinees with visual impairments, but for others it might be more appropriate to provide large-print testing materials, and for still others a reader or an audio tape with the questions. Look at each examinee individually and determine what his or her specific needs are. This information should serve as the basis for decisions about assessment accommodations. Since teachers work with students on a day-to-day basis, they are often the best qualified to help determine what types of assessment accommodations are indicated.

- *Accommodations that students routinely receive in their classroom instruction are generally appropriate for assessments.* In public schools if an accommodation is seen as appropriate and necessary for promoting learning during classroom instruction, it is likely that the same accommodation is appropriate and necessary for assessments. This applies to both classroom assessments and state and district assessment programs. For example, if a student with a visual handicap receives large-print instructional materials in class (e.g., large-print textbook, handouts, and other class materials), it would be logical to provide large-print versions of classroom assessments as well as standardized assessments. A reasonable set of questions to ask is (1) what type of instructional accommodations are being provided in the classroom, (2) are these same accommodations appropriate and necessary to allow the examinee to demonstrate their knowledge and skills on assessments, and (3) are any additional assessment accommodations indicated (Mastergeorge & Miyoshi, 1999)?

- *To the extent possible, select accommodations that promote independent functioning.* While you want to provide assessment accommodations that minimize the impact of irrelevant examinee characteristics, it is also good educational practice to promote the independent functioning of examinees (King et al., 1995). For example, if an examinee with a visual handicap can read large-print text this accommodation is likely preferable to providing a reader. Similarly, you might want to provide tape-recorded directions/items versus a reader or a word processor with a "read back function" versus a scribe. You want to provide accommodations needed to produce valid and reliable results, while also promoting examinee independence whenever possible.

- *Follow the publisher's guidelines when modifying standardized assessments.* Many authors and publishers provide guidelines regarding what accommodations are appropriate for their tests. When these guidelines are available, follow them strictly. This applies to both group and individually administered tests. Increasingly authors of individually administered tests are providing guidance about which accommodations are appropriate for their tests and which are inappropriate. For example, the *Interpretive Manual* for the Stanford-Binet Intelligence Scales, Fifth Edition (Roid, 2003) specifies appropriate accommodations and inappropriate modifications for each subtest in the battery (adopting the terminology that modifications imply changes that alter the construct being measured). As an example, on the "Memory for Sentences" subtest, which measures working auditory memory and language development, the author indicates it is appropriate to allow responses in writing or signs and to allow additional time for examinees to respond, but it is inappropriate to present the items in writing, to repeat items, or suggest memory strategies. Publishers of many group administered assessments also have guidelines for determining which accommodations are appropriate. For example, the College Board has a special division that handles requests for assessment accommodations and determines which accommodations are appropriate. Applicants must provide documentation that they have a disability and their need for special assessment accommodations (https://accommodations.collegeboard.org/typical-accommodations). Special Interest Topic 16.3 illustrates assessment accommodations that are allowed on one statewide assessment.

> Many publishers provide guidelines regarding what accommodations are appropriate for their tests.

- *Periodically reevaluate the needs of the examinee.* Over time needs of an examinee may change. In some cases, examinees will mature and develop new skills and abilities. In other situations there may be a loss of some abilities due to a progressive disorder. As a result, it is necessary to periodically reexamine the needs of the examinee and determine if the existing accommodations are still necessary and if any new modifications need to be added.

Again, we want to emphasize that when determining which accommodations to provide, you always want to assure that the reliability and validity of assessment results are maintained. As noted, we don't always have well-developed research-based information to help us make these decisions, so often we base them on professional judgment. In other words, you will have to carefully examine the needs of the examinee and the intended use of the assessment and make a decision about which accommodations are needed and appropriate. As an example, reading the test items to an examinee would clearly invalidate an assessment of reading comprehension. In contrast, administering the assessment in a quiet setting would not undermine the validity of the results (US Department of Education, 2001). Table 16.6 provides a summary of factors to consider when selecting assessment accommodations for examinees.

Special Interest Topic 16.3: Allowable Accommodations in a Statewide Curriculum and Assessment Program

The Texas student assessment program is designed to measure how well students have learned the knowledge and skills included in the Texas Essential Knowledge and Skills (TEKS) statewide curriculum. The Texas Education Agency (TEA) allows accessibility features (i.e., accommodations) for students taking the state tests. Decisions about what accommodations to provide should be based on the individual needs of the student and take into consideration if the student regularly receives the accommodation in the classroom. The TEA identifies a list of accessibility features that are allowed, including:

- Signing or translating test administration directions
- Allowing the use of a bilingual dictionary on mathematics, science, and social studies assessments
- Allowing a student to read the test aloud to facilitate comprehension
- Reading aloud or signing an expository or persuasive writing prompt
- Providing reading assistance on the Grade 3 mathematics test
- Typing a student's responses to a writing prompt for any Grade 4 student that cannot type proficiently
- Providing assistive tools when needed, such as:
  - Various types of scratch paper, dry erase boards, or any other medium that can be erased or destroyed
  - Colored overlays and changing color settings as needed for online tests
  - Blank place markers and the guideline tool for online tests
  - Magnifying devices and the zoom feature on online tests
  - Various types of highlighters, colored pencils, or any other tool that can be used to focus attention on text
  - Amplification devices (e.g., speakers, frequency-modulated systems)
  - Projection devices (e.g., closed-circuit televisions or LCD projectors for online tests)
- Giving permission for a student to use tools to minimize distractions (e.g., stress ball, noise-reducing headphones)
- Allowing individual test administration
- Allowing small-group test administrations
- Reminding students to stay on task
- Photocopying or enlarging nonsecure test materials

(continued)

Naturally, the testing program allows individuals to request accommodations that are not included in this list, and these will be evaluated on a one-by-one basis. Some accommodation requests require special approval by the TEA, such as complex transcribing (e.g., a teacher who enters a student's responses to writing prompts into an online testing system), allow an extra day to complete a test, providing a mathematics scribe, or some other request that is not covered by a listed accessibility feature.

In addition to the standard state tests, TEA also offers alternative assessments such as the STAAR (State of Texas Assessments of Academic Readiness) Alternate 2, which is designed for students with significant cognitive disabilities, and the STAAR Spanish, which is designed for students for whom a Spanish version of STAAR is the most appropriate measure of academic progress. These alternative versions are designed to help ensure that the TEA testing standards are compliant with federal education laws and requirements.

Table 16.6 Determining which accommodations to provide

- Tailor the modifications to meet the specific needs of the individual examinee (i.e., no "one-size-fits-all" accommodations)
- If an examinee routinely receives an accommodation in their classroom instruction, that accommodation is usually appropriate for assessments
- When possible, select accommodations that will promote independent functioning
- Follow the publisher's guidelines when modifying standardized assessments
- Periodically reevaluate the needs of the examinee (e.g., do they still need the accommodation, do they need additional accommodations)

16.6 Assessment of English Language Learners (ELLs)

When conducting an assessment in a language that isn't an examinee's first language, it's important to understand the potential impact such an administration can have on the interpretation of test results. The *Standards* (AERA et al., 2014) state "if a test is not intended to also be a measure of the ability to read in English, then test scores do not represent the same construct(s) for examinees who may have poorer reading skills, such as limited English proficient test takers, as they do for those who are fully proficient in reading English" (p. 60). Federal regulations (e.g., NCLB and ESSA) hold that when assessing (in English) students with limited English proficiency, educators should ensure that they are actually assessing the students' knowledge and skills and not their proficiency in English. For example, if a bilingual examinee with limited English proficiency is

> When assessing examinees with limited English proficiency, psychologists should ensure that they are actually assessing the examinees' knowledge and skills and not their proficiency in English.

unable to correctly answer a mathematics word problem that is presented in English, one must question if their failure reflects inadequate mathematical reasoning and computation skills, or insufficient proficiency in English. If the goal is to assess the examinees' English proficiency, it is appropriate to test in English. However, if the goal is to assess their achievement in an area other than English, you need to carefully consider the type of assessment or set of accommodations that might be needed to ensure a valid assessment. This often requires testing examinees in their primary or native language.

There are a number of factors that need to be considered when assessing examinees who are ELLs. First, when working with examinees with diverse linguistic backgrounds it is important to carefully assess their level of acculturation, language dominance, and language proficiency before initiating the formal assessment (Jacob & Hartshorne, 2007). This means you need to determine the examinee's dominant language (i.e., the preferred language) and their proficiency in both dominant and nondominant languages. It is also important to distinguish between conversational and cognitive/academic language skills. Conversational skills may develop in about 2 years, but cognitive/academic language skills may take 5 or more years to emerge (e.g., Cummins, 1984). The implication is that psychologists and teachers should not rely on their subjective impressions of English proficiency based on subjective observations of daily conversations, but should employ objective measures of written and spoken English proficiency.

> A number of strategies exist for assessing examinees with limited English proficiency.

A number of strategies exist for assessing examinees with limited English proficiency. These include:

- *Locating tests with directions and materials in the examinee's native language*: There are a number of commercial tests available in languages other than English. However, these tests vary considerably in quality depending on how they were developed. For example, a simple translation of a test from one language to another does not ensure test equivalence. In this context, equivalence means it is possible to make comparable inferences based on test performance. The question is: Does the translated test produce results that are comparable to the original test in terms of validity and reliability?
- *Deciding if it is possible to use a nonverbal test*: There are a number of nonverbal tests designed to reduce the influence of cultural and language factors. However, one should keep in mind that while these assessments reduce the influence of language and culture, they do not eliminate them. It is also possible they are not measuring the same construct as verbal tests designed for similar purposes.
- *Using a bilingual examiner to administer the test*: If it is not possible to locate a suitable translated test or a nonverbal test, a qualified bilingual examiner may conduct the assessment, administering the tests in the examinee's native language. When a qualified bilingual examiner is not available, an interpreter may be used. While this is a common practice, there are a number of inherent problems in the use of translators that may compromise the validity of the test results (AERA et al., 2014). Also, difficulty level of the vocabulary used may vary tre-

mendously across languages and may give the examinee undue advantage or create undue difficulty for the examinee—and, it is not at all intuitive as to which situation has been created by using a translation. Translators also have been trained, typically, to interpret, and not just translate which creates additional problem in determining scores accurately and in generalization of validity evidence. It is recommended that anyone considering this option consult the *Standards* (AERA et al., 2014) for additional information on the use of interpreters in assessing individuals with limited English proficiency.

Salvia, Ysseldyke, and Bolt (2007) provide suggestions for assessing students with limited English proficiency in terms of classroom achievement. First, they encourage teachers to ensure that they assess what is actually taught in class, not related content that relies on incidental learning. Students with different cultural and language backgrounds might not have had the same opportunities for incidental learning as native English speakers. Second, give students with limited English proficiency extra time to process their responses. They note that for a variety of reasons, these students may require additional time to process information and formulate a response. Finally, they suggest that teachers provide students who are ELLs with opportunities to demonstrate achievement in ways that do not rely exclusively on language.

16.7 Reporting Results of Modified Assessments

When psychologists modify an individually administered standardized test to accommodate the needs of an examinee with a disability, they typically document this in the psychological or educational assessment report. This is standard practice and is not the focus of serious debate. In contrast, there is considerable debate about the way scores of examinees receiving accommodations on large-scale standardized tests are reported. Some assessment organizations will use an asterisk or some other "flag" to denote a score resulting from a nonstandard administration. The *Standards* (AERA et al., 2014) note that this practice is promoted by some but seen as discriminatory by others. Proponents argue that without flags denoting nonstandard administrations, the scores may be misleading to those interpreting assessment results. That is, they will assume no accommodations were made when they actually were. Opponents hold that it unfairly labels and stigmatizes examinees with disabilities and potentially puts them at a disadvantage—it may also convey they have a disability without having obtained consent to release such information. The *Standards* suggest that two principles apply: (1) important information necessary to interpret scores accurately should be provided and (2) extraneous information that is not necessary to interpret scores accurately should be withheld. Based on this guidance, if there is adequate evidence demonstrating that scores are comparable both with and without accommodations, flagging is not necessary. When there is insufficient

> Some professionals support the use of "flags" to denote scores resulting from nonstandard assessments, whereas others feel this practice is unfair to examinees with disabilities and may place them at a disadvantage.

evidence regarding the comparability of test scores, flagging may be indicated. However, a simple flag denoting the use of accommodations is rather imprecise and when permissible by law it is better to provide specific information about the accommodations that were provided.

Different agencies providing professional assessment services handle this issue differently. The Educational Testing Service (ETS) indicates that when an approved assessment accommodation is thought to affect the construct being measured, they include a statement indicating that the assessment was taken under nonstandard testing conditions. However, if only minor accommodations are required the administration can be considered standard and the scores are not flagged. Minor accommodations include providing wheelchair access, the use of a sign language interpreter, or large-print test material. ETS provides information about the testing accommodations they provide at: https://www.ets.org/disabilities/test_takers/.

Special Interest Topic 16.4 provides a brief review of selected legal cases involving the provision of assessment accommodations.

Special Interest Topic 16.4: Assessment of Students with Disabilities: Selected Legal Issues

[A]n otherwise qualified student who is unable to disclose the degree of learning he actually possesses because of the test format or environment would be the object of discrimination solely on the basis of his handicap. – Chief Justice Cummings, U.S. 7th Circuit Court of Appeals[1]

Section 504 imposes no requirement upon an educational institution to lower or to effect substantial modifications of standards to accommodate a handicapped person. – Justice Powell, U.S. Supreme Court[2]

Phillips (1993) selected these quotes to illustrate the diversity in legal opinions that have been rendered regarding the provision of assessment accommodations for students with disabilities. Phillips wrote extensively in this area (e.g., 1993, 1994, 1996) and her writings provide some guidelines regarding the assessment of students with disabilities. Some of these guidelines are most directly applicable to high-stakes assessment programs, but they also have implications for other educational assessments.

Notice
Students should be given adequate notice when they will be required to engage in a high-stakes testing program (e.g., assessments required for graduation). While this requirement applies to all students, it is particularly important for students with disabilities to have adequate notice of any testing requirements since it may take them longer to prepare for the assessment. What constitutes "adequate notice?" With regard to a test required for graduation from high school one court found 1.5 years to be inadequate (*Brookhart v. Illinois State Board of Education*). Another court agreed, finding that approximately 1 year

(continued)

was inadequate, but suggested that 3 years was adequate (*Northport v. Ambach*).

Curricular Validity of the Test

If a state is going to implement a high-stakes assessment, they must be able to show that students have had adequate opportunities to acquire the knowledge and skills assessed by the assessment (*Debra P. v. Turlington*). This includes students with disabilities. One way to address this is to include the learning objectives measured by the assessment in a student's individualized education plan (IEP). One court ruled that parents and educators could decide not to include the skills and knowledge assessed by a mandatory graduation test on a student's IEP, but only if there was adequate time for the parents to evaluate the consequences of their child receiving a certificate of completion in lieu of a high school diploma (*Brookhart*).

Accommodations Must Be Individualized

Both IDEA and Section 504 require that educational programs and assessment accommodations be tailored to meet the unique needs of the individual student. For example, it is not acceptable for educators to decide that all students with a specific disability (e.g., learning disability) will receive the same assessment accommodations. Rulings by the federal Office of Civil Rights (OCR) maintain that decisions to provide specific assessment accommodations must be made on a case-by-case basis.

Invalid Accommodations

Courts have ruled that test administrators are not required to grant assessment accommodations that "substantially modify" a test or that "pervert" the purpose of the test (*Brookhart*). In psychometric terms, the accommodations should not invalidate the interpretation of test scores. Phillips (1994) suggests the following questions should be asked when considering a given accommodation:

1. Will format changes or accommodations in testing conditions change the skills being measured?
2. Will the scores of examinees tested under standard conditions have a different meaning than scores for examinees tested with the requested accommodation?
3. Would nondisabled examinees benefit if allowed the same accommodation?
4. Does the disabled examinee have any capability for adapting to standard test administration conditions?
5. Is the disability evidence or testing accommodation policy based on procedures with doubtful validity and reliability? (p. 104)

If the answer to any of these questions is "yes," Phillips suggests the accommodations are likely not appropriate.

Flagging

"Flagging" refers to administrators adding notations on score reports, transcripts, or diplomas indicating that assessment accommodations were

(continued)

provided (and in some cases what the accommodations were). Proponents of flagging hold that it protects the users of assessment information from making inaccurate interpretations of the results. Opponents of flagging hold that it unfairly labels and stigmatizes students with disabilities, breaches their confidentiality, and potentially puts them at a disadvantage. If there is substantial evidence that the accommodation does not detract from the validity of the interpretation of scores, flagging is not necessary. However, flagging may be indicated when there is incomplete evidence regarding the comparability of test scores. Phillips (1994) describes a process labeled "Self-selection with Informed Disclosure." Here administrators grant essentially any reasonable accommodation that is requested, even if it might invalidate the assessment results. Then, to protect users of assessment results, they add notations specifying what accommodations were provided. An essential element is that the examinee requesting the accommodations must be adequately informed that the assessment reports will contain information regarding any accommodations provided and the potential advantages and disadvantages of taking the test with accommodations. However, even when administrators get informed consent, disclosure of assessment accommodations may result in legal action.

Phillips (1993) notes that at times the goal of promoting valid and comparable test results and the legal and political goal of protecting the individual rights of students with disabilities may be at odds. She recommends that educators develop detailed policies and procedures regarding the provision of assessment accommodations, decide each case on an individual basis, and provide expeditious appeals when requested accommodations are denied. She notes:

> To protect the rights of both the public and individuals in a testing program, it will be necessary to balance the policy goal of maximum participation by the disabled against the need to provide valid and interpretable students test scores. (p. 32)

16.8 Summary

In this chapter we focus on the use of assessment accommodations with examinees with disabilities. Standard assessment procedures might not be appropriate for an examinee with a disability if the assessment requires the examinee to use an ability that is affected by their disability but is irrelevant to the construct being measured. In these situations, it may be necessary to modify the standard assessment procedures. Consider an examinee with a visual handicap taking a written test of computer science. While the examinee cannot read the material in its standard format, if they can read Braille an appropriate accommodation would be to convert the test to the Braille format. Since the test is designed to measure knowledge of computer science, not the ability to read standard print, this would be an appropriate accommodation. The goal of assessment accommodations is not simply to allow the examinee to obtain a higher score, but to provide the most reliable and valid assessment of the construct of interest. To this end, assessment accommodations should always increase the validity of the score interpretations so they more accurately reflect the examinee's true standing on the construct being measured.

There are three situations when assessment accommodations are not appropriate or necessary (AERA et al., 2014). These are (1) when the affected ability is directly relevant to the construct being measured, (2) when the purpose of the assessment is to assess the presence and degree of the disability, and (3) when the examinee does not actually need the accommodation.

A number of assessment accommodations have been developed to meet the needs of examinees with disabilities. These include:

- Modifications of presentation format (e.g., use of Braille or large print to replace standard text)
- Modifications of response format (e.g., allow an examinee to respond using sign language)
- Modifications of timing (e.g., extended time)
- Modifications of setting (e.g., preferential seating, study carrel to minimize distractions)
- Adaptive devices and supports (e.g., magnification and amplification devices)
- Using only a portion of the test (e.g., reducing test length)
- Using alternate assessments (e.g., tests specifically developed for examinees with disabilities)

There is a growing body of research on assessment accommodations that is partly due to Federal legislation that requires states to include students with disabilities when conducting statewide assessments. Some generally accepted principles about providing assessment accommodations include:

- Follow prescriptions regarding testing accommodations that are recommended in a student's IEP or Section 504 plan
- Tailor accommodations to meet the specific needs of the individual examinee
- Accommodations that examinees routinely receive in their classroom instruction are generally appropriate for assessments
- To the extent possible, select accommodations that promote independent functioning
- Follow the test publisher's guidelines when modifying standardized assessments
- Periodically reevaluate the needs of the student

In addition to examinees with disabilities, it may be appropriate to make assessment accommodations for ELLs. Both NCLB and ESSA require that when assessing examinees with limited English proficiency, we must ensure that we are actually assessing the students' knowledge and skills and not their proficiency in English. The same principle applies to assessments outside of the public schools. In terms of standardized assessments, typical accommodations include locating tests with directions and materials in the examinee's native language, substituting a nonverbal test designed to reduce the influence of cultural and language factors, and using a bilingual examiner or interpreter.

The final topic we address concerns reporting the results of modified assessments. In the context of individual psychological and educational assessments it is common for the clinician to report any modifications to the standardized assessment procedures. However, in the context of large-scale standardized assessments there is considerable debate. Some experts recommend use of "flags" to denote a score resulting from a modified administration of a test. Proponents of this practice suggest that without the use of flags, individuals interpreting the assessment results will assume that there was a standard administration and interpret the scores accordingly. Opponents feel that it unfairly labels and stigmatizes examinees with disabilities and may put them at a disadvantage.

References

American Educational Research Association, American Psychological Association, & National Council on Measurement in Education. (2014). *Standards for educational and psychological testing*. Washington, DC: American Educational Research Association.

Bolt, S. E., & Roach, A. T. (2009). *Inclusive assessment and accountability: A guide to accommodations for students with diverse needs*. New York, NY: Guilford Press.

Byrnes, M. A. (2008). Educator's interpretations of ambiguous accommodations. *Remedial and Special Education, 29*, 309–315.

Christensen, L. L., Braam, M., Scullin, S., & Thurlow, M. L. (2011). *2009 State policies on assessment participation and accommodations for students with disabilities* (Synthesis Report 83). Minneapolis, MN: University of Minnesota, National Center on Educational Outcomes.

Cummins, J. (1984). *Bilingualism and special education: Issues in assessment and pedagogy*. Clevedon: Multilingual Matters.

Fuchs, L. S. (2002). Best practices in providing accommodations for assessment. In A. Thomas & J. Grimes (Eds.), *Best practices in school psychology IV* (pp. 899–909). Bethesda, MD: NASP.

Fuchs, L. S., Fuchs, D., Eaton, S. B., Hamlett, C., Binkley, E., & Crouch, R. (2000). Using objective data sources to enhance teacher judgments about test accommodations. *Exceptional Children, 67*, 67–81.

Fuchs, L. S., Fuchs, D., Eaton, S. B., Hamlett, C. L., & Karns, K. M. (2000). Supplemental teacher judgments of mathematics test accommodations with objective data sources. *School Psychology Review, 29*, 65–85.

Gordon, M., Lewandowski, L., Murphy, K., & Dempsey, K. (2002). ADA-based accommodations in higher education: A survey of clinicians about documentation requirements of diagnostic standards. *Journal of Learning Disabilities, 35*, 357–363.

Jacob, S., & Hartshorne, T. (2007). *Ethics and law for school psychologists* (5th ed.). Hoboken, NJ: Wiley.

Kettler, R. J. (2012). Testing accommodations: Theory and research to inform practice. *International Journal of Disability, Development and Education, 59*, 53–66.

King, W. L., Baker, J., & Jarrow, J. E. (1995). *Testing accommodations for students with disabilities*. Columbus, OH: Association on Higher Education and Disability.

Lazarus, S. S., Thompson, S. J., & Thurlow, M. L. (2006, January). *How students access accommodations in assessment and instruction: Results of a survey of special education teachers* (Issue Brief No. 7). College Park, MD: Educational Policy and Reform Research Institute.

Lee, D., Reynolds, C., & Willson, V. (2003). Standardized test administration: Why bother? *Journal of Forensic Neuropsychology, 3*(3), 55–81.

Lovett, B. J., & Lewandowski, L. J. (2015). *Testing accommodations for students with disabilities: Research based practice*. Washington, DC: American Psychological Association.

Mastergeorge, A. M., & Miyoshi, J. N. (1999). *Accommodations for students with disabilities: A teacher's guide* (CSE Technical Report 508). Los Angeles, CA: National Center for Research on Evaluation, Standards, and Student Testing.

Northeast Technical Assistance Center. (1999). *Providing test accommodations. NETAC Teacher Tipsheet*. Rochester, NY: Author.

Phillips, S. E. (1993). Testing accommodations for disabled students. *Education Law Reporter,* *80,* 9–32.

Phillips, S. E. (1994). High-stakes testing accommodations: Validity versus disabled rights. *Applied Measurement in Education, 7*(2), 93–120.

Phillips, S. E. (1996). Legal defensibility of standards: Issues and policy perspectives. *Educational Measurement: Issues and Practice, 15*(2), 5–19.

Rickey, K. M. (2005). *Assessment accommodations for students with disabilities: A description of the decision-making process, perspectives of those affected, and current practices.* Unpublished doctoral dissertation, University of Iowa, Iowa City.

Roid, G. H. (2003). *Stanford-Binet intelligence scale-fifth edition.* Itasca, IL: Riverside.

Salvia, T., Ysseldyke, T. E., & Bolt, S. (2007). *Assessment in special and inclusive education* (10th ed.). Boston, MA: Houghton Mifflin.

Siskind, T. G. (1993). Teacher's knowledge about test modifications for students with disabilities. *Diagnostique, 18,* 145–157.

Thurlow, M. L., Christensen, L. L., & Lail, K. E. (2008). *An analysis of accommodations issues from the standards and assessments peer review* (Technical Report 51). Minneapolis, MN: University of Minnesota, National Center on Educational Outcomes.

Thurlow, M. L., Elliott, J. L., & Ysseldyke, J. E. (2003). *Testing students with disabilities: Practical strategies for complying with district and state requirements* (2nd ed.). Thousand Oaks, CA: Corwin Press.

U.S. Department of Education. (2001). *Guidance on standards, assessments, and accountability.* Retrieved from https://www2.ed.gov/policy/elsec/guid/standardsassessment/guidance_pg7.html.

Recommended Reading

American Educational Research Association, American Psychological Association, & National Council on Measurement in Education. (2014). *Standards for educational and psychological testing.* Washington, DC: AERA The Standards provide an excellent discussion of assessment accommodations.

Lovett, B. J., & Lewandowski, L. J. (2015). *Testing accommodations for students with disabilities: Research based practice.* Washington, DC: American Psychological Association This is a comprehensive source for a variety of issues related to assessment accommodations.

Luke, S., & Schwartz, A. (2007). Assessment and accommodations. *Evidence for Education, 2*(1), 1–12 This provides a good summary of testing accommodations, as well as resources for educational professionals.

Mastergeorge, A. M., & Miyoshi, J. N. (1999). *Accommodations for students with disabilities: A teacher's guide* (CSE Technical Report 508). Los Angeles, CA: National Center for Research on Evaluation, Standards, and Student Testing This guide provides some useful information on assessment accommodations specifically aimed towards teachers.

Phillips, S. E. (1994). High-stakes testing accommodations: Validity versus disabled rights. *Applied Measurement in Education, 7*(2), 93–120 An excellent discussion of some early legal cases involving assessment accommodations for students with disabilities.

Thurlow, M. L., Liu, K. K., Ward, J. M., & Christensen, L. L. (2013). *Assessment principles and guidelines for ELLs with disabilities.* Minneapolis, MN: University of Minnesota Improving the Validity of Assessment Results for English Language Learners with Disabilities (IVARED). Provides a summary of the essential principles of inclusive and valid assessments for English Language Learners with disabilities.

Turnbull, A., Turnbull, R., Shank, M., Smith, S., & Leal, D. (2020). *Exceptional lives: Practice, progress, & dignity in today's schools* (9th ed.). Hoboken, NJ: Pearson Education This is an excellent text that provides valuable information regarding the education of students with disabilities.

Best Practices: Legal and Ethical Issues

With power comes responsibility!

Abstract

In their professional roles, psychologists often use tests to make decisions that significantly impact their clients' lives. Moreover, tests are commonly used in research that affects science, public policy, and law. It is therefore imperative that psychologists and other test users ensure that the assessments they use are developed, administered, scored, and interpreted in a technically, ethically, and legally sound manner. This chapter presents guidelines based on existing professional codes of ethics and standards of professional practice to help assure professionals use tests responsibly. These guidelines address test development, selection, administration, scoring, and interpretation, as well the reporting of assessment results. The chapter concludes with a discussion of test taker responsibilities and a summary of assessment behaviors that professionals should avoid.

Electronic Supplementary Material The online version of this chapter (https://doi.org/10.1007/978-3-030-59455-8_17) contains supplementary material, which is available to authorized users.

Learning Objectives

After reading and studying this chapter, students should be able to:

1. Explain why the assessment practices of psychologists are held to high professional standards.
2. Identify major professional organizations that have written guidelines addressing psychological assessment issues.
3. Describe and give examples of the principles to consider when developing psychological and educational assessments.
4. Describe and give examples of the principles to consider when selecting psychological assessments.
5. Identify major resources that provide information about published tests and describe the type of information each one provides.
6. Describe and give examples of the principles to consider when administering psychological and educational assessments.
7. Describe and give examples of the principles to consider when interpreting, using, and communicating test results.
8. Describe and give examples of the primary responsibilities of test takers.
9. Describe ten assessment-related activities that psychologists should avoid.

While psychologists might not always be aware of it, their positions bestow them with considerable power. Psychologists make decisions in their professional roles that often significantly impact their clients, and many of these decisions involve information garnered from psychological assessments. Measurement devices are also used in research that affects science, public policy, law, and how groups of people and their behaviors are viewed and understood. As a result, it is our responsibility as psychologists to ensure that the assessments we use are developed, administered, scored, and interpreted in a technically, ethically, and legally sound manner regardless of where they are employed. This chapter provides some guidelines that will help you ensure that your assessment practices are sound.

Much of the information discussed in this chapter has been introduced in previous chapters. We will also incorporate guidelines that are presented in existing professional codes of ethics and standards of professional practice. The following guidelines reflect a compilation of principles presented in the *Standards for Educational and Psychological Testing* (American Educational Research Association, American Psychological Association, & National Council on Measurement in Education, 2014), the *Ethical Principles of Psychologists and Code of Conduct* (APA, 2002—hereafter referred to as the APA Ethics Code), and the *Rights and Responsibilities of Test Takers: Guidelines and Expectations* (JCTP, 1998).

17.1 Guidelines for Developing Assessments

The Joint Committee on Testing Practices (JCTP, 1998) notes that the most fundamental right of test takers is to be evaluated with assessments that meet high professional standards and that are valid for the intended purposes. Accordingly, psychologists who are involved in developing tests have a professional responsibility to develop instruments that meet or exceed all applicable technical, ethical, and legal standards. The most explicit and comprehensive guidelines for developing and evaluating tests are the *Standards for Educational and Psychological Testing*

> The most fundamental right of test takers is to be evaluated with assessments that meet high professional standards and that are valid for the intended purposes.

(AERA et al., 2014). While these standards apply most directly to professionally developed, standardized tests, they may be applied appropriately to less formal assessment procedures like those designed for research studies or to be used in classrooms. Below are some brief guidelines for the development of assessments that meet professional standards. For a more detailed discussion of test development principles, refer to Chap. 18.

1. *Clearly specify your assessment objectives and develop a table of specifications.* When developing any test, the first step is to specify the purpose of the test and the construct or domain to be measured. To this end, psychologists should begin by explicitly specifying the construct to be measured and developing a table of specifications (TOS) or test blueprint. The TOS should clearly define the content and format of the test and be directly linked to the construct being assessed (see Chap. 18 for more TOS information and examples). While the importance of this process should be obvious, in real-world situations it may be tempting to skip these steps and simply start writing the test. However, this is actually one of the most important steps in developing high-quality tests. If you have not clearly specified exactly what you want to measure, you are not likely to do a very effective job measuring it.

2. *Develop assessment procedures that are appropriate for measuring the specified construct.* Once the TOS is developed, it should be used to guide the development of items and scoring procedures. Guidelines for developing items of different types were presented in Chap. 6. Selected-response items and constructed-response items have their own specific strengths and weaknesses, and are appropriate for assessing some constructs and inappropriate for assessing others.

> The development of items and the scoring criteria should be an integrated process guided by a table of specifications (TOS) or test blueprint.

It is the test developer's responsibility to determine which procedures are most appropriate for the test they are developing.

3. *Develop explicit scoring criteria.* Practically all types of assessments require clearly stated criteria for scoring the items. This can range from fairly straightforward scoring keys for selected-response items and short-answer items to

detailed scoring rubrics for evaluating constructed-response items. Whatever the format, developing the items and the scoring criteria should be an integrated process guided by the TOS. Scoring procedures should be consistent with the purpose of the test and facilitate valid score interpretations (AERA et al., 2014).

4. *Specify a sampling plan for standardization and collect normative data.* It is important to clearly specify the target population and collect standardization data based on an appropriate sample. This area is discussed in more detail in Chap. 18.

5. *Develop clear guidelines for test administration.* All aspects of test administration should be clearly specified. This includes instructions to examinees taking the test, time limits, testing conditions (e.g., classroom or laboratory, individual or group), and any equipment that will be utilized. When applicable, it also includes detailing any background expertise or training that an examiner needs to administer the test. Psychologists should develop administration instructions in sufficient detail so that others will be able to administer the test in a standardized manner.

6. *Plan accommodations for test takers with disabilities and other special needs.* As discussed in Chap. 16, it is becoming more common for tests to be modified to accommodate the needs of individuals with disabilities or those with limited English proficiency. When developing assessments, some thought should be given to what types of accommodations may be necessary for these examinees. Universal design principles, aimed at making a test fully accessible to individuals with and without specialized needs, should be incorporated into test development whenever possible (Lovett & Lewandowski, 2015).

7. *Carefully review the assessment prior to administration.* Psychologists that develop tests should carefully review their tests to ensure technical accuracy. To this end it is beneficial to have a trusted colleague familiar with the measured construct review the test and scoring criteria prior to administration. In addition to reviewing for technical accuracy, assessments should be reviewed for potentially insensitive content or language and evidence of bias due to race, gender, or ethnic background. Bias in educational assessment is discussed in detail in Chap. 15.

8. *Evaluate the psychometric properties of assessments.* After administering the test, psychologists should use quantitative and qualitative item analysis procedures to evaluate and refine their assessments (discussed in Chap. 7). Psychologists should also perform analyses that will allow them to assess the reliability (Chap. 4) and validity (Chap. 5) of the scores obtained from their measurements. The extent of the reliability and validity studies depends on the application of the test. That is, tests being developed for commercial publication must have extensive evidence regarding the reliability of scores and validity of score interpretations. Less formal tests like those developed for research studies and classroom applications will require less extensive studies. While it might be difficult for psychologists working independently to perform some of the more complex reliability and validity analyses, at a minimum they should use some of the simplified procedures outlined in the appropriate chapters (Table 17.1).

Table 17.1 Checklist for developing assessments

1. Have the test objectives been clearly specified and a table of specifications (TOS) developed?
2. Are the assessment procedures appropriate for measuring the specified construct?
3. Have explicit scoring criteria been developed?
4. Was a sampling plan for standardization developed and appropriate data collected?
5. Have clear guidelines for test administration been developed?
6. Have accommodations for test takers with disabilities and other special needs been planned?
7. Has the assessment been reviewed for technical accuracy and potentially insensitive or biased content?
8. Have the technical properties of the assessment been evaluated?

17.2 Guidelines for Selecting Published Assessments

As we noted in Chap. 1, most psychologists will not specialize in test development. However, most psychologists that work in applied clinical or research settings will select published tests to administer to their clients or research participants. In selecting these tests, as when developing assessments, it is imperative to ensure that the assessments meet high professional standards and are valid for the intended purposes. Below are a few guidelines for selecting assessments that meet professional standards.

> Most psychologists who work in applied clinical or research settings will select published tests to administer to their clients or research participants.

1. *Select assessments that have been validated for the intended purpose.* As we have emphasized throughout this text, validity is a fundamental consideration when developing or selecting a test (see Chap. 5). Professionally developed assessments should clearly specify the recommended interpretations of test scores and provide a summary of the validity evidence supporting each interpretation. However, in the end it is the person selecting the test who is responsible for determining if the assessment is appropriate for use in their particular setting (AERA et al., 2014). The essential questions are how will the assessment information be used and have the proposed interpretations of the results of the test been validated for those uses?
2. *Select assessments with normative data that are representative of the target population.* The validity of norm-referenced interpretations is dependent on how representative the normative or standardization group is to the target population (see Chap. 3) or another reference group with whom examinees are to be compared. The fundamental question is does the normative sample adequately represent the type of examinees the test will be used with or alternatively a different reference sample to whom the examinees are to be compared. It is also important to consider how current the norms are since their usefulness diminishes over time (AERA et al., 2014).

3. *Select assessments that produce reliable scores.* It is important to select assessment procedures that produce reliable results. In Chap. 4 we presented guidelines regarding the levels of reliability recommended for different applications or uses. For example, when making high-stakes decisions it is important to use assessment results (i.e., test scores) that are highly reliable (e.g., $r_{xx} > 0.95$).

4. *Select tests that are fair.* While no assessment procedure is absolutely free from bias, efforts should be made to select assessments that have been shown to be relatively free from bias due to race, gender, or ethnic background. Bias in psychological assessment is discussed in detail in Chap. 15. It is important to note, however, that even when research demonstrates that reliability and validity evidence is generalizable across groups, a biased user can alter interpretations of test scores in ways that bias an otherwise fair and appropriate assessment.

5. *Select assessments based on a thorough review of the available literature.* The selection of assessment procedures can have significant consequences for a large number of individuals. As a result, the decision to select an assessment should be based on a careful and thorough review of the available information. It is appropriate to begin this review by examining information and material provided by the test publishers. This can include catalogs, test manuals, specimen test sets, score reports, and other supporting documentation. However, the search should not stop here and you should seek out independent evaluations and reviews of the tests you are considering. A natural question is "Where can I access information about assessments?" The following resources are ones we have found most helpful.

> Psychologists should select assessments based on a thorough review of the available literature.

  (a) *Mental Measurements Yearbook (MMY).* MMY is a series of volumes published every 3 years by the Buros Center for Testing. The MMY lists tests alphabetically by title and is an invaluable resource for researching published assessments. Each listing provides descriptive information about the test, including test author, publication dates, intended population, forms, prices, and publisher. It also contains additional information regarding the availability of reliability, validity, and normative data, as well as scoring and reporting services. Most listings include one or more critical reviews by qualified assessment experts.

  (b) *Tests in Print (TIP).* TIP is also published by the Buros Center for Testing. TIP is a bibliographic encyclopedia of information on practically every commercially available published test in psychology and education. Each listing includes the test title, intended population, publication date, author, publisher, and references. TIP does not contain critical reviews or psychometric information, but it does serve as a master index to the Buros Center's reference series on tests. In the TIP, tests are listed alphabetically within subjects (e.g., achievement tests, intelligence tests). There are also indexes that can help you locate specific tests. After locating a test that meets your criteria, you can turn to the Mental Measurements Yearbook for more detailed information on the test.

(c) *Test Collection at ETS*. The Test Collection at ETS provides a searchable electronic database that provides a listing of over 25,000 tests and other measurement devices. Summary information is provided about each test, along with a website URL directing you to where tests can be ordered or a reference to a journal article discussing the development of the test; links to downloadable versions of some tests are also provided.

(d) *Test Reviews Online*. Test Reviews Online is a web-based service of the Buros Center for Testing (www.Buros.org/test-reviews-information). This service makes test reviews available online to individuals precisely as they appear in the *Mental Measurements Yearbook*. For a relatively small fee (i.e., currently $15.00), users can download information on any of over 3500 tests that include specifics on test purpose, population, publication date, administration time, and descriptive test critiques.

(e) In addition to these traditional references, you should also search the scientific literature for reviews of tests published in refereed journals in addition to research on the use of specific tests. Information gained from literature review will almost always be more current and comprehensive than information contained in test reviews or test manuals.

6. *Select and use only assessments that you are qualified to administer, score, and interpret.* Since the administration, scoring, and interpretation of many psychological tests require advanced training, it is important to select and use only tests that you are qualified to use as a result of your education and training. For example, the administration of an individual intelligence test such as the Wechsler Intelligence Scale for

> It is important to select and use only tests that you are qualified to use as a result of your education and training.

Children, Fifth Edition (WISC-V) requires extensive training and supervision that is typically acquired in graduate psychology and education programs. Most test publication firms have established procedures that allow individuals and organizations to qualify to purchase tests based on specific criteria. For example, Psychological Assessment Resources (PAR) has a multitier system that classifies assessment products according to qualification requirements. In this system, Level A products require no special qualifications while Level C products require an advanced professional degree or license based on advanced training and experience in psychological and educational assessment practices. Before purchasing restricted tests, the potential buyer must provide documentation that they meet the necessary requirements. In some situations psychologists use what are referred to as technicians or psychological assistants to administer and score psychological tests under their supervision. In this context psychologists select the tests to be administered, interpret the results, and write the reports while the technicians actually administer and score the tests under the supervision of the psychologists. There are professional standards for the education and training of technicians, such as those published by the National Academy of Neuropsychology (Puente, Adams, Barr, Bush, & NANA Policy and Planning Committee, 2006).

7. *Guard against potential misuses and misinterpretations.* When selecting assessments, avoid selecting those that are likely to be used or interpreted in an invalid or biased manner. This is a difficult responsibility to discharge and requires continual vigilance. Nitko (2001) suggests that to meet this responsibility you must have a broad knowledge of how assessments are being used in your professional setting and any potential misuses or misinterpretations.

8. *Maintain test security.* For assessments to be valid, it is important that test security be maintained. Most commercially available tests are legally protected by various laws (e.g., copyright laws), which can include protection on test materials, test items, scoring algorithms, normative databases, etc. Individuals selecting, purchasing, and using standardized assessments have a professional and legal responsibility to maintain the security of assessments instruments. While each test publishing company has its own user agreements that cover test security, common restrictions include: (1) not providing test takers with access to testing materials or answers before taking the test; (2) prohibiting reproduction of materials without express written consent of the test publisher; (3) releasing assessment materials and results only to qualified individuals; and (4) limiting reviews of testing materials by test takers or parents/guardians to a setting supervised by a qualified representative of the organization conducting the assessment. Examples of breaches in the security of standardized tests include allowing clients to examine the test before taking it, using actual items from a test for preparation purposes, making and distributing copies of a test, and allowing test takers to take the test outside of a controlled environment (e.g., allowing them to take the test home to complete it).

9. *Before using tests as part of an assessment or other decision-making process, consider the consequences of testing as well as the consequences of not testing.* Are objective data needed to improve the decision-making process? In most cases the answer is yes, but a cost-benefit analysis may be necessary when one is in doubt. These guidelines are summarized in Table 17.2. Special Interest Topic 17.1 provides information on the controversial release of sensitive information about a popular projective technique.

Table 17.2 Checklist for selecting published assessments

1. Have the desired interpretations of performance on the selected assessments been validated for the intended purpose?
2. Do the selected assessments have normative data that are representative of the target population?
3. Do selected assessments produce reliable results?
4. Are interpretations of the selected assessments fair?
5. Was the selection process based on a thorough review of the available literature?
6. Are you qualified to administer, score, and interpret the selected assessments?
7. Have you screened assessments for likely misuses and misinterpretations?
8. Have steps been taken to maintain test security?
9. Have you considered the consequences of both testing and not testing?

Special Interest Topic 17.1: Wikipedia and the Rorschach Ink Blot Test

Most of you are likely familiar with Wikipedia, the web-based, free-of-charge encyclopedia that is written in a collaborative manner by contributors from throughout the world. Much to the chagrin of many college professors, it is often a first-line (and perhaps only) resource used by college students researching various study topics. At its best, Wikipedia serves to provide accessible information on a variety of subjects to a mass audience, helping to make information accessible to all those with access to the Internet. However, not everyone is supportive of all its content.

One content-related controversy emerged in 2009, when the ten Rorschach color plates were published in the Wikipedia article describing the Rorschach. Additionally the article contained information on the scoring and interpretation of the test along with information about popular responses. While detailed technical information on the scoring and interpretation of the Rorschach can be obtained in numerous psychological textbooks that are available for purchase by the public, we are not aware of the actual plates ever being reproduced and made available to the public. For example, we include inkblots similar to those used in the Rorschach in this textbook, but they were specifically created as examples and are not actual Rorschach inkblots.

On one side of the substantial debate are psychologists noting that the publication of these pictures undermines the utility of the Rorschach and is a clear violation of the ethics codes of major professional psychological associations like the American Psychological Association (APA). On the other side, it is argued that the Rorschach plates are in the public domain since they were initially published over 70 years ago, which exceeds the copyright term in many countries. While legal action against Wikipedia had been threatened to force removal of the plates, the Wikipedia article still contains the reproduced plates!

While it might not be illegal to reproduce these pictures and post them in the public domain, it is clearly unethical! It will never be known with certainty how much damage has been done to clinical utility of the test. It is clearly possible that clients might access this article prior to taking the Rorschach and exposure to the plates and accompanying information most certainly will impact their responses. Additionally, this makes "coaching" of clients by attorneys in forensic settings even more likely.

We see this as a clear example of an unethical breach of test security. While it is not clear who posted the plates or if they are a psychologist, in consideration of the public welfare we hope that in the future organizations like Wikipedia will respect and honor the ethics codes of major professions when it comes to publishing potentially damaging images and/or information.

17.3   Guidelines for Administering Assessments

So far, we have discussed your professional responsibilities related to developing and selecting tests. Clearly, your professional responsibilities do not stop there. Every step of the assessment process has its own important responsibilities, and now we turn to those associated with the administration of assessments. Subsequently we will address responsibilities related to scoring, interpreting, using, and communicating assessment results. The following guidelines describe your responsibilities when administering assessments.

1. *Provide information to examinees and obtain informed consent before administering any assessments.* In most situations, psychologists are ethically and legally required to obtain informed consent before providing professional services, including assessments. Informed consent is obtained when a psychologist (or other health professional) provides information to a prospective client about the services (i.e., assessment and/ or treatment) to be provided. The client

> In most situations, psychologists are ethically and legally required to obtain informed consent before providing professional services, including assessments.

then has the opportunity to carefully consider that information and decide if they want to receive the services. In terms of assessments, this information includes: (1) when and under what conditions the assessment will be administered, (2) the abilities and characteristics that will be assessed, (3) how the assessments will be scored and interpreted, (4) how the results will used, (5) confidentiality issues and who will have access to the results, and (6) how the results are likely to impact the client (APA, 2002; JCTP, 1998; Nitko, 2001). An excellent resource for all test takers is *Rights and Responsibilities of Tests Takers: Guidelines and Expectations* developed by the Joint Committee on Testing Practices (1998). Informed consent is mandated in both clinical (i.e., working with clients) and research (i.e., working with research participants) settings. Special Interest Topic 17.2 provides more information about various aspects of the informed consent process.

Special Interest Topic 17.2: Aspects of Informed Consent

As discussed earlier, psychologists must secure "informed consent" prior to providing professional services such as assessments or counseling. Most authorities on informed consent highlight the following four legal aspects:

1. *Capacity.* It is necessary that the individual providing consent to treatment has the mental capacity to understand all relevant information and what he/ she is agreeing to. This implies the individual is competent and rational. If the potential client does not have the mental capacity to provide the consent, other options must be pursued. For example, it may be necessary to have a custodian appointed by a court to make health care decisions for the

(continued)

individual. When the client is a minor, the parents are typically given the right to provide informed consent since minors are usually not considered to have the capacity to consent to psychological services. Many states allow minors to provide consent to psychological services in certain situations. For example, in the state of Texas minors may provide consent when there is suicide potential, when they have been abused, and when the treatment is for substance abuse or dependency.

2. *Sufficient information provided.* It is necessary that potential clients be given adequate information about the services to be provided in order to allow them to make an informed decision. That is, do they want these services? As we noted, clients need to know what assessments and interventions they are agreeing to and the potential consequences of these actions. This information must be provided in sufficient detail and in a manner that is easily understandable to the client.

3. *Voluntary.* Consent to treatment must be provided in a voluntary manner. There should be no coercion. In certain situations this is not as clear as it might initially appear. As described in Chap. 14 discussion of forensic assessment, in some situations failing to provide consent might be prejudicial to clients, so subtle pressure might be present even though their consent is technically voluntary.

4. *Documentation.* As our lawyer friends are fond of saying, "If it is not documented—it didn't happen!" In other words, the informed consent process should include a document that details the process and the client's agreement. This should be signed by the client signifying their acceptance of the arrangement. The client should be given a copy of the documents for their record and the original should be retained in their file.

2. *When minors are to be assessed, be sure to have legal written consent from the parent or legal guardian.* Minors should be asked to assent to the testing procedures; however, a minor cannot give consent for participation—this is true when conducting testing or survey research just as much as it is in clinical settings. Both assent from the minor and consent from the parent or legal guardian are ethical, and in many cases, legal requirements for assessing minors.

3. *Administer only those assessments for which you are qualified by education and training.* As noted previously, it is important to only select and use tests that you are qualified to use as a result of your education and training. Some assessments require extensive training and supervision before one is able to administer them independently.

4. *Administer the assessments in a standardized manner.* Assessments should be administered in the standardized manner specified in the test manual. This ensures fairness and promotes the reliability of scores and validity of their inter-

Table 17.3 Checklist for administering assessments

1. Did you provide information on the assessment and obtain informed consent before administering it?
2. *If a minor was assessed, did you obtain legal written consent from the parent or legal guardian?*
3. Are you qualified by education and training to administer the assessment?
4. Was the assessment administered in a standardized and fair manner?
5. When appropriate, was the assessment modified to accommodate the needs of test takers with disabilities?
6. Are proper test security measures followed?

pretations. Except in rare situations (see the next guideline), this requires that all examinees will take the assessment under the same conditions. For example, all examinees will receive the same materials and have access to the same resources (e.g., the use of calculators), receive the same instructions, and have the same time limits. Efforts should be made to ensure that the assessment environment is comfortable, quiet, and relatively free from distractions. Examinees should be given opportunities to ask reasonable questions.

5. *When appropriate, administration should be modified to accommodate the needs of examinees with disabilities.* As discussed in Chap. 16, when assessing examinees with disabilities it is often necessary and appropriate to modify the standard administration procedures to address the special needs of these students. Assessment accommodations are granted to minimize the impact of examinee characteristics that are irrelevant to the construct being measured by the assessment. A major consideration when selecting accommodations is to only select accommodations that do not undermine the reliability or validity of the assessment results. Many test publishers provide guidelines regarding what accommodations are permissible under specific conditions.

6. *Maintain test security.* As we noted previously it is important to maintain test security throughout the assessment process. Obviously, test administrations are a time when security can be breached. For example, it would be unethical to allow examinees to take the test outside of a controlled environment (e.g., allowing them to take the test home to complete it).

These guidelines are summarized in Table 17.3.

17.4 Guidelines for Scoring Assessments

As part of the test development and standardization process, explicit scoring procedures and instructions are developed to ensure correct, reliable, and unbiased scoring of test items. The following guidelines explain your responsibilities when scoring assessments.

1. *Make sure assessments are scored properly and recorded accurately.* It is a psychologist's professional responsibility to ensure the assessments are scored in an accurate manner. This applies to both commercially and personally developed assessments. With selected-response items this will involve carefully applying scoring keys and double checking errors. Better yet—use computer scoring when possible! With constructed-response items and performance assessments this involves the careful application scoring rubrics. The importance of double checking your calculations cannot be overemphasized. In Chap. 14 we noted that it is not uncommon to discover scoring and clerical errors in assessments submitted to the courts.

> It is a psychologist's professional responsibility to ensure their assessments are scored in an accurate manner.

2. *Make sure the scoring is fair.* An aspect of the previous guideline that deserves special attention involves fairness or the absence of bias in scoring. Whenever scoring involves subjective judgment, it is also important to take steps to ensure that the scoring is based solely on performance or content, and is not contaminated by ***expectancy effects*** related to examinees. That is, you don't want your personal impression of the examinee to influence your evaluation of their performance, in either a positive or negative manner. For example, in some situations it may be possible to score assessments without being aware of the examinee's identification.

3. *Keep assessment results confidential.* It is the responsibility of psychologists and others who score assessments to keep the results confidential. While different standards of confidentiality and privacy exist in different settings, it is the psychologist's professional, ethical, and legal responsibility to be aware of the laws and policies applicable in the settings where they provide services. For example, there are both state and federal laws that govern the confidentiality of psychological and medical test results. At the federal level the Health Information Portability and Accountability Act (HIPAA) and the Family Educational Rights and Privacy Act (FERPA) specify guidelines for maintaining the confidentiality of psychological test results in health and school settings, respectively. In summary, only in a limited number of situations (e.g., court order) can the results of a client's assessments be disclosed without their permission. As noted, information on the confidentiality of assessment results should be discussed with the client when obtaining informed consent.

> It is the responsibility of psychologists and others who score assessments to keep the results confidential.

These guidelines are summarized in Table 17.4.

Table 17.4 Checklist for scoring assessments

1. Are procedures in place to ensure that assessments are scored and the results are recorded accurately?
2. Are procedures in place to ensure the scoring is fair?
3. Are assessment results kept confidential?

17.5 Guidelines for Interpreting Assessment Results, Making Clinical Decisions, and Reporting Results

In Chap. 1 we stated that we advocate a model of assessment that incorporates psychometric sophistication, clinical insight, knowledge of psychological theory, and thoughtful reasoning. In this model, assessment involves a dynamic evaluation and synthesis of information that is obtained in a reliable and valid manner from multiple sources using multiple procedures. We noted that a psychologist conducting an assessment should assume the role of a "detective" that collects, evaluates, and synthesizes information and integrates that information with a thorough understanding of psychological theories of development, psychopathology, and individual differences (Kaufman, 1994). Below are some more specific guidelines.

1. *Use assessment results only for purposes for which they have been validated.* When interpreting assessment results, the issue of validity is the overriding concern. A primary consideration when interpreting and using assessment results is to determine if there is sufficient validity evidence to support the proposed interpretations and uses. When psychologists use assessment

   > Use assessment results only for purposes for which they have been validated.

   results it is their responsibility to promote valid interpretations and guard against invalid interpretations. Do not attach meaning to test scores or other indications of test performance for which there is no scientific support. We have encountered psychologists who have made unique interpretations of test performance and justified them (erroneously) by arguing there was no research to say the interpretation was not correct—validation of test score interpretations is an affirmative requirement.
2. *Use multiple sources and types of assessment information.* In this text we have described a wide variety of assessment procedures: cognitive tests (e.g., intelligence, achievement, and neuropsychological tests), self-report personality measures, behavior rating scales, interviews, and behavioral observations. All of these have a role to play in psychological assessment. Different assessment procedures have different strengths and weaknesses, and psychologists are encouraged to use the results of multiple assessments when making important decisions that impact their clients. It is not appropriate to base important decisions on the result of one assessment, particularly when it is difficult to take corrective action when the decision turns out to be incorrect.
3. *Stay close to the data.* This guideline holds that psychologists should remain evidence based in their test interpretations and not "overweight" their clinical judgment. There is a substantial amount of research demonstrating that an actuarial or statistical approach to interpreting assessment information is superior to a clinical or impressionistic approach. In the clinical/impressionistic approach, the clinician uses personal judgment and subjective processes to interpret the assessment information and make decisions. Often, such alterations in test score interpretation are based on faulty recollection of anecdotal data from years of

"clinical experience." While we will not review this research here, there is much evidence to indicate that clinicians and others tend to have selective recall of "facts" and cases that support a particular view and fail to recall as well or as accurately anecdotal data that disagree with their predispositions. In an actuarial/ statistical approach, human judgment is eliminated entirely and the interpretation is based solely on empirically established relationships (Dawes, Faust, & Meehl, 1989). Examples of these empirically based models include the use of regression equations, actuarial tables, and nomograms to facilitate clinical diagnosis and decision making. Grove and Meehl (1996) conclude that reliance on the least efficient of two decision-making models "... is not only unscientific and irrational, it is unethical" (p. 320). Actuarial models are not available to address many of the decisions professional psychologists are asked to make, but when they are available, we encourage their careful application. See Special Interest Topic 17.3 for more information on the actuarial versus clinical decision-making debate (see Special Interest Topic 17.3).

Special Interest Topic 17.3: The Accuracy of Clinical Versus Actuarial Approach to Interpreting Assessment Results

Almost 75 years ago, Sarbin (1943: as reported in Grove & Meehl, 1996) compared the accuracy of two very different approaches to interpreting assessment results. One approach involved a two-variable regression equation to predict college grade point average (GPA). The two variables were those most commonly used for predicting success in college: a college aptitude test score and high school GPA. The second approach was considerably more elaborate. In addition to the aptitude scores and high school GPA used in the linear equation, the counselor also had:

- Notes from an interviewer who had completed preliminary interviews
- Results of the Strong Vocational Interest Blank (i.e., an interest inventory)
- Results of a four-factor personality inventory
- Information from an 8-page questionnaire completed by the students
- Results of additional aptitude and achievement tests
- A personal interview with the students

The research question was—which approach is the most accurate? Can the counselor, with the benefit of all this additional information, make better predictions about student academic success than the two-variable equation? The answer might surprise you!

For female students, the two approaches were approximately equal. However, for male students the two-variable regression equation was significantly more accurate than the prediction of the counselor. If this was an isolated finding it would be easy to dismiss it as a chance happening. However, there has been a significant amount of research in the last 75 years that essentially supports these results—actuarial or statistical approaches to interpreting

(continued)

assessment data are more accurate than clinical or impressionistic approaches. Youngstrom, Freeman, and Jenkins (2009) noted that "The superiority of statistical approaches has been demonstrated more than 130 times in disciplines spanning economics and education as well as clinical decision making" (p. 363).

Two questions seem to jump to mind when considering these results: (1) Why are clinicians inferior to simple actuarial methods when interpreting assessment information? and (2) Why do most clinicians continue to rely on subjective impressionistic approaches in light of these findings? Although it is beyond the scope of this text to review all of the research addressing these questions, we can give you two quick responses:

- *Why are clinicians inferior to simple actuarial methods when interpreting assessment information?* From the beginning of this text we have emphasized that people are not very good at making subjective judgments about other people! This is behind our vigorous promotion of the use of objective assessment data to drive clinical decision making. The basis for our failure to accurately make judgments and predictions based on subjective impressions are likely the result internal biases (e.g., halo effect, self-fulfilling prophecy) and heuristics (i.e., mental short-cuts people use to rapidly process information). For those of you interested in learning more about this topic, examine the research in cognitive psychology regarding human judgment. The article by Grove and Meehl (1996) is a good place to start.
- *Why do most clinicians continue to rely on subjective impressionistic approaches in light of these findings?* Grove and Meehl (1996) identified a number of reasons why clinicians have not adopted actuarial approaches for interpreting assessment information. These include:
  - *Reason 1.* Fear of being replaced by a computer
  - *Reason 2.* Threat to self-concept if one acknowledges a simple regression equation is superior
  - *Reason 3.* Attachment to specific psychological theories
  - *Reason 4.* Belief that actuarial approaches dehumanize clients
  - *Reason 5.* Aversion to the idea of computers competing with humans on cognitive tasks
  - *Reason 6.* An education that did not instill a preference for scientific inquiry over subjective reasoning

  The authors suggest that *Reason 6* is probably the major culprit! We agree this is a major contributing factor, but believe *Reason 1* and *Reason 2* are also prominent. However, this is an empirical question that should be addressed using well-designed research!

4. *Be aware of the limitations of assessment results.* All assessments contain error, and some have more error than others. It is the responsibility of psychologists and other users of assessment results to be aware of the limitations of these

results and to take these limitations into consideration when interpreting and using them.

5. *Consider personal factors or extraneous events that might have influenced test performance.* This guideline holds that psychologists should be sensitive to factors that might have negatively influenced a student's performance. For example, was the examinee feeling ill or upset on the day of the assessment? Is the examinee prone to high levels of test anxiety? This guideline also extends to administrative and environmental events that might have impacted the examinee. For example, were there errors in administration that might have impacted the examinee's performance? Did any events occur during the administration that might have distracted the examinee or otherwise undermined performance? If it appears any factors compromised the examinee's performance, this should be considered when interpreting their assessment results.

6. *Consider any differences between the normative group and examinees or between the normative sample and the population to which examinees are compared.* If there are meaningful differences between the normative groups and the actual examinees, this must be taken into consideration when interpreting and using the assessment results. Likewise, if comparison to a specific population is necessary to which the examinee might not belong, be sure the standardization sample of the test adequately reflects the population parameters on important variables.

7. *Discuss assessment results with examinees in an easily understandable manner.* In most situations, examinees have the right to receive comprehensive information about assessment results that is presented in an understandable and timely manner. Additionally, it is the psychologist's responsibility to explain to examinees any likely consequences of the assessments, both positive and negative. Special situations that may preclude the explanation of test results include forensic evaluations and security screenings. In these situations psychologists must clearly explain the arrangements prior to obtaining informed consent and conducting the assessment (APA, 2002).

> It is the responsibility of psychologists to present assessment results in a timely and understandable manner.

These guidelines are summarized in Table 17.5.

Table 17.5 Checklist for interpreting, using, and communicating assessment results

1. Are assessment results used only for purposes for which they have been validated?
2. Were multiple sources and types of assessment information used when making high-stakes educational decisions?
3. Did you "stay close to the data" and minimize subjective inferences?
4. Did you take into consideration the limitations of the assessment results?
5. Have you considered personal factors or extraneous events that might have influenced test performance?
6. Are there any differences between the normative group and actual test takers that need to be considered?
7. Are results communicated in an easily understandable and timely manner?

17.6   Responsibilities of Test Takers

So far, we have emphasized guidelines that apply to those developing and using the tests. However, the *Standards* (AERA et al., 2014) note that test takers also have responsibilities. These responsibilities include:

1. *Examinees are responsible for preparing for the assessment.* Examinees have the right to have adequate information about the nature and use of assessments. In turn, examinees are responsible for preparing for the assessment.

2. *Examinees are responsible for following the directions of the individual administering the assessment.* Examinees are expected to follow the instructions provided by the individual administering the test or assessment. This includes behaviors such as showing up on time for the assessment, starting and stopping when instructed to do so, and recording responses as requested.

3. *Examinees are responsible for responding in a manner that accurately reflects their characteristics and abilities.* During assessments examinees should not misrepresent themselves in an effort to look more socially acceptable or to look more pathological. In other words, they should not engage in dissimulation. Cheating on tests is a related issue that is particularly problematic in academic settings. Cheating

> Examinees should not misrepresent themselves in an effort to look more socially acceptable or to look more pathological.

   includes copying from another examinee, using prohibited resources (e.g., notes or other unsanctioned aids), securing stolen copies of tests, or having someone else take the test for you. Any form of dissimulation or cheating reduces the validity of the test results. Special Interest Topic 17.4 provides guidelines for teachers to help prevent cheating in their classrooms, and Special Interest Topic 17.5 alerts us that cheating is not limited to students alone, but that at times those responsible for administering tests have been guilty of compromising the assessment process.

4. *In group testing situations, examinees are responsible for not interfering with the performance of other examinees.* Examinees should refrain from any activity that might be distracting to other examinees.

5. *Examinees are responsible for informing the psychologist or another professional if they believe the assessment results do not adequately represent their true abilities.* If, for any reason, examinees feel that the assessment results do not adequately represent their actual abilities, they should inform the psychologist. This should be done as soon as possible so the psychologists can take appropriate actions.

6. *Examinees should respect the copyright rights of test publishers.* Examinees should not be allowed to make copies or in any other way reproduce assessment materials.

7. *Examinees should not disclose information about the contents of a test.* While taking a test, examinees should not copy or write down specific information from a test, in an effort to try to share that information with others who will be taking the test in the future. It is an issue of test security, and likely will negatively impact the validity of the test scores!

These guidelines are summarized in Table 17.6.

Special Interest Topic 17.4: Steps to Prevent Student Cheating

Linn and Gronlund (2000) provide the following suggestions for teachers to help prevent cheating in their classrooms.
1. Take steps to keep the test secure before the testing date.
2. Prior to taking the test, have students clear off the top of their desks.
3. If students are allowed to use scratch paper, have them turn it in with their tests.
4. Carefully monitor the students during the test administration.
5. When possible provide an empty row of seats between students.
6. Use two forms of the test and alternate forms when distributing (you can use the same test items, just arranged in a different order).
7. Design your tests to have good face validity (i.e., so it appears relevant and fair).
8. Foster a positive attitude towards tests by emphasizing how assessments benefit students (e.g., students learn what they have and have not mastered; a fair way of assigning grades).

Special Interest Topic 17.5: Teachers Cheating?

Over 50 New York City educators may lose their job after an independent auditor produced evidence that they helped students cheat on state tests. (Hoff, 1999)

State officials charge that 71 Michigan schools might have cheated on state tests. (Keller, 2001)

Georgia education officials suspend state tests after 270 actual test questions were posted on an Internet site that was accessible to students, teachers, and parents. (Olson, 2003)

Cizek (1998) notes that the abuse of standardized assessments by educators has become a national scandal. With the advent of high-stakes assessments it should not be surprising that some educators would be inclined to cheat. When one's salary and possibly one's future employment is riding on how students perform on state mandated achievement tests, the pressure to ensure that those students perform well may override ethical and legal concerns for some people. Cannell (1988, 1989) was among the first to bring abusive test practices to the attention on the public. Cannell revealed that by using outdated versions of norm-referenced assessments, being lax with test security, and engaging in inappropriate test preparation practices all 50 states were able to report that their students were above the national average (this came to be referred to as the Lake Wobegon phenomenon). Other common "tricks" that have been employed by educators to inflate scores include using the same form of a test for a long period of time so that teachers could become familiar with the content; encouraging low-achieving students to skip school

(continued)

on the day of the test; selectively removing answer sheets of low performing students; and excluding limited-English and special education students from assessments (Cizek, 1998).

Don't be fooled into thinking that these unethical practices are limited to top administrators trying to make their schools look good—they also involve classroom teachers. Cizek (1998) reports that there are a number of recent cases where principals or other administrators have encouraged teachers to cheat by having students practice on the actual test items, and in some cases even erase and correct wrong responses on the answer sheet. Other unethical assessment practices engaged in by teachers included providing hints to the correct answer, reading questions that the students are supposed to read, answering questions about test content, rephrasing test questions, and sometimes simply giving the students the answers to items. Gay (1990) reported that 35% of the teachers responding to a survey had either witnessed or engaged in unethical assessment practices. The unethical behaviors included changing incorrect answers, revealing the correct answer, providing extra time, allowing the use of inappropriate aids (e.g., dictionaries), and using the actual test items when preparing students for the test.

Just because other professionals are engaging in unethical behavior does not make it right. Cheating, by administrators, teachers, or students, undermines the validity of the assessment results. If you need any additional incentive to avoid unethical test practices, be warned that the test publishers are watching! The states and other publishers of standardized tests have a vested interest in maintaining the validity of their assessments. As a result, they are continually scanning the results for evidence of cheating. For example, Cizek (1998) reports that unethical educators have been identified as the result of fairly obvious clues such as ordering an excessive number of blank answer sheets or a disproportionate number of erasures, to more subtle clues such as unusual patterns of increased scores. The fact is, educators that cheat are being caught and punished, and the punishment may include the loss of one's job and license to teach!

Table 17.6 Responsibilities of test takers

1. Examinees are responsible for preparing for the assessment.
2. Examinees are responsible for following the directions of the individual administering the assessment.
3. Examinees are responsible for responding in a manner that accurately reflects their characteristics and abilities.
4. In group testing situations, examinees are responsible for not interfering with the performance of other test takers.
5. Examinees are responsible for informing the psychologist if they believe the assessment results do not adequately represent their true abilities.
6. Examinees should respect the copyright rights of test publishers.
7. Examinees should not disclose information about the contents of a test.

17.7 Summary and Top 10 Assessment-Related Behaviors to Avoid

Psychologists have a responsibility to ensure that the assessments they use are developed, administered, scored, and interpreted in a technically, ethically, and legally sound manner. We are sometimes asked "Now that you have told us we should do, what are the most important things we should avoid?" To that end, here is our list of ten assessment-related behaviors that should be avoided.

1. Don't use assessments that produce poor quality data or scores (e.g., unreliable, lacking relevant validity data, inadequate normative data).
2. Don't use assessments that you are not qualified to administer, score, and interpret.
3. Don't base high-stakes decisions on the results of a single assessment.
4. Don't let your personal preferences and biases impact the scoring of assessments.
5. Don't breach confidentiality regarding assessment information.
6. Don't use technical jargon without a clear, common sense explanation when reporting the results of assessments.
7. Don't ignore the special assessment needs of persons with disabilities or diverse linguistic/cultural backgrounds.
8. Don't breach test security.
9. Don't make changes to standardized materials or to administration procedures without validation work indicating how these changes affect performance.
10. Don't assume that because an "expert" (you included) made up a set of test questions, they will work as intended—always collect evidence to support test applications.

References

American Educational Research Association, American Psychological Association, & National Council on Measurement in Education. (2014). *Standards for educational and psychological testing*. Washington, DC: American Educational Research Association.

American Psychological Association. (2002). Ethical principles of psychologists and code of conduct. *American Psychologist, 57,* 1060–1073.

Cannell, J. J. (1988). Nationally normed elementary achievement testing in America's public schools: How all 50 states are above average. *Educational Measurement: Issues and Practice, 7,* 5–9.

Cannell, J. J. (1989). *The "Lake Wobegon" report: How public educators cheat on standardized achievement tests*. Albuquerque, NM: Friends for Education.

Cizek, G. J. (1998). Filling in the blanks: Putting standardized tests to the test. *Fordham Report, 2*(11).

Dawes, R. M., Faust, D., & Meehl, P. E. (1989). Clinical versus actuarial judgment. *Science, 243,* 1668–1774.

Gay, G. H. (1990). Standardized tests: Irregularities in administering the test affect test results. *Journal of Instructional Psychology, 17,* 93–103.

Grove, W. M., & Meehl, P. E. (1996). Comparative efficiency of informal (subjective, impressionistic) and formal (mechanical, algorithmic) prediction procedures: The clinical-statistical controversy. *Psychology, Public Policy, and Law, 2,* 293–323.

Hoff, D. J. (1999). N.Y.C. probe levels test-cheating charges. *Education Week, 19*, 3.

Joint Committee on Testing Practices. (1998). *Rights and responsibilities of test takers: Guidelines and expectations*. Washington, DC: American Psychological Association.

Kaufman, A. S. (1994). *Intelligent testing with the WISC-III*. New York, NY: Wiley.

Keller, B. (2001). Dozens of Michigan schools under suspicion of cheating. *Education Week, 20*(18), 30.

Linn, R. L., & Gronlund, N. E. (2000). *Measurement and assessment in teaching* (8th ed.). Upper Saddle River, NJ: Prentice Hall.

Lovett, B. J., & Lewandowski, L. J. (2015). *Testing accommodations for students with disabilities: Research based practice*. Washington, DC: American Psychological Association.

Nitko, A. J. (2001). *Educational assessment of students*. Upper Saddle River, NJ: Merrill Prentice Hall.

Olson, L. (2003). Georgia suspends testing plans in key grades. *Education Week, 22*(1), 15.

Puente, A. E., Adams, R., Barr, W. B., Bush, S. S., & NANA Policy and Planning Committee. (2006). The use, education, training and supervisions of neuropsychological test technicians (psychometrists) in clinical practice official statement of the national academy of neuropsychology. *Archives of Clinical Neuropsychology, 21*, 837–839.

Youngstrom, E. A., Freeman, A. J., & Jenkins, M. M. (2009). The assessment of children and adolescents with bipolar disorder. *Child and Adolescent Psychiatry Clinics of North America, 18*(2), 353–390.

Suggested Reading

American Educational Research Association, American Psychological Association, & National Council on Measurement in Education. (2014). *Standards for educational and psychological testing*. Washington, DC: AERA This is the source for technical information on the development and use of tests in educational and psychological settings.

Internet Sites of Interest

http://www.apa.org This is the home of the American Psychological Association, a scientific and professional organization representing psychology in the United States. It offers a wealth of information on various psychological disorders, as well as references to numerous guidelines and standards that professionals must adhere to (e.g., Code of Fair Testing Practices in Education; Responsible Test Use: Case Studies for Assessing Human Behavior; Rights and Responsibilities of Test Takers: Guidelines and Expectations; etc.).

http://www.nanonline.org This is the home of the National Academy of Neuropsychology (NAN), a nonprofit professional association for experts in assessment and treatment of brain injuries and disorders. It offers a Professional Resources section that provides a number of helpful resources related to testing and test use.

How to Develop a Psychological Test: A Practical Approach

18

We have oft heard it said there are 3 things you should not watch being made: Laws, sausage, and psychological tests!

Abstract

Developing a good psychological test is not as easy as it may first appear. It involves a multistage process that typically takes a significant amount of time, research, patience, and perhaps most importantly, participants who are willing to take the test! This chapter provides an overview of the test development process, dividing it into four stages: test conceptualization, specification of its structure and format, planning standardization and psychometric studies, and plan implementation.

Supplementary Information The online version of this chapter (https://doi.org/10.1007/978-3-030-59455-8_18) contains supplementary material, which is available to authorized users.

Learning Objectives

After reading and studying this chapter, students should be able to:
1. Describe the process of developing a psychological test.
2. Understand the sequence of steps in designing and developing a psychological test.
3. Describe the importance of construct definition.
4. Explain the difference between conceptual and operational definitions of constructs.
5. Describe different types of common dissimulation scales and the purpose of each.
6. Design a table of specifications or blueprint for test content.
7. Describe the factors to consider in choosing a normative or standardization sample for a test.
8. Describe the factors to consider when choosing a type of score for a test.
9. Describe necessary reliability and validity studies for a new measure.
10. Draft a proposal for the development of a psychological test.
11. Carry out the plan for developing a new psychological test.

This chapter presents a practical approach to developing tests in the context of a general model that will apply to most types of tests. Some tests, such as those for employment, will have a few extra steps involved to satisfy certain legal criteria regarding their usage; however, you can learn about these if you go forward in the field of psychology as you begin to specialize. The chapter emphasizes the development of a strategic plan for test development over the day-to-day nuts and bolts of actually carrying out the plan—implementation of your plan will vary greatly depending upon the setting and the level of support you have available. However, our experience is that a strong, detailed plan leads to successful development. After all, would you expect a contactor to build a skyscraper without a blueprint? A careful plan must come first.

The validity of test score interpretations is ultimately the crux of quality of any test, and ensuring the validity of those interpretations begins when you begin the process of test development. This approach to test development is derived from the experiences of the authors of this text in actual commercial test development and from the practices of multiple test publishers of various sizes around the world, so does not reflect a pure model of any one company's approach. Neither is this approach purely psychometric nor idealized, but stems from our desire for you to understand how psychological tests are typically developed, when done well. We have chosen to focus on how commercial products are designed and implemented since commercial tests are by far the most likely tests you will encounter beyond classroom, teacher-made tests. However, this model also serves well those desiring to develop a test for limited research applications, though on a smaller scale of implementation.

Table 18.1   Phase one: steps in test conceptualization

1. Conduct a review of literature and develop a statement of need for the test.
2. Describe the proposed uses and interpretations of results from the test.
3. Who will use the test and why (including a statement of user qualifications).
4. Develop conceptual and operational definitions of constructs you intend to measure.
5. Determine whether measures of dissimulation are needed and if so, what kind.

To facilitate our presentation of this model we have separated the steps into four broad stages or phases: (1) test conceptualization, (2) specification of test structure and format, (3) planning standardization and psychometric studies, and (4) plan implementation. The first phase, test conceptualization, is designed to give you and others who may be working with you (test development is always a team effort) as much clarity as possible as to the nature of the test and what it is intended to measure as well as why and how it might be used. This knowledge will drive many of the later aspects of the design as you will see. Table 18.1 provides an outline for this first phase of the test development process. For a practical guide to the day-to-day aspects of carrying out such a plan, we recommend a chapter by Gary Robertson (2003), who was for many years in charge of developing and carrying out such plans for several major publishers and who generously has shared his expertise and experiences with the profession.

18.1   Phase I: Test Conceptualization

18.1.1   Conduct a Literature Review and Develop a Statement of Need for the Test

In developing a psychological or educational test, one first begins by identifying a need. This should include specifying the construct you want to measure and establishing that there is a need for a new way to measure it. There are literally thousands of psychological and educational tests available commercially. There are as many or more (no one is just sure how many) measures published in journal articles or on the Internet and designed for narrow or highly specific applications. Therefore, the first task of the test developer is to identify a need in the field. As psychology and education progress as sciences, new constructs are specified and old constructs are modified. As an example, intelligence was once measured via simple

> Test development begins with defining a need in the profession.

reaction time and measurements of sensory acuity. Next, knowledge became more important in the definitions of intelligence and informational items became more prominent among intelligence tests. Now, most intelligence tests emphasize problem-solving, and do so in two domains (some more): *crystallized intelligence*, which is the application of knowledge to problem-solving, and *fluid intelligence*, which is the ability to solve problems that are novel wherein no prior knowledge is required. So even though each era has seen the development and promulgation of many intelligence tests, the tests have changed as our thinking about intelligence has changed—some tests were revised and made modern in this sense while others simply could not be updated to current thinking and were put out of print. Entirely new tests of intelligence also were developed along the way to coincide with modern theories of intelligence. This same process occurs in areas such as personality, psychopathology, and even academic achievement as the curricula of schools changes and tests must be created to follow the curricula requirements.

At times, a clinician or researcher will have a need to measure a variable that is well defined and for which tests are available, but the quality of the available tests is suspect or the psychometric qualities of the test are simply outdated as reported in the test manual or relevant literature. In such instances, a test developer may

> Measurement is a set of rules for assigning numbers to objects, events, or behaviors.

decide to pursue the development of "a better mousetrap." As technology and theory advance in psychology, we also develop better or more exacting methods of measuring a construct via different methods or approaches or even items that were not available or feasible in earlier years, again leading one to devise an improved means of measuring a variable of interest. For example, measures of reaction time were once done via human observation and recording with a stopwatch. This is certainly crude compared to computer-controlled stimulus presentation and very accurate electronic measurement in milliseconds that are now commonplace in reaction time research.

Tests may assess clinically useful constructs but be impractical for real-world clinical application. The concept of sensation-seeking is a good example. Known in the research literature for many decades and believed to be of clinical interest with adolescents as well as with adult offender populations, in particular, the early measures of sensation-seeking were quite long and cumbersome although they measured the construct well. However, sensation-seeking was not widely assessed in clinical practice until the 1990s when Reynolds and Kamphaus (1992, 2004) devised a rapid, reliable measure of sensation-seeking that made the construct practical for application in clinical work with adolescents.

Standardization samples also may become dated and inapplicable to current examinees, and a test author or developer may have lost interest in updating and revising such a test, creating another opportunity for test development if there remains a need for measuring the constructs in question.

New constructs are sometimes defined in the fields of psychology and education as well. When this happens, the constructs are usually derived from theoretical observations and then must be studied and manipulated to be understood. To be studied, such constructs must be measured. And, measurement requires a set of rules for assigning numerical values to some observation—as you recall, that is essentially our definition of a test as a tool, a means of deriving numerical values to assign to observations of a construct or activity. There are thus always needs for new testing instruments in our field, whether it is to modernize existing instruments or to measure new constructs. Test developers and researchers can conduct very detailed and comprehension electronic literature searches for research on most any psychological construct and easily determine what instruments, if any, may be available for assessing a construct. These instruments can then be gathered and reviewed for quality and applicability. Only after such a review can need truly be determined. In addressing the question of need, we always like to ask as well: (1) Will the test I am considering developing improve practice or research in some area, and/or (2) will it enhance the human condition or our understanding of it?

18.1.2 Describe the Proposed Uses and Interpretations of Results From the Test

Once you have identified the need for a new test to measure a construct, you should describe the proposed uses and interpretations of the results. That is, assuming the test is well developed, how would it be used? In what settings and for what purposes would this instrument be employed? Once a user has the results of the test in hand, what purposes will have been served and what interpretations of these results are likely to be made?

The answers to these questions should flow logically from the preceding step. If you find them difficult to answer, there is a very good chance your conceptualization of the test and the constructs you intend to measure are too vague at this point. You should return to Step 1 and develop your ideas and conceptualization in more detail before proceeding.

Knowing how and in what setting a test may be used is crucial to many aspects of its development. For example, there are many omnibus personality tests available but they tend to emphasize different aspects of personality, emotion, and affect. Some emphasize normal personality and some emphasize psychopathological states. The setting (e.g., a psychiatric hospital versus employment selection) and intended use of the results will dictate different content and interpretive schemes.

It is common now for many public and private agencies, including the US Military, to conduct some form of personality screening for the hiring of public safety officers such as police, armed security forces, or even loss prevention specialists in department stores (who often dress as shoppers and simply roam the store watching for shoplifters and alerting security when thefts are observed). Tests designed specifically to assist in the selection of people who are likely to be happy and successful in such jobs and to work well with the public when in positions of authority appear on the surface to be highly similar to tests designed to diagnose psychopathology. However, during the development process, such tests are carefully scrutinized for items that are illegal to ask in preemployment screening and they emphasize normal range variations in personality traits over psychopathology in an attempt to match the responses of job applicants to those of prior employees who were very successful in the same job. Knowing the purpose of the test and the setting in which it will be used then influences the proper response to all of the remaining factors in the chapter, from who is the likely user of the test, to the proper normative sample, to the types of validity studies that must be done to validate the proposed interpretations of the scores.

18.1.3 Determine Who Will Use the Test and Why

Tests should be designed with specific users in mind. Here we refer to individuals who per-form specific functions that are facilitated by the use of psychological and/or educational

> Know whom you expect to use a test before it is developed.

tests as well as to the types of formal academic training and supervised experiences (if any) that might be required of users to apply test results appropriately. For most clinical tests, there are licensure and certification requirements put in place by vari-ous state laws that restrict use of tests to certain classes of professionals such as psychologists. However, these requirements vary a great deal from state to state. Many test manuals will devote a brief section to the description of test user qualifi-cations. Table 18.2 presents an example of the User Qualifications statement for the

Table 18.2 Example of a test manual's user qualifications section

Individuals using the Behavior Assessment System for Children, Third Edition (BASC-3) interpret its various components and use them in the evaluation, diagnosis, and treatment of developmental, learning, and behavioral disorders. Users are expected to have completed a recognized graduate training program in psychology; received formal academic training in the administration, scoring, and interpretation of behavior rating scales and personality scales; and, received supervised experience with such instruments. Most clinical, school, pediatric, counseling, neuro-, and applied developmental psychologists will have received such training. Administration and scoring of the various BASC-3 components may, with appropriate training and supervision, be completed by clerical staff. Individuals who use the BASC-3 with specialized populations (e.g., sensory impaired or recent immigrants from nonwestern cultures) are expected to have specialized training and experience in the use of such assessment devices and intervention materials with these populations.

Because of the wide variability across jurisdictions in certification requirements and the use of professional titles, it is not possible to determine solely by title, licensure, or certification, who is qualified to use the BASC-3. Consistent with the principles presented in the *Standards for Educational and Psychological Testing* (American Educational Research Association, American Psychological Association, & National Council on Measurement in Education, 2014), each individual practitioner must decide whether his or her formal academic training and supervised experience provide the necessary background and knowledge to use and interpret the BASC-3 appropriately. A variety of other professionally trained or certified staff (e.g., psychometrists, educational diagnosticians, clinical social workers, psychiatrists, and pediatricians) might have received the necessary formal academic training and supervised experience to use instruments like the BASC-3.

Source: Behavior Assessment System for Children, Third Edition (BASC-3). Copyright © 2015 NCS Pearson, Inc. Reproduced with permission. All rights reserved. "BASC" is a trademark, in the USA and/or other countries, of Pearson Education, Inc. or its affiliate(s)

Behavior Assessment System for Children, Third Edition (Reynolds & Kamphaus, 2015). You will see an example of how the authors deal with the variability in licensure and certification issues by relying more upon formal academic training and supervised experience for use of the BASC-3, both of which are considered crucial because the BASC-3 is used so widely for clinical diagnosis and eligibility determination. The authors here rely more upon competencies expected of individuals with such training than job titles. We think all test manuals should include a section like this one, that explains expectations of the authors and publisher of the test for the education and training of those who would use the test.

It is also helpful at this stage to determine just which individuals in what settings are most likely to find the proposed test helpful in their roles. Hopefully, this flows directly from the purpose of the test and the proposed interpretations of results. If the purpose of the test is to diagnose the presence of a clinical condition such as pediatric bipolar disorder, the targeted user will most likely be a clinical or pediatric psychologist or perhaps even a psychiatrist. However, a test being designed to screen large numbers of children to see if they have elevated risk levels for emotional and behavior disorders in order to determine whether a follow-up evaluation of their mental health or behavioral or emotional status is warranted, might be designed so that it can be administered and scored by a teacher or a mental health aide or even a nurse. Knowing the anticipated user will result in design changes, particularly related to the complexity of the test's administration, scoring, and interpretation since different classes of test users will have different skill levels.

18.1.4 Develop Conceptual and Operational Definitions of Constructs You Intend to Measure

Often we think we understand the meaning of constructs like depression, anxiety, crystallized intelligence, fluid intelligence, aggression, agreeableness, and the like until we try to put them into words. Then, we may realize that we are not as clear on such constructs as we originally thought! Putting them into words assures we understand them and that others can see our intended meaning—which is very important to measurement because, often, people will understand or interpret construct names differently. Frequently, we find our first attempts at writing a definition of a construct we think we understand quite well to be awkward and several rewrites are usually necessary. Writing a clear description of what we intend to measure also forces us to clarify to ourselves what we intend to measure so that we can explain it more clearly to others as well. Having such definitions in mind and on documents to which we can refer throughout the test development process also helps us in item writing, item selection, and test score interpretation later in the process. We recommend writing two types of definitions—a conceptual one and an operational one.

A *conceptual definition* explains our construct at a theoretical level and may use many interpretive words. An *operational definition* tells others exactly how our test will define or measure the construct. This is better illustrated through example. Let's consider the common psychological term depression.

A possible conceptual definition might read: Depression is a state of melancholy, sadness, and low energy levels that leads to anhedonia, feelings of worthlessness, and chronic fatigue.

An operational definition might read: On the Student's Rating Scale of Depression, depression will be assessed by summing ratings in the scored direction on observations of behavior such as expressions of feelings of sadness, feelings of loneliness, of being misunderstood, and being not liked, a lack of engagement in pleasurable activities, too much or too little sleep, tearfulness at inappropriate times, and complaints of fatigue.

So, the conceptual definition tells us what it is you want to measure in the abstract and the operational definition tells us more directly and specifically how the construct score will be derived. Some may find these efforts tedious for scales that have many constructs, however, the more constructs that are present on a test, the more we find such definitions useful.

18.1.5 Determine Whether Measures of Dissimulation Are Needed and If So, What Kind

Dissimulation is the presentation of one's self in a manner that is different from how you really are—presenting yourself through a disguise of sorts or under pretense. For example, if you are really feeling very sad but do not want to admit it to others, you might respond "false"

> Dissimulation means presenting oneself in a disguise or under pretense.

to a personality test question such as "I feel sad" to conceal your feelings from others. It is also possible for you to engage in dissimulation about others if, for example, you are completing a rating scale about another person such as your child, spouse, or an elderly parent.

Why do people engage in dissimulation? There are many reasons. People will deny symptoms on an assessment of personality or psychopathology because they do not want to be seen as having what they consider to be undesirable traits or do not want to admit to behaviors others may find unacceptable. This phenomenon even occurs among people seeking treatment! In employment settings, it is not uncommon for job applicants to try and answer the questions in the way they think is most likely to get them the job they are seeking.

People will also report symptoms they do not have to make themselves look far more impaired than is actually the case. This too occurs for a variety of reasons and is termed *malingering* when they have something to gain by making such a false presentation. For example, people may fake personality and behavior problems as well as cognitive deficits to obtain disability benefits, to enhance damage rewards in lawsuits over a personal injury, or to avoid punishments such as prosecution for crimes they may have committed. In the case of cognitive assessments, dissimulation evaluations are often accomplished through effort testing, that is, giving tests that are easily accomplished by nearly anyone as long as they try to complete the task accurately. Effort testing is recommended in nearly all forensic matters and whenever a patient has something to gain by feigning cognitive deficits (Bush et al., 2005).

Exaggerated endorsement of problems may also occur at times when a person really is experiencing a great deal of intrapsychic pain and wants to be sure to get the clinician's attention right away. Teachers sometimes endorse emotional and behavioral problems in more extreme ways than are present with a student when completing behavior rating scales in order to get the attention of the school psychologist and to be sure to obtain help as soon as possible in managing the student's behavior.

Dissimulation can take many forms and sometimes you will see more specific definitions of certain types of dissimulation. For example, Bush et al. (2005, p. 420) offer the following definitions of terms, all of which are relevant to the more general umbrella of dissimulation:

- *Symptom validity*: The accuracy or truthfulness of the examinee's behavioral presentation (signs), self-reported symptoms (including their cause and course), or performance.
- *Response bias*: An attempt to mislead the examiner through inaccurate or incomplete responses or effort.
- *Effort*: Investment in performing at capacity levels. Although often not specified in discussions of *effort testing*, this term refers to the examinee's effort to perform well—that is, to *pass* an effort test is to do well on the test.
- *Malingering*: The intentional production of false or exaggerated symptoms, motivated by external incentives. Although symptom validity tests are commonly referred to as *malingering tests*, malingering is just one possible cause of invalid performance.
- *Dissimulation*: The intentional misrepresentation or falsification of symptoms, by overrepresentation or underrepresentation of a true set of symptoms in an attempt to appear dissimilar from one's true state.

If you understand the purpose of your test as well as who will be using it and in what circumstances, you will then know if you need to include scales to detect dissimulation of various types. The field of psychology has expended great effort over the years to develop sophisticated means of detecting dissimulation and we will now turn to an explanation of the most common methods.

18.1.5.1 Scales for Detecting Dissimulation on Assessments of Personality and Behavior

The most common scales of dissimulation (also known commonly as validity scales) on measures of personality and behavior are F-scales, L-scales, and inconsistency indexes. These are briefly described here:

> Dissimulation scales are often referred to as validity scales.

F-Scales *F-scales* are also known as Infrequency scales and are sometimes referred to as "Fake Bad" scales. The latter usage is because F-scales are designed to detect exaggerated symptom presentation. Items included on Infrequency or F-scales have two common characteristics. First, they reflect symptoms that are very rarely endorsed as present even by persons with significant levels of psychopathology or represent extreme endorsements of common symptoms that are also rare, hence the name Infrequency Scale. And second, they have low average intercorrelations, i.e., they are unrelated to each other so do not cluster together well enough to form a coherent construct. Because these items represent infrequent responses that are poorly associated with each other, examinees who indicate they experience a large number of these symptoms are likely exhibiting an exaggerated presentation of psychopathology. A cutoff score that indicates high probability of an exaggerated presentation is determined by examining the responses of the standardization sample to these rarely endorsed items to determine the distribution of the total item scores.

L-Scales *L-scales* are often termed ***Social Desirability*** scales. They are also referred to as "Fake Good" scales. The name L-scale comes from the original name of these scales—Lie Scales—a term now seen as pejorative and considered archaic. L-scales are designed to detect the inaccurate denial of symptoms that are really present, detecting the opposite response bias of the F-scale. L-scales typically are developed by including special items along with extreme responses to traditional items that reflect commonplace flaws that nearly everyone experiences at some time. For example, on an item that reads "I have feelings of sadness," a person who wants to deny symptoms might respond with "Never." Since at least occasional feelings of sadness are a common human experience, such a response would earn the examinee a point on the L-scale. No single item response will get someone tagged as engaging in dissimulation; rather it is the cumulative response pattern that is examined just as with the F-scale.

Inconsistency Scales *Inconsistency scales* are designed to detect inconsistencies in responses to item stems on personality and behavior scales. When a respondent is not consistent in responding to similar items, the results are not considered to be reliable. For example, an examinee who endorses the item "I am full of energy" and also endorses the item "I feel fatigued" may be responding inconsistently. One reason for inconsistent responding may be dissimulation but other reasons are plausible in many cases as well. For example, a respondent who is having difficulty understanding or reading the questions may produce an elevated score on an Inconsistency scale. An individual who is not motivated and so randomly responds to questions may also produce elevated inconsistency scores. Inconsistency scales are derived by examining first the correlation matrix of all of the items on a test to see which items are the most similar in terms of their response patterns—that is, if we know the answer to one item, does it predict well the answer to another item? Items are then chosen in pairs for the Inconsistency scale by choosing items that correlate highly with one another and that have similar content. Once the item pairs are chosen, the scores on each item in the pairs are subtracted to create a difference score for each pair of items. These difference scores are converted to their absolute values and then summed. Next, the standardization sample data are examined to find the distribution of the difference in scores between each item in each pair in order to establish a cutoff for inconsistency in responding.

For certain types of tests, it may be useful to derive other dissimulation scales for special purposes. It is common when developing measures for the selection of public safety personnel, for example, to include more advanced and subtle indicators of response biases since this applicant pool tends to deny most common problems and to minimize any emotional discord they may experience when responding to personality tests.

Although not measures of dissimulation, test authors sometimes also include scales that look at the comprehension of the items and cooperation level of the examinee on self-report and rating scales. These scales go by various names and are sometimes referred to just as a V-scale or **Validity Scale**. These scales typically contain nonsensical items where the answer is the same for everyone who takes the test seriously, cooperates with the exam process, and can comprehend the items. For example, one of the items on a V-scale might be "I drink at least 100 glasses of water every day." Of course, no one does this, so anyone who answers yes or true to such an item most likely is either not cooperating with the evaluation process or cannot comprehend the items on the test. A V-scale will contain multiple items to ensure against false positives since anyone can mark one item incorrectly by mistake. Such scales might be considered "effort testing" for personality and behavior rating scales.

18.1.5.2 Scales for Detecting Dissimulation on Assessments of Aptitude and Achievement

As we have noted, some individuals will not make an effort to do well on tests of aptitude or achievement for reasons of gain and such a lack of effort is commonly seen as malingering, though other reasons are plausible. For example, individuals with a traumatic injury to certain locations in the frontal regions of the brain may experience *amotivational syndrome* as a consequence of the injury—this syndrome causes them to have difficulty putting forth good effort and recognizing when effort is needed to succeed. Amotivation and avolition are also common in psychiatric disorders such as schizophrenia (Strauss et al., 2018) and can contribute to diminished effort when completing psychological tests.

Few cognitive measures have built-in measures of dissimulation or lack of effort. (We do not worry about people "faking good" on such performance measures since you cannot be smarter than you really are!) However, some do build in scales or items to detect lack of effort. Most often, malingering on cognitive measures is evaluated by assessing the following (Bush et al., 2005):

- Performance patterns on ability measures indicative of invalid responding
- Inconsistencies between test results and known patterns of brain functioning
- Inconsistencies between test results and observed behavior
- Inconsistencies between test results and reliable collateral reports
- Inconsistency between test results and documented background information

Built-in scales for detecting effort can also be useful when they have been demonstrated empirically to reflect a lack of effort. For example, on the Test of Memory and Learning-Second edition (Reynolds & Voress, 2007), one of the subtests contains sets of word pairs an examinee has to recall. The examiner reads a list of word pairs and then gives the examinee one of the words from the pair and the examinee is to recall the other word in the pair. Half of the word pairs on the list are extremely easy however, and it is rare for anyone, even very young children, to respond incorrectly on the "easy pairs." On some measures, such as parts of the Halstead-Reitan Neuropsychological Test Battery, an early item set is presented to teach the examinee how to respond to the test that will be administered. It is rare for anyone, even those with significant brain injuries, to respond incorrectly to more than one or two of these types of items if they are truly attempting to do them accurately.

Often in the cognitive domains however, there are entire tests devoted to detection of lack of effort or malingering. These types of tasks also may be built into a larger test battery. In the following sections, we discuss two of the most popular methods to detect lack of effort, Symptom Validity Tests, and Forced-Choice Tests.

Symptom Validity Tests (SVTs) *Symptom Validity Tests* (SVTs) are tests designed to look very difficult but that are in fact very easy and on which most people who put forth effort to succeed do so. The instructions for such tests are also important. On occasion, the instructions provided to the examinee indicate the task is going to be quite hard and not to get upset if they cannot perform well. For example,

> Symptom validity tests are designed to look very difficult but that are in fact very easy.

one such test presents an examinee with 15 items to memorize in only 10 s. As part of the instructions, the examinee is told they are about to take a memory test that is very difficult because they will be asked to memorize 15 things on a page but will only have 10 s to do so. However, the items for memorization are logically related in such a way they are very easy to memorize in even less than the allotted time and it is rare that anyone putting forth reasonable effort does not recall 10–11 of the stimuli, and most people recall all 15 correctly. On such SVTs, performance below established cutoff scores on one or more well-validated test designed to measure exaggeration or fabrication of cognitive deficits suggests insufficient effort to do well.

Forced-Choice Tests *Forced-choice tests* as measures of malingering are simply multiple-choice tests that have true–false, yes–no, or more possible response options. If we know the number of choices per item and the number of items, we can calculate the chance level of responding. For example, on a 40 item 4-choice multiple-choice test, a person who knew none of the answers should get about 10 items correct purely by chance alone. If the number correct deviates below chance at a significant level on forced-choice tests we know that either the person is extremely unlucky or they actually knew the correct answers and responded incorrectly so as to look impaired. One of the authors of this text (CRR) in a forensic examination some years ago gave such a test to an examinee claiming a particular brain injury—on this 40-item, 4-choice multiple-choice test, the examinee earned a raw score of zero. The odds of this happening are extremely low on a chance basis and the best explanation of this low level of performance was that the examinee did in fact know the answers but chose to respond incorrectly. Performance on one or more forced-choice measures of cognitive functioning that falls below chance to a statistically significant degree typically is interpreted to indicate biased responding.

18.2   Phase II: Specification of Test Structure and Format

During this phase of test development, the author should prepare a detailed description of the proposed test and the testing materials. Table 18.3 provides an outline of the numerous steps to be completed during this phase.

18.2.1 Designate the Age Range Appropriate for the Measure

Be sure to determine the appropriate age range for the assessment at the very beginning of the test description. The age of the examinees for whom the test is intended will also dictate a variety of design features. Young children, for example, cannot perform some tasks that older children can perform and need more interaction with an examiner. Tests that require the child to read and respond to test items (unless it is a test of reading) do not work very well before the age of 8 or 9 years. Tests for the elderly that require rapid motor responses or good coordination skills usually are not a good idea (unless measuring these factors is the purpose of the test) and will confound the interpretation of the results of the test. Younger as well as older examinees also may require more time for testing, and bonus points for quick performance are often a poor idea for tests with these populations.

Table 18.3 Phase II: specification of test structure and format

During this phase the goal is to clearly describe the proposed test, including information on the following:

1. Age range appropriate for this measure
2. Testing format (e.g., individual or group; print or computerized); who will complete the test? (e.g., the examiner, the examinee, or some other informant)
3. The structure of the test (e.g., subscales, composite scores, etc.) and how the items and subscales (if any) will be organized
4. Written table of specifications
5. Item formats (given by subtests or subscales if any, with sample items illustrating ideal items) and a summary of instructions for administration and scoring
   (a) Indicate the likely number of items required for each subtest or scale
   (b) Indicate the type of medium required for each test (e.g., verbal cue, visual cue, physically manipulated objects or puzzle parts, etc.)
6. Written explanation of methods for item development (how will items be determined—will you need content experts to help write or review items?), tryout, and final item selection

18.2.2 Determine and Describe the Testing Format

The first key consideration here is to determine whether the test will be administered only to individuals by an examiner or whether groups of people can be tested with minimal examiner interaction. (A test designed for group administration typically can be administered to individuals as well.) Will the test be presented in a print or computerized format? Who will actually complete the test or answer sheet? Will it be the examiner, the examinee, or some other third-party informant such as occurs with behavior rating scales (e.g., parent, teacher)?

18.2.3 Describe the Structure of the Test

Will the test yield just one score as a sum of all of the item responses or will it need to be broken into subscales? The structure of the test most often is dictated by the constructs you intend to measure, so the definitions you have written are quite important to consult in making this determination. If there are subscales or subtests then will there also be composite scores that provide summary indexes of the subtest groupings? Explain here how the items and subscales (if any) will be organized and if it is not clearly apparent from your rationale for the test and discussion of the underlying constructs, it is important to address here just why this specific organization of the items and subtests is the most appropriate (recognizing, of course, that research you conduct during the test development process may result in alterations to your intended structure if dictated by the actual data).

18.2.4 Develop a Table of Specifications (TOS)

The content of tests should emphasize what was emphasized in the definitions of constructs. The method of ensuring congruence among the construct definitions, operational definitions, and test content is the development and applica-

> A table of specifications is a blueprint to the content of the test.

tion of a table of specifications (TOS), which is also referred to as a test blueprint. Traditionally a TOS is developed for measures of achievement to ensure congruence with a curriculum or field of study in which academic accomplishment is to be assessed. An example is given in Table 18.4. The column on the left, labeled *Content Areas*, lists the major content areas to be covered in the test. These content areas are derived by carefully reviewing the educational objectives and selecting major content areas to be included in the test. Across the top of the two-way table, we list the levels of Bloom's cognitive taxonomy (see Special Interest Topic 18.1 for a brief description of *Bloom's Taxonomy*). The inclusion of this section encourages us to consider the complexity of the cognitive processes we want to measure. There is a tendency for authors to rely heavily on lower-level processes (e.g., rote memory) on achievement tests in particular, and to under emphasize higher-level cognitive

Special Interest Topic 18.1: Bloom's Taxonomy of Cognitive Objectives
Bloom, Engelhart, Furst, Hill, and Krathwohl (1956) developed a taxonomy of cognitive objectives that are commonly referred to as *"Bloom's Taxonomy."* This taxonomy provides a useful way of describing the complexity of an objective by classifying it into one of six hierarchical categories ranging from the most simple to the most complex. These categories are briefly described below.

1. *Knowledge.* The simplest level of the taxonomy is **knowledge**. Objectives at the knowledge level involve learning or memorizing specific facts, terms, names, dates, etc. Examples of educational objectives in the knowledge category include:
   (a) *The student will be able to name each state capital.*
   (b) *The student will be able to list U.S. presidents in the order they served.*
2. *Comprehension.* Objectives at the **comprehension** level require understanding, not simply rote memorization. Objectives at this level often use verbs like interpret, translate, explain, or summarize. Examples of educational objectives at the comprehension level include:
   (a) *The student will be able to describe the use of each symbol on a U.S. Geographical Survey map.*
   (b) *The student will be able to explain how interest rates affect unemployment.*
3. *Application.* Objectives at the **application** level involve the use of general rules, principles, or abstract concepts to solve a problem not previously encountered. Examples of objectives at the application level include:
   (a) *The student will be able to write directions for traveling by numbered roads from any city on a map to any other city.*
   (b) *The student will be able to apply multiplication and division of double digits in applied math problems.*
4. *Analysis.* Objectives at the **analysis** level require the student to reduce or break down a complex concept into its basic parts or elements in a manner that illustrates the relationship of parts to whole. Examples of educational objectives at this level include:
   (a) *The student will describe maps in terms of function and form.*
   (b) *The student will distinguish the different approaches to establishing validity and illustrate their relationship to each other.*
5. *Synthesis.* Objectives at the **synthesis** level require the student to blend existing elements in such a way that they form new structures or patterns. Examples of objectives at the synthesis level include:
   (a) *The student will construct a map of a hypothetical country with given characteristics.*
   (b) *The student will propose a viable plan for establishing the validity of an assessment instrument following the guidelines presented in the Standards for Psychological and Educational Testing* (AERA et al., 2014).

(continued)

6. *Evaluation.* Objectives at the ***evaluation*** level require the student to make evaluative judgments regarding the quality, value, or worth of something for a stated purpose. Examples of objectives at the evaluation level include:

   (a) *The student will evaluate the usefulness of a map to enable him/her to travel from one place to another.*

   (b) *The student will judge the quality of validity evidence for a specified assessment instrument.*

Although somewhat dated, we believe Bloom's Taxonomy is helpful because it presents a framework that helps remind test developers to include items reflecting more complex educational objectives in their tests. This is not to imply that lower-level objectives are trivial and should be ignored. For each objective in your curriculum, you must decide at what level you expect students to perform. In a brief introduction to a topic, it may be sufficient to expect only knowledge and comprehension of major concepts. In a more detailed study of a topic, higher more complex levels of mastery will typically be required. However, it is often not possible to master high-level objectives without first having mastered low-level objectives. While we strongly encourage the development of higher-level objectives, it is not realistic to require high-level mastery of everything. Education is a pragmatic process of choosing what is most important to emphasize in a limited amount of instructional time. Our culture helps us make some of these choices, as do legislative bodies, school boards, administrators, and even occasionally parents and students. In some school districts, the cognitive objectives are provided in great detail, whereas in others they are practically nonexistent. As noted earlier, the current trend is for federal and state lawmakers to exert more and more control over curriculum content.

processes. By incorporating these categories in our TOS, we are reminded to incorporate a wider range of cognitive processes into our tests.

The numbers in the body of the table reflect the number of items to be devoted to assessing each content area at each cognitive taxonomic level. Table 18.4 depicts specifications for a 30-item test. If you examine the first content area in Table 18.4 (Scales of measurement) you see two *knowledge* level items, two *comprehension* level items, and two *analysis* level items will be devoted to assessing this content area. The next content area (Measures of central tendency) will be assessed by three *knowledge* level items and three *comprehension* level items. The number of items dedicated to assessing each objective should reflect the importance of the objective in the curriculum and how much instructional time was devoted to it. In our TOS, we determined the number of items dedicated to each content area/objective by examining how much material was devoted to each topic in the text, how much time we typically spend on each topic in class lectures, and the relative importance we give the topic.

Some experts recommend using percentages instead of the number of items when developing a TOS, since the final number of test items might vary from your initial estimates. To do this, simply replace the number of items in each cell with the percentage of items you wish to fall into each category. When done this way, it also becomes apparent how your items will weight the test in any particular direction. For example, you might determine that approximately 20% of your instruction involved the different scales of measurement. You would like to reflect this weighting in your test so you devote 20% of the test to this content area. If you are developing a 30-item test this means you will write 6 items to assess objectives related to scales of measurement ($0.20 \times 30 = 6$). If you are developing a 40-item test this will mean you write 8 items to assess objectives related to scales of measurement ($0.20 \times 40 = 8$).

While TOSs traditionally are built for tests of achievement and aptitude, they are also immensely helpful with tests of personality and behavior. For example, depression is a multifaceted problem. If I want to develop a measure of depression, I must be sure my test items sample the broad domain of depressive symptoms accurately

Table 18.4 Table of specifications for test on a chapter on basic statistics (number of items by content area and level of objective)

Content areas	Level of objective						Total
	Knowledge	Comprehension	Application	Analysis	Synthesis	Evaluation	
Scales of measurement	2	2		2			6
Measures of central tendency	3	3					6
Measures of variability	3	3	3				9
Correlation and regression	2	3		2	2		9

Table 18.5 Table of specifications for a measure of depression

Types of behavior	Facets of depression (%)						Totals
	Melancholy	Physiological symptoms	Isolationism	Anhedonia	Cognitive issues (attention, concentration, decision-- making)	Thoughts of death or self-harm	
Overt behaviors associated with depression	10%	10%	5%	10%	10%	5%	50%
Covert behaviors associated with depression	10%	10%	5%	10%	10%	5%	50%
Total	20%	20%	10%	20%	20%	10%	100%

and that different facets of depression are covered in reasonable percentages. Otherwise, I may overemphasize some aspects of depression to the exclusion of others. Table 18.5 gives an example of what a TOS for a measure of depression might look like. Here we see the areas or facets of depressive symptoms we want to assess along the top and the headings on the side denote types of behaviors, overt (those easily observable by others) and covert (those usually known only to the individual). Since depression has both overt behaviors that are recognized by others as well as internal thoughts and feelings that are considered important to diagnosis, I want to be sure to cover both areas in each facet or dimension of depression. My TOS helps me to write items that reflect all of these cells in the table—it is my blueprint to content coverage!

18.2.5 Determine and Describe the Item Formats and Write Instructions for Administration and Scoring

Different types of items are useful in different circumstances and can be used to measure different characteristics in different ways. For example, assessment of feelings, thoughts, self-talk, and other covert behaviors is usually

> Different item formats serve different purposes and are not always interchangeable.

best accomplished via self-report. Once the self-report format is selected, a decision is then made about the self-report item format, since there are a number of self-report item options. Many self-report scales use a simple true–false or yes–no response option. However, self-report scales can also use rating scales. Take the item, "I feel sad," for instance. In the following example by altering the response format, we change the intent and interpretation of the item responses.

1.	I feel sad.	True	False			
2.	I feel sad.	Never	Sometimes	Often	Almost always	
3.	I feel sad.	Daily	Weekly	Monthly	Once a year or less	Never

The first option asks more about a current state (i.e., how I feel right now), while the other options look at longer-term trends in feelings. So even on a self-report scale, changes in item formats will influence how well we have implemented our operational definitions. If our intent was to develop a self-report scale the reflected current level of depression, Option 1 is the preferred item format. However, if we were interested in levels of depression over a longer period of time, we would give preference to the formats presented in Options 2 and 3. It is crucial to consider how the item format will impact factors like administration and scoring, but even more so, how the chosen item formats may affect the validity of our proposed test score interpretations as well as the degree of construct consistency between our item formats and our conceptual and operational definitions of constructs.

We have reviewed and discussed item formats and item types in several other areas of this book, so we will not focus on them here. However, it is crucial to a successful test development project that item formats be specified no later than this stage of the planning process and that they are evaluated logically for construct consistency. Item formats should be chosen first for construct consistency and next for efficiency of the test-taking process, including ease and accuracy of administration and scoring. It is important to be aware of the psychometric characteristics of different item formats as well. For example, for rating scales, either four or five response options seem to be optimal in developing reliability without unduly lengthening the time required to complete the ratings. Rating scales with more than four or five options rarely improve reliability or validity of test score interpretation and take longer for raters to complete. Unnecessary length is always an undesirable attribute for a test.

In developing item formats, it is also important to address several other questions. The testing medium must be specified for each item format. Will visual cues be provided such as pictures? Will the items require the examinee to manipulate objects physically as in puzzle-solving tasks or tests of dexterity? Will verbal cues be the item format and if so, will the examinee read the cue or will the examiner read it? If the latter, will the examinee read along with the examiner? Is the item format appropriate for the construct within the target population? For example, individuals with autism spectrum disorders often have language difficulties, so items that are verbal and require good oral or expressive language that is intended to measure anything other than expressive language, will be poor choices for such a population. Consider a measure developed to assess intelligence in children with autism and ask yourself whether the following test item would be useful "Explain why it is important for everyone to follow the rules when playing a game." For children with autism, such an item is just too confounded with verbal comprehension and expression abilities to be a good measure of the construct of interest, i.e., the ability to solve the question and deduce the answer.

Once you have chosen the proper item formats, write sample items for each format you plan to use on your test. In writing items, it is important to follow solid principles of item writing such as those outlined in Chap. 6. In writing your items, also write what you believe will be the correctly keyed response according to what you are attempting to measure and the direction of scoring of the test (i.e., will a high score be positively or negatively valued by the recipient of the scores?). Some tests score errors so that a high score means poor performance, whereas others score numbers correct so that a high score means good performance.

Next, you are ready to write the instructions for administration and scoring of the test items. Begin this process by drafting the instructions for the examiner to follow in administration of the test followed by the instructions to be conveyed to the examinee. Our experience is that initial drafts of such instructions, no matter how hard we try or how many times we have done this, are not very good! They tend to be overly long and detailed or too short and leave out crucial information. Once you draft the instructions, sit with them and the test materials you have drafted so far, and attempt to both administer and to take the test. You will almost certainly find problems within this first draft. Redraft the instructions at this point and then give the materials to someone unfamiliar with the test and see if they can give the test to you without making mistakes. Following this exercise, continue to revise the directions for administration and scoring until someone unfamiliar with the test can administer and score it accurately. To assess the scoring accuracy, have more than one person score the responses of several examinees and calculate the interscorer reliability coefficients—this likely will have to wait until a tryout version of all of the items is available, but will be worthwhile to complete before going to a larger tryout.

This is also a good time to estimate the number of items you think will be required to assess the construct(s) reliably. Keep in mind the rule of thumb that has been verified repeatedly over decades of test development experience—you should initially write a minimum of twice as many items as you expect to end up needing on

> When writing items for a new test, always draft at least twice as many items as you think will be necessary to measure the construct reliably.

the test. For constructs that are lesser known or difficult to measure, three times the final targeted number of items is a reasonable goal for the first draft. This will not be wasteful of anyone's time. Many items will drop out due to poor item statistics, item bias issues, and ambiguity, just to name a few of the issues you will encounter. This rule is followed by very experienced item writers. Having an advance estimate of the number of items is useful for a variety of reasons. The number of items obviously will be related to the length of time it takes to administer and score the test as well as the time required of the examinee. Some target populations for tests are far more sensitive to the time a test takes to complete than others, especially younger examinees and older examinees. Individuals with certain disorders, such as ADHD and many of the pervasive developmental disorders among others, have limited attention spans, and unless the items are intended to measure attention, lengthy scales may be confounded by the attentional problems inherent to such populations.

18.2.6 Develop an Explanation of Methods for Item Development, Tryout, and Final Item Selection

Now you are ready to build your plan for actually writing the test items that form the foundation for the test proper. In preparing this plan, determine what theory if any you will be following, refer back once again to your initial conceptualization and definitions to be sure you are on target, and keep your TOS handy! The next real issue is to determine who will be writing the item drafts and what kind of background and training they will need. You will also need to supply the item writer(s) with all of the information you have written so far.

For virtually any test except those of very narrow constructs where you are the leading researcher, content area experts will be needed to help write effective items. While this is most obvious for academic achievement tests, we have found it to be true in every category of test we have developed. No clinician, for example, no matter how good, can be an expert in writing test items in all aspects of psychopathology, for all aspects of aptitude, intelligence, and related cognitive processes, or for all personnel selection or interest measures. Also, as we noted indirectly in the section preceding this one, item writers will need to have knowledge of the target population since some groups of individuals will be unable or ill equipped to respond appropriately to certain item types. In these cases, inappropriate item types will introduce confounds into the assessment of the construct you want to measure.

This is also the time to set down the methods for choosing items for the test. A series of procedures will be necessary in determining the final items for any test. We recommend the following:

1. *Have a panel of experts in the area of the test chosen from different ethnic, religious, and gender groups review the items for cultural ambiguity and offensiveness.* Although some advocate this procedure for detecting culturally biased items, research (see Chap. 15) indicates that expert reviewers are no better than chance at such tasks. However, such experts are necessary to determine whether an item contains content that might be seen ambiguously or with different meanings in other cultures or might contain material that is fine in one cultural setting but considered offensive in others.

2. *Designate a plan for an item tryout.* Choose a small sample of the target population and have the test administered and scored so you can receive feedback on all aspects of the test including the item content and formats, instructions, scoring, and the stimulus materials. Apply statistical methods for item analysis to detect any items that perform poorly at this stage and either rewrite or eliminate these items before going forward.

3. *Designate the statistical methods you will employ for item selection.* There are multiple approaches to item selection such as determining the correlation each item has with the total score on the measure, reviewing the item score distributions and percentage of responses in the keyed direction, comparing the mean item scores of different groups predicted to differ on the items, and so on. While each of these methods will select many of the same items, it is rare these methods overlap completely in their selection of items. Different item selection criteria are most appropriate for different types of tests with different purposes, so be sure to match your item selection procedure to your purpose and target population.

4. *Designate the statistical methods you will use to assess items for differential item functioning (DIF) across ethnicity and gender (i.e., what statistical assessments of item bias will you perform).* Methods for detecting item bias are discussed in more detail in Chap. 15; however, a priori planning for item bias studies is important for several reasons. The first has to do with sample size. Certain methods (e.g., models based in item response theory) require larger samples to stabilize than do other approaches. Disproportional sample sizes across the groups being compared (e.g., comparing responses of White and Black samples) adversely affects some statistical procedures while others are robust to such issues if they are not too extreme. Knowing what methods you are going to employ in advance ensures adequate sampling to carry out the analyses.

As we have noted throughout this chapter, planning each step in advance is far more likely to produce tests with reliable scores and interpretations that are consistent with the initial intent of developing the measure.

18.3   Phase III: Planning Standardization and Psychometric Studies

In the next phase of test development the author should describe the standardization procedures that will be used, describe the reliability and validity studies that will be pursued, and describe any special studies that might be needed to support the test interpretations. Table 18.6 provides an outline of these steps.

18.3.1 Specify a Sampling Plan for Standardization

Describing the target population for the test is the first step in deciding upon a sampling plan. The standardization sample for a test determines the normative scores, also known as norms, and forms the reference group to whom examinees are compared in a norm-referenced

> Describing the target population for the test is the first step in deciding on a sampling plan.

test. In other types of tests (e.g., criterion-referenced tests), the performance of target populations will also be important is designating cut scores and related decision-making concerning performance on the measure. Once you have defined the target population, that is, the reference group for each person who takes the test, you are ready to develop a sampling plan.

It would be best always to obtain a true random sample of the target population for the test, but this is a near impossibility. We typically cannot know all members of the population and even if we could, we could not force all randomly selected members of the population to take our test! Anyone we choose to take the test as part of our sample has the right to refuse, even if we could identify the complete population. Nevertheless, we need to ensure that our sample is representative of the targeted population. The current best method for doing so is to write out a population proportionate stratified random sampling plan. To do this, we first determine

Table 18.6 Phase III: planning, standardization, and psychometric studies

1. Describe the reference or norm group and sampling plan for standardization.
2. Describe your choice of scaling methods and the rationale for this choice.
3. Outline the reliability studies to be performed and their rationale.
4. Outline the validity studies to be performed and their rationale.
5. Any special studies that may be needed for development of this test or to support proposed interpretations of performance.
6. List the components of the test (e.g., manual, record forms, any test booklets or stimulus materials, etc.).

what characteristics (strata) of our population are salient for ensuring the representativeness of the sample. Then we determine what percentages of people with each of those characteristics are needed to make our sample representative. This is best understood with an example.

On most measures of general aptitude or general intelligence, the target reference group is "persons living in the United States and who are fluent in English." We know the United States is composed of people from many different ethnic backgrounds, different levels of socioeconomic status, different regions of the country, and different levels of population density. Since these variables are relevant to establishing how well our sample mimics the population, we will want to sample people from all of these groups according to their relative proportions in the population at large. If 1% of our target population was African American women living in the northeast region of the United States in cities with a population of more than 100,000 and with an educational level of high school graduate, we would want 1% of our sample to include people who match this description. Statistics on population demographics are gathered and maintained by the U.S. Bureau of the Census and are typically available for numerous demographic characteristics on the bureau's website. In the measurement of constructs that are affected by aging or human development, we also need to decide if age-corrected scores are to be provided and if so, include age as a variable in our stratification table. For most tests, the samples are not a perfect match to the population on the variables chosen; it is important to look at the representation of the samples to determine how close they are. Comparing the actual outcomes to the idealized outcomes provides us with evidence of a reasonable effort to create such a sample and makes users aware of any discrepancies between our sample of the population and the ideal sample.

Next, you will need to determine the appropriate size of the sample overall. This is determined by many different factors including the item statistics and other statistical analyses you will be conducting, as some require larger samples for stability than do others, as well as very practical matters such as the costs to obtain the samples in both time and money. The relative precision required of the normative data will also be a factor. For example, tests designed for applications in clinical diagnosis, personnel selection, and other instances that strongly affect peoples' lives, require larger, more accurate samples than might a scale designated purely for research purposes.

18.3.2 Determine Your Choice of Scaling Methods and Rationale

There are many different types of scores that can be determined for a test and they are not all the same—they have different purposes, answer different types of questions about the examinees, and have different psychometric characteristics. So, what scores should you use? Just as different reference groups or standardization

> Just as different standardization samples provide us with different kinds of information, different types of test scores answer different questions.

samples provide us with different kinds of information and allow us to answer different questions, different types of test scores answer different questions. Prior to being able to answer our question of which scores we should use, we need to know what it is we want the test score to tell us. Below are some brief descriptions of major types of scores.

- *Raw scores*: **Raw Scores** tell us the number of points accumulated by a person on a measure and can tell us their relative rank among test takers, assuming we know everyone's raw score, but typically provide us only with ordinal scale measurement.
- *Standard scores*: Traditional **standard scores** address the general question of how this person's performance compares to the performance of some specified reference group and typically reflect interval scale measurement.
- *IRT Scores*: **Rasch** or **IRT-based scores** are on an equal-interval scale that reflects position on some underlying or latent trait. These scores are particularly useful in evaluating the degree of change in scores over time and in comparing scores across tests of a common latent trait.
- *Criterion-referenced scores*: **Criterion-referenced scores** tell us whether or not or to what extent a person's performance has approached a desired level of proficiency.

To illustrate how the use of different types of test scores might address different questions, consider the issue of whether or not a student's performance in reading has changed following the introduction of specialized teaching methods after it was discovered the student was having great difficulty acquiring reading skills. In such a circumstance, a student, John, would be administered a reading test prior to initiating an intervention or specialized reading methods to obtain a baseline level of performance. After some period of specialized instruction, John would be tested a second time to determine whether or not his skills in reading had changed. If the test used provided one of the four types of scores noted above, what would each of these scores tell us about John's change in reading skill?

- Common standard scores that are norm-referenced by age group would answer the following question: *How has John's reading performance changed relative to the average rate of change of other children the same age?*
- Rasch-type scores would answer the question: *How has John's reading performance changed relative to the starting point of his specialized instruction?*
- Raw scores would answer this question as well but are not on an equal-interval scale and make it difficult to estimate by how much John's reading performance has changed. The advantage of a Rasch-type score in this circumstance is that the distance between each score point is the same throughout the entire range of scores.
- Criterion-referenced scores answer a different question. Criterion-referenced scores address the question: *Has John's performance in reading reached a predetermined level of proficiency or a set goal for his instructional progress?*

All of these questions may be important, but they are in fact quite different, and different types of scores are required to answer each one. To understand the difference in the types of information provided, consider if John were running a race instead of learning to read. Norm-referenced standard scores would reflect John's position in the race relative to all other runners at any given time. Rasch-type scores would indicate accurately his distance from the starting point (or any other designated point) but would not allow us to assess his progress relative to other runners without also knowing their Rasch score. Raw scores would indicate distance from the starting point as well, but unlike being measured in feet or meters in a race, when used with psychological or educational variables, they would not indicate the distance accurately at each point of progress. A criterion-referenced score would let us know when John had passed specific points on the racetrack or had reached the finish line. So here we see that each type of score provides us with a different type of information. Which score we should use is dependent upon the type of information we desire.

For purposes of evaluating change, in some circumstances, standard scores that are age corrected are the most appropriate but in other circumstances, criterion-referenced scores or even Rasch scores may be more appropriate. In an educational environment where we are looking to assess improvement in academic achievement levels of an individual student, the question of acquisition of academic skills relative to an age-appropriate peer group would be the most appropriate question to address in nearly all instances. That is, it is important to know if a student is making progress or keeping pace relative to other students the same age and not just relative to the starting point. If we only considered progress relative to a starting point and thus only looked at changes in raw scores or some other form of growth score such as reflected in a Rasch scale, we could certainly determine if a student was making progress. However, the student may be progressing at a rate that is less than that of classmates and so is falling further and further behind. By using age-corrected standard scores, we see easily whether the student is progressing at a lesser rate, the same pace, or more quickly than other students of the same age.

In a therapeutic environment, we have very different concerns. A person who is in psychotherapy being treated for depressive symptoms may be making progress. However, we would not want to discontinue therapy until a specific criterion point had been reached. In such cases, we would be more interested in the absolute level of symptomatology present or absolute level of distress experienced by the patient as opposed to their relative level of change compared to some peer group, and tests designed for this purpose may require a different scaling option.

Once we know what type of score we want to use, in the case of norm-referenced scores, we need to address whether to use normalized (a type of nonlinear score transformation) scores or linear transformations of these scores. This choice may be made once data have been collected. The rationale for each choice is discussed in Chap. 3 of this text and also in Reynolds and Kamphaus (2015).

18.3.3 Briefly Outline the Reliability Studies to Be Performed and Their Rationale

Tests designed for different purposes as well as tests of different types (most notably speeded versus nonspeeded tests) produce scores that should be evaluated differently for relative reliability. For most tests, one should examine the relative accuracy of the domain sampling of the

> Tests designed for different purposes produce scores that should be evaluated differently for relative reliability.

items and coherency of the items with one another. Most often this is done through calculation of internal consistency reliability coefficients, the most popular and widely applicable being Cronbach's alpha (also see Chap. 4 for details on reliability estimation). If a goal is to develop alternate forms of a test, that is, two or more versions of a test intended to measure the same constructs, then the correlation between the two forms can serve as an estimate of the internal consistency reliability of the scores yielded by the different forms of the test. However, this is only true if the different forms actually measure the same construct. The stability of the scores over time should also be assessed except in unusual circumstances. Assessment of the stability of the scores over time is typically termed "test-retest reliability," and tells us the extent to which scores on the test change or remain the same over a specified period of time. Whether change in scores over time is due to issues with the test or reflects true change in the construct is an important distinction when interpreting test-retest or stability coefficients. Test-retest studies also afford the opportunity to assess practice or testing effects—that is, the effects on future scores of having taken the test on a previous occasion. Such information is quite valuable when interpreting scores for a person who has taken the same test on more than one occasion. In planning test-retest studies, these issues need to be considered when determining the appropriate time interval between the initial and follow-up testing. Are practice or testing effects anticipated and should the underlying construct being measured be expected to change in this time period? As mentioned previously, when scoring involves subjective judgment, it is also important to evaluate inter-rater reliability. If the test requires someone to time responses with a high degree of accuracy, it is useful to establish the inter-rater reliability of the timing of responses as well.

18.3.4 Briefly Outline the Validity Studies to Be Performed and Their Rationale

As with reliability studies, it is crucial to plan validity studies in advance. Also, it is vital that the validity studies be conceptualized and designed in a way that allows assessment of the appropriateness of the proposed interpretations of the test once the test is completed. We dis-

> Be certain the validity studies target the proposed interpretations of the scores as well as their intended application.

cussed five basic categories or classifications of validity evidence in Chap. 5 and each area will need to be addressed. However, the emphasis and level of detail of the validity evidence will (or should) vary depending upon the constructs assessed, the proposed interpretations of test scores, and purposes for which the scores will be applied. For an intelligence test intended for use as a predictor of academic success, predictive studies of the criterion chosen to reflect academic success (e.g., graduation rate, ACT scores, etc.) should be emphasized and receive the highest priority. Similarly, tests for personnel selection should undergo studies of the predictive accuracy of the scores with regard to job success (however the user defines this—which should be on an a priori basis) over some specified period of time. Job success can have many definitions by the way, so criterion definitions also must be specified. Some users might define job success as number of years with one employer, some according to supervisor ratings of job performance, some according to number of items produced on an assembly line, or in the case of sales workers, the number of dollars in sales generated over a quarter, year, or more. Different tests might be necessary to predict each such criterion variable although all might be called job success.

A measure of developmental psychopathology that is intended to result in enhanced diagnostic accuracy among the various Autism Spectrum Disorders (ASD) would receive a different emphasis. Here, validity studies should emphasize the ability of the test scores to discriminate among groups of individuals diagnosed (independently of the test) with each of the relevant disorders. Often, journal editors will see "validity studies" of tests designed to assist in the diagnosis of clinical disorders that only look at the ability of the test scores to distinguish diagnosed groups from non-diagnosed or normal samples. This type of research is seldom helpful because almost any test will distinguish normal from non-normal given good test score reliability and large samples. The real issue is distinguishing among the correct diagnoses within a referral sample, such as distinguishing children with ASD from those with ADHD or depression. Seldom do clinicians attempt to determine if a person has one specific disorder such as depression versus an absence of any disorder.

The bottom line is to be certain the validity studies target the proposed interpretations of the scores as well as their intended application. There is no limit to what can be designed as validity studies. Some legal requirements exist for certain types of tests such as personnel selection or classification measures, but for the most part, validity studies are limited only by the creativity of the researcher and their knowledge of the construct and relevant theories that embody the construct they are measuring.

18.3.5 Determine If There Are Any Special Studies That May Be Needed for Development of This Test or to Support Proposed Interpretations of Performance

Depending upon the uniqueness of the measure or the construct targeted for measurement, there may be some very specialized studies required that do not routinely appear in test manuals. Reconsider the proposed applications of the test at this point and try to think of at least one such study that would enhance the application of the measure. You may decide there is nothing unusual required, but this is the time to think outside of traditional validity evidence to see if there are any unique approaches, methods, or research designs you can implement to support applications of your proposed measure.

18.3.6 List the Components of the Test

Before implementing any part of the testing or tryouts of the materials, items, instructions, and the like, make a complete list of all the physical components of the test and review it carefully to be sure you will have all the necessary parts. This also gives you a better idea of the potential cumbersomeness of the proposed test and a preview of its costs! At this point, you will also note if there are any special manufacturing needs for the proposed test or any special software considerations.

18.4   Phase 4: Plan Implementation

18.4.1 Reevaluate the Test Content and Structure

The final phase of the test development process is where the author actually implements the test plan. At this point, we might paraphrase a famous old English story, and remind you that "… the best laid plans of mice and men oft go astray." As you implement your developmental

> As a great piece of literature stated, "the best laid plans of mice and men oft go astray."

plan, you will undoubtedly note changes that need to be made in the items and perhaps even the structure of the test. As you carry out the necessary developmental research, you will find the data do not support all of your assumptions about the test 100%. It is a wise and more likely successful test developer and author who after each phase of the project reevaluates the remaining steps to see if any modifications are necessary to produce the desired end product. Never be afraid to make changes dictated by the data or the feedback received from those involved in administering tryout versions of the test. In the end, it will make for a better test. Flexible development plans and flexibility in implementation guided by the ongoing data collection process are necessary to success.

18.4.2 Prepare the Test Manual

Once the test development process is complete, it is time to prepare the manual for the test. Test manuals should contain a description of the test development process that is sufficient to allow others to replicate what has been accomplished and for users to make accurate determinations as to the usefulness of the test for their purposes. Generally, a test manual should contain chapters that introduce and describe the measure and its conceptual and theoretical foundations, detailed instructions for administration and scoring of the test, an interpretive schema that is supported by validity evidence developed during the test development process, detailed information on the item development process and the standardization and related psychometric characteristics of the test, its score, and its interpretation, including information on test score reliability and evidence for the proposed interpretations of performance on the test. Limitations and cautions in using the measure as well as any special applications of the measure in the field should also be noted. The *Standards* (AERA, et al., 2014) provide additional and in some cases more detailed guidance concerning the information that should be provided in the professional manual for psychological and educational tests. The above is a general outline of the content of the manual and the specific contents will vary according to the type of test and its applications. Keep in mind that some measures (e.g., tests for personnel selection) may have special legal requirements for information that must be available prior to their usage.

18.4.3   Submit a Test Proposal

If you want to have your test published, you will need to submit a test proposal to an appropriate publisher. The major test publishers have slightly different guidelines for developing and submitting a test proposal or prospectus. The test proposal guide used by Psychological Assessment Resources (PAR) can be found online at: https://www.parinc.com/Publish-with-PAR#94149-publishing-opportunities.

18.5   Summary

In this chapter, we provide a practical description of what we have experienced and many others have recommended as the necessary steps and components of the test development process. Throughout this textbook, we introduced or provided additional details on certain constructs such as dissimulation scales and how to determine their necessity. The chapter emphasizes the early conceptual phases of test development as critical to a successful project, especially determining the need for a new test and developing conceptual and operational definitions of constructs you intend to measure. We also emphasize the necessity of describing in advance of initiating the development of a new measure its intended uses and interpretations of results, as well as who will use the test and why.

The largest section of the chapter is devoted to instructions for preparing a detailed description of the test, including a table of specifications, or test blueprint. We give examples of a publisher's requirements for submission of proposals for new commercial psychological tests. Last, we give a general description of the content covered in typical test manuals, noting that some specialized tests may have additional requirements for information that must be available prior to their legal and ethical application in practice.

Careful review of all of these materials as well as the preceding chapters of this text will prepare you well to embark on what can be a truly interesting but, at times, trying endeavor of psychological and educational test development.

References

American Educational Research Association, American Psychological Association, & National Council on Measurement in Education. (2014). *Standards for educational and psychological testing*. Washington, DC: American Educational Research Association.

Bloom, B. S., Engelhart, M. D., Furst, E. J., Hill, W. H., & Krathwohl, D. R. (1956). *Taxonomy of educational objectives: The classification of educational goals: Handbook. Cognitive domain*. White Plains, NY: Longman.

Bush, S., Ruff, R., Troster, A., Barth, J., Koffler, S., Pliskin, N., ... Silver, C. (2005). Symptom validity assessment: Practice issues and medical necessity. *Archives of Clinical Neuropsychology, 20*, 419–426.

Reynolds, C. R., & Kamphaus, R. W. (1992). *Behavior assessment system for children: Manual*. Circle Pines, MN: American Guidance Service.

Reynolds, C. R., & Kamphaus, R. W. (2004). *Behavior assessment system for children* (2nd ed.). Circle Pines, MN: American Guidance Service.

Reynolds, C. R., & Kamphaus, R. W. (2015). *Behavior assessment system for children* (3rd ed.). Bloomington, MN: NCS Pearson.

Reynolds, C. R., & Voress, J. (2007). *Test of memory and learning-second edition (TOMAL-2)*. Austin, TX: Pro-Ed.

Robertson, G. J. (2003). A practical model for test development. In C. R. Reynolds & R. W. Kamphaus (Eds.), *Handbook of psychological and educational assessment of children: Vol. 1. Intelligence, aptitude, and achievement* (2nd ed., pp. 24–57). New York, NY: Guilford Press.

Strauss, G. P., Nuñez, A., Ahmed, A. O., Brachard, K., Granholm, E., Kirkpatrick, B., ... Allen, D. N. (2018). Latent structure of negative symptoms in schizophrenia. *JAMA Psychiatry, 75*(12), 1271–1279.

Recommended Reading

Bush, S., Ruff, R., Troster, A., Barth, J., Koffler, S., Pliskin, N., ... Silver, C. (2005). Symptom validity assessment: Practice issues and medical necessity. *Archives of Clinical Neuropsychology, 20*, 419–426.

Kaufman, A. S., & Kaufman, N. L. (1983). *Kaufman assessment battery for children: Examiner manual and technical manual*. Circle Pines, MN: American Guidance Service.

Reynolds, C. R., & Kamphaus, R. W. (2003). *Reynolds intellectual assessment scales and Reynolds intellectual screening test: Professional manual*. Lutz, FL: Psychological Assessment Resources, Inc..

Robertson, G. J. (2003). A practical model for test development. In C. R. Reynolds & R. W. Kamphaus (Eds.), *Handbook of psychological and educational assessment of children, Vol. 1: Intelligence, aptitude, and achievement* (2nd ed., pp. 24–57). New York, NY: Guilford.

Appendix: Calculation (Table A.1)

Table A.1 Proportions of area under the normal curve

Value of + (−) z	Area under the curve between the distribution mean and the corresponding z score	Area under the curve that is above a positive (or below a negative) corresponding z score
0.00	0.0000	0.5000
0.01	0.0040	0.4960
0.02	0.0080	0.4920
0.03	0.0120	0.4880
0.04	0.0160	0.4840
0.05	0.0199	0.4801
0.06	0.0239	0.4761
0.07	0.0279	0.4721
0.08	0.0319	0.4681
0.09	0.0359	0.4641
0.10	0.0398	0.4602
0.11	0.0438	0.4562
0.12	0.0478	0.4522
0.13	0.0517	0.4483
0.14	0.0557	0.4443
0.15	0.0596	0.4404
0.16	0.0636	0.4364
0.17	0.0675	0.4325
0.18	0.0714	0.4286
0.19	0.0753	0.4247
0.20	0.0793	0.4207
0.21	0.0832	0.4168
0.22	0.0871	0.4129
0.23	0.0910	0.4090
0.24	0.0948	0.4052
0.25	0.0987	0.4013
0.26	0.1026	0.3974
0.27	0.1064	0.3936

(continued)

© Springer Nature Switzerland AG 2021
C. R. Reynolds et al., *Mastering Modern Psychological Testing*,
https://doi.org/10.1007/978-3-030-59455-8

Value of + (−) z	Area under the curve between the distribution mean and the corresponding z score	Area under the curve that is above a positive (or below a negative) corresponding z score
0.28	0.1103	0.3897
0.29	0.1141	0.3859
0.30	0.1179	0.3821
0.31	0.1217	0.3783
0.32	0.1255	0.3745
0.33	0.1293	0.3707
0.34	0.1331	0.3669
0.35	0.1368	0.3632
0.36	0.1406	0.3594
0.37	0.1443	0.3557
0.38	0.1480	0.3520
0.39	0.1517	0.3483
0.40	0.1554	0.3446
0.41	0.1591	0.3409
0.42	0.1628	0.3372
0.43	0.1664	0.3336
0.44	0.1700	0.3300
0.45	0.1736	0.3264
0.46	0.1772	0.3228
0.47	0.1808	0.3192
0.48	0.1844	0.3156
0.49	0.1879	0.3121
0.50	0.1915	0.3085
0.51	0.1950	0.3050
0.52	0.1985	0.3015
0.53	0.2019	0.2981
0.54	0.2054	0.2946
0.55	0.2088	0.2912
0.56	0.2123	0.2877
0.57	0.2157	0.2843
0.58	0.2190	0.2810
0.59	0.2224	0.2776
0.60	0.2257	0.2743
0.61	0.2291	0.2709
0.62	0.2324	0.2676
0.63	0.2357	0.2643
0.64	0.2389	0.2611
0.65	0.2422	0.2578
0.66	0.2454	0.2546
0.67	0.2486	0.2514
0.68	0.2517	0.2483
0.69	0.2549	0.2451
0.70	0.2580	0.2420

(continued)

Table A.1 (continued)

Value of + (−) z	Area under the curve between the distribution mean and the corresponding z score	Area under the curve that is above a positive (or below a negative) corresponding z score
0.71	0.2611	0.2389
0.72	0.2642	0.2358
0.73	0.2673	0.2327
0.74	0.2704	0.2296
0.75	0.2734	0.2266
0.76	0.2764	0.2236
0.77	0.2794	0.2206
0.78	0.2823	0.2177
0.79	0.2852	0.2148
0.80	0.2881	0.2119
0.81	0.2910	0.2090
0.82	0.2939	0.2061
0.83	0.2967	0.2033
0.84	0.2995	0.2005
0.85	0.3023	0.1977
0.86	0.3051	0.1949
0.87	0.3078	0.1922
0.88	0.3106	0.1894
0.89	0.3133	0.1867
0.90	0.3159	0.1841
0.91	0.3186	0.1814
0.92	0.3212	0.1788
0.93	0.3238	0.1762
0.94	0.3264	0.1736
0.95	0.3289	0.1711
0.96	0.3315	0.1685
0.97	0.3340	0.1660
0.98	0.3365	0.1635
0.99	0.3389	0.1611
1.00	0.3413	0.1587
1.01	0.3438	0.1562
1.02	0.3461	0.1539
1.03	0.3485	0.1515
1.04	0.3508	0.1492
1.05	0.3531	0.1469
1.06	0.3554	0.1446
1.07	0.3577	0.1423
1.08	0.3599	0.1401
1.09	0.3621	0.1379
1.10	0.3643	0.1357
1.11	0.3665	0.1335
1.12	0.3686	0.1314

(continued)

Table A.1 (continued)

Value of + (−) z	Area under the curve between the distribution mean and the corresponding z score	Area under the curve that is above a positive (or below a negative) corresponding z score
1.13	0.3708	0.1292
1.14	0.3729	0.1271
1.15	0.3749	0.1251
1.16	0.3770	0.1230
1.17	0.3790	0.1210
1.18	0.3810	0.1190
1.19	0.3830	0.1170
1.20	0.3849	0.1151
1.21	0.3869	0.1131
1.22	0.3888	0.1112
1.23	0.3907	0.1093
1.24	0.3925	0.1075
1.25	0.3944	0.1056
1.26	0.3962	0.1038
1.27	0.3980	0.1020
1.28	0.3997	0.1003
1.29	0.4015	0.0985
1.30	0.4032	0.0968
1.31	0.4049	0.0951
1.32	0.4066	0.0934
1.33	0.4082	0.0918
1.34	0.4099	0.0901
1.35	0.4115	0.0885
1.36	0.4131	0.0869
1.37	0.4147	0.0853
1.38	0.4162	0.0838
1.39	0.4177	0.0823
1.40	0.4192	0.0808
1.41	0.4207	0.0793
1.42	0.4222	0.0778
1.43	0.4236	0.0764
1.44	0.4251	0.0749
1.45	0.4265	0.0735
1.46	0.4279	0.0721
1.47	0.4292	0.0708
1.48	0.4306	0.0694
1.49	0.4319	0.0681
1.50	0.4332	0.0668
1.51	0.4345	0.0655
1.52	0.4357	0.0643
1.53	0.4370	0.0630
1.54	0.4382	0.0618

(continued)

Table A.1 (continued)

Value of + (−) z	Area under the curve between the distribution mean and the corresponding z score	Area under the curve that is above a positive (or below a negative) corresponding z score
1.55	0.4394	0.0606
1.56	0.4406	0.0594
1.57	0.4418	0.0582
1.58	0.4429	0.0571
1.59	0.4441	0.0559
1.60	0.4452	0.0548
1.61	0.4463	0.0537
1.62	0.4474	0.0526
1.63	0.4484	0.0516
1.64	0.4495	0.0505
1.65	0.4505	0.0495
1.66	0.4515	0.0485
1.67	0.4525	0.0475
1.68	0.4535	0.0465
1.69	0.4545	0.0455
1.70	0.4554	0.0446
1.71	0.4564	0.0436
1.72	0.4573	0.0427
1.73	0.4582	0.0418
1.74	0.4591	0.0409
1.75	0.4599	0.0401
1.76	0.4608	0.0392
1.77	0.4616	0.0384
1.78	0.4625	0.0375
1.79	0.4633	0.0367
1.80	0.4641	0.0359
1.81	0.4649	0.0351
1.82	0.4656	0.0344
1.83	0.4664	0.0336
1.84	0.4671	0.0329
1.85	0.4678	0.0322
1.86	0.4686	0.0314
1.87	0.4693	0.0307
1.88	0.4699	0.0301
1.89	0.4706	0.0294
1.90	0.4713	0.0287
1.91	0.4719	0.0281
1.92	0.4726	0.0274
1.93	0.4732	0.0268
1.94	0.4738	0.0262
1.95	0.4744	0.0256
1.96	0.4750	0.0250

(continued)

Table A.1 (continued)

Value of + (−) z	Area under the curve between the distribution mean and the corresponding z score	Area under the curve that is above a positive (or below a negative) corresponding z score
1.97	0.4756	0.0244
1.98	0.4761	0.0239
1.99	0.4767	0.0233
2.00	0.4772	0.0228
2.01	0.4778	0.0222
2.02	0.4783	0.0217
2.03	0.4788	0.0212
2.04	0.4793	0.0207
2.05	0.4798	0.0202
2.06	0.4803	0.0197
2.07	0.4808	0.0192
2.08	0.4812	0.0188
2.09	0.4817	0.0183
2.10	0.4821	0.0179
2.11	0.4826	0.0174
2.12	0.4830	0.0170
2.13	0.4834	0.0166
2.14	0.4838	0.0162
2.15	0.4842	0.0158
2.16	0.4846	0.0154
2.17	0.4850	0.0150
2.18	0.4854	0.0146
2.19	0.4857	0.0143
2.20	0.4861	0.0139
2.21	0.4864	0.0136
2.22	0.4868	0.0132
2.23	0.4871	0.0129
2.24	0.4875	0.0125
2.25	0.4878	0.0122
2.26	0.4881	0.0119
2.27	0.4884	0.0116
2.28	0.4887	0.0113
2.29	0.4890	0.0110
2.30	0.4893	0.0107
2.31	0.4896	0.0104
2.32	0.4898	0.0102
2.33	0.4901	0.0099
2.34	0.4904	0.0096
2.35	0.4906	0.0094
2.36	0.4909	0.0091
2.37	0.4911	0.0089
2.38	0.4913	0.0087

(continued)

Table A.1 (continued)

Value of + (−) z	Area under the curve between the distribution mean and the corresponding z score	Area under the curve that is above a positive (or below a negative) corresponding z score
2.39	0.4916	0.0084
2.40	0.4918	0.0082
2.41	0.4920	0.0080
2.42	0.4922	0.0078
2.43	0.4925	0.0075
2.44	0.4927	0.0073
2.45	0.4929	0.0071
2.46	0.4931	0.0069
2.47	0.4932	0.0068
2.48	0.4934	0.0066
2.49	0.4936	0.0064
2.50	0.4938	0.0062
2.51	0.4940	0.0060
2.52	0.4941	0.0059
2.53	0.4943	0.0057
2.54	0.4945	0.0055
2.55	0.4946	0.0054
2.56	0.4948	0.0052
2.57	0.4949	0.0051
2.58	0.4951	0.0049
2.59	0.4952	0.0048
2.60	0.4953	0.0047
2.61	0.4955	0.0045
2.62	0.4956	0.0044
2.63	0.4957	0.0043
2.64	0.4959	0.0041
2.65	0.4960	0.0040
2.66	0.4961	0.0039
2.67	0.4962	0.0038
2.68	0.4963	0.0037
2.69	0.4964	0.0036
2.70	0.4965	0.0035
2.71	0.4966	0.0034
2.72	0.4967	0.0033
2.73	0.4968	0.0032
2.74	0.4969	0.0031
2.75	0.4970	0.0030
2.76	0.4971	0.0029
2.77	0.4972	0.0028
2.78	0.4973	0.0027
2.79	0.4974	0.0026
2.80	0.4974	0.0026

(continued)

Table A.1 (continued)

Value of + (−) z	Area under the curve between the distribution mean and the corresponding z score	Area under the curve that is above a positive (or below a negative) corresponding z score
2.81	0.4975	0.0025
2.82	0.4976	0.0024
2.83	0.4977	0.0023
2.84	0.4977	0.0023
2.85	0.4978	0.0022
2.86	0.4979	0.0021
2.87	0.4979	0.0021
2.88	0.4980	0.0020
2.89	0.4981	0.0019
2.90	0.4981	0.0019
2.91	0.4982	0.0018
2.92	0.4982	0.0018
2.93	0.4983	0.0017
2.94	0.4984	0.0016
2.95	0.4984	0.0016
2.96	0.4985	0.0015
2.97	0.4985	0.0015
2.98	0.4986	0.0014
2.99	0.4986	0.0014
3.00	0.4987	0.0013
3.01	0.4987	0.0013
3.02	0.4987	0.0013
3.03	0.4988	0.0012
3.04	0.4988	0.0012
3.05	0.4989	0.0011
3.06	0.4989	0.0011
3.07	0.4989	0.0011
3.08	0.4990	0.0010
3.09	0.4990	0.0010
3.10	0.4990	0.0010
3.11	0.4991	0.0009
3.12	0.4991	0.0009
3.13	0.4991	0.0009
3.14	0.4992	0.0008
3.15	0.4992	0.0008
3.16	0.4992	0.0008
3.17	0.4992	0.0008

Index

© Springer Nature Switzerland AG 2021
C. R. Reynolds et al., *Mastering Modern Psychological Testing*,
https://doi.org/10.1007/978-3-030-59455-8